"Swati Chattopadhyay and Jeremy White have done a superb job in delineating a critical field for understanding contemporary architecture. With the contributors, they weave together a set of narratives that offers a strong sense of place and time in crisis that is at once global and local. The result is an excellent assemblage of recent thoughts and concerns about the place of contemporary architecture in society. Wide-ranging, incisive and yet accessible, the essays in this book lead us to firmly believe that architecture matters, for its ways of impacting the ethico-political problems of our time, and how it may now be engaged to deal with the crisis of the twenty-first century."

Abidin Kusno, *Professor, Environmental Studies, York University, Canada*

"At the core of this important volume is an essential questioning of structural violence and its emergent spatial and material embodiments at all scales in contemporary architecture. Disassembling binaries, unsettling systems of power, and countering formal narratives, this collection of deft authors signals how architectural discourse today is an essential mode for confronting the now ... and never again."

Sean Anderson, *Associate Curator, Department of Architecture and Design, The Museum of Modern Art, USA*

The Routledge Companion to Critical Approaches to Contemporary Architecture

The Routledge Companion to Critical Approaches to Contemporary Architecture convenes a wide array of critical voices from architecture, art history, urbanism, geography, anthropology, media and performance studies, computer science, bio-engineering, environmental studies, and sociology that help us understand the meaning and significance of global architecture of the twenty-first century. New chapters by 36 contributors illustrated with over 140 black-and-white images are assembled in six parts concerning both real and virtual spaces: design, materiality, alterity, technologies, cityscapes, and practice.

Swati Chattopadhyay is Professor in the Department of History of Art and Architecture at the University of California, Santa Barbara. She is the author of *Representing Calcutta: Modernity, Nationalism, and the Colonial Uncanny* (Routledge 2005); *Unlearning the City: Infrastructure in a New Optical Field* (Minnesota 2012); and co-editor of *City Halls and Civic Materialism: Towards a Global History of Urban Public Space* (Routledge 2014).

Jeremy White is an architect and a game designer, and a lecturer in the Department of History of Art and Architecture at the University of California, Santa Barbara. He is the co-editor of *City Halls and Civic Materialism: Towards a Global History of Urban Public Space* (Routledge 2014).

The Routledge Companion to Critical Approaches to Contemporary Architecture

Edited by Swati Chattopadhyay and Jeremy White

LONDON AND NEW YORK

First published 2020 by Routledge

2 Park Square, Milton Park, Abingdon, Oxon, OX14 4RN
605 Third Avenue, New York, NY 10017

First issued in paperback 2021

Routledge is an imprint of the Taylor & Francis Group, an informa business

Copyright © 2020 Taylor & Francis

The right of Swati Chattopadhyay and Jeremy White to be identified as the authors of the editorial matter, and of the authors for their individual chapters, has been asserted in accordance with sections 77 and 78 of the Copyright, Designs and Patents Act 1988.

All rights reserved. No part of this book may be reprinted or reproduced or utilized in any form or by any electronic, mechanical, or other means, now known or hereafter invented, including photocopying and recording, or in any information storage or retrieval system, without permission in writing from the publishers.

Trademark notice: Product or corporate names may be trademarks or registered trademarks, and are used only for identification and explanation without intent to infringe.

Publisher's Note
The publisher has gone to great lengths to ensure the quality of this reprint but points out that some imperfections in the original copies may be apparent.

Library of Congress Cataloging-in-Publication Data
Names: Chattopadhyay, Swati, 1962- editor. | White, Jeremy (Jeremy Scott), editor.
Title: The Routledge companion to critical approaches to contemporary architecture / edited by Swati Chattopadhyay and Jeremy White.
Description: New York : Routledge, 2019. | Includes bibliographical references and index.
Identifiers: LCCN 2019011652 | ISBN 9781138917569 (hardback)
Subjects: LCSH: Architecture and society—History—21st century.
Classification: LCC NA2543.S6 R685 2019 | DDC 720.1/03—dc23
LC record available at https://lccn.loc.gov/2019011652

ISBN 13: 978−1−03−209034−4 (pbk)
ISBN 13: 978−1−138−91756−9 (hbk)

Typeset in Bembo
by Wearset Ltd, Boldon, Tyne and Wear

To our students present and future

Contents

List of Figures   *xiii*
Notes on Contributors   *xviii*
Acknowledgments   *xxiii*

1 Introduction: Contemporary Architecture, Crisis, and Critique   1
    Swati Chattopadhyay and Jeremy White

PART I
Design   9

2 Public Face and Private Space in the Design of Contemporary Houses   11
    Alice T. Friedman

3 Designs on Disaster: Humanitarianism and Contemporary Architecture   25
    Andrew Herscher

4 Architectures of Risk and Resiliency: "Embedded Security" in the Redesign of Sandy Hook Elementary School   36
    Rachel Hall

5 When the Megaproject Meets the Village: Formal and Informal Urbanization in Southern China   46
    Max Hirsh and Dorothy Tang

6 After the Counter-monument: Commemoration in the Expanded Field   57
    Mechtild Widrich

PART II
Materiality   69

7 Architectures of Memory, Past and Future   71
    Abby Smith Rumsey

Contents

8 Life and Death in the Anthropocene 80
   Heather Davis

9 The Space of Relation: Body, Emotion, and Empathy in Architectural
   Experience 91
   Sarah Robinson

10 Edges: Body, Space, and Design 102
   Jeremy White

11 Habit's *Remainder* 117
   Aron Vinegar

12 Ephemeral Architecture: Toward Radical Contingency 138
   Swati Chattopadhyay

PART III
Alterity **161**

13 Inhabiting Ruins: The Ministry of Defense and the Limits of
   Occupation in Monrovia, Liberia 163
   Danny Hoffman

14 Border Architecture: Territories, Commons, and Breathing-Spaces 175
   George F. Flaherty

15 Camps: Contemporary Environments of Autonomy, Necessity, and
   Control 187
   Charlie Hailey

16 Defensive Alterity in Contemporary Sri Lankan Architecture 200
   Anoma Pieris

17 Recasting the Ethnic Retail Street: Analyzing Contemporary
   Immigrant Architecture in the United States 215
   Arijit Sen

PART IV
Technologies **229**

18 Obsolescence and Its Futures 231
   Daniel M. Abramson

19	Intelligent Architectural Settings *Christopher Beorkrem and Eric Sauda*	244
20	Future Architecture: Biohybrid Structures and Intelligent Materials *Ljiljana Fruk and Veljko Armano Linta*	256
21	Networked Urbanism: Definition, Scholarship, Directions *T. F. Tierney*	270
22	The Architecture of Water *Karen Piper*	287

PART V
Cityscapes — 301

23	What Might Be: Re-describing Urbanscapes of the Global South *AbdouMaliq Simone*	303
24	Watching the City: A Genealogy of Media Urbanism *Joshua Neves*	311
25	The Singapore Flyer: View, Movement, Time, and Contemporaneity *Iain Borden*	323
26	Bi-Space: The Original Social Networking Site *Craig L. Wilkins*	337
27	Urchins in the Infrastructure: Building with Hedgehogs in the Multispecies City *Laura McLauchlan*	351
28	Unsettling Formal Power Systems *Saskia Sassen*	363

PART VI
Practice — 373

29	Is It Really that Bad? The Status of Women in Architecture and the Gender Equity Movement *Despina Stratigakos*	375
30	Where Is the Social Project? *Kenny Cupers*	387

Contents

31 Collaboration: Unresolved Forms of Working Together in Contemporary
    Architectural Practice   393
    Sony Devabhaktuni and Min Kyung Lee

32 Starchitecture: Starchitect   405
    Jeremy White

33 A Eulogy for the Present: *The Death of Architecture, c.2000* Exhibition 424
    Rohan Shivkumar

34 Architects "Getting Real": On Present-Day Professional Fictions   439
    Arindam Dutta

Index   454

Figures

2.1	Marc-Antoine Laugier: *Essai sur l'architecture*, Paris: N. B. Duchesne, 1755	12
2.2	Philip Johnson, The Glass House and Brick Guest House, New Canaan, CT, 1949	14
2.3	David Adjaye, Dirty House, London, England, 2002	17
2.4	Rick Joy, Jax House/Desert Nomad, Tucson, AZ, 2003–2005	19
2.5	Michael Maltzan, Pittman Dowell House, La Crescentia, CA, 2009	21
3.1	Shigeru Ban, emergency shelters at Gihembe Refugee Camp, Rwanda, 1999	26
3.2	Gihembe Refugee Camp, Rwanda, 2015	28
3.3	Shop using mVISA, Gihembe Refugee Camp, Rwanda, 2015	31
5.1	An aerial view of Xiaoguwei Island, home to the Guangzhou Higher Education Mega Center and four villages	48
5.2	Typical campus architecture in Guangzhou's University Town	49
5.3	Beigang's marketplace and "food street" are popular among the university students who live in the dormitories surrounding the village	51
5.4	The Silver Sky Guesthouse is located inside a decommissioned ancestor hall	53
5.5	Students from Sun Yat-sen University and the Guangdong Academy of Fine Arts teamed up to convert a former village house into Beigang's first co-working space	54
6.1	*Mothers of Macedonia* fountain and *Warrior Monument*, Skopje, Macedonia, 2014	58
6.2	Michael Arad and Peter Walker, *Reflecting Absence*, National September 11 Memorial and Museum, New York	59
6.3	Ai Weiwei, *F. Lotus*, Belvedere Palace, Vienna, 2016	61
6.4	Site of Jochen Gerz's and Esther Shalev-Gerz's *Monument against Fascism*, 2009	63
6.5	Replica of Palmyra's Triumphal Arch at Trafalgar Square, London, April 2016	64
6.6	Jonas Dahlberg, *July 22 Memorial*, Sørbråten site opposite Utøya, rendering studio Dahlberg	65
8.1	Ivanhoe Reservoir looking northeast from the west side, showing outlet tower	81
8.2	Ivanhoe Reservoir, detail of northwestern corner	88
9.1	Peter Zumthor, Silk curtains at Kolomba Museum, Cologne, Germany	96
9.2	Tomás Saraceno, *Poetic Cosmos of the Breath*, 2013. Installation view, Mobile M+:Inflation!, Hong Kong, China. Commissioned by M+ Gunpowder and Arts Catalyst	98

Figures

9.3	Anja Thierfelder, *Lightscapes*, Installation at the 2016 Venice Biennale	99
9.4	Crepuscular light, Khao Yai National Park Thailand	100
10.1	Approach to the Ed Roberts Campus. Note the change in paving in the lowest image, a variation in texture to guide the visually impaired	104
11.1	*Remainder*, Tom in the bathroom at a party on Plato Road	118
11.2	*Remainder*, Tom hit by falling debris	119
11.3	*Remainder*, Tom's jerking motions in the London underground	120
11.4	*Remainder*, Tom with blood dripping off his nose after being hit by fallen debris	121
11.5	*Remainder*, Tom barely visible within the heap of falling debris	122
11.6	*Remainder*, Tom's odd grip as he is making a cardboard model of Madlyn Mansions	123
11.7	*Remainder*, Tom with milk spilling out of its container	124
11.8	*Remainder*, Cardboard model of Madlyn Mansions	125
11.9	*Remainder*, The liver lady	127
11.10	*Remainder*, Opening credits of the film	128
11.11	*Remainder*, The last of the evicted tenants from Madlyn Mansions	129
11.12	*Remainder*, Re-enactors "frozen" in place	130
11.13	*Remainder*, Tom smashing the cardboard model of Madlyn Mansions	131
11.14	*Remainder*, Tom choosing the re-enactors assembled by his "facilitator" Nazrul Ram Vyas (Arsher Ali)	131
11.15	*Remainder*, Furniture covered in generic brown wrapping paper	132
11.16	*Remainder*, Tom drawing his finger over an "inner eight" scratched into the window pane of a phone booth	133
11.17	*Remainder*, Re-enactors for the bank robbery trip over a "material kink" in the carpet	134
11.18	*Remainder*, Tom gripping the "material kink" in the carpet	134
11.19	*Remainder*, Re-enactors tripping over the "ghost kink" in the carpet	135
12.1	Rasheed Araeen, *Rite/Right of Passage*, Dhaka Art Summit, 2018	139
12.2	Rasheed Araeen, Plan of *Rite/Right of Passage*, 2017	140
12.3	Street before construction of the *pandal* of Badamtala Ashar Sangha, 2017	144
12.4	Purnendu Dey and Snehasish Maity, *pandal* of Badamtala Ashar Sangha, 2017	145
12.5	Bimal Samanta, *pandal* of Bakulbagan Sarbojanin, 2017	146
12.6	Small low-budget *pandal* on narrow lane near Hedua; note the *ro'ak* of residences for use as seating space, 2017	146
12.7	Purnendu Dey and Snehasish Maity, Scaffolding of *pandal* of Badamtala Ashar Sangha, 2017	148
12.8	Bimal Samanta, Panel detail of *pandal* of Bakulbagan Sarbojanin, 2017	152
12.9	Bimal Samanta, Wall detail of *pandal* of Bakulbagan Sarbojanin, 2017	154
12.10	Bimal Samanta, Ceiling over outdoor lounge, *pandal* of Bakulbagan Sarbojanin, 2017	155
12.11	Bimal Samanta, Sketch for *pandal* of Bakulbagan Sarbojanin, 2017	156
13.1	The interior courtyard of Monrovia's Ministry of Defense	164
13.2	Exterior of the Ministry of Defense from across what was intended to be the parade grounds	168
13.3	The Ministry's viewing stands	169
13.4	The ambiguous and disproportionate front entrance to the Ministry building	170

Figures

13.5	Former inhabitants of the Ministry of Defense on the structure's roof	172
14.1	Javier Téllez, *One Flew over the Void (Bala perdida)*, 2005, Las Playas, Tijuana, Mexico/Imperial Beach, San Diego, U.S., photographic documentation of performance	177
14.2	Estudio Teddy Cruz + Fonna Forman, *Casa Familiar: Living Rooms at the Border*, San Ysidro, California, 2001, maquete	179
14.3	Estudio Teddy Cruz + Fonna Forman, *Manufactured Sites: A Housing Urbanism Made of Waste/Maquiladora*, 2005–2008, maquete	180
14.4	Estudio Teddy Cruz + Fonna Forman, *Non-Stop Sprawl: McMansion Retrofitted Project*, 2008, maquete set in mirrored box	181
14.5	Yona Friedman, *Spatial City over Paris*, 1960, collage on a postcard, collection of Musée National d'Art Moderne, Centre Georges Pompidou	183
14.6	Ron Herron, *Walking City Project on Ocean*, exterior perspective, 1966, cut-and-pasted printed and photographic papers and graphite, collection of Museum of Modern Art, New York	184
15.1a	Aerial view of Burning Man, 2015	190
15.1b	Installation by Michael Garlington, *Totem of Confessions*, Burning Man, 2015	190
15.2a	Aerial view of Dadaab's Ifo 2 camp with original Ifo camp in background, 2011	193
15.2b	Shelters built at the edge of Ifo camp in Dadaab, July 2011	193
15.3a	Aerial view of Camp Bondsteel, Kosovo	195
15.3b	Dining facilities and Burger King at Camp Bondsteel	195
16.1	Geoffrey Bawa, Sri Lanka Parliament 1979–1982	202
16.2	Anuradhapura, Ruvanwelisaya stupa	205
16.3	War related destruction, homes in Jaffna	207
16.4	Geoffrey Bawa, former Edward Reid & Begg Office, entrance courtyard (Gallery Café) designed as a house for Bartholomeusz 1961–1963	209
16.5	Geoffrey Bawa, Triton Hotel (Heritance Ahungalle) 1978–1981	211
17.1	Map of Chicago showing Morton Grove, Devon Avenue, and the University of Illinois campus	216
17.2	Interior layout of Ghareeb Nawaz, Drawing by Travis Olson, Center for Historic Architecture and Design	219
17.3	Exterior advertisements on the storefront, Ghareeb Nawaz	220
17.4	Prayer room inside Ghareeb Nawaz before new renovation	221
17.5	Front façade of commercial buildings along Devon Avenue	223
18.1	Northwick Park Hospital, growing end, Harrow (England), Richard Llewelyn Davies and John Weeks, 1961–1976	233
18.2	McCormick Tribune Campus Center, Illinois Institute of Technology, Chicago, Rem Koolhaas, 1997–2003	236
18.3	Prada Boutique, Tokyo, Herzog + DeMeuron, 2003	237
18.4	Asia Society Hong Kong Center, Hong Kong, Tod Williams Billie Tsien, 2011	240
18.5	Building 23 rehabilitation, Zlín (Czech Republic), Pavel Mudřík and Pavel Míček, 2006	241
19.1	VALSE flowchart	250
19.2	Top: Heat Map view. Bottom: Event Selection view	251
19.3	Prototype of the VALSE interface	253

Figures

20.1	Nanostructure (nanoflower) made of DNA biomolecule and gold nanoparticles used for design of light triggered memory devices	257
20.2	Molecular structures of carbon nanomaterials. C60 Fullerene (upper left), carbon nanotube (upper right), and graphene (bottom)	259
20.3	Night image of Lloyd's Building by Richard Rogers, London	261
20.4	3D chemical structure of polyethylene made of repeatable carbon units	263
20.5	Variety of protein structures	265
20.6	The three classes of virus capsids (shells). All canonical capsids made up from trapezoidal subunits can be built from a single type of pentagon and different hexamers (shown in distinct shades)	266
20.7	(A) A male Eastern Bluebird; (B) Plum Throated Cotinga; (C) and (D) Their respective keratin and air nanostructures	268
21.1	Urban habitants shown as a percentage of total national population	271
21.2	Re-programmable surface, BIG Audi Urban Future Initiative 2010	279
22.1	The Los Angeles Aqueduct	289
22.2	Map of Central Valley Project and State Water Project, San Joaquin Valley, CA. U.S. Bureau of Reclamation	290
22.3	Robert M. Brereton's proposed irrigation canals, Charles Nordhoff, *California: A Book for Travellers and Settlers*, New York: Harper & Brothers, 1874	291
24.1	Images of the city increasingly forming everyday urban architectures and experience. A construction site in Beijing's Doncheng District is fenced in with images of a future park, left, while cars and cyclists pass by, right	313
24.2a and 24.2b	Wang Wo's *Outside* focuses on street-level practices, like fighting or dancing, before zooming out to reveal the larger urban fabric and the cinematographer's distant position	318
24.3	The LED Sky Screen at The Place shopping mall in Beijing's Chaoyang District shows looping nature videos and live TV broadcasts	320
24.4	A migrant worker watches broadcast TV on a large screen attached to Beijing's Worker's stadium ahead of the 2008 Olympic Games	321
25.1	Exterior view	324
25.2	View towards Downtown	327
25.3	View over the Gardens by the Bay project towards the Singapore Strait	327
25.4	Cabin at top of the Flyer	332
27.1	Hedgehog footprints from Redcliffe, Bristol	351
27.2	Hazards for modern hedgehogs: some of the many dangers hedgehogs face when living near humans	353
27.3	*Umwelt* mysteries: hog and human senses	355
27.4	An abandoned hibernaculum built inside a hedgehog house from the back garden of hedgehog champion, Kay	357
27.5	St Agnes hedgehog	360
28.1	Hilary Koob-Sassen, *When the Material Becomes Speech*	364
28.2	Hilary Koob-Sassen, *Incompleteness*	366
31.1	Community gardens, Spreefeld Spreeacker, id22, 2015	394
31.2	"Estimating value" workshop, Wittenberge Town Hall, subsolar, 2015	397
31.3	Brainstorming discussion, New York, SO-IL, 2015	398
31.4	*Fountain House*, Montreal, raumlabor, 2014	401

32.1	Scheme 1: Artist–Object relationship. Scheme 2: Artist–Object relationship in context	407
32.2	Scheme 3: Artist–Object relationships in separate contexts. Scheme 4: Artist–Object relationships in a shared context	408
32.3	Scheme 5: Impossible Artist–Object relationships	409
32.4	Scheme 6: Starchitect (artist)–Starchitecture (object) relationship. The table below indicates the background, or negative space, framing the object as a function of context	410
32.5	The visually striking Walt Disney Concert Hall, 2016	411
32.6	Scheme 7: Starchitect–Builders–Starchitecture relationship	412
32.7	Scheme 8: Starchitect–Starchitecture relationship (hiding other designers and design influencers)	413
32.8	Author's photograph of water damage on the underside of the roof inside Frank Gehry's Stata Center on M.I.T. campus, 2016	415
32.9	Architecture as Sign. Author's photograph of the 1977 edition of *Learning from Las Vegas* set against the blank screen of a local drive-through theater in Goleta, California (empty sign). Inset detail: Photograph adorning the first two editions of *Learning from Las Vegas*, depicting the "Tan Hawaiian with Tanya" billboard that became an iconic reference to the book (Vinegar 2008)	419
33.1	M/s Prabhakar B Bhagwat, bas relief, *Death of Architecture*	427
33.2	M/s Prabhakar B Bhagwat, one of the fingerprints of texts concerning Indian nationalism, *Death of Architecture*	427
33.3	Arya Architects, panel showing ways of drawing water from the ground, *Death of Architecture*	428
33.4	BARD Studio, drawings of some of the "Transactional Objects" proposed for the city of Mumbai, *Death of Architecture*	430
33.5	INformalities, "Hundred Hands," *Death of Architecture*	431
33.6	Busride, "End of the Local," *Death of Architecture*	432
33.7	Anthill Studio, illustration for "Terrestrial Time," *Death of Architecture*	434
33.8	Samira Rathod Design Associates, some of the objects reconstructed from the residue of demolitions in the town of Bhadran, *Death of Architecture*	435
33.9	Location of the firms participating in the *Death of Architecture* exhibition	437

Contributors

Daniel M. Abramson is Professor of Architectural History and Director of Architectural Studies at Boston University. He is the author of *Obsolescence: An Architectural History* (Chicago 2016); *Building the Bank of England: Money, Architecture, Society, 1694–1942* (Yale 2005); and *Skyscraper Rivals: The AIG Building and the Architecture of Wall Street* (Princeton Architectural Press 2001).

Christopher Beorkrem is an Associate Professor in the School of Architecture at the University of North Carolina at Charlotte. He currently serves as coordinator of the DesComp Dual Master's Degree in Architecture and Computer Science, and as Co-Director of the Digital Arts Center. He teaches studios and workshops in computational design and fabrication. The second edition of his book, *Material Strategies in Digital Fabrication* (Routledge) came out in 2017.

Iain Borden is Professor of Architecture and Urban Culture, and Vice-Dean Education, at The Bartlett, University College London. His most recent book is *Skateboarding and the City: a Complete History* (Bloomsbury 2019).

Swati Chattopadhyay is Professor in the Department of History of Art and Architecture at the University of California, Santa Barbara. She is the author of *Representing Calcutta: Modernity, Nationalism, and the Colonial Uncanny* (Routledge 2005); *Unlearning the City: Infrastructure in a New Optical Field* (Minnesota 2012); and co-editor of *City Halls and Civic Materialism: Towards a Global History of Urban Public Space* (Routledge 2014).

Kenny Cupers is an Associate Professor in the History and Theory of Architecture and Urbanism at the Faculty of the Humanities and Social Sciences of the University of Basel, where he co-founded and leads its new division of Urban Studies. His publications include: *The Social Project: Housing Postwar France* (Minnesota 2014), *Use Matters: An Alternative History of Architecture* (Routledge 2013), and *Spaces of Uncertainty: Berlin Revisited* (Birkhäuser 2018).

Heather Davis is an Assistant Professor of Culture and Media at The New School. She is the co-editor of *Art in the Anthropocene: Encounters among Aesthetics, Politics, Environments and Epistemologies* (Open Humanities Press 2015) and editor of *Desire Change: Contemporary Feminist Art in Canada* (MAWA and McGill Queen's University Press 2017).

Sony Devabhaktuni is an Assistant Professor in the Department of Architecture at the University of Hong Kong. His research focuses on the capacity of architectural drawing to address cultural, socio-political, and economic issues and has been supported by grants from the Graham

Foundation for Advanced Studies in the Fine Arts, the Fulbright Scholar Program, and the General Research Fund of the government of Hong Kong.

Arindam Dutta is a Professor of Architectural History at MIT's Department of Architecture. He is the author of *A Bureaucracy of Beauty: Design in the Age of its Global Reproducibility* (Routledge 2007), in addition to a number of essays and edited volumes on the relationships of technology, knowledge production, economic thought, and globalization.

George F. Flaherty is an Associate Professor of Art History at the University of Texas at Austin. Specializing in contemporary art, architecture, and cinema from Latin America and the Latinx United States, he is the author of *Hotel Mexico: Dwelling on the '68 Movement* (California 2016).

Alice T. Friedman is the Grace Slack McNeil Professor of the History of American Art and Co-Director of the Architecture Program at Wellesley College. She is the author of numerous articles and books, including *Women and the Making of the Modern House* (Harry N. Abrams 1998) and *American Glamour and the Evolution of Modern Architecture* (Yale 2010). Friedman is currently working on a book entitled *Poker Faces: Architecture, Public Identity and Private Life*, which focuses on houses that conceal the activities and life choices of queer and other non-conforming clients behind blank walls or stylistically conventional façades.

Ljiljana Fruk is a lecturer in bionanotechnology at the Department of Chemical Engineering and Biotechnology, University of Cambridge. She works on development of bio-nano hybrids for biomedical applications, green catalysis, and water remediation. Besides her scientific work, she is an active science popularizer, art-science exhibition curator, book author (*Molecular Aesthetics* [MIT Press 2011]; *Molecules That Changed the World* [Artresor 2016]), and, most importantly, Molecular Chocolates designer.

Charlie Hailey is Professor in the School of Architecture at the University of Florida, where he teaches design, history-theory, and design/build. His books include *Camps* (MIT 2009), *Design/Build with Jersey Devil* (Princeton 2016), and most recently, with photographer Donovan Wylie, *Slab City* (MIT 2018). Hailey is a 2018 Guggenheim Fellow.

Rachel Hall is an Associate Professor of Communication and Rhetorical Studies at Syracuse University. She is the author of *The Transparent Traveler: The Performance and Culture of Airport Security* (Duke 2015) and *Wanted: The Outlaw in American Visual Culture* (Virginia 2009). Hall is currently working on a new book entitled *The Future Comes Home: Everyday Restorations of Possibility*.

Andrew Herscher is cofounder of a number of militant research collectives, including Detroit Resists and the We the People of Detroit Community Research Collective, and is Associate Professor at the University of Michigan. His publications include *Violence Taking Place: The Architecture of the Kosovo Conflict* (Stanford 2010), *The Unreal Estate Guide to Detroit* (Michigan 2012), and *Displacements: Architecture and Refugee* (Sternberg 2017).

Max Hirsh is a Professor at the University of Hong Kong and a leading expert on airports and urban infrastructure. He is the author of *Airport Urbanism: Infrastructure and Mobility in Asia* (Minnesota 2016).

Contributors

Danny Hoffman is Professor of Anthropology at the University of Washington. He is the author of two books on West Africa's Mano River region, *The War Machines: Young Men and Violence in Sierra Leone and Liberia* (Duke 2011) and *Monrovia Modern: Urban Form and Political Imagination in Liberia* (Duke 2017).

Min Kyung Lee is an Assistant Professor in the Growth and Structure of Cities Program at Bryn Mawr College. Her research concerns histories of mapping modern cities and social theories of architectural practices.

Veljko Armano Linta is the lead architect at Armano Linta studio, Zagreb, Croatia. He studied in Norway (United World College), USA (Middlebury College) and graduated as M. Arch in 2009 at the Faculty of Architecture in Zagreb and is a Gaia Education certified trainer for sustainable design and communities.

Laura McLauchlan teaches Environmental Justice with the Environmental Humanities program at the University of New South Wales and Eco-criticism at NYU Sydney. Her research interests are centered around urban multispecies ethnography, feminist materialist approaches to key issues of sustainability of practices of environmental activism and questions of radical kindness.

Joshua Neves is an Assistant Professor of Film Studies at Concordia University, and is the Director of the Global Emergent Media (GEM) Lab. His monograph, *Underglobalization: Beijing's Media Urbanism and the Chimera of Legitimacy* is forthcoming with Duke University Press (2020). He is the co-editor, with Bhaskar Sarkar, of *Asian Video Cultures: In the Penumbra of the Global* (Duke 2017).

Anoma Pieris is a Professor at the Faculty of Architecture Building and Planning. Her publications include, *Architecture and Nationalism in Sri Lanka: The Trouser under the Cloth* (Routledge 2012); *Assembling the Centre: Architecture for Indigenous Cultures: Australia and Beyond* (Routledge 2014) with Janet McGaw and *Architecture on the Borderline: Boundary Politics and Built Space* (forthcoming, Routledge, Architext 2019).

Karen Piper is the author of *The Price of Thirst* (Minnesota 2014), *Left in the Dust* (Palgrave 2006), and *Cartographic Fictions* (Rutgers 2002). She has also published a memoir entitled *A Girl's Guide to Missiles* (Viking Penguin 2018). She currently teaches at the University of Missouri.

Sarah Robinson is an architect practicing in San Francisco and Italy. She holds degrees in philosophy with honors from the University of Wisconsin-Madison and University of Fribourg in Switzerland and an M.Arch from Taliesin, the Frank Lloyd Wright School of Architecture, where she served as the founding president of the Board of Trustees. She has written *Nesting: Body, Dwelling, Mind in Architecture: Neuroscience, Embodiment and the Future of Design*, with Juhani Pallasmaa, in addition to numerous literary and critical essays. She cofounded and edits the journal *Intertwining* and teaches in the NAAD program at IUAV in Venice.

Abby Smith Rumsey is a historian of ideas focusing on the creation, preservation, and use of the cultural record in all media. Her latest book is *When We Are No More: How Digital Memory Is Shaping Our Future* (Bloomsbury 2016). She holds a BA from Radcliffe College and MA and PhD degrees in history from Harvard University. She has been a Fulbright Fellow and taught at Harvard and Johns Hopkins Universities.

Contributors

Saskia Sassen is the Robert S. Lynd Professor of Sociology at Columbia University and a Member of its Committee on Global Thought, which she chaired till 2015. She is the author of eight books and the editor or co-editor of three books. Her two most recent books are *Expulsions: Brutality and Complexity in the Global Economy* (Harvard/Belknap 2014), and *Ungoverned Territories?* (Harvard 2018).

Eric Sauda is a registered architect who specializes in the use of digital and computational technologies and their transformative effect on architecture. He is Director of the Digital Arts Center at the College of Arts and Architecture at the University of North Carolina at Charlotte. His research has focused on the areas of urban visualization and interactive architecture. He works closely with the Urban Visualization Research Group, the Charlotte Visualization Center at the College of Computing and Informatics, the ComputingInPlace Research Group and the Vice Chancellor for Information Technology.

Arijit Sen is an architect and historian who writes, teaches, and studies urban cultural landscapes. He directs the Buildings-Landscapes-Cultures field school, a national award winning participatory action-research project that explores history and heritage of local neighborhoods in Milwaukee. He has co-edited *Landscapes of Mobility: Culture, Politics and Placemaking* (Ashgate 2013); and *Making Place: Space and Embodiment in the City* (Indiana 2013).

Rohan Shivkumar is a Mumbai-based architect and filmmaker. He is currently the Dean of Research and Academic Development at the Kamla Raheja Vidyanidhi Institute of Architecture and Environmental Studies. His work ranges from architectural projects, academia, urban research, and advocacy, along with film-related projects including multidisciplinary explorations into the overlaps between art, cinema, and architecture. He also curates films for various forums in the city.

AbdouMaliq Simone is an urbanist with particular interest in emerging forms of collective life across cities of the so-called Global South. Simone is presently Senior Professorial Fellow, the Urban Institute, University of Sheffield , Visiting Professor of Sociology, Goldsmiths College, University of London and Visiting Professor of Urban Studies at the African Centre for Cities, University of Cape Town. His most recent book is *Improvised Lives: Rhythms of Endurance in an Urban South* (Polity 2018).

Despina Stratigakos is an architectural historian and Vice Provost for Inclusive Excellence at the University at Buffalo. She is the author of three books that explore the intersections of power and architecture. Her most recent book, *Where Are the Women Architects?* (Princeton 2016), confronts the challenges women face in the architectural profession.

Dorothy Tang is an adjunct assistant professor of landscape architecture at the University of Hong Kong and a doctoral candidate at MIT's Department of Urban Studies and Planning. Her practice and research explores the intersections of infrastructure and everyday life, especially communities confronting large-scale landscape and environmental change.

T. F. Tierney is an Associate Professor of Architecture and Chair of the Urbanism + Theory Program at the University of Illinois, Urbana Champaign. In addition to teaching, Tierney directs URL: Urban Research Lab. Her recent publications include *Intelligent Infrastructure* (Virginia 2017) and *The Public Space of Social Media* (Routledge 2013), which was a finalist for the Jane Jacobs Urban Communication Award.

Contributors

Aron Vinegar is Professor of Art History in the Department of Philosophy, Classics, History of Art and Ideas (IFIKK) at the University of Oslo, Norway. His publications include *I AM A MONUMENT: On Learning from Las Vegas* (MIT Press 2008); *Heidegger and the Work of Art History* (co-edited) (Ashgate 2014). He is currently completing a book entitled *Subject Matter: On the Art, Architecture, and Aesthetics of Habit.*

Jeremy White is an architect and a game designer, and a lecturer in the Department of History of Art and Architecture at the University of California, Santa Barbara. He is the co-editor of *City Halls and Civic Materialism: Towards a Global History of Urban Public Space* (Routledge 2014).

Mechtild Widrich teaches in the Art History, Theory and Criticism Department at the School of the Art Institute of Chicago. She is the author of *Performative Monuments: The Rematerialisation of Public Art* (Manchester 2014). Her research focuses on the intersection of art and architecture, on performance art, and on global art geographies.

Craig L. Wilkins, architect, author, and activist, serves on the University of Michigan Taubman College of Architecture and Urban Planning faculty. A 2017 Smithsonian Cooper-Hewitt Museum National Design Award winner and Hip Hop architectural theorist, he is the director of the Wilkins project, a creative practice that includes both written and built work.

Acknowledgments

This book has been four years in the making. We thank the contributors for their willingness to collaborate on this project and for their patience. Thanks to the editors at Routledge for entrusting us with this project and to the editorial assistants for shepherding the volume through its various stages. And if it were not for Mallorie Chase helping with the last push in bringing this volume together, it might not have seen the light of day. Thanks Mallorie.

1

Introduction
Contemporary Architecture, Crisis, and Critique

Swati Chattopadhyay and Jeremy White

Premise

The term "contemporary" has become a common parlance in architecture, and in many respects, seems to have supplanted the terms modern and postmodern. Yet there is no agreement on what the term means. Mimicking the discourse on contemporary art, some scholars use it to invoke post-WWII architecture, which then becomes a surrogate for mid-century modernism and the backlash of postmodernism. Or, it extends the modern into the present moment, implicitly asserting fundamental continuity. For others, the substitution of contemporary for modern simply implies jettisoning the ideology of twentieth-century -isms and their grand narratives. Some critics use it to represent the fashionable trends in current-day architecture—dynamic building forms with luminous skins that defy the imagination of the organic—with some scattered references to sustainability, new materials, and digital media. No critical unraveling of the term takes place; its apparent self-evidence becomes tautological. The widespread yet inconsistent use of the term, however, suggests a need for critical examination.

Most of the books published in the last two decades on contemporary architecture are architect-centric lavishly illustrated volumes—architectural monographs or compilations of works by various architects.[1] The only volume that attempts an historical perspective, *A Critical History of Contemporary Architecture, 1960–2010* (2014), edited by Elie G. Haddad and David Rifkind, is a collection of essays that portray the plurality of modernisms around the world since 1959. It makes no attempt to interrogate the notion of the contemporary and contains none of the issues that pertain to the digital revolution or multiple global crises that concern this volume.

In this book, we convene a wide array of critical voices from architecture, art history, urbanism, geography, media studies, bio-engineering, environmental studies, and sociology to help us understand the meaning and significance of contemporary architecture, that is, architecture of the twenty-first century. By "architecture" we mean the full range of built environments from the scale of the building component to the scale of the city and landscape. It allows for "real" and "virtual" spaces and habitations, and is global in its scope. It also allows for everyday spaces as well as the exceptional, encompassing more than mere art-architecture. The other term, "contemporary," is more problematic.

What is the "contemporary" in contemporary architecture? Is it merely a temporal signifier? Since the early twentieth century, the term has referred to the architecture of the writer's present day: the Russian Constructivists described their architecture as contemporary, their "now" inaugurated by the Bolshevik Revolution. They were not alone. The art-minded writers and architects in the 1930s and 1940s, were keen to give expression to the present day, asserting a modernist architecture that had its roots in Europe between the two world wars. This deliberate emphasis on the present marked a conceptual and spatial break with the past, although the preference for European source material was hardly new.

Nearly a century has gone by since the formulation of a modernist architectural ontology, disseminated across the globe via colonial and imperialist power relationships. It seems appropriate, given the temporal distance, to pose what may seem like the implicit if simplistic question: Is the modern of the twentieth century the modern of the twenty-first? Today, as architectural historians in the West are busy bringing the entire repertoire of practices since WWII under the rubric of "contemporary" (Haddad and Rifkind 2014), architects and architectural critics in China insist on describing their cutting-edge contemporary architecture as "modern" architecture (Ding 2014). To allow for a repertoire of divergent modernisms was at odds with the universalizing manifestoes of the early and mid-twentieth century. This alone, if we take a narrow stylistic approach, would seem to give credence to a new descriptor. We do not, however, propose one all-encompassing contemporary that has somehow replaced twentieth-century modernism. The many fissures and inconsistencies in posing a pan-contemporary make it as unsuitable as insisting upon a consistent and persistent notion of modern.

If we turn to the philosophers, we encounter a more nuanced understanding of the "nowness" of the contemporary. For them, contemporariness as a temporal concept is more concerned with the "untimely" rather than timeliness. In "What Is the Contemporary," Georgio Agamben describes contemporariness as a "singular relationship with one's own time, which adheres to it and at the same time, keeps a distance from it" (Agamben 2009: 41). This kind of temporality, defined by anachronism and disjuncture, suggests a way of seeing that extends beyond architecture and yet informs it: "The contemporary is the one who is struck by the darkness that comes from his own time" (Agamben 2009: 45). If we take Agamben's cue that to understand the contemporary we need to confront the beam of darkness that emanates from an epoch and attend to its obscurity, a useful starting point may be the many crises of the present century that are constitutive of how we build and inhabit the architectural landscape of today and sets the parameters for how we think about what is built.

Thus far, the twenty-first seems a century of anxieties. Besides 9/11 and the prolonged state response to it, this anxiety has been deepened by a financial crisis, a housing crisis, a ballot-box crisis, an environmental crisis, a food security crisis, not to mention the crisis of the Westphalian state whose sovereignty is increasingly adumbrated by multinational corporations and non-state actors: migrants, immigrants, guest workers, and aliens. Wars in Afghanistan, Iraq, Syria, Yemen, heightened racism and ethnic cleansing, and border wars in a dozen states continue unabated. Assassination by drone, that long arm of the state extending well beyond national borders, constitutes a new type of warfare. This technological revolution of the twenty-first century is fired by the digital age. It has not just revolutionized warfare but everyday life at its core. State surveillance of its own citizens alternates with corporate surveillance of the consumer public, challenging the conception of civil rights and democracy. The prospect of living in privately managed smart cities fundamentally alters notions of public space by blurring what was once the finely articulated line of privacy. Digital communication has opened up wonderful opportunities for forming new communities and accelerating development of new construction technologies. It has, however, also fragmented communities and communications between proximate groups.

Instead of treating these crises and revolutions as incidental, outside, or merely incentives or departure points for architectural form-making, we ask: How can we see these crises as informing and contributing to architecture in the twenty-first century? How might the practice of architecture and architectural history and urbanism responsibly engage with these crises?

When we think of architecture in the broadest sense—all of the built environment and spatial practice—connections between larger crises and architectural production become clear. For example, the financial crisis of 2008 was part of the housing crisis in the U.S. and was implicated in a global real-estate crisis; global climate change casts a shadow over the growing reliance on concrete as a building material because concrete manufacturing produces 10 percent of the world's carbon dioxide that aggravates the green-house effect on the planet. The recent flurry of tall construction in Asia and the Middle East—often claiming to be energy-efficient—has been accomplished in large measure by the design work of American and European architecture and engineering teams who crisscross the globe in vehicles burning jet fuel, one of the most notorious contributors to climate change.

Or let us take the example of the digital revolution that has fundamentally transformed the way we communicate, imagine, and represent our ideas of architecture and design. Building information modeling (BIM) is supplanting computer-aided design (CAD) and focus seems fixed on the digital as a technology, but it also is an environment, one scarcely imagined by modernist and even postmodernist thinkers of the previous century. The digital environment has spawned its own calculus of aggregates: it absorbs labor hours in the billions and even operates as a surrogate habitation for millions around the globe. As economist Edward Castronova argued over ten years ago in *Exodus to the Virtual World* (2008), the virtual realm of gaming and social media shapes the way we conceive of the real world. Given that designing for the virtual world has become as compelling as for the real world, questions arise anew about what constitutes architecture. Perhaps it is not a specious question in the contemporary world to ask an architect, what is your avatar? The significance of architecture and the materiality of space that shape social practice is not only fundamentally different today than it was three decades ago, this significance registers differently in various parts of the globe. It is also important to understand the points of view of different constituencies as well as different disciplines: it is a dizzying puzzle.

This book is not a solution to the puzzle. No single book could be. Instead, we present essays from disparate academic disciplines, each representing the voice of a scholar who has given some thought to a piece of the puzzle that has intrigued them in some way. Only some of these writers have made an academic career in architecture, many hail from other scholarly disciplines, thus lending this volume a variety of approaches that we hope will stimulate the conversation if not complicate the puzzle.

Plan of the Book

In response to the confusion caused by the term contemporary, this volume addresses the paucity of studies that bring social, economic, technological, and environmental concerns to understand architecture in the twenty-first century. Here we look to different disciplines to aid our approach by providing multiple perspectives on the subject. However, our goal is not to codify contemporary architecture. We aim to provide the grounds for critique. Despite the breadth of disciplinary perspectives and the historical and global sense we bring to this project, this is not an encyclopedia of contemporary architecture. A comprehensive account of contemporary architecture, even if it were possible, is beyond the scope of this volume. Instead we asked our contributors to focus on what distinguishes this epoch and its architecture and spatial practice from their disciplinary point of view. Aimed primarily at undergraduate students, and secondarily at graduate students and faculty, we expect the book's approach to be instructive in terms of method. We hope the volume will urge students—would-be architects, designers, historians, and preservationists—to rethink how the larger world of socio-politics and habitation is related to form-making. The essays in this volume, we hope, will help them question their assumptions about the contemporaneity of architecture in the twenty-first century, and recognize there are histories of their contemporary. Some of these are too stark to ignore: camps confining immigrants and ethnic minorities along the U.S.–Mexico border in 2018 repeat the dreadful legacy of the twentieth century. Camps as the nomos of twentieth-century modernity also defines their contemporary (Agamben 1998).

The book is organized in six parts—Design, Materiality, Alterity, Technologies, Cityscapes, Practice—although many of the essays cross-cut this parcelization. The rubrics stand for the key concerns expressed in the essays. Under Part I: Design, five authors offer divergent understandings of what constitutes design in the twenty-first century. Alice Friedman's and Rachel Hall's essays concern issues of privacy, publicness, and security. Friedman investigates how the changing notions of privacy and domesticity have cast an impress on residential design in the U.S., examining recent designs that tackle efforts by queer and unconventional clients to resist public voyeurism. Hall's essay analyzes design strategies that attempt to mitigate "risk" in school building design in the face of gun violence. The design features "embedded security" that "nests the cultural refusal to enact gun control within nostalgic design tropes," alluding to a past when schools were considered relatively safe spaces. Hall's critique of such design strategies echoes Andrew Herscher's concerns about the claims of humanitarian architecture and how housing for refugees has produced a new politics of global segregation. The essay by Max Hirsh and Dorothy Tang on the transformational dynamics of a peri-urban region in the Pearl River Delta in China conveys successful strategies of informal production of space in the wake of the failure of the planned university town to provide adequate facilities for the student population. Mechtild Widrich revisits the idea of the counter-monument to show how recent designs to memorialize lost lives in war and mass murders address the complex terrain of viewership in a multi-media world that memorials encounter in the present. In analyzing the design decisions made by architects, these essays pay particular attention to the use of construction materials and the materiality of privacy, violence, displacement, refuge, and loss. The next section extends this discussion to a larger set of concerns about the materiality of architecture.

In Part II: Materiality, Abby Smith Rumsey asks what is the function and materiality of memory in the present as we cross the digital divide into a supposedly "immaterial" realm of digital networks. The "immaterial" domain is after all carefully grounded in the imposing materiality of a new building type: the server plant. Humans are scarce in this new building type. As architects learn to design new knowledge environments they also encounter the changing parameters of the body that is fundamental to architecture. Jeremy White's essay in this section argues that there is very little that is self-evident in the idea of body as it relates to architecture and explains the shifts from the idea of a universal body of the modernists to the idea of universal access by rethinking the relation between the boundaries of bodies and space in real and virtual environments. The boundaries between the body and the environment is also the subject of Sarah Robinson's essay where using the findings of neuroscience she explores the role of design to engage human empathy. Aron Vinegar's essay in this section raises a different set of questions about the body by challenging the idea of habit, habitus, and habitation as these have been traditionally understood in architectural and social theory. His essay counters the idea of "flows" that permeates the discourse on contemporary architecture and space. The recalcitrance that Vinegar discusses with respect to the body extending into the environment shows up with a different urgency in Heather Davis's essay on the role of plastic—its "pervasiveness, banality, and longevity"—and the imagination of ecology, duration, and finitude that ensues from our encounter with this recalcitrant matter. Swati Chattopadhyay's essay critiques the idea of permanence that afflicts architecture and suggests we rethink the idea of duration in reimagining how the built fabric is put together.

The concern over agency and identity that pervades the essays in the first two parts of the book is brought front and center under Part III: Alterity. Borders, edges, duration, permanence, recalcitrance, memorial, informality, and urban infills here appear in other forms. In Danny Hoffman's essay material recalcitrance appears as a defense building that "resists" reclamation and new fantasies of urban incorporation. The Brutalist architecture of the mid-twentieth century as a detritus of modernism here becomes a different site for thinking about architecture, violence, and occupation that is the subject of Anoma Pieris's meditation on the failure of the architecture profession in Sri Lanka to come to terms with the legacy of the nation's protracted civil war. Pieris wants us to think of alterity as self-scrutiny rather than as self-affirmation. Charlie Hailey, Arijit Sen and George Flaherty examine issues of mobility and (im)migration. Flaherty considers how militarized borderlands might be reconfigured as commons, and shares some concerns with Sen's essay that sees immigrant architecture as a "dramaturgical performance of emplacement" enabling immigrants to straddle multiple worlds. Hailey's essay sheds light on the contradictory formulations that support the building and containment in camps to address the enormity of human displacement—over 60 million people—in the contemporary world. The scarcity of materials and new digital technologies that define the lifeworlds of the refugees in camps, Hailey notes, is not contradictory but the mark of the contemporary.

Part IV: Technologies elaborates on many of the issues raised in the first three sections: the imagination of temporality, materiality, and built fabric when new technologies and knowledge systems are confronted by architects, developers, and planners. Daniel Abramson historicizes sustainability in the light of the long twentieth century's experimentations with obsolescence. Bringing the dominant paradigm of sustainability with planned and unplanned obsolescence is intended to help us think critically about the future of sustainable design. Karen Piper's essay on water infrastructure raises some similar concerns as she looks for possible approaches that move beyond the technocratic visions of modern and contemporary mega-water infrastructure projects. The remaining essays in this section suggest possible utilization of digital technologies to imagine intelligent designs. Christopher Beorkrem and Eric Sauda propose new models for conducting post-occupancy evaluations using new sensing and data analysis technologies. Ljiljana Fruk and Veljko Linta stage a conversation between a nanoscientist and an architect to think of the revolutionary potential of building materials and structures that may be engineered at the nano scale with biohybrid materials. T. F. Tierney explains the promise of intelligent infrastructure of cities and what constitutes networked urbanism as spaces of contestation and creativity.

Part V: Cityscapes presents six essays that explain the creative capacity of cities if they can be reimagined and reconceptualized. AbdouMaliq Simone's, Craig Wilkins's and Saskia Sassen's essays offer strategies of redescription, bringing attention to processes that remain opaque to planners and urbanists. Simone aims to engage with not what the city is, but what it can be, through a "technology of detachment" (as a prototype is detached from propriety) as a mode of "constant unsettling." Wilkins argues against a "zero-sum" functionalist model of cities to consider possibilities of a new aesthetics arising out of community creativity. Sassen sees in the new formations of bottom-up informal politics in cities across the globe the creative potential of the powerless for hacking power, and advocates an "open-source urbanism." Joshua Neves, Iain Borden, and Laura McLauchlan argue for viewing cities differently—as spaces mediated by televisuality, new time–space rhythms, and beyond the human-centric perspective to incorporate the non-human animal world as shared occupants. Neves shifts the attention to models of urban visuality beyond the Euro-American city, invoking the concept of "media urbanism." Both Borden and McLauchlan bring attention to the ethics of city experience, forcing us to think of our responsibility as citizens, critics, and designers.

The last part, Part VI: Practice, returns to the designs and designers and to the profession of architecture. The profession, many would argue, is in an acute state of crisis—it has little to say in what gets built, has little political impact, and is upstaged by new financial, political, and technological instruments (Deamer et al. 2016). Some problems are old and persistent. As Despina Stratigakos notes, the gender inequity in the architecture profession remains embarrassing. Architecture schools and educators are complicit in this, she argues. And it is not the only thing that architecture schools are helping perpetuate. Both Rohan Shivkumar's and Arindam Dutta's essays point out that architecture schools and faculties aid the profession in producing their own irrelevance and obsolescence. Jeremy White's essay on starchitects traces the history of the obscurationist tendency in celebrity architecture, while Dutta explains the problem from the perspective of global real-estate investment in which the fiction of design follows financial speculation. Shivkumar's placement of architecture exhibitions in India against the backdrop of the loss of nationalist/modernist privilege demonstrates a hollowing out of responsibility among practicing architects and educators. The social project of architecture has been in crises for a while and now has to be rescued by a handful of practitioners who try to imagine a new way of practicing. Essays by Kenny Cupers as well as Sony Devabhaktuni and Min Kyung Lee suggest new ways of negotiating this crisis through community-based participatory design and collaborative work respectively.

We intentionally begin with questions about design and conclude with the designers by bookending the collection with Design and Practice. There has been no effort here to portray the celebrated works of contemporary architecture or laud the great practitioners. The contributors instead have assumed a critical stance to speak to the urgency of the now. We want our readers to rethink what architects do, how are they trained, who are they trained by, and with whom. Indeed, what is the role of architecture and design in contemporary society? What could and should be architecture's task? Themes of "duration," "edges/borders," "violence," "unsettling," "infrastructure," and thinking beyond Anthropocentrism (and the Anthropocene) shift emphasis off the architect to the inhabitor. These themes are the findings, so called, of our collective deliberation on the crisis of our contemporary.

In this collection of stories there are sites and subjects from across the globe—ghost towns and informal urbanization in China, immigrant architecture in Chicago, besieged rivers in India, and hedgehogs in Bristol—negotiating and subjected to hardware and software, examples that we hope will provide students of architecture and (would-be) architects much material for thought. Despite the breadth of this collective deliberation, we have made no attempt to be representative. There are many other sites that could perhaps provide additional fodder or counter-arguments, and if this collection in any way helps generate those counter-arguments we would consider our goal accomplished.

Note

1 These include G. de Bure, *Talk about Contemporary Architecture* (2009), the collation of manifestoes in C. Jencks and K. Kropf (eds) *Theories and Manifestoes of Contemporary Architecture* (1997), excerpts from the writings of architects as in G. Wingårdh and R. Wærn, *Crucial Words* (2007), lectures by designers

such as in N. Spiller and P. Cook (eds) *The Lowe Lectures: Paradox of Contemporary Architecture* (2001), or reflections on modern and contemporary architectural imagination and utopias such as N. Spiller, *Visionary Architecture* (2007).

References

Agamben, G. (1998) *Homo Sacer*, D. Heller-Roazen trans., Palo Alto: Stanford University Press.

Agamben, G. (2009) *What Is an Apparatus and Other Essays*, trans. David Kishik and Stefan Pedatella, Palo Alto: Stanford University Press.

Castronova, E. (2008) *Exodus to the Virtual World: How Online Fun Is Changing Reality*, New York: Palgrave Macmillan.

Deamer, P., Cayer, A., Korsh, S., Peterson, E., and Shvartzberg, M. (2016) *Asymmetric Labor: The Economy of Architecture in Theory and Practice*, New York: The Architecture Lobby.

Ding, G. (2014) "'Experimental Architecture' in China," *Journal of the Society of Architectural Historians* 73, 1: 28–37.

Haddad, E. and Rifkind, D. (eds) (2014) *A Critical History of Contemporary Architecture, 1960–2010*, New York: Routledge.

Jencks, C. and Kropf, K. (eds) (1997) *Theories and Manifestoes of Contemporary Architecture*, London: Thames and Hudson.

Spiller, N. (2007) *Visionary Architecture: Blueprints of the Modern Imagination*, London: Thames and Hudson.

Spiller, N. and Cook, P. (2001) *The Lowe Lectures: Paradox of Contemporary Architecture*, Chichester, West Sussex: John Wiley.

Wingårdh, G. and Wærn, R. (2007) *Crucial Words: Conditions for Contemporary Architecture*, Basel: Birkhäuser Verlag AG.

Part I
Design

2
Public Face and Private Space in the Design of Contemporary Houses

Alice T. Friedman

Introduction: Architecture and Domestic Privacy in a "Hyperpublic" World

Following the convention established by the Roman architect Vitruvius and elaborated by European theorists from the Renaissance until the advent of Modernism, it is customary to trace the origins of architecture back to the so-called "primitive hut," represented as a post and beam, gabled structure. As shown in the well-known frontispiece to Marc-Antoine [Père] Laugier's *Essai sur l'architecture* (1755) (Figure 2.1), the image was intended to illustrate the origin of the classical Orders and to serve as a short-hand statement about architecture's essential function as shelter and its capacity to put a roof over our heads. With these theoretical constructs at its core, the history of architecture in Europe and the U.S. over the last three centuries might well be described as an extended engagement with the challenges presented by the structural frame, the floor plane, and the roof (e.g., in well-known examples such as the detached columns of the Neoclassical Panthéon in Paris, the steel skeleton of the American skyscraper, or Le Corbusier's Maison Dom-ino) accompanied by the increasing lightness, transparency, and virtual elimination of the load-bearing wall. In this narrative, the significance of the wall's role as boundary, screen, or filter, whether in domestic, institutional, or religious typologies, was largely framed as a side bar of cultural, rather than architectural, significance—that is, as an element of program rather than form.

As designers of Modern houses in the 1920s, architects such as Le Corbusier and Mies van der Rohe celebrated the advent of the transparent glass wall and the open plan not only as key elements in mass-produced housing, but also as essential ingredients in the modern liberation of the individual citizen in the industrialized world, a citizen who was tacitly assumed to be European, white, and heterosexual. This man was imagined as the head of a family unit whose private leisure and personal comfort were the corollaries of their public labor as workers in the well-run state. According to the Modernist schema, bourgeois notions of individual privacy and the concomitant design elements in single-family houses that facilitated them, such as thresholds, lobbies, halls, or other devices for screening and separating public from private or servant from served spaces, would become obsolete (Perrot 1990; Bryson 2010). As Le Corbusier explained at the conclusion of *Vers une architecture* (1923), the challenge for modern policymakers came down to a choice between "Architecture or Revolution": the promise of available

Alice T. Friedman

Figure 2.1 Marc-Antoine Laugier: *Essai sur l'architecture*, Paris: N.B. Duchesne, 1755
Source: Frontispiece.

housing, improved hygiene, and a universal, machine-like response to the demands of everyday life were what gave meaning and value to the "machine à habiter" (McLeod 1983 and 1985; Frampton 2001: Chaps. 7 and 8). Standard type forms, regularization of household and daily life, and the use of industrial materials like concrete and plate glass would usher in a new physical and social transparency.

Such notions, together with prevailing heteronormativity and gender bias among members of the professional classes and in the artistic circles to which these architects belonged, contributed to the valorization of conventional planning and typology, and to a virtual silence about Modern architecture's capacity—or obligation—to accommodate social and cultural difference. Despite the evident lessons of Le Corbusier's own custom-designed and highly individualized studios and houses of the 1920s, including the Villa La Roche (for a gay art collector) and Stein-de Monzie (for a married American couple in late middle age, their best friend, and her grown daughter), Modern housing became, in theory and often in practice, synonymous with standardization, both socio-political and formal (Friedman 1998: Chap. 3). Modern domestic architecture was offered as a universal and placeless solution, with easily constructed skeletal structures, thin glass or stucco walls, and horizontally stacked planes that left their stark interiors open to examination by passersby.

Although these narratives and the values that underlay them proved to be remarkably durable within the culture of architecture, they have been eroding over the past 30 years. Three major shifts in contemporary culture underlie these changes: (1) shifting demographics of the family and the increasing prevalence of single-person households, particularly in cities; (2) the feminist and queer liberation movements and the legitimization (in Europe and America especially) of gay and lesbian voices in architecture; and (3) the revolution in digital technology and communication that has profoundly altered not only online communication, but also the status of the home, the individual, and of the boundaries between public and private space (Wacks 2015). Conversations about privacy, and thus about the shape and status of the boundary wall and the partition in contemporary architecture, appear to have supplanted the preoccupation with transparency and social engineering at the center of architectural discourse (Colomina 2009; 2011; Ockman 2009: 49 and 51).

Fears about government and work-place surveillance, wide-spread hacking of email, bank accounts, and credit cards, and increasing anxiety about the status and meaning of public information on social media like Facebook and Instagram have also contributed to these developments. Rising anxiety about identity theft and the status of public reputation have forced both clients and architects to respond with an increasing focus on the wall, the screen, and the interior. Celebrity culture and the creation of a fast-moving "hyperpublic" digital realm—here, as elsewhere, a "new world" that is described in spatial and architectural metaphors—of texts, images, and sounds underscore the need for new perspectives on the function and status of boundaries, thresholds, closets, and private space in general. Though concerns about privacy and surveillance have been under discussion since the Cold War and the introduction of "Big Brother" in George Orwell's *1984* (published in 1949), there is a new urgency in regard to these issues in twenty-first-century architectural design and planning. Moreover, changes in the core questions asked by architectural historians and critics, particularly in the area of domestic architecture, suggest a profound realignment of values and priorities (Heynen and Baydar 2005).

The new architectural historiography of the past two decades has yielded both significant critical concepts and new historical information. Placing clients and their programmatic requirements at the center of the narrative and analytical stage changes the way in which decision-making is understood: design planning is now widely analyzed as a series of trade-offs between formal or conceptual concerns on the one hand and real-world challenges (habits of living, gender, sexual orientation, household structure, engagement with community, social acceptance or exclusion, economic constraints, and environmental concerns) on the other (Sanders 1996). As a result, studies of the architectures of both past and present have become both more complex and also more narrowly specific: engagement with and analysis of place, region, and individual conditions of identity and beliefs have largely supplanted notions of universality and uniformity at the heart of contemporary design, encouraging a more flexible and responsive architecture, whether in new construction or in renovation/retrofit.

Indeed, recent historical research has shed new light on the contradictions inherent both in mid-century Modern architecture and in broadly accepted notions of domestic privacy, contradictions that contain lessons for contemporary architects (Friedman 1998: Chap. 4). For example, the well-known pairing of two of the best known Modernist sites in the United States—Philip Johnson's Glass House/Brick House complex in New Canaan, CT of 1945–1948/1953 (Figure 2.2) and Mies van der Rohe's Farnsworth House in Plano, Illinois of 1945–1951—yields a far more complex picture of the American domesticities when viewed from a queer or feminist perspective. Cast in this new light, Johnson's New Canaan complex can be read as an artfully composed architectural essay about the conflicts between Modernist theory, understood as a utopian ideal of universal form and social engineering, and the particularities of social/cultural values and client-centered conditions that shape real-world projects. These include the relationship between privacy and spectacle, transparency and opacity, and the coherence of inside and

Alice T. Friedman

Figure 2.2 Philip Johnson, The Glass House and Brick Guest House, New Canaan, CT, 1949
Source: Copyright Alice T. Friedman.

outside, both in the built environment and in the social realm—public face and private space. By pairing a house of glass in which the activities of daily life can be viewed by casual observers (in theory if not in practice: the New Canaan estate is in fact secluded behind stone walls in what was then a rural town) with a house of brick that completely encloses its interior in a mute and uninflected wall, Johnson offered a starting point for a conversation not only about the limits of form and materials, but about the sorts of differences in private life (notably of gender identity and sexual orientation) that lay behind the boundary walls of his estate.

Johnson's architectural ruminations should also be recognized as a pointed and somewhat mischievous response to Mies's Farnsworth House, a house that had recently been featured in an exhibition at the Museum of Modern Art (where Johnson was the Curator of Architecture) and was widely regarded as Mies's masterwork, the crowning achievement of the Modernist project. Given that the client, a prominent Chicago-based woman doctor, would later describe the house as an "x-ray" in which she felt exposed—and in a period in which female sexuality was barely acknowledged, it is telling that she focused on the shameful fact that her garbage pail would be visible to outsiders—Johnson's New Canaan essay represented a very prescient interrogation of the mid-century social and cultural conventions on which Modernism's formal language was predicated.

In the Brick House, where the interior is cut off both structurally and stylistically from the exterior, the limits of professional/architectural and personal deviance are explored through a coded language of architectural forms and historical references. One enters the house directly into the bedroom (created in the 1953 renovation), a fantasy stage set ringed all around by tall, white, "Moorish" arches and moveable panels of luxurious, pink and gold Fortuny silk. The low bed and round ottomans are covered in soft woolen fabric and a rheostat (a new technology at the time) allowed the user to dim the lighting system for maximum theatrical effect. Floating ceiling vaults and indirect lighting complete the mise-en-scène. Unlike the Glass House, the Brick House contravenes both Modernism's rules and American social norms.

This brilliant "camp" interior thus makes a strong statement: it not only encodes messages about feminized gay sexuality that were well understood by informed observers, but also offended the Modernist orthodoxies of the time by deploying multiple design heresies, including atectonic, non-structural, arches, surface ornamentation (in pink and gold no less), and historical quotations. Given that the rules of "International Style" Modernism design had been codified by Johnson himself in the 1932 "Modern Architecture" exhibition at MoMA, it is clear that the New Canaan complex contained particularly significant provocations, yet these remained largely unexplored until feminist and queer studies legitimated the sort of client-centered and archival research that decoded the extended meanings of Johnson's paired houses (Hitchcock and Johnson 1997).

Similar initiatives in interdisciplinary, critical analysis of the history of the built environment have been advanced elsewhere, notably in Renaissance Studies (e.g., Musacchio 2009), but the most profound implications for the practice of contemporary architecture are contained in new perspectives on twentieth-century building types and ideologies (Lasner 2012; Abramson 2016). For example, recent examinations of the use and history of industrial materials, notably glass, have opened new fissures in the Modernist narrative. Among the most provocative of these is an essay by architectural historian Joan Ockman, entitled "A Crystal World: Between Reason and Spectacle" which explores the contradictions between the Modernist valorization of transparency and the harsh political realities of the twentieth century (Ockman 2009). In her study, Ockman cites comments by Walter Benjamin from an early essay on "Surrealism" (1929) which follow the broadly accepted equation between morality and Modernist transparency; she then goes on to examine the postwar response offered by the philosopher Ernest Bloch in 1959: "In another metaphor extension," Ockman explains,

> the transparent environment was seen [by Benjamin and many of his avant-garde contemporaries] as a necessary training ground for life in a modern society predicated on the enlightened values of democracy, openness, egalitarianism, and freedom. As Walter Benjamin put it in the late 1920s in his essay "Surrealism": "to live in a glass house is a revolutionary virtue par excellence. It is also an intoxication, a moral exhibitionism that we badly need."
>
> *(Ockman 2009: 51)*

Ockman then quotes Bloch's more worldly, and chilling, response to this fantasy: "the wide window filled with a noisy outside world needs an outside filled with attractive strangers, not full of Nazis; the glass door down to the floor really presupposes sunshine … not the Gestapo" (Bloch 1988: 187). This sort of critical investigation clearly opens up questions about surveillance, violence, and political power that have been largely suppressed by the broad acceptance of Modernist orthodoxies (Colomina 2009; Martin 2009).

Architects, designers, and curators have been exploring these challenges through the language of built form for two decades. In 1999, an exhibition entitled "The Unprivate House" brought together a number of projects that focused on walls, partitions, and screens in a world of newly popular digital technologies for time-based recording, image projection, and information retrieval (Riley 1999). Among the most provocative of these were Shigeru Ban's "Curtain Wall House" (Tokyo, 1997) and Rem Koolhaas's "Maison à Bordeaux" (1998), both of which confronted Modernist orthodoxies head on. In his sardonic Tokyo project, Ban threw down the gauntlet by enclosing the principal façades of an urban house with a two-story canvas curtain that can literally be drawn shut or left open to expose the interior living spaces (although not the bedrooms or toilets) (Riley 1999: 72–75). In Koolhaas's house, the hierarchies of interior and exterior zones, fixed and flexible spaces, and the status of the floor planes are completely reordered and called into question: designed for a family in which the father uses a wheelchair, the house is sunken into the ground and consists of a perforated cast-concrete upper level for private use, a glazed lower level for family use, and a triple-height glass atrium on the interior with a "floor" that can move up and down to traverse the entire vertical section of the space: it is in fact an over-sized elevator platform (Riley 1999: 92–95) that stops on each level of the house. Spatial flexibility, complexities of program, and the diverse bodily experiences of users are clearly engaged in this way, casting further doubt on the status of Modernism's "everyman" subject.

Another project in the MoMA exhibition raises more profound questions: in Joel Sanders's unbuilt "House for a Bachelor," a 1950s, single-family tract house in Minneapolis was repurposed as a home for a single, professional man, exposing the shifts that had taken place in the social and cultural status of the "bachelor" in the period since the original residence was built (Riley 1999: 100–103; Potvin 2014). Here a sunken garden, an Astroturf exercise area, a terrarium, and an "underground spa" at the back of the house provide privacy and encode messages about gay "lifestyle" in a condition of suburban density, while a large, projection television and reflective screens on the interior create a glamorous, high-tech ambiance. These space-dividing features also enable the occupant to gain information about the public world at large from within the private sphere of the home. A "hanging wall" for digital projections permits the user to lay out his clothing and thus to "fabricate identity" before going outside.

Sanders's unbuilt project, published alongside Michael Maltzan's Hergott Shepard Residence (Beverly Hills, 1999) for a gay, professional couple, were among the first projects by well-known architects to publically engage the issues of sexuality and privacy raised by the New Canaan complex. In the sleek, modern Maltzan-designed home, interior circulation between public and private spaces, significant sight lines through glass walls, and the relationship between the house and the surrounding urban context are handled in ways that subtly shift the terms of twentieth-century domesticity. In Sanders's unbuilt project, which has come to be recognized as a turning point in the discourse, the politics of diversity and the poetics of bodily experience are explored more in a forward-looking, technologically sophisticated, architectural language (Riley 1999: 76–79).

A handful of contemporary houses, discussed in depth below, suggest some of the ways in which these core issues—privacy, sexuality, surveillance, digital technologies, high density, adaptive reuse and flexibility, changing household composition, community vs. solitude, and bodily engagement with the built and natural sensoria—have been explored within the context of the global, urbanized, hyperpublic culture of the twenty-first century. These projects all highlight the changing nature of the wall—as boundary, as scrim, as a screen for projection (in every sense) in a period of intense scrutiny and public image-making.

Urban Boundaries

At the Dirty House (Figure 2.3), two 18-foot high studios and associated living quarters on three floors were designed by David Adjaye for an artist couple, Tim Noble and Susan Webster

Public Face and Private Space in House Design

Figure 2.3 David Adjaye, Dirty House, London, England, 2002
Source: Copyright Alice T. Friedman.

(Allison 2005: 26–41). Here the inhabited, private spaces are completely concealed behind thick brown walls covered in dark, anti-graffiti paint, creating a tactile outer surface reminiscent of mud brick. High above the street, a wooden balcony protected by a cantilevered roof, painted white on the underside of the eaves, floats above the solid, dark block. Square mirror-glass windows punctuate the first floor of the exterior façade yet provide no visual access to what lies within: instead, their shiny, black surfaces, deeply recessed on the upper floor to reveal the thickness of the wall, reflect the light of the sky and street along with the graffiti-covered walls of nearby buildings, maintaining the scale and rhythm of the London street yet pushing back both the real and imaginary boundary of the home. These "windows" read as empty signifiers of conventional architectural forms (rather like the windows on Venturi's "Mother's House," 1964, a touchstone in the interrogation of Modernism) and, here as there, are drained of meaning—they are vestigial survivors of outmoded social behaviors (looking in on one's neighbors or out at the street) and urban conditions. By contrast, the entry door is hidden, set flush with the wall surface and thus camouflaged by both color and texture. These devices effectively neutralize any attempt at intrusion, surveillance, or physical penetration of the boundary between public and private, creating a mute, uninflected, and impassive display of muscle, rather like the immense and immovable form of a security guard or a mono-syllabic "bouncer" at a Soho club.

The house's now widely published exterior resulted from the conversion of an abandoned furniture warehouse in an East London neighborhood increasingly sought after by artists for live/work studio space. Adjaye's decision to conserve the irregular brick exterior wall of the original building and to demolish and rebuild everything that lay behind it reflects a contemporary tendency—one that is often brilliantly exploited in Adjaye's work—to conceive of architectural form not in terms of interior and exterior spaces created by orthogonal partition walls and floor planes creating interior voids, but instead as a series of concentric thick and thin layers separated by interstitial voids. Thus the studios and living spaces at Dirty House are illuminated by a variety of ingenious devices: by the square exterior window openings that bring bright light to the interior entrance lobby, by clerestory lighting in one studio, by skylights in the roof, and by large glass window-walls which open onto a deep wooden balcony terrace on the top floor. These theatrical lighting scenarios create a series of diverse, monumental, light-filled, and emphatically private spaces, cut off from the surrounding city.

This spatial organization and the resulting condition of interiority were described by design critic Deyan Sudjic in 2002:

> Floating on top is a white lid, seemingly poised weightless over the heavy mass of the dark cube below. It's the studio's living area, but the floor-to-ceiling glass walls are invisible from the street, set back behind a terrace and screened from view by a brick wall. It's like a glass pavilion, full of light, with impressive views over the City skyline and its burgeoning crop of new skyscrapers. From the street, it's impossible to understand the nature of the building. It's only inside that it begins to show how it works.
>
> *(Sudjic 2002)*

An equally significant intervention into the conventional notion of the boundary wall is made at Sou Fujimoto's "House N," in Oita, Japan, 2008 (Rosenfield 2015; Gregory 2009). Here the relationship between the public street and the inhabited space of the interior is mediated by a series of layered screening walls perforated by irregular openings that distort the views and create a maze-like perambulation across zones of increasing privacy. Some of these perforations are glazed and some are open, creating a series of boxes within boxes rather than a fixed line between interior and exterior. The interstitial spaces between the walls, including an open-air courtyard that can be viewed from the street, further problematize the notions of the door and the threshold, boundaries that become increasingly ambiguous as the layers of the house are explored.

Another comparative example, though located in a very different context, is Allied Works Weekend House in Dutchess County, New York of 2012. The house lies at the center of a wooded, 400-acre estate and art park commissioned by a New York-based couple, both of whom are prominent art collectors; the site was extensively modified by landscape architect Michael van Valkenburgh. As in the Dirty House and House N, what is most distinctive about the project is the handling of the glazed wall surface: here the main volumes of the house are bounded by a skin of opaque and transparent panels which enable the owners to completely enclose the interior with a series of screens on which a 360-degree video installation by Doug Aitken, entitled "Lighthouse," can be projected (Browne 2014). Composed of changing, high-color images shot in and around the estate, this installation functions not only as a privacy screen but also as a means of altering the surrounding views through the use of time-based media.

Given the vagaries of image-production in a world of social media voyeurism, "Facebook envy," and fluid identity presentation, the implications for the use of such media walls in domestic architecture are intriguing, to say the least (Williams 2013). One can easily imagine new strategies for the dissemination of a range of texts and images through projection on both interior and exterior wall surfaces. In a world of coded marketing campaigns such as Subaru's use of insider knowledge in its choice texts (references to Provincetown or to being "out," for example) and images that might be recognized by certain gay and lesbian car buyers as "winks and nudges" signaling shared values, the making of such messages would be simple, while their

Public Face and Private Space in House Design

meaning remains highly problematic. As we know from the study of targeted communication strategies, including the use of quotes and memes in what the media critic Dahna Boyd has called "self steganography" among teenagers, the possibilities for manipulating both public and private audiences are thrilling, challenging, and troubling in equal measure (Mayyasi 2016; Boyd 2011). The coded messages deployed in the language of architectural form by Philip Johnson in his mid-century projects, or the subtle ironies of Postmodern historicism pale by comparison.

Rural Privacy and Regional Landscape

Like Rick Joy's many later houses, Jax House—an early work by the then-emerging architect—orchestrates the relationship between outside and inside through a sequence of carefully sited boundary walls and window openings that draw on the regional traditions of the American southwest. While Jax House highlights characteristic poetics of tactility and sensual experience in materials, lighting, and circulation, and his deep engagement with the desert landscape, the house stands out among the architect's works because it was commissioned by a single man as a private, rustic retreat with limited access to, and by, the outside world (Figure 2.4).

The house is located in the Sonoran Desert outside Tucson, AZ. Constrained by the limited budget of the client, the project was left unfinished for a number of years before a new owner, a San Francisco art dealer, stepped forward to complete it according to his own program (Joy 2006, 2015; Pearson 2005). Three metal boxes, raised above the desert floor and clad in weathered steel plates, are scaled to provide intimate shelters in direct contact with the changing landscape and light of the desert valley. Each box houses a separate element of the stripped-down domestic program: sleeping; living/dining; and study/guest room. More reminiscent of abandoned shipping

Figure 2.4 Rick Joy, Jax House/Desert Nomad, Tucson, AZ, 2003–2005
Source: Copyright Jeff Goldberg/ESTO.

Alice T. Friedman

containers or discarded and displaced industrial detritus (though their meticulously crafted surfaces, both inside and out, are clearly evident when viewed at close range) than elements in a custom-designed home, these forms have a contingent quality. The architect compared them to "hunter's blinds," signaled by the exposed metal fasteners that anchor their steel skins. When it was first published, with its unfinished interior walls exposed and its rooms still empty, the house had the roughness of an abandoned bunker; later images give an impression of warmth, elegance, and comfort, enhanced by the maple veneer that now lines the interiors and strategically placed apertures to let in views and changing natural light. Recent photos show the owner's extensive collection of African and Pacific Island sculpture bathed in light and framed by the window openings. A separate carport is sited a short distance away.

A rectangular aperture cut out of one side of each box offers "a singular view for each primary space," as Joy explained it, and each vista highlights a different time of day, enclosing the evening view of the desert landscape and the twinkling city lights through the living room window, focusing on the dawn sunlight that illuminates a mountain hillside from the bedroom, and framing "a still life of rock outcropping a saguaro for the small den" (Joy 2002). Each box and its openings are also oriented to create maximum opportunities for privacy and reflection. Underscoring the fragility of the site and the immediacy of the experience, the boxes are connected by simple, open-air gravel paths; there is no covered walkway between the units. A small terrace, large enough for only one or two chairs, is located off the back of the den (Pallasmaa 2002). Here as elsewhere the space is scaled for privacy, quiet conversation, and reflection.

What sets Jax House apart is the focus on solitude and simplicity that permit an intense sensation of time and place in the desert landscape. This specificity of location and region clearly breaks with the conventions of Modernism. Moreover, its very contingency, particularly as originally designed, flies in the face of contemporary standards of luxury and individual comfort. Like Sanders's House for a Bachelor, or the Glass House/Guest House complex, Jax House upends conventions of household order and heteronormative ideologies of domesticity, to make alternative ways of living possible. In contrast to an earlier neighboring home, Joy's "Tucson Mountain House" (2001), which is built of traditional "rammed earth" and sited on a wide-open plateau, Jax's House/Desert Nomad eloquently expresses its program through dispersed elements, clustered in secluded hollow. Here the poetics of privacy in the Sonoran Desert landscape are expressed in a unique and profound language of form in dialogue with nature.

Privacy in the Urban Megacity

In 1997, Lari Pittman and Roy Dowell, artists and educators, purchased the 1952 Dorothy Serulnik House, a glass house with an open plan designed by the mid-twentieth-century architect Richard Neutra for his secretary and her husband (Pearson 2010). The Serulnik house occupies one of three plots in a 6-acre compound, intended by Neutra and his clients to accommodate future growth and investment; the site remained undeveloped, however, until one of the adjacent parcels was transformed by the present clients into an extensive garden and outdoor pavilion. Transparent, light, and compact, the Serulnik house reflects its architect's characteristic fusion of interior and exterior spaces by visually extending the living room into the back garden via a large, transparent glass wall. A classic example of mid-century Modern California glamour, the Serulnik house is currently used as a guest house for the newly designed complex; its sleek lines, openness, and light, rectilinear forms continually challenge Michael Maltzan's intensely contained, polygonal enclosure on the steep hillside below.

In the new 2500 sq. foot house, which responds to both the increased density of the suburban California site and the steep hillside on which the complex is located, thick diagonal walls,

Public Face and Private Space in House Design

layered openings, and a substantial interior courtyard turn the logic of Neutra's on its head: here the focus is on boundary and enclosure, and while there are dramatic views to the valley and surrounding landscape via carefully choreographed exterior platforms and window openings, there are few opportunities for visual or physical access to the private space of the home (Figure 2.5). High, clerestory windows and small, randomly placed circular openings offer little relief from the mute, futuristic form of the plain, white exterior. Once inside, however, the house opens up in a series of animated, light-filled vistas that crisscross along oblique lines that pass through the glass walls of the court. Here domesticity is reinvented through the elimination of thresholds and boundaries: clearly no children or servants intrude into the cool order of this elegant living room, study, and master bedroom.

This layered sequence of visual experiences and architectural conditions took the innovative planning of the 1952 Serulnik house as its starting point:

> By slicing and dissecting his seven-sided structure into a series of triangles and polygons, Maltzan creates a geometry that challenges conventional notions of household order. As soon as you enter, you can look into the master bathroom on one side or to the living room in front. From the living room, you can walk out to a covered balcony overlooking the valley or up one step to the courtyard. The bedroom on the other side of the court faces the living room with floor-to-ceiling glass (though shades can be pulled down). A galley kitchen occupies an interstitial space between the dining room and a library. Noting that the Serulnic house broke many rules when it was built, Pittman says that living in it for many years "radicalized" us.
>
> *(Pearson 2010)*

Figure 2.5 Michael Maltzan, Pittman Dowell House, La Crescentia, CA, 2009
Source: Copyright Iwan Baan.

Here the poetic exploration of the character and meaning of the enclosing wall and the interstitial volumes of the interior again recall the dialogue between the Glass House and the Brick House at New Canaan: in both projects, privacy, propriety and the capacity of architecture to accommodate new forms of domestic organization are highlighted by breaking apart the Modernist glass box. In both projects, the status of the clients as gay men is suggested through a series of slippages in which conventional forms and domestic categories are eliminated or distorted. As in the English country house or Renaissance villa, here leisure, reflection, and social life supplant the messy activities of conventional family life and labor.

In a number of interviews, the couple talked about their desire to reorder the hierarchies of traditional American houses, increasing visual privacy (there are no doors except on the bathroom) and reducing the kitchen—an ever-expanding element in the increasingly over-scaled, open-plan "family rooms" or "great rooms" provided by conventional new homes—to a secondary, functional space (Rappaport 2010: 79). The clients' goals are described in an article in *Architectural Record*:

> "As a same-sex couple, we felt that the old nomenclature of residential space didn't apply to us," states Lari Pittman, who, with his partner, Roy Dowell, challenged Michael Maltzan, FAIA, to explore the architectural ramifications of nontraditional relationships. For example, they wanted no doors or partitions between rooms. Instead, they asked Maltzan to "disrupt and dismantle the hierarchy of spaces" found in other houses and rethink conventions of privacy.
>
> *(Pearson 2010)*

In Maltzan's project, the congruence of architectural and social alterity offered both the clients and the architect an opportunity to explore new ways of shaping and inhabiting domestic space. By responding to these challenges in such original ways, and by emphasizing both the boundary wall and the openness of interior space, the Pittman Dowell House offers a virtual primer of ideas and design strategies for contemporary architecture, particularly when it is analyzed and understood within the context of the Serulnik House nearby. Like Johnson's New Canaan complex, this grouping of buildings opens up significant questions and offers a wide array of architectural answers.

The Future of Domesticity, Privacy, and Public Space

How might the insights and innovations of these high-budget projects be applied to the design of houses on a broader scale? Among the many lessons offered by these projects, the most significant focus attention on the uncoupling of structure and spatial organization, freeing the interior from the conventions of orthogonal projection and Modernist tectonics. Walls conceived as thick boundaries, walls as thin or perforated screens, walls as large-scale information devices and protective surfaces—all of these options are very much in play and easily adaptable to a variety of physical, political, and economic conditions. Devises such as slicing, layering, perforating, and stacking are explored in all of the projects discussed here to create the sort of flexible, imaginative interiors that can accommodate live/work programs and changing household structures that do not remain fixed across time. Moreover, adaptive reuse of existing buildings, building parts, and especially the rhythms and scales of existing conditions such as we saw in Adjaye's Dirty House, suggests engagement with the particularities of place, whether real or virtual, and a disruption of Modernist narratives of universality and coherence.

Digital projection, pattern printing, such as one sees in the graphic data-protection imagery explored by the artist Jurgen Mayer H., and information technologies have transformed the nature of private and public space, making surveillance a political reality, identity a fluid representation, and voyeurism a popular game (Colomina 2011; Mayer H. 2016). Yet social media also create new realities of community that silently cross the physical boundaries of the built environment, liberating humans to communicate and inhabit spaces, both real and virtual, in previously unimagined ways. Contemporary architecture engages with this new order through its capacity to transform physical spaces and thus to shape both the conscious and unconscious experience of the diverse groups of people who use them. Now more than ever the power of place and the politics of space are understood to be not only linked but inseparable.

Acknowledgments

I am grateful to Reed Kroloff for helping me to identify and think about these contemporary houses, and to Hannah Townsend for her research assistance.

References

Abramson, D. (2016) *Obsolescence: An Architectural History*, Chicago: University of Chicago Press.
Allison, P. (2005) *David Adjaye Houses: Recycling, Reconfiguring, Rebuilding*, London and New York: Thames and Hudson.
Benjamin, W. (1929) "Surrealism: the last snapshot of the European intelligentsia," in *Selected Writings*, Vol. 2, *1927–34*, Cambridge, MA: Harvard University Press, 47–56.
Bloch, E. (1959) "Building in empty spaces," in Ernest Bloch (1988) *The Utopian Function of Art and Literature: Selected Essays*, trans. J. Zipes and F. Mecklenburg, Cambridge, MA: MIT Press, 186–199.
Boyd, D. (2011) "Teen privacy strategies in networked publics," Presented at "Hyperpublic: Privacy and Public Space," Harvard University, Berkman Kline Center for Internet and Society. June 10. www.youtube.com/watch?v=bdLCKdjClFw.
Browne, A. (2014) "Ant Farm," *W Magazine*, January 1. www.wmagazine.com/story/hudson-valley-art-barn.
Bryson, B. (2010) *At Home: A Short History of Private Life*, London: Doubleday.
Colomina, B. (2009) "Unclear vision: architectures of surveillance," in Michael Bell and Jeannie Kim (eds) *Engineered Transparency: The Technical, Visual and Spatial Effects of Glass*, New York: Princeton Architectural Press, 78–87.
Colomina, B. (2011) "Architectures of surveillance," Presented at "Hyperpublic: Privacy and Public Space," Harvard University, Berkman Kline Center for Internet and Society. June 10. www.youtube.com/watch?v=UuOHtNwspGg.
Frampton, K. (2001) *Le Corbusier*, New York: Thames and Hudson.
Friedman, A. T. (1998) *Women and the Making of the Modern House*, New York: Abrams.
Gregory, R. (2009) "House N," *Architectural Review* (April): 49–53.
Heynen, H. and Baydar, G. (eds) (2005) *Negotiating Domesticity: Spatial Productions of Gender in Modern Architecture*, London and New York: Routledge.
Hitchcock, H.-R. and Johnson, P. (1997) *The International Style*, New York: W. W. Norton. [Museum of Modern Art, 1932].
Joy, R. (2002) *Rick Joy Desert Works*, introduction by Juhani Pallasmaa, New York: Princeton Architectural Press.
Joy, R. (2006) "Desert Nomad [Jax] House." www.moderndesign.org/2006/03/rick-joy-nomad-house-tour.html.
Joy, R. (2015) "Conversation with Marlon Blackwell," Architectural League, New York. http://archleague.org/2015/03/in-conversation-marlon-blackwell-and-rick-joy/.
Lasner, M. G. (2012) *High Life: Condo Living in the Suburban Century*, New Haven: Yale University Press.
Laugier, M.-A. (1755) *Essai sur l'architecture*, Paris.
Le Corbusier (Jeanneret, C.-E.) (1923) *Vers une architecture*, Paris: G. Crès et cie.
Martin, R. (2009) "Mirror glass (a fragment)," in M. Bell and J. Kim (eds) *Engineered Transparency: The Technical, Visual and Spatial Effects of Glass*, New York: Princeton Architectural Press, 39–44.
Mayer, H. J. (2016) https://en.wikipedia.org/wiki/J%C3%BCrgen_Mayer_(architect).

Mayyasi, A. (2016) "How an ad campaign made lesbians fall in love with Subaru," *Priceonomics*, May 23. http://priceonomics.com/how-an-ad-campaignmade-lesbians-fall-in-love-with/.

McLeod, M. (1983) "Architecture or revolution: Taylorism, technocracy and social change," *Art Journal* 43, 2: 132–147.

McLeod, M. (1985) *Urbanism and Utopia: Le Corbusier from Radical Syndicalism to Vichy*, PhD thesis, Princeton University, Ann Arbor: University Microfilms.

Musacchio, J. (2009) *Art, Marriage and the Family in the Florentine Renaissance Palace*, New Haven: Yale University Press.

Ockman, J. (2009) "A crystal world: between reason and spectacle," in M. Bell and J. Kim (eds) *Engineered Transparency: The Technical, Visual and Spatial Effects of Glass*, New York: Princeton Architectural Press, 45–54.

Pallasmaa, J. (2002) "Thought and experience in Rick Joy's desert architecture," Introduction to Rick Joy, *Desert Works*, New York: Princeton Architectural Press, 10–21.

Pearson, C. A. (2005) "Among saguaro cacti, Rick Joy plants a cluster of vividly rusted steel boxes, forming Desert Nomad House for an itinerant art dealer," *Architectural Record* 193, 4 (April): 146–153.

Pearson, C. A. (2010) "Pittman Dowell residence: breaking conventions," *Architectural Record* (April 19): 72–75. www.architecturalrecord.com/articles/8780-pittman-dowell-residence.

Perrot, M. (ed.) (1990) *A History of Private Life*, Vol. IV: *From the Fires of Revolution to the Great War*, Cambridge, MA: Belknap Press.

Potvin, J. (2014) *Bachelors of a Different Sort: Queer Aesthetics, Material Culture and the Modern Interior in Britain*, Manchester: Manchester University Press.

Rappaport, M. (2010) "Houses of light," *Apollo* (September): 75–79.

Riley, T. (1999) *The Unprivate House*, New York: MoMA.

Rosenfield, K. (2015) "Video: House N by Sou Fujimoto," *Arch Daily*, April 30. www.archdaily.com/626020/video-house-n-by-sou-fujimoto.

Sanders, J. (ed.) (1996) *Stud: Architectures of Masculinity*, New York: Princeton Architectural Press.

Sudjic, D. (2002) "Alchemy in a dilapidated furniture factory," *Observer*, December 1. www.theguardian.com/theobserver/2002/dec/01/1.

Wacks, R. (2015) *Privacy: A Very Short Introduction*, 2nd edition, Oxford: Oxford University Press.

Williams, A. (2013) "The agony of Instagram," *New York Times*, December 13: ST1.

3
Designs on Disaster
Humanitarianism and Contemporary Architecture

Andrew Herscher

In 2014, Shigeru Ban was awarded the Pritzker Architecture Prize, typically described as the highest honor a contemporary architect can receive. In the announcement of Ban's award, the Pritzker jury made much of Ban's "humanitarian efforts" (Pritzker Architecture Prize 2014). For that jury, it seemed, Ban's achievement was to extend the benefits of architecture from the select group of entitled people who could afford to hire an architect to the recipients of humanitarian assistance—among the most disadvantaged people on the globe.

This extension was an iteration of a relationship between professional architecture and humanitarian relief that has existed throughout the history of humanitarianism. Since its emergence in the mid-nineteenth century, humanitarianism has often manifested itself in relation to buildings or the built environment. Whether understood in relation to the slums of cities, or relief facilities for victims of famines and epidemics constructed by colonial administrations, or camps for displaced people erected by nongovernmental and intergovernmental organizations, humanitarianism has frequently involved the design of spaces—camps, shelters, emergency housing, and still others—to which architects have contributed their disciplinary expertise or have subsequently claimed as their disciplinary patrimony.

Throughout much of this history, architecture's engagement with humanitarianism was not marked as exceptional; modernism in architecture can be understood as, among other things, an attempt to reorganize architecture according to some of the imperatives that also organized humanitarianism.[1] And so, refugee camps accommodating people displaced by the violence of World War I appeared along with other buildings in the pages of *Der Architekt* during the war; the issue of mass housing emerged in CIAM after the war to contend with the consequences of a mass war waged against a mass subject; and emergency shelters accommodating citizens of English cities unhoused by German aerial warfare appeared along with other buildings in the pages of the *Journal of the Royal Institute of British Architects* during World War II (Herscher 2017).

The career of the paradigmatic "modern" architect, Le Corbusier, perhaps epitomizes the intersection of modernism, architecture, and humanitarianism (Herscher 2017: 43–46, 68–70). Le Corbusier's Maison Dom-ino, usually considered in terms of the development of "purist architecture," was conceived in 1914, amid the devastation of Belgian cities in the beginning of World War I; the abstract Dom-ino frame was intended to facilitate the rapid and efficient reconstruction of Belgian housing. After the war, Le Corbusier continued to approach the needs of the displaced and unhoused as resources for architectural innovation; his 1929 project for a "Floating Asylum," commissioned by the French branch of the Salvation Army for a barge on the Seine, provided the physical space for a new community that would take homeless people off Parisian streets. During World War II, Le Corbusier developed the "murondin" system of dry construction to quickly and efficiently build shelters for displaced people and designed settlements based on this system to house up to 1000 people. "Architecture or revolution?" Le Corbusier's famous question at the conclusion of his 1923 manifesto, *Towards an Architecture*, suggested that revolution could be avoided by architecture, but it was humanitarian needs that provided Le Corbusier with many of the specific programs for architecture to pre-empt revolution by assimilating potentially restive sections of the urban population into the social status quo.

By Ban's 2014 Pritzker Prize, however, the relationship between architecture and humanitarianism was different: the post-World War II emergence of an international humanitarian regime and consequent specialization of humanitarian architecture now rendered traffic between client-based practice and relief work as extraordinary (Siddiqi 2017). As one critic wrote about Ban's 1999 "emergency shelters" at the Gihembe Refugee Camp in Rwanda, this project "made him famous and particularly admired … in a field where humanitarian relief work isn't exactly commonplace" (Kimmelman 2007) (Figure 3.1).

The architectural history of Gihembe Refugee Camp registers two of the most salient dynamics of the field of contemporary humanitarian architecture: first, the application of architectural expertise to the refugee camp and, second, the application of digital technology to the problem of refugee accommodation. The salience of these dynamics, I suggest, comes from their parallel effectiveness at displacing recognition of one of the most intractable issues facing both contemporary architecture and contemporary politics: the shelter crisis that leaves vast swathes of the world's population under- or unhoused on what Mike Davis has termed "the planet of slums" (Davis 2007).

Cardboard for Humanity: Ban at Gihembe[2]

The residents of the Gihembe Refugee Camp are descendants of Rwandan Tutsis who found sanctuary in the neighboring Belgian Congo when anti-Tutsi violence swept Rwanda between

Figure 3.1 Shigeru Ban, emergency shelters at Gihembe Refugee Camp, Rwanda, 1999
Source: Photograph courtesy of Shigeru Ban Architects.

1959 and 1961.³ Those refugees subsequently received citizenship in what became Zaire, where many built secure and prosperous lives. But with the collapse of Zaire in the aftermath of the Rwandan Genocide and Civil War, their citizenship was revoked and they were forced to return to Rwanda. Many refugees were forced to turn over all their possessions to Congolese soldiers or militia members as they fled, and therefore arrived in Rwanda with little or nothing of value (Wakabi and Kigambo 2012).

The United Nations High Commissioner for Refugees (UNHCR) first housed these refugees close to the border between Rwanda and the Democratic Republic of the Congo—Zaire's successor state—in a refugee camp at Mudende. In the months after this camp was established, however, Interahamwe militias launched a series of attacks on it, killing an estimated 3000 refugees. The UNHCR then moved the surviving refugees further from the border, to Gihembe, at the end of 1997, where Ban's prototype emergency shelters were erected about a year later (Lynch 2013). His shelters accommodated newly arriving refugees at the camp, which from its founding lacked sufficient housing to accommodate all of its residents.

In 1998, the first year of Gihembe's operation, the UNHCR provided incoming refugees with plastic sheets and aluminum poles to use for shelter, but refugees would often cut down trees to use as supports for the plastic sheets and sell the aluminum poles in the adjacent town of Byumba. While this entrepreneurialism provided refugees a rare opportunity to produce value and accumulate capital, it also led to what the UNHCR called "deforestation" around the camp, despite the fact that the building of the camp initiated the process of deforestation in the first place.⁴ The question was actually who at Gihembe had the right to deforest. In response to this question, Ban created a prototype shelter that used recycled cardboard tubes, which refugees could not sell, in place of aluminum poles to support the plastic sheets. Fifty of these prototypes were erected at Gihembe in 1999.

Following his work in post-earthquake Kobe in 1995, Ban's project at Gihembe extended his architectural practice to sites and problems that had become the domain of a specialized architectural humanitarianism.⁵ Ban subsequently carried out a series of other projects using recycled materials for post-disaster shelter—in the post-typhoon Philippines, post-earthquake Nepal, Japan, and Haiti, and post-hurricane New Orleans—alongside other architectural work in the field's more conventional contexts.

In the announcement of Ban's Pritzker Prize, the Pritzker jury declared that Ban "uses the same inventive and resourceful design approach for his extensive humanitarian efforts" as he does in his "elegant, innovative work for private clients" (Pritzker Prize 2014). But this claim should be understood differently with the recognition that, at Gihembe, *the architect's invention and resourcefulness replaced the invention and resourcefulness of refugees*. The architecture that Ban provided at Gihembe may have been minimal, just as in his "elegant, innovative work for private clients," but it was precisely this minimal architecture that limited the capacity of refugees to build their own spaces and their own lives. That precisely this act of limitation is read as humanitarian is more than irony. This reading points to a politics of inequity embedded in humanitarian architecture—if not humanitarianism more generally—that mystifies the notion of a common humanity.

And yet, the dominant reading of Ban's project in architectural discourse is much more than a fiction of architecture as an art of equality in which "the same design approach" subtends the shelters of refugees and the refuges of the tax sheltering class. Just this same fiction testifies to the actual inequality that motivates the staging of fictions of equality, the recruitment of the refugee as the human figure by means of which architecture seeks redemption, and, perhaps most importantly, the relationship between the refugee's performance in architectural narratives of humanitarian intervention and her actual life in the humanitarian space of the refugee camp. I want to suggest, then, that the impact of Ban's emergency shelters at Gihembe lay in the way they furthered the helplessness of refugees and received acclaim for providing assistance to the helpless.

The humanitarian emergency at stake was the lack of accommodation for refugees at Gihembe. Ban's shelters responded to this lack by conjoining and supplanting it with another emergency that humanitarianism itself was accomplice to: the normalized emergency in which stateless refugees indefinitely occupy refugee camps and depend on humanitarian assistance for their survival.[6] The refugee residents of Gihembe are unable to be repatriated to the Democratic Republic of Congo, where they are considered to be Rwandan; they are unable to be repatriated in Rwanda, where they are considered to be Congolese; and very few of them have been able to secure resettlement in a third country (UNHCR Rwanda 2014). The refugee camp at Gihembe therefore exists as a permanently temporary space where the threshold conditions of bare life extend indefinitely into the future (Kabeera 2012).

Indeed, it was the *punctual* emergency that Ban's shelters aimed to ameliorate that inaugurated the *protracted* emergency of everyday life in Gihembe—an emergency in which Gihembe's refugees "live in the conditions of the camp that further immobilize, demoralize, and often extend their experiences of brutality on a daily basis" (Lynch 2013: 8). Yet Ban's shelters did not only introduce refugees to Gihembe; through the exchange of valuable aluminum poles for valueless cardboard tubes, those shelters also introduced refugees to the abjection that humanitarian assistance at Gihembe entailed.

Ban's shelters, intended for short-term use, have long since been replaced by more durable houses at Gihembe (Figure 3.2). Sometimes with the assistance of aid workers, the camp's long-term residents have built themselves houses with wood frames and mud-plaster walls. The wood harvesting that Ban's temporary shelters were designed to forestall has surreptitiously continued to yield building material for these permanently temporary houses (UNHCR Rwanda 2009). The only part of Ban's emergency shelters that could be recycled for these houses was the part that Ban inherited from the UNHCR's emergency shelters: the plastic sheet, which provides the roof for houses whose residents cannot afford corrugated metal. Many houses lack windows and no house is supplied with water or electricity. Around 12 square meters in size, the houses

Figure 3.2 Gihembe Refugee Camp, Rwanda, 2015
Source: Photograph by Sam Ngendahimana.

accommodate families that can include many children, the latter being among the only sanctioned objects of (re)production at Gihembe.

The Camp as Politics

The repeated display of images of Ban's emergency shelters in exhibitions and texts about humanitarian architecture from 1999 to the present should be viewed in relation to the protracted emergency in which Gihembe's refugee residents reside. As Ban's shelters appear and re-appear amid professional architecture's conjoined expressions of guilt and self-congratulation, the residents of Gihembe still live in an emergency. No longer crowded under tents, they are now crowded into houses. The fact that there are no new architectural images of Gihembe does not mean that Ban's emergency shelters solved the shelter problem (as Ban himself would no doubt admit), but the continuous replay of his initial response undoubtedly obscures the fact that the shelter problem persists as refugees are forced to occupy camps that they cannot leave—a phenomenon that is increasingly typical in camps across the globe (Davies and Isakjee 2015).

And yet, from 1999 to the present, professional architecture has been preoccupied with punctual responses to punctual emergencies like those that faced incoming refugees to Gihembe. The exemplars of "humanity" that "humanitarian architecture" has recognized and responded to occupy *situations* of abjection and distress amid wars, disasters, and displacements, rather than the *conditions* of abjection and distress that characterize everyday life for the vast majority of humans on the planet (Architecture for Humanity 2006). According to Saskia Sassen, this bifurcated attention to social suffering demands that the language and policies of humanitarianism be replaced by languages and policies adequate to the slow violence of everyday life experienced by many communities across the globe (Sassen 2014). Until this replacement, however, what the humanitarian rescue of human beings from situations of abjection and distress in many cases accomplishes is a restoration of those humans to the conditions that made them vulnerable to those situations in the first place. This is why Slavoj Žižek argues that "much more than a refugee, a slum-dweller is a *homo sacer*, the systematically generated 'living dead' of global capitalism. The slum-dweller is a kind of negative of the refugee: a refugee from his own community" (Žižek 2009).

In 2016, the Museum of Modern Art (MoMA) in New York displayed the exhibition "Insecurities: Tracing Displacement and Shelter." "Bringing together works by architects, designers, and artists in a range of mediums and scales that respond to the complex circumstances brought about by forced displacement," the press release announced that "the exhibition focuses on conditions that disrupt conventional images of the built environment as an arbiter of modernity and globalization" (Museum of Modern Art Department of Communications 2016). Locating itself in the context of recent and contemporary humanitarianism, the exhibition can be located in a related but different context, as well.

In 1986 Shigeru Ban was commissioned by MoMA to design an exhibition in Tokyo of Alvar Aalto's furniture and glasswork. In Ban's words:

> in order to avoid the expense and the inevitable waste of resources, recycled paper tubing was adopted as alternative material and was used to create ceiling panels, partitions, and display stands. The material explorations in this exhibit design mark the beginning of "paper architecture."

(Shigeru Ban Architects 1986)

Ban famously brought this paper architecture to humanitarianism at Gihembe and, in so doing, directed architectural attention to spaces and activities hitherto on the periphery of the discipline.

From 1999 to the present, this attention has steadily grown.[7] MoMA's "Insecurities" exhibition marked what might be taken as the full unfolding of this attention—the circulation of paper architecture from MoMA exhibition material, through humanitarian architecture, to a MoMA exhibition on humanitarian architecture. That these sorts of circulations take place is, of course, old news. What is of interest in this case is the way in which the stasis of refugees at Gihembe is on some level sustained by the continuous global circulation of images of temporary architecture that some of these refugees briefly inhabited.

In "The Decline of the Nation-State and the End of the Rights of Man," an essay written in the years following World War II, Hannah Arendt probed the contradictions that statelessness posed to humanitarian and human rights politics. In the course of her analysis, she anticipated what is now the reality of refugee life in places like Gihembe—the way in which the camp became "the only 'country' the world had to offer the stateless" (Arendt 1958). For Arendt, however, it was clear that the fundamental problem of the camp was less architectural than political:

> The first loss which the rightless suffered was the loss of their homes.... This calamity is far from unprecedented; in the long memory of history, forced migrations of individuals or whole groups of people for political or economic reasons look like everyday occurrences. What is unprecedented is not the loss of a home but the impossibility of finding a new one.... [I]t was a problem not of space but of political organization.
>
> *(Arendt 1958: 293–294)*

To the extent that humanitarian architecture is *only* understood as "a problem of space" in the context of the punctual emergency, Arendt suggests, it will be inadequate both to the punctual emergency that seems to disrupt social order and to the enduring emergency that is that order. To put it differently, one could ask: "is it possible to design a 'better' refugee camp?"

From Voucher Humanitarianism to Digital Shelter

If Arendt suggests the impossibility of building a better refugee camp, digital technology is in the process of rendering the question of the better refugee camp moot, while displacing the problem of political organization yet again. In 2014, the year in which Ban was awarded the Pritzker Prize, the World Food Program and Visa Inc. selected Gihembe Refugee Camp as the site to launch mVISA, a digital humanitarian relief program. One of a proliferating number of similar examples of "voucher humanitarianism" developed through collaborations between humanitarian institutions and the financial services sector, "mVISA is a bank account in the form of a virtual wallet linked to a mobile phone number" (González 2015). The World Food Program distributed mobile phones to heads of households at Gihembe and then, through mVISA, transferred 6,300 RWF (US$8.60) per month to those heads of households, allowing them to use these funds to make purchases (Figure 3.3).

The voucher humanitarianism of which mVISA is an early example has led to another important intersection of contemporary architecture and humanitarianism. Emerging from an ongoing privatization of humanitarianism, voucher humanitarianism has yielded "digital shelter," the posing of the housing market as a "solution" to the housing needs of displaced populations, and the potential end of the camp as the primary humanitarian spatial technology.

The privatization of humanitarianism received its institutional mandate in 1999 when the United Nation's "Global Compact," released at the World Economic Forum in Davos, announced an intention to "harness the energy and influence of multinational corporations to

Figure 3.3 Shop using mVISA, Gihembe Refugee Camp, Rwanda, 2015
Source: Photograph courtesy of World Food Programme.

act as good corporate citizens" (United Nations 1999). Following such partnerships as those between the Coca-Cola Company and the United Nations Development Program, the Pfizer Corporation and the United Nations Children's Fund, and the United Parcel Service and CARE International, humanitarianism became a target of corporate expertise (White 2012).

Among other places, this targeting played out in the context of the refugee camp, with the Ikea Foundation establishing a partnership with the UNHCR to develop a new form of temporary shelter. The resulting "Refugee Housing Unit"—ultimately re-branded as the "Better Shelter"—was designed to be shipped in flat packs, assembled without additional tools and equipment, and last for three years, two and a half years longer than the tarpaulin shelters it was intended to replace (Ikea Foundation 2015). In March 2015 the Ikea Foundation announced that the UNHCR ordered 10,000 "Better Shelters" for immediate deployment in the following summer (United Nations High Commissioner for Refugees 2012). Applying techniques of consumer furniture design, construction, and delivery to refugee housing, this deployment normalized that housing by integrating it into the housing market. Not at all incidentally, an Ikea "Better Shelter" formed the centerpiece of MoMA's 2016 "Insecurities" exhibition.

The integration of refugee housing into the housing market was enormously furthered with the almost simultaneous advent of voucher humanitarianism: a technique by means of which humanitarian assistance takes the form of vouchers distributed by automated teller machines and credit card readers (Harvey 2005; Smith et al. 2011). Voucher humanitarianism has been developed by the UNHCR and the World Food Program, which have partnered with credit card companies, mobile phone companies, banks, and other businesses to provide digitally accessed funding to Syrian refugees in Lebanon, Jordan, and Turkey with which to purchase food and rent shelter.[8] Architecturally, voucher humanitarianism gives refugees "digital shelter"—digitally distributed funds with which to purchase physical shelter.

In 2013, in one of the most recent innovations in voucher humanitarianism, all Syrian refugees arriving in Jordan were added to a biometric database (Sundelin 2013). At Jordanian ATMs equipped with iris scanners, these refugees could be identified by iris scans rather than by ATM cards and PIN codes:

> Instead of receiving food packages, money vouchers or bank cards from the UNHCR, refugees in the iris-identification system receive a monthly text message saying money has been placed in their accounts. Then, they walk up to an ATM owned by Cairo Amman Bank, and, rather than insert a card and punch in a pass code, they look into a specially designed iris camera. Once ID'd, a refugee would be able to withdraw his or her monthly allotment of cash.
>
> *(Maron 2013)*

Two rationales were offered for iris scanning, each based on the increased efficiency of aid distribution that this scanning presumably permits: first, refugees can "access their money in a secure way without having to keep track of a card and number," and second, scanning will "help thwart refugee fraud" (Maron 2013). And yet, voucher humanitarianism also brought about a new relationship between humanitarianism, refugee, and the housing market. With the control of refugee bodies no longer predicated on the spatial boundaries of the refugee camp, the development of a system of housing vouchers for refugees allowed the housing market to at least notionally accommodate the provision of shelter even in states of humanitarian emergency.

The smoothing of distinctions between humanitarianism and capitalist consumerism is typically regarded—from the perspectives of humanitarianism and capitalism alike—as "progress." As a typical claim asserts,

> with significant logistical abilities, massive resources invested in R&D and highly capable personnel, many within the aid community hope that businesses can do for humanitarian aid what Amazon did for the world of retail or what Microsoft and Apple did for personal computing.
>
> *(Zyck and Armstrong 2014)*

But "businesses" exists not only as facilitators of and contributors to humanitarian aid, but also as instigators of the emergencies to which humanitarianism responds. It is this status of "business"—which is to say, the status of capitalism's structural violence—which is effaced in the privatization of humanitarianism. The inequalities, deprivations, and oppressions of this violence, business as usual in the frame of capitalism, thereby become business as usual in the frame of humanitarianism, as well (Žižek 2008).

In this sense, it is not accidental that the technological innovation of digital shelter, which forces refugees to compete for substandard housing with working-class renters, brings precise economic benefits to property owners, in the form of increased housing demand, along with increased social suffering to communities denied affordable housing. This became apparent in Jordan, where for a time an estimated 80 percent of registered Syrian refugees were residing outside of refugee camps, for the most part in the country's most impoverished municipalities. There, refugees competed with poor and working-class residents for affordable housing. In the summer of 2014, according to one NGO,

> The rapid influx of Syrian refugees into northern Jordan has directly impacted the housing market, driving up rental prices and exacerbating an already acute lack of housing. This challenging situation has forced many to resort to coping strategies such as sharing living quarters … and improvising makeshift shelters with limited access to basic services.
>
> *(REACH 2014)*

Subsequently, in the beginning of 2015, reports began to emerge of Syrian refugees moving from Jordanian cities back into refugee camps: *these were camps that began to provide refuge not from war zones, but from cities without affordable housing* (Walsh 2015). The disaggregation of humanitarianism and architecture through the advent of digital shelter has thereby returned to the housing question that solicited their aggregation almost 100 years earlier in the context of architectural modernism. While slums were a target of modernism's ameliorative efforts, that is, they are supposed to be ameliorative in the context of digital shelter.

The architectural labor performed by Syrian refugees in repurposing a refugee camp into affordable housing in Jordan is also a critique of the predominant model of architectural humanitarianism, if not humanitarianism more generally. Predicated on the management of punctual emergencies, humanitarianism normalizes emergencies of inequality, oppression, and unequal exposure to danger and violence that are commonplace in global capitalism and ongoing colonialism; on a planet of slums, what humanitarianism offers as a refugee camp is less of a refuge than affordable housing. Designs in response to the slow disasters of inequality, exploitation, and exclusion that are normalized in capitalism and colonialism transcend the given terms of architectural humanitarianism but also address the core emergencies from which humanitarian emergencies arise.

Notes

1 As Daniel Bertrand Monk and I have suggested, "whatever else it aspired to attain, the architectural modernism of the interwar period also envisioned itself as a humanitarian practice of sorts, of necessity preoccupied with the unhoused and underhoused": see "The new universalism: refuges and refugees between global history and voucher humanitarianism," *Grey Room* 61 (2015), 74.
2 This section draws upon Andrew Herscher, "Cardboard for humanity," in Nick Axel, Beatriz Colomina, Nikolaus Hirsch, Anton Vidokle, and Mark Wigley (eds) *Superhumanity* (Minneapolis: University of Minnesota Press, 2018), 34–41.
3 On the prehistory of Gihembe, see René Lemarchand, *The Dynamics of Violence in Central Africa* (Philadelphia: University of Pennsylvania Press, 2009); Gerard Prunier, *Africa's World War: Congo, the Rwandan Genocide, and the Making of a Continental Catastrophe* (New York: Oxford University Press, 2009); and Filip Reyntjens, *The Great African War: Congo and Regional Geopolitics, 1996–2006* (Cambridge, UK: Cambridge University Press, 2009).
4 In December 1998, UNHCR reported that, in Rwanda, it

> supports the forestry programme that is redressing damage done to the environment by massive shelter programmes and refugee camps. In addition to reforestation programmes, UNHCR has also introduced, in both camps and settlement sites, energy-saving stoves that reduce energy lost by open cooking fires by at least 60 per cent. The use of 'paper poles' for shelter construction is also being investigated.
>
> *(UNHCR, "UNHCR Global Appeal 1999—Rwanda," December 1, 1998, www.unhcr. org/3eaff44124.html)*

5 Anooradha Iyer Siddiqi identifies Fred Cuny and Ian Davis as protagonists in this specialization: see Siddiqi, "Architecture culture, humanitarian expertise: from the tropics to shelter, 1953–1993," *Journal of the Society of Architectural Historians* 76, 3.
6 In Rwandan refugee camps like Gihembe, "nearly every Congolese refugee relied exclusively on UNHCR for basic needs, including food, water, health care, education, and clothing": see United

States Committee for Refugees and Immigrants, "U.S. Committee for Refugees World Refugee Survey 2003 – Rwanda," June 1, 2003, www.refworld.org/docid/3eddc48b8.html.
7 Among its contemporary manifestations is the 2016 Venice Biennale of Architecture; oriented around the theme of "Reporting from the Front," the Biennale attends to architecture's encounter with refugees in the national pavilions of Austria and Germany as well as in a number of other projects.
8 For example, through the "Digital Food" program, MasterCard and the World Food Programme have partnered to develop pre-paid debit cards for Syrian refugees in Turkey and Lebanon; see MasterCard, "MasterCard and the United Nations World Food Programme in partnership to deliver 'Digital Food'," press release, September 13, 2012, http://newsroom.mastercard.com/press-releases/mastercard-and-the-united-nations-world-food-programme-in-partnership-to-deliver-digital-food-4/ and World Food Programme, "Meet our partners," www.wfp.org/partners/private-sector/meet-our-partners/mastercard.

References

Architecture for Humanity (2006) *Design Like You Give a Damn: Architectural Responses to Humanitarian Crises*, New York: Metropolis Books.
Arendt, H. (1958) "The decline of the nation-state and the end of the rights of man," in *The Origins of Totalitarianism*, New York: Meridian.
Davies, T. and Isakjee, A. (2015) "Geography, migration, and abandonment in the Calais refugee camp," *Political Geography* 49.
Davis, M. (2007) *Planet of Slums*, New York: Verso.
González, E. (2015) "Working with the private sector through cash-based interventions," Inter Agency Working Group on Disaster Preparedness for East and Central Africa, https://humanitarianpartnership-conference.wordpress.com/presentations-3/.
Harvey, P. (2005) *Cash and Vouchers in Emergencies*, London: Overseas Development Institute.
Herscher, A. (2017) *Displacements: Architecture and Refugee*, Berlin: Sternberg Press.
Herscher, A. (2018) "Cardboard for humanity," in N. Axel, B. Colomina, N. Hirsch, A. Vidokle, and M. Wigley (eds) *Superhumanity*, Minneapolis: University of Minnesota Press, 34–41.
Ikea Foundation (2015) "A home away from home," www.ikeafoundation.org/better-shelter/.
Kabeera, E. (2012) "Life inside Gihembe Refugee Camp," *New Times*, www.newtimes.co.rw/section/article/2012-06-25/54353/.
Kimmelman, M. (2007) "Shigeru Ban: building to last, just long enough," *New York Times*, www.nytimes.com/2007/05/22/travel/22iht-arch.1.5820314.html.
Lemarchand, R. (2009) *The Dynamics of Violence in Central Africa*, Philadelphia: University of Pennsylvania Press.
Lynch, E. A. (2013) "Mudende: trauma and massacre in a refugee camp," *Oral History Forum* 33.
Maron, D. F. (2013) "Eye-imaging ID unlocks aid dollars for Syrian Civil War refugees," *Scientific American*, www.scientificAmerican.com/article/eye-imaging-id-unlocks-aid/.
MasterCard (2012) "MasterCard and the United Nations World Food Programme in partnership to deliver 'Digital Food'," http://newsroom.mastercard.com/press-releases/mastercard-and-the-united-nations-world-food-programme-in-partnership-to-deliver-digital-food-4/.
Monk, D. and Herscher, A. (2015) "The new universalism: refuges and refugees between global history and voucher humanitarianism," *Grey Room* 61.
Museum of Modern Art Department of Communications (2016) "Insecurities press announcement," http://press.moma.org/wp-content/files_mf/insecurities_pressannouncement_final.pdf.
Pritzker Architecture Prize (2014) "Announcement," www.pritzkerprize.com/2014/announcement.
Prunier, G. (2009) *Africa's World War: Congo, the Rwandan Genocide, and the Making of a Continental Catastrophe*, New York: Oxford University Press.
REACH (2014) *Housing and Tensions in Jordanian Communities Hosting Syrian Refugees*, www.reachinitiative.org/?s=housing+and+tensions+in+jordanian+ communities.
Reyntjens, F. (2009) *The Great African War: Congo and Regional Geopolitics, 1996–2006*, Cambridge, UK: Cambridge University Press.
Sassen, S. (2014) *Expulsions: Brutality and Complexity in the Global Economy*, Cambridge, MA: Harvard University Press.
Shigeru Ban Architects (1986) "Alvar Aalto—Tokyo, Japan, 1986," www.shigerubanarchitects.com/works/1986_alvar-aalto/index.html.

Siddiqi, A. I. (2017) "Architecture culture, humanitarian expertise: from the tropics to shelter, 1953–1993," *Journal of the Society of Architectural Historians* 76, 3.

Smith, G., Macauslan, I., Butters, S., and Tromme, M. (2011) *New Technologies in Cash Transfer Programming and Humanitarian Assistance*, Oxford: Cash Learning Partnership.

Sundelin, G. (2013) "Iris-scanning technology streamlines refugee registration process—UNHCR," *Jordan Times*, http://jordantimes.com/iris-scanning-technology-streamlines-refugee-registration-process-unhcr.

United Nations (1999) "Secretary-General proposes global compact on human rights, labour, environment, Address to World Economic Forum in Davos," press release SG/SM/688, www.un.org/press/en/1999/19990201.sgsm6881.html.

United Nations High Commissioner for Refugees (1998) "UNHCR Global Appeal 1999—Rwanda," www.unhcr.org/3eaff44124.html.

United Nations High Commissioner for Refugees (2012) "A safe place to call home," www.unhcr.org/pages/52a5c44f6.html.

United Nations High Commissioner of Refugees Rwanda (2009) "Environmental management in refugee situations learning workshop," www.humanitarianresponse.info/system/files/documents/files/Environmental%20Management%20in%20Refugee%20Situations%20Learning%20Workshop.pdf.

United Nations High Commissioner for Refugees Rwanda (2014) "Resettlement: a life-changing journey," https://data2.unhcr.org/en/documents/download/48473.

United States Committee for Refugees and Immigrants (2003) "U.S. Committee for Refugees World Refugee Survey 2003 – Rwanda," www.refworld.org/docid/3eddc48b8.html.

Wakabi, M. and Kigambo, G. (2012) "Congo: refugee life and the cycle of war," *The East African*, www.theeastafrican.co.ke/magazine/Refugee-life-and-the-cycle-of-war/.

Walsh, T. (2015) "Syrian refugees move back to camps in Jordan," *US News and World Report*, www.usnews.com/news/articles/2015/01/28/syrian-refugees-move-back-to-camps-in-jordan.

White, S. (2012) *Corporate Engagement in Natural Disaster Response: Piecing Together the Value Chain*, Washington, DC: Center for Strategic and International Studies.

World Food Programme (2012) "Meet our partners," www.wfp.org/partners/private-sector/meet-our-partners/mastercard.

Žižek, S. (2008) *Violence: Six Sideways Reflections*, New York: Picador.

Žižek, S. (2009) *In Defense of Lost Causes*, New York: Verso.

Zyck, S. A. and Armstrong, J. (2014) *Humanitarian Crises, Emergency Preparedness and Response: The Role of Business and the Private Sector*, London: Overseas Development Institute.

4
Architectures of Risk and Resiliency
"Embedded Security" in the Redesign of Sandy Hook Elementary School

Rachel Hall

In August 2016, school officials invited members of the press to tour the newly redesigned Sandy Hook Elementary School in Newton, Connecticut. It was a preemptive measure. School officials wanted to ensure students a peaceful start to the 2016–2017 school year. In particular, officials did not want a frenzy of media attention to disturb the students' introduction to the facility. Nor did they want to risk having the new campus shrouded in the tragic events of December 14, 2012, when 20-year-old Adam Lanza shot his way through the locked entrance to the school and fatally shot 20 children between six and seven years old and six staff members in less than five minutes. The community had long ago chosen to demolish the old structure, as if the traumatic memories associated with that place could not be overcome in situ. The school's public relations strategy was largely successful. Reports published from the press conference and tour treat the events of December 14, 2012 as implicit material, briefly mentioning it, short-handing it, or altogether side stepping any direct allusion to it and trusting readers to fill in the missing contextual details from cultural memory.

Sunny photographs of an inviting, whimsical, and naturalistic campus dominate the publications. Reporters and architectural critics relay surprise at how little the school resembles a fortress or bunker. They describe being drawn in by the openness of the structure and the "warm and calming environment" (Hussey and Foderaro 2016). They also make much of the gradual, sustainably landscaped approach to the school, and the way that the building is reassuringly tucked into its surroundings (Sisson 2016). While broadly enthusiastic about the school's redesign, journalists eagerly reassure readers that security has not been sacrificed for design. To the contrary, they present ample evidence that the school is "the latest in high security," where the trend is to nest high-security features inside beautiful design (Weller 2016). Indeed, the Sandy Hook redesign is perhaps best described as risk design nested within resilient design.

As a response to gun violence on school campuses, "embedded security" nests the cultural refusal to enact gun control within nostalgic design tropes that harken back to a time when (some) schools were imagined as relatively safe spaces. Of course, nostalgia for how schools used to feel is not universally available to parents, students, and teachers. In particular, nostalgia for the way "our" schools used to feel eludes those communities in which the schools have long since been "securitized" because the entire student body is presumed capable of criminal activity. Educators and cultural criminologists, among others, have used the phrase, "school-to-prison pipeline," as a way of calling out the state's disregard for some populations of children, save to discipline and punish them. Whether parents desire and/or expect their child's public school to resemble a well-funded children's museum or a juvenile detention center has everything to do with the demographics and tax base of their community, as well as how the threat of gun violence is constructed across different communities in the United States. It matters whether the threat is assumed to issue from within or without the school population. Such presumptions carry historical and racial implications regarding what types of children are treated as potential victims of gun violence (innocents) and what types of children are treated as perpetrators of gun violence (criminals).

While anti-violence advocates, educators, and parents working within communities long plagued by gun violence have been calling for stricter gun control legislation for decades, national outrage over gun violence did not register until predominantly white communities in Colorado and Connecticut were affected. The attention garnered by Sandy Hook, in particular, has to do with how young the victims were, the heightened dramatic impact and all-at-once-ness of mass shootings (in comparison to the slow, steady death toll of gun violence in poorer communities), and the presumption of safety enjoyed by those privileged to live in relatively affluent school districts. The everyday presence of gun violence in lower-income communities has not garnered national outrage that might push for the implementation and enforcement of stricter gun control laws. Rather, it is used to argue for more surveillance of the student body, armed guards on campus, and zero-tolerance disciplinary policies. Another way to express this difference is in terms of neo-segregation in the United States, which informally supports the policing and fortification of white spaces in ways that participates in a racialized aesthetics of security (Massey, TenHoor, and Korsh 2015). As part of this same spatial imaginary, nonwhite spaces are contained, policed, and/ or abandoned by the state and neighboring communities. There is a hard feel and zero-degree security aesthetic to the policing of nonwhite communities, which are not likely to become candidates for high-profile architectural experiments in resilient design.

Within the relatively well-off community of Newton, Connecticut, though, the national failure to enact adequate gun control legislation in response to the mass shooting at Sandy Hook Elementary falls back on (1) the State of Connecticut, which passed legislation requiring new and renovated schools to implement infrastructural fixes, and (2) the local community, where it registered *as a design problem*. The architects charged with the school's redesign, Svigals + Partners, had to comply with the preventative infrastructure design techniques outlined in the *Report of the School Safety Infrastructure Council* (Currey 2015). But the team had to meet the new requirements in a manner that respected the Newton community's (and nation's) desire to move on from their bad feelings about the tragic events of 2012. Svigals + Partners delivered on both fronts by nesting risk design within resilient design, which journalists covering the project describe as "embedded security."

"Embedded security" renders risk design invisible to children, even as it promises interpretive pleasures for adults in the know. In the media coverage of journalists' tours of the new Sandy Hook facility and campus, writers delight in the subtlety of now-you-see-it-now-you-don't security features. Likewise, journalists emphasize the "polyvalent" character of prominent landscape design elements, which promise to achieve sustainable natural beauty while promoting security. A reporter for *Business Insider* notes that

> When parents and buses begin to drop kids off next month, they'll pass through multiple security checkpoints on the way to the entrance. They'll also pass by several bioswales, which are angled landscapes that direct storm run-off and keep outside people at a distance.
>
> *(Weller 2016)*

A reporter for the *New York Times* informs readers that the "bioswales" are planted out with native species. These reports resonate with the popular appeal of behind-the-scenes access (Hussey and Foderaro 2016). Once you are in the know, design features oscillate between signifying risk and resiliency: it's a rabbit … it's a duck … it's a rabbit…. Each fleeting appearance comforts in its way. Reports of a target that has been "hardened" reassure those with cultural fears and anxieties regarding mass shootings. Open, naturalistic, and playful design elements conjure up romantic associations with childhood. The beauty of nesting the one within the other is that once you know the security features are there, you can relax out of the oscillation and settle on the side of unfettered childhood … at least for a while.

As a design solution to the political stalemate over gun violence in the United States, "embedded security" does important cultural work because it enables users of the space and consumers of its design to shift between the contradictory value systems represented by risk and resilient design, respectively. Risk design accedes to the worst-case scenario. It anticipates more episodes of gun violence on school campuses in the near future and, consequently, endeavors to "harden" schools deemed worthy of protection, which are re-conceptualized as "targets" of roving, armed, and dangerous persons. Risk design remakes the built environment of some communities in preparation for the next attack, embedding the armature for future attacks (made in the image of historical attacks) within a building's infrastructure. Like risk design, resilient design accedes to the worst-case scenario, but its tense is the future anterior. Resilient design is located on the far side of the near future, where additional episodes of gun violence will have already occurred. Resilient design remakes the built environment in a manner that supports the ability of some communities to "bounce back" from gun violence in their schools. Instead of giving in completely to a bunker mentality, resilient design endeavors to make schools feel contemplative, welcoming, and warm. Each approach: risk and resilient design, hedges the bets laid by the other. Rather than stake a position on the side of either (1) retreating behind defensive architectures or (2) remaining naively open to the wider world, architects and journalists act as though smart, good-looking design makes it possible to move between positions and states as circumstances dictate.

Resilient Design

In contemporary usage, the term "resiliency" carries the positive connotation of having survived hardship and learned to thrive again. But the term's definition is not so clearly located on the after side of trauma, where one can finally exhale. Nor is it uniformly celebratory. The *Oxford English Dictionary* defines resiliency as: "1. Rebound or recoil; 2. Elasticity; 3. Tendency to revert to a state; and 4. Capacity to recover from misfortune, shock, illness." Like a coiled spring, resiliency implies two possible positions: retreat and expansion. And it connotes the flexibility and energy of resistance and release or the ability to "bounce back." Understood temporally, rather than in terms of physics, resiliency contains the threat of regression and the possibility of healing from past wounds. We might say, then, that "resiliency" is the capacity to move between states or positions (for good or ill) and, as such, a tensely paradoxical (and perhaps appropriately humble) concept on which to stake our collective futures.

Resilient design began as a response to climate change (Fehrenbacher 2013). In this context, resiliency connotes both the elasticity required of those living in hurricane alleys and the capacity to recover from the terrible misfortune, shock, and devastation of being hit by a big storm. While architects used to engage environmental concerns via sustainable design, there has been a shift in key terms over the last ten years or so from "sustainability" to "resiliency" (Minnery 2015). "Resiliency" refers to architectural designs invented in response to natural disasters (e.g., Brad Pitt's high-profile "Make It Right" project to rebuild neighborhoods in New Orleans's Lower Ninth Ward and, more recently, designs inspired by Hurricane Sandy) (Feireiss 2009). In the context of contemporary architectural design, "resiliency" modifies buildings—their ability to withstand natural disasters, extreme weather conditions, and perhaps also explosions. Rendered by prestige architectural firms, resilient designs often impose a purportedly universally appealing but historically white modernist and postmodernist aesthetics onto any and all of the communities served (Rollo 2016). In the context of climate change more broadly construed, "resiliency" is a term used to signal the quality that individuals, families, communities, cities, and city systems must cultivate in order to survive the presumably harsher conditions of the near future. It is consistent with a neoliberal politics that shifts the burden of responsibility for managing and emerging from crises, from the federal government to local communities, families, and individuals.

The Sandy Hook Elementary School redesign stands out as worthy of close study, in part, because it extends the architecture of resiliency into the terrain of therapeutic design. In the context of traumatic events like mass shootings, "resiliency" refers to the human capacity for emotional recovery in the wake of those events. It should be said that extending resiliency, from the buildings in question to the people that use them, creates a metaphoric linkage between gun violence on school campuses and terrifying weather events. The implication is that gun violence is as unstoppable as a level-four hurricane. Even as the genealogy of resilient design naturalizes gun violence, the Sandy Hook redesign, in particular, treats the natural world as imbued with the spirit of resiliency. "Nature" becomes both a model and a natural resource of resiliency for humans, who might need to turn to its healing properties in the wake of traumatic events. The Sandy Hook Redesign website brands the project as nature therapy: "Exploring regenerative, restorative, and healing elements of nature as they serve to foster an environment of learning, environmental stewardship, and community involvement" ("The New Sandy Hook School" 2016). Themes explored include: "canopies that connect; bridges and thresholds; tree houses and a new horizon; the inner forest; layers of transparency; and the building as book" ("The New Sandy Hook School" 2016). That is to say, the redesign intentionally addresses itself to the communal, physical, environmental, and psychological dimensions of the term "resiliency," blending these aspects together like the watercolor aesthetic and soft lines used in architectural renderings.

The Sandy Hook redesign includes allusions to historical concepts of childhood as a state of resiliency and children as particularly resilient—an often-repeated assertion of common sense among adults today. It does so via the design concept and cultural ideal of a pastoral childhood. Plucky characters out of literary history feel present in the wooded campus, including Mark Twain's nineteenth-century runaway (Twain 1996) and Sigmund Freud's twentieth-century feral child/artist (Freud 2003). Creativity is a product of necessity in the former (resourcefulness and practical know-how on the run) and refreshing wildness in the latter (the unfettered expressions of those discontented with civilization). A contemporary riff on these anachronistic and semi-primitivist notions of Euro-American childhood, the Sandy Hook redesign incorporates whimsical, modernist aesthetics into a rustic, naturalistic setting.

The building "brings the outdoors inside," with its generous use of glass and brightly colored window shades. The school's atrium, which looks out onto the amphitheater facing the woods, exudes brightness and warmth. Floor to ceiling windows bathe the space in natural light. The inclusion of red, yellow, and orange panes of glass arranged to resemble the randomness of children's artwork lends the space a playful sensibility. Twenty-foot aluminum trees reach up to sturdy hardwood ceilings, drawing the eyes upward to the whimsical, metallic mobiles dangling far overhead. Bean-shaped, brightly colored seating at ground level resembles the shapes and colors that one might see in an Alexander Calder mobile. Here, resilient design invites children to be contemplative and to bask in the space's spirit of buoyancy.

The layout of the campus incarnates the romantic idea that the entire world is both a child's playground and her classroom. Prominent design motifs include forests, animals, tree houses, brightly colored glass, gardens, rain water, mobiles, and sunshine. These motifs are woven throughout the interior and exterior spaces of the forested campus along fluid modernist curves. Writing for *Curbed*, Patrick Sisson provides an elegant description of how the building achieves a sense of flow with the landscape: "Arrayed in three distinct wings, the school wraps around a series of outdoor spaces, including an amphitheater and two playgrounds that run right up to the forested edge of the school property" (Sisson 2016). An ethos of sustainability is reinforced by the building materials used on the project: "The building exterior reflects back upon the surroundings, with planks of machiche and garapa hardwoods arrayed in a wavy pattern suggesting the surrounding trees and hills" (Sisson 2016). The grounds are planted out with sustainable native species and feature foot bridges for traversing the bioswales designed to catch storm run-off and nourish nearby plant life. "Tree house" break-out rooms face the forest and literally hang out over the grounds.

Christopher Hawthorne, architectural critic for the *LA Times*, admits that it may be too much to ask a modestly state-funded elementary school building to make a symbolic statement, but he argues that something approaching this happens with the forest-facing tree-house elements on the back side of the structure. He criticizes the school's façade for being a little too on the nose, citing some of the more saccharine design elements: the obligatory nods to regional aesthetics and expectations. But the back of the structure, which abuts the woods, is where something inspired happens. He writes,

> Though it never captures it fully, their design gestures toward a surprising and bracing idea: that in contemporary American culture we can no longer find reliable security by turning away from the wild, metaphorical or otherwise, and toward the civilized.
>
> *(Hawthorne 2016)*

The brilliance of the school's design, according to Hawthorne, is in its return to a complex, rather than a naïve, understanding of American pastoralism: "American architecture—and New England architecture in particular—has its roots in a kind of self-sufficiency, often exaggerated or theatrical, that requires uncultivated nature as a foil" (Hawthorne 2016). Of course, in contemporary North America, safe spaces designed for children who wish to play at self-sufficiency have as their foil all of those unsafe spaces in which other children have no choice but to operate in a self-sufficient manner, due to the fact that their communities have been abandoned by the state and are policed in a manner that represents an active threat to their well-being, rather than a source of protection. In other words, the romance of American pastoralism is every bit as (if differently) racialized in its contemporary, nostalgic designs of children's play spaces as in its expressions in nineteenth-century American literature.

Hawthorne's read of the Sandy Hook redesign raises the question of what a return to the cultural ideal of a pastoral childhood accomplishes in the present context. Those who subscribed to the nineteenth-century version of pastoralism resented the intrusion of modern technologies on the rural idyll (Marx 2000). A design concept that pays homage to a nineteenth-century pastoral childhood resists—at least on a symbolic level—the historical intrusion of an active-shooter into the metaphoric and literal spaces of idealized childhoods. And yet, nesting high security within resilient design anticipates the shooter's return, acquiescing to a nightmare scenario in which the creative children nestled in their tree houses become sitting ducks once more.

Hawthorne finds hints of a fresh, critical perspective on pastoralism in the redesign. But as a design motif, contemporary American pastoralism does not approach the complexity or nuance that it once achieved in American literature. More specifically, it loses a sophisticated sense of irony, regarding what the intrusion of history onto the rural idyll portends.

Embedded Security

The new Sandy Hook Elementary School building is embedded within the natural landscape such that it achieves a sense of flow with the environment. This design achievement *feels* good because it expresses the cultural ideal of a pastoral childhood. Embedded means protected in the sense that the embedded object is physically surrounded, as the root system of a plant must be embedded in soil so that it might take root and flourish. Gardening metaphors are often used to symbolize the process of tending to children, educating them, and, thereby, seeding change in future generations. Here embedding promises expansion and growth over many years: resilient design.

In contemporary parlance, though, "embedded" increasingly means invisible to the naked eye. If a feature is embedded, it is protected because people don't know that it's there. This is the sense in which embedded is used in computing and military contexts. So, for example, one code is embedded within another or a journalist is embedded with a military unit. Embedded security asks us to embrace the spirit of resiliency in an era of risk by reminding us that security measures are in place even if we cannot see them. In this respect, embedded security is paternalistic. Security measures are embedded, or disguised, so as not to communicate the anticipation of threat to persons using the space on a daily basis. The "gentle fortress" is intended to spare the feelings of the building's inhabitants by avoiding triggers of traumatic memories for returning staff and/or suggestions of possible future injury or harm to students.

The Sandy Hook Redesign is an exemplar of embedded security. Funded by a $50 million grant from the State of Connecticut, the new campus is, in part, a product of risk design (Phippen 2016). State funding for the project means that the new structure and campus must comply with the security standards outlined in the State of Connecticut's *Report of the School Safety Infrastructure Council*. The four major goals of the school security assessment and subsequent compliance measures outlined are to: improve "deterrence," "detection," "delay," and "response" (Currey 2015: 10). The report advocates Crime Prevention Through Environmental Design (CPTED) or using "architectural design, landscape planning, security systems, and visual surveillance to create a potentially crime free environment by influencing human behavior" (Currey 2015: 18). And it advocates the inclusion of "controlled hiding spaces" (33). Other examples of design features required for compliance with state security standards include: "lockable doors on every classroom, having unobstructed ground-level views outside, separating kindergarten and pre-K play areas from the other grades, and locating playgrounds at least 50 feet away from areas that public vehicles access" (Budds 2016). The recommendations outlined in the report conjure up nightmare scenarios in which school campuses become sites of gun violence once again. The report is bracing and demands that state schools brace themselves for the unwanted near-future attacks that it envisions.

Architecture historian Jonathan Massey uses the term risk design to describe the process by which contemporary architecture engages risk imaginaries: "the discourses, representations, and practices through which we understand and conceptualize risks" (Massey 2014: 9). In Massey's study of the Gherkin in London, the concept of risk design is meant to reflect the fact that architecture is not merely an effect of economics and politics but a medium of risk management, by which he means that architecture exerts an influence on economics and politics "as design instantiates power" (Massey 2014: 10). London first turned to design as a response to terrorism in the early 1990s, when the city had to rethink its approach to security in light of the Provisional Irish Republican Army bombings (Massey 2014: 18). In prestige architectural projects like those of Foster + Partners in London, designing out terrorism involves "target hardening," which Massey describes as "a carefully modulated combination of overt and implicit strategies" (Massey 2014: 20). Examples of visible strategies include bollards, mounted surveillance cameras, and airport-style security checks at the building's entrances. Implicit strategies would include the incorporation of materials capable of absorbing blast energy or the use of decentralized ventilation systems as a means of mitigating the risks associated with chemical or biological attack (Massey 2014: 19). A selling point in architectural projects designed for businesses and governmental agencies, overt security strategies are not so desirable in spaces designed for children's education and play. Bollards, for example, do not have a place in the design concept of a pastoral childhood.

Embedded security is "subtle," if not entirely invisible. It delivers risk design without the armored aesthetics and paramilitary vibe. This did not happen overnight in the U.S. context, where risk design took shape in response to the threat of international terrorism. The most reliable risk management choice for schools, according to the Department of Homeland Security and the Federal Emergency Management Agency, is "target hardening." Target hardening implies a definable territory to be guarded. In the case of school architecture and concern with children's safety, interiors are conceived of as "safe havens" and "safe rooms," or islands of "life safety systems" amid the threat of death looming all around. The document cautions against taking the bunker mentality too far because of the unique vulnerabilities associated with that approach. As a result, tensions arise between a desire for protective barriers versus the appeal of open vistas that enable surveillance of the grounds by school personnel; designed enclaves (or defensible areas) and threats associated with a greater concentration of "assets" ("clustered versus dispersed functions"); partitioning as a mitigation technique vs. the potential for isolation and loss of surveillance capacity. The primer suggests that schools hedge their bets ("Primer" 2003).

The architects working on the Sandy Hook redesign nest covert risk mitigation features within a design concept that communicates resiliency via tropes of childlike whimsy and natural wonderment. When members of the press describe the Sandy Hook redesign in terms of "embedded security," they are referencing the design team's avoidance of overt strategies of risk management in favor of implicit strategies. Embedded security attempts to resolve the conflicts that arise when designers consider the potential uses of a space even as they attempt to deliver design for security's sake. When engaging in risk design, the Federal Emergency Management Agency (FEMA) admits that "conflicts sometimes arise between security-oriented site design and conventional site design. For example, open circulation and common spaces (which are desirable for conventional design) may be detrimental to certain aspects of security" ("Primer" 2003: 2–2). Landscape design may have to be compromised in the name of greater security because vegetation may provide "a cover or screen for covert activity" (2–4). The first edition of FEMA's primer on safe school design advocates a "holistic" approach that integrates form and function and treats security and "more traditional design tasks" as complementary (2–4). In the intervening years between the publication of the first edition of the FEMA primer (2003) and the Sandy Hook redesign project (2016), the key word shifts from "integration" to "embedded," where the emphasis shifts from mixing competing design functions to hiding one function within another form or function.

Embedded security naturalizes risk design. The Sandy Hook redesign communicates serenity and non-defensiveness via its openness to nature and the dynamic sense of flow between the campus's interior and exterior spaces. The literal transparency of glass makes this possible. But, the glass is impact-resistant and was intended to provide expansive views of the school grounds from inside so that teachers and administrators might act as sentries, monitoring the campus for intruders. Indeed, the earliest usage of the term "resiliency" (in the fifteenth century) is in terms of the manumission theory of sight. "Why those things that are to be seen must of necessity be enlightened? because sight is the resiliencie [L. *resilientia*] of the light from the object to the eye" ("Resilience," Oxford English Dictionary 2010: 1651). Ironically, this outdated understanding of how vision works resonates with the concept of "natural" or "organic" surveillance liberally employed in the Sandy Hook redesign. "Natural surveillance" is a crime prevention method in which city planners modify environments in a manner that heightens the visibility of the people moving through and using those spaces. The environment and its condition of visibility deter potential offenders by communicating the likelihood that wrongful acts will be observed by others using the space. In short, the environment's design and lighting conditions make a person with the intent to do harm feel conspicuous, as if that person was illuminated and rays of light were passing from his body directly into the eyes of nearby persons, turning them into witnesses.

Contemporary applications of natural surveillance depict embodied practices of surveillance as an organic effect of smart design. This reflects the term's drift from its roots in neighborhood and community activism to law-and-order and design solutions to crime. Urban planner and neighborhood activist Jane Jacobs coined the term in her groundbreaking book *The Death and Life of American Cities*, written with inspiration from her Greenwich Village neighborhood and published in 1961. Natural surveillance refers to Jacobs's idea that the best way to promote neighborhood safety is to nurture the cultural and social life of those spaces. The more active and engaged a community is, the more that there is going on in a neighborhood, the more the people who live there will remain curious about goings on and actively engage in people watching. A vibrant community translates into "eyes on the street," not because people are socialized into peer surveillance as, for example, in contemporary neighborhood watch programs or the Department of Homeland Security's "If You See Something, Say Something" campaign. A lively community draws eyes and ears because of human curiosity and social impulse, rather than savvy skepticism and widespread fear or mistrust of others (Goodyear 2013). In Jacobs's words:

> You can't make people watch streets they do not want to watch. Safety on the streets by surveillance and mutual policing of one another sounds grim, but in real life it is not grim. The safety of the street works best, most casually, and with least frequent taint of hostility or suspicion precisely where people are using and most enjoying the streets voluntarily and are least conscious, normally, that they are policing.
>
> *(Goodyear 2013)*

In contemporary usage, the concept of natural surveillance has been stripped of pleasure and curiosity and is imbued with hostility and suspicion in keeping with peer surveillance and neighborhood watch programs, which implore citizens to vigilantly manage the risk of international terrorism and engage in the paranoid policing of white spaces, respectively.

The Sandy Hook redesign supports natural surveillance. The design offers "plenty of sight lines from inside the building to the surrounding campus and also within the structure. This essentially turns everyone in the building into a sentry that can alert the administrative staff if anything seems amiss" (Budds 2016). The contemporary, stripped-down version of natural surveillance puts additional pressure on educators and administrators, who are expected to vigilantly surveil the school grounds for intruders while also performing the duties outlined in their contracts. While natural surveillance claims to be an organic effect of well-designed spaces, in practice it puts educators and administrative staff in the role of lookout, which shifts the responsibility for stopping gun violence in schools from perpetrators and legislators to educators and students.

Conclusion

Embedding risk design within resilient design does not pretend to resolve the contradiction in cultural values presented by these two approaches. Take for example, the Newtown community's careful approach to reopening its doors, which is consistent with its decision to site a memorial to the mass shooting downtown and at a considerable remove from the school grounds. With an emphasis on resiliency over memorialization, the community decided that only after the new school was back in operation and some semblance of normalcy had returned to the community ("moving on") would Newton turn its attention to a memorial ("reflecting back"). But risk design is inherently historical insofar as it outfits buildings for unwanted futures by modeling those unwanted futures on traumatic historical events. Still, there is no denying the school's charm. Most parents would be delighted to send their young children there.

A design that recovers less fearful and relatively untethered concepts of childhood is a bold and inspirational move in the context of contemporary moral panics over child safety, offering an example of how design might challenge forth and inspire change even as it charms. But embedded security represents a doubling down on design—on behalf of some communities and not others—in an historical context in which adults lack the political will to pass adequate gun control legislation. Because we refuse to prevent gun violence, we remake the school environments of privileged kids such that they serve two diametrically opposed functions: security and openness. In the contemporary context, design vies with law-and-order as a favorite go-to solution for the social problems that plague us. There is a racial politics to which solution is deemed appropriate in a given context. But the Sandy Hook redesign, in particular, begs the question: what or whom is being protected by the brilliance of "embedded security"? The obvious answer to this question is: children in affluent school districts. The less obvious but no less true answer is: gun manufacturers and enthusiasts. Embedded security buries cultural memories of the last mass shooting in the infrastructural details of new and retrofitted school buildings with clever landscape designs. If preparedness means readying oneself and one's community for the worst-case scenario, then the gun owner's right to be prepared (an armed citizenry) demands that administrators, educators, and students master another version of preparedness. Like so many coiled springs, the "education corps" must be prepared to be resilient, if and when they fail to prevent future acts of gun violence against their communities.

References

Budds, D. (2016) "The School an entire town designed: rebuilding Sandy Hook Elementary," *CO. DESIGN*. www.fastcodesign.com/3062562/the-school-an-entire-town-designed-rebuilding-sandy-hook-elementary (May 1, 2017).

Currey, M. (2015) *Report of the School Safety Infrastructure Council*. (2014) Online. http://das.ct.gov/images/1090/ssic_final_draft_report.pdf (May 1, 2017).

Fehrenbacher, J. (2013) "Resilient design: is resilience the new sustainability?" *Inhabitat*. https://inhabitat.com/resilient-design-is-resilience-the-new-sustainability/ (May 1, 2017).

Feireiss, K. (2009) *Architecture in Times of Need: Make It Right Rebuilding the Lower Ninth Ward*, New York: Prestel.

Freud, Sigmund. (2003) *Totem and Taboo*, Abingdon, Oxon: Routledge.

Goodyear, S. (2013) "A new way of understanding 'eyes on the street'," *Citylab*. www.citylab.com/equity/2013/07/new-way-understanding-eyes-street/6276/ (May 1, 2017).

Hawthorne, C. (2016) "At Sandy Hook Elementary, a new campus and a new start at a site of horror," *Los Angeles Times*. www.latimes.com/entertainment/arts/la-et-cm-sandy-hook-school-20160827-snap-story.html (May 1, 2017).

Hussey, K. and Foderaro, L. (2016) "New Sandy Hook School is ready nearly 4 years after massacre," *New York Times*. www.nytimes.com/2016/07/30/nyregion/new-sandy-hook-school-is-ready-nearly-4-years-after-massacre.html (May 1, 2017).

Jacobs, J. (1992) *The Death and Life of Great American Cities*, New York: Vintage.

Marx, Leo. (2000) *The Machine in the Garden: Technology and the Pastoral Ideal in America*, New York: Oxford University Press.

Massey, J. (2014) "Risk Design," *Grey Room* 54 (Winter): 9.

Massey, J. TenHoor, M., and Korsh, S. (2015) "Introduction: Black Lives Matter," *Aggregate*. http://we-aggregate.org/piece/black-lives-matter (May 1, 2017).

Minnery, R. (2015) "Resilience to adaptation: a crucible for ethical practice in architecture," *Architect*. www.architectmagazine.com/aia-architect/aiafeature/resilience-to-adaptation_o (May 1, 2017).

Phippen, J. (2016) "A New Sandy Hook Elementary School," *The Atlantic Monthly*. www.theatlantic.com/news/archive/2016/07/new-sandy-hook-elementary-school/493586/ (May 1, 2017).

"Primer to design safe school projects in case of terrorist attacks: providing protection to people and buildings" (2003) *Risk Management Series*. Federal Emergency Management Agency 428. https://permanent.access.gpo.gov/lps44537/fema428.pdf (May 1, 2017).

"Resilience." (2010) *Oxford English Dictionary*. www.oed.com.libezproxy2.syr.edu/view/Entry/163619?redirectedFrom=resilience#eid (May 1, 2017).

Rollo, D. (2016) "Rendering disaster architecture: remodeling citizenship in post-Katrina New Orleans," Dissertations – ALL. Paper 503.

Sisson, Patrick. (2016) "New Sandy Hook Elementary School design finds safety, security in openness," *Curbed*. www.curbed.com/2018/2/22/17042004/sandy-hook-elementary-school-design-security-safety (May 1, 2017).

"The New Sandy Hook School" (2016). www.sandyhook2016.com (May 1, 2017).

Twain, M. (1996) *Adventures of Huckleberry Finn*, New York: Random House.

Weller, Chris. (2016) "The New Sandy Hook Elementary School hides high security in beautiful design," *Business Insider*. www.businessinsider.com/new-sandy-hook-elementary-design-2016-8 (May 1, 2017).

5

When the Megaproject Meets the Village

Formal and Informal Urbanization in Southern China

Max Hirsh and Dorothy Tang

Many accounts of contemporary architecture in China focus on the country's urban megaprojects, executed at a scale and speed that are unfathomable in the developed world (Wu and Gaubatz 2012).[1] Other scholars, meanwhile, have drawn attention to the hyperdense urban villages that have become the default home for the millions of migrant workers who power China's service and manufacturing industries (Bach 2010; Kochan 2015). These two settlement forms are emblematic of the two modes of urbanization that have characterized China's post-Mao development over the past three decades. The central government's top-down planning approach is evident in China's myriad megaprojects, whose construction typically entails large-scale demolition of the existing built environment, an accelerated design process aimed at delivering bombastic results, and scant contemplation of the needs of their intended users. Urban villages, on the other hand, are enclaves ruled by rural land governance policies and evince a bottom-up accretion of urban functions that is predicated on a haphazard juxtaposition of programmatic elements, widespread disregard for health and safety regulations, and a pragmatic repurposing of existing village typologies to match the changing demands of the urban economy.

Architectural analyses of these two settlement forms have often been written in order to highlight the relative merits of, and purported conflict between, top-down and bottom-up modes of urban development in contemporary Chinese cities. By contrast, this essay studies the interaction between megaprojects and villages in order to better understand how the creative combination of formal and informal architectural strategies can produce outcomes that are both complementary and beneficial. In this essay—which is part of a larger project on village redevelopment strategies in southern China—we study how the construction of a new "higher education mega center" on the edge of Guangzhou's urban area transformed the economy of previously rural villages. At the same time, we demonstrate how entrepreneurship at the village level compensated for structural and programmatic deficits in the megaproject's master plan. To do so, we investigate three traditional village building typologies—and their programmatic transformations over the past decade—in order to shed light on the productive potential of integrating formal and informal modes of urban design in the contemporary Chinese context.

In so doing, we seek to draw attention to the social and spatial experiments that are being conducted in suburban villages located on the margins of major urban centers in southern China: creative approaches, borne of pragmatism and ingenuity, that open up the possibility of alternative architectural models and urban futures for China as a whole.

In 2000, the Guangzhou Planning Bureau commissioned a study to identify the site for a new Guangzhou Higher Education Mega Center (GZHMC). The colossal project was one of dozens of "university cities" that were built across China over the past two decades (Li, Li, and Wang 2014; Ye et al. 2014). These university cities are physical evidence of the central government's ambition to expand access to higher education, a goal first articulated under a 1995 policy called "Science and Education Leading the Country to Prosperity"; and subsequently formalized in China's 10th five-year plan on education. At the turn of the twenty-first century, these policy innovations led to a five-fold increase in the number of new university students in less than a decade (Liu 2008: 29).

To address the unprecedented expansion of China's student population, local governments across the country were instructed to build new higher education districts that were designed at the scale of mid-sized cities. Combining up to a dozen campuses on one site, these residential "university cities" aimed to accommodate hundreds of thousands of students in a comprehensive teaching, learning, and living environment. For many municipalities, university towns also served two additional purposes. First, university towns are a typical example of so-called "face" projects: bombastic megaprojects such as opera houses, airports, stadiums, and new central business districts (CBDs) that are designed to increase a city's visibility and prestige. The timely completion of these "face" projects within the cycle of the five-year plan is essential for securing future promotions for mayors and provincial governors throughout China. Second, as urban land became an increasingly valuable commodity, universities found it difficult to expand existing inner-city facilities, as planners re-zoned these downtown locations for more lucrative functions. Relocating campuses to peripheral education districts would both free up space in the inner city, and help to develop less desirable locations on the suburban fringe. By 2015, more than 40 university cities had been built across China.

The construction of Guangzhou's University Town needs to be understood within this broader urban development paradigm. Completed in 19 months, it was designed to accommodate a population of up to 400,000 students enrolled at ten institutions of higher learning spread across an island on the southeastern edge of Guangzhou called Xiaoguwei (Figure 5.1). Prior to its redevelopment, Xiaoguwei had been home to a rural population of about 14,000 people living in six villages, who derived their livelihood from fishing, agriculture, and forestry (Liu 2008: 121). Two villages were located on the site of the University Town's future central axis, and were thus demolished, their inhabitants relocated to a new public housing development near the island (Liu 2008: 123). The four remaining villages were incorporated into the Higher Education Mega Center's master plan. However, as the architect Liu Heng notes, the villages' integration into University Town took place without any study of the settlements' social characteristics and topographic conditions. Existing spatial and economic practices were consequently ignored and disrupted. In one village, for example, an elevated highway was built on top of an eighteenth-century ancestor hall; elsewhere, a 50-meter ring road sliced through a fishing village, disconnecting it from its waterfront jetties (Liu 2008: 128–129). More problematically, little thought was given to how these villages might interact—socially, spatially, economically—with a projected population of nearly half a million students. Regarding villagers as an unfortunate impediment to future development, planners envisioned that the four remaining villages would function as autonomous islands, sealed off from University Town by six-lane boulevards and two-meter high separation walls.

Max Hirsh and Dorothy Tang

Figure 5.1 An aerial view of Xiaoguwei Island, home to the Guangzhou Higher Education Mega Center and four villages
Source: Photograph by Dorothy Tang.

The inattention to detail, both formal and programmatic, is not surprising, given that planners were tasked with designing a city from scratch within an extremely short time frame. Specifically, they were required to plan and design ten campuses, with a total of 300 buildings, in a design phase that lasted less than three months. A hastily organized competition, officiated by the Guangzhou Planning Bureau, determined each building's design. In the final selection process, jurors were allocated a maximum of five seconds to evaluate each of more than 1000 detailed design proposals (Liu 2008: 90–92). The results are emblematic of early twenty-first-century institutional architecture in China (Figure 5.2). University Town's ten campuses are characterized by an unremitting reductiveness, formalized by a relentless repetition of massing, building alignments, and stylistic details. The resulting impression of emptiness and abstraction is reinforced by the Higher Education Mega Center's geographically extensive scale. Driving across the island on one of University Town's three major ring roads, visitors encounter an endless array of sports complexes, administrative buildings, and formal plazas that alternate with rigidly aligned dormitories, arranged in groups of ten or more. The ring roads divide the island into three concentric zones, each measuring up to 1 kilometer across. Traveling from one campus to another, or transferring to one of the two subway stations located on University Island's central axis, can take up to 45 minutes by bus.

Although Guanghzhou's Higher Education Mega Center was designed as a self-sufficient city, the interstitial spaces between the dormitories, boulevards, and classrooms are notable for the complete absence of urban programming. When the first batch of students moved in to University Town in 2004, they quickly discovered that it was impossible to find food late in the evening and on weekends, when university canteens were closed. Entertainment facilities were nonexistent. Dormitory rules forbade couples from living together. Perhaps more surprisingly,

When the Megaproject Meets the Village

Figure 5.2 Typical campus architecture in Guangzhou's University Town
Source: Photograph by Dorothy Tang.

students found it difficult to locate a quiet place to study, especially during exam periods. University libraries lacked sufficient seating, dormitories proved too noisy, and most campus facilities were locked down by the late afternoon.

University Town is thus perhaps most notable for its lack of services and spaces that cater to the basic needs of its primary users: students. In order to fill these formal and programmatic voids, the four villages that remained on Xiaoguwei Island have developed a symbiotic relationship with the university campuses that surround them. Within a few short years, these villages have transitioned from traditional rural settlements into densely populated enclaves tailored to the needs of students. Through a process of what the urban scholar He Shenjing terms "studentification," these villages compensate for structural and programmatic deficiencies in University Town's master plan by supplying flexible and affordable living, work, and leisure spaces for students and recent graduates, many of whom remain on the island after graduation (He 2015). While these practices were initially condemned by university officials—who criticized the proliferation of illicit "love hotels" and other forms of unsupervised entertainment—the process of "studentification" has been increasingly formalized, evidenced by the construction of higher quality retail environments and by the programmatic adaptation of traditional rural typologies to meet the villages' changing social and economic profile. In the process, these villages have evolved into a new settlement form that cannot be accurately described as either rural or urban. Surrounded by a low-density institutional environment, they are not comparable to the hyperdense "villages in the city" that have been entirely engulfed by rapid urbanization, and that have been the subject of much academic inquiry in the past decade. Nor do these villages resemble the traditional rural settlement forms out of which they emerged. Instead, the villages located inside University Town occupy an in-between space, on the outskirts of Guangzhou, where the forms and functions of city and country life co-exist in close proximity.

Beigang: Becoming a "College Village"

An investigation of the architecture of Beigang, a village located between the campuses of Sun Yat-sen University and the Guangdong University of Foreign Studies, sheds light on the productive interaction between the megaproject and the village, and on the concomitant typological innovations that have taken place throughout University Town. A walk through Beigang reveals some of the typical features of the in-between villages located in suburban Guangzhou. More than 5000 rental units and 500 stores are packed into the village's warren of alleyways. Pedestrians need to be mindful of the electrical wires that sway precariously just above their heads, the dogs languishing at their feet, and the motorcycles that whiz through the narrow streets at breakneck speed. Asphalted walkways give way to patches of muddy earth at regular intervals. Against this backdrop of haphazard development, we study Beigang's "studentification" through an analysis of three traditional village typologies: the ancestor hall, the village house, and the marketplace.

From Marketplace to Food Street

Beigang's popularity among students has been the driving force behind the village's rapid redevelopment over the past decade. Soon after University Town opened, Beigang became known for its concentration of affordable restaurants offering tasty food, operated by migrants out of hastily repurposed village homes. Entrepreneurs who lacked sufficient start-up capital rented metallic push carts on a seasonal basis, returning to their home villages at the end of each semester. In 2011, in an attempt to capitalize on Beigang's culinary reputation, the village committee hired a local developer to build an outdoor "food street" with higher quality finishes and centralized sanitation facilities (Figure 5.3). At night and on weekends, throngs of students stroll along the heavily trafficked arcade, which is located along the road that marks the boundary between Beigang and the campus of Sun Yat-sen University. Dozens of cooks tend to steaming pots, griddles, and bamboo baskets, selling street snacks and more substantial meals to University Town's hungry inhabitants. The street's remarkable culinary variety testifies to the geographic diversity of Beigang's migrant workers who have been attracted to the village and its ever-replenishing supply of young, middle-income customers, from all over China. Shops serving typical Cantonese cuisine—congee, roast goose, barbecued pork—compete with hawkers offering dishes of more distant progeny: Lanzhou beef noodles, lamb kebabs from Xinjiang, Fujianese pork rib soup. Other restaurants dish out sinified approximations of Western, Korean, and Japanese cuisine. In between the food stalls, barbers, beauticians, and clothing designers cater to the notoriously fickle fashion sensibilities of the undergraduate crowd. The food street's cosmopolitan attributes, both real and imagined, are thus reflected in the consumption practices of the meandering students who, strolling languidly between stalls, buy sizzling halal *chuan* from women in headscarves and indulge in makeovers that promise to make them look like their favorite K-pop stars.

From Ancestor Hall to Hotel

Ancestor halls are a common feature of villages throughout southern China. They formalize the Confucian practice of ancestor worship, and are important sites of pilgrimage and donation for relatives making return visits from overseas. These halls also operate as communal village spaces, hosting weddings, festivals, and performances. Beigang village originally contained two ancestor halls, maintained by two separate clans with the surname Siu. When University Town was built, part of the village was demolished to make way for the surrounding dormitories, and one of the two Siu clans was resettled in a new housing estate south of Xiaoguwei Island. Responding pragmatically to their forced relocation, the clan decided to rent out their ancestor hall and distribute the income among the resettled villagers. They found a taker in Mr. Ye, a young

Figure 5.3 Beigang's marketplace and "food street" are popular among the university students who live in the dormitories surrounding the village

Source: Photograph by Dorothy Tang.

migrant entrepreneur from eastern Guangdong province who was one of the pioneers of Beigang's thriving guest house industry (He and Su 2015). When Ye first arrived in the village in 2008, he discovered that local university students suffered from a lack of privacy in the dormitories, and that young couples had nowhere to spend time alone. Working together with the Siu clan, Ye converted the ancestor hall into the Silver Sky Guesthouse. He demolished the interior spaces but kept its impressive gateway, and then built a three-floor addition onto the back, which Ye outfitted with 20 guest rooms that can be rented by the hour, day, or week. At the same time, the Siu clan rented out the remaining areas of the ancestor hall to two other migrant entrepreneurs, who converted the hall's side wing and forecourt into an all-you-can-eat hotpot buffet and a bicycle rental shop, respectively (Figure 5.4).

The Silver Sky is one of the more than 80 guesthouses that have proliferated in Beigang's narrow alleyways. During the academic year, they serve as de facto love hotels, where young couples can enjoy a few hours away from the prying eyes of classmates and teachers. More upmarket lodges like the Silver Sky are also popular among parents who visit their college-age children during holidays and at graduation. In the summer months, guest houses like the Silver Sky transform once again, in keeping with Beigang's evolving role as a site not only for entertainment, but also as an ancillary zone for professional development, intellectual creativity, and the incubation of new ideas.

From Village House to Co-Working Space

These evolving functions are evident in a village house behind the ancestor hall that is managed by a recent university graduate from Fujian province. Like many of his classmates at Sun Yat-sen University, Chen Xiaowei often complained about University Town's lack of informal spaces where he could study, chat, hang out with friends, or work on group projects (Chen 2016). Chen found this particularly frustrating in the evening and on weekends, when most campus buildings are closed. During a vacation to Beijing, he chanced upon on a café/co-working space geared towards the needs of college students, offering inexpensive beverages, free wi-fi, long hours, and an atmosphere that was conducive to both studying and socializing. Chen decided to replicate that model in Beigang. A classmate provided the introduction to a local villager who was looking to rent out his family's home, which Chen repurposed into the Fangjian Co-Working Space (Figure 5.5). To do so, Chen hired students from the Guangzhou Academy of Fine Arts—which is also located in University Town—to redesign the interior of an historic village courtyard house. The converted courtyard hosts a tea lounge and a communal study space. A glass ceiling covers the courtyard with a shifting grid of pre-cast concrete panels on the ground, interspersed with plants that thrive on natural light. The lounge's interior features naturally finished laminated wood shelves and a long work bench equipped with electrical outlets and a grid of bookshelves. The lounge is a popular hangout for current students, and for the many recent graduates—notably product and fashion designers—who have opened small shops in the village. Rooms towards the back of the small complex are equipped with laminated wood conference tables and projectors. The human resource departments of local companies frequently organize recruiting sessions for graduating students inside these smaller spaces. During the summer months, the co-working space hosts freehand drawing and 3D modeling studios organized by professors from the Guangzhou College of Technology and Business. The college is not located anywhere near University Town: in fact, it is about 60 kms away. Nevertheless, the instructors found that Beigang village—with its abundance of cheap housing and flexible work spaces—offered a favorable atmosphere for teaching and learning that was markedly different from the austere and highly regimented environment of their own campus (Zhou 2016).

Figure 5.4 The Silver Sky Guesthouse is located inside a decommissioned ancestor hall

Source: Photograph by Dorothy Tang.

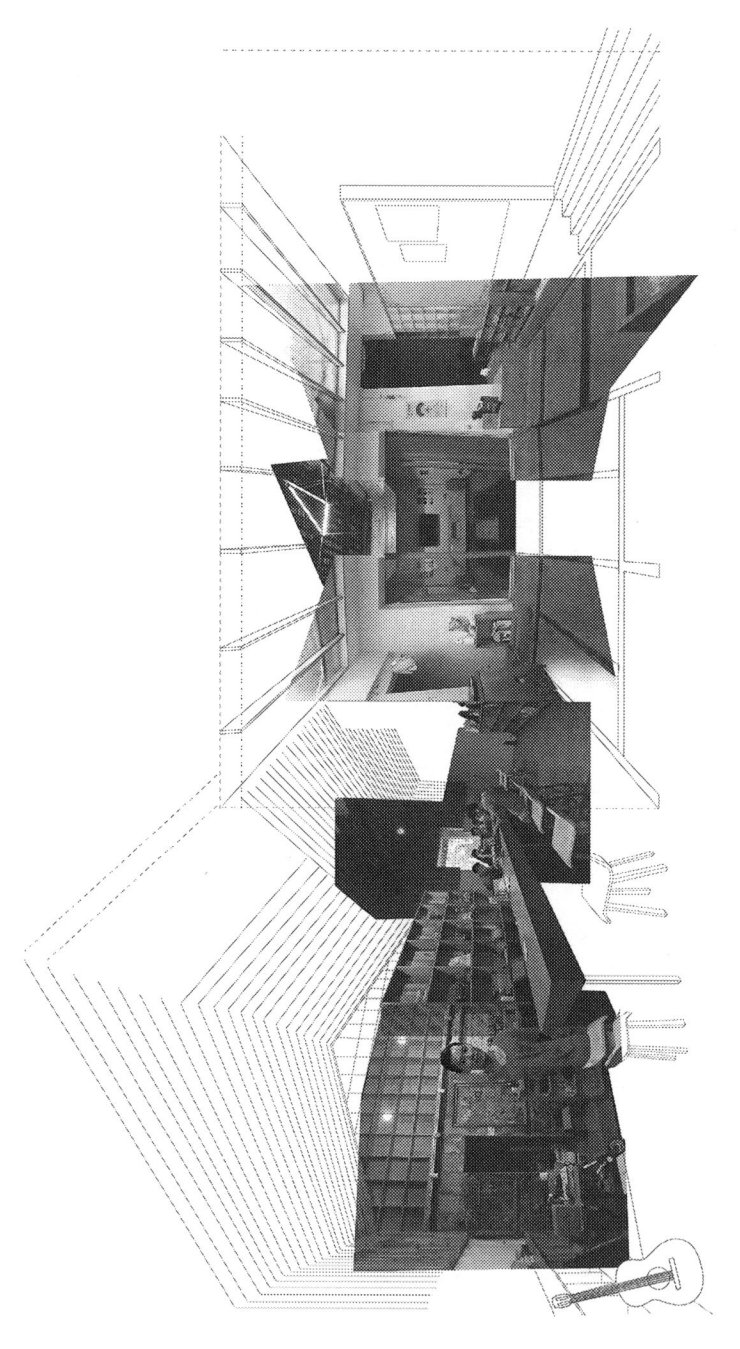

Figure 5.5 Students from Sun Yat-sen University and the Guangdong Academy of Fine Arts teamed up to convert a former village house into Beigang's first co-working space

Source: Photograph by Dorothy Tang.

Conclusion

Beigang's lively public spaces and dynamic economy arise from the productive interaction between university students and migrants who operate small student-oriented businesses such as restaurants, dessert cafés, hotels, snack stalls, clothing stores, and beauty salons. The spatial dialogue between students and migrant entrepreneurs is moderated by Beigang's original village population, who have rented out their homes and partnered with real estate developers in order to formalize Beigang's role as a service center for university students, and to continuously upgrade and intensify the process of "studentification" taking place in their home village. The three typologies discussed above shed light on the formal and functional implications of that process. On the one hand, the ancestor hall hotel is indicative of the rather unsentimental way in which the village's architectural heritage has been repurposed to meet Beigang's shifting programmatic needs. In effect, the ancestor hall's conversion emblematizes a pragmatic approach to rapidly changing circumstances that emphasizes a frugal adaptation of existing village typologies.

More broadly, we can discern two larger themes that emerge out of our typological study of village transformation in Guangzhou's University Town. First, we argue that the village needs to be understood as both a service center for university students and as a low-cost incubator for start-up firms and creative industries that are connected to University Town's institutions of higher learning. Beigang's migrant entrepreneurs play a critical role in providing the basic necessities of daily life, such as food and clothing, to the thousands of students in University Town. At the same time, the redesigned village homes offer transitional living and work spaces where recent university graduates can transition from student life into the adult world: a place where they can hone their design skills, test out new product ideas, meet potential employers, and experiment with running a business. Beigang thus functions as a locus of creativity and economic development in a much more organic and ultimately effective way than master-planned "creative industry districts" that aestheticize rather than actualize knowledge-intensive economic innovation. In effect, Beigang can be read as a vernacular innovation district where highly talented individuals from the nearby university campuses take advantage of the freedom and flexibility afforded by the less regulated environment of the village. The insertion of these young people into the village not only improves the educational experience and career prospects of the students themselves, but also produces a vast supply of service-sector jobs for migrant workers as well as a reliable source of rental income for the original villagers. The University Town master plan's original intention to segregate the villages from the surrounding universities is thus turned upside down, providing benefits to both.

This leads to our second conclusion: namely, that megaprojects like Guangzhou's Higher Education Mega Center can only operate effectively in tandem with informal "in-fill." In effect, Beigang compensates for some of University Town's basic design flaws by providing for the everyday needs of students, which were somehow overlooked by the megaproject's master plan. That includes both basic life necessities, such as food, as well as the typical accoutrements of university life in a consumption-oriented society, such as fashionable clothing and entertainment. At the same time, the village overcomes larger flaws in the campuses' conceptual framework by acting as a bridge between education and industry. Neither of these issues—one quotidian, the other existential—was addressed by the megaproject's master plan.

Beigang is just one of hundreds of villages across China that have been rapidly transformed by their proximity to large-scale megaprojects. These "megaproject villages," for lack of an existing term, exhibit an entrepreneurial spirit that permits them to adapt quickly and efficiently to changing social, spatial, and economic circumstances. In so doing, they compensate for significant functional gaps in the master plans of urban megaprojects, and are able to approach unforeseen challenges—which often emerge only after the projects are complete—in a flexible and responsive manner. Rather than regarding villages as an unfortunate vestige of the past and impediment to growth, architects and planners would be well advised to incorporate these existing settlements into the design process of future urban development projects.

Note

1 The authors would like to thank Margaret Crawford and Liu Heng for their helpful comments and suggestions; as well as Jin Jiayi and Peng Yixuan for their research assistance. Unless otherwise noted, the essay is based on fieldwork conducted at Guangzhou Higher Education Mega Center between September 2015 and November 2016. The project was funded through the generous support of the Division of Landscape Architecture at the University of Hong Kong and the Hang Seng Bank Golden Jubilee Education Fund for Research.

References

Bach, J. (2010) "'They come in peasants and leave citizens': urban villages and the making of Shenzhen, China," *Cultural Anthropology* 25: 421–458.
Chen, X. (2016) Interview with the authors at Fangjian Co-Working Space, Beigang Village, Guangzhou, June 21.
He, D. and Su, J. (2015) "Beigang: University Town made it rich (Beigang: Daxuecheng Rang Ta Fu Qilai)," *Guangzhou Daily*, January 15.
He, S. (2015) "Consuming urban living in 'villages in the city': studentification in Guangzhou, China," *Urban Studies* 52, 15 (November): 2849–2873.
Kochan, D. (2015) "Placing the urban village: a spatial perspective on the development process of urban villages in contemporary China," *International Journal of Urban and Regional Research* 39: 927–947.
Li, Z., Li, X., and Wang, L. (2014) "Speculative urbanism and the making of university towns in China: A case of Guangzhou University Town," *Habitat International* 44: 422–431.
Liu, H. (2008) "Instant urbanization: the making of Guangzhou University City," Unpublished Thesis (Doctor of Design), Harvard University.
Wu, W. and Gaubatz, P. (2012) *The Chinese City*, London: Routledge.
Ye, C., Chen, M., Chen, R., and Guo, Z. (2014) "Multi-scalar separations: land use and production of space in Xianlin, a university town in Nanjing," *Habitat International* 42: 264–272.
Zhou, L. (2016) Interview with the authors at Fangjian Co-Working Space, Beigang Village, Guangzhou, July 22.

6

After the Counter-monument
Commemoration in the Expanded Field

Mechtild Widrich

Is there anything distinctive about contemporary memorials or monuments? Commemoration remains, as it always has been, a retrieval of past events for the present. According to writer Robert Musil, who described the "job" of monuments in the 1920s, memorials or monuments typically use objects and spatial settings to "kick-start" commemoration (Musil 1978: 507). And yet, the form, function, and setting of monuments have changed rapidly over the last decades. This shift has been felt so distinctively, that the prestigious *Encyclopedia of Aesthetics*, published in 1998, found it necessary to have two entries under the rubric "Monument." The editor's comment on this decision was as follows: "to appreciate the relevance of monuments as subjects of aesthetic inquiry, this entry comprises two essays: Historical Overview, Twentieth Century counter-monuments."[1] The somewhat unwieldy term "counter-monument," used primarily for European Holocaust memorials, must have seemed fitting to describe a then-new, "democratic," ostensibly antiauthoritarian model of commemoration, embodied in monuments whose formal qualities, from jagged and scored surfaces to immersive or open formats (rather than monoliths on plinths), symbolized loss, disappearance, and fragmentation. Gone was the gesture of victory conveyed by an erect, stable permanence. In the United States, Maya Lin's *Vietnam Veterans Memorial* (1982), whose commission and execution in fact preceded the popularization of the counter-monument concept, is often put in this category. Indeed it has become the exemplary counter-monument for the subtle yet powerful way it suggests grief and loss on an enormous scale. While melding into the severe landscape of the Washington Mall, it allows for the tracing of the name of casualties inscribed in the black basaltic stone. This interaction has become so much part of the work that most printed photographs of the monument show some sort of "engaged visitor" touching the stone while being reflected in the dark surface (see Johnson 1998: 213ff.); volunteers organized by the U.S. National Parks Service hand out tracing paper and pencils. Kirk Savage has defined Lin's project, which faced aesthetic and political resistance before becoming the most widely acclaimed American memorial (indeed, a mobile half-size replica travels the country) as "the nation's first 'therapeutic' memorial," meaning by this both the monument's cathartic effect on visitors and, more critically, the tendency to use (counter-)monuments to heal rather than thematize conflict (Savage 2009: 267).

Let me be clear. The traditional victory monument is alive and well. In the United States it is evidenced in the 2004 *National World War II Memorial* on the Washington Mall. Elsewhere it takes a more dramatic form. In Skopje, the capital of Macedonia, for example, much of the city's socialist-modernist fabric (an earthquake in 1963 had destroyed many of the historical buildings) has been torn out by the conservative twenty-first-century government in a megalomaniacal effort to recall the glories of a "Macedonian nation" extending back in time to Alexander the Great. Forty new monuments and 20 historicist buildings will reshape the perception of this region's history for generations to come (Figure 6.1). But there is no doubt that these kinds of unregenerate "monumentality" are a strange leftover from past centuries, ignoring not only the queasy indifference that Musil diagnosed in responses to urban statuary (he thought this an outdated model), but also the postmodern critique of historical master narratives. The latter, coupled with growing demands for after taking political responsibility for acts of injustice ranging from slavery to the Shoah, led to the institution of memorials meant to engage individuals subjectively rather than attempting to instill heavy-handed moral or political lessons. In that sense, it is Lin's memorial and not the bronze trio of soldiers plopped down near it (*The Three Soldiers* by Frederick Hart) at the behest of conservative congressmen, nor Skopje, that embodies the early twenty-first-century consensus on how the past, and in particular the traumatic past, should be remembered.

The term counter-monument itself, introduced by the American literary scholar James E. Young (1992)—who also wrote the corresponding entry in the *Encyclopedia of Aesthetics*—has thus proven useful to identify the shift in artistic practices of commemoration that took place in

Figure 6.1 *Mothers of Macedonia* fountain and *Warrior Monument*, Skopje, Macedonia, 2014
Source: Copyright Mechtild Widrich.

the late twentieth century. It has also, unfortunately, overshadowed the complex debate about a larger change in the way we understand historical consciousness, which includes the various attempts to involve people in history instead of "feeding" them an official narrative of progress and national success; moreover, as a coinage that seems to describe a particular genre of public art and architecture fairly well, it has obscured the unstable links of recent memorials with practices ranging from landscape design to performance art and the use of social media. Young himself was concerned primarily with projects that commemorate the victims of wrongdoings of states, from the colonial period to the Cold War, and most prominently with the German and Austrian efforts to commemorate the victims of the Holocaust. The complicated question of how to find a form for monuments dedicated to groups that had suffered at the hands of the society commemorating them led to discussions that, however compelling, tended to focus on the formal choices—from the comic-book Holocaust memoir of Art Spiegelman's *Maus* (1980–1991) to the architectural memorials of Peter Eisenman in Berlin and Rachel Whiteread in Vienna. Eisenman's *Memorial to the Murdered Jews of Europe* (finished 2004) with its concrete slabs of different heights on a sloping ground openly embraced experiential buzz words such as "labyrinth," "destabilization of the body," and "disorientation"; much was made of the width between the stones, which was to prevent people from walking next to each other. The monumentality was described as fragmented, dispersed in space, or even broken, in favor of corporeal experience. Old heroic forms *had* to fall by the wayside in this narrative, but could not erase the inherent tension in these "exculpatory" monuments between those who are remembered and those seeking active commemoration as a public, globally visible sign of catharsis, reform, or closure. Cognate forms are more easily and less controversially employed in the *National 9/11 Memorial and Museum* in New York on the site of the former World Trade Centers, which combines traces of the minimalist aesthetic of Maya Lin with a symbolic use of the void. Under the title *Reflecting Absence* (Figure 6.2), the design by architect Michael Arad and landscape

Figure 6.2 Michael Arad and Peter Walker, *Reflecting Absence,* National September 11 Memorial and Museum, New York

Source: Photograph by Sascha Porsche, 2011/Commons Wikimedia.

designer Peter Walker turns the footprints of the former buildings literally into two pools with waterfalls descending along the edges. The names of the victims are engraved on the sides and the negative forms are surrounded by deciduous trees. The creation of a memorial landscape in the otherwise dense fabric of downtown Manhattan could have been a welcome invitation to slow down and reflect. Yet at the beginning of the new millennium such a design is already uncontroversial, even predictable, and few see a contradiction between the longing for individual contemplation, nationalist self-praise, and compliance with the anticipated national and international memorial tourism.[2]

From a twenty-first-century point of view and a more global perspective, we see an even more complex memorial imperative, in which old forms re-emerge, and the counter-monuments of the memory boom of the 1980s and 1990s have themselves come under scrutiny. Their putative democracy and inclusiveness, if not universality, has been challenged by the introduction of new epochal concepts like the Anthropocene that draws attention to the fact that humans live their lives within a geological and meteorological theater that impacts and is impacted by their presence. This has resulted in a broader, but also a more sober view of memorials as geographical and ideological landscapes than what the subject-centered architecture of the "memorial boom" allowed for. Just as the way we understand and remember our past is sensitive to the changes of the world and how we treat it, we can say that monuments are indeed indicators of a contemporary state of affairs. With a growing emphasis on a world *beyond* the memorial, and stretching out beyond the visitor's immediate perception in space as well as in time, a corresponding shift in the stakes of commemoration has, almost imperceptibly, taken place. *Processes* rather than *events* have come to assume more prominence in today's memorial landscapes. In a very literal sense, contemporary monuments have come to handle contemporary or contemporaneous themes and problems in a way that opens up the monument's presumed strict orientation to the past.[3]

To provide a vivid sense of just how commemoration has changed since the beginning of the twenty-first century, I want to discuss Ai Weiwei's controversial 2016 installation *F. Lotus* (Figure 6.3) at the baroque Belvedere Palace in Vienna. It consists of lifejackets collected from the Greek island of Lesbos, the leftovers of refugees journeying to Europe in overloaded boats in grueling, often lethal conditions. The life-vests are arranged in groups of five, in the form of decorative flowers, floating in the reflecting pool leading to the main façade of the palace of Prince Eugene of Savoy, a great collector of art and a military leader most noted for fighting back the Ottoman Empire from central Europe at the end of the seventeenth and the beginning of the eighteenth centuries.[4] Formally blending into this *Gesamtkunstwerk* of architecture and garden design, *F. Lotus* is an act of subversive decorum that addresses the current state of a world of war, migration, and climate change. The material itself is in a way recycled, as the jackets were discarded on the island after the journey over the sea. Their change from utilitarian object to decoration disrupts the complacent consumption of beauty in the formal garden through the "authentic" roughness of the material, and at the same time conscripts what would be mere garbage into a new cycle of symbolic value—the value of political commemoration.[5] Is *F. Lotus* a contemporary monument in the double sense I suggested above—not just a monument of the present, but one that reflects on that present? I think so, for the most significant shift of the 1980s might not have consisted in the various formal changes overtaking the genre of the monument, nor in the loss of authority on the part of designers and commissioners (which is something of an alibi for administrators anxious to take the moral high ground), but rather in a shift in the social life of the monument. The old mode of interaction between monument and pedestrian, which as Musil pointed out too often took the form of obstacle avoidance, gave way to a call for *performative* interaction of the visitor(s) with the monument. By this I mean more

Figure 6.3 Ai Weiwei, *F. Lotus*, Belvedere Palace, Vienna, 2016
Source: Copyright Mechtild Widrich.

than the general call for reflection and subjective feeling discussed above: the word "performative" in linguistic theory means doing something by representing it to be so (a phenomenon familiar in signatures and other legally binding ceremonies). Many monuments, in their design and mode of use, called directly for visitors to take a stand or act publicly, whether by signing, reading, or just standing in a particular relation to the monument: thus the celebrated *Monument against Fascism* in Hamburg-Harburg by Jochen Gerz and Esther Shalev-Gerz (1986) asked visitors to sign a lead-faced column if they vowed to remain vigilant against fascism. Over the course of several years, the signed column was lowered into the ground and ultimately no longer visible (Figure 6.4). On the rationale of performative monuments, even acts of refusal and vandalism, like carving a swastika into the column, were contextualized as part of the social fabric of the monument and its community, however sinister the act.[6] It is telling that the two most prominent projects to commemorate the peaceful protests that led to the fall of the communist East German government in 1989 and the German unification in 1990 have either been rejected for execution after initial praise, or are still under debate. Both projects relied on the participation of the audience in a playful way: the memorial in Leipzig (competition won by M+M in 2012) under the title *70.000* involved that parts of the design, 70.000 metal pedestals dispersed on a soccer-field-size basin (symbolizing the peaceful protesters in 1989 that lead to the fall of the communist regime), could be taken "anywhere"—be it to another site in public space or simply home as a souvenir. In Berlin (competition won in 2011 by Milla & Partner and Sasha Waltz, a choreographer), the project was conceived as some kind of oversized seesaw to be used by the audience to symbolize the power of the people to shift history. These projects show that a celebratory counter-monument can easily become a superficial playground-art. Instead of symbolic responsibility, there is play; instead of historical consciousness, there is entertainment.

However, the implicit social link the counter-monument wanted to achieve is by no means a thing of the past, but neither is it, nor has it ever been, anti-authoritative: rather, new forms of authority, from democratic activism to visions of life in the *longue durée* are evoked by new forms of public art. As audiences multiply through becoming engaged via photographs or social media, the objects or sites of commemoration are being adapted accordingly. New questions arise: How does the construction of history travel through time, and space, via photographs and other means, how does it change meaning and what is its force? The destruction of statues and parts of ancient buildings in Palmyra in Syria through ISIS (Islamic State) in 2015 and 2016 is in its vandalism a potent showing that authoritarian regimes still see relevance in the marking of sites (also in the negative through destruction), but also in changing its audiences. The destruction was first broadcast proudly by the destroyers themselves; proof came to the world from satellite images, and started a debate about creating replicas of parts of the destroyed structure through digital imaging to be presented in London and New York—one such restored arch, manufactured without any direct contact with the site from photographs, was shown in Trafalgar Square, London, in 2016 (Figure 6.5) and stood there both as a *pars pro toto* symbol of the respect we should show former and different cultures, and as a memorial of resistance to recent terrorism.[7] More pertinently, the globally conducted discussion about reconstructing Palmyra goes way beyond issues of preservation. As art historian and preservationist Alois Riegl noted in his celebrated 1903 essay, "The Modern Cult of Monuments," memorials change their meaning and purpose as history flows past them. They may be "willed" monuments (built to be such), or they might become monuments due to the particular story they are able to tell: Riegl claimed that even a "torn piece of paper" could come to assume a memorial function and thus serve as a monument (Riegl 1982). Palmyra and other sites affected by current world politics (as were the Buddhas of Bamiyan in Afghanistan, destroyed by the Taliban in 2001) show not only how right Riegl was about the shifting function of monuments, but that their symbolic value is as

Figure 6.4 Site of Jochen Gerz's and Esther Shalev-Gerz's *Monument against Fascism*, 2009
Source: Copyright Mechtild Widrich.

Mechtild Widrich

Figure 6.5 Replica of Palmyra's Triumphal Arch at Trafalgar Square, London, April 2016
Source: Copyright Creative Commons, photograph by Garry Knight.

important as ever. It also shows, and this is new, that their change into signs of resistance, or victory, their participation in a fight for territory, is now even more important as it is broadcast to an audience worldwide through digital media. Still I would think that there is no break with the history of traditional monuments, but rather modifications that go hand in hand with shifts in the way society sees commemoration—Riegl already discussed such shifts in regard to changing audiences in the Habsburg Empire of his time. Commemoration, and this is probably why it is much less stable than the old-fashioned claim to eternity in monuments would lead us to believe, as a reclamation of the past has to change with the way humans change their approach to the process of mourning, cathartic healing, or the celebration of past events.

One of the demands of late twentieth-century monuments was to the authenticity of a commemorative site or its materials. This assumed correlation between what should be remembered and the geographical location of the object or relic triggering commemoration was then new, at least when it comes to newly commissioned memorials. Riegl already noted the thirst for authenticity in debates about then contemporary restorations. But the nineteenth century also experienced an extension and deterritorialization in the understanding of historically important places, from the spread of the photographic postcard to commemorative urban constructions like London's Trafalgar Square (named after the cape in southern Spain where Horatio Nelson decisively beat Napoleon's fleet). Thus, it seems likely that the felt need for a memorial to conform to a resonant place is part of a larger postmodern shift that sees a connection between personal memory and history, and the need to involve individuals in the telling of both personal and collective stories.[8] French historian Pierre Nora has during the 1980s and 1990s described the *lieux de mémoire*, which are places (they can be real or imagined, objects or myths) that crystallize memory for a particular community, while urban theorist Françoise Choay has insisted around the same time on the relevance of authentic geography by declaring Auschwitz the only true monument of the twentieth century (Nora 1984f; Choay 1992). Ai Weiwei shows that the assertion of the "authenticity" of the material is still important, but ideas of site and audience have changed; thus he transposes the fate of individuals in a particular place and time into more general themes of migration and global responsibility.

Many of the more ambitious contemporary memorials understand that actions humans perceive as history are always also changing the earth as a whole. Issues of economics (monument tourism), of the environment (the role of nature as memorial, and its precarious status in urban and rural civilization), and of representation (not only national or ethnic, but just as often global and cross-generational), must be kept in mind in order to evaluate current debates and designs. This is true even for memorials that seem to be dealing with very specific events and their strictly human consequences. Jonas Dahlberg's winning proposal for the Norwegian *07/22 Memorial* to commemorate the victims of the attack of right-wing extremist Anders Behring Breivik in 2011 seems, at first sight, to take up many of the formal and ideological tropes of the late twentieth century (Figure 6.6). The memorial has three parts: (1) a massive intervention into the landscape opposite of the island Utøya, where 69 mostly young people were shot in the massacre, (2) a temporary memorial in the government center of Oslo, which was the target of several bombs by the same terrorist, (3) a more permanent memorial in the same location once the fate of the damaged modernist buildings has been decided. The Swedish artist is best known as the maker of films and video installations that question perception and reality and show strange architectural settings and desolated cityscapes. His theme is the construction of reality in our minds—a peculiar choice perhaps for a memorial to a brutal terrorist attack, but, possibly a sign of current memorial culture. The work in progress, whose opening has been postponed, at the time of writing, due to protests from the local population, seeks to disconnect the tongue of land opposite the island from the mainland by a kind of sea canal, thus preventing visitors from looking too closely at the authentic location

Figure 6.6 Jonas Dahlberg, *July 22 Memorial*, Sørbråten site opposite Utøya, rendering studio Dahlberg

of the massacre. The walls of the earth cut would be engraved with the names of the victims, making them visible, yet out of reach, as would be the disconnected plot of land at the end of the peninsula, which would essentially be inaccessible. Symbolically, the cut also reduces the size of Norway, and makes clear that the wound cut into the territory will remain forever. Dahlberg says he wants to prevent a tourist spectacle, which seems like the expected means to memorialize a catastrophe in the twenty-first century. In a way, he thus works with, but also against, Nora's and Choay's conceptions of *lieux de mémoire* and authenticity. Access to history, which was the demand of the 1980s, has been replaced by monument tourism, and he subtly opposes such a view, even as he takes for granted the primacy of place by intervening in it. Notably, I think, Dahlberg proposes to use the excavated earth and stones for the memorial site in Oslo, reminding us that commemoration today is not just about national feelings or catharsis, meditation, and solitude, but that it is part of what drives history at least equally as much as national sentiment these days: economy and exploitation of resources, and our need for a cautious handling of the world at large, if we want to prevent catastrophic scenarios in the future. Feelings and resources are both excavated from the ground, which moves the debate from interaction between humans and history to one in which the tension between individual demands and its consequences for the globe need to be addressed. That Dahlberg's proposal won, and that it has faced public resistance, also tells us much about Norway: a highly educated nation whose affluence depends in great part on the exploitation of natural resources, notably petroleum and fish.

That a monument intended to mourn the victims of a mass murder could reach beyond this quite difficult task to consider the sites of violence, but also the structure of the place, nation, and the world it inhabits, might seem like a tall order, but it is typical of the way twenty-first-century monuments appropriate the dominant model of the counter-monument, with its performative appeal to spectators and visitors, and use it as the platform for an expanded reflection on ongoing processes beyond the human subject doing the commemorating. National history, the message in the best cases of contemporary monuments, is only part of a global situation. Personal interaction, while still at the center of commemoration, has been reassessed, often merging political activism with the representational values and historical depth (or search thereof) of commemoration. Monuments and memorials have been about the power to be able to make present a theme in public space—be they installed from the government or pushed through via community engagement. To make space for the bigger picture and to conceive history globally, understood not in the routine sense of global politics but comprising earth's ecosystems and geological and physical structures, might be the task for the memorials still to come. If so, it should keep artists and architects meaningfully occupied and vigorously challenged, for it will not be an easy one.

Notes

1 *Encyclopedia of Aesthetics*, vol. 3, edited by Michael Kelly (Oxford: Oxford University Press, 1998), 272; the entry "counter-monument" is authored by James E. Young.
2 An insightful and critical account of the memorial boom in the United States and its political implications, including a chapter on "Terrorism Memorials and Security Narratives," is Doss (2010).
3 This should not be taken as an endorsement, of course, as the past remains important, for example in the *Steilneset Memorial* by Peter Zumthor and Louise Bourgeois in Norway (2011), commemorating the victims of the witch trials of the seventeenth century. Also, monuments "to the Future" (Joseph Beuys's 1976 contribution to the Venice Biennial) and "for Historical Change" (Clegg and Guttman, 2004), both engaging various relics from the environment, are not strictly a new phenomenon, though as I argue here, they are a growing trend.
4 One might also think of Eugene, in his conquest of the Balkan states for the Habsburg Empire, as a precursor of the multi-ethnic, multi-religious Europe that conservatives find so threatening in today's refugee crisis.

5 Ai Weiwei had mounted similar life jackets in Berlin on the pilasters of a concert hall a few months earlier, and, in 2009, had arranged the backpacks of children who died in the 2008 earthquake in Sichuan (partially due to negligent construction of school buildings) on the façade of the Haus der Kunst in Munich. This work was entitled *Remembering*.
6 For more on this social interaction with monuments, see Widrich (2014).
7 One important protagonist making possible these reconstructions was software developer and activist Bassel Khartabil, who was executed by the Syrian government in 2015. On the role of social media and the destruction of cultural heritage in the Middle East, see Karimi and Nasser (2016).
8 Here again there is an early twentieth-century predecessor, the French *Annales* historian Maurice Halbwachs.

References

Choay, F. (1992) *L'Allégorie du patrimoine*, Paris: Seuil; trans. as *The Invention of the Historic Monument*, Cambridge, UK: Cambridge University Press, 2001.
Doss, E. (2010) *Memorial Mania: Public Feeling in America*, Chicago: University of Chicago Press.
Johnson, G. A. (1998) "Sculpture, photography, and the politics of public Space: Serra's *Tilted Arc* and Lin's *Vietnam Veterans Memorial*," in Geraldine A. Johnson (ed.) *Sculpture and Photography: Envisioning the Third Dimension*, Cambridge, UK: Cambridge University Press.
Karimi, P. and Nasser, R. (2016) "The demise and afterlife of artifacts", Aggregate, December 12. http://we-aggregate.org/piece/the-demise-and-afterlife-of-artifacts.
Kelly, M. (ed.) (1998) *Encyclopedia of Aesthetics*, vol. 3, Oxford: Oxford University Press.
Musil, R. (1978) "Denkmale," *Nachlass zu Lebzeiten* in A. Frisé (ed.) *Gesammelte Werke* vol. 7, Reinbek bei Hamburg: Rowohlt.
Nora, P. (1984) *Les Lieux de mémoire*. Paris: Gallimard; translated as *Realms of Memory*, New York: Columbia University Press, 1996–1998.
Riegl, A. (1982 [1903]) "The modern cult of monuments: its character and origin," translated by K. W. Forster and D. Ghirardo, *Oppositions* 25: 20–51.
Savage, K. (2009) *Monument Wars: Washington D.C., the National Mall, and the Transformation of the Memorial Landscape*, Berkeley: University of California Press.
Widrich, M. (2014) *Performative Monuments: The Rematerialisation of Public Art*, Manchester: Manchester University Press.
Young, J. E. (1992) "The counter-monument: memory against itself in Germany today," *Critical Inquiry* 18, 2 (Winter): 267–296.

Part II
Materiality

7

Architectures of Memory, Past and Future

Abby Smith Rumsey

Among the species of the earth, humans are not the strongest or fastest. Nor do we have the biggest brains. Yet we are dominant over the planet—dangerously so. By what power do we thrive in even the most inhospitable environment? It is our collective memory, a bank of knowledge and know-how built over generations. This renewable resource is augmented and amplified by technologies that store knowledge in durable physical objects, shared across time and space. From cuneiform and codex to GPS satellite and supercomputer, memory technologies enable us to exert ever greater control over nature and other humans. Often casually referred to as information technology, our knowledge infrastructure is the cornerstone of the built environment.

What will happen to this infrastructure in the contemporary era? Beginning roughly in 2000, we have been besotted with data and captivated by notions of innovation and disruption for their own sake. Hyperbole aside, digital technologies are just the latest chapter in the story of a grand information inflation that began 200 years ago with the shift from print-on-paper to multimedia. The invention of image capture in the 1830s and audio recording in the 1870s were responses to the emerging consensus among Western scientists that evidence-based knowledge alone has a legitimate truth claim (Rumsey 2016). The demand for evidence kicked off a treasure hunt for data and specimens from all over the globe. The building trade responded by erecting museums, libraries, and archives to house and serve collections. Professional cadres sprung up to service these resources—librarians, archivists, curators, conservators, and preservation scientists. The reverence for applied knowledge as the engine of progress led to rapid specialization among disciplines. We are now in possession of so much knowledge that a professional—engineer, architect, chemist, surgeon, designer, historian, economist—spends 25+ years under formal instruction to master a field. This, in turn, dramatically alters the demographics of marriage and child-rearing in developed countries.

We are moving from artifact-based analog infrastructure to digital networks. This period of transition will come to a close around mid-century, when the first two generations of digital natives have reached maturity. By 2050 the development of technologies, practices, and core digital infrastructure will slow to an equilibrium evolving by incremental change. Which digital tools will be developed, which come to market, which communities adopt them and how—all this is yet to be determined. What is certain is that adaptation to new tools necessitates co-evolution, both the tools and the humans using them evolving together. There will be a blending of artifact and virtual in the ways we interact with our past. That said, the default search mode for knowledge is digital. The way to discover knowledge that was "born analog" will be through digital finding aids, including but not limited to digital surrogates. To ensure access to knowledge in the twenty-first century we must remediate the analog past for digital discovery and access as quickly as possible.

The salient challenge to a safe porting of the analog past to the digital present is a common prejudice that we are moving so fast into the future that the past has lost its value. The notion that the present, let alone the future could ever supersede the past is ideologically dangerous. The totalitarian utopianisms of the twentieth century demonstrated that. Stipulating a bright and shining future meant that censors needed to vigilantly control what stories were told about a nation's past and by whom. When justifications of present-day difficulties were required, state-owned media were not shy about making up facts about the past. After all, the most effective way to command people's expectations of the future is to control what they believe happened in the past.

From the perspective of human biology, the notion that the past lacks intrinsic value is simply incompetent. To live without memory is impossible. Memory is not about the past, it is about the future. Amnesia, both personal and cultural, does more than erase the past and erode our sense of identity. It robs us of the future. For imagination is no more than memory in the future tense.

How the Past Creates the Future

Nature endows all life with two types of memory. The most basic is the genome, the genetic material that stores information on how to grow up to be an anteater or an aardvark, a human or humpback whale. Our collective cultural memory operates in analogous ways. Culture instructs children living in Japan, for example, that their native linguistic potential will enable fluent, idiomatic Japanese, not Portuguese or Urdu. Culture determines what music we hear, what literature we read, which foods we taste. Each of us has personal preferences, but culture sets the parameters of our choices.

The genome is commodious and conservative, cheerfully carrying baggage from the ancient history of the species. We now understand that obsolete or superfluous genetic information can come in very handy when a creature has to adapt to a radically changing environment. For example, marine creatures with vestigial leg-like appendages of little use in the water had an advantage when they were stranded on land: they developed legs. Fortunate, too, are the cultures that conscientiously preserve their past. Conservation of obsolete knowledge and know-how offers people an ever renewable resource of ideas and solutions to present-day problems. Try to imagine how the engineers and architects, painters and writers of late medieval Europe would have reinvented themselves and their crafts without access to the physical ruins and orphaned texts of classical Rome and Greece.

Nature also endows individuals with the ability to learn and remember. Learning is the capacity to be modified by experience and environment. Each creature, from amoeba to zebra, acquires information about its physical and social worlds in which they must survive and procreate. This information is stored in memory, embodied and literally encoded in the nervous system and muscles. It is spatialized in the brain—geocoded, in effect. Spatial arrangement of memory allows speedy recall, just like the shelf order of books expedites retrieval of a specific volume. Spatialization does something more important, though. It creates meaning. Where a memory is placed within a network of associated memories constitutes its significance, creates its emotional valence—that is, its value (Dolan 2002).

From this memory bank of meaning and affect we construct a mental model of the world, the reference model we use to navigate our world in safety. After a good night's sleep, during which our brain has been busy sorting through the happenings of the day, we awake each morning with up-to-date knowledge of how the world works. When we encounter something new, bright and shiny, enticing or frightening, the unconscious anticipates what to expect. The sound of an explosion, the smell of smoke, a concussive shock on an eardrum—we don't have time to process this consciously in real time if we are going to save our skin. But our body knows because it remembers.

That is why the content of memory is the past, but it is about the future. Our memories are not designed to be photographic or optimized for perfect recall. Memory does not map onto facts. On the contrary, we endlessly update our model of the world as the world changes. Good memory shapes the past to make it more useful in the present. Its job is to guide our decision-making, evaluate what is of long-term value, distinguish signal from noise, and purge useless data from our system.

With access to our personal memory and the collective memory of culture, humans have temporal depth perception unique among species and are able to imagine a deep past and a future that unfolds indefinitely. We routinely infer patterns of cause and effect almost everywhere. That is what we call sense-making. We pose questions about how the world works, then apply the answers to change the world. Designing a shelter, engineering a bridge, developing a pest-resistant strain of wheat, planning a round-trip voyage to the moon—these are all feats that rely crucially on the stewardship of knowledge. Because to be useful, knowledge must be fixed, unchanging, trustworthy. Natural memory is anything but. And so we invented a third memory.

What Happened When We Invented a Third Memory

We would not be dominant over the planet if we relied exclusively on sharing knowledge person to person, body to body, through dance, music, or recitation. The invention of writing about 6000 years ago liberated knowledge from the frailties of human memory and of mortality itself. Writing was invented in multiple places at multiple times, evidence of the crucial role recorded knowledge plays in cultures that develop complex societies (Wolf 2007: 43). As we moved from agricultural to industrial economies, the need for recorded knowledge and the literacy to make use of it kept growing (Morris 2015). By all measures, we grow ever more dependent on knowledge and robust architectures of memory. Our post-industrial economy is deep into the process of shaping the culture of knowledge it needs.

Development and domestication of digital technologies will follow a path similar to the recording technologies of yore. Take cuneiforms, among the oldest forms of writing. These clay tablets were originally invented for accounting. Sumerian rulers wanted their scribes to keep track of flocks of sheep and vats of oil. The tablets evolved into physical tokens that warranted contracts and trades between perfect strangers over long distances. Clay tablets are a cunning way to compensate for the inherent weakness of human memory (and moral character, in the case of cheats and fraudsters). They are impossible to tamper with without leaving traces of attempted forgery. These objects, in fact, are so durable that they are not damaged by fire, like books and digital tapes, but actually become stronger. The British Museum alone has about 130,000 tablets, some dating to the fourth century BC (British Museum 2017).

Succeeding technologies such as the codex and the compact disc store more information and are more portable. But they are far less durable or tamper-proof. Our current preferred memory tool, the smart phone, is the most capacious and portable yet, able carry our words, our music, and our images in our pockets. But the hardware demands frequent upgrades and the software even more frequent updates just to remain stable. They have proven far easier than clay tablets to steal or tamper with without detection.

Sturdy and secure as cuneiforms may be, nobody uses them anymore. We are more than willing to make the trade-off between durability and capacity. Each new recording medium has lowered barriers to create, share, and consume information. Each has accelerated the reach and speed of communication. And each taps into human potentials unanticipated by its creators.

Technologies have no intrinsic power of their own, only those their creators and users cede to them. Over time cuneiforms went from being the monopoly of palace administrators to appropriation by the populace, used for propaganda, poetry, and prophecy. Computers, too, were invented for purely instrumental use—in this case for the military in World War II to calculate missile trajectories. They have since been repurposed for comparison shopping, finding mates, booking restaurant reservations, and viewing movies and TV shows. As augmented reality (AR) and virtual reality (VR) are developed, users will invent new modes of discovery and scholarship, art and entertainment, narration and presentation. The next decades will be a time of exploring the potentials of computers, testing their powers, learning from their failures and ours, and devising laws and codes of behavior that maximize their power and minimize their abuse.

What Long-Term Value Looks Like

If the past is so important for the future, what will happen to the present moment as it turns tomorrow into the digital yesterday? How will we know what is important to preserve? Until the twenty-first century, the volume of publication was constrained by the costs of production. Publishing houses, film studios, and recording companies determined who got access to the means of production, acting in effect as primary filtering systems. In the developed world, the Internet has few such barriers. Online, the first order of filtering is done by search engines, apps, and social media sites that funnel our attention to specific spheres of content. They tend to reward content's currency over long-term value. Filtering is often captive to commercial incentives. It is easily manipulated without transparency to the user, and its goal is to monopolize our attention by offering a convenient one-stop destination for personal updates, sports scores, political reporting, consumer recommendations, and so forth (Winkler and Mullins 2015). The metric for value? Clicks, likes, retweets, and links.

One of the unanticipated consequences of our precipitous adoption of digital inscription is that our personal and collective knowledge is now committed to a form of memory that is even more ephemeral and unstable than human memory itself. Web pages, for example, which last an average of 100 days, cannot persist without active maintenance, unlike paper pages that endure passive management and benign neglect with little harm (Rumsey 2016: 65). If we want to preserve information for the future, we need to capture and stabilize it now. But how do we know what information will have value in the future?

The crude filtering of search and social media aside, we have yet to discover enough about the potential uses of digital data to confidently predict what will matter. New types of data, new uses, and new techniques of extracting information from bits will generate their own paradigms of long-term value. Ten years ago it was hard to discern historical value in something as trifling as a tweet. We now know that an individual tweet may have limited intrinsic value, but in context, at the scale of an entire Twitter stream, and analyzed by the right algorithms of pattern recognition, 280 characters can yield meaningful indicators of change over time in demographics, public health, political attitudes, or evolution of the language.

There are two questions to ask about long-term value in the face of such uncertainty: What will people need to know? And what do we want people to know about us? There are categories of information people require to survive and go about their business, records produced by government agencies and critical for accountability to citizens, for example. This would include military service records, birth and death certificates, voter registration lists, legislative history, court records, tax filings, as well as scientific evidence such as scans of the sky, climate data, formulae for antibiotics, the chemical model of insulin, the inventories of nuclear waste, and so forth. Ensuring future access to these records requires well-funded public institutions. In this century there has been a systematic disinvestment of the public sector that impoverishes public archives, libraries, and museums, the very institutions we rely on to preserve cultural content for present and future access. This trend is accompanied by increasing privatization of critical infrastructure such as weather satellites, data storage, and records management. By mid-century, if we continue to outsource our culture to the private sector nearly all digital culture will be managed by private entities, even those created at public expense. And the fate of analog culture will be in the hands of perilously underfunded libraries and museums.

The second question about long-term value seems simpler to answer: What do we want people to know about us? But here, too, we have less control over leaving a legacy we shape than we might assume. The content we create—it's ours, and we can do with it what we want, right? But think about where our content resides. Our biography is on LinkedIn or Facebook. Our communication through "free" services like Gmail and Twitter is on company servers. Our photos reside in a cloud owned by commercial services like Amazon, Apple, or Instagram. These are the traces of ourselves. To preserve them, we must negotiate with the platforms to which we entrust our content and ourselves. In market capitalism, private enterprise has the resources to create and disseminate the content that constitutes our cultural heritage. Copyright law serves the dual purpose of providing incentives to creators to circulate their works; and, by limiting the terms of copyright privileges, ensuring the transfer of content to the public domain. We have not revised copyright quickly enough to secure these dual purposes in the digital realm. We need the copyright holders of the works of Chuck Berry and Beyoncé, Marvel comics and the Star Wars films to preserve their digital content and deed them to the public domain. The next decades will determine the fate of the public domain. If the public domain shrinks, so, too will cultural memory, our essential engine of creativity.

In the end, long-term value will be determined not by contemporaries but by future generations when they re-use content we produce today. But they will use only what we make available to them. We create content at such a scale and on such a variety of platforms that come and go, in so many codes that are proprietary that it is impractical to preserve everything. Nor should we try. We must choose what to save and what to lose, or risk certain loss through negligence or malevolence.

We cannot dodge our responsibility to be ethical stewards of knowledge. The more rapidly we modify the world, the more urgent the need to document to the world today as it changes. The gases in the atmosphere, levels of acidification in the oceans, population migrations, species growth and extinction—if we do not capture and preserve information about them today, it will not be available in 20 years' time, let alone 50 or 100. We need to accelerate building the digital infrastructure. That begins by examining why memory cannot exist without matter and how space itself produces meaning.

Why Memory Has Materiality

Digital memory implies an untethering from the physical, if only because time and space no longer constrain the sharing of information. Information becomes ubiquitous, available through our machines anytime, anywhere. But its immateriality is an optical illusion. All cognition is physically embodied. Consciousness itself is an emergent property of life and memory is incarnate in muscle and nerve. Our artificial, externalized memory also exists only through matter. Networks of machines freighting digital assets point to point, packet by packet, even wirelessly, have very specific materiality, though of a substance less visible than bound volumes of paper standing shoulder to shoulder on bookshelves. What is referred to whimsically as the cloud is not a vaporous element permeating the sky. It comprises server farms scattered across the global landscape, often remote from cities, seismic threats, and flood plains. They have an imposing footprint on the ground. For while they employ a limited number of personnel, they consume prodigious watts to run machines and yet more watts to cool them down. Racks of servers holding petabytes of data face the same physical threats as book repositories—excessive cold and heat, floods, mold, fire, theft, intrusion, and vandalism. On top of that, security threats can come through networks on the other side of the planet, not only a nefarious intruder into the server room. Data are never stored in only one location. A storage unit is one node of a distributed system connected by cables and wireless networks, entangled in a complex matrix of dependencies that begin and end with secure flows of energy. Digital information is not "green," any more than books are friends to forests. The digital memory of humanity will only be as secure as our sources of energy.

When the nineteenth century experienced its information inflation, it remade the landscape of cities and towns. The cheap manufacture of books, invention of photography and audio recording, and expeditions around the globe to gather natural and anthropological specimens placed great pressure on the existing infrastructure. Brand new libraries, museums, and archives went up in urban centers to accommodate burgeoning collections and provide access to them. These structures articulated contemporary ideas of the value of knowledge. For the high-tech library at Ste Geneviève in Paris, opened in 1850, the architect Henri Labrouste used that newfangled material cast-iron to raise the ceiling, let in more light, and reduce the risk of fire to books—all in the service of spreading enlightenment. The neo-Renaissance Library of Congress building, opened in 1897 and sited directly behind the U.S. Capitol, was fashioned as a temple of learning to advertise America's new prosperity and sophistication, akin to the Florence of the Medicis. Today these and other libraries are retrofitted for the twenty-first century with wireless networks and computer catalogs. Yet they still stand as monuments to an antique view of knowledge in a world where proximity to knowledge required proximity to the artifacts of memory themselves.

Why Memory Is Spatialized

Digital materiality radically changes our spatial relationship with each other and our shared knowledge. We are networked to the world. But the world is also networked to us and we are very easy to find. Until the twenty-first century, we had to go to the library to get information. Now information chases us and begs for attention. If we allow our apps, subscriptions, and platforms to alert us, then we are pestered all day by vibrations and noises that hijack our scarcest resource—attention.

Despite the ubiquity of data, there will be spaces—physical and virtual—comparable to Ste Geneviève and the Library of Congress in the digital realm. Even virtual knowledge must be spatialized. Both ancient practice and contemporary neuroscience speak to the importance of spatial orientation in the formation and retrieval of memory. Neuroscientists have discovered that a single organ in the brain, the hippocampus, initiates memory formation and functions as an internal GPS by mapping our environment (Underwood 2014). Alzheimer's disease causes damage to the hippocampus, and as a consequence sufferers lose access to their memories. Just as tellingly, they lose a sense of where they are in the world and how they got there. Treatment centers can palliate the painful anxiety that afflicts their patients by recreating a physical space similar to one in their recent past.

Without the benefit of neuroscience, Greek and Roman orators figured out a technique of recall, mnemonics, that operates by spatializing knowledge. As Cicero, a devotee of the method, described it in *De Orate*:

> [P]ersons desiring to train this faculty [of memory] must select places and form mental images of the things they wish to remember and store those images in the places, so that the order of the places will preserve the order of the things, and the image of the things will denote the things themselves, and we shall employ the places and images respectively as a wax writing-tablet and the letters written on it.
>
> *(Yates 2001: 17)*

So the Greek and Roman orators set about building memory palaces, imaginary—virtual—structures populated with physical cues that would prompt emotion and content. Using mnemonics, they could dazzle listeners with their rhetorical skills without notes.

Through neuronal networks, information abides in us located within specified webs of meaning. Our social and mental lives reflect this architecture of consciousness. We cannot negotiate personal relationships, understand abstract concepts, let alone remember things without spatializing what we know. Understanding relationships among aunts, uncles, fathers, and mothers, ranking family members by birth order, grasping the logic of action and reaction, cause and effect, if X then Y—these are all ways we make sense by seeing patterns. And what is a pattern but a consistency of spatial arrangement, whether in one dimension or four?

Like this essay, contemporary discourse is studded with biological metaphors, as the tapestry of nineteenth-century intellectual and aesthetic culture was richly woven with mechanistic metaphors and the twentieth with relativity and atomic physics. Biological models of memory will increasingly inform the design of the digital infrastructure as science gains greater knowledge of how nature organizes itself (Laughlin 2005: 76). It will inform the development of artificial intelligence and the design of the objects we call robots that operate within that infrastructure. We know very little about how we affectively attach ourselves to—or project ourselves onto—the objects we create and the tools we use. At an unconscious level, we understand them as extensions of ourselves, just as we understand our data as extensions of ourselves, even if it resides in a desktop computer or in the cloud.

The next decades will witness further exploration of the capacities of virtual and augmented reality, which in turn will reveal their value in haptic learning, narrative formation, annotation, and mediation of the real world with its past, and more which remains at present unknowable. These tools will evolve as we use them, as we in turn will evolve with them.

For Now, a Close Encounter with the Past

With a bravado that masks acute anxiety, we judge ourselves so powerful that we deserve our own geological epoch, the Anthropocene, to brand our impact on earth. Paradoxically, this christening echoes the twentieth-century notion of the modern, born in the wake of World War I and the dissolution of European empires, when a traumatized generation sensed an irreparable rupture between their experience and all history before them. Like a scorned lover, the modern rejected the past with its reassuring chronologies, ideologies, sense-making paradigms, and artistic forms. That legacy seemed a cruel joke at best, and the joke became crueler and deadlier during World War II and the atomic era. The postmodern sensibility doesn't even take the past seriously enough to rail against it. It makes light of the very notions of style, canonicity, sincerity, and seriousness. The modern was nothing if not dead serious.

The ethos of the present era is still evolving, but it is marked already by an unsettling swing between techno-optimism and dystopian gloom. We are painfully aware that we are using our powers to radically and permanently alter the biosphere, that we do so out of a desire to fashion the planet into a cocoon optimized for Homo sapiens, and that we will not stop soon. We map the genome to engineer it and create chemical and nuclear weapons to eradicate enemies, be they pests or people. In the face of anthropogenic climate change, bioengineering, and genetic manipulation, we have no choice but to be scrupulous stewards of human memory as well as our planet's resources or risk an amnesia we cannot afford. Designers and builders are determining what this era will be as they shape the built environment. Their work has long faced a functionality test few other aesthetic forms do. But now, beyond the familiar demands to make spaces that are livable, efficient, safe, durable, and beautiful, there is a more urgent test to pass: How green, how nonlethal is what we build?

Each generation confronts the past and fashions its own interpretation of how we got here from there. Confrontation with history will never end as long as we believe the origins of the present lie in the past. In some instances the call for reinterpretation follows discovery of new evidence. More often we examine the past because we are having trouble accounting for the present—our particular present—in the context of planning for the future. We are creating a human monoculture at a scale that has no precedence—the globe. The faster we create tools to explore, control, and ultimately remake the world, the closer our encounter with our past will be.

In the future, people will nominate various names for this era, names we might reject as irrelevant and alien to our subjective experience of it. But the meaning of any given moment or epoch is determined only by what happens afterwards. In this, memory instructs us again that things have meaning only in context. What will that context look like? What will people be able to discover about us? That is the question. We alone have the answer. We have the technologies to document the present and design the digital infrastructure to carry the sum of human memory forward in time. We are now the stewards who decide what traces of ourselves and all those before us will be left for others to make sense of.

References

British Museum (2017) "Studying cuneiform tablets," www.britishmuseum.org/about_us/departments/middle_east/facilities_and_services/study_room/studying_cuneiform_tablets.aspx (April 21, 2017).

Dolan, R. J. (2002) "Emotion, cognition, and behavior," *Science* 298 (November 8): 1991–1994. http://science.sciencemag.org/content/298/5596/1191.full.

Laughlin, R. B. (2005) *A Different Universe: Reinventing Physics from the Bottom Down*, New York: Basic Books.

Morris, I. (2015) *Foragers, Farmers, and Fossil Fuels: How Human Values Evolve*, Princeton: Princeton University Press.

Rumsey, A. R. (2016) *When We Are No More: How Digital Memory Is Shaping Our Future*, New York: Bloomsbury Press.

Underwood, E. (2014) "Brain's GPS finds top honor," *Science* 346 (October 10): 149. http://science.sciencemag.org/content/346/6206/149.1.full.
Winkler, R. and Mullins, B. (2015) "How Google skewed search results," *Wall Street Journal*, March 19.
Wolf, M. (2007) *Proust and the Squid: The Story and Science of the Reading Brain*, New York: Harper Perennial.
Yates, F. A. (2001) *The Art of Memory*, London: Pimlico.

8
Life and Death in the Anthropocene

Heather Davis

> The present is conditioned by the accumulated traces of the past, and the future of the earth will bear the marks of our present. While the manufacture of plastics destroys the archives of life on the earth, its waste will constitute the archives of the twentieth century and beyond.
> *(Bernadette Bensaude-Vincent)*

In 2007, the Los Angeles Department of Water and Power (LADWP) detected high levels of bromate, a carcinogen, in Los Angeles's Silver Lake and Elysian Reservoirs (Figure 8.1). Bromide is found naturally in groundwater, and chlorine is added to drinking water in order to kill bacteria. But when exposed to sunlight, as was the case in these open-air reservoirs, the two chemicals react and carcinogenic bromate forms. The facilities serve about 600,000 people in downtown and South Los Angeles, and the city was forced to dump the water (Helfand 2007). The municipal government began to build a new underground facility, but until its completion they needed a way to control this chemical reaction on the other major reservoir, Ivanhoe Reservoir. The temporary solution was to put 3.4 million black plastic balls onto the surface of the reservoir, with the idea that they would absorb sunlight, drastically reduce water evaporation, and also lessen algae growth, while stopping the chemical reaction and thus the formation of bromate (Vara-Orta 2008). The four-inch-diameter polyethylene balls covered the surface of the reservoir, sealing out the sunlight. The newspaper images associated with this event—thousands of plastic balls being poured down a cement embankment to re-surface the water—bore a striking resemblance to contemporary art, such as the earth works and land art of the 1960s and 1970s. Viewers could easily be forgiven if they accidentally thought the event was a new piece by a contemporary landscape or installation artist, such as Olafur Eliasson or Maya Lin. But, in this case, the relationship to contemporary art was entirely accidental, speaking both to the state of art practice today and to environmental aesthetics. This phenomenon, of accidental or incidental aesthetics, is a hallmark of what is being called the Anthropocene—the era in which extractivist logic and capitalist economics have drastically reshaped the chemical, geological, and biospheric conditions of the earth. From the extraordinarily beautiful colors made from tar for the World Exhibition in 1862 (Leslie 2005: 75–78), to the London smog that inspired Monet and other impressionists (Mirzoeff 2014: 220–226), to the trash vortex, "the largest water architecture of the twenty-first century" (Preciado

Life and Death in the Anthropocene

Figure 8.1 Ivanhoe Reservoir looking northeast from the west side, showing outlet tower
Source: Copyright Junkyardsparkle.

2013: 33), the re-shaping of the earth by humans has also meant the birth of entirely new colors and aesthetics. The aesthetic effects—as in *aisthesis*, or affects produced by our sensorial experience of the environment—have been entirely re-ordered by the presence of plastic. The use of the term "plastic arts" was first recorded in 1624 (OED). Until the invention of the synthetic polymer that we have come to know as plastic, the arts held a virtually monopoly on artifice; now it is chemical engineers who re-make and re-fashion the earth.

The inadvertent aesthetics produced by the event of covering the Ivanhoe Reservoir in plastic balls draws attention to the larger ways in which aesthetics is shifting under the conditions of the Anthropocene. These "shade balls," as they are called, are typically used to keep birds out of water near industrial facilities and airports and to stop water evaporation in petroleum operations. The LADWP initially bought three million balls to cover the Ivanhoe Reservoir (after the initial phase of introducing 400,000 balls), then nine million more for two other reservoirs in the city, and is scheduled to blanket the L.A. Reservoir, which has a surface area of 176 acres, with 80 million balls, permanently (Kavanaugh 2014). These procedures reveal what plastic does best: it acts as a sealant, a barrier, both literally sealing something off from its surrounding environment—in this case, a reservoir—while also materializing the desire for impenetrability, for objects, bodies, and selves to be discrete, for categories not to mix, for a monadic identity separated from its environment.

Plastic: The Substrate of Advanced Capitalism

The first synthetic polymer, Bakelite, was created in 1907 and patented in 1909 by Leo Baekeland. It was invented to fill consumer demand for items that were becoming more difficult to get—such as ivory and silk—as anti-colonial resistance movements started simmering, and as the earlier pillaging of resources made these items increasingly unavailable and expensive (Meikle 1995: 26). Lauded as the material of 1000 uses, plastic became the cheap alternative, the perfect substance for a burgeoning commodity society that would emerge full force in the post-WWII era. Plastic has always been a thoroughly profit-driven material. Even when the category of what we now think of as plastics was still in formation, its nature was more "commercial than scientific," as Jeffrey Meikle argues in his illuminating and far-reaching cultural history, *American Plastic* (1995: 5). In other words, the invention and proliferation of plastics was driven less by a need to develop new technologies, such as medical or warfare applications (although WWII boosted the use of plastics greatly), than to simply replace the objects we already had—but at a price and in a quantity that helped to instantiate a middle class defined by consumption.

Plastic created the conditions for global trade and consumerism, while these systems themselves became increasingly reliant upon various forms of plastic. As Andrea Westermann notes in her study of PVC (or vinyl) in Germany:

> Plastic packaging, in particular, facilitated mass consumption.... The new ways of handling and distributing commodities in retail and wholesale were not only based on plastic containers and plastic bags, but also required an improved stackability of goods, achieved by material innovations like shrink-wrap.
>
> *(Westermann 2013: 76–77)*

Indeed, the infrastructure and speed of advanced capitalism, and the fantasy of unending economic growth fueled by extractivist policies and mass consumerism depend upon plastic. This explains why 280 million tons of plastic was produced worldwide in 2012, with a projected increase to 33 billion tons annually by 2050 (Rochman et al. 2013).

Plastic can be considered the substrata of advanced capitalism. It reveals our utter dependency upon petrochemicals. But its role in our life, unlike the more abstract relationship that we have with other oil products, such as gasoline or electricity, is intimate. We use plastics to eat, clothe ourselves, as sex toys, as soothers for babies. Our computers and phones, those objects we seemingly cannot do without, could not exist without plastics as the lightweight portable devices that they are. Nor could the Internet, with thousands of underwater and underground cables sealed from the elements with plastic coating (Starosielski 2015). Plastic is ubiquitous and infiltrates so many aspects of our daily lives that its presence is easy to take for granted and also hard to fathom. It has introduced entirely new sensorial regimes with its smooth surfaces and bright colors. It also implicates us: there is no way to extract one's life in the twentieth century from plastic. This is true for people across economic classes and geographies, even if the objects we interact with and the ways we do it remain stratified. Plastic is a problem that cannot be externalized. However, the value attributed to plastic, as Gay Hawkins reminds us, is not intrinsic to the material, but is enacted. As Hawkins writes,

> Plastic is represented as something that seems to have an unfolding logic already within it—it is an instrument for capital accumulation. The assumption is that plastic has intrinsic economic values that are realized in processes of industrial research or market application.
>
> *(Hawkins 2013: 49)*

It accumulates value precisely because of how it is used, what it enables, and how it circulates through the economy.

Plastic represents the promises of modernity: the promise of sealed, perfected, clean, smooth abundance. It encapsulates the fantasy of ridding ourselves of the dirt of the world, of decay, of malfeasance. As Westermann argues, vinyl's plasticity and its chemical creation captured what high modernity expected from technology at large: a world freed from the material restrictions that nature traditionally imposed on humanity. By implication, we would also have a world freed of scarcity, a world of plenty.

(Westermann 2013: 69)

Plastic represents a shiny new world, one that removes people from the cycles of life and death, one that supersedes the troublesome, leaky, amorphous, and porous demands of our ancestors, our bodies, and the earth. Ridding ourselves of the demands of the earth seemed to promise a world of prosperity through scientific control. In 1941, chemist V. E. Yarsley and research manager of B.X. Plastics Ltd., E. G. Couzens, wrote that the plastic future would be shiny and bright:

> "Plastic Man," will come into a world of colour and bright shining surfaces.... He is surrounded on every side by this tough, safe, clean material which human thought has created.... [W]e shall see growing up around us a new, brighter cleaner and more beautiful world, an environment not subject to the haphazard distribution of nations' resources but built to order, the perfect expression of the new spirit of planned scientific control, the Plastics Age.
>
> *(Yarsley and Couzens 1941: 149–152)*

This idealist dream, or dream of transcendental idealism, represents the apex of the Cartesian split, as matter itself is dictated and rearranged by the human mind. Planned scientific control envisions this clean, smooth world, sealed off from the outside—it is not just the barriers of a hazmat suit or the miracles of Tyvek house wrap, but the basic building blocks of matter that are manipulated and re-built. As Bernadette Bensaude-Vincent writes:

> Matter came to be presented as a malleable and docile partner of creation—a kind of Play-Doh in the hands of the clever designer who informs matter with intelligence and intentionality. Just like the *demiurgos* in Plato's *Timaeus*, the material engineer can impose forms on a passive, malleable *chora*.
>
> *(Bensaude-Vincent 2013: 22)*

This dream of the ultimate passivity of nature, pliable to the wills and whims of the modern subject, has had horrifying implications. Plastic—in its production, distribution, and waste cycles—represents the inevitable corollary to unfettered economic growth: it is both intensely resource-depleting (8 percent of world oil production goes into the manufacture and production of plastics) and ecologically devastating. Indeed, plastic brings together some of the most abiding environmental concerns of our time because of its pervasiveness, banality, and longevity.

For although plastic maintains its identity under virtually all conditions, impervious to what surrounds it, all the matter that exists outside of the logic of chemical engineering (everything that existed prior to 1850, say) has been radically altered by the presence of plastic. At the present moment, nowhere on earth can be considered free of plastic. And no one in Canada, the United States, and many other countries who has been tested has been found to be free of plastic chemicals (Liboiron 2013: 134). Plastic not only spreads while maintaining its molecular form, but the plasticizers that are added to plastic (one or more of a possible 80,000 chemicals added to make plastic pliable or pink or heat-resistant) leach and off-gas; detached from the polymer bond, they are able to move into the surrounding environment and whatever bodies may be found there. These chemicals are having untold effects on the bodies and ecologies that they are now composing. In addition, "various plasticizers have been correlated with infertility, recurrent miscarriages, feminization of male fetuses, early-onset puberty, obesity, diabetes, reduced brain development, cancer and neurological disorders such as early onset senility in adults and reduced brain development in children" (Liboiron 2013: 142). This is only the list of possible effects on the human body, without even beginning to account for all the other bodies affected by plastic and their associated chemicals.

Plastics also accumulate. They gather in the environment in the forms of blighted landscapes, bags fluttering in the wind, or lighters and wrappers are found in ditches, masses of untold plastic items piled in garbage dumps, and in the gyres of the ocean, where they swirl and are eaten by many forms of marine life, from bacteria to birds, tortoises to whales. Plastics also accumulate what is around them, particularly by adsorbing persistent organic pollutants, which due to a similar chemical structure, tend to latch on to oil-based plastics. Once this happens their toxicity grows, and the threat to anything that might mistakenly take it for food also amplifies, bioaccumulating up the food chain. As plastics gain in toxicity their value depletes, they are cast off, re-entering market chains for what little profit can be made from recycling, spreading their accumulated toxins wherever they go.

They are then sifted, filtered through, recognized for their worth by those who cannot afford to participate in this throw-away culture, for those who are also placed elsewhere, out of sight of the markets of capital that rely on invisible labor in order to perpetuate this system. Recycling—first-world atonement for single-use plastics and unfettered consumption—is, for the most part, a highly costly and dangerous process. As Gay Hawkins reminds us, "What makes recycling such a labor-intensive practice, and therefore often concentrated where labor is cheap, is the demands … plastic makes on the human, the ways in which it refuses to cooperate in processes of dematerialization and requalification" (Hawkins 2013: 64). The stubbornness of the material of plastic is worked through the body, and the poisons that it harbors are also transferred. It spreads its reign of death as it refuses to go away. These problems get shipped to places with fewer regulations, such as Wen'an, China, which, after 25 years of operating as a plastics recycling village, is effectively a dead zone with rampant and pervasive negative health effects for the population and local ecology (Minter 2014). This can be understood within the framework of what Rob Nixon calls "slow violence," the violence enacted by chemical industries, late capitalism, and paradigms of Western economic growth on the rest of the planet. That is, a "violence that occurs gradually and out of sight, a violence of delayed destruction that is dispersed across time and space, an attritional violence that is typically not viewed as violence at all" (Nixon 2011: 2).

Recalcitrant Matter

Plastic has an unfortunate metaphorical connotation. For although plastic is often thought of as a malleable material, as in the common use of the term "plasticity," or in the case of Catherine Malabou's conceptualization of the functioning of the brain, it is perhaps the hardest material there is (Malabou 2008, 2010, 2012). It is hard, because it refuses its environment, creating a sealant or barrier that remains impermeable to what surrounds it. It influences its environment while remaining mute to that environment's influence. Instead, plastic serves as a container, both literally and metaphorically, as about 35 percent of plastic produced is for the purposes of packaging. These items are then cast off, placed elsewhere, re-appearing as unsightly objects of debris and refuse. As James Marriott and Mika Minio-Paluello from Platform London—a group of activists and artists who track the relationship of oil to violence and conflict—illustrate, in a typical bucket of ice cream, we can:

> recognize a remarkable lifespan: crude oil formed 3.4 million years ago in rocks under the Caspian comes to rest on the bed of the Atlantic [as a fragment of a plastic container] for the next 10,000 years. Between these two stretches is a tiny window of transformation. It might take just 22 days for Azeri oil to be transported from beneath the Caspian to the Munchmunster plastics factory. Then the container could be moulded, filled, sold and discarded in the span of the following 40 days. In the space of only two months, this oil is extracted, transported, traded, transformed and transformed again before it is sold and ultimately trashed.
>
> *(Marriott and Minio-Paluello 2013: 180–181)*

Not only are the lifespans of plastic products often extremely short, synthetic polymers, derived from oil, are a kind of living dead among us. After digging up the remains of ancient plants and animals, we are now stuck with the consequences of these undead molecules, the ones that refuse to interact with other carbon-dependent life forms. For although plastics photodegrade and break apart, they do not biodegrade. That is, the pieces may get smaller and smaller, but they do not turn into something else. They do not go away. The molecules themselves remain intact, holding onto their identity. In her excellent book on the relation of the chemical industry to our notions of art, artifice, and nature, Esther Leslie writes:

> What is revealed ... is the drive of the chemical industry towards "the impersonation of life," "from death to death transfigured." Refuse turns into worth in an act worthy of alchemy, but rather than cracking the code of life itself, all that has been achieved ... is the polymerization of a few dead molecules.... Death imitates life and reinforces its domain.
>
> *(Leslie 2005: 8)*

And, in its proliferation and accumulation, it does indeed extend death outwards, transforming the ecologies that it now composes. Mimicking the properties of many substances that have a relation to the cycles of life and death, such as endocrines and Persistent Organic Pollutants (POPs), plastic survives, lives on, and accumulates for a projected 10,000 years.[1] This quality of the undead is what plastic is often used for: to package and preserve, to seal off bacteria and other organisms to prevent the decay of fruits, vegetables, and other organic matter, and, of course, reservoirs.

This recalcitrance of matter, plastic's non-plasticity, is illustrated perfectly by an advertisement for Wemco, a laminating firm in Austin, Texas, used in July 1985: "Plastic is forever ... and a lot cheaper than diamonds" (Meikle 1995: 25). Mike Michael reflects on the fact that plastic is an entirely industrial material, existing outside of craft or domestic circuits, and he also comments on the relationship between the metaphor and material of plastic. He writes,

> In a word, there is little plasticity in plastic, especially if we take plasticity to connote the potential for new or renewed connections to be rendered domestically (i.e., outside of a professional or industrial setting) and thus for the functions of plastic to be recovered or altered or adapted or invented.
>
> *(Michael 2013: 33)*

Plastic, once it has been formed through the miracles of the chemical industry, remains recalcitrant both to biological processes as well as to human creativity. It is the materialization of the horror of identity, of the stability of form, of a futurity without change. As Luce Irigaray writes in *This Sex Which Is Not One*: "Because you need/want to believe in 'objects' that are already solidly determined. That is, again, in yourself(-selves), accepting the silent work of death as a condition of remaining indefectibly 'subject'" (Irigaray 1985: 115). Here, the materiality of plastic takes this epistemological framing too seriously, the relationship between the solidity of the object accepts the silent work of death by existing outside of death and life. It seals off the cyclical mechanisms of circulating matter, clinging desperately to an identity that reaches far beyond biological time and into geologic time. Plastic suggests that we in the post-Kantian world have become voracious and solipsistic subjectivities driven by a dangerously self-interested will.

Finitude

Plastic, in this sense, represents the fundamental logic of finitude, carrying the horrifying implications of the inability to decompose, to enter back into systems of decay and regrowth. In our quest to escape death, we have created systems of real finitude that mean the extinguishment of many forms of life. Finitude represents a Western metaphysics of understanding death as the end of a carbon-based life form. Finitude represents the drama of existence played out in relationship to the teleological orientation of time towards our own end: a one-way trajectory from birth to growth to death, focused on the individual. Jean Baudrillard also remarks that, as we are increasingly "[p]lunged by chance [or by a blind design] into an abnormal uncertainty, we have responded with an excess of causality and finality" (Baudrillard 1990: 12). This drama of finitude is intimately tied to our notions of existence, as an individual and as a species, and is seen explicitly in some current narrations of apocalypse within the discourse of the Anthropocene.

The Anthropocene, by relying upon the oft-cited and problematic use of the *anthropos*, seems to fulfill this narrative teleology by advancing a notion of the human as the masculinist technological agent doomed to bring about humanity's own end. What is troubling in this scenario is both the logic of finitude that it proposes—that there will be a clear, clean, and defined end, rather than the much more probable scenario of ongoing devastation, species extinction, and mutation towards a future that will become increasingly toxic but otherwise difficult to predict—and that Man will finally burn through his own glory.

This undifferentiated drama of the end is evidenced in Benjamin Bratton's explication of what he calls the "post-Anthropocenic" (2013); it is also seen in a more sinister form in those who embrace the current conditions as an opportunity to create more money and promote unfettered growth. And these are the kinds of politics associated with what Clive Hamilton has identified as the "good Anthropocene." He writes:

> A new breed of ecopragmatists welcomed the epoch as an opportunity. They have gathered around the Breakthrough Institute, a "neogreen" think tank founded by Michael Shellenberger and Ted Nordhaus, the authors of a controversial 2004 paper, "The Death of Environmentalism." They do not deny global warming; instead they skate over the top of it, insisting that whatever limits and tipping points the Earth system might throw up, human technology and ingenuity will transcend them.
>
> *(Hamilton 2014)*

This techno-utopianism is precisely the kind of logic deployed to divorce us from the conditions of being earth-bound creatures in the first place. It is interested only in the extension of a particular way of life, and the individuals who benefit from it, instead of understanding the cyclical, processual, and transformative nature of life itself.

The reign of death already spread through our naivety in believing that we could control and dominate earth systems should be enough to dissuade us from pursuing this path any further. Plastic materializes the desire to give complete freedom to the mind and to control our environment:

> [P]lastic established unprecedented control over the material environment. Taken to extreme, such control implied the possibility of stifling humanity in a rigidly ordered artificial cocoon, or, in the event of a loss of control, the possibility, as a retired Du Pont chemist predicated in 1988, that humanity would "perish by being smothered in plastic."
>
> *(Meikle 1995: 9)*

What we have seen is that it was exactly the rigidly ordered artificial cocoon of plastics, as well as other fallouts from chemical engineering, that are causing humanity to perish. This holding onto itself that most clearly and molecularly differentiates plastic—a materialized wish to exit the cyclical processes of becoming to which all matter is subject—has inaugurated an era where "men shall seek death, but death shall flee from them," as Werner Herzog says at the end of *Lessons of Darkness* (1992). It is a form of nihilistic lust that pulls, like a black hole, so many of the biological organisms on earth, even as it differentially affects those who benefit from the uses of plastic and those who suffer its consequences.

Extinguishment

As an alternative framework to finitude, extinguishment recognizes that things live and die, recomposing in a different form, but without the drama of *the end* (Figure 8.2). Particular configurations of matter, politics, ideas, and organisms obviously cease to exist, while others come into being. However, extinguishment abandons the teleological impulse by recognizing the circularity and fecundity of living systems. *This* civilization may die, but within that death is the possibility for a reconfiguration with what may be left. Humanity will most certainly one day die off, and it wouldn't be a great surprise if that happened in the relatively near future, but that doesn't mean that species won't evolve or mutate, or that our descendants, even if primarily bacterial, won't inherit the world we leave behind. Apocalypse or the "end of Man" rids us of the questions of inheritance, of a sense of obligation and responsibility to a future, however bleak, too easily. With the concept of extinguishment comes both an acknowledgment of biological, technological, and social limits, but without the drama that would have those neatly encapsulated into a clean break. The framework of extinguishment then recognizes the fact that plastic is killing off *particular* worlds through its proliferation, even as plastic itself remains a materialization of the drama of finitude, refusing to participate in the cycles of extinguishment.

To return again to the black plastic balls in the Ivanhoe Reservoir, I want to think about the fact of their blackness, what their blackness might open up in parallel to the concept of extinguishment. Fred Moten, in a lecture titled "Black Kant (pronounced Chant)," discusses the regulatory framework that Kant applies to the aesthetic and moral regime (2014). He argues that the categories of moral and aesthetic judgment have been deployed to regulate the overabundance of the nonhuman world, the threatening fecundity that then gets displaced through racist logic onto the bodies of black people. In "Blackness and Nothingness," Moten elaborates on these themes; he writes "blackness is ontologically prior to the logistic and regulative power that is supposed to have brought it into existence but that blackness is prior to ontology"

Figure 8.2 Ivanhoe Reservoir, detail of northwestern corner
Source: Copyright Junkyardsparkle.

(Moten 2013: 739). Although Moten is writing specifically from the point of view of thinking about the unthinkable conditions of slavery and its continuation into contemporary black life, there seems to be a necessary reworking of the category of ontology, and the relationship to exhaustion, that bears on what it means to live with toxicity, to live in a time of mass extinctions, a time that arises precisely due to the same kinds of ontological positions that excluded blackness, and black people, from ontology to begin with. What would it mean, then, to return blackness to the black plastic balls? What new relations might we humans have to plastic if we thought of its emerging in blackness, from the black of oil, to the black of these balls? Certainly, if the fantasy of separation were abandoned, plastic might be seen as a powerful and in some respects ancient material that does not separate, but that connects us to an unforeseeable future. This future is not one that is then filled with optimism, but rather one that seeks to elide or overturn the comfort of transcendental subjectivity, and instead finds a way to live with "existence without standing" (Wagner 2009: 1).

> [It] is not only to *reside* in an unlivability, an exhaustion that is always already given as foreshadowing afterlife, as a life in some absolutely proximate and unbridgeable distance from the living death of subjection, but also to *discover and to enter* it.
>
> (Moten 2013: 746)

We must learn to enter into an untenable world, instead of operating from the fantasy that it can be barricaded against.

If we simply give in to the drama of finitude then there is no point in fighting, in organizing, in creating new economic and political systems that will allow us, or allow other species, to continue. Extinguishment offers another narrative framework for recognizing the horrors of species death but without seeing this as a pre-ordained or necessary movement. It embraces both the fecundity of life as well as the complete randomness of its systems, while proposing a model within which humans can begin to take responsibility for what we have done—but without tying this to the destiny of humanity. Exhaustion is the understanding of the cyclical movement and transformation of life through death. Exhaustion is the way in which different beings come into the world and pass through it, transforming into something else. For although, as Peter Sloterdijk reminds us, we are "condemned to being-in, even if the containers and atmospheres in which we are forced to surround ourselves can no longer be taken for granted as being good in nature," we must find ways of living without the categories and fantasies of containment, either in relation to time or in relation to matter (Sloterdijk 2009: 108). We must recognize the porousness of our bodies and thoughts that leach into economics and materials, that transfer our wastes across the planet and into the deep future. We must allow for a certain doubt in our thought, one that eschews mastery in favor of the idiot, and insists on practices of slowing down, of hesitation, as Isabelle Stengers suggests in her cosmopolitical proposal.[2] It is not by neatly announcing the end of days that we can begin to change the path that we are on: and even in its inevitability, we have a responsibility to account for the slow violence enacted on the poorest in the world as well as other creatures. We must finally break free of the logic of plastic.

Notes

1 This is the number given by Anthony Andrady, a chemical engineer and leading expert in plastics (Weisman 2007: 16). However, one of the troubling things about plastic is that its lifespan is unknown, although certain forms of bacteria and fungi have evolved to be able to successfully biodegrade plastic.
2 Stengers insists that this process of slowing down thought is necessary to the composition of politically livable worlds. She writes:

> It is a matter of imbuing political voices with the feeling that they do not master the situation they discuss, that the political arena is peopled with shadows of that which does not have a political voice, cannot have or does not want to have one…. The cosmopolitical proposal therefore has nothing to do with a program and far more to do with a passing fright that scares self-assurance, however justified.
>
> *(2005: 996)*

References

Baudrillard, J. (1990) *Fatal Strategies: The Crystal Revenge*, New York: Semiotext(e).
Bensaude-Vincent, B. (2013) "Plastics, materials and dreams of dematerialization," in J. Gabrys, G. Hawkins, and M. Michael (eds) *Accumulation: The Material Politics of Plastic*, London: Routledge, 17–29.
Bratton, B. (2013) "Some trace effects of the post-anthropocene: on accelerationist geopolitical aesthetics," *e-flux* 46. www.e-flux.com/journal/some-trace-effects-of-the-post-anthropocene-on-accelerationist-geopolitical-aesthetics.
Hamilton, C. (2014) "The new environmentalism will lead us to disaster," *Scientific American*. www.scientificAmerican.com/article/the-new-environmentalism-will-lead-us-to-disaster.
Hawkins, G. (2013) "Made to be wasted: PET and the topologies of disposability," in J. Gabrys, G. Hawkins, and M. Michael (eds) *Accumulation: The Material Politics of Plastic*, London: Routledge, 49–67.
Helfand, D. (2007) "L.A. must dump water from two reservoirs," *Los Angeles Times*, December 15. www.latimes.com/local/la-me-water15dec15-story.html.
Herzog, W. (1992) *Lessons of Darkness*.

Irigaray, L. (1985) *This Sex Which Is Not One*, Ithaca, NY: Cornell University Press.
Kavanaugh, C. (2014) "Plastic balls protect California reservoirs," *Plastic News*, January 3. www.plasticsnews.com/article/20140103/NEWS/140109973/plastic-balls-protect-california-reservoirs.
Leslie, E. (2005) *Synthetic Worlds: Nature, Art and the Chemical Industry*, London: Reaktion Books.
Liboiron, M. (2013) "Plasticizers: a twenty-first-century miasma," in J. Gabrys, G. Hawkins, and M. Michael (eds) *Accumulation: The Material Politics of Plastic*, London: Routledge, 134–149.
Malabou, C. (2008) *What Should We Do with Our Brain?* New York: Fordham University Press.
Malabou, C. (2010) *Plasticity at the Dusk of Writing: Dialectic, Destruction, Deconstruction*, New York: Columbia University Press.
Malabou, C. (2012) *Ontology of the Accident: An Essay on Destructive Plasticity*, Cambridge, UK: Polity.
Marriott, J. and Minio-Paluello, M. (2013) "Where does this stuff come from?" in J. Gabrys, G. Hawkins, and M. Michael (eds) *Accumulation: The Material Politics of Plastic*, London: Routledge, 171–183.
Meikle, J. (1995) *American Plastic: A Cultural History*, New Brunswick, NJ: Rutgers University Press.
Michael, M. (2013) "Process and plasticity: printing, prototyping and the prospects of plastic," in J. Gabrys, G. Hawkins, and M. Michael (eds) *Accumulation: The Material Politics of Plastic*, London: Routledge, 30–44.
Minter, A. (2014) "Plastic, poverty and pollution in China's recycling dead zone," *Guardian*, July 16. www.theguardian.com/lifeandsytle/2014/jul/16/plastic-poverty-pollution-china-recycling-dead-zone.
Mirzoeff, N. (2014) "Visualizing the Anthropocene," *Public Culture* 26, 2: 220–226.
Moten, F. (2013) "Blackness and nothingness (mysticism in the flesh)," *The South Atlantic Quarterly* 112, 4: 739.
Moten, F. (2014) "Black Kant (pronounced chant)," paper presented at the California Institute of the Arts, Valencia, California, March 18.
Nixon, R. (2011) *Slow Violence and the Environmentalism of the Poor*, Cambridge, MA: Harvard University Press.
Preciado, B. (2013) *Testo Junkie: Sex, Drugs, and Biopolitics in the Pharmacopornographic Era*, New York: Feminist Press.
Rochman, C., Browne, M. A., Halpern, B. S., et al. (2013) "Policy: classify plastic waste as hazardous," *Nature* 494: 169–171.
Sloterdijk, P. (2009) *Terror from the Air*, Los Angeles: Semiotext(e).
Starosielski, N. (2015) *The Undersea Network*, Durham, NC: Duke University Press.
Stengers, I. (2005) "The cosmopolitical proposal," in B. Latour and P. Weibel (eds) *Making Things Public: Atmospheres of Democracy*, Cambridge, MA: MIT Press, 994–1003.
Vara-Orta, F. (2008) "A reservoir goes undercover," *Los Angeles Times*, June 10. articles.latimes.com/2008/jun/10/local/me-balls10.
Wagner, B. (2009) *Disturbing the Peace: Black Culture and the Police Power after Slavery*, Cambridge, MA: Harvard University Press.
Weisman, A. (2007) "Polymers are forever," *Orion* 26, 3. www.orionmagazine.org/index.php/articles/article/270.
Westermann, A. (2013) "The material politics of vinyl: how the state, industry and citizens created and transformed West Germany's consumer democracy," in J. Gabrys, G. Hawkins, and M. Michael (eds) *Accumulation: The Material Politics of Plastic*, London: Routledge, 68–86.
Yarsley, V. E. and Couzens, E. G. (1941) *Plastics*, Harmondsworth, Middlesex: Penguin.

9

The Space of Relation

Body, Emotion, and Empathy in Architectural Experience

Sarah Robinson

As architects, our primary medium is space, but what exactly is space? Answering that question depends largely on who we ask. From the point of view of classical physics, space is a neutral container defined by Euclidean coordinates. Newtonian space is absolute and unaffected by anything external—space is immutable and immoveable (Newton 1687). According to Einstein, space is neither empty, nor immutable, but moves and bends and curves relative to the weight, shape, and movements of surrounding bodies—space is not absolute; space is responsive, flexible, and inseparable from time. Space is not a void, space is a substance, it is one of the material components of the universe (Rovelli 2014).

This physical understanding of space, this sense of space as a something rather than a nothing is much closer to the way a sculptor, a Japanese gardener, a neuroscientist, or a phenomenologist would understand space. For them, space is not an abstraction or a question of inert geometry, but an essential source of meaning and presence. And while Einstein introduced an entirely different conception of the cosmos than the one Newton had imagined, it has taken thinkers in these diverse disciplines to work out the implications of his theories in the human realm.

Existential Space

While many philosophers had become obsessed with the question of time in response to Einstein's Special Theory of Relativity, three important works by phenomenologists appeared in the middle of the last century, which dealt primarily with the inseparable notion of space. Otto Friedrich Bollnow's *Lived Space* (1961) was a direct response to Eugene Minkowski's *Lived Time* (1933) and in it he investigated the nature of the space in which we actually live, the space that is conditioned by our daily habits and conscious engagement (Bollnow 1961). Martin Heidegger famously elaborated on lived space in his "Building, Dwelling, Thinking," in which he equated being with dwelling. According to him, our existence depends upon and is made possible by the space in which we dwell. Space and dwelling are interdependent and born of one another, the actions of building and dwelling "create space" (Heidegger 1951). And finally, Gaston Bachelard's monumental work, *The Poetics of Space* (1964) investigates the mental, imaginative, and psychological dimensions of our intimate milieu, which of course was the precursor to Foucault's later formulations of heterotopic space (Foucault 1986). These works collectively flesh out the reality of existential space and provide a poignant contrast to the notion of space as merely a mathematical construct.

Embodiment: Body as Origin

These thinkers laid the groundwork for an understanding of space as a dynamic, interactive atmosphere latent with potentiality. Yet no one went farther than the phenomenologist Maurice Merleau-Ponty, who insisted that space is not only fundamentally existential, and existence is fundamentally spatial, but that space originates in the human body. The body is not in space and time, but rather is space and time, the body belongs to the fabric of space and time in an indistinguishable embrace. Bodily experience is the primary and fundamental ground of our being, "I am my body," he declared (Merleau-Ponty 1945).

The intention of the often used term embodiment is to correct centuries of thinking that have displaced and dismissed the body as the primary source of being and knowing. Descartes' famous *cogito ergo sum*, "I think, therefore I am," fails to capture the manner in which we actually exist in the world. And, in an effort to right this fatal wrong, Merleau-Ponty insisted that the body is the primary medium for perception of the world. We understand the world, others and ourselves through the whole of our bodily experiences. We do not arrive at knowledge merely through thinking, but through full bodied experience, feeling, intuition, conscious and unconscious apprehension. He insisted that the body is our primary source of signification and meaning—our primary expression of space.

Neuroscience: The Extension of the Body in Space

The indissoluble nature of the body and space is now being corroborated by neuroscientists, who, like Merleau-Ponty before them, describe space in terms of the body and consider the body to be the locus of space. They use the term peripersonal space to describe the envelope that immediately surrounds your body. This invisible envelope is plastic and modulates according to the tools, objects, intentions, and affordances that are present within its field. In their seminal investigations of peripersonal space, the neuroscientists Giacomo Rizzolati and Vittorio Gallese concur with Merleau-Ponty, who noticed that space is "not a sort of ether in which all things float…. The points in space mark, in our vicinity, the varying range of our aims and our gestures" (Rizzolati et al. 1997). The envelope surrounding our body is not neutral, but conditioned by our mental and physical presence. It is now generally accepted that the body considers the tool, pencil, bicycle, or chair to be part of itself (Holmes et al. 2006). Our body extends into surrounding space through the means of both inanimate objects and our intentions, our aims and desires.

We know too that animals, including us, are endowed with "place-cells" in our brains that correspond to physical locations in the surrounding environment (O'Keefe et al. 1998). Our brain maps our surrounding terrain into its intimate convolutions. Research in neuroscience, coupled with a rich history of phenomenological investigation together reveal space to be many layered, multidimensional, and highly personal. The Newtonian paradigm of empty space was a mathematical construct and was never intended to describe daily life, the limits of its application need to finally be acknowledged. Space, as Einstein realized a century ago, is a physical component of the universe, like light and matter—the space outside of us wraps into our most inner folds. Where we end and the world begins is an open question.

Empathy: Affective Space

Like our newly rendered and enriched understanding of space, contemporary interest in the notion of empathy is the fruit of the cross-pollination of philosophical insight and scientific research. Empathy is the translation of the German *Einfühlung*, a word coined by the philosopher Theodor Lipps in the second half of the nineteenth century, to describe the aesthetic experience of "feeling oneself" into a work of art (Lipps 1913). The experience of empathy, according to Lipps, was not only the projection of one's feelings into an object, but an interactive emotional participation with and in the work. And in this sense, empathy extends one's imagination and consciousness in space. His invention of empathy offered a radical alternative to the commonly held understanding of aesthetic experience as a purely cognitive enterprise. Empathy implicitly questioned the rigidity of the subject/object duality between the observer and the work of art.

Aesthetic experience as an inherently participatory, empathic, and spatial phenomenon has since been born out by experimental neuroscience. In studying the work of Lucio Fontana and Franz Kline, the art historian David Freedberg and the neuroscientist Vittorio Gallese showed that these artworks activate our innate mirror systems, and that through the process of embodied simulation we experience the bodily movements and emotional sensations of the artist that went into creating the work. We sense the violence of Fontana's cut canvas as if the knife were tearing our own skin, Kline's muscular brush marks activate the motor schema in our own bodies that originally stained the canvas black (Freedberg and Gallese 2007). Similarly, the neuroscientists Hanna and Antonio Damasio and their colleagues showed that when we observe objects touching, our brain responds as if ours were the body being touched (Damasio et al. 2011). In this way, art works and objects in general lose their strict objectivity and mingle with our inner worlds. These studies affirm Bachelard's statement that indeed, objects have no reality apart from their relations (Bachelard 1984: 56).

The Integrative Role of Emotion

Findings in the cognitive and neurosciences have upended the long-cherished certainty of Western divides. Dualisms such as mind/body, subject/object, outer/inner, like the notion of absolute space, are finally being placed within their proper limits. We are beginning to understand the subtle and complex interpenetrations and overlaps that connect such ostensible polarities. For example, the tired segregation between and privileging of reason over feeling has given way to a much richer and nuanced understanding of the evolutionary importance of emotion. The philosopher Giovanna Colombetti understands emotions to be sources of meaning that ground the more elaborate modes of sense making in complex organisms, arguing, "The richer and more differentiated emotions that one finds in animal and human lives are enrichments of the primordial capacity to be sensitive to the world." (Colombetti 2014: 19).

Emotion is an all-pervasive sensory capacity and like all of our senses, emotion is not limited to a specific circuit or region of the brain. After an extensive research of the literature on brain regions traditionally associated with emotion and those for cognition, the neuroscientist Luiz Pessoa concluded that, "Parceling the brain into cognitive and affective regions is inherently problematic and ultimately untenable" (Pessoa 2008). Emotion and cognition are interdependent dimensions of behavior that result from the activity of multiple brain regions that are neither intrinsically emotional nor cognitive, but contribute to behavior in distinct ways depending on the broader neural context in which they participate. According to the developmental psychologist and neuroscientist Kenneth Dodge, "All information processing is emotional, in that emotion is the energy that drives, organizes, amplifies, and attenuates cognitive activity and in turn is the experience and expression of this activity" (Siegel 2015: 147).

Neuroscientists and philosophers are converging upon an understanding of emotion which broadens its meaning and importance beyond the strictly subjective. That is, our emotions not only monitor and express our inner states, our emotions make us continually aware of the threats, pleasures, potentials, and affordances of the surrounding environment. Emotion is an internal response to an external situation, and in this sense not only integrates the many-layered modes of knowing within our bodies, but also serves to integrate our organism with the environment on which our lives depend.

This enriched understanding of emotion threatens the hard boundaries we typically take to exist between our isolated selves and surrounding space. Like empathy, our sense of emotion enables and allows us to navigate and flourish in the network of our relations; both emotion and empathy are crucial for finding meaning and value in our surrounding worlds. In his *Lived Space*, O. F. Bollnow acknowledged the breakdown between the notion of purely subjective interior states and wholly external situations in writing about the mood of a space. "Mood," Bollnow wrote, "is not something subjective 'in' an individual and not something objective that could be found 'outside' in his surroundings, but it concerns the individual in his still undivided unity with his surroundings" (Bollnow 2011: 217). The reality of existential space assumes the continuity between individual and environment, and therefore supersedes the fiction of the isolated self. The emotional dimension, the mood, is a critical layer of existential space, a dimension which has been all too neglected in the architecture of our recent past.

Engaging Emotion

One of the great insights of neuroscience is the basic principle of neural plasticity, which means that our sensory, affective, and cognitive faculties develop and flourish to the extent that they are engaged—the bottom line of neural plasticity is: use it or lose it. Our immediate environment reinforces and exercises certain capacities, while ignoring others. Consequently, our organism develops or atrophies in response to the richness or poverty of the environment we inhabit. An example of neural plasticity is the fact that European's who walk regularly on cobblestone streets that stimulate the vestibular nerves in the soles of their feet retain their sense of balance far longer than their American counterparts who walk on smooth surfaces (Robinson 2011). In this instance the environment provides stimulation to the nervous system in a simple, integrated, time-honored fashion. Body, mind, and world influence one another dynamically and reciprocally.

The architecture and urban environments of the last half-century have been amply criticized as exhibiting an ocularcentric, rational bias, and consequently failing to engage our emotions, elicit our empathy, or captivate our imagination (Pallasmaa 1996). According to the principle of neural plasticity, it would not be a stretch to speculate that such environments contribute to an atrophy of emotional wholeness, and serve to reinforce a culture of autism. In fact, generational increases in depression, anxiety, and behavioral disorders have been well documented in North America and have been occurring in tandem with generational increases in narcissism, and significant declines in empathy and concern for others (Twenge et al. 2013). Of course, innumerable factors have collectively contributed to such declines, but it would be difficult to deny the coincidence that we now spend 90 percent of our lives inside buildings, and if the built environment fails to nurture our capacities for emotional and empathetic intelligence, that environment is in some measure contributing to such deterioration.

How can we design to engage the emotions so that we might correct this damaging atrophy? We would do well to start, as Merleau-Ponty did, with the whole of our body, to design with the acute awareness that, "I am my body." The needs and desires of the body that have been sorely neglected must now be invited fully into design. We now know that emotion does not reside in one region of the brain but is distributed throughout our entire nervous system. Further, like all sensory systems, our capacity for emotion is intimately intertwined with every other sense. The way we speak about emotion as "feeling" betrays this natural integration. When we design for the sense of touch, we also enhance our sense of feeling.

Consider the word, emotion itself: emotion comes from the Latin *emovere*, which means "to move out, to agitate." Emotion conjures the image of moving energy, and is the very counterpoint to stillness. Vittorio Gallese's work on mirror systems and embodied simulation repeatedly correlates the activation of empathy with movement (Gallese 2009). We instinctively identify and relate to other living things, and the presence of movement, of breathing is the surest indication that something is alive. Yet, architecture is certainly the most stable of the arts, how can we introduce movement into something ostensibly static like a building, whose very ontology implies being rooted, motionlessly to the ground. How exactly do we animate that which is inanimate?

Animate Space

If the very definition of emotion is the stirring up of an otherwise even state, then one might venture to suggest that physical movements against a backdrop of stillness would be emotionally evocative. That is, if emotions are inner eruptions in response to exterior perturbations, then their analogue would be physical displacements in the surrounding environment. Movement depends on stillness: we recognize movement against a background of stillness, the flight of birds across the quiet of blue, the rustle of a squirrel in the tranquility of the forest. These movements activate a latent atmosphere, awaken an emotional response, expressing the overall mood of the setting. Even the most humble movement, the wavering of leaves in a soft breeze, the brush of a fabric curtain against the weight of a solid wall, can be activations and awakenings. In his Kolomba Museum in Cologne, Germany for example, Peter Zumthor added hand sewn silk curtains to the monumental windows. The delicate tissue of the fabric that moves with the slightest touch enlivens the stoic solidity in which it is framed. The contrasting textures speak to our own human fragility and strength (Figure 9.1).

European languages lack a vocabulary to speak of the vital necessity of such interdependencies and tend to quickly resort to dualisms. In contrast, the Japanese have a rich vocabulary in this regard; the potential for the subtlest of movements to evoke feeling tones is wonderfully captured, for example, with their word "fuzei," which is written with the characters meaning "wind" and "emotion." Rich with ambiguity, "fuzei" means both atmosphere and taste, and is often used in reference to garden design (Slawson 1987). Evoking emotion through contrast depends on subtlety and suggestion, a fitting paradigm for such an approach would be the Japanese garden and not the Las Vegas strip.

Working with contrasts has long been the domain of the artist, "Weight is the best way to express weightlessness," said the sculptor Isamu Noguchi. He also reported that when it came time for him to work with larger spaces, he "conceived them as gardens, not as sites with objects, but as relations to a whole" (Noguchi 1968: 15). Engaging emotion and animating space have very much to do with invoking relations, and as Noguchi noticed, reinforcing relationships often takes the emphasis away from centralized objects. Japanese garden design, whose aim is to create evocative overall atmospheres, for example, eschews orthogonal, central pathways and domineering, hard-edged perspectives. In the Japanese garden, context is stronger than object, it is not that the teahouse or the pavilion are trivialized, but rather their presence

Figure 9.1 Peter Zumthor, Silk curtains at Kolomba Museum, Cologne, Germany
Source: Photograph courtesy of Dorothee Dubois.

does not make their surroundings subservient to them, instead, the many finely rendered details of their surroundings serve to quietly reinforce, rather than diminish their presence.

The Space of Relation

A space of relation emphasizes interdependencies and values the quality of context over the dominance of the isolated object. Objects cease to lose their absolute independence, but not their individuality. Think about the word "individual": it actually means unable to be divided, and suggests wholeness rather than complete independence. Noguchi did not consider his sculptures to be isolated objects, the essence of sculpture for him was not so much the formation of the object, it was "the perception of space, the continuum of our existence" (Noguchi 1968: 52). Taking our cue from his inspiration in the Japanese garden, shifting our attention away from the isolated object, to develop and accentuate the context in which it is embedded is inherently an act of connection—an acknowledgment and celebration of relation.

As architects, we are not without references in this regard. Consider the enduring analogy between architecture and music, for example. We have hardly considered the extent to which music is a fully immersive experience of space. Music animates space, moving sound waves through the air to vibrate the fluid filled channels in our inner ear, and in this way very literally moves us. Our auditory system is multidirectional and inherently immersive, and therefore essentially spatial—we can close our eyes, but we cannot close our ears. Our auditory sense is receptive, rather than commanding, like our visual sense.

Music is not only an immersive experience of space, when listening to music we feel an overwhelming sense of movement: pulses, rhythms, contractions, expansions, rising, falling, swelling, fading, and so on. We perceive music as moving, and researchers in the psychology of music take this as a basic presupposition. Researchers Noël Carroll and Margaret Moore claim that we perceive vicariously the movement in music, which is why it feels natural to respond physically to music by dancing, citing fMRI studies showing that listening to music is processed in the same parts of the brain that are responsible for processing movement, and that both actually listening to or imagining music activates the pre-motor cortex (Carroll and Moore 2011).

Music is an art of relationships—it is as much about the notes as the gaps between them. Music is an art of proportion, and proportion too, is all about relationship; the measure of the part as related to the whole. Architectural theory and practice has been greatly enriched in its analogy to musical proportion, but those proportions have tended to be applied to the elements of the building itself, rather than extended into the surroundings, or applied to those inhabiting the space. And, when proportion has been related to the human body, the body is considered as an ideal and an abstraction, but not a concrete, physical reality whose vulnerabilities and strengths are the domain of both architecture's creative expression and ethical responsibility.

Architects are becoming ever more sensitive to the contexts and situations in which they build. Working with and finding the poetry and texture in local identities and histories has greatly enriched recent architectural work. Intensifying relationships with the local environment has been a rich source of inspiration, but what I am suggesting here is not only looking without for such inspiration, but also looking within, within our own bodies and minds. Engaging the limits and affordances of human sensory perception has scarcely been considered in architectural design.

Affirming the Breath

Breathing is the sign of life. The most fundamental expression of our interdependence with our surroundings is the air that enters our body—air is warmed, enriched, and exhaled only to start

Figure 9.2 Tomás Saraceno, *Poetic Cosmos of the Breath*, 2013. Installation view, Mobile M+:Inflation!, Hong Kong, China. Commissioned by M+ Gunpowder and Arts Catalyst
Source: Copyright Studio Tomás Saraceno. Photograph courtesy of Tomás Saraceno.

the cycle anew. This most basic reality also takes place inside our buildings—without the constant exchange of air, our buildings are no longer fit to be habitats for humans. How easily this essential fact of our embodiment is overlooked. The air is everywhere, yet how rarely do we use it as a design element. The architect Tomás Saraceno in his astonishingly simple experiment, *Poetic Cosmos of the Breath*, used paper-thin fabric, a few sandbags, and a handful of participants to celebrate the vital presence of the air. Staged at dawn when temperature conditions naturally shift, the air inside the enormous hot air balloon is warmed by the greenhouse effect, with no mechanical aid, and the lightweight material lifts from the ground, creating a stunning shimmer that seems to saturate the air in a rainbow iridescence (Figure 9.2).

Sensualizing Space

Working at the intersection of art, architecture, and science, through making latent relationships visible and concrete, Tomás Saraceno expresses the materiality of space. Space is a material component of the universe, but it is difficult to consider it as such when the very word connotes a sense of the neutral and the inert. Here again, it is helpful to turn to the Japanese, whose word "ma," can mean space, gap, or pause and is very closely related to the meaning of the interval in music, the pause between the notes, or the opening between two distinct parts. "Ma" is not a geometric designation, but an extension of human consciousness, a medium in which relationships cohere. "Ma" combines the characters for door and for moon, and graphically evokes the crevice in a door through which moonlight peeks in. The association with the moon is especially evocative as the reflected light of the moon has long been a cross-cultural symbol of the emotions.

The polyvalent meaning of the word "ma" suggests the latent dynamism of space, the manner in which space becomes animated through contrast. The weight and presence of the door serve to strengthen and stabilize the faltering light of the moon. In her installation, *Lightscapes* at the

The Space of Relation

Figure 9.3 Anja Thierfelder, *Lightscapes*, Installation at the 2016 Venice Biennale
Source: Copyright Sarah Robinson.

2016 Venice Biennale, the architect Anja Thierfelder captures the sense of the word, "ma," by reproducing the atmospheric optical phenomenon of crepuscular light rays (Figure 9.3). The startling rays of sunlight that are made visible when they blaze through a dense forest or thick cloud cover are called crepuscular rays (Figure 9.4). The rays of light become visible through contrast, the obfuscation of dense clouds, or the solidity around the opening in a door, or the biomass of the forest canopy. Sunlight is reflected from microscopic airborne particles, and is made visible through its obscuration.

Light is a powerful determinant of emotion and mood. Few things shift our mood as much as a change in the weather, as Marcel Proust so rightly noticed (Proust 1920). We architects love the light, but have scarcely considered its full, multi-sensory, physiological, and poetic potential. Consider the daily experience of light touching your skin: the light that makes its way through a window not only warms your skin, it expands the space around you, making both it and you feel a little larger. The light shifts your mood as it regulates your hormone levels and tunes your body to seasonal and cosmic cycles. The light filtering through a room captures your imagination in multiple directions—unveiling the hidden, light invites the imagination to trace its path; without your awareness your mind begins to fill in the shadows the light has brought newly into relief. At the same time, the light tugs your mind outward, towards the opening, inviting you to seek the source of this sure and quiet power. Here, in a single experiential incident, countless subtle shifts and nuances have transpired, the light has touched not only your skin, it has touched

Figure 9.4 Crepuscular light, Khao Yai National Park Thailand
Source: Copyright Sarah Robinson.

your mind and reminded you of your place on the ground, your position in the larger scheme of things.

Architecture: An Interactive Perceptual Field

Thanks to breakthroughs in the physical and biological sciences we have traveled far from the Newtonian/Cartesian dichotomies that impoverished our understanding of our interdependence with the surrounding world. Yet, unfortunately many of us continue to behave according to an obsolete paradigm, assuming that the world outside and the world inside stop at the surface of the skin. We persist in thinking of buildings as objects with an independent existence, when in truth they are interdependent, interactive, developmental fields (Robinson 2015). Buildings are not isolated objects, they are spaces of relation, and it is up to us architects to find how and with whom we can make them connect.

References

Bachelard, G. (1964) *The Poetics of Space*, trans., Maria Jolas, Paris: Presses Universitaires de France.
Bachelard, G. (1984) *The New Scientific Spirit*, Boston: Beacon Press.
Bollnow, O. F. (1961) *Lived Space*, trans. D. Gerlach, *Philosophy Today* 5(1/4): 31–39.
Bollnow, O. F. (2011) *Human Space*, ed. J. Kohlmaier, trans. C. Shuttleworth. London: Hyphen Press.
Carroll, N. and Moore M. (2011) "Moving in concert: dance and music," in Elisabeth Schellekens and Peter Goldie (eds) *The Aesthetic Mind: Philosophy and Psychology*, Oxford: Oxford University Press, 333–345.
Colombetti, G. (2014) *The Feeling Body*, Cambridge: MIT Press.
Damasio, H. et al. (2011) "Seeing touch is correlated with content-specific activity in primary somatosensory cortex," *Cerebral Cortex* 21(9): 2113–2121.
Foucault, M. (1986) "Of other spaces," *Diacritics* 16: 22–27.
Freedberg, D. and Gallese, V. (2007) "Motion, emotion and empathy in aesthetic experience," *Trends in Cognitive Science* 11(5): 197–203.
Gallese, V. (2009) "Mirror neurons, embodied simulation, and the neural basis of social identification," *Psychoanalytic Dialogues* 19: 519–536.
Heidegger, M. (1971 [1951]) "Building dwelling thinking," in *Poetry, Language, Thought*, New York: Harper & Row, 145–61.
Holmes, N. et al. (2006) "The body schema and the multisensory representations of peripersonal space," *Cognitive Process* 5(2): 94–105.

Lipps, T. (1913) "Zur Einfühlung," *Psychologische Untersuchungen* vol. 2, Leipzig: Engelmann.
Merleau-Ponty, M. (1945) *Phénoménologie de la Perception*, Paris: Gallimard.
Minkowski, E. (1933) *Lived Time*, London: E. K. Ledermann.
Newton, I. (1687) *Philosophiae Naturalis Principia Mathematica*.
Noguchi, I. (1968) *Noguchi*, New York: Whitney Museum.
O'Keefe, J. et al. (1998) "Place cells, navigational accuracy and the human hippocampus," *Philosophical Transactions of the Royal Society B: Biological Sciences*, 353(1373): 1333–1340.
Pallasmaa, J. (1996) *The Eyes of the Skin: Architecture and the Senses*, London: Wiley.
Pessoa, L. (2008) "On the relationship between emotion and cognition," *Neuroscience* 9: 158.
Proust, M. (1920) *In Search of Lost Time*, vol. 6, trans. C. K. Scott Moncrieff, London: Penguin.
Rizzolati, G. et al. (1997) "The space around us: peripersonal space, definitions and implications," *Science* July 11; 277(5323): 190–191.
Robinson, S. (2011) *Nesting: Body, Dwelling, Mind*, Richmond, CA: William Stout Publishers.
Robinson, S. (2015) "John Dewey and the dialogue between neuroscience and architecture," *Architecture Research Quarterly* 19(4): 361–367.
Rovelli, C. (2014) *Sette Lezione Breve della Fisica*, Milano: Adelphi.
Siegel, D. J. (2015) *The Developing Mind: How Relationships and the Brain Interact to Shape Who We Are*, 2nd edition, New York: Guilford Press.
Slawson, D. (1987) *Secret Teachings in the Art of Japanese Gardens*, New York: Kodansha USA.
Twenge, J. M. et al. (2013) "Overwhelming evidence for generation Me," *Emerging Adulthood* 1: 21–26.

10
Edges
Body, Space, and Design

Jeremy White

In the twentieth century, a generation of Modernist architects conceptualized the body as an actor in space. Le Corbusier's famous Modulor Man was perhaps the most iconic expression of the architecture profession's obsession with designing space to suit the scale of the human body (Le Corbusier 1954). During that dramatic era of architectural design, consideration of the spatial edge became central to the artist's intervention in the landscape. As "space" superseded "room," "edge" became a subject to think about and redefine. Spatial flow from inside to outside became *de rigueur* in architectural parlance, and the body's passage from one interior space to another could be accomplished without confronting that body with a door. While the edge between one space and another could be reduced to a whisper or a suggestion, a change in floor finish or the ascent of one or two risers, the architect never questioned the clear boundary between space and the body. In that relationship, space received the architect's full attention, while the body was taken for granted. The body remained an actor in space, playing a key role, but the body itself was never the target of rethinking. That held true for the distinction between body and space; the edge between them was never blurred.

This essay concerns the built environment's relationship to the body. Specifically, it treats the edge between user and space as a relatively new field of transformation and design. I consider this edge in four ways, beginning with the manipulation of the built environment in order to accommodate bodies that would, until recently, fall outside a "normal" category of mobility and action. Bodies outside that range include those that cannot walk, see, hear, or require augmentation in order to accomplish tasks such as entering a building. The second part of the essay focuses quite literally on the edge between body and space by exploring recent experimentation in body modification that includes mechanical augmentation in the form of prosthetic limbs. In this second section, architecture crosses the limits of environment to reside on the body. The third section explores the remotest boundary of that kind of experimentation. It deals with the recent trend towards the promulgation of virtual bodies, exploring "avatarchitecture" and the parallel modeling of real buildings in virtual space both before and after they are constructed in the real world. There is much to consider in that similarity. The final section of this essay returns to the corporeal. It deals with ideas about the body and their influence on identity, focusing on the conceptual edge of gender and its extension in space. Although contentious debate about this edge would seem to be cultural and political, beyond the purview of architectural design, that debate often centers on the most mundane yet necessary of spaces in the architectural landscape, the public bathroom. Underlying these four sections, each a view into a changing parameter of everyday life, is this assertion: the contemporary realm tests core definitions about the body upon which human identity is founded. Physical boundaries are vulnerable to conceptual verity, and vice versa. Architecture has always played a role in forging and filtering a sense of self, and these recent explorations and transformations affirm that role.

Expanding the Normal

When the United States Congress passed the Americans with Disabilities Act (ADA) in the early 1990s, it extended civil rights to bodies that were considered to lie outside the normative range (Hamrale 2017). "Disability" meant unable to walk, stand, climb, or otherwise traverse and act in space "normally." The term "normal" was key, and that act of Congress made it illegal to discriminate against "disabled" or "challenged" bodies. In order to comply with this new civil rights legislation, the environment itself needed to be modified. It not only required there be a ramp available to the person who cannot make use of the risers and treads of stairs, it mandated that the ramp be situated so that it allows that person to come and go not by a secondary or back route, but through the front door. Just as the 1964 Civil Rights Act did away with back entrances for African Americans, the ADA of 1990 did the same for wheelchair-bound individuals. The implications were similar. The Civil Rights Act asserted no difference between a person of color and anyone else, abolishing the second-class status of African Americans in the United States. Likewise, the ADA expanded the category of the normal body to include those without legs or other corporeal variations affecting mobility and physical action. Normal was legally expanded to include disabled, and this conceptual move necessitated environmental follow-through that could only be managed by the designer and the contractor. This strategy to create barrier-free design, often referred to as design for all, inclusive design, or universal design, is now commonplace in architectural education and practice.

The Ed Roberts Campus in Berkeley, California, is one of the more ambitious attempts to create an accessible environment (Figure 10.1). Opened in 2011 it was designed by Leddy Maytum Stacy Architects (LMS) in collaboration with universal design consultant Mikiten Architects (Pearson 2011). LMS centered their design around a helical ramp bathed in natural light from an oculus roof. Connected to a local subway station, the building is intended to house tenants devoted to access or allied missions, and to serve as a fully operating model of universal design. This environment is an arena where a delicate game of accommodation is played out by designers. Bodies unable to walk, bound to a motorized chair or one propelled by the labor of biceps and triceps, transit from space to space without ever encountering a curb or step. Bodies with impaired or unusable vision are able to move through those same spaces, navigating by use of textures and sounds designed into surfaces and devices. Herein lurks a problem.

A feature intended to accommodate one challenge can pose an obstacle to another accommodation. The bottom of the ramp signals its incline with small bumps intended to be "read" by a visually impaired body tapping with a walking stick, and yet, not so bumpy that the wheelchair's access is deterred or barred. The practical challenge of accommodating a range of normality is commensurate with the expansion of the definition of the normal body. At times this necessitates duplication of access. For example, the call button of an elevator is located a foot off the floor, in order to accommodate a wheel chair-bound body negotiating that space. Another is located in easy reach of a standing adult. Intended to comply with the ADA, Division 2 of the 2016 California Building Code demands that 50 percent of drinking fountains in public space accommodate seated bodies while the other 50 percent accommodate the standing adult body.

Figure 10.1 Approach to the Ed Roberts Campus. Note the change in paving in the lowest image, a variation in texture to guide the visually impaired

Source: Photographs by Mallorie Chase.

Design may be effective here, but no design will have the desired effect without maintenance. A fragrance-free workplace policy is in effect in the building, in order to accommodate the sensitivities of some workers, and visitors are discouraged from wearing perfume or cologne. Body meets environment; volatile organic compounds rate at the lowest end of the spectrum in this building, thanks to the selection of floor and wall coverings, as well as a HEPA filter integrated into the ventilation system. Natural ventilation is balanced with mechanically pushed and filtered air, fueled in part by the electricity harvested from a photovoltaic array installed on the nearly flat roof. Carpets include 39 percent recycled products while the marmoleum bathroom flooring is manufactured with raw materials such as linseed oil and pigments free of heavy metals and installed with solvent-free adhesives. The bulletin boards in this transit-oriented and information-rich environment were made from 50 percent post-industrial recycled product. The materials and assemblies accommodate a host of certifications: The Forest Stewardship Council, the U.S. Access Board, the Carpet and Rug Institute's Green Label, and the U.S. Green Building Council's Leadership in Energy and Environmental Design (LEED) Gold certificate standard. When moving in, tenants are handed a list of cleaning products conforming to LEED standards, and the goal is to maintain a campus accommodating every human body regardless of allergies, sensitivities, and disabilities.

The Ed Roberts Campus provides an example of an environment shaped to accommodate an expanded range of the "normal" body. In this regard, the body itself was re-conceptualized first in legal terms and then in terms of how the body occupies and moves through space. The new conception drove many of the choices made by the design team. In this space, the edge between body and environment is brought into focus. The interface between body and space was configured to allow greater mobility and access, and perhaps in the walking stick and the wheelchair we begin to see an overlap between environment and body. The chair moves with the wheelchair-bound body and thus flirts with the category of "body," but it is also a designed and manufactured assemblage and therefore may also be categorized as "artifact," thereby flirting with the category of "space." As we shall see, this sort of conceptual overlap can get more involved.

Edges of Body/Space

When architects think about the interface between body and environment, their training and disposition prompt them to focus on the environment. As we saw with the Ed Roberts Campus, the environment is designed to accommodate the body, and the category of "normal body" was broadly defined. This focus can be turned around, although doing so would seem to move the discussion out of the architect's realm into robotics. Rather than employ design to shape the environment, it is possible to apply the art and science of design to shape the body. The edge between environment and body can be thought of as a zone of interaction. Rather than see the two as distinct, body and space, architecture can be thought of as an extension of the designed environment onto the body.

Body modification is a practice that might belong in this category of architectural strategy. It often refers to the tattoo, body piercing, and cosmetic surgery (DeMello 2000; Atkinson 2003). As of this writing, Americans who are in their thirties are more likely than not to sport a tattoo, images needled into their skin. Pierced ears and tattoos can be categorized as decorative expressions of self, adornment to the natural body, and in this way can occupy the same category as styled hair, foundation, false or painted nails, and T-shirts printed with images of dragons, Star Wars vehicles, or pithy statements such as "I work hard so my cat can have a better life." In many cases, body modification is meaningful even when temporary or decorative, as in the styling of hair, a renewable and naturally changing feature. Although the decorative is body modification's primary order, other forms of body modification make the decorative its second purpose.

The design of a limb is usually instigated by tragedy. An accident in a moving vehicle, for example, or an arm accidentally lodged in a basement furnace, or some other unlikely and unexpected event resulting in the medical necessity to remove the limb (Brooker 2012; Ziegler-Graham et al. 2008). Disease such as diabetes, or infection, can also invoke this necessity. Many amputees get on with their lives without a prosthetic replacement, but a privileged few replace that which was lost. These patients reside primarily in the Global North and elsewhere in markets where healthcare reaches the middle class and beyond.[1] The prosthetic replacement can be realistic, such as those sculpted by artist Sophie De Oliveira Barata, who trained in the creation of special effects in film. She can match the hue, texture, hair, and random imperfections of the patient's natural skin (Anthony 2013). This replacement strategy constitutes an envelope covering a mechanical attachment to the body, restoring the limb's visual presence and some of its functionality.

Although many amputees can afford nothing more than a hook or a peg, the twenty-first-century market caters to clients who demand complete functionality. The prosthetic becomes one of many. Just as a shirt for running is tucked away in a drawer or hangs in a closet, alongside a shirt for the workplace and another shirt for an evening out, the privileged amputee is likely to store limbs for a range of functions: a realistic limb for the office or that special night out, a "blade runner" leg for the marathon (it looks more like the rotor of a machine than a human limb), and a waterproof limb for the swimming pool. Although the mechanical limb has a prolonged history reaching back centuries, the computerized and robotic prosthetic is a development local to this century. Nerves surgically rerouted from the control of lost muscle tissue to new mechanical apparatus in the prosthetic replicate the range of action lost by the amputation. Computerized knees and wrists work with transducers to restore functionality. Identity is rooted in the body, and as long as a prosthetic simulates the form and flesh of the human part, replicating and restoring original body function, it can effectively preserve that sense of self.

What if the prosthetic is not finished with material simulating human skin? What if the prosthetic arm has more digits than the human original it replaces, or digits that bear little resemblance to natural human fingers? Popular fiction featuring the cyborg, such as Marrisa Meyer's youth novel *Cinder*, explore the identity crisis of a person who must come to terms with the self-realization that their body is only fractionally natural.

The well-publicized case of Viktoria Modesta, a voluntary amputee, reveals how the boundary between leg and shoe can blur (Saner 2014). One of her custom-made prosthetics is a black spike, an artful extension of the delicate spike of a glamorous shoe, the shoe reimagined as the spike itself, and in turn, the leg itself reimagined as the spiked heel. She can swap that out for a leg sporting a light, and another with stereo speakers operated via Bluetooth connection. Veronika Pete, an amputee who was medically forced to lose a leg, contracted with Barata to create a prosthetic equipped with storage compartments, and a battery for charging small electronic devices. It is not merely a replacement leg; it is storage, thereby conceptually shifting that limb out of the category of body and into environment (Mason 2014). Is it a leg or a dresser? The answer is yes, both. Rethinking the purpose of a leg to extend its functionality expands that purpose beyond the normative range.

Architects often think of the exterior limit of a building as an "envelope," applying the metaphor of skin to architecture. Pete requested her prosthetic look like a mechanical device. Rather than human skin, she wanted to think of the exterior limit of her prosthetic as a building or automobile envelope, selecting shiny metal (Mason 2014). This is an architectural finish that

Open Bionics, a robotic prosthetics start-up in the United Kingdom is hoping to bank on, offering affordably priced limbs that embrace the popular aesthetics of iconic movies such as *Star Wars* (Light Saber hand), Disney's *Frozen* (the Snowflake hand), and the many films based on Marvel comics heroes (Iron Man hand). Their advertising features young boys and girls holding up metallic and light-embedded arms, the license donated by Disney and Lucasfilms (Jakupsstovu 2018). Characters from video games also feature prominently, as do the user's options to create variations of their own prosthetics using a 3D printer (Birrell 2017). This is a significant development, because it expands more than merely the normative range of the body. It indicates an expansion of identity as based on the body, or at least, it flirts with the inclusion of the mechanical as part of the organic.

If the natural body can be modified such that it sports robotic legs, why not put wheels at the ends of those mechanical limbs? Think roller blades, but add an electric-powered engine. At a larger architectural scale of the automobile, the autonomous car extends functionality further, and stretches the reach of the prosthetic further as well. The autonomous automobile is a mobile space, but in this era of prosthetic revolution, it can also be thought of as an extension of the body, and no loss of an organic part is required. While inhabited, the automobile encloses and maintains a layer of personal space bounded by skin and clothing, while metal, glass, and paint present a perimeter of defense and public presentation; a space suit for the street. The self-driven car is both machine and clothing, a mode of transportation and climate control (not to mention conspicuous consumption). At the time of this writing, companies such as Uber, United Postal Service (UPS), and Waymo, are exploring implementation of autonomous vehicles, while car manufacturers plan for a street network populated with automobiles performing the function of dumbwaiters zigzagging horizontally across the urban fabric. The Ford Motor Company calls it "on-demand vehicles," for passengers or their goods (Ohnsman 2017).

Telepresence and Avatarchitecture

If the self-driving automobile can be reconceptualized as architectural space, and the artificial limb can be thought of as an extreme form of body modification, an architecting of the body as it were, can the edge between body and environment be reconceptualized further? Can an artificial limb subsume the entire body; a remotely operated body, standing in as a surrogate for the owner as it interacts with its environment? This might be called "telepresence," a fringe element of contemporary space. And what of the recent development of the digital avatar? That is, a digital surrogate standing in for the user? It has curious implications for the body and architecture.

A timid but implemented example of telepresence is the machine called the Beam, produced by Suitable Technologies in the Silicon Valley of California. Intended for a market where workers telecommute, this machine augments conference calling and the videophone. The Beam is a screen, microphone, and camera mounted on a tripod that is set on motorized wheels, and it moves through real space controlled by the remote worker miles away (Stevenson 2014). Because it can move, the remote operator can see and hear an environment and its denizens, such as an office space, much like a gamer interacts with a digital space by operating an avatar. However, by virtue of occupying space in a real environment, the Beam can stand in for the body of the remote worker, thereby projecting the worker's presence in an environment the worker does not occupy.

A more extreme version of telepresence, but one not yet implemented except as crude prototypes exhibited at expos and trade fairs, is the Geminoid, a surrogate produced by Hiroshi Ishiguro of the Intelligent Robotics Laboratory in Osaka, Japan. Susumu Tachi of Tachi Labs in

Tokyo has also been experimenting with telepresence for decades, and his recent focus on real-time remote robotics seems motivated by social concerns rather than merely by physical challenges. The Tachi Lab website explains that a CEO in one city could store a remote robotic version of themselves in another city's branch office (Jervis 2016). Occupying its own office, when necessary, the CEO could remotely activate it and operate it, "inhabiting" the robot to attend a meeting or inspect a manufacturing floor. Sculpted to look and sound just like the living CEO, even wearing the CEO's own clothing, this physical avatar could presumably stand in for the CEO and project his immediate presence in a space he does not actually occupy. Other scenarios are driven by fear. A child's Geminoid gets on a school bus, sparing the actual child the dangers of public space and school shootings. Two Geminoid avatars meet at a coffee shop on a first date.

Geminoid is an extreme and probably unrealizable prototype that seems more fiction than science, but its technological development stems from a demographic trend driving the development of social robots. According to the United Nations Population Division in 2010, the elderly population in Japan is increasing faster than the rest of the population. Dr. Tachi is an emeritus professor in the Department of Gerontology, where he helped develop solutions to the vexing problem of declining birthrates and increasing life expectancy, a problem developing in other countries such as China and the U.S. (DESA 2017). Declining mobility and cognition makes living independently a challenge, requiring support at home. That support might come from the family, but with generations living independently, often in places miles apart, support increasingly is sought from the environment. Removing barriers is one strategy, and adding robotic functionality to the environment is another.

The robotic solution is looked to by some as a means of providing care as well as independence to the elderly population. Robotic nurses, or "nursebots," have been in the experimental stage for several years, but are far from widespread implementation (Harrington 2016). Will they replace human help, and will they be affordable only for the wealthy? Besides solving the problem of mobility, cleaning, and food production, robots are being developed for less mechanical functions. Can a robot, or artificial intelligence, fulfill the social need of companionship? Japan's Advanced Institute of Industrial Science and Technology developed PARO, a "therapeutic robot." It looks like a small white seal, is soft, furry, and coos when spoken to, touched, stroked, or picked up. It learns by the owner's speech, responding to the pet-name given it and by common physical gestures (Knickman and Snell 2002). PARO can only serve as a surrogate cat or bunny, or some other breed of pet; it cannot fetch medicine or shop for groceries. The Beam's primary function of serving as an interface between individuals separated by great distance, also seems to serve primarily a social function.

While operating the Beam, the remote worker experiences the machine's environment via headphones and a screen, hearing and seeing through a mediated apparatus. There is little opportunity for the remote operator to experience the feeling of immediacy that comes with occupying space, of actually interacting with coworkers. Like the telephone and the videophone, this remote connection does not destabilize the operator's experience of space. The operator is not likely to become confused, thinking they are actually in the office instead of their remote location. There is also little opportunity for the remote operator to project their sense of identity onto that kind of machine surrogate, which means workers interacting with that machine are unlikely to confuse the Beam for the remote operator.

The ambition to create Geminoid as a likeness of its operator, however, flirts with the possibility of confusing identity and spatial experience, especially if combined with "telexistence," the real-time experience of being somewhere else. Operating the limbs of the surrogate requires the remote operator wear a suit equipped with sensors so that the surrogate's movements approximate those of the operator's. The information flow from the remote operator to the surrogate would comprise an information loop, from the surrogate machine to the remote operator and back again. Hypothetically, augmenting this loop with a virtual reality suit would convey so much information about the surrogate's environment, conveyed not merely as a visual experience but potentially as a multi-sensory experience, which the remote operator's experience would shift from vicarious to immediate. Likewise, the remote operator's reactions would appear genuine to those interacting with the surrogate. Where the Beam adds mobility to the videophone interface, the combination of anthropomorphic likeness with virtual reality would seem to breach a new category of experience.

NASA has been using virtual reality (VR) technology for some time, training astronauts for the experience beyond the Earth's atmosphere. Wearing VR goggles over their eyes and haptic sensors on their arms and legs, astronauts on Earth can train in simulated orbit (NASA 2018). The United States Army trains soldiers using VR as well, often augmented with a digital interface resembling the experience of violent video games. Goggles and headphones deliver visual and aural data to trainees either in a confined booth or in a larger space. An empty white-walled room in Fort Benning thereby transforms in the trainee's mind into a street in Kabul, where an entire platoon of trainees performs a mock patrol (Mead 2013). The difference for Tachi Labs is that the VR operator controls a surrogate, thereby doing more than merely immersing the wearer in an alternate spatial experience. The data loop delivers information to the operator not merely to afford immersion in a space, but to do two other functions: deliver real-time mechanical information to the surrogate, thereby controlling its movement in space, and immerse the operator in the surrogate itself. In the parlance of digital game culture, Geminoid is an avatar.

There are social implications. Experiments with people interacting with each other through digital avatars, conducted at Stanford University and elsewhere, indicate that the avatar can reduce the anxiety induced by social interaction in real space (Won, Bailenson, and Lanier 2015). Awkward mannerisms such as excessive hand movements or other habits or "ticks" can be programmed out of the avatar's behavior, filtering the movements of its operator. Besides dampening anxiety, interactions through avatars have other potentialities. In a group situation where people interact in the same digital space, each operator can look the speaker in the eye, through their avatars, and experience the speaker looking back at them, fostering a greater sense of personal contact despite the group "environment." A speaker therefore enjoys the sensation of commanding an audience's attention.

Digital simulations of space populated with avatars operated by "users," such as those in the digital game *Second Life* created by Linden Labs of San Francisco, grew in popularity and made mainstream news in the first decade of the twenty-first century (Ring 2007). The digital world hosted on its servers were used by several universities to conduct remote classrooms, the instructor represented as an avatar and each student likewise represented as avatars of their own design. As a social media platform, and as a creative space, systems like *Second Life* were hailed as a new and undeniable trend in the way humans interact socially (Castronova 2005). Space-based social interaction without space; a space-less venue. The bold pronouncements about contemporary transformation of social interaction and public space seem to have quieted since the first decade of the new century, and the hubris and noise masked another transformation that has been underway for decades.

The programming that goes into the construction of digital avatars and the digital worlds they inhabit is part of a larger technological development that transformed even architectural drawing. Back in the first half of the twentieth century, the design environment was equipped with drafting tables appointed with table lamps and a parallel edge rule. Design happened as lines were drawn on those vinyl covered tables, and computations would soon be tapped out on calculators, replacing slide-rules. In our twenty-first century, that computing and drawing environment is now harbored on hard-drives located in expansive data centers, buildings that shelter 100,000 square feet of machinery and occupied by only a handful of technicians operating a redundancy of HVAC systems. Reduced to the binary language of the toggle-switching computer, architectural design is reduced to numbers made sensible to the designer via software and a physical interface granting access to that software. The design environment is now a digital environment created and mediated by that software and its guild of programmers (Craven 2018; Quirk 2012).

This has been standard operating procedure for decades, and is the way physical objects, Light Saber limbs and autonomous vehicles alike, or any consumer product, enters the world. For quite some time computer aided design drawing (CADD) replicated, replaced, and improved upon hand-drafting, but the latest incarnation of digital design belongs in a different category. Engineers do not merely draw lines anymore, and certainly the contemporary architect does not either. They augment CADD with form-based software, or modeling software. Instead of drawing lines to represent walls and columns, they create digital models of walls and columns, inputting a variety of information beyond length and thickness into that model. A wall "drawn" today models brick or concrete block or an assembly of lightweight steel channels, gypsum board, and plywood with a stucco exterior finish. The model is not there to be measured or merely gazed upon, as a representation of what the actual building will look like, it can be tested for stress and strain, lateral forces, and the transference of heat. The data-rich digitized model of a column is loaded by a digital model of gravity, or tested by a digital model of a lateral force simulating a seismic event, digitally concocted in the synthetic realm inside the hard drive's reality. The building model can be situated in a digital replica of the 100 plus degree heat of Tucson, Arizona in July, and then transported to a replica of a below freezing environment near Fairbanks, Alaska in January, tested in each locale. The effects of the sun can be made to digitally beat down on the digital model of the building, and its performance can be assessed before nailing even one real 2×12 joist to a 2×6 top-plate in the real world. Preceding the real building, the testable digital model possesses an uncanny ontological presence, unlike the old architectural drawings that merely represented an architect's design. The digital model is a virtual building. As such, its form-based "construction" abides by the same rules as the avatar.

The virtual building can be populated with avatars. It can even be experienced vicariously by programming a walk-through or fly-by, allowing the viewer to see what the building and its features will be like through the computer screen. This innovation has developed further, where the "viewer" can don VR goggles and a VR suit, shifting the experience of the virtual building from vicarious to immediate (Beaman 2016). A client in VR gear walking through a building is not much different from a VR-equipped gamer interacting with a virtual environment, despite a difference in motivation.

Unlike the architect's drawing, the virtual building is usable during the life of the building. After construction, the real building equipped with sensors and alarms can send data to the building information model (BIM), alerting a security company that its downstairs window has been broken or that sprinklers suspended from the ceiling have been triggered (Bremer 2011). In this scenario, the blurry edge between body and environment is nothing compared to the fuzziness between information and the environment. The data encoded in the digital realm crosses the divide into the real world and has enacted a new term, the "smart environment."

Imagine hopping out of an autonomous vehicle to shop for vitamins and enjoy a soda with a friend. As soon as you enter the retail space you unknowingly encounter a space made smart by radio frequency identification sensors, global positioning system transmitters, laser range finders, and cameras. Your smartphone is recognized, which is why you notice an electronic poster advertising a product similar to the one you purchased online a couple of hours ago, and why a Beam-like robot emerges from the crowd to tell you about a new soda shop that just opened nearby. It has a basket and offers to carry the items you purchase for a nominal fee that will be waived when you purchase an item from the right store. You have entered a "ubiquitous network" that is part robot, part smart space, and part data harvester (Sato et al. 2011). The robots are not plastic objects in space ("plastic" in the sense of Modernist aesthetics), but integrated into a variety of physical features all around you. The environment itself is robotic, or has robotic characteristics. The phone you carry is co-opted by that environment, and maybe your car is too. Supporting this smart environment is a virtual realm connecting and organizing and transmitting data, allowing the environment to react to human presence. In that realm, the body occupying physical space is read as an avatar occupying virtual space.

The avatar, as a representation of the body and the self, can be quite dynamic and unexpected. In digital games such as the popular *World of Warcraft*, and many others, it is standard operating procedure for the user's avatar to be something other than human; an elf, an orc, a half-orc, or as in *Second Life*, one's avatar can even be an automobile or a deer, or anything the user is capable of constructing using Linden Labs' coding tools. The space-less realm of the virtual world affords an unprecedented ability to shape one's surrogate body, and thus, to explore and reflect upon images of the self. The body has become a fertile realm for design and representation.

Transbody/Transpace

Picking up the telephone to call customer service, or initiating a company's chat function on their website, puts the human customer into contact with artificial intelligence. Is that voice emanating from a human body or generated by software? Knowing what is a robot and what is human is already a little tricky, and reconceptualizing the autonomous car as both robot and space complicates matters even more. We need not enter the robot realm to feel the boundaries blur and transform. Being capable of seeing the disabled body as a normal body effectively dissolves the stark boundary definition of "normal." Other boundaries of body-centered identity are being tested as well. Crossing cultural categories often stirs up anxiety, as was evident in the United States during the second half of the twentieth century when African Americans crossed lines of segregation. In the 1950s, brave individuals who passed through doorways barred to them by custom propelled the Civil Rights Movement (Branch 1988). They sat at lunch counters prohibited to them, and drank at water fountains legally inaccessible to them. Some whites' fears of miscegenation and a mental reorientation to the idea of equality despite skin color fueled resistance against the Civil Rights Movement. For white supremacists, ending Jim Crow segregation posed a crisis of identity, and the surge of white supremacist rallies after the election of Donald Trump in 2016 is perhaps an indication that this crisis is not yet fully resolved (Heim 2017).

By the 1950s, the movement to tear down custom and law limiting the rights and actions of African Americans was propelled by a number of allied organizations that successfully maintained national focus on their issues. Other issues were also brought into focus on the fringe of that movement. In the 1960s, in Los Angeles, San Francisco, and New York, confrontations with police and property owners flared as LGBTQ individuals asserted their rights as equal citizens (Stryker 2008). The Compton Cafeteria Riot of 1966 in San Francisco and the Stonewall Riot three years later in New York are perhaps the best-known clashes, but they were accompanied by picketing and other public petitions asserting civil rights in the United States. By the second decade of the twenty-first century, the LGBTQ Movement stood upon the foundation of a substantial history of activism. As it was with the Civil Rights Movement in the previous decade, the fundamental issue was body and environment; which body is allowed in which space?[2]

The public bathroom is a communal yet private space, where the focus of activity centers on the human body. The relationship between body and environment comes into focus in that space, with the skin of the body literally coming into contact with the physical material of the space. It is therefore a multi-sensory space, and an environment of vulnerability. It is a space where being partly undressed is allowed, and where the body is cleansed. Typically, one expects the public bathroom in the United States to have toilets and sinks, both with running water. Approximately half will also have urinals intended for the male body as it urinates. Mirrors are also common as are dispensers for paper products, the former literally reflecting the body's image while the latter intended for application to the body's skin. In the past decade, it has become common for such spaces to accommodate the changing of an infant's diapers, even in those spaces designated for men only, a trend subverting the patriarchal prejudice defining the mother as the principal child-caretaker (Vinopal 2016). Above all, the public bathroom is a space in duplicate, one reserved for females, the other for males. That division is stark, made physical and spatial, reifying the conceptual categories of male and female.

A haven from the opposite sex, the men's and women's room are the product of cultural notions about gender, sex, and identity. They are duality spaces that make gender-opposites tangible. For some, when a male enters a public bathroom set aside for women, the feeling of transgression is palpable. The resistance against allowing transgendered individuals to use the gender designation that they identity with can be explained partly by the challenge that this spatial transgression represents. For those who see gender identity tied to assignment of sex at birth, clarity between male space and female space is greatly desired. A broader view of gender can allow for designations to change, and in the United States, approximately 1.4 million adults identify as transgender. Their use of the bathroom designated for the gender they identify with is often met with the claim that it violates privacy (Flores 2016).

In 2015, a 14-year-old informed his mother that he identified as a boy, and four months later he was at the center of a lawsuit about privacy violation. The 14-year-old was barred from using the boy's locker room in the school gym. For his Fitness for Life class, the boy was required to use a unisex bathroom two flights of stairs away from the locker room and gymnasium. After petitioning the school to allow him to use the boys' locker room in the gym, and granted permission, parents mounted a case against the school on the grounds that it violated other students' privacy. This assertion was predicated on their idea that a transgender boy is not an equivalent gender as their own sons. Three years later, a federal judge in Portland dismissed the parents' case ruling in favor of the boy's right to use the bathroom corresponding to the gender he identified with. Similar cases bubbled into public view across the United States, triggering debates about Title IX, legislation originally created by Congress in 1972 to protect women's equal access to school programs, funding, and facilities (Zaveri 2018).

For resisters, allowing transgender choice casts doubt on the very oppositional nature of male/female and masculine/feminine, and fuels a political divide with implications and complexities beyond the mundane realm of public bathrooms. To them, this transgression of space represents a contempt for category, and the contentious political battles fought over transgender access to public bathrooms exhibits some of the same fire evident when blacks tested the edge of white space.

Architectural solutions have been offered to alleviate the privacy problem without denying transgendered individuals their civic rights, and even work around the political debate about those rights (Sisson 2018). That solution is to replace communal bathroom space with individuated space. That is, instead of a large room with a row of sinks and another row of toilets, enclose a toilet, sink, mirror, and dispensers in a private and secure space accommodating only a single body. The other strategy is to combine the two separate spaces, one dedicated for females the other for males, into a communal unisex space where privacy is organized spatially in zones. The most private or closed zone for elimination, less closed and less private for washing, and so forth. This would mean the sinks and mirrors are accessible to all, simultaneously, but the toilets/urinals are each enclosed in a smaller private space accommodating only a single body.

Popular culture has explored the combined communal bathroom. The television show *Ally McBeal*, which aired in the late 1990s produced by Twentieth-Century Fox, regularly featured its communal unisex bathroom as a space where characters stepped away from the office space and interacted with each other socially. Rather than a space where men retreated into male space or women withdrew to female space, it was a space where workers seemed to retreat from work, an all-social space devoted as much to social interaction as to grooming or elimination. It became an amusing environment fostering arguments, singing and dancing, gossip, and character and plot development. Many of the characters were ridiculous and exaggerated in their social mannerisms, and the mundane office social environment was made exotic and dramatic by the occasional interruption of a song and dance number, often played out in the bathroom. The unusual unisex function of that space added to the exotic character of the television show itself, which often featured fantasy scenes involving a dancing baby and other hallucination-like images and interactions (Asimow 2014). The mere fact that men and women interacted together in the same public bathroom seemed fantastical enough, and that exotic space aptly fostered the titillating romantic relationships that the show focused on. The absurdity of a dancing baby and of lawyers dancing and singing in the bathroom together normalized the absurdity of men and women sharing the same public bathroom. The thematic setting of *Ally McBeal* was a law office, a rather prophetic setting given how perceived transgressions of gendered space have become such a divisive legal issue.

The public bathroom is a contentious legal space where dirt and cleanliness operate as both physical and moral conditions. Opponents of transgender access to that space often base their argument on a skepticism of transgendering itself. That is, they dispute the blurring of gender and sex, believing in a narrowly defined system of body identity (Bettcher 2013). Readings of space influence readings of social category (gender), and vice versa. When the boundary between categories blurs, it necessitates reconceptualization of space. Fear of a male entering a space designated for women, or vice versa, is possible only when denying the verity of a blurred gender definition.

Conclusion

The body, spatial experience, and identity are not what they used to be. Imagine Le Corbusier hopping forward in his time machine. His amorphously masculine modular scale figure might work in the era of contemporary architecture, but does his adage about machines and houses as machines account for the digital and the virtual? Perhaps minimalist abstraction continues to work in this era of transformation and transgression, but would Corbusier be ready to see the body as a machine or as an extension of the environment? Would he be ready to see the rules and parameters of the digital realm assert themselves in the real world? Would he be prepared to design bathrooms without regard for gender boundaries?

Lines have been crossed. If there is any question that the contemporary world is categorically different from the world in which Modernist architecture and aesthetics arose and flourished, one need only look to four thematic areas. First, universal design now posits an expanded range of the normative body, requiring the shaping of the architectural environment to accommodate not an average body, once defined as an adult male and fully ambulatory body, but a range of bodies. Second, environmental design now extends to the body itself. Body modification is so broad a category that it can encompass hair styling, tattooing, and prosthetic arms. Third, the digital realm now harbors avatars expressing their user, as well as models of buildings and environments that not only precede the actual construction of buildings they represent but survive the construction process to become an integral part of the experienced environment. Fourth, the reconceptualization of the body as an expression of gender identity extends to public space in the real world, triggering political battles in the United States and other places about which bodies may go where.

These four areas are mutually supportive. The expanded range of the normal body in universal design opens the door to reconceptualizing the function of an arm when designing a prosthetic limb. Body modification inevitably involves the expression of the self as the body is sculpted, either reaffirming one's identity or reimagining it. The questioning of gender identity assigned at birth is buoyed by experiments in body modification, and those experiments can be accomplished much more easily in digital space located on the body of the avatar. The technological tools employed to devise avatars are the same used to construct digital environments as well as digital models of buildings. Although Light Saber limbs may be the exception, designing virtual buildings in digital space is now the norm in architectural practice, and with virtual reality, the experience of digital space is also now competitive with the experience of real space.

Admittedly, a sizable portion of this chapter dealt with science fiction; not realized actualities but merely envisioned potentialities. As of this writing, the autonomous car is a controversial prototype with pilot programs cautiously emerging in a variety of places. The Geminoid is more theory than practice, and VR experience is following the tail of the digital revolution but complete telexistence immersion is not reality. An even larger portion of this essay, however, concerned already realized situations and developments. Universal design is enforced by ordinance in many places, and gender neutral public bathrooms are too. What was once taken for granted, the normal body and the extreme clarity between male and female, has undergone reconceptualization. Body modification occasionally entails the reconceptualization of a piece of human anatomy, thereby calling into question the edge where body and mechanical environment meet, or the boundary between categories such as male and female. That edge is also shown to be fluid when we consider data and the data-rich environment. Small pockets of smart space exist here and there, and corporations and governments ponder the capitalist potential of the smart city and its promise of disciplining public space and the consumer market.

Corbusier and his fellow Modernists devoted considerable attention to envisioning the world of the future, as did writers such as Alvin Toffler who believed the future would be so different that it would stress an individual's ability to cope (Toffler 1970). For imagineers of the twentieth century, their vision centered on materials. High-strength steel, concrete, glass, and especially plastic, and the acceleration of industrial manufacturing and transportation lit up their crystal balls as they looked to the future. By the end of the twentieth century, visions of the imminent world supplanted information for materiality. At the end of the second decade of the twenty-first century, in a world of avatars, VR, BIM, and the testing of gender boundaries in a universally designed landscape, the very materiality of the world seems capable of reconceptualization.

Notes

1 Limb Loss Statistics, Amputee Coalition, Amputee-Coalition.org (accessed August 17, 2017).
2 The "T" of LGBTQ refers to transgender, individuals who identify or express their gender differing from the gender assigned to them at birth. It is the most spatial and identity-rich letter of LGBTQ. In

2016, the state legislature of North Carolina banned ordinances intended to allow transgender people using the public bathroom corresponding to their gender identification. This was a response to the city of Charlottesville that had just established an ordinance preventing property owners and public entities from barring a transgendered person's use of the bathroom corresponding to their gender identification. This inspired other state legislatures to enact their own laws forcing transgendered people to use public bathrooms corresponding to one's sex indicated on their birth certificate. By then, nearly 20 states passed civil rights legislation protecting a transgendered person's right to use the bathroom whose gender they identify with, starting with Maine's law passed in 2005. Maine's Human Rights Act of 1995 was amended in 2005 to expand the definition of sexual orientation to include "gender identity or expression" (Ch. 337, 9-C).

References

Anthony, A. (2013) "Meet the woman who turns artificial limbs into works of art," *Guardian*, December 28.
Asimow, M. (2014) "*Ally McBeal* and subjective narration," in Michael Asimow, Kathryn Brown, and David Ray Papke (eds) *Law and Popular Culture: International Perspectives*, Newcastle upon Tyne: Cambridge Scholars Publishing, 11–26.
Atkinson, M. (2003) *Tattooed: The Sociogenesis of a Body Art*, Toronto and Buffalo: University of Toronto Press.
Beaman, M. (2016) "Virtual reality and architecture," *Architectural Record*, November 1.
Bettcher, T. (2013) "Evil deceivers and make-believers: on transphobic violence and the politics of illusion," in Susan Styker and Aren Z. Aizura (eds) *The Transgender Studies Reader 2*, New York: Routledge, 278–290.
Birrell, I. (2017) "3D printed prosthetic limbs: the next revolution in medicine," *Guardian*, February 19.
Branch, T. (1988) *Parting the Waters: America in the King Years, 1954–63*, New York: Simon and Schuster.
Bremer, D. (2011) "BIM and security system design," *Electrical Contractor Newsletter*, accessed February 10, 2018, www.ecmag.com/section/systems/bim-and-security-system-design.
Brooker, G. (2012) *Introduction to Biomechatronics*, Raleigh: SciTech Pub.
Castronova, E. (2005) *Synthetic Worlds: The Business and Culture of Online Games*, Chicago: University of Chicago Press.
Craven, J. (2018) "CAD and BIM architecture and design software: computer applications for architects and builders," accessed February 11, 2018, www.thoughtco.com/what-is-cad-or-bim-178399.
DeMello, M. (2000) *Bodies of Inscription: A Cultural History of the Modern Tattoo Community*, Durham, NC: Duke University Press.
DESA (2017) "World population prospects, the 2017 revision, key findings and advance tables," *Working Paper No. ESA/P/WP/248*, New York: United Nations, Population Division.
Flores, A. et al. (2016) *How Many Adults Identify as Transgender in the United States?*, The Williams Institute.
Hamrale, L. (2017) *Building Access: Universal Design and the Politics of Disability*, Minneapolis: University of Minnesota Press.
Harrington, E. (2016) "Feds spend $999,946 building robot nurses," *Washington Free Beacon*, January 13.
Heim, J. (2017) "Recounting a day of rage, hate, violence and death: how a rally of white nationalists and supremacists at the University of Virginia turned into a 'tragic, tragic weekend'," *Washington Post*, August 14.
Jakupsstovu, G. (2018) "Open bionic's prosthetic hero arm is now available in the UK, Tech Network," accessed July 2, 2018, https://thenextweb.com/insider/2018/04/25/open-bionics-prosthetic-hero-arm-is-now-available-in-the-uk/.
Jervis, R. (2016) "Forget the robots – here come the geminoids!," *USA Today*, March 13.
Knickman, J. and Snell, E. (2002) "The 2030 problem: caring for aging baby boomers," *Health Services Research* 37(4): 849–884.
Le Corbusier (1954) *The Modulor: A Harmonious Measure to the Human Scale Universally Applicable to Architecture and Mechanics*, Cambridge, MA: Harvard University Press.
Mason, L. (2014) "Veronika Pete: Human 2.0: technologies of enhancement," *Cybersalon*, accessed September 1, 2018, www.youtube.com/watch?v=xzCFRVeM1yk.
Mead, C. (2013) *War Play: Video Games and the Future of Armed Conflict*, Boston and New York: Houghton Mifflin Harcourt.

NASA (2018) "Virtual reality training," accessed March 26, 2018, NASA.gov.

Ohnsman, A. (2017) "Ford's 2021 self-driving ride-share goal expands to include delivery services," *Forbes*, August 22.

Pearson, C. (2011) Ed Roberts Campus, *Architectural Record*, accessed January 12, 2018, www.architecturalrecord.com/articles/7868-ed-roberts-campus?v=preview.

Quirk, V. (2012) "A brief history of BIM," *ArchDaily*, accessed September 1 2018, www.archdaily.com/302490/a-brief-history-of-bim.

Ring, H. (2007) "Architecture's Second Life," *Archinect*, January 9, accessed January 15, 2018, http://archinect.com/features/article/47037/architecture-s-second-life.

Saner, E. (2014) "Viktoria Modesta, the world's first amputee pop star," *Guardian* December 20.

Sato, M., Kamei, K., Nishio, S., and Hagita, N. (2011) "The Ubiquitous Network Robot Platform: Common platform for continuous daily robotic services," IEEE/SICE International Symposium on System Integration.

Sisson, Patrick (2018) "How bathroom design can be a bridge to more accessible architecture," *Curbed*, July 31, www.curbed.com/2018/7/31/17636872/transgender-bathroom-accessibility-design-stalled.

Stevenson, S. (2014) "Wish I were there: The Beam telepresence robot lets you be in two places at once," *Slate*, May 14. www.slate.com/articles/technology/technology/2014/05/beam_pro_telepresence_robot_how_it_works_and_why_it_is_strangely_alluring.html.

Stryker, S. (2008) *Transgender History*, Berkeley: Seal Press.

Toffler, A. (1970) *Future Shock*, New York: Random House.

Vinopal, L. (2016) "Changing tables now required by law in Federal building men's rooms," *Fatherly*, October 12, www.fatherly.com/news/new-law-baby-changing-tables-mens-rooms/.

Won, A. S., Bailenson, J. N., and Lanier, J. (2015) "Appearance and task success in novel avatars," *PRESENCE, Teleoperators and Virtual Environments* (24)4: 335–346.

Zaveri, M. (2018) "Oregon judge rules in favor of transgender students in Oregon Bathroom Case," *New York Times*, July 26.

Ziegler-Graham, K., MacKenzie, E., Ephraim, P., Travison, T., and Brookmeyer, R. (2008) "Estimating the prevalence of limb loss in the United States: 2005 to 2050," *Archives of Physical Medicine and Rehabilitation* 89(3): 422–429.

11

Habit's *Remainder*

Aron Vinegar

> [T]his messy, irksome matter that had no respect for millions, didn't know its place. My undoing: matter.
>
> *(McCarthy 2005: 17)*

In this essay, I want to emphasize three issues: the relationship of habit to matter; subject to substance; and fluidity to its remainders, grounds, and precipitates. Notions of fluidity course through all discussions of habit, and this emphasis offers us a way to think more critically about contemporary architectural culture. If the contemporary fetish is no longer reified substance but rather fluidity (Žižek 2017), an attention to the recalcitrances, viscosities, and automaticities at the heart of habit are crucial for thinking the contemporary in and out of architecture. In this light, habit offers us a way to rethink contemporary architecture's relationships to capitalism; subjectivity; its particular commitments to topology, parametrics, networks, and new materialisms; the increasing automaticity of intelligence in our era; and the very subject matter of architecture itself.

Instead of offering a summary or synoptic overview of the relationship of habit to contemporary architectural theory and practice, or exploring how this nexus might relate to recent developments within the humanities and natural sciences,[1] I want to engage in a detailed and somewhat idiosyncratic reading of Tom McCarthy's influential novel *Remainder* (McCarthy 2005/2007), and the equally complex feature-length film interpretation of the novel with the same title, directed by the video-artist Omer Fast (Fast 2015).[2] My aim is to demonstrate a particular sense of habit and architecture that is fully attentive to its subject matter.[3]

Synopsis of *Remainder*

At the beginning of *Remainder*, the unnamed narrator is involved in a terrible accident. He is hit by falling debris from the sky, and subsequently loses most of his habitual actions that we take for granted. After some moving descriptions of having to visualize and plan out every step in order to achieve simple acts that we take for granted, like walking or picking up a carrot, he has

Aron Vinegar

Figure 11.1 Remainder, Tom in the bathroom at a party on Plato Road
Source: Production still by Chris Harris.

a Proustian moment at a party in an acquaintance's apartment.[4] It is triggered by a small crack in the plaster wall of a bathroom, which invokes an intense feeling of a time before his accident when he had a sense of fluidity that was seemingly disengaged from the kinds of detours, delays, and re-routings that he must now go through in order to undertake even simple actions (Figure 11.1).[5]

After this event, the narrator spends all the money he receives as settlement for the accident to reenact this intense, specific, but also generic memory when he had more familiar habits and modes of habitation. He buys an apartment block, Madlyn Mansions, in the Brixton area of London, and hires people to replicate the exact conditions that triggered the experience. As the novel proceeds, the narrator's compulsion to repeat intensifies to dizzying degrees, both within the apartment building, and extending to many other scenes and events outside it. As he does so, these repetitions generate more anomalies, excesses, recalcitrant substances, and remainders that need to be taken up in further repetitions. After the "final" reenactment—a bank robbery that takes place in an actual bank during working hours—the narrator eventually tries to erase all remainders, including the annihilation of himself, as an absolute remainder.

The Subject as A Sum of Accidents

> The individual is essentially nothing but a sum of accidents and, what is more, that sum is itself accidental.
>
> *(Bachelard 2013: 41)*

Remainder begins with a terrible "ACCIDENT." The unnamed narrator of the novel—played by Tom Sturridge in Omer Fast's film and named Tom—is hit by "something falling from the sky. Technology. Parts, bits" (McCarthy 2007: 3). A catastrophe literally befalls him, but we are never given the source from which these parts and bits have broken off, and thus we can never locate the determinate cause of this disaster in the novel (Figure 11.2). Is it a satellite, crane,

Figure 11.2 Remainder, Tom hit by falling debris
Source: Copyright Omer Fast. Film still by Aron Vinegar.

plane, or falling debris from a construction site? Although this event takes place in a specific city, London, and more specifically a typical glass atrium in a business district (the narrator was a "market analyst" before the accident), the indeterminate nature of the accident suggests that this inaugural trauma does not simply come from the outside: the subject is not primarily shattered from an external source. Rather, we are witnessing the traumatic emergence of subjectivity itself in and through its dissolution. Simply put, the subject arrives by falling outside itself (Nancy 2000: 19).[6] It is important to note that the narrator never heals and restores himself through habit. If habit is the conversion of the particular or contingent accident into a nominal universality that then becomes an internal necessity, this trajectory never seems to be accomplished. The narrator is unable to convert or internalize that accident into a stable form of life, despite all his attempts to do so (Malabou 2008: 70–75, 2005: 73).[7] In *Remainder*, habit as a way of being seems to be haunted by being's waywardness. What is at stake here is how this subject as a sum of accidents and contingency is elaborated into a persistent yet *unsettling conatus* (Comay 2018: 43; Comay and Ruda 2018: 4).[8] To be sure, there is a certain force of the outside involved here, but that is also a force of the immanent outside, which I want to call habit.

It is tempting to call *Remainder* a disaster novel/film, in which the constellations and coordinates that structure the protagonist's world come crashing down. It is as if McCarthy, in his own preposterous way, has purposely overturned the famous sentences engraved on Kant's tombstone that mark out the wondrous coordinates of that philosopher's world: "the starry heavens above me and the moral law within me" (Kant 1788: 203).[9] Instead of creating meaningful constellations, both astral and bodily, the accident creates "a white slate," "a black hole," or a "crater," from which the novel takes its inaugural and compulsive repetitions (McCarthy 2007: 3). The accident that blows a crater in the narrator is also a crater of matter itself, and thus, in a repetition of a repetition, we have a crater emerging from a crater. This double convulsion and dislocation inaugurates the novel's compulsive repetitions, which persistently spew forth the intractable bits and pieces of stuff; the myriad sticky and viscous substances in which the narrator is caught up but which he is never able to inhabit in any stable way.

The novel does not only disgorge surplus matter, it also simultaneously voids or de-substantializes this matter. The compulsive repetitions and reenactments are the mode of emptying out and filling up in *Remainder*. In doing so, the "sub" in substance and subject is constantly absolving, never definitely solving or resolving, let alone accomplishing the complete solubility of matter by spirit that is intrinsic to the notions of fluidity and grace that are always at stake when issues of habit, inhabitation, and dwelling are raised. As a consequence, subject and substance are mutually dislocated, never quite finding their proper place or co-imbrication: "[T]his messy, irksome matter that had no respect for millions, didn't know its place. My undoing: matter" (McCarthy 2007: 17). McCarthy has called attention to a "material negative" in his writing, which is his way of emphasizing the fact that immaterial processes are always material (McCarthy 2016: 54). But the phrase "material negative" also suggests the opposite: that material processes are always insubstantial, transubstantial, immaterial, and virtual. McCarthy calls this "un-matter" in the novel (McCarthy 2007: 171). The strange and unsettling matter in *Remainder* is always cracking, warping, kinking, dissolving, absolving, and desubstantializing itself into a "dense areality" (Nancy 2008: 93). As such, it is never completely sublatable into any given world, organic body, communication, loop, network, dispositif, or orthopedic structure, up to and including any construction, whether as a self or an architectonic structure. From the beginning of *Remainder*, the narrator is possessed and convulsed by the agonistic weight of intractable and intransitive matter that contracts, buckles, and wracks the body and "trips" him up into a subject that is then constituted by all these fault lines, fissures, cracks, and coagulations. Needless to say, this material negative does not serve as a stable construction

Figure 11.3 *Remainder*, Tom's jerking motions in the London underground
Source: Copyright Omer Fast. Film still by Aron Vinegar.

material for the smooth conversion of *bildung* into building, habit into habitation, *ethos* into edification.[10]

The riveting electronic soundtrack to the film, composed by Schneider TM (Dirk Dresselhaus) is an incessant, repetitive, noisy, machinic, static, and glitchy score. Its short-circuiting tonality gives an acousmatic pitch to the tensed, contracted, and machinic tonus of the "buffeting," "short-circuits," and "jerking" that possess Tom's bodily gestures and comportment as he moves through urban and architectural environments, as well as his dis-connection with people and things (Figure 11.3). Although the narrator's automaticity, rigidity, and fixity are never resolved, that should not be seen as the failure of habit. Rather it is an overemphasis on one side of habit's dialectic between addiction and grace, hardness and fluidity, that throws that dialectic out of whack, and which can never be corrected or balanced out in a rhythm of making and breaking habits. The genius of the novel and film is that they expose the hyperbolic logic of habit via a trenchant critique of the role of fluidity in its capacity to smooth over units into unity; how habit propels us along a chain of events, such that the metaphor of chain and links is fused, and that fusion is then converted into an organic whole or continuous stream that effortlessly draws us forward.

Death Becomes You

> But the life of Spirit is not the life that shrinks from death and keeps itself untouched by devastation, but rather the life that endures it and maintains itself in it.
>
> *(Hegel 1977: 19)*

After the bits and pieces crash through the glass atrium onto Tom Sturridge—and after a significant temporal delay in the film—he is flattened out on the pavement, blood dripping from his nose onto the sidewalk and barely visible within the heap of fallen debris (Figures 11.4 and 11.5). He is indeed flattened out—almost buried alive—but he has not flat-lined. After he is

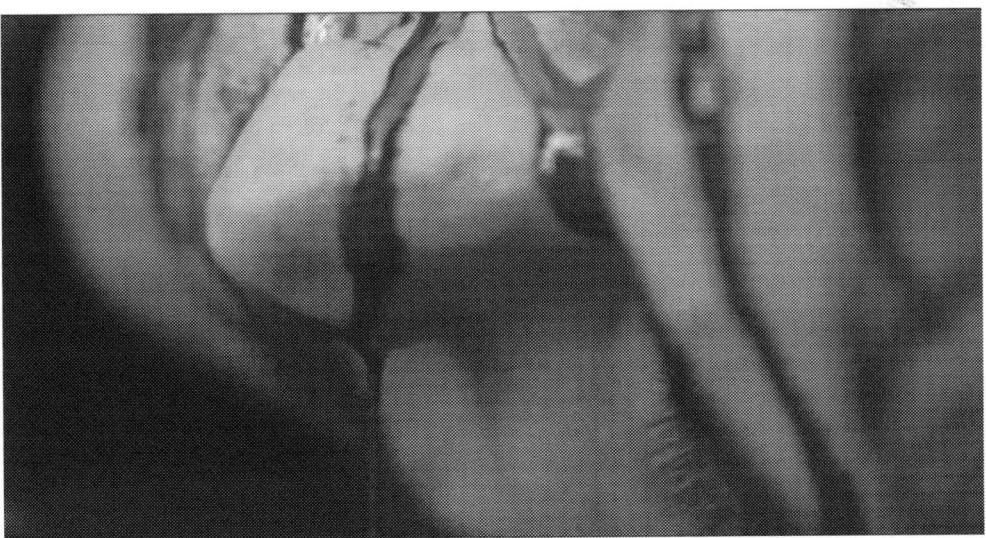

Figure 11.4 **Remainder**, Tom with blood dripping off his nose after being hit by fallen debris
Source: Copyright Omer Fast. Film still by Aron Vinegar.

Aron Vinegar

Figure 11.5 *Remainder,* Tom barely visible within the heap of falling debris
Source: Copyright Omer Fast. Film still by Aron Vinegar.

taken to the hospital and hooked up to bits and pieces of medical technology, which keep him alive, we learn that he is "not dead, clinically speaking" (Fast 2015). This is a body that has tarried with death; we encounter a *form of life* that, as Hegel has described in some infamous lines in the *Phenomenology of Spirit*, "maintains itself in devastation," and literally dwells in it, thus demonstrating a certain capacity to incorporate death, and to repeat it (Hegel 1977: 19).[11] These inaugural scenes in the novel and film offer us a body that is seized at the point where the threshold of death, passivity, automaticity, and inertia wrack the body as a force of death in life, beyond dying, survival, or mere living. As a result of the accident, the protagonist is rendered in a state of living rigor mortis, in which his jerky bodily movements, odd gestures, and stiffness are seemingly set against the fluidity of habitual action that we so desperately count on for all our daily tasks, such as eating, gripping, walking, driving, speaking, not to mention dwelling and inhabiting (Figure 11.6).

In some influential theories about the origin of life in the organism or subject, such as Freud or Hegel, the inaugural outer crust that precipitates the organism's separation into inside and outside—its primal separation and abstraction from the environment—requires a literal sacrifice of its own living matter for the sake of life. Although, that crust can harden into a rigid carapace, shell, or thick wall, in *Remainder* there is a sap of life that oozes out of its cracks. The narrator is inundated by that *stickiness* throughout the novel. If in the high modernist tradition from Walter Pater to Viktor Shklovsky to Samuel Beckett habit is often seen as the lightning rod that dampens the jolt of particularity, smothering our sensitivity, and deadening us to the world, it would seem that in a different light that deadening is also a site that gives way to a procedure of undeadening. If repetition and binding constitute and contract all drives, then it is clear that the death drive is the paradoxical *effect* of habit. Thus, habit germinates the indeterminate substance of the body, at the very site of its recurrent binding. The narrator is driven by an incessant

Habit's Remainder

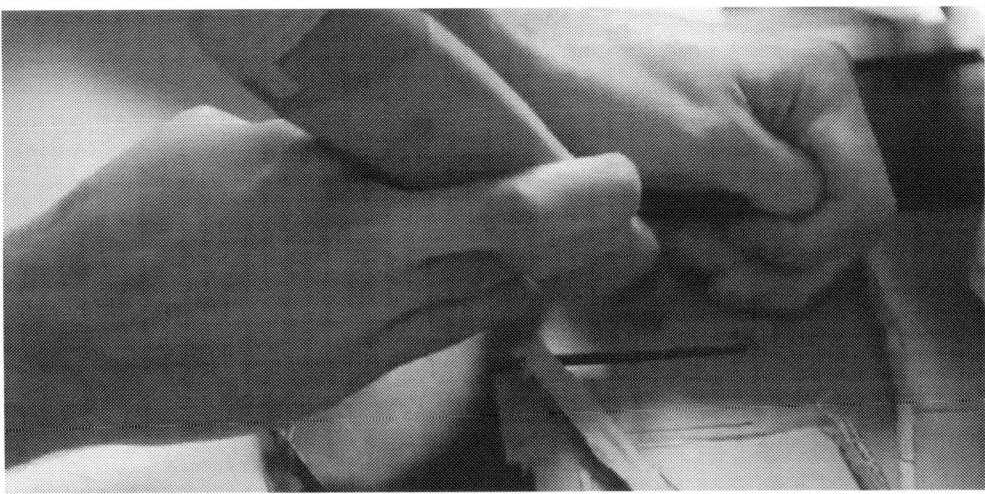

Figure 11.6 Remainder, Tom's odd grip as he is making a cardboard model of Madlyn Mansions
Source: Copyright Omer Fast. Film still by Aron Vinegar.

repetition compulsion that dissolves all given determinations … all the way to the end of the novel when the narrator tries to erase the material traces of his own position as an absolute remainder.

On Stuckness and Repetition

> Massive substance is supported only by a spreading, not by interiority or by a foundation.
> *(Nancy 1993: 199)*

In habit, as Hegel points out, a series of units is reduced to unity, such that the "single details" comprising any activity have become "infected … with its universality" (Hegel 1971: §410 A).[12] In habit, the body is rendered pliant and fluid, and is able to convert thought into action without the recourse to consciousness, reflection, or representation … so the story goes. We think of an inculcated habit that has permeated the body in terms of a graceful gesture that has shed all excess, inertia, energy, time, and complication, as if spirit had permeated matter through and through rendering it *soluble*. Within philosophies of habit, architecture is this act of inhabitation *and* the sedimentation of this carrying of being—what Hegel has termed, "This being-at-home-with-oneself we call habit"—and a primary exemplar of habit as a mode of bodily proximity and self-feeling without hindrance, distance, or recalcitrance, as in Michael Ondaatje's poem *Her House*: "When you can move through a house blindfolded it belongs to you. You are moving like blood within calmly in your own body" (Hegel 1971: §410 A; Ondaatje 1997: 87). In contrast, we should recall that the opening scene of the film begins with blood flowing outside of the body, and that coagulation is extended to all kinds of sticky substances spilling out from their containers (see Figure 11.4; Figure 11.7).

In *Remainder*, the repetition at the heart of habit is never sublated and bound into unity but rather persists as a compulsion to repeat that is often rendered as an eternal repetition of the same gesture that never accomplishes and incorporates itself as a stable tendency or disposition to act. The narrator needs to consciously think about everything he does and go through *every* step in

123

Aron Vinegar

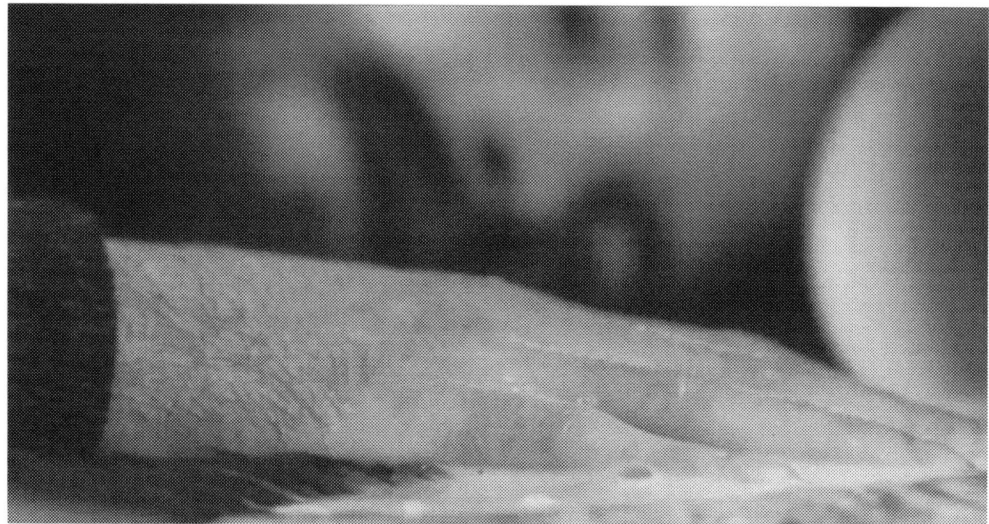

Figure 11.7 Remainder, Tom with milk spilling out of its container
Source: Copyright Omer Fast. Film still by Aron Vinegar.

his mind and watch himself do it, before he can attempt even the simplest of actions. In contrast to Bergson's claim that habit is the ability to undertake an action without calling up its representation, that is precisely what is not available to him. He has to look and think about every movement. Because of this, the character must construct and rehearse detailed written or mental lists of each individual step required in the sequence of actions required to engage in a simple task like eating. These detailed accounts of the travails in having to think about everything before doing it are particularly intense near the beginning of the novel, when the narrator is trying to regain that lost sense of fluidity and ease, but they never really abate.

He will list how many steps and sequences it takes to accomplish the simplest of movements, in which he must pay attention to "each footstep, how the knees bend, how to swing my arms" (McCarthy 2007: 14). His "rerouting" physiotherapy is based on visualizing these sequential steps "in his head" before actually doing them. For example, he is asked to visualize all the movements involved in picking up a carrot as a preparation for actually picking up the carrot, which he notes involves "twenty-seven" movements, just as there are "seventy-five" required, he claims, in order to take a single step when walking (McCarthy 2007: 19–22). I will return to the carrot example, but these examples are slightly misleading. It is easy to assume that what we are getting here is a contrast between the speed of habit and the slowness of conscious thinking. But these delays, detours, fixations, and frenetic repetitions are also internal to the logic and ontology of habit itself no matter how fully contracted or incorporated. This detour is not merely a detour of understanding or thinking interrupting the speed and flow of habit. There is a persistent automaticity and stuckness at the core of habitual action no matter how fast or fluidly it moves. Although the narrator tries to recover a sense of grace that he remembers *feeling* before the accident, that is a constitutive impossibility for him. First, he never recovers his ease of movement, due to the damage to his proprioception, even if he almost gets up to speed—"(m)aybe ninety" percent of his pre-accident state (McCarthy 2007: 22). But the point here is that this 10 percent remainder allows us to see that his state is not an exceptional one.

When the narrator has recovered most of his damaged proprioception, he engages in a discussion with his friend Greg about Robert De Niro's acting in *Mean Streets*. He is full of admiration for how De Niro is "just being"—naturally immersed in his actions like lighting up a cigarette, opening a fridge door, or walking down a street: "every move he made, each gesture was perfect, seamless," such that he "merged with it until he was it and it was him and there was nothing in between" (McCarthy 2007: 23). Greg responds that he could never "just be" even before the accident, as the first wisp of smoke gets in your eyes "and makes you wince," or the fridge door catches and "milk slops over" and that it is the automaticity and artificiality of film that creates this fluidity. Greg notes that his friend is not unusual but rather "just more usual than everyone else" (McCarthy 2007: 23–24). This is reaffirmed, by the narrator's last clear memory of before the accident of being "buffeted by wind" (McCarthy 2007: 7). This buffeting—which is then repeated throughout the novel and film—suggests a kind of turbulence, an intransitive transitivity. Even the "tingling" feeling he gets throughout the novel when he has fleeting glimpses of the "fluid and unforced" movement he had before the accident, and triggered by his reenactments, is ambivalent (McCarthy 2007: 67). Early on in the novel that "tingling" feeling is specifically linked to his last clear memory, such that this self-feeling is also a low-level electricity that is of a piece with his surges of short-circuited movement.

In a conversation with his lawyer Marc Daubenay, the narrator cannot confirm that his memory of the apartment building was somewhere he had actually "lived." There is no pure pre-reflective or pre-predicative embodied experience to be had here, as his recall is constructed of bits and pieces of "memories, imaginings, novels, films" that are glued together, and that are just as "fragile" as the crude model and sketches that he constructs of the apartment building out of letters, bills, Blu Tack, cardboard, tape, glue, and markers (McCarthy 2007: 73; Fast 2015) (Figure 11.8, see Figure 11.6). Fragile, yet insistent and persistent. After his "facilitator" Nazrul Ram Vyas, who handles all the logistics of the narrator's reenactments, asks him if one particular reiteration was a success, he replies that it was up to a point, but that the "detour" that separated him from his dream of seamless movement could not simply be "cut off" (McCarthy 2007: 152). Indeed, as that cut is internal to habit itself and the incessant cuts—repeating reenactments and reenacting repetitions—produces ever more excesses of matter and remainders.

Figure 11.8 Remainder, Cardboard model of Madlyn Mansions
Source: Copyright Omer Fast. Film still by Aron Vinegar.

Perhaps the most exemplary aspect of the convergence of repetition and stuckness in the film and novel are the "glitches" where the narrator/Tom is jerking back and forward as he is caught up in his own gestural tautology (see Figure 11.3). It is as if the body is searching for itself in a coil of precipitation and delay, perpetually catching up and running too far ahead, and thus in a constant state of bodily dispossession. The riveting soundtrack suggests that self-feeling is always haunted by mechanism, in which habit is not the carrying of being, or the possession of being, but a being carried away by the body's intractability. These glitches—sonic, bodily, electronic, digital, economic—in *Remainder*, bring us into contact with an exteriority, objecthood, rigidity, and automaticity that is in us in itself, and never simply as a means towards self-possession. If the habitual subject does not weld together individual movements as all commentators on habit argue, the language used to describe habit as an embodied and "concrete universality" often resorts to the same machinic metaphors, as in Hegel's definition of habit as the "mechanism of self-feeling" (Hegel 1971: §410). The unity of habit would seem to *rivet* us to our body, or as this is stated in a slightly different way by Rudi Visker: "we are more than the direct object of the word to be. It *sticks* [my emphasis] to the one who is supposed to conjugate it in the first person singular" (Visker 2009: 165–166).

Subject Matter and Infinite Absolving

> The moment one tries to define what habit is, one is led to the fundamental properties of matter.
>
> *(James 1950: 104)*

It is important to get a feel for the viscous sense of unruly matter in the novel. When the narrator in *Remainder* has practiced visualizing grasping the carrot—has gone through all the steps and sequences in his process of neural "rerouting," and lifted more than 1000 imaginary carrots to his mouth—he attempts to actually hold this "gnarled, dirty, and irregular" thing in his hands (McCarthy 2007: 20). At this point his physiotherapist backs away to watch, as if he was "a house of cards" that might collapse at any moment. When the carrot is finally in his hand, the narrator is shattered by its materiality and thingness that can not be grasped or controlled. He calls it the "surge of active carrot," which starts to "short-circuit the operation." The carrot rolls and slips away. "At least it didn't fall on anyone" (McCarthy 2007: 21). In contrast to this goal-oriented activity, as exemplified by the proverbial carrot, the narrator is forever caught up by the materiality of the carrot, partially engendered by his incessant repetitions, which short-circuits these smooth movements. Right before this rerouting section in the novel, he enters Green Park tube stop, where he observes a disassembled escalator lying in pieces awaiting to be overhauled:

> You think of an escalator as one object, a looped, moving bracelet, but in fact it's made of loads of individual, separate steps woven together into one smooth system. Articulated. These ones had been dis-articulated, and were lying messily around.
>
> *(McCarthy 2007: 16)*

It is important to note that the escalator in pieces is never put back seamlessly for the narrator; it remains there in pieces, and also as a greasy stain on his coat sleeve, due to his retrieval of a ticket extracted from two cog-wheels at the turnstile: "this messy, irksome matter that ... didn't know its place. My undoing: matter" (McCarthy 2007: 17).[13] Later on in the novel when the narrator's health is deteriorating due to his "reenactment addiction," a doctor diagnoses his "cog-wheel rigidity," as an autonomic symptom of his traumatic state (McCarthy 2007: 220).

There are many other examples to work through in the novel and film that involve spilling liquids that overflow their containers—blood from bodies; grime from surfaces; windshield wiper fluid from automotive encasings; "sticky black goop and tar" from coffee cups; a leaking garbage bag that leaves a "sticky-looking patch on the floor"; wine and beer sloshing from glasses onto tables, floors, and clothes; "bits of plaster, plastic, wire, and dust wires" spilling from walls; grease from machine parts. As the narrator notes, matter is being tracked everywhere. Instead of habit as a carrying or having of being, subject matter is *being-carried-away* from its having, and the narrator is constantly caught up and stained by this matter. The perturbations in the novel unsettle him through acts of *grounding* that produce literal precipitates—solids from fluids, or better, coagulations—that never settle in place or completely settle to the bottom as ground or foundation. One might say they are suspended.

In *Remainder*, the immanent loop of habit is always cracking, opening up, and overflowing with accruals and irruptions of substance. Perhaps this is a reminder that habit is not simply about the movement between fluidity and hardness, grace and addiction. It would seem that habit is not the frictionless, smooth, running of things, or even the stumbling over of things, but the eruption of substance produced by mobilized inertias. The incessant delays, repetitions, loops, and short-circuits in the novel and film do not bind any preexisting excesses, accruals of substance, or accidents but rather engender them (I will return to this in the section on the figure eight). A prime example of this is the liver lady, who features prominently in the reenactments in Madlyn Mansions (Figure 11.9). She is required to fry liver—which "spat and sizzled and smelled rich and brown and oily"—over and over again, such that the "vaporized fat" accumulates and eventually clogs up the extraction fan that is meant to waft its odor up to the narrator in the apartment above (McCarthy 2007: 70 and 155).

Although one might be inclined to read the escalator or carrot passages as a vivid, if not a crude and literal image, that is meant to exemplify all the steps required to think about before undertaking any task, or as an exemplification of Heidegger's "broken tool" revealing itself *as such*, or as analogs to his damaged and disrupted neural circuitry, I think that misses the point. Rather they suggest that a certain sense of habit as fluidity can tend to mask that irruption of matter and create the appearance of a smoothly operational loop. These passages reveal the grounds and precipitate of the fantasy of habit as the balanced solubility, permeation, and transparency of matter and spirit, action and object, body and environment.

Figure 11.9 Remainder, The liver lady
Source: Copyright Omer Fast. Film still by Aron Vinegar.

This attentiveness to precipitates and remainders is also a political critique of neo-liberal capitalism. Instead of financial liquidity we are given infinite absolution and the inertias and persistencies that refuse to be mobilized and put into circulation. Instead of the socio-structural role of capitalism in converting elements into series that cement the structural laws governing the circulation of everything, we get the resurgence of those elements and particularities that *do* circulate but in ways that reaffirm them in and as remainders (Lyotard 1991: 48–49).[14] If the narrator's monetary settlement is supposed to provide a final settlement between the respective "bodies"—the narrator, his lawyer, the ones responsible for the accident—this does not offer a resolution to the case; it never closes the loop or ends the process (McCarthy 2007: 4). Even the word *Remainder* in the opening credits of the film is absolved into bits and pieces, re-main-der (Figure 11.10), just as the protagonist literally "gags" on the "-l-" in "settlement" in the early pages of the novel, alluding simultaneously to that word's legal dimensions, his monetary recompense for the accident, and his own infinite grounding, which never reaches any kind of settlement, even when he tries to let the feeling induced by the crack in the wall "settle down" in him (McCarthy 2007: 4 and 68). If the contemporary fetish is not reified substance but rather fluidity, then *Remainder* is also a process of defetishization alerting us to the precipitations and grounds that are virtual within all fluids and fluidity. As Jason Barker has noted, the system of contemporary capitalism is one with all the redundancy left in (Barker 2017: 150). *Remainder* is a recalcitrant if not resistant exploration of that condition.

The novel, however, never gives into the temptation of equating habit *tout court* with ideology in the form of a positivity, custom, habitus, or dispositive that is imposed on the subject in and through the social order. The narrator's automatic, jerky, and compulsive movements are, oddly enough, what is most alive in him, and what prevents him from being merely another "remainder" within the economic and libidinal circuitries of neo-liberal capitalism he has both suffered and profited by.

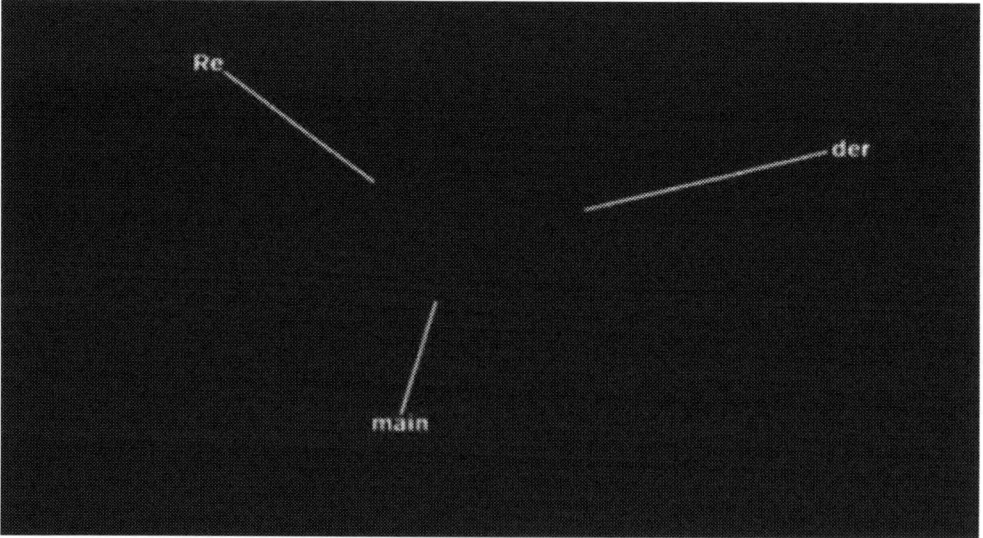

Figure 11.10 *Remainder,* Opening credits of the film
Source: Copyright Omer Fast. Film still by Aron Vinegar.

Being Carried Away vs The House of Being

> Habit is the point at which a subjectivity seeks to make itself a master of being, the place in which, with a perfect circularity, having, which derives from being, appropriates the latter to itself. Having is nothing but the appropriation of being.
>
> *(Agamben 2016: 61)*

Habit always plays a central role in issues of self-preservation, the consolidation and shoring up of a self. The Latin and Greek nominatives for habit, *hexis* and *habitus*, are derived from Greek verbs *echein* and *habere* meaning to have or to hold. They indicate habit's ability to endure; to impart a degree of stability and continuity—or rigidity as the case may be—to our character, bearing, and mode of doing things. Habit is a way of appropriating and stabilizing being. Thus, habit is always linked to issues of property and possession. In the novel and film these issues take on their most emphatically architectonic dimension with the purchase of Madlyn Mansions and the eviction of its previous tenants (Figure 11.11). The narrator's fragility, which seems to be concomitant with a receptive attentiveness to matter that we are contracted by in habit and which provides our contact and connection with all other kinds of matter, both organic and inorganic, is increasingly subsumed into an attempt to literally *construct* a clearly demarcated place to reenact his lost spontaneity through a hyper-control of his environment, and every single action and object within it. As he informs Naz: "we'll need complete … jurisdiction over all the space," in order to have absolute control of the reenactors performances (McCarthy 2007: 88). As the Madlyn Mansions reenactments get ever more complex, the narrator hardly leaves the apartment block, and the reenactments are extended for ever longer periods of time. The indentured "enactors" he hires are "on" more often than "off," and often "frozen" in place for hours, while he either walks around specific sections of the apartment building or is immersed in his bathtub (his prosthetic fluidity) staring at the re-constructed "crack" in the wall (Figure 11.12).

If the apartment building's foundation is a literal crack which triggers the narrator's Proustian moment, that crack seems to be plastered over in increasing acts of orthopedic rigidity and domination. The narrator's "undoing" by matter is not simply a matter of the joys of pure becoming, nor does it result in the further nurturing of his self as a "house of cards." Although

Figure 11.11 **Remainder,** The last of the evicted tenants from Madlyn Mansions
Source: Copyright Omer Fast. Film still by Aron Vinegar.

Aron Vinegar

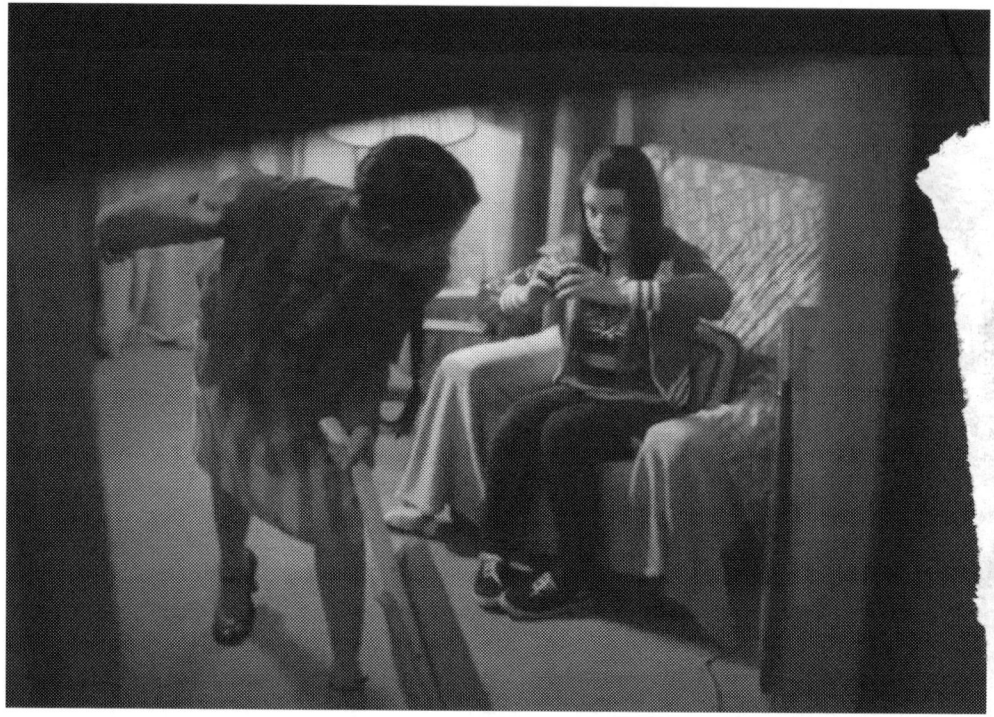

Figure 11.12 *Remainder*, Re-enactors "frozen" in place
Source: Copyright Omer Fast. Film still by Aron Vinegar.

Tom's rough cardboard model in the film is clearly marked with a visible sticker that reads "fragile," that does not prevent him from smashing it in a fit of rage (see Figure 11.8; Figure 11.13). But in many ways, these acts of domination, control, and possession, which are part of the logic of habit, and one of its bodily, social, and political possibilities, are not the whole picture. The narrator constantly returns to the crack he has carefully re-constructed in the bathroom of the apartment block, as if to keep tearing it open, which is often described as "fleshy," and that perpetually spills forth the matter that he is also bent on plastering over and containing. The tendency of habit to smooth over discontinuity can always pitch towards absolute enclosure and suffocation, but the constant repetitions in *Remainder* produce ever more glitches, opacities, and sticky reservoirs of recalcitrant matter that both trigger and short-circuit the drive for aesthetic totality.

The traditional gathering function of architecture—its capacity to create a world by constructing the walls that separate the house of Being from all the beings and myriad stuff of the ontic world—is never fully accomplished. The narrator's attempt to subsume all gesture, actions, time, parts, units, and matter into his possession is bound to failure. He can never manage to coordinate all these elements in a satisfactory way, and there are parts of his memory that he can never recall, which include all the other "neutral" or "less specific" inhabitants of the building, who wear goaltender-like hockey masks during the reenactments in the novel and full body and face stockings in the film, and the "blank" parts of the building and its furnishings that he can't remember in detail, which are left neutral, indeterminate or, in the film, covered with generic brown wrapping paper (Figures 11.14 and 11.15). Nor is his passion for repetition even contained by the walls of the apartment, as some of his reenactors escape without his notice, and his compulsion to repeat spills out into ever wider

Figure 11.13   *Remainder*, Tom smashing the cardboard model of Madlyn Mansions
Source: Copyright Omer Fast. Film still by Aron Vinegar.

Figure 11.14   *Remainder*, Tom choosing the re-enactors assembled by his "facilitator" Nazrul Ram Vyas (Arsher Ali)
Source: Copyright Omer Fast. Film still by Aron Vinegar.

domains of the city itself as it always had. Matter continues to trip him up, and his attempts to incorporate all remainders produce ever more stuff. The narrator's drive to possess is thus also repeated in that he is possessed by his possession, which recoils away from him in his very attempts to have it. In *Remainder*, habit or habitation is precisely *not* "the place in which, with a perfect circularity, having, which derives from being, appropriates the latter to itself" (Agamben 2016: 61).

Figure 11.15 Remainder, Furniture covered in generic brown wrapping paper
Source: Copyright Omer Fast. Film still by Aron Vinegar.

Figure Eight, Viscous Circles, Grounding, and the Topology of the Subject

> What, then, would be the ego, where would it be, given its topological distinction from the Id, if not at the crossing of the 8, at the point of connection between these two intersecting asymmetrical circles, the circle of real objects and that of the virtual objects or centres.
>
> *(Deleuze 1994: 100)*

The figure eight is a persistent *topologerie* in *Remainder* (Nasio 2004: 102).[15] From the beginning of the novel the narrator is drawn towards and disturbed by the figure awarded for the settlement of his injury, eight and a half million pounds: "The eight was perfect, neat: a curved figure infinitely turning back into itself." Although that amount is excessive in itself, it is the half million that brings out the logic of its too muchness: "But then the half. Why had they added the half? It seemed to me so messy, this half: a leftover fragment, a shard of detritus" (McCarthy 2007: 8). While the narrator is pondering this figure, he is simultaneously moving in a figure eight pattern through the city, as he searches for a phone booth to call his lawyer. After tracing this path several times, he stops, pauses, and jerks back and forth at the crossing of the pattern traced by his kinky movements ("kinking" is a word that comes up more than a few times in the novel). Even his Proustian moment is engendered by this figure: at the party he moves through the apartment "in the pattern of an eight," and the bathroom, "this extra room," where he encounters the crack, "popped up beside it like the half had in my Settlement: offset, an extra" (Figure 11.1) (McCarthy 2007: 64). Subsequently, he finds Madlyn Mansions through a similar movement of overshooting and looping back through the city after this epiphany. In the film, Tom draws his finger over a figure eight, or, more accurately an "inner eight," scratched onto the window pane of a phone booth (Figure 11.16). The topology of the figure eight also features prominently in all the reenactments and is specifically named as such, or, is alluded to by McCarthy's precise descriptions of the narrator's looping and circuitous movements. These moments are also accompanied by sticky patches that pop up in conjunction with the "figure of eight." The final figure eight in the novel is produced from the vapor trails left by the plane, "(t)urning back, then turning out. Then turning back again," that the narrator hires to "vaporize" all remainders, including himself, from his last reenactment of a bank robbery staged in an actual

Figure 11.16 *Remainder*, Tom drawing his finger over an "inner eight" scratched into the window pane of a phone booth
Source: Copyright Omer Fast. Film still by Aron Vinegar.

bank during working hours (McCarthy 2007: 305–308). In the film, this loop comes back to the beginning of the novel and film, with the narrator "*about* to be—hit by something falling from the sky," while the camera circles around Tom Sturridge in a slow 360-degree close-up shot.

In every instance the figure eight movement engenders these sticky, material remainders, and thus they are never merely a subsequent addition to it. The narrator's incessant repetitious and looping movements—which are simultaneously fast and slow, precipitous and delayed, transitive and intransitive—open up the closed circle by doubling, crossing, and twisting it, thus preventing its tendency to absolute immanence, self-closure and from definitively settling down as a solid ground or foundation. "In effect, to ground is always to bend, to curve, and recurve" (Deleuze 1994: 273). In *Remainder*, matter is continuously agitated—its parts, moments, and subject matter subjected to a movement of infinite grounding that suspends matter rather than settling it. The figure eight is a "circle of circles" that repeats, extends, and intersects with itself, and the crossing of the two circles is simultaneously an accumulation of substance and its evacuation or voiding; the accumulation of matter always accompanying that voiding and a voiding or virtualization that always accompanies matter in its positive traits. The figure eight marks the crossing of both the excess of matter *and* "un-matter," just as one of the kinks in the novel is both a "material kink" in a carpet and a "ghost kink" that is tripped over due to the recalcitrance lurking at the very heart of habit (Figures 11.17, 11.18, and 11.19) (McCarthy 2007: 296). The logic, materiality, temporality, and movement of habit engenders a subject matter that is both virtually present and materially insistent; a *remainder* that doggedly persists even as it is sublimated into tenuous wisps of vapor. Habit is up to the task of entering into the contemporary movements of that strange and persistent subject matter we call architecture and unsettling any attempt to do away with the subject.[16]

Figure 11.17 *Remainder*, Re-enactors for the bank robbery trip over a "material kink" in the carpet
Source: Copyright Omer Fast. Film still by Aron Vinegar.

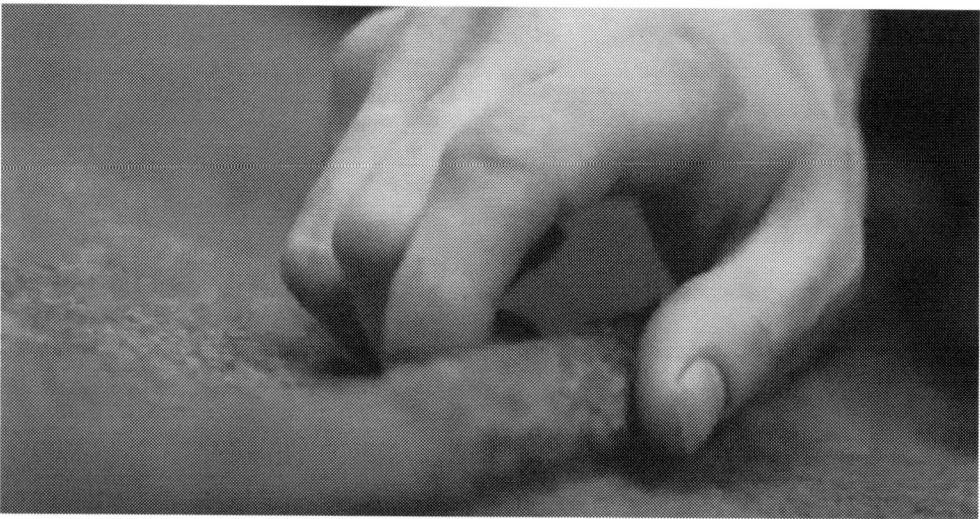

Figure 11.18 *Remainder*, Tom gripping the "material kink" in the carpet
Source: Copyright Omer Fast. Film still by Aron Vinegar.

Habit's *Remainder*

Figure 11.19 *Remainder*, Re-enactors tripping over the "ghost kink" in the carpet
Source: Copyright Omer Fast. Film still by Aron Vinegar.

Notes

1 Most of the contemporary work on habit has developed within or draws upon writings in philosophies of mind and cognition that emphasize the imbrication of mind, body, and environment (extended mind, enactivism, distributed cognition, material engagement theory), developments in neuroscience, neurophilosophy, and neuro art/architecture (plasticity, epigenesis, empathy theory), issues related to the mechanization and automaticity of intelligence, for example algorithms and infrastructures, or with certain strands of philosophy that have been prominent within architectural theory, such as new and speculative realism, object-oriented ontology, actor–network theory, phenomenology, various forms of monism, Deleuze's transcendental empiricism, and writings on technology, media, and science within the humanities that engage with habit directly or indirectly.

2 *Remainder* was originally published in 2005 with Metronome Press. Since this book is not readily accessible for most readers, I will use the Vintage edition published in 2007. I had the privilege of talking about habit in *Remainder* with Tom McCarthy and Omer Fast in Oslo in the form of a public conversation that took place between the three of us at the Literaturhuset in the fall of 2016 and during their visit to a course I was teaching on habit at the University of Oslo. Thankfully, they were intrigued by my request to engage with their work in this way, and of course they are invested in all the issues that habit raises—repetition, matter, politics, bodies, institutions, social positivities, control, exploitation, freedom—but I do not believe that they explicitly think about their work in terms of habit in a comprehensive way. I can only say that for me it has been crucial. A special thank you to Alex Potts who suggested that I read *Remainder* quite a few years back.

3 I mean *subject matter* to refer to the relationship between Subject and Substance in the Hegelian sense of their "grounding circularity." Also, Subject here should not necessarily be read as subjectivity although that might be one of Subject's moments. This reference to Hegel indicates that what I claim to be the contemporary pertinence of habit to architecture draws on some "older" philosophical material that is generally avoided within architectural circles. This is not to say that I am uninterested in or do not engage with the domains of thought listed in note 1. Accounts of habit in relationship to architecture are few and far between and they inevitably draw on the bodies of knowledge that I list above.

4 The Proustian moment refers to the famous scene in Marcel Proust's *Swann's Way*, the first of Proust's seven volumes of *In Search of Lost Time* (*A la rechereche du temps perdu*), in which the narrator involuntarily recalls a memory from his childhood after tasting a small cake (madeleine) dipped in tea. The crack in the bathroom wall in *Remainder* is the narrator's Proustian moment, which takes place in the

apartment block that he finds/constructs and is called Madlyn Mansions. A longer essay would have to pay closer attention to the fundamental contortions that McCarthy gives to these Proustian coordinates.

5 In the film, the physical crack in the bathroom wall is deemphasized, and the figure of a child who appears to Tom in the bathroom is the primary attachment to his "memory" of the gestures and scenes in Madlyn Mansions. This child recurs at important points in the film, and it would take a much longer essay to do justice to its persistence. It should be noted that the film does pay sensual attention to the scars on Tom's body.

6 In this opening scene we witness what Lacan has called the "premature birth of man"; a condition that is always haunted by the body in pieces, and an inability to coordinate bodily movements, and which subsequently requires all modes of orthopedic structures that would render us stable, upright, and whole. I should hasten to add this prematurity persists beyond infancy despite the lure of all manner of stabilizing imagos that are meant to "quadrate the ego"—from mirrors to habit to architecture. See Lacan (2006: 3–9).

7 Catherine Malabou has emphasized the role of accident in regard to habit in terms of the relationships between contingency and necessity, the universal and the individual, genus and species. But the narrator in *Remainder* never seems to achieve the kind of plasticity of self she describes; he cannot self-generate in a way that is able to negotiate between the drive for preservation and an exposure to the outside, and thus "accidentalize" himself or become an "insistent accident" in the way she accounts for in her important writings on plasticity and habit. See Malabou (2008: 70–75); Malabou (2005: 73).

8 Rebecca Comay calls it a "strange conatus." My wording is derived from hers, as is the notion of "strange resolving." See Comay (2018: 43); Comay and Ruda (2018: 4).

9 This passage is taken from the Conclusion of Kant's *Critique of Practical Reason*.

10 Here I am trying to argue that the movement from habit to architecture, from action to object, from the intransitive to transitive, is complicated by habit. There is no clear sedimentation and conversion of habit into a stable and solid entity "out there," as a way to compensate for how habit *itself* creates a gap or division within being, as the subject matters from which both habit and architecture are mutually constituted are always already fissured, holey, aerated, cracked, and insubstantial.

11 See the note for the epigraph in this section for the complete sentence. There are many more rich thoughts on this single page that could be elaborated on here in regards to the relationship of death and habit.

12 The important section on habit is found on pp. 139–147.

13 These sticky matters that do not know their place is instantiated in the writing itself. All of these incidents are displaced and tracked through the novel as stains, which are generated from the incessant "grounding circle" of McCarthy's *ethos* of writing. In fact, they spill out and stain his subsequent novel as well, including its graphic design. See McCarthy (2015).

14 Many of the essays in this book contain astute considerations of habit. I am still coming to grips with them.

15 Nasio has coined the term *topologerie* to refer to mathematical topology and the psychoanalyst's particular twisting of this topology in theorizing and writing. I am using it in the same sense here. It is through the figure eight that Lacan and Deleuze engage with Hegel's "circle of circles," which is the latter's figure of the absolute.

16 My main points of reference with regard to the figure eight are primarily Hegel, Deleuze and Lacan, and some of their most astute commenters. The issue of the "circle of circles" (Hegel), "the crossing of the 8" and "grounding circle" (Deleuze), and the "interior eight" (Lacan) is complex and these figures are in conversation with each other. But their subtle differences—often due to the choice of prepositions—are crucial. Most discussions of topology in architecture tend to avoid the speculative dimensions that I am emphasizing here.

References

Agamben, G. (2016) *The Use of Bodies*, trans. A. Kotsko, Stanford: Stanford University Press.
Bachelard, G. (2013) *Intuition of the Instant*, trans. E. Rizo-Patron, Evanston: Northwestern University Press.
Barker, J. (2017) "Schizonanalytic cartographies: on maps and models of capitalism," *Filozofski vestnik* 38, 1: 133–151.
Comay, R. (2018) "Resistance and repetition: Hegel and Freud," in R. Comay and B. Zantvoort (eds) *Hegel and Resistance: History, Politics and Dialectics*, London: Bloomsbury, 35–58.

Comay, R. and Ruda, F. (2018) *The Dash—: The Other Side of Absolute Knowing*, Cambridge, MA: MIT Press.

Deleuze, G. (1994) *Difference and Repetition*, trans. P. Patton, New York: Columbia University Press.

Fast, O. (2015) *Remainder*, film produced by British Film Institute, Soda Film + Art, Phi Films, Deutscher Filmförderfonds (DFFF), Filmförderung Hamburg Schleswig-Holstein, Medienboard Berlin-Brandenburg, Zweites Deutsches Fernsehen (ZDF), ARTE, Tigerlily Films, Amusement Park Films.

Hegel. G. W. F. (1971) *Philosophy of Mind (Part Three of Encyclopedia of the Philosophical Sciences (1830))*, trans. W. Wallace and A. V. Miller, Oxford: Clarendon Press.

Hegel. G. W. F. (1977) *Phenomenology of Spirit*, trans. A. V. Miller, Oxford: Oxford University Press.

James, W. (1950) *The Principles of Psychology*, vol. 1, New York: Dover Publications.

Kant, I. (2002 [1788]) *Critique of Practical Reason*, trans. W. Pluhar, New York: Hackett Publishing.

Lacan, J. (2006) "The mirror stage as formative of the I function as revealed in psychoanalytic experience," in *Écrits: The First Complete Edition in English*, trans. B. Fink, New York: W. W. Norton, 75–81.

Lyotard, J.-F. (1991) *The Inhuman: Reflections on Time*, trans. G. Bennington and R. Bowlby, Stanford: Stanford University Press.

Malabou, C. (2005) *The Future of Hegel: Plasticity, Temporality and Dialectic*, trans. L. During, London: Routledge.

Malabou, C. (2008) *What Should We Do with Our Brain*, trans. Sebastian Rand, New York: Fordham University Press.

McCarthy, T. (2007) *Remainder*, New York: Vintage; and Omer Fast, *Remainder*, film released in 2015.

McCarthy, T. (2015) *Satin Island*, London: Jonathan Cape.

McCarthy, T. (2016) *Recessional—OR, The TIME OF THE HAMMER*, Zurich and Berlin: Diaphanes.

Nancy, J.-L. (1993) "Corpus," in *The Birth to Presence*, trans. B. Holmes and others, Stanford: Stanford University Press.

Nancy, J.-L. (2000) *Being Singular Plural*, trans. R. Richardson and A. O'Byrne, Stanford: Stanford University Press.

Nancy, J.-L. (2008) *Corpus*, trans. R. A. Rand, New York: Fordham University Press.

Nasio, J.-D. (2004) "Objet a and the cross-cap," in E. Ragland and D. Milovanovic (eds) *Lacan Topologically Speaking*, New York: Other Press, 98–116.

Ondaatje, M. (1997) *The Cinnamon Peeler*, New York: Vintage.

Visker, R. (2009) "Intransitive facticity," in F. Raffoul and E. S. Nelson (eds) *Rethinking Facticity*, Albany: SUNY Press, 149–192.

Žižek, S. (2017) "Fictitious capital and the return of personal domination," https://thephilosophicalsalon.com/fictitious-capital-and-the-return-of-personal-domination/.

12
Ephemeral Architecture
Toward Radical Contingency

Swati Chattopadhyay

Transformative Connections

Rasheed Araeen's monumental installation *Rite/Right of Passage*, located in the forecourt of the Bangladesh Shilpakala Academy welcomed visitors to the 2018 Dhaka Art Summit (Figure 12.1). You could walk through the passage created by the bamboo lattice work, painted vivid red, for a dramatic entry into the exhibition complex. For the organizers of the Dhaka Art Summit the choice of Araeen's "bright red improvised geometry" was intended as a defiance of Western hegemony:

> [to] invite visitors to enter a rite of passage into a new mode of thinking with Bangladesh at the center of its own existence, rather than at the periphery of someone else's, while also looking back at the philosophies that informed the long history of internationalist thought in politics and aesthetics in the region.
>
> *(DAS 18 Exhibition Guide: 25–26)*

Araeen's installation served as a fitting ensemble to a venue that connected ideas, works, and people in imaginative ways. We could construct additional meanings from Araeen's installation, however, given its deliberate deployment of an ordinary material set to a repetitive non-hierarchical set of formal relationships in which distinctions between center/periphery are eschewed. In Dhaka Araeen worked with a narrow site and in his drawings he specified the location, form, dimension and material for the installation (Figure 12.2). The mode of construction was left to the local builders, thus retaining a trace of the artisanal hand characteristic of vernacular bamboo construction. At the same time the brilliant vermillion paint on the structure erased the distinctions between post and joint, cross-piece and tie, lending it a unifying theme.

London-based writer and artist, Araeen, has worked with structural components assembled as sculptural form since 1965. Trained as a civil engineer, Araeen took to using truss-like structures, reminiscent of the Constructivists' penchant for engineering form, to move beyond the representational hegemony and compositional hierarchy of Western art (Martin 2011: 126).[1] His drawings and minimally modified prefabricated structural elements such as I-beams placed in various configurations elicit the geometrical beauty inherent in these structural members and

Figure 12.1 Rasheed Araeen, *Rite/Right of Passage*. Dhaka Art Summit, 2018

Source: Copyright Pablo Bartholomew. Commissioned and produced by Samdani Art Foundation for Dhaka Art Summit 2018. www.dhakaartsummit.org.

Swati Chattopadhyay

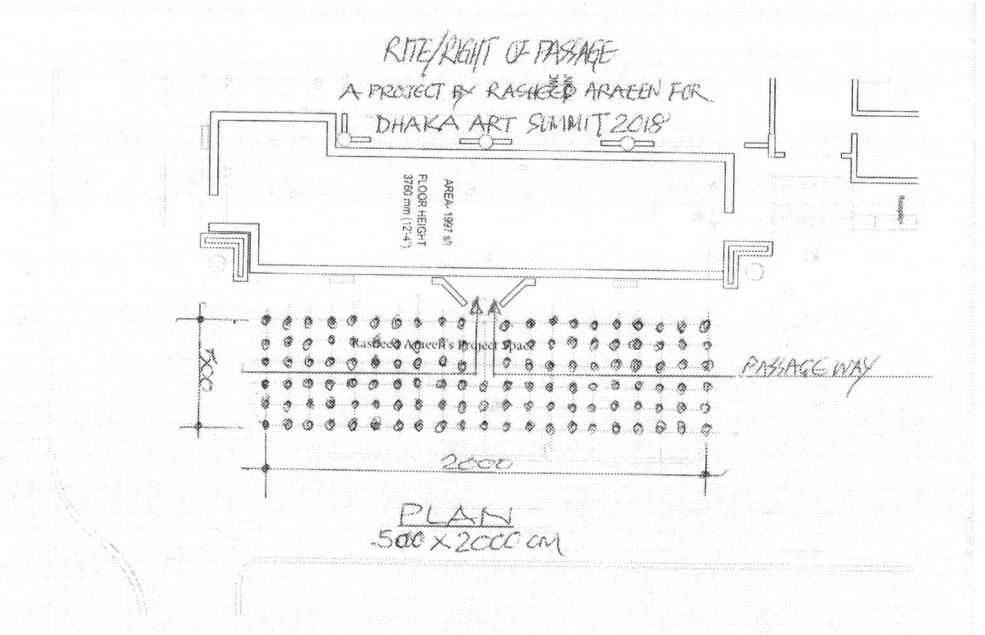

Figure 12.2 Rasheed Araeen, Plan of *Rite/Right of Passage*, 2017
Source: Copyright Rasheed Araeen.

the open-ended possibilities of generating patterns through formal permutations and combinations. By 1968 he was conferring upon such "universal" structural forms specific cultural connotations of practice, use, and belonging. He named them, *Homage to Tatlin*, *Char Yaar*, *Char Yaar I*, *Char Yaar II*, *Mile Gaye Phir Chaaron Yaar*, and *Milap*. All of these played on themes of conversation and friendship, while the following year he increased the formal complexity of the tower-like works, bringing attention to the role of color in form-making: *Lal Kona* and *Rang Baranga* (Araeen 1984; Aikens 2017). Most of these have since been recreated as museum pieces. Since the mid-1990s he has also done outdoor installations with an explicit commitment to visitor participation. The scale of the structures has correspondingly increased: *To Whom It May Concern* (1996) and *When There Is a Will There's a Way* (1998) used steel scaffolding rods to create large installations. The use of commonly available material distinguishes his work as does a certain openness to artisanal improvisation, despite the dimensional specificity that is at the core of these artworks. In two recent venues, Hong Kong (2017) and Dhaka (2018), he turned to a locally available material, bamboo, which opens up a new set of conversations about "site-specific" work, even as the monumental forms of the installations exceed the definition of structure/sculpture to become temporary spaces of habitation. The lashed joints peculiar of bamboo construction were still apparent underneath the coat of paint in *Rite/Right of Passage*, however, and produced a distinctive feature that is not found in Araeen's previous experiments with structural forms that were nailed or welded together without much of a seam.

Bamboo structures are a common mode of building in many parts of South and East Asia. The specific tradition of building with bamboo in eastern India is old and venerable: the bent bamboo form that lent the village houses in Bengal (*bangla*) their distinctive curved roofs were mimicked in masonry forms in terracotta temples of medieval Bengal and Mughal and Rajput pavilions in northern and western India. Centuries later the elegant simplicity of the house form would be translated into the colonial bungalow. These formal translations and attendant structural transformations were recognitions of a delectable affinity between lashed bamboo roofs and masonry vaults, between the so-called impermanent and permanent modes of construction. In some ways, Araeen's *Rite/Right of Passage*, a commentary on migrant passages, struggles, and desires, may be seen as a link that facilitates recognition of this tradition. What might have been a "normal occurrence" in this milieu is given a transformational capacity in this installation by its location, formal treatment, and citation, offering a structural opening into new opportunities and critical commentaries.[2]

I wish to use this reading of Araeen's architectural installation as an entrée into another contemporary art/architectural phenomenon that uses bamboo as the primary building material to create spectacular venues for a festive event: Durgapuja or worship of the goddess Durga and her entourage, in Kolkata. An annual Hindu religious event held in September–October, it is the biggest festival in the state of West Bengal, but is also celebrated in other parts of India, Bangladesh, and across the world of the Bengali diaspora. In Kolkata, a temporary pavilion, or *pandal* as it is called, is constructed to host each community *puja* for the five days of the event. Often lasting longer, the *pandals* in Kolkata in terms of sheer novelty can put any architectural biennale to shame. But more important is the story of urban materiality that these temporary structures evince. The construction philosophy in these short-lived, time-bound works is not to pre-determine every aspect of the construction process ahead of time for quick installation, but to build upon and give shape to the contingent possibilities of the material at hand, the skills of the workers on site, and the urban context. In their selective appropriation of built space—buildings, streets, sidewalks, parks—the pavilions set up a conversation between the ephemeral and the perennial, between permanence and impermanence, between hard and soft interventions. Durgapuja pavilions, I propose, have transformative capacity and provide learning opportunities for grappling with the *temporal horizons* that govern architectural production.

Im/Permanence

Permanence is the defining prejudice of the architecture profession. This prejudice has been nurtured by generations of architects and patrons who imagined the artistic merit of their buildings as their legacy to posterity. Adolf Loos remarked that only tombs and monuments deserve the appellation of "art"; other buildings that necessitated everyday use were not deemed worthy of serious artistic consideration (Bonnemaison and Macy 2008: 2). The violent changes in time-space resulting from the Industrial Revolution, and the plethora of time-saving and light-weight construction techniques invented to meet the demands of capitalist production might have hardened such prejudices.

As architects and scholars we have not moved sufficiently beyond this prejudice. We presume that permanent structures that occupy cities—durable wood and masonry buildings, the networks of concrete road, canal, and steel infrastructure—are the real stuff of architecture and urbanism. This is despite the fact that all built works, including those that are understood to be permanent, have a limited temporal horizon (Chow 2018): some last for a few years and some for decades; residential buildings are planned to last a shorter duration than road infrastructure; office and commercial spaces face quick turnovers for reasons that have nothing to do with their structural integrity. Against the imagination of permanence is set everything that is presumed to be short-lived. The terms that describe structures lasting for a few days to a few months or that which are vulnerable to weather conditions—impermanent, temporary, and ephemeral—are used interchangeably, without attending to their differential architectural, infrastructural, and political import.

Durational thinking typical of the profession affects every aspect of design and its futures, and is structurally related to how contingency is imagined and negotiated. As architects, we are keen on innovation, but we hope to achieve this by abating all contingencies, rather than seeing the potential in a play of contingencies (Chattopadhyay 2012). Let me be clear: to plan is to abate contingency, no matter who does the planning. What I am questioning here is not "plan" (decision making that projects an outcome) and planning as a mode of action, but disciplinary practices that aim to foreclose all contingencies and therefore the productive potential of "conflict, ambiguity and indeterminacy" (Holston and Appadurai 1996). Similarly, while fungibility as obsolescence is integral to modern architecture (Abramson 2016), fungibility as reversibility is not.[3] While digital technology enables architects to imagine forms otherwise not possible, attention to the relation between soft and hard technologies and architectonic softness remain exception rather than the norm.

A growing body of scholarship on ephemeral architecture and urbanism, in the shape of camps (Hailey 2009; Herscher 2017), festival and coronation architecture (Hosagrahar 1992; Bonnemaison and Macy 2008), "ephemeral megacity" (Mehrotra and Vera 2015, 2016), and urban popular culture (Henkin 1998; San-Juan 2001; Simone 2004; Chattopadhyay 2012) have brought attention to the unstable meaning of im/permanence in architecture.[4] In this literature, the term ephemeral is used to describe the *materiality* of architecture and space but refers to a number of distinct phenomena: (a) destructible medium—paper architecture or designs on paper that were/are never realized as built forms; (b) sensations such as smell, sound, touch, thermal comfort; (c) experience of momentary economic and social exchanges in an urban milieu such as hustling on the street; (d) affect of collectivity as in a soccer match or a protest march; (e) short-lived interventions such as posters and bills pasted on walls or wall-writing which will be washed away or painted over in the near future; (f) illumination and waterworks that are turned off after a certain duration; (g) structures built for festive events or as emergency shelters that are meant to be dismantled after their immediate purpose is served, even if there is no material decay of the building components. The techniques of negotiating inadequate infrastructure—discontinuous supply of water, electricity, and gas, as well as uneven roads and temporary bridges—are often folded into the category of temporary habitation, even if neither the habitation (squatter settlements and slums) nor the techniques in practice last for a short duration. That some such structures indeed have a shelf-life longer than planned, or are rebuilt with more long-term ambitions elsewhere, adds to the difficulties of reorienting a temporal imagination that assumes permanence as the desirable norm.

Agency

The resurgence of ephemerality in urban studies is related to investigations of urban formations in the Global South, and the recognition that infrastructural patchworks, short-lived structures, exchanges and sensations hold the key to understanding how political agency is shaped in such cities (Simone 2004, 2014; Simone and Pieterse 2017; Bayat 1997; Holston 2009; Hou 2010; Chattopadhyay 2012). The historical literature, however, reveals a comparable scenario for cities in other parts of the world (Henkin 1998; Chase, Crawford, and Kaliski 1999; Upton 2008; Bonnemaison and Macy 2008; Hazan 2015; Sen 2017).

Claims of permanence and impermanence are inherently political and define possibilities of inclusion and exclusion. This has to do with not only which space and how much space is occupied but how long and in what form and by whom. Permanence linked to the modern Western conception of property rights, a legacy of Enlightenment thought, has historically been used by European colonial and metropolitan powers against peoples whose mode of living did not require the construction of masonry structures. Inattentive to or ignorant of how temporality, property, and territorial occupation were understood by indigenous peoples and tribal populations (Banerjee 2006), the absence of "durable" structures became an excuse for dispossessing millions of people across the world.

Indeed there is a long tradition going back to antiquity of temporary structures being constructed for festive celebrations in Europe. The recorded history suggests that such ephemeral architectural events were typically organized and planned by the state or by city authorities as celebratory events. One architect or a small group of architects would be responsible for the design of the temporary architecture, not unlike the building ethos of world fairs and expositions of the nineteenth and twentieth centuries.[5] Less attention has been given in architectural histories to the non-state-sponsored structures and popular appropriations of urban space for pagan rituals, cults of saints, games, and entertainment that had scant state sanction.

The pavilions built for Durgapuja in Kolkata fall into this latter realm of popular architecture. Just as the everyday infrastructures in cities in the Global South do not always follow the logic of state planning and responsibility, the pavilions differ essentially from these state- or city-sponsored events. No central authority determines the design and planning of the pavilions, although the builders work within some nominal safety ground rules set by the police and fire marshal. In other words, the labor of the numerous agents that enable the construction of the pavilions and unfolding of Durgapuja as an event is sufficiently varied and each intervention sufficiently particularized to defy a unifying or a totalizing view.

A comparison with the mega religious event, Kumbh Mela, held at the pilgrimage site at Prayag (Allahabad), would help explain the uniqueness of Kolkata's Durgapuja landscape. First, the Kumbh Mela ground is constructed as a separate "temporary city" every 12 years next to the city of Allahabad, whereas Durgapuja is an annual event in which a temporary infrastructure is superimposed on an existing city. In terms of urban design, the Durgapuja pavilions work as urban "infill," and the city-level infrastructural planning by the police and the municipality must consider the daily interface between everyday city infrastructure and the additional burden of *puja* infrastructure. They must anticipate the impact of a few thousand of these pavilions by a few thousand different agencies. For Durgapuja organizers and residents, the *puja* pavilion as temporary occupation of urban space affects their daily lives for a variable duration—anywhere between three months for the elaborate pavilions to a week or two for the smaller ones—and constitutes an investment in their immediate community. Second, the structures at the Kumbh Mela are fairly simple in terms of construction, and their aesthetic character is not prioritized, whereas in the Durgapuja pavilion, aesthetics and architectonics are prime considerations. Third, given the desire for novelty and the myriad agencies at work, the pavilions and therefore the overall infrastructure of Durgapuja are different each year. In contrast, the Kumbh Mela has a "master plan" worked out by a central planning authority which sets down the basic infrastructural framework. Every 12 years this framework is adjusted to meet the changing contours of the riverine topography and the anticipated number—several million—of fair attendees. From the scale of the pavilion to the scale of the city, the architectural and infrastructural conditions of these two festive events are fundamentally different in terms of temporality and spatiality. The Kumbh Mela planning, Mehrotra and Vera have correctly pointed out, has flexibility and a certain open-endedness that enable inhabitation by different groups by giving these groups the agency to work out specific arrangements within an allocated space. The ephemeral architecture and infrastructure of Kolkata's Durgapuja suggests a process that is more complex and relies on contingency as a creative factor in its success.

Urban Infill

Consider a street about 20 or 40 feet wide in a primarily residential neighborhood, lined with mid-rise townhouses (Figure 12.3). These early-mid twentieth-century buildings abut the street and have verandahs, front steps, *ro'aks* (stoop) that facilitate street-watching and conversation, creating an inhabitable street edge. It is common for trees on sidewalks to have a seating arrangement around the tree trunk. Light fabric or tarpaulin hung across two trees or from lamp posts provide shelter for occasional sidewalk vendors—perhaps a green grocer or the neighborhood *dhobi* who makes a living by ironing clothes for residents in the locality. Maintenance of the sidewalk as well as the buildings varies a great deal, with the water stains of a prolonged monsoon visible on the building walls.

During the five-day Durgapuja celebration, organized by a neighborhood association or club, such a street is entirely transformed. Here you may walk into a slice of New York City with its iconic skyline, complemented by a Gehryesque pavilion (Figure 12.4). Or you may discover a finely engineered bamboo structure that selectively closes and discloses the street as habitat (Figure 12.5). Alternatively, the *pandal* may be very modest and low-budget, and incorporate the wide *ro'ak* or raised platform of a building into the pavilion space as a practical, space-, time-, and cost-saving measure (Figure 12.6).

Figure 12.3 Street before construction of the *pandal* of Badamtala Ashar Sangha, 2017
Source: Copyright Swati Chattopadhyay.

Figure 12.4 Purnendu Dey and Snehasish Maity, *pandal* of Badamtala Ashar Sangha, 2017
Source: Copyright Swati Chattopadhyay.

Figure 12.5 Bimal Samanta, *pandal* of Bakulbagan Sarbojanin, 2017
Source: Copyright Swati Chattopadhyay.

Figure 12.6 Small low-budget *pandal* on narrow lane near Hedua; note the *ro'ak* of residences for use as seating space, 2017
Source: Copyright Swati Chattopadhyay.

Not all the pavilions are built on the street: parks and playgrounds, vacant lots, forecourts of buildings, green islands, and a combination thereof are used for these site-specific constructions. The simplest *pandal* is a square or rectangular construction of bamboo poles lashed together with coconut coir or fabric ties. A "wall" of fabric and plywood creates an enclosure covered by a lean-to or gable roof covered with tarpaulin. Nearby buildings, boundary walls, lamp posts, and street furniture are cannily incorporated into these pavilions. The bamboo poles may be tied to verandah railings or columns of an adjacent building for structural support. The *ro'ak* adjoining a residential building admirably answers the spatial need of a *puja* pavilion. The raised platform may be used for placing the Durgapuja idols, while the street space in front shaded by a bamboo pavilion forms the congregation space, often without obstructing pedestrian traffic. In some instances, depending on the dimensional capacity of the street, sidewalk, and adjacent buildings, the existing *ro'ak* continues to support its everyday sitting and gathering function during the festival while a raised platform on the opposite sidewalk answers the space requirements of a *puja* pavilion. In one instance of a pavilion in 2018 the deity was hosted in the hall of a school building while the "*pandal*" constituted the uncovered lane that led to this space—the adjoining walls of the buildings on this lane were brightly painted to produce a festive atmosphere with little cost.

To construct the larger more glamorous pavilions on the street, the roadway has to be partially or fully closed off to vehicular traffic for one to three months between mid-monsoon and fall, the duration of closure depending on the scale and design ambition of the organizers. The New York skyline created by Badamtala Ashar Sangha in 2017 was situated on a vacant lot and incorporated the street in front in its design by making it the pedestrian path that cut through one edge of the venue. Once visitors entered the "gateway" constructed for the pavilion ensemble the structure came into full view, rising up to 100 feet in places, completely obscuring the everyday environment of the neighborhood. The visual feast was created out of nothing more precious or permanent than paper and fabric on a bamboo scaffold. Here the usual building materials of such pavilions were transformed into an unusual stage set to fundamentally alter the ambiance of that neighborhood for a few days. The bamboo scaffold was only visible at the back where visitors were not expected to go (Figure 12.7). Those from the neighborhood were privy to this backspace, where the structure was exposed and untrimmed, although nothing forbid visitors to enter the back purlieus: urban commonsense understood this back space as off-limits to visitors.

In contrast, the bamboo structure of Bakulbagan Sarbojanin in 2017 engaged and interacted with the buildings on site visibly yet lightly. Located on the street near a T-junction, the pavilion space was distributed into three distinct components: the main space that hosted the deity and occupied the sidewalk and half the main thoroughfare, leaving a narrow vehicular access; and two subsidiary spaces separate from the main pavilion—one on the sidewalk on the opposite side and the other on a vacant lot. These subsidiary spaces were meant for volunteers, residents, and club members. Gateways on three streets were nominal gestures of defining the pavilion territory and these barely touched the surrounding buildings (see Figure 12.5). The pavilion could have been located on the narrow street (thereby blocking it) leaving the main street open to full vehicular access, but keeping access to all streets and buildings (distributing the access load) was considered important by the designer.

Thus the Durgapuja pavilion as a temporary urban infill responds to the particularities of the neighborhood, the site, and traffic pattern. After the celebrations are over, the structures are dismantled, a process that takes from a day to a week before the street and locality are returned to their "normal" routines. And now imagine about 2000 of these pavilions built at the same time, each one with a different design, a good many—about 400—of which are very large, with

Figure 12.7 Purnendu Dey and Snehasish Maity, Scaffolding of *pandal* of Badamtala Ashar Sangha, 2017

Source: Copyright Swati Chattopadhyay.

the most well-known ones attracting crowds of 100,000 or more every day. In addition, about 500 *pujas* are organized within housing estates, apartment complexes, and gated communities, and about the same number are held in private residences, many of which are accessible to the public. This stunning bottom-up mobilization of urban space and city life is made possible by the successful deployment of an urban ethos that is underlined by a radical notion of contingency.

Radical Contingency

Contingency is fundamental to human agency: "to understand oneself as agent is to understand the contingency of *all* human practices" (Mapel 1990). As unpredictability of a future event, as an unplanned/unforeseen occurrence, it is the potential for change and improvisation inherent in our interaction with the world. It is the silver lining in the negative connotation of uncertainty and the possibility of newness in our reading of the world.

In spatial organization, the multiplication of contingencies that in a particular view of planning might appear unstructured/incoherent/risky is the basis for the emergence of fresh structures that gather meaning within particular conjunctures of time, location, and milieu. Rather than attempting to abate all contingencies and thereby stilling the temporal horizon (acting like a fixed object of universal validity in empty homogenous time), spatial actions that leverage contingency as a productive moment are mindful of various overlapping temporalities and the permeability of temporal boundaries.

In much of the Global South, the canny reading/appropriation of minimal resources and inadequate public infrastructure is a necessary response to the multiplication of contingencies resulting from the planned and unplanned limitations of the state. In this form contingency is the lifeblood of popular agency that often has a contestory relation with civil society and its elite-centric predeterminations. City authorities tend to read such negotiations of contingency variously as "encroachment" (on public space), "illegal occupation" (of private property), "poaching" of civic infrastructure (through drawing off water from the mains or electricity from the nearest transformer). Whether one opposes or approves these appropriations there is an implicit understanding that these actions are *transformative*, in a manner that digital piracy can be transformative (Philip 2005; Liang 2011). What is overlooked in the denunciations and defense of these actions is the *spatial process* these actions entail—and that it might serve as a useful model to learn about architecture and urban interventions if we are to be serious about heeding durational claims, fungibility, relation between soft and hard materials and technologies, and reversibility. The process that relies on contingency and its affordances elicit modes of innovation/inventiveness that deserve careful analysis. In the balance of the essay I will briefly touch upon these affordances, taking the example of the Bakulbagan Sarbojanin pavilion design of 2017 as the key example.

Ground Rules

Durgapuja is a five-day festival based on the lunar calendar. Traditionally, planning for the fall festival began about mid-year. Idol-makers started preparing in summer, and *puja* committees would meet in August to make plans and commission the idols. *Pandal* making started at most a week prior to the beginning of festivities and lighting was installed and last-minute decorative touches added on the evening of *sashti*, the first day of the *puja*. On *dashami*, the concluding day of the *puja*, the idols were immersed in a nearby water body.

In the last 20 years, Durgapuja has witnessed a major shift in scale—both the number of *pujas* has increased (doubled in the last 20 years) and the size, budget and design of a large number of these *pujas* have increased manifold (Chattopadhyay 2012). Durgapuja has become an art venue (Guha-Thakurta 2015). For the largest *pujas* now artists are commissioned even before the previous year's Durgapuja concludes, thus making the planning process and fund-raising a year-long affair. By February, artists have sourced their materials and sketched out their design plans. The prefabricated parts of the *pandal* produced in workshops scattered across the city and provinces go to work from that time. After the laborers and construction crew leave the site, having made the space ready for the religious event, the secular time of the festival (shopping, cultural performances, feasting, *pandal* hopping) continues to intersect with the ritual time of the ceremony that consists of daily offerings and lengthy liturgical practices in the mornings and evenings.

The municipality allows *puja* committees two months lead time to occupy public space in the city. The permission process requires approval from multiple agencies—the police, fire services, power supply companies, municipal bodies who control urban land use and allocation, and the environmental control board—now conducted through a single-window e-portal. Construction of the large pavilions begins two or three months prior to the commencement of the *pujas*, and this extended time in excess of two months must have the approval of the police authorities. Most venues take from a month to a few days to be completed, creating a heterogeneous temporal pattern of *pandal* construction. The three months during which the venues take shape and the few days to a week after the conclusion of the *puja* when the pavilions remain on the site in the process of being dismantled—a total duration of about three and a half months–produce recognizable if unevenly distributed spatial knots in the city fabric.

In terms of traffic circulation, as roads get increasingly closed off with the approach of the event, the most affected areas are the northern and southern parts of the city that have a preponderance of *pujas* on the street. In comparison, most *pujas* in the outermost wards in the south, west, and east are held in parks, open spaces, and vacant lots. It is important to note that there are fewer per square kilometer of streets in these outermost wards than in the inner city. Immediately prior to the five days of festivities the Kolkata Police overlays on this micro-scale changes in traffic pattern additional traffic regulations at the macro level. For example, vehicular traffic is restricted on a large number of streets; car parking is not allowed along major arteries (these roads have restricted parking in any case), and vehicular space is cordoned off from sidewalks with temporary bamboo "fences" to prevent indiscriminate jay walking; bus routes are altered; goods vehicles are barred from the city during peak hours; and special police arrangements are made particularly in view of the "big *pujas*" (Nesakumar 2017).[6]

The changes in patterns of access impact the daily lives of residents beyond their impact on commuting time. For a couple of months, a closed off street in a neighborhood might become a parking space and/or a play space for children. When a *pandal* is located in a daily market area which does not have a permanent infrastructure, the *pandal* under construction might provide that infrastructure—the platform is used by vendors and the bamboo structure used for displaying wares. In other words, the *pandal* structure is simply incorporated into the daily life and rhythm of the residents who come to view it as much an affordance to inhabitation as an obstacle to movement.

This mode of crafting and utilizing space is dependent on cultivating a certain habit of seeing the urban fabric that does not settle for one or the other, but one *and* the other. From the perspective of the neighborhood community and the organizers the street is not merely appropriable space but one that is shared and has overlapping claims. The infringement on everyday vehicular circulation or interruption of business is not seen as a right, but as something that needs to be tolerated and accommodated.

Ephemeral Architecture: Radical Contingency

Fungibility

The art of *pandal* making relies on this view of public space as fungible—changeable as the need arises—and culls together fragments of the urban fabric to create a venue that remains open-ended in its construction logic. Crafting the *puja* venue means particularizing it for a short duration, investing it with meaning without foreclosing its transformative potential for another as yet unanticipated purpose. This approach is not to be confused with creating a "multi-purpose" space that has only generic attributes. The space occupied by the *pandal* is open to other uses *and* it is given over to a particular task during a specific duration when that task is given priority over others.

The favoring of bamboo as the primary material of construction serves this principle of fungibility—its ability to sustain infinite interchangeability *and* specific articulation. In that sense bamboo is doubly fungible. The short life span of the *pandal* enables this dual attribute to be maintained, and it is here that it differs from more permanent construction in bamboo (e.g., bamboo house construction).

The choice of bamboo at first may seem largely pragmatic—its light weight and soft technology lessens capital and transportation costs. Bamboo structures do not necessitate elaborate foundation work and rely on their mesh-like structural arrangement for strength. Thus bamboo is suitable for temporary structures where a certain amount of risk is considered acceptable. The festival season is known for tropical storms, and the *pandals* must protect against heavy rainfall and wind force. As in post-hole construction, bamboo poles are inserted in holes a few inches (3–6") deep for the basic structural support. In substantial pavilions *sal* timber posts are used intermittently for vertical support to ensure that the roof load is safely carried to the ground. Typically, the bamboo poles are used with minimal sizing and dressing both as a cost-saving measure and to retain its reusability. They are highly interchangeable and the longest pieces are kept for roofing. In the last two decades finishing the bamboo structure with wooden battens that give the structure a more regular profile has become popular. Once the enclosure and roof is defined, wooden planks on a bamboo/*sal* base are used to create the floor, stairs, and ramps, and light wall materials (fabric or corrugated iron sheets) are augmented with additional layers to give the decorative effect: thermacol, paper, glass, clay, plastic, wrought iron, etc.

The versatility of bamboo that contributes to the artistry of the structures resides in its flexibility that helps in shaping a vast array of forms, often in impressively improvisatory ways, within a short time. Unlike prefabricated construction materials, the bamboo pieces are not used as modular elements. The kind of modularity that characterizes modernist architecture and avant-garde autoconstruction would restrict its possibilities. It is its iterative capacity (as opposed to modularity) that maximizes the potential for a large variety of forms. In some *pandals* wood and to a lesser extent steel members are used, but in a manner that obeys the construction rules of light bamboo construction.

Innovation

In today's Durgapuja milieu that places a premium on artistry, designers have to validate their ideas and prove their worth by winning awards. The desire for innovation has turned designer Bimal Samanta to focus on the multiple possibilities in the materials of construction. Bucking the trend of *pandal* design, he insists on a monochromatic palette to "surprise" the viewer with a presentation of spaces and surfaces that lifts the ordinary way of seeing materials such as bamboo and iron from their usual modes into works of architectonic virtuosity. For Samanta planning begins right after the conclusion of the previous year's festivities.

For the Bakul Bagan Sarbojanin *pandal* in 2017, Samanta sourced a special type of bamboo from the state of Tripura. According to him, the material suggested the design (Figure 12.8).

Figure 12.8 Bimal Samanta, Panel detail of *pandal* of Bakulbagan Sarbojanin, 2017
Source: Copyright Swati Chattopadhyay.

Several months of experiment with the strength and design potential of the material in his workshop yielded a panoply of patterns which when arranged in panels constituted the spatial ensemble. At one level, the *pandal* became a sheer display of creative treatment of the material and skilled workmanship: vertical sections cut through the center of the bamboo arranged in layers to create a sense of depth, round cross-sections of various diameters and members of various widths arranged in patterns to produce definition and contrast. At another level, it was an essay on the ethics of production that heeds the time-sense of Durgapuja as an event and the role of the *pandal* as an urban infill.

While Samanta had a design conception and a plan in mind, the majority of the design decisions evolved as the construction continued, allowing him to change his mind in response to the craftsmen's work, fix mistakes, and fine-tune the design. He considered this ability to react and redesign on the spot a virtue of *pandal* design. His designs are labor intensive and resource conscious, but predicated on discovering new potential during the construction process. Among the 14–16 workers who worked on site a good many were taught skills or taught themselves skills that they had never practiced before. Someone with no experience in welding steel or chiseling bamboo would learn the skills in a few days and improvise methods to produce unplanned visual effects.

The bamboo was treated with a fire retardant but otherwise left unpainted. It changed color and tone during the six months it took from sourcing the material to the completion of construction, and the lighting design picked up on these unpredictable nuances. The extraordinary attention given to details and finishing and the open-endedness of the design process yielded a product that even the designer could not have envisioned at the outset. Indeed, there is no expectation that the product would be fully designed before construction begins. Designers are hired by organizers without any sense of the actual plan and what the product form and construction might be. The contingency of the process and the context are prime ingredients of innovation.

Softness

The structural frame for this *pandal* was made of narrow-gauged steel bars that were welded on site to form a cage that carried the roof load. The thinness of the steel members also meant minimal damage to the sidewalk and street on which these steel bars rested as in post-hole construction. Around these steel bars Samanta planned wall sections of varying thickness by introducing layers of patterned bamboo, each wall section being designed differently (Figure 12.9). The layered depth of these enclosing walls and partitions allowed introduction of hidden lights to further articulate the design and enhance the lightness—ephemeral nature—of the structure.

The lightness of the pavilion as an urban intervention was evident in the manner in which the gateways and the subsidiary spaces were designed. The sitting space—an outdoor lounge of sorts—was located in a rather unsightly unpaved vacant lot, used for parking cars during the remainder of the year. Whereas a typical design response might have been to enclose the space with colored fabric to hide the peeling paint of the boundary walls and the unfinished look of the lot, Samanta's design focused on the ceiling of the sitting space. The intriguing filigree pattern of the ceiling moved attention away from the site's unsightliness and towards the sky, taking advantage of a tree that brightened the corner of the lot (Figure 12.10).

For those who noticed, Samanta's pavilion carried the impress of his signature, and he was self-conscious of the parameters of the design process that produced his signature design. Every

Figure 12.9 Bimal Samanta, Wall detail of *pandal* of Bakulbagan Sarbojanin, 2017
Source: Copyright Swati Chattopadhyay.

Figure 12.10 Bimal Samanta, Ceiling over outdoor lounge, *pandal* of Bakulbagan Sarbojanin, 2017

Source: Copyright Swati Chattopadhyay.

conversation brought forth comparisons with the previous year's award-winning *pandal* of Shibmandir Sarbonjanin and the other *pandal* he designed in 2017 in iron and steel for Ajeya Sanghati. The latter was entirely constructed of recycled wrought iron and scrap steel, but was assembled in a manner that did not differ substantially from the all-bamboo construction. The softness of his approach was encouraged by the short duration of the event, and the premise of leaving the site as is at the completion of the event.

One could also argue that the deployment of soft and hard materials and the softness of the edges that gave character to his design at Bakulbagan Sarbojanin were drawing upon a vocabulary of the everyday spaces of cities such as Kolkata. His structure touched the surroundings gently but as in most other *pandals* it relied on the neighboring buildings for structural support and formal coherence (Figure 12.11). It also required buy-in from the residents of these buildings for the permission process and for the ensuing construction to proceed. When the *pandal* was dismantled, the holes made on the ground were filled in, and very few traces remained of its emplacement on the streets or side walks. This soft approach to the urban fabric is enabled by the corresponding softness—give—of the street edges and sidewalks as they are inhabited. There is a level of accommodation and acceptance of yielding to a new purpose in the use of neighborhood infrastructure, without forfeiting the present occupation of space for good, that makes these temporary infills possible.

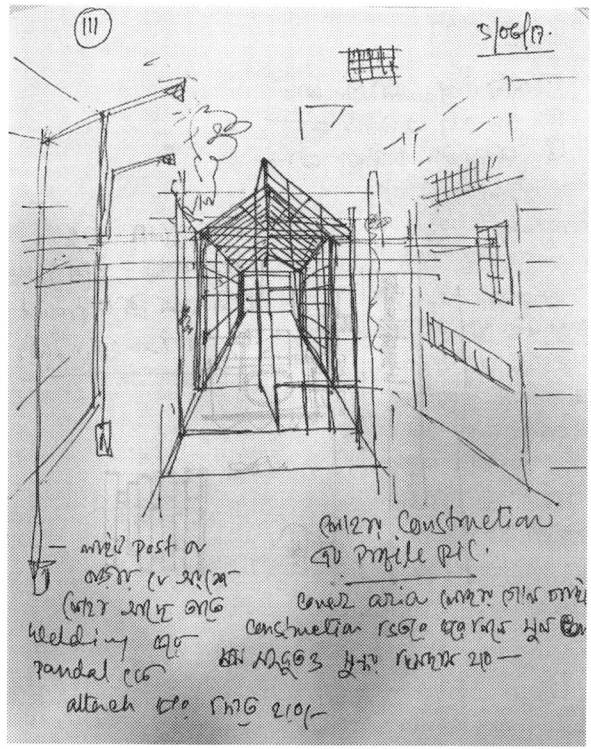

Figure 12.11 Bimal Samanta, Sketch for *pandal* of Bakulbagan Sarbojanin, 2017
Source: Courtesy Bimal Samanta.

Reversibility

As the concluding event of the festivities, the Kolkata Police oversees the immersion of the deities in the Hooghly River and attempts to regulate the sorting of insoluble and toxic materials before the clay idols are taken mid-stream and plunged in the water. Police boats ensure that the flotsam from the frames of the idols do not create a logjam. While the materials used for building the structures are typically recyclable, the application of decorative materials that use lead-based paints and components that do not easily up-cycle or down-cycle remains a public concern.

Nevertheless, Durgapuja *pandals* are designed on the principle of reversibility, and have been so, long before reversibility became a watchword in sustainability discourse. Once the event has concluded, the ropes are untied, the components are sorted, and all materials including the bamboo and wood piles are moved from the site. The structural materials used for construction are reused for other purposes, primarily for similar constructions for other festive events. It helps that the mode of assembly requires minimal alteration of the structural components: the coconut coir and fabric cords that are used to tie the bamboo and timber members are undone without damaging either the ropes or the bamboo/timber. *Pandals* such as the ones designed by Samanta are often bought by organizations in part or whole to be reused in another venue, and the designer may or may not have much say in how the components are reassembled.

If this sounds like the reinstallation of public artworks in other parts of the world, it is well to remember that Durgapuja *pandals* as "installation art" far predates the concept of installation art as it is used in the contemporary art world. But more important perhaps is to remember that its dual characteristics—context specificity and structural generalizability, its reversibility and cyclicity in anticipation of future return—makes it exceptional as installation art. Araeen's bamboo installation with which I began this essay could not be relocated without doing substantial damage to the structure. Indeed, it would be more efficient and cheaper to construct Araeen's bamboo structure anew if it were to be reinstalled in a different site. Most bamboo *pandal* structures avoid this eventuality as the reuse of its structural components is also a source of revenue.

The event leaves marks on the physical and social fabric in multiple ways, however. Painted patterns on the asphalt and stray decorations linger as do some Sunday morning and evening gatherings of neighbors to mull over this year's event, and to plan for the next year. The Kolkata Police do their briefing of Durgapuja policing immediately at the conclusion of the event. But for the most part, the changes in the rules of traffic arrangement and the return of the *puja* site to its everyday purpose of street, sidewalk, park, and vacant lot occurs without fanfare as normal busyness returns to these locations.

Concluding Traces

The short duration of the event brings to the fore socio-spatial relations and spatial affordance that might otherwise remain unnoticed, and generates new claims to space and recognition that would not have been otherwise possible. This includes the capacity of a dense urban fabric to absorb the stress of road closure, infrastructural overload (transportation/electricity/water supply/garbage disposal) and additional footfalls by stretching its existing infrastructure. Or it may be a low-income neighborhood claiming equivalence with its upper-class brethren through inventive design schemes made possible by the agency of clubs, celebrities, and political parties.

Durgapuja is a major source of income and upward mobility for a large number of artisans, designers, and suppliers, and the public focus of the event makes it an important venue for mobilizing community and political aspirations. Several current politicians from center and center-right parties have honed their organizing skills by acting as *puja* organizers. And those without any such prior experience, from the municipal to the state level, are eager to get into the organizing fray as they view the experience of managing a Durgapuja, and the social connections one makes in the process, as crucial to creating their political profile and shaping their voting constituencies. Such constituencies need not be local, and the imagination of a larger public—a larger political community—is always implicit in the assumption of Durgapuja as a platform for constructing or bolstering one's political profile or the agenda of a political party.

In terms of the urban fabric, ephemeral architecture of this kind, allied with the annual nature of the event, anticipates future returns and in some ways the site remains prepared to foster such anticipation. For many organizations, the *pandal* is built in the same location every year. While the design may be different each year, the urban context to a large extent dictates the *pandal*'s size and emplacement. The ephemeral and the perennial congeal as points of recognition and acquire legitimacy through representation. It is not difficult to notice that community organizers foresee more permanent impact on the community through these means. A club may decide to take a more "permanent" possession of a green island they had occupied during the *puja*, aided by political backing, or refurbish their club house if they had managed to save some resources from the festival proceedings. A tea-stall on the sidewalk that popped up during the event may become a favored site of gatherings, giving it a longer lease on life.

Such outcomes are not entirely accidental. Durgapuja *pandals* have morphological and temporal semblance with the myriad ephemeral structures that define public spaces in cities such as

Kolkata: food carts, hawker stalls, wall writings, billboards, street games, and gatherings. As an event of short duration they enhance and highlight as they build upon the affordances of this ordinary perennial fabric which is the sourcebook of radical contingency.

Notes

1 Even those who used structural components for their sculptures such as Anthony Caro, Araeen noted, were invested in composition in which hierarchy of size and shape described the form.
2 In this context see, the description of one of Rasheed Araeen's exhibition proposals as "normal occurrence, albeit within a particular milieu" in Rasheed Araeen, *Making Myself Visible* (1984: 15).
3 See Daniel Abramson's essay in this volume.
4 To this we may add a longer history of scholarship going back to the 1980s on world fairs and their critical role in shaping architectural and political discourse. For more on ephemerality and obsolescence see Daniel Abramson's, AbdouMaliq Simone's, and Arijit Sen's essays in this volume.
5 This bias in the literature—with its emphasis on the role of the state and architect/planners—might well be a product of what scholars have chosen as their investigative focus. The reverse side of the urban weave would probably elicit stories of popular appropriation of urban space for pagan rituals, cults of saints, games, and entertainment that had scant state sanction.
6 In 2017 the Kolkata Police planned for 156 of these "big *pujas*" among the approximately 2499 community *pujas*.

References

Abramson, D. M. (2016) *Obsolescence*, Chicago: University of Chicago Press.
Aikens, N. (ed.) (2017) *Rasheed Araeen*, Zurich: JRP/Ringier.
Araeen, R. (1984) *Making Myself Visible*, London.
Banerjee, P. (2006) *The Politics of Time: Primitives and History Writing in a Colonial Society*, New Delhi: Oxford University Press.
Bayat, A. (1997) "Un-civil society: the politics of the 'informal people'," *Third World Quarterly* 18, 1: 53–72.
Bonnemaison, C. and Macy, C. (eds) (2008) *Festival Architecture*, London: Routledge.
Chase, J. L., Crawford, M., and Kaliski, J. (1999) *Everyday Urbanism*, New York: Monacelli Press.
Chattopadhyay, S. (2012) *Unlearning the City: Infrastructure in a New Optical Field*, Minneapolis: University of Minnesota Press.
Chow, R. (2018) "In the field," Mapping Urban Materiality Symposium, University of California, Santa Barbara, April.
Dhaka Art Summit (2018) "Bearing point 1, politics: the most architectural thing to do," Dhaka Art Summit '18 Exhibition Guide.
Guha-Thakurta, T. (2015) *In the Name of the Goddess: The Durga Pujas of Contemporary Kolkata*, Delhi: Primus Books.
Hailey, C. (2009) *Camps: A Guide to 21st-Century Space*, Cambridge: MIT Press.
Hazan, E. (2015) *A History of the Barricade*, New York: Verso.
Henkin, D. (1998) *City Reading: Written Words and Public Space in Antebellum New York*, New York: Columbia University Press.
Herscher, A. (2017) *Displacements: Architecture and Refugee*, Berlin: Sternberg Press.
Holston, J. (2009) *Insurgent Citizenship: Disjunctions of Modernity and Democracy in Brazil*, Princeton: Princeton University Press.
Holston, J. and Appadurai, A. (1996), "Cities and citizenship," *Public Culture* 2, 6: 187–204.
Hosagrahar, J. (1992) "The city as durbar: theater and power in imperial Delhi," in Nezar Alsayyad (ed.) *Forms of Dominance: On the Architecture and Urbanism of the Colonial Experience*, London: Avebury & Grower, 83–105.
Hou, J. (2010) *Guerilla Urbanism and the Remaking of Contemporary Cities*, New York: Routledge.
Liang, L. (2011) "Beyond representation: the figure of the pirate," in Mario Biagioli, Peter Jaszi, and Martha Woodmansee (eds) *Making and Unmaking Intellectual Property: Creative Production in Legal and Cultural Perspective*, Chicago: University of Chicago Press, 353–376.

Mapel, D. R. (1990) "Civil association and the idea of contingency," *Political Theory* 18, 3 (August): 392–410.

Martin, C. J. (2011) "'Non-compositional and non-hierarchical', Rasheed Araeen's search for the conceptual and the political in British sculpture," in Rebecca Peabody (eds) *Anglo-American Exchange in Sculpture, 1945–1975*, Los Angeles: J. Paul Getty Museum.

Mehrotra, R. and Vera, F. (eds) (2015) *Kumbh Mela: Mapping the Ephemeral Megacity*, Ostfildern, Germany: Hatje Cantz Verlag.

Mehrotra, R. and Vera, F. (2016) *Ephemeral Urbanism: Cities in Constant Flux*, Santiago, Chile: ARQ Ediciones.

Nesakumar, V.S., Deputy Commissioner of Police, Traffic Department, Kolkata (2017) *Kolkata Traffic Police. Police Arrangements: Durga Puja and Lakshmi Puja, 2017*, September 17.

Philip, K. (2005) "What is a technological author? The pirate function and intellectual property," *Postcolonial Studies* 8, 2: 199–218.

San Juan, R. M. (2001) *Rome: A City Out of Print*, Minneapolis: University of Minnesota Press.

Sen, A. (2017) "Discarding Corb's shoes: marginal voices and local histories from the urban edge," in Manu Sobti (ed.) *Chandigarh Rethink: Transforming Ruralities and Edge(ness) in Global Urbanities*, San Francisco: ORA Editions, 64–74.

Simone, A. (2004) *For a City Yet to Come: Changing African Lives in Four African Cities*, Durham, NC: Duke University Press.

Simone, A. (2014) *Jakarta: Drawing the City Near*, Minneapolis: University of Minnesota Press.

Simone, A. and Pieterse, E. (2017) *New Urban Worlds: Inhabiting Dissonant Times*, London: Wiley.

Upton, D. (2008) *Another City: Urban Life and Spaces in the New Republic*, New Haven, CT: Yale University Press.

Part III
Alterity

13

Inhabiting Ruins

The Ministry of Defense and the Limits of Occupation in Monrovia, Liberia

Danny Hoffman

In 2012, the Ministry of Defense building in the Liberian capital, Monrovia, was a vast, empty landscape (Figure 13.1).[1] The hulking structure originated with a modernizing campaign launched by Samuel Doe, the junior military officer who took over the Liberian presidency following a 1980 coup d'état. Monumental architecture, for Doe as for so many other political leaders, was a project of state making and personal aggrandizement. The Ministry of Defense, however, was never finished. War broke out in Liberia at the end of 1989. The Israeli firm contracted to design and construct the building completed its concrete supports but little more. Even before the fighting reached Monrovia, the Ministry was a skeleton, though a structurally sound one.

For more than a decade, hundreds of fighters with the Government of Liberia Armed Forces squatted in the Ministry's ruins, ostensibly to defend the man who ultimately succeeded Doe, Liberia's warlord president Charles Taylor. They created within the space a vibrant if crowded community. When Taylor was ousted in 2003, the men remained in the building and maintained the roughly built vertical community.

When the government of Taylor's successor, Ellen Johnson Sirleaf, ordered the building's occupants to leave by mid-2010, most of the young men who had occupied the space had few options. Monrovia's existing slum settlements are grossly overcrowded. Many of those evicted from the Ministry of Defense now live on the beach, in garbage dumps, in graveyards, in the swamp, or in other unfinished buildings around town.

By the start of the 2016 rainy season, six years after their eviction, the Ministry of Defense remained virtually empty. Major Sandi was one of very few residents allowed to stay in the empty Ministry of Defense as caretaker and night watchman. Sandi has now spent more than a decade and a half as a "temporary" resident of the building. Today he lives virtually alone in a closet, surrounded by thousands of vacant square feet of reinforced concrete.

When I asked Major Sandi what he hopes will be done with the building, he pauses. This, apparently, is not a question he has ever been asked before. "Maybe a hotel. It would make a nice hotel." My conversation with Major Sandi was one that was repeated, in various forms, throughout Monrovia in the decades during and after the war. Large communities of ex-combatants and their dependents informally occupied a range of structures in the city. Government ministries, factories, schools, hospitals, and hotels had all served as barrack spaces, refugee

163

Figure 13.1 The interior courtyard of Monrovia's Ministry of Defense
Source: Copyright Danny Hoffman.

camps, and as squatter settlements in a city in which housing stock has always been limited, a city that experienced a radical population influx during the war.

By 2012, much of that population was being evicted. In a few instances the Liberian government did undertake renovation projects on the reclaimed structures. More often, however, the buildings sat empty, the subject of wild rumors and protracted legal contests. Their former occupants, meanwhile, struggled to find habitable places within the city. Like the displaced population of the Ministry of Defense, many found themselves in the city's interstitial spaces, leading a semi-nomadic urban existence as they occupied and were then forced out of one space after another.

Extraordinarily, these displacements generated little if any active resistance. Though the young men who found themselves adrift in the city were frequently veterans of one or more armed forces, and though a rhetoric of militarism and a return to war pervaded everyday conversations, forceful claims to the occupied buildings they had inhabited for years were simply not part of the post-war politics of Monrovia.

It is a striking absence given the global context in which these dynamics occurred. This was, after all, a moment in which citizens of cities around the globe articulated forceful demands for their rights to the city through various manifestations of the "occupy" movement. The so-called Arab Spring that swept North Africa and the Middle East was both attributed to, and largely expressed through, conflicts over rights to the city. Land invasions and squatters' rights movements took place across the African continent simultaneously. All of this was well known, and closely followed, by Monrovia's urban residents. And yet in this city, a city facing a state of emergency vis-à-vis its built environment and with a recent history of communal violence, a popular claim on the city's available built forms failed to materialize. Why this apparent failure of a popular urban politics in Monrovia? Why, when as David Harvey put it, there was "a spirit of protest and revolt that spread contagiously through urban networks" (2012: 116) around the globe, why did that same fervor to claim the ruin forms of global modernism not take hold in this post-war African city?

In this chapter, I approach this absence as a problem of, and for, contemporary architecture. In contrast to such celebrated case studies as the Torre David in Caracas or Rome's Corviale, the Ministry of Defense never served as a site for staking political claims on urban territory. While on the surface the Ministry would seem the perfect embodiment of what Edensor and others have called the modernist ruin's potential to "provoke the speculation about how space and materiality might be interpreted, experienced and imagined otherwise" (2005: 330), the Ministry of Defense remained, even after more than a decade of occupation, a structure stubbornly unavailable as a site for articulating new urban visions. The building was a ruin, but not a blank canvas on which to project novel or enduring claims to urban belonging.

A significant factor in that obstinacy lay in the material form of the building itself. Slavoj Žižek (1997: 3–4) has argued that the contradictions and fictions of a political ideology can be read in the architecture that it inspires. But the corollary is that, contradictory though it may be, some architectures express their ideology so completely that they can be impossible to reinterpret or resist. A growing literature in architecture, urban design, and planning argues that the future of architecture lies not in "making buildings" but in "a politics of selectively taking them apart" (Stoner 2012). This is especially the case in cities of the Global South, cities with a large and growing population of urban poor and cities dominated by an aging or ruined modernist infrastructure. An "architectural" reading of Monrovia's Ministry of Defense, however, serves as a useful starting point for asking how built forms themselves might resist such deconstruction, and what the limits of such a politics might be.

Danny Hoffman

Excessive Architecture

Despite its half-finished and badly damaged state, the Ministry of Defense is an unmistakably brutalist building. Often used to describe (or decry) any monumental concrete structure, brutalism, or more accurately "The New Brutalism," has a more specific history that, in the Ministry of Defense at least, is not easily shed.

The architects most strongly associated with brutalism as an architectural movement are the British designers Alison and Peter Smithson. Though they built surprisingly little, their extensive body of writing and paper architecture had an outsized influence on the development of modern design from the 1950s well into the 1980s, and a disproportionate impact on African architecture in particular (see Elleh 1997).

The Smithsons began their interventions in modern architecture with a radical vision for devastated post-war London. For the Smithsons and their cohort of young architects, the English architectural establishment's program for rebuilding British cities was a betrayal of both the progressive politics and the internationalism of early modern masters like Le Corbusier and Mies van der Rohe (Banham 2011 [1955]: 15–18, 1966; Crosby 2011 [1955]: 17–18; Smithson 2001: 41). Their response was a severe design program that they considered an ethical rather than an aesthetic intervention. Architecture should not be a tool for rebuilding the state. It was an opportunity to retool post-war subjectivity for the modern world. "Brutalism tries to face up to a mass-produced society," they famously wrote, and "drag a rough poetry out of the confused and powerful forces which are at work" (Smithson and Smithson 2011 [1957]: 37).

In an extensive analysis of what this meant in practice, Reyner Banham (2011 [1955]) describes an architecture based on the idea that a building's lay-out should be immediately clear, ("formal legibility of plan"); that its physical support structures should be obvious ("clear exhibition of structure"); and that its materials should be undecorated ("valuation of materials for their inherent qualities 'as found'"). This tripartite definition of brutalism was a consequence of the Marxian understanding of class antagonism that circulated among the Smithsons' artistic circles. Freedom for the working classes needed to begin with truth telling and dismantling Marx's "camera obscura of ideology," the masking of the real conditions (partly through architecture) that made it impossible for workers to perceive the causes of their exploitation. Formal symmetry and the undisguised exhibition of structure and material were part of a larger project of peeling back all manner of dishonesty, projecting instead a more truthful and more powerful image, an unsubtle declaration of "the inherent nobility of man" (Smithson 2001: 42).

Inside and out, brutalist structures were meant to make visible the raw essence of their materials in a consistent statement, a statement selling a singular idea. It is an architecture of "surfaces" (Leatherbarrow and Mostafavi 2002), meaning an architecture that leaves little space for ambiguous or indeterminate experiences. Brutalist architecture should intervene into the everyday worlds of those who come into contact with it by clearly broadcasting unmistakable messages. Modernist architecture as a machine for the production of images is a theme that has run through much of the critical literature (see, for example, Forty 2012; Zimmerman 2004). But in brutalism, with its emphasis on the potential in both form and material to communicate political messages, the logic of the image is particularly dominating.

Though explicitly anti-statist in its application in Britain, ironically it was largely in the service of the state that the network of architects and designers in dialogue with the Smithsons carried the brutalist aesthetic outside of Europe—most notably to cities in the colonial and early postcolonial Global South (Chalfin 2014; Fry and Drew 1956; Hess 2000; Liscombe 2006; le Roux 2003; le Roux and Uduku 2004; Uduku 2006). Brutalism's philosophical underpinnings fit with the ethos of independence and modernization sweeping Africa, and its muscularity and heavy-handedness mirrored the drive of African elites to consolidate and advertise their new authority. What began as a politically progressive, avant-garde architectural movement in postwar European housing quickly spread outward to become a major component in the complex function of modern infrastructure in Africa. While it bequeaths its "modernity" on African cities, it does so within highly prescribed limits and at the cost of uncompromising and unsparing political subjection (Larkin 2008: 245).

When Samuel Doe contracted to have Defense built, what he sought was the advertising potential inherent in the building. Doe needed an architecture that would immediately confirm a simple but uncontestable message: that his soldiers had, through force of arms, seized the state and that they had the strength to keep it. This was in no way a building for the Liberian people. The Ministry of Defense was about militarized state authority.

What are the consequences of an architecture so saturated with the message of state? All architecture is communicative. But what of architecture whose sole message is that of the power and authority of martial sovereignty? Given that militarized state authority is the singular *parti pris* of the Ministry of Defense, its strongest analogies are not the architecture of other postcolonial ministry buildings, even those in cities such as Chandigarh, Brasilia, Dodoma, or Abuja that adhere to the principles of the Modern Movement. A closer built analog is, rather, the tectonic logic in the total control architecture of the postmodern prison.

In her book on Supermax prisons in the U.S., Lorna Rhodes (2004) describes spaces in which architecture becomes a tool for exercising sovereignty in the most absolute terms. The result is not a space of discipline, as in the Foucauldian reading of the modern prison. Prisoners subject to this total confinement do not emerge as social beings. "The prison environment," Rhodes writes, "could not be better designed to activate a sense of threat to the coherence of the self" (2004: 56).

This post-disciplinary prison succeeds, if that is the correct term, because it creates an environment that is uninhabitable. It is "non-subject" producing (Butler 2004) because those who are subject to it do not know how to live there. They can move through these spaces, even reside in them for extended periods. But they cannot dwell in them in any meaningful way. These are spaces that do not allow their inhabitants to imagine alternative futures. It is an architecture that works actively to mitigate the human capacity for imagination and experimentation.

There is no question that the Ministry of Defense building is inhospitable. But its excessiveness goes much further. The way in which the building amplifies its brutalist aesthetics creates a space of Supermax-like control, a singularity of (state) purpose. The rigid set of formal characteristics, envisioned by the Smithsons and their cohort, became, in the Liberian context, the scene of the violence of authoritarianism and urban subjugation, a site of non-subject-producing, alien space in which even long-term occupants of the building could never fully learn to dwell (Heidegger 1993).

An Aesthetics of Images

In plan, the Ministry is an almost perfect square. Identical octagonal turrets stand at each outside corner. A massive inner courtyard at the heart of the structure exaggerates the rigid geometry. Though the façades of the building are badly scarred (and in some cases incomplete), the intended design was clearly a repetitive pattern of windows set in shallow bays. A viewer would be able to immediately understand the lay-out of the structure, interior and exterior, from virtually any vantage point. Like all brutalist buildings the Ministry of Defense would have no secrets and no internal hierarchy. The hierarchy the Ministry establishes is with the world around it (Figure 13.2).

Figure 13.2 Exterior of the Ministry of Defense from across what was intended to be the parade grounds
Source: Copyright Danny Hoffman.

The Ministry of Defense does so by making visibility a crucial part of its program. But it inverts the politics of vision. This is a building that reserves for itself the right to look. Set on a slight hill, it is impossible to view the Ministry from anywhere except below it. There are no window openings of any kind until what would effectively be the structure's second floor. Recessing the repetitive glazing on the façade de-emphasizes them as visual access points into the building, but exaggerates their eye-like function. They look out much more effectively than they look in. Consistent with brutalist image-logic, the building is immediately visually graspable from any angle, but anyone within sight of the building is also powerfully aware of being simultaneously caught in the building's gaze.

Only two elements break the symmetry. Perversely, both underscore, rather than disrupt, the sense of an unassailable sovereign that stands apart from the people below. The first is a massive viewing stand on the top floor of the building (Figure 13.3). The sculptural stairs and benches are positioned to give a commanding view of the large open ground in front, a perch over the parade field from which Doe and his senior military officers could personally inspect their troops.

Here again the form and placement of this architectural feature would seem to work against it being understood, and appropriated, as anything other than an artifact of a state of emergency and the imposition of military authority. The steps and seating are outsized and inhumanly shaped. They seem deliberately distorted or caricatured, as though sculpted to accommodate what Mbembe (1992) once called the "vulgar" aesthetics of the African big man with his swollen body and grossly scaled appetites. The viewing stand is positioned so high above the earth that it establishes no relationship to the ground; it would be strikingly impractical and

Inhabiting Ruins

Figure 13.3 The Ministry's viewing stands
Source: Copyright Danny Hoffman.

ineffective as a space for publicly dramatizing the connection between a military leader and his troops. The view from the stand is sweeping and imperial, but it creates no interface between exterior and interior. It offers only a god's eye view of seemingly unlimited surveillance.

The second break in the symmetry of the Ministry is an inexplicable protrusion from the front of the building (Figure 13.4). It is possible that the sculpted form was intended to support some elaborate *porte cochère* in the original building design. More likely, however, it was simply intended as a strong sculptural element, the sole decorative feature on an otherwise Spartan façade. Regardless of its intended use, however, the impact is much the same as with the viewing platform: it relates to something larger than human. Its scale is disproportionate to those who might occupy the space. As a result it has none of the effect of mediating inside and outside at the building's entry. If it is proportionate to anything recognizable, it is to the superhuman persona cultivated by big men rulers like Doe and, even more so, his successor Charles Taylor. Once again, this is an excessive architecture that renders even the most mundane of functions, entry and exit from a building, absurd.

This problem of scale runs throughout the building. The rooftop of the Ministry was allegedly designed to offer multiple landing pads for the helicopters of the president and his chief ministers. The towers of the corner stairwells are massive fortifications rather than simple passageways. The interior courtyard is so dwarfed by the surrounding edifice that it feels more like a gladiatorial arena than an inner sanctum. These outsized capacities are reflected in the way Monrovians describe the building. General Henry Dubah, a former chief of staff for the Liberian Army, claimed improbably that the roof of the building was large enough to serve as a runway for planes. Speaking during a court case that challenged proposals to demolish the Ministry, Monrovia lawyer T. Dempster Brown alleged that an enormous tunnel leads out from the

Figure 13.4 The ambiguous and disproportionate front entrance to the Ministry building
Source: Copyright Danny Hoffman.

basement, a tunnel so large and long that it could be used to load huge caches of weaponry into submarines. During interviews with the building's former inhabitants in 2012, one militia fighter, Hassan, told me simply, "It was a city by itself."

In press accounts of the Ministry of Defense the building is most often characterized as "bulletproof," a term ex-combatants used as well.[2] It is a telling metaphor. The structure seemed impregnable in virtually every sense. Its tectonics, Kenneth Frampton's (1990) term for the poetics of construction, the union of the engineering and art required to make a building both stand up and mean something, seemed impervious to intervention—including the interventions that came with ten years of squatter occupation.

Like many large structures in the postcolonial tropics, the Ministry of Defense is made from rough concrete. Only the support columns are reinforced with steel. Otherwise most of the façade is simple concrete block infill, relatively thin, cheaply made and assembled without forms or skilled labor. As a result, the structural, reinforced concrete pillars read as solid supporting masses, whereas the small block infill reads as less substantial, even flimsy by comparison. In a completed building this difference between the two forms of concrete would likely be masked (though doing so would not be orthodox New Brutalism). Without that mask it is difficult to make the two elements cohere. The structural support appears overwhelming in proportion to the materials that define the space, the more human, domestic side of the construction. In the Ministry most of this infill is gone, leaving only the muscular supports. Hence the need for residents to import their own building materials to carve the massive space. As a result, the occupied space of the Ministry consisted of two kinds of material: a raw and permanent structure that held the building up and the more ephemeral and bricolaged materials that divide its interior space. The way these materials meet one another is the building's tectonics, and there a significant part of its meaning as a human habitat lies.

Just as the plan of the Ministry and its scale made it a structure that seemed to relate only to the sovereign power of the Liberian state, so too, the tectonics of the building challenge the idea that the space can be meaningfully appropriated and claimed by anyone operating with human material or at a merely human scale. The reinforced concrete columns of the building belong to a different tectonic order than the plastic sheeting, zinc, cardboard, and wood scraps out of which squatters could fashion their own infill walls, floors, and ceilings. There was no way to join these elements in a unified and meaningful synthesis. The building's bones, its basic structure, would always stand apart from anything the residents might do to it or within it. Their own efforts would always be provisional and transitory; those of the Liberian state would always have an aura of permanence.

It need not be this way. The bricolage, ad hoc aesthetics of colonized structures can develop their own logic of assembly and coherent, meaningful tectonic orders. The residents of the Torre David in Caracas, for example, used locally produced concrete blocks to subdivide the spaces of the 45-floor tower that was structurally very similar to the Ministry of Defense. But at Torre David an infill of concrete block used in concert with other more transitory materials like wood, zinc, and plastic became an architecture of permanence. In the barrios of Caracas such ad hoc infill is part of the local building vocabulary; it is an architecture in its own right, made meaningful by the mass waves of urban migrants and by the Chavez regime's rhetoric of rights to the city for the urban poor (Urban Think Tank 2013). Once joined to existing infrastructure it marks a rightful claim on space. This is its tectonics. So when residents began to join materials to the existing concrete skeleton of the massive tower, the details of these joints read as an appropriation by its new inhabitants. By accreting their own materials onto the structural framework of the tower, the residents signified their intention to remain. The two materials together read singularly and, at least conceptually, the building became theirs. It is a claim they have already proven willing to fight for and to defend (see Urban Think Tank 2013; Anderson 2013).

This is not the case in Monrovia. There is in Monrovia an architectural vocabulary of appropriated space. But unlike Torre David, it is more unstable, less permanent. There is no material vocabulary for marking the permanent appropriation of infrastructure, no tectonic vocabulary that would allow for colonized spaces to be read as fully integrated and fully appropriated. In a brief but telling anecdote about the historic instability of architecture in Monrovia, anthropologist Merran Fraenkel described in 1964 how one of the best known and most financially successful shops in the city was a zinc shack that had existed on the same spot for almost 100 years. Despite its long tenure on the site, residents "read" the building not as a successful colonization of space but as an architecture of impermanence, since the legal ambiguities of land ownership meant that it could be swept away at any moment (see Fraenkel 1964: 49).

Half a century later, the Ministry was marked by the same dichotomy: the permanence of the state was broadcast through the structure, while the residents' infill remained saddled with a sense of impermanence and transitoriness. The Ministry housed a large community, but it never allowed them to claim the building or permitted them to see within it a way to claim for themselves a stable foothold in this city. Despite the fact that many of them had resided in the building for a decade, this remained true until the day the ex-combatants were told to leave. And, largely without resistance, they did.

Impossible New Bodies

In a famous essay on postmodernity, Fredric Jameson (1991) argued that John Portman's Westin Bonaventure Hotel in Los Angeles was the perfect embodiment of postmodern architecture. It

Figure 13.5 Former inhabitants of the Ministry of Defense on the structure's roof
Source: Copyright Danny Hoffman.

was a building to be passed through, a building impossible to know how to inhabit. To dwell in the Bonaventure would require radical imagination and a whole new social landscape. Until Angelenos learned to "grow new organs, to expand our sensorium and our body to some new, yet unimaginable, perhaps ultimately impossible, dimensions" (1991: 39), the Bonaventure would be a relay station in the networks moving bodies and commodities through the city.

The Ministry of Defense is Monrovia's Westin Bonaventure. Not because it shares the Bonaventure's postmodern aesthetic, but because like the Bonaventure its architecture is impossible to comprehend. The Ministry housed a population of ex-combatants and their dependents for more than a decade, but it was a population in transit, never a political community that could or would stake a more permanent, meaningful claim to the space around it. No one in the Ministry of Defense was actively seeking to "grow new organs" (Figure 13.5).

There are, however, two important parentheticals to add to the story of the Ministry's excessive architecture.

The first is that the Ministry's inaccessibility has nothing to do with being ill-suited to an African city. Modern architecture belongs in and to African cities no less than to cities anywhere. Whether or not there are more meaningful or appropriate architectures better suited to life on the continent is a separate debate. But there is nothing distinctly African about being unable to lay claim to a space like the Ministry of Defense. If there are structures in Monrovia in which it is impossible to know how to live, it is not because those forced to move through them are ill-suited to modernity. It is because the modernity those forms represent is by definition uninhabitable.

A second note of caution lies in Major Sandi's odd proposition that the Ministry of Defense might someday make a fine hotel. There is, of course, sad poetry in a man squatting in a vast ruin imagining the building might someday house more affluent transients. But there is also a hint of possibility. The ex-combatants who resided in the Ministry of Defense could not imagine it as a space that belonged properly to them, a space that they could ever lay claim to and make their own. Certainly it was not a space they could imagine outside the terms established by Monrovia's modern political economy, in which the movement of young men and the labors of their bodies have become their sole productive resources (see Hoffman 2011).

But in her book on Supermax prisons, the ultimate excessive architecture, Rhodes describes how even there, making space uninhabitable is a project that requires constant invention (2004: 90). The control prison may never become subject-producing space, but those contained within find ways to communicate with one another; dream new ways to attack their jailers; discover new weapons in the alien architecture that surrounds them. In response, an entire industry generates new prison architectures that mitigate the potential of inmates to experiment. Nothing on this landscape is fixed.

Imagining that the Ministry of Defense might one day house a luxury hotel is not a political claim on the building, not an act of resistance on behalf of a population violently excluded from the modern city. If anything it replicates the logic that produced such marginality, a logic of inventing new ways to produce precarity among Monrovia's ex-combatant youth. Hardly the material from which to build popular resistance, let alone a political community. But it contains, at least, the hint that even here there may yet be an as yet unimagined urban future.

Notes

1 Portions of this chapter were published in an early version in the introduction and first chapter of Hoffman (2017).
2 See, for example, Winston Parley, "Liberia: government targets unfinished Defense Ministry," *The New Dawn* November 18, 2013. Accessed March 25. http://allafrica.com/stories/201311180879.html.

References

Anderson, J. L. (2013) "Slumlord," *The New Yorker*, January 28. www.newyorker.com/.
Banham, R. (1966) *The New Brutalism: Ethic or Aesthetic?*, New York: Reinhold.
Banham, R. 2011 [1955]. "The New Brutalism," *October* 136: 19–28.
Butler, J. (2004) *Precarious Life: The Powers of Mourning and Violence*, New York: Verso.
Chalfin, B. (2014) "Public things, excremental politics, and the infrastructure of bare life in Ghana's city of Tema," *American Ethnologist* 41, 1: 92–109.
Crosby, T. (2011) [1955] "The New Brutalism," *October* 136: 17–18.
Edensor, T. (2005) "Waste matter: the debris of industrial ruins and the disordering of the material world," *Journal of Material Culture* 10, 3: 311–312.
Elleh, N. (1997) *African Architecture: Evolution and Transformation*, New York: McGraw-Hill.
Forty, A. (2012) *Concrete and Culture: A Material History*, London: Reaktion Press.
Fraenkel, M. (1964) *Tribe and Class in Monrovia*, London: Oxford University Press.
Frampton, K. (1990) "Rappel à l'ordre, the case for the tectonic," *Architectural Design* 60, 3–4: 19–25.
Fry, M. and Drew, J. (1956) *Tropical Architecture in the Humid Zone*, New York: Reinhold.
Harvey, D. (2012) *Rebel Cities: From the Right to the City to the Urban Revolution*, New York: Verso.
Heidegger, M. (1993) "Building dwelling thinking," in *Basic Writings*, New York: HarperCollins.
Hess, J. B. (2000) "Imagining architecture: the structure of nationalism in Accra, Ghana," *Africa Today* 47, 2: 35–58.
Hoffman, D. (2011) *The War Machines: Young Men and Violence in Sierra Leone and Liberia*, Durham, NC: Duke University Press.
Hoffman, D. (2017) *Monrovia Modern: Urban Form and Political Imagination in Liberia*. Durham, NC: Duke University Press.

Jameson, F. (1991) *Postmodernism, or, the Cultural Logic of Late Capitalism*, Durham, NC: Duke University Press.
Larkin, B. (2008) *Signal and Noise: Media, Infrastructure, and Urban Culture in Nigeria*. Durham, NC: Duke University Press.
le Roux, H. (2003) "The networks of tropical architecture," *The Journal of Architecture* 8, 3: 337–354.
le Roux, H. and Uduku, O. (2004) "The media and the modern movement in Nigeria and the Gold Coast," *Nka: Journal of Contemporary African Art* 19 (Summer): 46–49.
Leatherbarrow, D. and Mostafavi, M. (2002) *Surface Architecture*, Cambridge, MA: MIT Press.
Liscombe, R. W. (2006) "Modernism in late imperial British West Africa," *Journal of the Society of Architectural Historians* 65, 2: 188–215.
Mbembe, A. (1992) "The banality of power and the aesthetics of vulgarity in the postcolony," *Public Culture* 4, 2: 1–30.
Rhodes, L. (2004) *Total Confinement: Madness and Region in the Maximum Security Prison*, Berkeley: University of California Press.
Smithson, P. (2001) *The Charged Void: Architecture*, New York: Monacelli Press.
Smithson, A. and Smithson, P. (2011) [1957] "The New Brutalism," *October* 136: 37.
Stoner, J. (2012) *Toward a Minor Architecture*, Cambridge, MA: MIT Press.
Uduku, O. (2006) "Modernist architecture and "the tropical" in West Africa: the Tropical Architecture movement in West Africa, 1948–1970," *Habitat international* 30, 3: 396–411.
Urban Think Tank (2013) *Torre David: Informal Vertical Communities*, Zurich: Lars Müller.
Zimmerman, C. (2004) "Photographic modern architecture: inside 'the New Deep'," *Journal of Architecture* 9: 331–354.
Žižek, S. (1997) *The Plague of Fantasies*, New York: Verso.

14

Border Architecture

Territories, Commons, and Breathing-Spaces

George F. Flaherty

What, if anything, is border architecture? Is it architecture at or near geopolitical boundaries? Is 10 miles too far to qualify? What about 100 miles? Borders tend to be analyzed in terms of state sovereignty and world economic systems, as the meeting points of territories that must be settled, exploited, and controlled. These processes are often administered by remote metropoles that view the borderlands with a combination of interested suspicion and ignorant disdain. At the same time, capitalism demands that goods and bodies flow without friction. As David Harvey has argued, the territorial logics of the state and capital are overlapping but never fully congruent (Harvey 2003). Borders, of course, are not limited to international boundaries and are created and maintained within nations by racial, socioeconomic, environmental injustices, among other factors. Architectural histories of the borderlands are few in comparison to those of their metropoles, and they tend to reproduce rather than complicate such logics. These narratives generally fail to recognize, let alone account for, the negotiations among border dwellers and the various local and global forces that seek to give their home shape. How might the analysis of borders and their built environments proceed if we analyze these spaces not only as territories but as *commons*?

By "commons" I refer to shared resources (water, air, food, fuel) that serve as the base to human existence and vitality, overseen by the communities that use them. Commons also refers to the history of industrialization in the North Atlantic world, which transformed communal lands into "wastes" that required enclosure—and which transformed the people who subsisted from those lands into perpetual border dwellers, living at the boundaries of property. The enclosure process continues. We can observe it in the casual and systematic privatization of public space in cities, resource extraction from national parks and lands held by indigenous populations, and bio-piracy. This process is not limited to the land but also, as Michael Hardt and Antonio Negri argue, "the languages we create, the social practices we establish, the modes of sociality that define our relationships, and so forth" (Hardt and Negri 2010: 139).[1] Critics, and recently even some champions of this process, foundational to capitalism, have turned to the historical commons as well as more recent extensions, such as the liberalization of intellectual property laws and the "open access" of knowledge, to respond to the political economy of neoliberal transition and planetary climate change and envision potential correctives to these intertwining trajectories.[2]

George F. Flaherty

To return to my initial question about the expanse of so-called border architecture, if looking through the lens of the terrestrial and intellectual commons, then border architecture is ultimately something mobile and mutable, as much built environments as a set of portable ideas and tactics that engage the multitude of boundaries and disparities. Indeed, some architects working in the Global North are beginning to exercise the commons concept. British architect David Chipperfield convened the 2012 Venice Biennial of Architecture with the theme "Common Ground," calling for his peers to approach collaboration critically rather than as a means of producing surplus value, and to encroach on the social, political, and economic enclosures of our day. This essay focuses on a cluster of test cases of border architecture in the spaces between Tijuana (Mexico) and San Diego (United States), from the 1990s to the present. They highlight the local but also transnational flows of construction materials, building techniques, and urban policy. Since the mid 1990s, architect-scholar Teddy Cruz and colleagues at his San Diego-based firm, Estudio Teddy Cruz + Forman, have researched informal settlements in the "waste" spaces produced by industrialization in Tijuana, the inefficiencies and unsustainability of sprawl and obsolescence in San Diego, and the increasing militarization of the international boundary by both countries.[3] These investigations, often drawing from actors and sources not usually included in urban planning, serve as the basis for redevelopment proposals, for the twin cities and beyond. Their proposals update utopian architectures of the 1960s and 1970s, which explored mobility and adaptability amid postwar destruction in Europe and the industrial boom but also growing awareness of environmental degradation in the U.S. Cruz and his colleagues' research has drawn interest from curators at major museums, the press, and private organizations that fund social service and public policy.

Mobility and adaptability of architectural materials and knowledges is ultimately what will define contemporary borderlands architectures, and perhaps contribute to a decolonization of architectural knowledge, recognizing that some of the most vital ideas and tactics for human dwelling originate from its "peripheral" zones.[4] Although among the most discussed border zones, Tijuana–San Diego is not meant to be universally representative. At the same time, as a journalist recently described, the cities are a "crucible of new ideas, just as the fault lines between tectonic plates on the ocean floor are breeding-grounds of new life" (McGuirk 2014: 276). Border architecture may well be our future global architecture.

A Border/less World

English-language discourse about the U.S.–Mexico border has often been dominated by racist/xenophobic worldviews. This has intensified with the presidential campaign and election of Donald Trump.[5] Given his much-publicized rhetoric, the uninformed citizen might be forgiven for thinking that architecture in the borderlands is limited to walls. At the same time, dozens of border walls have been erected or are under construction globally since 2000, including one announced by the Mexican government for its southern border with Guatemala (*The Economist* 2016). The momentous fall of the Berlin Wall in 1989 did not mark the so-called "end of history," nor did it mark the end of walls as props for assuaging states' and reactionary societies' anxieties over immigration, drug trafficking, and sovereignty (Fukuyama 1989). Rather, the incongruency of the territorial logics of state and capital has only grown. As Wendy Brown argues, with globalization we see "increasingly liberalized borders, on the one hand, and the devotion of unprecedented funds, energies, and technologies to border fortification, on the other" (Brown 2010: 8). More and more walls are being deployed even as they grow less and less effective, in spite of their technological embellishments (sensors, drones, etc.), a testament not to their functionality but their rhetoric and affect.

This dematerialization and rematerialization of border walls, geopolitical and technological, finds parallel—and challenge—in smaller-scale negotiations by several prominent artists. In 2011, Ana Teresa Fernández and collaborators "erased" the Imperial Beach fence, which extends out into the Pacific Ocean, by painting the Mexico side with bright blue paint that matched the sky on most days, producing an illusion of transparency (if not permeability). In another well-known intervention at Imperial Beach, Javier Téllez organized the shooting of a human cannonball over the fence from Tijuana, in a 2005 performance titled *One Flew Over the Void (Bala perdida)* as part of a binational art festival, InSite (Figure 14.1). For the 1997 iteration of InSite, Francis Alÿs used his commission fee to travel from Tijuana to San Diego, albeit without crossing the Mexico–U.S. border: passing instead through Baja California to Australia and then tracing the Pacific Rim, and entering the U.S. through the much less intensively policed border with Canada (and sending postcards all along the way). These interventions, while incubated by a cosmopolitan art world, gesture to residents in Tijuana and San Diego that come up with and make do with creative and informal solutions to everyday problems of mobility, place-making, sustenance, and politicking.[6] Architects play a leading role in the narrative that follows but they are not the key actors; everyday people are, along with the knowledge they carry in their bodies, movements, and words. They do not need theorists like Cruz to make their way in life. However, because I am interested in how their tactics might travel beyond the borderlands, such mediators become part of the story. The goal here is not to romanticize these spaces of precariousness but to call attention to how we might learn from one another given that emergency, whether economic or ecological, is capitalist modernity's norm (Benjamin 1969: 257).

Figure 14.1 Javier Téllez, *One Flew over the Void (Bala perdida)*, 2005, Las Playas, Tijuana, Mexico/Imperial Beach, San Diego, U.S., photographic documentation of performance

Source: Courtesy Javier Téllez and Koenig & Clinton, New York.

Territories and commons are not mutually exclusive categories but their relationship needs rebalancing. A cultural approach to architecture, which accounts for built environment as a material practice and an imaginative one, offers some counterweight. This is because not only buildings but social, political, and economic structures will require revision if we are to address modernity's permanent state of emergency. Raymond Williams, in his study of the dialectical literatures of rural and urban life in modernizing Britain, offered an expansive definition of the commons. With the historical commons enclosed, marginal and emergent cultures develop new strategies for dwelling that refuse hegemony. Williams writes, "When the pressure of a system is great and is increasing, it matters to find a breathing-space, a fortunate distance, from the immediate and visible controls ... Community, to survive, has then to change its terms" (Williams 1975: 107).[7] The cultural critic insists on a physical and/or intellectual space of dwelling within and potentially in resistance to an apparently dominant system or inevitable process. Neither commons nor communities that form around are places for nostalgia. The commons urbanism currently practiced between Tijuana and San Diego is oriented to the future.

Breathing-Spaces

Teddy Cruz is an advocate of not only a permeable border wall but also a movable one. Cruz is interested in the everyday spatiality of people on the ground, and how political and economic structures might be reworked to grant them even more room for maneuver and recourse. While Cruz and colleagues' proposals have not always been fully executed, they draw from and contribute to an emerging commons of architectural ideas and tactics that negotiate dwelling in borderlands and emergencies, including organizations like ToroLab in Tijuana. Circulating well beyond the Mexico–U.S. borderlands, thanks to press coverage and without strict copyright, these proposals are available to those who care to consider them.

Until the early 1990s, another form of commons was regularly practiced in Mexico. One of the major, if frequently corrupted, outcomes of the Mexican Revolution (1910–1920) were *ejidos*. These parcels, designated for agriculture and held communally, total roughly one-half of the country's arable land held by three million people, were the backbone of agrarian reform and rural politics in Mexico. Preparing to ratify the North American Free Trade Agreement (NAFTA), the state modified the constitution to destabilize the *ejido* system, permitting its privatization and later dropping tariffs and subsidies that protected communal production (Yetman 2000). In preparation for neoliberal industrialization in the borderlands in the 1960s and 1970s, the state began to acquire and expropriate parcels in cities like Tijuana in order to develop industrial parks for binational assembly plants (*maquiladora*) and related infrastructure. Long-term residents of Tijuana and more recent arrivals have refused to accept the total privatization of the landscape, and a considerable percentage of housing in Tijuana is auto-constructed on spaces left over by industrialization, absentee property owners, and ineffective urban planning. With limited land, expansion occurs vertically and public and private lives and spaces frequently overlap. Any space too small for domestic construction is occupied by commercial activities. Municipal services are negotiated over time, often allowed to exist in a zone of indeterminate legality.

Homes and businesses in Tijuana's *colonias* are sometimes built using found and recycled materials. These include, as Cruz has documented, components harvested from San Diego and greater southern California. Professional and amateur pickers truck the materials across the border: plywood, aluminum windows, and refrigerator doors. Discarded garage doors become walls for a house, what Cruz calls "residential ready-made" (Cruz 2010), echoing Marcel Duchamp. Car tires, which are notoriously difficult to recycle, are cut and interlocked to form retaining walls in sloping neighborhoods. Street-level living spaces might be elevated above the ground on posts to create a loggia for recreational or commercial activity. At times, whole bungalows, which dotted San Diego's first-ring neighborhoods from the 1920s through the 1950s, are lifted off their foundations and cross the border. The flow resembles the "just in time" supply chain of the *maquiladoras*.

These components are the waste products of urban sprawl and planned obsolescence in the U.S. housing market. They are also the product of subprime home loans, at least before the U.S. housing bubble burst beginning in 2006. San Diego was disproportionately hit among American cities, becoming a real estate "dead zone" according to one business magazine (Tully 2006). Ironically, it was the loose financial market and the illusion of perpetual home value growth that facilitated the apparent obsolescence of the bungalows, so-called starter homes (often financed by the Federal Housing Agency to house military families). Mexican workers in San Diego were also hurt by the crisis, returning to Tijuana as economic opportunities tightened, leading to a crunch in housing stock there.

Learning from the borderlands, Cruz and colleagues have put forward plans for small-scale redevelopment in greater Tijuana and San Diego. In San Ysidro, California, located just north of the border crossing by the same name, Cruz partnered with Casa Familiar in 2001, a local non-profit and social service center, to develop a small parcel with an old church. San Ysidro was founded by the Little Landers in 1908, a group led by the utopian journalist-activist William Ellsworth Smythe that sought to establish "colonies" of yeoman farmers (self-sufficient yet cooperative) in arid parts of California and Idaho. Today just over 30,000 mostly Latino residents live there with an annual median income of less than half the rest of the county. It also suffers from severe air pollution due to idling trucks at the world's busiest land border crossing.

Twenty-three units of housing were planned, including apartments for seniors that also included space for childcare that would serve working families (Figure 14.2). The church would

Figure 14.2 Estudio Teddy Cruz + Fonna Forman, *Casa Familiar: Living Rooms at the Border*, San Ysidro, California, 2001, maquete

serve as a community cultural center. In order to fully actualize the project Cruz and Casa Familiar sought permission to encroach on neighboring underutilized land, including an alleyway, for circulation and informal commerce. They also sought more density than the area was currently zoned for, although conceptualized outside of the "mixed-use" pursued by for-profit developers, which comprises market-rate housing and formula retail. This led to significant back and forth with town officials. As Cruz notes, design based on commons is difficult for existing planning regulations, which are based on property law as much on public good, to accommodate. Little progress was made. In 2016, the PARC Foundation, run by New York-based artist David Deutsch, provided funding for the cultural center, which Casa Familiar leaders acknowledged was a more philanthropically expedient (and less risky) proposition for donors (quoted in Morlan 2017).

For their "Manufactured Sites" proposal from 2005, Estudio Teddy Cruz + Forman focused on a nimbler process, and more incremental and improvisational urban change instead. They explored the redevelopment possibilities of off-the-shelf and recycled joists, hinges, braces, scaffolding, and other mass-produced construction tools (Figure 14.3). These tools were meant to serve as the framework for fast and responsive construction of residential and commercial buildings, or a combination of the two uses. Design beyond the superstructure was left up to the users and their community. The tools are also more portable than plans for a specific plot of land.

Museums and universities have served as important seed banks for Cruz's proposals, although not without treading on the cultural politics of such institutions. For the Museum of Modern Art in New York in 2009, Estudio Teddy Cruz + Forman turned their attention to the McMansion and "gated community" phenomena of San Diego's suburbs. Gated communities have replaced racially exclusive covenants and so-called "sun-down towns" that excluded people of color through a combination of law, custom, and force. They presented "Non-Stop Sprawl,"

Figure 14.3 Estudio Teddy Cruz + Fonna Forman, *Manufactured Sites: A Housing Urbanism Made of Waste/Maquiladora*, 2005–2008, maquete

a multimedia installation consisting of two parts. The first, was a single scale model of a typical McMansion—beige stucco, red ceramic roof tiles, vaguely Spanish colonial revival—placed in a box ringed with mirrors and without a top (Figure 14.4).[8] The viewer peered down at this microcosm that appears to rapidly expand out of nothing, an endless yet hermetic landscape of overbuilt homes. The infinity McMansion is joined by a two-channel video that envisions how the housing type might be retrofitted not to address the issues of "quality" or "good taste" but to respond to the changing demographic and socioeconomic makeup of suburbs with greater density.[9] In the near not distant future, global warming will render such sprawl not only reckless but impossible. The "Non-Stop Sprawl" video shows, through photographs and animations, how a McMansion or any large single-family home might be converted into townhomes, expanded to encompass more multi-family units, two houses combined to produce more residential density or land use revised to include retail and other work-consumption spaces. The plans and techniques are creative but rudimentary, the video meant to serve more as inspiration rather than as a how-to procedural. While a home for avant-gardist architecture interventions, New York's Museum of Modern Art (MoMA) has in the past struggled to make sense of vernacular building. Its 1964 *Architecture without Architects* exhibition, curated by Bernard Rudofsky, indulged in primitivism and paternalism even as it attempted to celebrate "non-pedigreed" builders' "humane" and "more intelligent" ways of living (Rudofsky 1964). Even more recent MoMA exhibitions, such as *Small Scale, Big Change: New Architectures of Social Engagement* (2010), reproduce certain metropolitan assumptions about architecture in the Global South, expressing wonder that "successful" projects manage to emerge under such difficult economic or political conditions. If elite institutions are to serve as seed banks for architectures to address the world's toughest challenges, then it will have to continue to welcome mediators like Cruz.

Figure 14.4 Estudio Teddy Cruz + Fonna Forman, *Non-Stop Sprawl: McMansion Retrofitted Project, 2008,* maquete set in mirrored box

Across their projects, Estudio Teddy Cruz + Forman seeks to intervene on what have been bedrock concepts of capitalist urbanization. For the McMansion project, for example, he asks viewers to "rethink ownership" and "co-own resources" when it comes to sub-dividing residential lots for density (Estudio Cruz + Forman 2012). Cruz is not calling for the wholesale redistribution of wealth but at least a municipal-scale acknowledgment that as climate change progresses, the same owners and speculators that oppose such tactics will call for their coastal and other vulnerably located property be protected at public cost.[10] These calls are likely to be promoted by these constituencies and their brokers in government as "common sense," part of a long-standing self-image among accommodated San Diegans that the city is somehow exempt from broader regional and transfrontier problems.[11]

Cruz and colleagues have themselves tried to transplant their commons urbanism to locations beyond geopolitical border zones—and museums. In Hudson, New York, they collaborated with the PARC Foundation starting in 2008 to redevelop a series of lots located off the town's main street acquired by the foundation. On a smaller, more consolidated scale Hudson shares some urban and social issues with Tijuana–San Diego. The former whaling town has just over 64,000 residents but is home to sizable poor and immigrant communities while at the same time catering to affluent weekend residents from New York City. A narrow linear park was at the core of their plan for affordable housing, seeking to link the neighborhood to an emerging corridor of antiques dealers, "creative retail," and high-end restaurants (Thomas 2016: TR9). Although the *New York Times* architecture critic noted the ambition with the headline, "Learning from Tijuana," the national real estate crisis, by then full-blown, stopped the project in its tracks (Ouroussoff 2008: E1).[12] Despite this failure, Hudson was an opportunity to test the portability and adaptability of Estudio Teddy Cruz + Forman's border thinking. Failure is central to utopian projects, because their merit cannot always be recognized in their historical moment or is short-lived. During the 1973 international oil crisis, for example, environmentally sustainable architecture was of great interest in the mainstream only as long as prices remained high and supplies scarce (Borasi and Zardini 2007).

Indeed, we can understand Cruz and colleagues as contributing to a tradition of utopian urbanism in Europe and the U.S., which put forward prefabricated and mobile architecture as solutions to the pressing social and environmental issues of the 1950s through 1970s. Prefabrication, whereby the components of a building are machined in a factory and delivered for assembly on site, promised to accommodate those displaced by housing shortages more efficiently and to bring modernist design to remote areas. Observing the speed and transience—and alienation—of the industrial world, some architects experimented with designs that would continue to move and change once they reached their (initial) destination. At the 1956 meeting of the Congrès International d'Architecture Moderne in Dubrovnik, Hungarian-French architect Yona Friedman sought out interlocutors for his growing interest in cities designed and continually redesigned by its inhabitants.[13] Friedman saw existing cities as too embedded in a fixed place (foundations, basements, etc.) and too slow to respond to society's needs. With "Ville Spatiale" (1958), he proposed a superstructure erected above the urban fabric that would serve as a framework at the disposal of residents to build and rebuild dwellings (from prefab components) (Figure 14.5). (Homes elevated on beams in Tijuana are a local solution to a shared urban problem.) British architect Ron Herron proposed five years later what he called a "Walking City," a nomadic urban exoskeleton with retractable legs that could seek out resources as needed (Figure 14.6). Around the same time fellow Archigram collective member Peter Cook put forward a "Plug-in City," where modular units were added and subtracted by crane. Not unlike recent interest in these collectives and other mid-century neo-avant-gardes, such ideas have a tendency to return. They return, translated for the times by their conjurers, because they seek to address social contradictions at the heart of capitalist modernity that remain unresolved (by design).

Figure 14.5 Yona Friedman, *Spatial City over Paris*, 1960, collage on a postcard, collection of Musée National d'Art Moderne, Centre Georges Pompidou

Source: Courtesy Yona Friedman.

George F. Flaherty

Figure 14.6 Ron Herron, *Walking City Project on Ocean*, exterior perspective, 1966, cut-and-pasted printed and photographic papers and graphite, collection of Museum of Modern Art, New York

Source: Courtesy Simon Herron.

As Simon Sadler has written of Archigram, we have in these examples and those of Estudio Teddy Cruz + Forman an "aesthetic of incompleteness" (Sadler 2005: 14). These proposals, in their portability and mutability, look forward and invite us to change the way we live, just as climate change is doing (insisting) the same. They place greater and necessary emphasis on density, work with rather than against environmental conditions, reject planned obsolescence to stretch the boundaries of recycling, and disseminate local knowledges. This amounts to a renegotiation of the commons of modernist architecture, giving up the power and grandness but not the influence of articulating a future from the bottom up as much as the top down. A commons urbanism, perhaps never outside of the territorial logics of the state and capital, must confront territorialities within and outside of architecture itself. As Cruz has argued,

> It is out of socio-cultural and economic tensions and from territories of political conflict, such as the San Diego–Tijuana border region, that critical architectural practices can emerge. These are territorial projects whose main focus is not the object of architecture, but the subversion of the information imprinted artificially on the land, the alteration of the boundaries and limits established by the institutions of official development.
>
> *(Cruz 2005)*

Some scholars have celebrated Tijuana as a laboratory of postmodernism for its cultural hybridity but increasingly the city, along with San Diego, is a laboratory for negotiating our future on earth. The two cities are in the words of Williams, a "fortunate distance" from one another, close enough to learn from and support one another. For those of us who continue to live at and learn from the commons, breathing-spaces endure border walls.

Notes

1. Most modern commentators on the commons have gone back and forth on how to balance public and private interests, although mostly as mediated by political, economic, and cultural elites. Even Harvey, the Marxist geographer, has proposed that the commons requires a mix of individual and collective action and of private and public decision-making if it is to operate at any scale larger than the hyperlocal (Harvey 2011).
2. These commons—historical, legal, conceptual, and artistic—might be interconnected in order to effect social change (Elias 2016).
3. Since 2012, Cruz has partnered with Fonna Forman, a political theorist at the University of California at San Diego, where Cruz teaches as well. Forman's earlier academic work sought to recuperate an ethics from Adam Smith's economic philosophy.
4. On border thinking as a method of decolonization, see Walter Mignolo (2000).
5. Trump's call for a "border wall" and delivery of prototypes by the U.S. government is beyond the scope of this essay.
6. However, the expediency of culture as yet another resource to be managed and leveraged under globalization should not be underestimated, with site-specific biennials such as InSite susceptible to becoming a "network of assembly sites" not so different from *maquiladoras* (Yúdice 2004: 288).
7. In similar vein, José Esteban Muñoz sought to map a "brown commons," where queer people of color could realize a "being-in-common" in the Los Angeles punk music scene, surpassing "the limits of the individual and the subject" (Muñoz 2013).
8. There is no standard definition for the McMansion but they are generally large, built up to property lines, with cookie-cutter façades, layouts, and finishes, sometimes with a profusion of secondary masses (gables, garages, etc.), and out of scale compared to surrounding structures.
9. Households below the federal poverty line are migrating outwards from city centers (Berube 2010).
10. Such expectations are not unrelated to their preference for abatement rather than prevention, the latter requiring structural transformations of society and economy (Davis 1995). San Diego is beginning to plan for climate change with a recently adopted city-planning document, its "Climate Action Plan" (City of San Diego 2016).
11. In 1974, architects Kevin Lynch and Donald Appleyard conducted a study of the San Diego area for the city's planning department. They titled it "Temporary Paradise?," which assumed that San Diego was a paradise but left unsaid the dominant classes greatest anxiety: that "their" city might become Los Angeles or Tijuana—an unplanned, brown metropolis (Lynch and Appleyard 1990).
12. The foundation sold off most of the parcels it owned in 2016.
13. Friedman would correspond with Le Corbusier, Jan Trapman, Jacob Bakema, Garrit Rietveld, Jerzy Soltan, John Habrakan, Constant Nieuwenhuys, Jean Prouvé, and Kenzo Tange (Friedman 1970; Busbea 2007).

References

Benjamin, W. (1969) "Theses on the philosophy of history," in *Illuminations*, ed. Hannah Arendt, trans. Harry Zohn, New York: Schocken Books.
Berube, A. et al. (2010) "State of metropolitan America: on the frontlines of demographic transformation," Washington, DC: Brookings Institution, www.brookings.edu/wp-content/uploads/2016/06/metro_america_report.pdf (November 14, 2016).
Borasi, G. and Zardini, M. (2007) *Sorry, Out of Gas: Architecture's Response to the 1973 Oil Crisis*, Montreal: Canadian Centre for Architecture.
Brown, W. (2010) *Walled States, Waning Sovereignty*, Cambridge, MA: MIT Press.
Busbea, L. (2007) *Topologies: The Urban Utopia in France, 1960–1970*, Cambridge, MA: MIT Press.

City of San Diego (2016) "Climate Action Plan," July 12, www.sandiego.gov/sites/default/files/final_july_2016_cap.pdf (June 15, 2018).
Cruz, T. (2005) "Border postcards: chronicles from the edge," recorded lecture, London School of Economics, delivered March 11, https://digital.library.lse.ac.uk/objects/lse:riz725hac (June 15, 2018).
Cruz, T. (2010) "Mapping non-conformity: post-bubble urban strategies," *E-misférica* 7, 1, http://hemisphericinstitute.org/hemi/en/e-misferica-71/cruz (November 14, 2016).
Davis, M. (1995) "The case for letting Malibu burn," *Environmental History Review* 19, 2: 1–36.
The Economist (2016) "More neighbours make more fences," January 7, www.economist.com/blogs/graphicdetail/2016/01/daily-chart-5 (November 14, 2016).
Elias, A. J. (2016) "The commons as network," *ASAP/Journal* 1, 1: 25–50.
Estudio Cruz + Forman (2012) "Rethinking ownership," https://vimeo.com/36577968 (November 14, 2016).
Friedman, Y. (1970) *L'Archtecture mobile: vers une cité conçue par ses habitants*, Tournai: Casterman.
Fukuyama, F. (1989) "The end of history," *National Interest* 16: 3–8.
Hardt, M. and Negri, A. (2010) *Commonwealth*, Cambridge, MA: Harvard University Press.
Harvey, D. (2003) *The New Imperialism*, New York: Oxford University Press.
Harvey, D. (2011) "The future of the common," *Radical History Review* 109: 101–107.
Lynch, K. and Appleyard, D. (1990 [1974]) "Temporary paradise? A look at the special landscape of the San Diego region," in T. Banerjee and M. Southworth (eds) *City Sense and City Design: Writings and Projects of Kevin Lynch*, Cambridge, MA: MIT Press, 721–764.
McGuirk, J. (2014) *Radical Cities: Across Latin American in Search of a New Architecture*, New York: Verso.
Mignolo, W. (2000) *Local Histories/Global Designs: Coloniality, Subaltern Knowledge, and Border Thinking*, Princeton: Princeton University Press.
Morlan, K. (2017) "Carving out community space in San Ysidro," *Voice of San Diego*, February 14, www.voiceofsandiego.org/topics/arts/culture-report-carving-out-community-space-in-san-ysidro/ (June 15, 2018).
Muñoz, J. E. (2013) "'Gimme gimme this … gimme gimme that': annihilation and innovation in the punk rock commons," *Social Text* 31, 3: 95–110.
Ouroussoff, N. (2008) "Learning from Tijuana: Hudson, N.Y., considers different housing model," *New York Times*, February 19, E1.
Rudofsky, B. (1964) *Architecture without Architects: A Short Introduction to Non-Pedigreed Architecture*, Albuquerque: University of New Mexico Press.
Sadler, S. (2005) *Archigram: Architecture without Architecture*, Cambridge, MA: MIT Press.
Thomas, A. (2016) "An old river town is elegantly transformed," *New York Times*, July 27, TR9.
Tully, S. (2006) "Welcome to the dead zone," *Fortune*, May 5, http://archive.fortune.com/2006/05/03/news/economy/realestateguide_fortune/index.htm?iid=sr-link1 (November 14, 2016).
Williams, R. (1975) *The Country and the City*, New York: Oxford University Press.
Yetman, D. (2000) "*Ejidos*, land sales, and free trade in northwest Mexico: will globalization affect the commons?," *American Studies* 41, 2–3: 211–234.
Yúdice, G. (2004) *The Expediency of Culture: Uses of Culture in the Global Era*, Durham, NC: Duke University Press.

15

Camps

Contemporary Environments of Autonomy, Necessity, and Control

Charlie Hailey

Arriving

The little aluminum pot perched on three stones above a meagre fire.
(Rawlence 2016: 111)

To perceive in the darkness of the present, this light that strives to reach us but cannot—this is what it means to be contemporary.
(Agamben 2009: 46)

The present includes the immediacy of what we see as well as the exigency of what we do not. The present does not require presence. Televisual images stream disparate events—gamers queuing for the most recent release, blue tarpaulins spread across post-disaster landscapes, and informal settlements pressed along closed borders. Despite their contrasting programs, all of these events occur in camps. Though founded in urgency, exigencies might remain remote as our attention readily courses from disaster to conflict to entertainment, but their presence has depth—whether experiential or historical—and urgent situations recall the word's Latin root *exigere* with its demand to perform thoroughly. With precision and duration. In spite of their ephemeral foundations, camps have a long history, and their deployment interrogates environmental, socio-political, and cultural concerns, measuring the forces at work.

Speed, globalism, and climate have complicated how, what, and where we build. Given the paradoxes of present and presence, a key question is how to understand that which resists visibility and clarity? How to negotiate immediacy with distance, dislocation with locality, and exigency with response? These questions become particularly difficult considering the physical presence of the built environment. Few constructed spaces have the capacity to hold such paradox and obscurity, and still fewer spaces can channel current forces and indicate future directions, while recalling—even if anachronistically—historical precedents. At the start of the twenty-first century, camps are contemporary environments that bring the present into contact with presence.

Seeking the contemporary, Giorgio Agamben reminds us that the sky's darkness holds light. There are stars we see, and there are also stars that remain invisible as their receding galaxies outpace incoming starlight. Like someone emerging from a light-filled room, looking skyward at night, Agamben asks us not to wait for our eyes to adjust, but to embrace the momentary obscurities of stars and darkness alike.[1] Rereading Agamben's essay, a reciprocal image comes to mind. NASA's satellite images of earth at night enthrall with their tracery of lights that mark cities, highways, and conurbations. Initially developed to study clouds by moonlight, these images now visualize infrastructural systems, global development, and light pollution. Imagine this array of lights turned off and consider the previously unlit spaces along its edges, inland from the coast, along secondary and tertiary routes, next to invisible but reinforced borders. In the wake of dimmed electrification, cooking fires and low-voltage lighting would emit a soft glow, revealing an archipelago of camps, many of them larger than their urbanized counterparts.

Out of this obscurity and darkness is the contemporary tenancy of global space, a displaced population of more than 60 million people.[2] Some of these dimly lit spaces host internally displaced persons (IDPs); others hold refugees who have crossed borders. All of them are camps. Not cities, they are settlements decreed temporary but made permanent by necessity.[3] Others mark the transient locations of more than ten million recreational vehicles, many of which serve a burgeoning North American demographic identified by the acronym UHE, or usual home elsewhere (Curtin 2011). Making up for fewer occupants with wider global distribution, still others identify strategic locations of military camps where tens of thousands of soldiers reside on islands, within inland conflict zones, along veins of energy extraction. Whether nomadic by choice or because of need, this is the contemporary megalopolis. Where NASA's Earth's City Lights map elides borders, a map of camps reminds us of them. As the former highlights connecting corridors, the camps—particularly those driven by necessity and conflict—occur in remote, even largely inaccessible, areas. While city lights burning into the night indicate excess, surplus, and waste, other factors like austerity and conservation calibrate camps' output.

Detail and Territory

Though an alternative to the City Lights map and an inversion of its conventions, this map of camps relies on a mode of visualization that often oversimplifies, occasionally sanitizes, realities of the camp. Apparent order from above belies chaotic circumstances on the ground, what looks like an overview of a city reveals a lack of infrastructure at street level, and military camps that may appear like suburban greenfields disclose islands of control on the ground. Aerial views remain important means for planners to understand a camp's dynamic systems, but the flyover is also how the rest of the world comes to know the camp, through media tropes that approximate the scope of disaster and displacement. In this essay, each set of illustrations pairs aerial and ground views of a particular camp. Each photograph serves only as a fleeting glimpse of a built environment caught between transience and permanence. The disjunction between vignette and overview is also the tension between detail and territory that binds the conception, construction, and occupation of camps. Camps work between the tent peg and the campsite, between modular shelter and infrastructural layout, between the mark and the field. Each scale, each end of the visual field has a role to play in revealing present conditions of the camp, which can also be extended to the broader forces of contemporary life.

Above Dadaab's camps, the view of Ifo 2's grid invokes organization, suggests containment, and regiments districts, its wide streets buffering tribal distinctions and facilitating aid distribution. On the ground, cooking fires burn. In his book *City of Thorns*, Ben Rawlence describes a cooking fire lit by Isha and Ahmed, refugees who came to Dadaab to escape the 2011 famine in Somalia and who live in the area known as N Zero on the outskirts of Dadaab's Ifo camps. Wood expected from aid agencies has not arrived so that walking miles across a desert of stumps is necessary to gather thorn bush branches for shelter and fuel. When he describes the fire, Rawlence emphasizes smallness—"little," "stone," "meagre"—within the camp's immensity and its extended field. The tension between this cooking fire and the unforgiving territory required to provide its wood maps the contemporary situation of camps.

Adaptation

Camps are exceedingly adaptable environments that provide two key modes to understand the contemporary. Camps accommodate conditions that might otherwise remain without space. And they indicate local as well as global changes at their earliest stages. Consequently, camps make present future trajectories of migration, trace invisible flows of capital, make room for tacit aspirations of shifting demographics, and demonstrate archaic yet quotidian and ultimately relevant definitions of dwelling itself. As camps anticipate change, their adaptability is agility in movement and ideology. Camps accommodate the nomadic, while they embrace foundational and elemental aspects of shelter. Just as the term "camp" also denotes a political position, camps are open to transformations of objectives, values, and meaning. This combination of efficacy and vulnerability engenders a taxonomic strategy to organize the different responses of the camp. Patterns in the arrays and complexities of camps yield three categories: autonomy, necessity, and control (Hailey 2009). Autonomous camps arise from choice, and need underpins camps of necessity. Camps of control hold people or territories by force. A camp's mobility holds latent permanence, and its purpose is often as labile as its location is transient. Objectives driven by necessity—such as humanitarian aid—might be complicated by controlling forces. A drive for autonomy—such as a self-regulated community—might be freighted with public obligations as well as obscure but persistent regulations. Camps' agility also facilitates tactical shifts from conditions of need to power or between autonomy and necessity. Camps inevitably touch on all three categories, just as each camp offers its own version of the contemporary.

Autonomy

Camps of autonomy register desire. Campers long for closeness to nature, seek communal life, look for sites to practice alternative identities (even if as temporary avatars), and aspire for places that are quite simply free. But these new proximities often require distance. Some might find isolation in a backyard camp—outside of quotidian domestic space; but others seek greater separation, across a geographic expanse, in remote sites such as Europe's wild camps or the U.S. Bureau of Land Management's Long Term Visitor Area camps. Choosing to camp negotiates proximity and distance—camping offers freedom *from*, while it is also a return *to* (Hailey and Wylie 2018). Autonomous campers want to be free from power, rules, routines. Concurrently, what they seek elicits—whether intended or not—a return to basics, elemental forms of living, even surviving. You give something up when you decide to go camping. Nostalgia, ennui, resistance, asceticism, and aesthetics all might play a part in this camping process. Nowhere are these features more intertwined than in the festival camp of Burning Man. The arc of this camp's history also points toward the commodification of autonomous camping as a privileged process and as an image (Figures 15.1a and 15.1b).

Burning Man is a well-known camp of autonomy. The festival camp's origins extend back to 1986 when Larry Harvey, Jerry James, and friends convened to burn the "man" on California's Baker Beach. Four years later, the Cacophony Society's Zone Trip #4 inaugurated the annual event with an apocryphal journey to Nevada's Black Rock Desert. In spite of commodification and higher costs (tickets to the 2016 festival approached $400), Burning Man's central

Figure 15.1a Aerial view of Burning Man, 2015
Source: Photograph Copyright Scott London.

Figure 15.1b Installation by Michael Garlington, *Totem of Confessions*, Burning Man, 2015
Source: Photograph Copyright Scott London.

purpose remains, quite simply, to camp. Not the musical performances at Coachella and other festival camps, just themed sub-camps where participants (and participate you must) practice self-expression and self-reliance. Two types of images identify the camp: on-ground photographs that highlight the hedonism but also recall—nostalgically—polaroid-era selfies, and the equally obligatory aerial photograph from a three-quarter birds-eye view that places the two-thirds camping circle in the foreground and the Jackson Mountains in the background.

With each annual meeting, the camp's population has increased (70,000 in 2015) along with exposure to media and socio-cultural influence (BLM 2015). At the festival, you can still only buy and sell ice and coffee; but now after-festival installations sell Lexus cars and advertising spoofs adapt Burning Man's image and theme.[4] In its first decade, many of its festival-goers were urbanites traveling from northern California and leaving one city for another. Anachronistically, Burning Man is a secularized camp meeting. Its neo-primitives engage in aesthetic performances throughout the week in late summer, and at the end they perform a now entirely ritualized clean-up to practice Leave No Trace (LNT) principles across the playa, looking for Matter out of Place (MOOP). Quasi-scientific acronyms proliferate as clothing lessens, so that the camp meeting combines with nudist camp and research field station. Organizers have long prohibited traditional campfires, and festival-goers must use elevated burn platforms to protect the sensitive playa. So, the overall camp has its own outsized fire when the "man" is burned at the center of its 3-kilometer diameter. In this way, Black Rock City, as the event is known, comes to symbolize the romance and pragmatics of the archetypal camping experience—summer camp, Boy Scout and Girl Scout camps, and even the backyard camp (if the camp is considered broadly in its Western, regional context). Complementing its smaller-scale, aesthetic experiments, Burning Man's didactic layout applies practical rules of camping writ large across the desert landscape: note the prevailing breeze and pitch your tents upwind of the campfire. A tithe to the environment, one-third of the camp remains open to exhaust smoke from the burning "man"—further dramatizing a conflagration that temporarily and symbolically rejects what its participants have all accepted (Hailey 2011).

Necessity

Camps also accommodate need amid increased population displacement. Lodged between autonomy and control, camps of necessity occur in the wake of crisis. Natural disasters, economic disruptions, political conflicts, and societal changes generate provisional but often obdurate settlements of refugees, homeless persons, relief workers, gypsies, hobos, and even survivalists. Camps of necessity negotiate the need *for* and the response *to*. This disjunction means that conditions of need may become protracted, and a lack of responsiveness can yield other camps of protest, whether they target migration policies, as in the case of Europe's No Border Camps, or address homelessness and the loss of housing in urban and suburban environments, as with SDF (Sans Domicile Fixé) camps in Paris and the Occupy Our Homes movement in North America (Hailey 2013). Consequently, camps of necessity challenge definitions of borders and public space alike.

This disconnect also means that displaced populations are at risk of being ignored, misunderstood, isolated, exploited, or dominated. Reference guides, manuals, and handbooks have sought to address this disjunction. UNHCR guides remain the standard for refugee camps, but other reference handbooks have tested the economic viability of exceeding the minimum standards, have served as antidotes to the planned obsolescence of camps of necessity, have further reconciled gaps between safety and assistance, and have sought alternatives of social sustainability.[5] Aid does not always fit a camp's urgent situation, and identities of those in the camps do not always match the perception of outsiders. UNHCR includes both assistance and protection in its mandate for relief but can sometimes only deliver one or the other. In the latter cases, necessity shifts toward control. The range of response is as diverse as the displaced persons' experiences are varied. In the early 1990s, UNHCR introduced the phrase "persons of concern" to establish a broader framework—legal and logistical—to support those not necessarily identified as refugees, including asylum seekers, stateless persons, and IDPs.[6] With refugee settlements in particular, camps evidence previously invisible scales of displacement. In the mid-1990s, at the height of the Rwandan crisis, more than a quarter of the population in Tanzania's Kasulu district lived in camps. Such camps are typically set up on marginal land, far from urban centers and not suitable for agriculture. In addition to conflict, camps of necessity often accommodate those affected by earthquakes, hurricanes, and sea level rise; but camps of this size strain local environments and natural resources. And refugees, by definition, face a double displacement—away from ancestral homeland and within a new home country (Figures 15.2a and 15.2b).

The five camps of Dadaab exemplify this disconnect. International media perennially cites Dadaab as the "world's largest refugee camp," and it remains the most populous. Somalia's civil war in the late 1980s and early 1990s and the 2011 drought combined with continuing conflict have spurred two main waves of displaced persons to enter the semi-arid landscape of Kenya's North Eastern Province. The first three camps—Ifo, Dagahaley, and Hagadera—are each the equivalent of placing a version of New York City's Bronx borough in the desert of the American southwest. Ifo 2 and Kambioos were added 19 years later in 2011 to alleviate pressures of overcrowding at Dadaab. This complex of camps reflects the realities of post-colonialism, twenty-first-century geopolitical intervention, mobile money's new capitalism, and environmental degradation, within a surrogate state of half a million refugees, a generation of whom have known nothing but camp life (Hailey 2011, 2014; Kagan 2011; Slaughter and Crisp 2006; Stevens 2006). Kenya and earlier British occupying governments have historically sought to limit mobility in this area where nomadic pastoralists have traditionally herded and camped. The Kenyan government has retained emergency rules and extrajudicial powers in the region and, most recently, has threatened to close Dadaab amid fears that the camp hosts members of the terrorist group Al-Shabaab.

The camps at Dadaab generate informal economies that range from mobile money's virtual presence to firewood's more tangible absence. With "M" for mobile and Swahili "Pesa" for money, M-Pesa allows for transactions to be executed over mobile phones by those who do not have access to traditional banks. This economic work-around eases the flow of remittances from outside the camp and complements other internal modes of payment like bartering and Kenyan shilling notes. Firewood is a commodity that must be gathered. Refugees at Dadaab travel beyond the camp's perimeter to look for wood, sometimes on roundtrips as long as 30 kilometers (Giles and Hyndman 2004).[7] This range of resource extraction extends even further when UNHCR provides firewood, which regularly moves hundreds of kilometers for a delivery. As a result, aid agencies have sought to introduce alternative fuels and cookers.[8] But many of the refugees want to use traditional Somalian methods of cooking of which wood fires are an integral part, just as traditions of nomadism have long been at odds with the colonial, and now camp-related, forces in the region. The demand for wood has created its own economy, with firewood as the tangible commodity in contrast to the more ephemeral transfer of mobile money. And all of these informal activities play out across the formalized warp and weft of gridded plans. The grid facilitates closure and reflects agencies' need to organize space so that aid can be effectively distributed, as it also lattices under the spontaneous self-settlement that still occurs across the rectilinear blocks. Indicating another version of the contemporary, Dadaab is an emergency space that remains emergent but has long since become too permanent to still be considered temporary.

Figure 15.2a Aerial view of Dadaab's Ifo 2 camp with original Ifo camp in background, 2011
Source: Photograph Copyright United Nations.

Figure 15.2b Shelters built at the edge of Ifo camp in Dadaab, July 2011
Source: Photograph Copyright United Nations.

Control

Camps of control seek to establish power over regions and populations. In terms of strategy, camps operate by location and force; and in terms of space, they utilize containment. If openness typifies autonomous camps and indeterminacy characterizes camps of necessity, then controlled camps are purportedly closed spaces. In some cases, these camps remain largely invisible, cloaked in their remoteness or their embeddedness, like France's *zones d'attente* where immigrants are held in airports. In other cases, they are in full view, but their intentions are obscure, like twenty-first-century permutations of U.S. overseas military facilities. Camps of control might be singular, like the Marine Corps' two boot camps for training soldiers, but typically form a larger network, like the United Kingdom's Transit Processing Centers, Australia's offshore camps, and Europe's detention camps for migrants. Camps of control also tie into environmental concerns. Permanent Accommodation Camps and Man Camps harbor laborers and oversee resource extraction, while the U.S. military's North American camps hold more than 25 million acres of ecologically sensitive and culturally significant land.

Camp Bondsteel in southeastern Kosovo reflects contemporary fluidities of military planning. The camp demonstrates how places held by force can be fleeting but not ephemeral. In 1999, Camp Bondsteel was constructed in three months as a primary base for NATO-led, multi national brigades and battle groups of the Kosovo force deployed in response to the Kosovo crisis. As the Balkan conflict waned, the immediacy of the base as a "light-switch facility" became a longer-term Forward Operating Station (FOS). This indeterminate terminology reflects the camp's flexibility in the easy shift from peace-keeping mission to broader strategic presence. The camp's size, amenities, and facilities belie its transience and indicate a lasting installation—a system of more permanent ephemera. Military operations appropriated 1000 acres, moved a half-million cubic yards of earth, and assembled building materials equivalent to a 355-house subdivision (Hailey 2009: 274–276). Only in this type of environment can the anachronisms of Roman castrum and suburban development coexist, and at such a large scale. At the time of its completion, Camp Bondsteel was the largest U.S. military camp constructed since the Vietnam War (Figures 15.3a and 15.3b).[9]

Military engineers and planners have presented this camp as the "Bondsteel template." This naming convention alludes to the mutability and paradoxes of contemporary camps of control. Named for James L. Bondsteel, who served in the Vietnam War and received the Medal of Honor, "Bondsteel template" recalls war's heroism and its workaday utilitarianism (McClure 2000: 6–11). When separated from the context of naming a place for a person, the term points toward a firmness and fixity—"bond" and "steel"—meshed with the openness necessitated by daily life—what the military calls QOL (quality of life). Just as "Camp Bondsteel" pairs the general and specific, its invocation as a template engages the universal as well as the particular. And perhaps most significantly, the pairing of a proper name with an open-ended tag echoes the growing privatization of the American military's logistical operations. The private firm Kellogg Brown and Root built Camp Bondsteel for more than 35 million dollars and continued to operate the camp under a contract that approaches 200 million dollars annually (Johnson 2004: 143).[10] As Chalmers Johnson and other analysts have also noted, Camp Bondsteel's location along the route of proposed trans-Balkan oil pipelines points toward strategic protection and control of economic interests. Back in the camp, soldiers can eat at Burger King, Anthony's Pizza, and Taco Bell.

Figure 15.3a Aerial view of Camp Bondsteel, Kosovo
Source: Photograph Copyright United Nations.

Figure 15.3b Dining facilities and Burger King at Camp Bondsteel
Source: Photograph Copyright Sherry Crum.

Charlie Hailey

Breaking Camp

> When a flash of lightning illumines a dark landscape, there is a momentary recognition of objects. But the recognition is not itself a mere point in time. It is the focal culmination of a long, slow process of maturation. It is the manifestation of the continuity of an ordered temporal experience in a sudden discrete instant of climax.
>
> *(Dewey 2005: 24)*

The flash urbanism of Burning Man, the protracted surrogate state of Dadaab, and the flexible military template of Camp Bondsteel. These camps resonate with John Dewey's "focal culminations" as specific events and particular places cast in a historical framework of temporary built environments and, more broadly, within the shifting questions of how and why we build. Camps are witnesses to conflicted histories and complicated aspirations. The unsettling range of camps' permutations—from freedom to need to power—requires consideration even if resolution remains impossible. If we are looking for Dewey's "momentary recognition," camps span near and far, making present previously distant events. Camps also bridge the temporary and the permanent. Neither completely transient nor fully immoveable, camps occur as moments in a continuum. Their relevance as contemporary spaces lies in their capacity to hold chronological and episodic time—what Agamben (2009: 52) presents as the chronological indeterminacy of the contemporary.

Camps are kairotic spaces. Typically translated as opportune and appropriate time, *kairos* has its origins in the mythological figure of Zeus' youngest divine son who represented the spirit of opportunity that must be grasped before it passes.[11] Luck and fortune also characterize *kairos*, linking to anachronism's anomalies of chronological errors and displacements. Agamben (2005: 68–69) contends that *chronos* and *kairos* are nested within one another, and camps allow access to the disjunctions of near and far, as well as temporary and permanent, through the "contracted and abridged" time of *kairos*.[12] In each case, camps present kairotic spaces for localized events tied to past settlement patterns that endure in spite of their obscurity and to global forces that point toward future systems. Though they might remain unstable, camps provide momentary insight to understand the meaning of value-laden—even if destabilizing—forces in the contemporary built environment. This is the "grounding without ground" that architect Ignasi de Solà-Morales deftly extracted from Nietzsche's discussion of dilemmas in building the modern home on his way to defining weak architecture's productive yet unstable events (Solà-Morales 1997: 64–65).[13] Camps are weak, but they can also be instruments of power.

Ostensibly, a camp might be established with objectives for autonomy, opening up opportunities for freedom. But lifting the veil of how it changes over time and how it functions in the present reveals systems that also include necessity and control. Burning Man satisfies a need for escape and belonging, and the event's organizers now offer this gratification behind a fence, with an entry fee. Autonomy is not necessarily free. And camps of control come in many forms, sometimes veiled in the name of freedom. As Burning Man strictly moderates and curates its image base, from on-the-ground vignettes to aerial photographs, military camps like Bondsteel use imaging and surveillance for security. And FOBs, aggressive projections of power as well as vulnerable outposts—the "forward" in Forward Operating Base—also harbor the choices (and fast food) of American suburban life, albeit behind perimeters. These double-displacements contract distinctions of here and there, now and then, open and closed. Meanwhile Dadaab's traditional cooking fires burn with imported wood and its informal economy moves with mobile money between cell phones, while its residents are officially denied movement outside the camp.

Within this contracted time, camps offer insights to the dilemmas of the twenty-first century's built environments. Like Dewey's flash of lightning, such insight is both fleeting and practical (Heidegger 1962: 401).[14] In terms of the former, the camp's relations between exceptional and everyday float within its geographic, political, and cultural territories; and with the latter, it requires concrete responses for shelter, livelihood, and infrastructure. Most critically for its contemporaneity, the camp models these relations and these practices *through* its displacement. The camp models a temporary house, while it also displaces home. In camps, such paradoxes are not contradictory but are instead contemporary.

Acknowledgments

The author would like to thank Bahar Aktuna for assistance with preparation of the manuscript and Sanford Kwinter for critical feedback on the origins and meaning of *kairos*.

Notes

1 Throughout his essay "What Is the Contemporary," Agamben (2009: 39–54) works between disjunctions and anachronisms and between exigencies of urgent need and shadows of the past—ideas that have served as a departure point for this essay. Agamben also presents these ideas through the figure of the contemporary philosopher: "The contemporary is he who firmly holds his gaze on his own time so as to perceive not its light, but rather its darkness" (2009: 46).
2 In a December 18, 2015 news release, the United Nations High Commissioner for Refugees (UNHCR) announced that the number of forcefully displaced persons exceeded 60 million in 2015, ten million more than World War II's levels of displacement. See Tim Gaynor, "2015 likely to break records for forced displacement," www.unhcr.org.
3 National Aeronautics and Space Administration (NASA) notes that "the brightest areas of the Earth are the most urbanized, but not necessarily the most populated." See NASA Visible Earth. "Earth's City Lights." Online. Available at: http://visibleearth.nasa.gov/view.php?id=55167 (April 14, 2016).
4 The Burning Man artists who created *Uchronia: Message Out of the Future* at the 2006 camp refashioned a similar sculpture for party stage sets to exhibit and promote Lexus automobiles. More recently in 2015, the restaurant Quiznos released a video spoofing the festival to promote its sandwiches. In each case, Burning Man organizers considered legal action.
5 Manuals include the following: Sphere Project, *Humanitarian Charter and Minimum Standards for Disaster Response* (2011); UNHCR, *Handbook for Emergencies* (2007); UNHCR, *Practical Guide to the Systematic Use of Standards and Indicators in UNHCR Operations* (2006); and Corsellis and Vitale, *Transitional Settlement* (2005).
6 UNHCR's document (1992) "Protection of persons of concern to UNHCR who fall outside the 1951 Convention: a discussion note EC/1992/SCP/CRP.5" outlined the preliminary approach for "persons of concern":

> Bridging the gap between these two sets of responsibilities [protection and assistance] in a way which ensures adequate protection of persons of concern to UNHCR who fall outside the 1951 Convention, while maintaining the international consensus on protection of refugees, remains a major humanitarian challenge both for UNHCR and for States generally.

See also UNHCR (August 1, 2005) "An introduction to international protection: protecting persons of concern to UNHCR: self-study module 1." Switzerland: Office of the United Nations High Commissioner for Refugees. Online. Available at: www.unhcr.org/3ae6bd5a0.pdf (April 2, 2016).
7 Most of those who gather firewood are women, and their trips out of camp leave them vulnerable to attacks. For a detailed discussion, see Giles and Hyndman (2004: 198–199).
8 Alternatives to three-stone cooking fires include liquefied petroleum gas (LPG) stoves, fuel-saving stoves that reduce the amount of firewood needed, sustainably sourced wood (as in South Sudanese camps in Ethiopia, where environmental forest harvesting occurs in its northern regions), and advanced firewood cook stoves and clean-cooking stoves like the Norwegian company Safi's bioethanol stoves.

9 Johnson (2004: 143) notes that "Army wags say facetiously that there are only two man-made objects that can be seen from outer space"—the Great Wall of China and Camp Bondsteel.
10 The contract includes supplies, service, and maintenance, only excluding military duties.
11 *Kairos* stands in contrast to *chronos*, which is more measured, linear time.
12 Discussing Agamben's work, Gary Shapiro (2013: 135) notes that *kairos* is a "temporal contraction, the time that ushers in the event." For origins of Agamben's discussion of *kairos*, see Detienne and Vernant, (1991 [1978]).
13 Solà-Morales invokes the contemporary to expand his working definition of weak architecture: "The proposals of contemporary art are to be constructed not on the basis of any immovable reference, but under the obligation to posit for every step both its goal and its grounding." And then "contemporary architecture, in conjunction with the other arts, is confronted with the need to build on air, to build in the void" (1997: 59). Nietzsche (1996: 24) places this contemporary crisis between the current "agitated ephemeral existence and the slow-breathing repose of metaphysical ages." See also Hailey (2008: 113, 252–253, 261–262).
14 Heidegger's discussion of "moment of vision" and the term *Augenblick* (literally "glance of the eye") parallels the meaning of *kairos*. Dreyfus (2005) notes the connections between *Augenblick* and *kairos* in "Can there be a better source of meaning than everyday practices? Reinterpreting Division I of *Being and Time* in the Light of Division II." See also Ward (2016); and see Nussbaum (1990: 305) for a sustained discussion of "practical insight" in *The Fragility of Goodness*.

References

Agamben, G. (2005) *The Time That Remains*, trans. P. Dailey, Stanford: Stanford University Press.
Agamben, G. (2009) "What Is the contemporary?," in *What Is an Apparatus? and Other Essays*, Stanford: Stanford University Press.
BLM (Bureau of Land Management) (2015) "Burning Man 2015: special recreation permit stipulations." August 7. http://burningman.org/wp-content/uploads/2015_blm_srp_decision.pdf (March 28, 2016).
Corsellis, T. and Vitale. A. (2005) *Transitional Settlement: Displaced Populations*, Oxford: Oxfam GB.
Curtin, R. T. (2011) "The RV consumer in 2011," Surveys of Consumers, University of Michigan. https://data.sca.isr.umich.edu/fetchdoc.php?docid=49063 (April 5, 2016).
Detienne, M. and Vernant, J.-P. (1991 [1978]) *Cunning Intelligence in Greek Culture and Society*, trans. J. Lloyd, Chicago: University of Chicago Press.
Dewey, J. (2005) *Art as Experience*, New York: Perigree.
Dreyfus, H. L. (2005) "Can there be a better source of meaning than everyday practices? Reinterpreting Division I of *Being and Time* in the Light of Division II," in R. Polt (ed.) *Heidegger's Being and Time: Critical Essays*, New York: Rowman & Littlefield, 141–155.
Giles, W. M. and Hyndman, J. (eds) (2004) *Sites of Violence: Gender and Conflict Zones*, Berkeley: University of California Press.
Hailey, C. (2008) *Campsite: Architectures of Duration and Place*, Baton Rouge: Louisiana State University Press.
Hailey, C. (2009) *Camps: A Guide to 21st-Century Space*, Cambridge, MA: MIT Press.
Hailey, C. (2011) "Burn after building," *Icon* 102 (December): 62–69.
Hailey, C. (2013) "Occupying is camping," in J.-F. Prost (ed.) *Adaptive Actions: Heteropolis*, Montreal: Leonard & Bina Ellen Art Gallery/Concordia University.
Hailey, C. (2014) "Camps, corridors, and clouds: inland ways to the ocean," *Harvard Design Magazine* 39 (Winter): 24–30.
Hailey, C. and Wylie, D. (2018) *Slab City: Dispatches from the Last Free Place*, Cambridge, MA: MIT Press.
Heidegger, M. (1962) *Being and Time*, New York: Harper.
Johnson, C. (2004) *Sorrows of Empire: Militarism, Secrecy, and the End of the Republic*, London: Verso.
Kagan, M. (2011) "We live in a country of UNHCR: the UN surrogate state and refugee policy in the Middle East," in *The UN Refugee Agency: Policy Development and Evaluation Service Research Paper No. 201* (February 1) UNLV William S. Boyd School of Law Legal Studies Research Paper Series.
McClure, R. L. (2000) "The engineer regiment in Kosovo," *Engineer: The Professional Bulletin for Army Engineers* 30, 2 (April): 6.
Nietzsche, F. (1996) *Human, All Too Human*, trans. R. J. Hollingdale, New York: Cambridge University Press.

Nussbaum, M. C. (1990) *The Fragility of Goodness*, Cambridge, UK: Cambridge University Press.
Rawlence, B. (2016) *City of Thorns*, New York: Picador.
Shapiro, G. (2013) "Kairos and chronos: Nietzsche and the time of the multitude," in K. Ansell-Pearson (ed.) *Nietzsche and Political Thought*, London: Bloomsbury, 123–140.
Slaughter, A. and Crisp, J. (2006) "A surrogate state? The role of UNHCR in protracted refugee situations," in *New Issues in Refugee Research*, Research Paper No. 168 (November/December).
Solà-Morales, I. (1997) *Differences: Topographies of Contemporary Architecture*, Cambridge, MA: MIT Press.
Sphere Project (2011) *Humanitarian Charter and Minimum Standards for Disaster Response*, revised edition, Oxford: Oxfam.
Stevens, J. (2006) "Prisons of the stateless," *New Left Review* 42 (November/December).
UNHCR (2006) *Practical Guide to the Systematic Use of Standards and Indicators in UNHCR Operations*, 2nd edition, Geneva.
UNHCR (2007) *Handbook for Emergencies*, 3rd edition, Geneva.
Ward, K. (2016) *Augenblick: The Concept of the Decisive Moment in 19th and 20th Century Western Philosophy*, London: Routledge.

16
Defensive Alterity in Contemporary Sri Lankan Architecture

Anoma Pieris

Since its development by continental philosophers such as Emmanuel Levinas and Gabriel Marcel, the concept of "otherness" has fueled numerous discourses on absolute or relative interpretations of difference and similitude (Treanor 2006: 5, 8).[1] Postmodern and poststructuralist cultural discourses have likewise influenced architectural interest in uncanny, liminal, or interstitial forms of spatial alterity that reject canonical metanarratives drawn from Euro-American modernism. Alterity has been spatialized on increasingly polemical terms beyond its "disruption of the homological relation between form and function," and resultant production of antithetical architectural meanings—for example, anti-monuments or anti-institutions (Benjamin, 2000: 11; see also Stevens, Franck, and Fazakerley 2012).[2] The concept has expanded to include conditions of duality such as interiority and exteriority, and utopian or dystopian experiences; alternative spatial practices such as self-organization and performativity; and resistant positions that are piratical, hedonistic, or counter-hegemonic.[3] Transnational identities or hybrid and multiple readings of canonical urban or architectural phenomena are seen as challenging binary interpretations of alterity. The term "alterities" has been used as an invented term for describing altering practices—the multiple possibilities of feminist architectural praxis (Petrescu 2007).

These approaches appear salient for professional practice. Michael Jensen's "Mapping the Global Architect of Alterity" (2014: ch. 1), for example, provides new frames of reference across several contemporary debates that might address the radical deterritorialization of cultural spaces through globalization. Jensen examines these frames of reference across critical aesthetic practice, professionalization, and pedagogy. Others have followed suit. Brent Allpress (2015) uses the concept in developing proposals for the adaptive reuse of iconic modern buildings thus challenging the modernist architects' claim to autonomy. Thomas Mical (2012) argues that by dealing with spatial alterity we are better equipped for reconciling or anticipating future spatial transformations.[4] Their translation of alterity into a design tool is underscored by a crisis of extant pedagogy in the face of globalization's social proximities and homogenizing forces. The relevance for Asia is somewhat different.

As theorized in *Orientalism* by Edward Said (1978), through their literary and aesthetic practices orientalist scholars supported the colonial production of alterity for dominance over subject races. Postcolonial societies have had to decolonize these asymmetrical orientalist representations, self-orientalizing practices, and constructions of the "self" and "other" in order to restore cultural confidence. Both exotic and abhorrent constructions of alterity have thereby entered architectural production, differentiating local architectural traditions from their modern counterparts. Such dialectical cultural framings have been propagated through orientalist material practices such as expositions, publications, archaeological surveys, museology, photography, and the fine arts, which form substantial portions of the recorded histories of many postcolonial nations. A generation of scholars has since decolonized this legacy by indigenizing, complicating, and diversifying the East–West polemic around the objects and subjects of modernity, most notably the urban and architectural spaces introduced via colonialism (Pieris 2010). However, these orientalist themes persist in the many vanity publications that celebrate exotic Asian architectures. William Lim's *Asian Alterity* (2008) operates across these multiple discourses, reducing Asia and the West to contentious polemical categories and outlining new Cultural Studies-based interpretive parameters, while simultaneously invoking those earlier sensorial themes. The economic empowerment and "Rise of Asia," the need for interdisciplinary cross-fertilization, and the notion of multiple or plural modernities anchor his rebuttal of hegemonic Westernization. Lim's approach is largely prescriptive, focused on the role of professionals in the transformation of an increasingly prosperous Asia rather than the *Other Asias* beyond their purview (with reference to Spivak 2008: ch. 4).

This chapter uses the concept of alterity to discuss the exclusionary construction of normative spaces around polemical postcolonial categories of "self" and "other." The example explored is an extreme one of architectural production during the Sri Lankan civil war. However, this case is no exception if we acknowledge how inter-Asian and global conflicts have transformed Asia, producing militarized cultures, and military and militant regimes, and have sustained Western military interventions. Utopian projections of the region and its nations conceal volatile internal and external pressures unacknowledged by architects. Their discursive silences become apparent, in this example, when we juxtapose selective national spatial projections with their more abject wartime counterparts. This chapter's dual purpose is to examine the conceptual utility of alterity when internalized for self scrutiny, and to expose the fallacy of seemingly *a*political architectural representations. I suggest that Sri Lanka's design practitioners have constructed a *defensive alterity*.

Dystopian Politics

In July 1983, one year after the completion of the celebrated new Sri Lankan parliament by architect Geoffrey Bawa (Figure 16.1), the island was rocked by an anti-Tamil pogrom and was plunged into a state of bitter civil war. Official estimates vary from between 400 to 3000 deaths among the minority Tamil population and many thousand properties destroyed (Dissanayaka 1983: 93; Sharvananda, Sahabandu, and Zuhair 2002). Black July, as it was commemorated, was the climax of simmering anti-Tamil urban sentiment and provocative Tamil separatist politics, but was not unprecedented. Anti-Tamil violence had occurred at a much smaller scale following ethno-linguistic nationalist policies in 1958 and immediately after the 1977 elections that brought the market-oriented United National Party (under Prime Minister later President J. R. Jayewardene) into government. This election placed the minority Tamil United Liberation Front with separatist ambitions as the parliamentary Opposition. Growing animosity between Sinhala and Tamil parliamentarians became evident when, in 1981, the Jaffna Public Library, the foremost institution for an erudite minority in a historically Tamil city, was burnt to the ground. The involvement of government officials and police in incidents leading to this heinous act presaged violence to come.

Political theorists (Tambiah 1996; Gunasinghe 1988b; Winslow and Woost 2004; Bastian 2008: 151–164) have attributed the reasons behind these early targeted attacks to competition

Figure 16.1 Geoffrey Bawa, Sri Lanka Parliament 1979–1982

Source: Copyright Anoma Pieris.

over resources made available through economic liberalization, the asymmetrical distribution of developmental projects (their neglect of Tamil areas), and the majoritarian politics of successive postcolonial governments, which favored the approximately 75 percent Sinhala-Buddhist majority constituents over the Tamil-speaking Tamil and Muslim minorities (the Tamil population was around 18 percent).[5] While the nuanced details of these various interest groups are too complex to discuss in this chapter, allegations that the July 1983 pogrom was instigated by the government suggested the insidious undercurrents of targeted victimization (Paul Sieghart 1984: section 2.7; Gunasinghe 1984, 1988a; Piyadasa 1984). The failure of the government to protect its Tamil voters, to provide them with adequate and timely compensation, or indeed to recognize and admit neglect suggested its culpability.

The severity of the July 1983 pogrom highlighted the bitter undercurrents of postcolonial subjectivity that underwrote Jayewardene's ascendance, his liberalization of the economy, embrace of marketization, and reconfiguration of the constitution through several amendments to accommodate an executive presidency.[6] This political change was spatially manifested as the new legislative capital at Sri Jayewardenepura with its parliamentary complex (discussed previously in Pieris 2014). By reducing the significance of the former colonial capital, Colombo, to a commercial capital, opening up suburban spaces to its immediate southeast and rejuvenating the lost heritage of a sixteenth-century Sinhala kingdom (that had unified the island by defeating northern Tamils), Jayewardene placated Sinhalese voters, who were envious of minority advancement and suspicious of capitalist goals.[7] Jayewardene couched this transformation in the language of Buddhist justice—advocating "A free and just society" as his election platform. Sovereign claims expressed through the capital and parliament reinforced Sinhala-Buddhist political hegemony.

The urban plan of Sri Jayewardenepura did not incorporate the extant ruins of the precolonial kingdom, which were overtaken by suburban sprawl. The plan was governed by Western models of the Garden City adopted by local planners. Despite this disjunction between political will and professional practice, the new capital fulfilled the ideological inscription of a Sinhala-Buddhist history. Its creation was a strategic move by a president whose party had been rejected at successive elections, due to its Western leanings, and was a means for swaying a population made overly nationalistic through insular socialist policies. Sri Jayewardenepura became a city largely of Sinhalese suburban residents, while Tamils and Muslims favored its congested postcolonial counterpart.

These two utopian transformations that were institutional and suburban reinvented the national space in substantial ways, just as the destruction of the Jaffna Library and burning of Tamil homes hollowed out the spaces of minority cultures. They articulated the normative subjectivity of the preferred Sri Lankan subject who would be ideologically and economically supported. Meanwhile the social structures that might challenge it were neglected or destroyed. The new capital of Sri Jayewardenepura rose out of the marshlands while Tamil homes and institutions were reduced to ashes. Such evocative parallel images, although unconnected to the architectural profession's aims, inadvertently sustained it. Their utopian projections of a bucolic Sri Lankan lifestyle appeared all the more powerful in this dystopian present. The suburban lands opened up by Sri Jayewardenepura provided ample opportunities for spacious villa-style homes. Nevertheless, the parliament's moment of glory was short-lived. Tamil separatists who launched successive attacks on Colombo and its institutions saw these as the representative spaces of a mono-cultural majoritarian democracy. They targeted them as reprisals for aerial bombardment in the north. Sensitive institutions and neighborhoods would be defensively barricaded, streets would be closed off, and homes would be converted to fortresses against armed suicidal attacks. Much of the plan for expanding Sri Jayewardenepura was delayed due to its vulnerability and embassies and institutions remained in the fortified commercial capital. The parliament, impacted by multiple security measures, would become inaccessible to the public behind barbed wire and iron palisades.

This chapter interrogates this oppressive image of alterity, as it unraveled and was reproduced across the many spatial scenarios of the Sri Lankan civil war. It asks why prevailing discourses on Sri Lankan architecture failed to recognize its "other," focusing instead on varied postcolonial efforts to subordinate its colonial past. Throughout the civil war period, publications on local vernacular and religious monuments fueled architectural thinking's resilient cultural dialectic (Lewcock, Sansoni, and Senanayake 1998). Monographs on the first generation of local architects—Geoffrey Bawa (Taylor 1986; Robson 2002), Minnette de Silva (1998), Valentine Gunasekara (Pieris 2007), and the Danish architect, Ulrik Plesner (2013)—were revealed as stances for or against European modernism. The precolonial vernacular became a celebratory source of cultural dignity and hospitality expressed through indigenized design templates for elite residential and hotel architectures. Meanwhile, the war, a grim specter of dispossession and displacement was absent from these representations of "Sri Lankan" architecture, even while serving as a subtext to their salubrious imagery. On the one hand, news of the war was censored so that the immediacy of this violence was removed for the elite consumers of these ideas. On the other hand, Colombo was a defensive city and recipient of the war-related refugee influx. These circumstances mutually fashioned the profession, its new recruits, and its products.

The initial segregation of the parliament, due to its island setting, was incongruent with the liberal ethos of the Jayewardene regime. This was the government that had opened up the economy after decades of socialist policies and import substitution.[8] Foreign investment, marketization, Free Trade Zones, and the exportation of labor carved unprecedented global networks of capital. The parliament's defensive fortification implied the price of this freedom, even as inequitable resource allocation and constitutionalized biases towards Buddhist institutions continued to modify the terms of democracy. These biases were pronounced in one of the most impressive projects to mobilize architectural expertise during the 1980s, the UNESCO nomination for Sri Lanka's historic sites.

Utopian Histories

The nomination structure set up by UNESCO has served a particular historical purpose useful for the cultural reinvention of postcolonial nation-states. Where heritage sites were instrumentalized in culturally hegemonic nation-building exercises UNESCO unwittingly provided the stamp of authority. Inequitable political agendas underlying state formation were animated by their response. Furthermore, as nations embraced marketization, UNESCO listings were critical for internationalizing tourism by providing the organizational frameworks that exemplified global heritage practice. This was the case in Sri Lanka, where the UNESCO Cultural Triangle Project's international campaign in 1978 coincided with the election of the Jayewardene government and subsequent internationalization of the tourism industry. The significance of the Buddhist sites, including Anuradhapura, Polonnaruwa, Sigiriya, Dambulla, and Kandy, was articulated as forming the country's "historical core" giving "supreme expression to its religious values, national identity and artistic creativity … as a centre of Buddhist tradition" (Prematilleke 1994). The sites were impressive. Anuradhapura and Polonnaruwa comprised hundreds of monument sites with evidence of both Buddhist and Hindu pasts (Figure 16.2). Funding for the $44-million project came from multiple sources, predominantly Japan, Britain, and China. The international campaign involved lengthy processes, careful restorative work, mobilization of labor and resources. The project was responsible for elevating archaeology, nationally and internationally, and was a training ground for a generation of experts. Many of the publications on

Figure 16.2 Anuradhapura, Ruvanwelisaya stupa
Source: Copyright Anoma Pieris.

Sri Lankan architecture and archaeology occurred under its auspices, and many architects pursued careers in archaeology.

The Cultural Triangle Project inserted Sri Lanka into the UNESCO community, ensuring its participation in other venues of the International Council on Monuments and Sites (ICOMOS). It created the ground for lobbying for the protection of monuments that would otherwise have been destroyed. Yet the internationalization of the Cultural Triangle Project recuperated colonial archaeological preferences through its revisionist histories. As argued by several scholars (Jeganathan 2009: 108–136; Jazeel 2013: 50), colonial archaeology had historically privileged, excavated, and reproduced an Aryan Buddhist past that proved useful for Sinhala-Buddhist revivalist campaigns (Tamils were differentiated as Dravidians). Historical texts, written by Buddhist clergy and translated and legitimized by orientalist scholars, reinforced the politics of custodianship based on the Buddha's legendary visits to the island, his selection of it for the continuation of his doctrine, proselytization of prehistoric Aboriginal clans, and appointment of guardian deities (Kemper 1991: ch. 4). The subsequent colonization of the island by Aryans for a Buddhist imperial project was justified, dynastic lineages were established, and the Dravidian enemy was named.

Buddhist imperial ideologies of that early period were constructed against successive Hindu colonizers from the Indian subcontinent. Later, regional competition with Hindu, Cera, and Chola kingdoms of South India and immigration from there between the thirteenth and fifteenth centuries hardened Buddhist notions of sovereignty. While Hindu deities were accommodated within the Buddhist pantheon and Brahminic practices and Tamil language use persisted in court culture, such syncretic practices remained subordinate to the authority of Buddhism. European Christian conquest, iconoclastic practices, and proselytization under the Portuguese and Dutch preceded the proliferation of British urban institutions provoking a defensive anti-colonial Buddhist revival during the nineteenth century. After independence these same archaeological praxes were aestheticized and commodified for political purposes producing an ideology inimical to pluralism (Jazeel 2013: 52–54). Buddhism took center stage. It fed a hierarchy of entitlements which favored the Sinhala-Buddhist majority, elevating their language and protecting their religion due to the island's purported custodianship of the Buddhist doctrine (Kemper 1991: ch. 4). The accretion of these histories of Sinhala-Buddhist cultural victimization in the colonial period and political resistance and resurgence underscored contemporary ethnic hostilities.

These asymmetrical values dominated the 1982 listings for the initial two sites of the UNESCO Cultural Triangle: The Sacred City of Anuradhapura established in 4 BCE and lasting ten centuries and its successor, the Ancient City of Polonnaruwa (CE 12–13). Criterion III of the ICOMOS evaluations, on which the online descriptions were based (until their revision in 2015) were biased towards the Sinhala perspective. Having established the "Tree of Enlightenment" (the cutting of the fig tree under which the Buddha sat), and a religious topography shaped by the relics of Siddhartha embedded in stupas, as foundational elements, they claimed:

> Anuradhapura attests in a unique and specific way to the Sinhalese civilization. On numerous occasions the city was submitted to the assaults of invaders from southern India—Tamils, Pandyas, Cholas, etc. It stands as a permanent manifesto of the culture of Sri Lanka, impervious to outside influences.

While …

> Polonnaruwa bears witness to several civilizations, notably that of the conquering Cholas, disciples of Brahminism, and that of the Sinhalese sovereigns during the 12th and 13th centuries.
>
> *(ICOMOS 1982a and b)*[9]

The biases of this state-led discourse cast the architecture of Tamil minorities as objects of alterity and created few if any spaces for plural celebration of their many contributions to heritage discourse. Muslim, Veddah (Aboriginal), and Burgher heritage—the other, minor players in the Sri Lankan polity—was likewise marginalized. Tamil calls for secession hardened against such exclusionary perspectives. This was the inimical context that erupted into civil war.

Displacement

The Sri Lankan civil war (1983–2009) was an ethnic intrastate conflict provoked by increasingly ethnocratic policies of the postcolonial nation-state. Linguistic nationalism and university standardization increasingly marginalized ethnic Tamil, Muslim, and Burgher minorities provoking calls for federalism and eventually militancy by members of the Tamil minority. Once government troops were deployed to suppress them, the Tamil-speaking minorities in the northern and eastern war zones suffered unprecedented levels of violence and displacement. The Cultural Triangle Project developed alongside these hostilities historicizing political claims for sovereignty by articulating the magnitude of the Sinhala-Buddhist domain. However, the city of Anuradhapura was also the political boundary of the escalating conflict with important military and air force bases. Sites in Anuradhapura such as the Sri Maha Bodhi, the historic fig tree described above, were subject to separatist attacks.[10] Tourists to the Cultural Triangle confronted these harsher realities in the forms of vehicle, baggage, and body searches as they traveled through the sacred precinct.

The physical destruction in the warzone was never far from the sacred center (the nearest border town, Vavuniya, being 49 kilometers to the north), but its details were kept from local residents due to a moratorium on military news. Numbers reported were frequently manipulated and news readers depended on external sources. The careful preparation of the sacred cities for international audiences, the conservation of monuments and regulation of traffic occurred alongside the shelling, evacuation, and militarization of cities in the north and east. The region saw mass displacements of Tamils during escalating conflict between the Liberation Tigers of Tamil Eelam (LTTE), the Sri Lankan Security Forces, and the Indian Peace Keeping Force, of Muslims expelled by the LITE in 1990, an exodus out of Jaffna in the face of the advancing Sri Lankan army in 1995, and the piecemeal attrition of districts and villages due to the creation of 18 Israeli-style High Security Zones (HSZ). Some 90,000 people were displaced internally, 130,000 persons due to the creation of HSZs, and 146,098 Sri Lankans registered as refugees in 64 countries (IDMC 2014).[11]

The magnification of Anuradhapura through a massive injection of government funding and the destruction of the north and east through parallel increases in defense expenditure may seem unconnected, but they occurred in tandem during the first heated decades of the civil war. The cost of this destruction to Jaffna's heritage monuments went unaccounted, although they featured in the appeals made by the overseas Tamil diaspora. A list of 1342 damaged temples and 93 damaged churches in the north and east were published by diasporic lobbies in 2004 (Tamil Centre for Human Rights 2004).

The extent of damage in the war zone is better communicated by the Resettlement and Rehabilitation Authority of the North. They estimated that 30 percent of housing was completely destroyed, 40 percent badly damaged, and the remaining 30 percent slightly damaged (RRAN 1998: 56, cited by van Horen 2002) (Figure 16.3). IDPs were enumerated at the end of the war.

Figure 16.3 War related destruction, homes in Jaffna
Source: Copyright Anoma Pieris.

Those who could do so, fled by boat, rail, or air to southern cities, to India, or to sympathetic nations in the West. Their abandoned homes would be occupied or requisitioned by the various combat groups—the LTTE, the Indian Peace Keeping Force, or Sri Lankan government forces—and would gradually fall to ruin or be salvaged by neighbors as the war wore on. Many made homes in the derelict structures of former institutions. Others made their way to the government refugee camps.

This history of wartime displacement was the second example of an interiorized alterity that entered architectural discourse in subversive ways. On the surface, Sri Lankan house design blossomed with the growing international reputation of Geoffrey Bawa (Figure 16.4). The general framing for its popularity was a discourse on the tropical climate obsessively pursued in Southeast Asian architectural publications as the defining feature of both colonial and postcolonial Asian architectures. The revival of this discourse and its regionalist framing was supported by a number of key players: the Geneva-based Aga Khan Foundation with its awards and MIMAR publications, the tropical conferences revived by Alexander Tzonis, Liane Lefaivre, and Bruno Stagno (2001), and the House Books of Robert Powell that placed Sri Lanka within this utopian frame (1993, 1996, 1998, 2001, 2015). The MIMAR monograph on Geoffrey Bawa (Taylor 1986), three years into the conflict, depicted an island paradise. So it was with the many picturesque homes that were featured in House Books focusing on their formal organization around courtyards and gardens, where modernist forms and traditional workmanship were framed by lush tropical surrounds. They influenced many of the homes that were constructed in suburban Sri Jayewardenepura modeled after feudal *walavvas* (elaborate homes of indigenous elites) with deep overhanging roofs and spacious verandahs. A generation of Sri Lankan architects influenced by Bawa and Plesner dedicated their talents to achieving a sophisticated synthesis of indigenous and modern elements, captivating for their phenomenological qualities, and cultivated a sophisticated architecture of hospitality based on local design features.

The burgeoning international interest in Sri Lankan architecture fed the island's own projections of utopian content. Opportunities for publishing came via vanity publications which deliberately foregrounded positive imagery. Their projections of Asian homes and tropical living were largely sentimental reconstructions of lifestyles appealing to expatriate audiences. In fact many of these style books featured expatriate homes. Second, although national projections or advocacy of these preferences did not produce the global discourse, they identified individuals or artifacts deemed representative of Sri Lankan character. These choices were often contentious, depending on the politics of the local professional fraternity. However, by the end of the twentieth century, when the war was still raging, vernacular architecture and its derivative contemporary styles dominated local design culture and promoted Sri Lankan aesthetics. The style won Bawa national and international accolades.[12]

Despite this wholehearted affirmation of a particular utopian ambience as characterizing Sri Lankan architecture, a closer look at the urban houses of the generation after Bawa hints at trouble in paradise. Houses were surrounded by exceptionally high exterior walls, indeed perimeter walls become the building envelope. Radically different from the sprawling bungalows of an earlier era, these involuted spaces suggest general withdrawal from public activity. The familiar vernacular vocabulary of pitched terracotta tile roofs graced with carved timber doors, windows, and verandahs were no longer evident. Few openings punctured the exterior envelope. These inhospitable translations of urban architecture provided a fortified utopia against the dual threats of urban poverty and political unrest. Occupation of the entire site area denied the public reciprocity that build neighborhood character, while the minimalist façade was both defensive and offensive. The interiors, in contrast, were delightful escapes into multiple tropical stage sets enhanced by bright Mediterranean color schemes; salient features of the growing practice of defensive alterity.

Figure 16.4 Geoffrey Bawa, former Edward Reid & Begg Office, entrance courtyard (Gallery Café) designed as a house for Bartholomeusz 1961–1963

Source: Copyright Anoma Pieris.

This interiority of urban architecture in fortified Colombo responded to multiple factors including the scarcity of land in a growing city, urban unrest, and insurrection during the early 1970s and late 1980s and, in the last example, the need for security for an elite clientele. Each stage of this retraction from hospitable engagement to a hostile perception of urban environs paralleled historic changes in the city outside. Colonial bungalows and country villas were no longer tenable in the embattled city where everyday life adapted and reacted to various phases of the civil war.

The houses featured in architectural publications failed to document harsher urban realities faced by refugees from the warzone. The means for their accommodation were far from ambient, but they too catered to different economic capacities ranging from luxury apartments for returning expatriates to high-rise slums. Packed together in small land parcels in the congested minority suburbs of Kotahena and Wellawatte, these structures either replaced ruined homes abandoned after the pogrom, or gave way to the pressures of real estate developers. The worst of these buildings had poor amenities and ventilation and were rented for exorbitant rates. Whole families crowded into single room apartments, treating them as transitory accommodation and carrying their former homes with them as title deeds or photographs. Documentation of these fragments in *The Incomplete Thombu* by artist/art historian T. Shanaathanan (2011), in the form of sketches by displaced Tamil homeowners redrawn as architectural plans, made these absences and alterities visible.

Hospitality

The homes of urban elites or dispossessed minorities were minor histories in the domestic upheavals produced by civil war. The large-scale multiplication of dwelling spaces formed more substantial architectural interventions, both in the north and the south of the country, and inserted incongruent forms of urbanization into rural environs. The most successful among these were the tourist hotels, built in Colombo by multinational hotel chains, their scale ironically mirrored in the high-rise refugee accommodation of minority suburbs. The Intercontinental, Ramada, Galadari, and Taj Samudra hotels dominated the Central Business District, overpowering the former parliament, later used as the Presidential Secretariat, and the contiguous arcaded colonial buildings. However, these hotels were predictable environments designed to emplace world travelers through homogenized aesthetic themes. Hotels along the southern coast of Sri Lanka immediately north and south of Colombo were more intimate extensions of local architectural discourse.

The hotels designed by Geoffrey Bawa and by those who adopted his architectural style were the flag bearers of the utopian and idealized program (Pieris 2012: ch. 7) (Figure 16.5). More significantly, their consumption by international tourists made these environments simultaneously local and global. The hotels bore and cultivated all the aspects of the Sri Lankan style already tested in the domestic arena, multiplying it 100-fold for expansive resort hotels. Their architectural elements entered style books of the era reciprocally influencing domestic architecture. Staged living learned from resort environments influenced elite homes. The consumers for these experiences were the urban elites and expatriates who ventured out of beleaguered southern cities for temporal respite, or the Western tourists who, despite their governments' warnings traveled to Sri Lanka and were momentarily transported into a tropical colonial past. The elegant surroundings and servility of staff perfected their experience, providing temporary relief from harsher wartime realities.

The hotels designed by Sri Lankan architects exemplify defensive forms of alterity, since their insulation from imminent danger was part of their appeal. Seclusion, tropical ambience, high

Defensive Alterity in Sri Lankan Architecture

Figure 16.5 Geoffrey Bawa, Triton Hotel (Heritance Ahungalle) 1978–1981
Source: Copyright Anoma Pieris.

boundary walls, and picturesque aspects concretized the values of peaceful habitation, no longer possible in everyday domestic spaces. Exceptional outpourings of architectural talent preserved this fantasy, extending the hospitality withheld from Lankan minorities to transient visitors from overseas. In contrast, the forcibly mobilized internally displaced minority citizens were confined to numerous government camps. Menik farm, the largest of several in the Vavuniya area reported a population of 225,000 persons in 2009 (Perera 2012).

Admittedly, these tent cities were inaccessible to all but government or international aid workers and the Sri Lankan military for a large part of the war. However, given the opportunity, architects might have intervened to provide better housing conditions or developed ethical practices and design guidelines for alleviating human distress. If built projects were too risky then paper-architecture, research studios, and publications should have swelled this space. The profession, ill-equipped to confront socially compelling questions, appeared diverted by more insular interests at the time. Humanitarian issues surfaced after the 2004 Indian Ocean tsunami displaced large numbers of coastal residents in Sri Lanka's south and east. The news media's juxtaposition of damaged resort hotels and derelict fisher villages exposed the nation's troubling socio-economic alterity. International non-governmental organizations injected large sums of foreign-aid for post-tsunami housing enabling a number of renowned practitioners to experiment in this domain. Few would commit to projects in the war-ensconced northeast. In fact, barring a few dedicated individuals who persisted in this arena, humanitarian architectural agendas remained relatively muted until the last five years of the 26-year-long conflict.

This chapter has provided a troubling account of architectural preferences in a nation defined and transformed by war. Even as its architects contributed substantially to the visibility of Asian architecture, as an environmentally sensitive, hospitality-oriented, and indigenizing practice, they persistently neglected the humane responses required of professionals during conflict. The becalming ambience of Buddhist architecture, a quality seemingly captured by Bawa, masked other violent undercurrents that persisted out of sight. Did deliberate withdrawal from the horrors of conflict produce this architecture of exceptional ambience? Was this resilient culture of hospitality a defensive response to surrounding social suffering? Or were there other pressing political or economic reasons for professional preferences?

Apart from a few individuals committed to humanitarian work, war-related interrogation of critical ethical questions are muted in Sri Lanka's design portfolios, as in Asia, a region beset by border conflicts and political unrest. These omissions appear symptomatic of graver exclusions whereby design education feeds national strains of cultural hegemony. Professional practices insulate themselves from the disruptive evidence of those "others" who cannot enter the aesthetic utopias they perpetuate. Such choices made by architects pose vexing questions about architecture, its operative canon, and its ethical limits.

Notes

1 Levinas challenged philosophies based on ontological foundations (notions of the self) and proposed an understanding of the other as absolute (wholly other). Marcel, however, proposed a relative understanding of the other (in relation to the self).
2 Claes Oldenburg's anti-monuments are examples of this perspective.
3 A symposium "Architecture of Alterity" held at the University of Edinburgh on May 25–27, 2015 included papers that interpreted alterity in these diverse ways. https://archofalterity.wordpress.com/.
4 See also Ameri (2015) on the cultural imperatives of secular institutions.
5 Population in percentages in 2012: Sinhalese 74.9, Sri Lanka Tamil 11.1, Indian Tamil 4.1, Sri Lanka Moor 9.2, Burgher 0.18, and Malay 0.21 (Census of Population and Housing Sri Lanka 2012, online).
6 Opportunities given to educated Tamils by the colonial government are frequently cited by Sinhala sources as a reason for the relative advancement of this minority group.
7 The sixteenth-century King Parakrama Bahu VI was the last to unify the island as a Sinhala kingdom and was invoked by politicians for this achievement. Following the arrival of the Portuguese in 1505, Lanka was colonized successively by them and the Dutch until independence in 1948.
8 A previous era of social welfare policies in 1956–1965 and 1970–1977 favored majoritarian constituencies and strengthened Sinhala-Buddhist ideological positions. These were periods of increasing import-substitution industrialization with a brief interval (1965–1969) when import substitution was combined with liberal economic policies.
9 UNESCO, State Parties, Sri Lanka, Sacred City of Anuradhapura and Ancient City of Polonnaruwa. http://whc.unesco.org/en/list/200 and 201 (December 10, 2014).
10 The LTTE in this scenario are the Liberation Tigers of Tamil Eelam.
11 The total population figures recorded in the 1981 and 2001 census data were 14.85 million and 19.4 million persons, respectively.
12 Bawa was awarded the Vidya Jyoti (Light of Science) 1985 and Deshamanya (Pride of the Nation) 1993 awards by the president of Sri Lanka and awarded the Aga Khan Foundation's Chairman's Award in 2001.

References

Allpress, B. (2015) "Alteration and alterity: the adaptive reuse of modern architecture," *Architect Victoria*, 5. http://archvicmag.com.au/2015-summer/alteration-and-alterity-the-adaptive-reuse-of-modern-architecture/ (July 28, 2016).
Ameri, A. H. (2015) *The Architecture of the Elusive Distance*, Farnham, UK: Ashgate.
Bastian, S. (2008) "Political economy of ethnic violence in Sri Lanka: the July 1983 riots," in J. Uyangoda (ed.) *Matters of Violence: Reflections on Social and Political Violence in Sri Lanka*, Colombo: Social Scientists Association, Colombo.
Benjamin, A. (2000) *Architectural Philosophy*, London: The Athlone Press.

de Silva, M. (1998) *The Life and Work of an Asian Woman Architect*, Colombo: Smart Media Productions.
Department of Census and Statistics, Sri Lanka (2012) Census of Population and Housing, Preliminary Report, Colombo. www.statistics.-gov.lk/PopHouSat/CPH2011/Pages/sm/CPH%202011_R1.pdf (March 30, 2015).
Dissanayaka, T. D. S. A. (1983) *The Agony of Sri Lanka: An In-depth Account of the Racial Riots of 1983*, Colombo: Swastika Press.
Gunasinghe, N. (1984) "May Day after the July holocaust," *Lanka Guardian*, May 1, reprinted in *Newton Gunasinghe: Selected Essays*, ed. S. Perera, Colombo: Social Scientists Association, 1996, 2nd edition 2011, 197–200.
Gunasinghe, N. (1988a) "Anti Tamil riots and the political crisis," *Lanka Guardian*, May 1, reprinted in *Newton Gunasinghe: Selected Essays*, ed. S. Perera, Social Scientists Association, Colombo, 1996, 2nd edition 2011, 166–175.
Gunasinghe, N. (1988b) "The open economy and its impact on ethnic relations in Sri Lanka," *Lanka Guardian*, November 15, reprinted in *Newton Gunasinghe: Selected Essays*, ed. S Perera, Social Scientists Association, Colombo, 1996, 2nd edition 2011, 176–196.
ICOMOS (1982a) International Council for Monuments and Sites, World Heritage List No. 200. http://whc.unesco.org/archive/advisory_body_evaluation/200.pdf (July 29, 2016).
ICOMOS (1982b) International Council for Monuments and Sites, World Heritage List No. 201. http://whc.unesco.org/archive/advisory_body_evaluation/201.pdf (July 29, 2016).
IDMC (2014) Internal Displacement Monitoring Centre, May, Sri Lanka, IDMC figures analysis as of May 2014. www.internal-displacement.org/south-and-south-east-asia/sri-lanka/figures-analysis (June 1, 2014).
Jazeel, T. (2013) *Sacred Modernity: Nature, Environment, and the Postcolonial Geographies of Sri Lankan Nationhood*, Liverpool: Liverpool University Press.
Jeganathan, P. (2009 [1995]) "Authorising history, ordering land: the conquest of Anuradhapura," in P. Jeganathan and Q. Ismail (eds) *Unmaking the Nation: The Politics of Identity and History in Modern Sri Lanka*, New York: South Focus Press, 108–137, 1st edition, Colombo: Social Scientists Association.
Jensen, M. (2014) "Introduction: mapping the global architect of alterity," in M. Jensen, *Mapping the Emergence of the Global Architect: Essays in Practice, Representation and Education*, New York: Routledge.
Kemper, S (1991) *The Presence of the Past: Chronicles, Politics and Culture in Sinhala Life*, Ithaca, NY: Cornell University Press.
Lewcock, R., Sansoni, B., and Senanayake, L. (1998) *The Architecture of an Island: The Living Legacy of Sri Lanka, a Thousand Years of Architecture Illustrated by Outstanding Examples of Religious, Public and Domestic Buildings*, Colombo: Barefoot.
Lim, W. S. W. (2008) *Asian Alterity: With Special Reference to Architecture + Urbanism through the Lens of Cultural Studies*, Singapore and Hackensack, NJ: World Scientific.
Mical, T. (2012) "Spatial alterity: the importance of unusual and unfamiliar spaces in everyday life," *Knowledge Works*, November 7, University of South Australia. www.unisa.edu.au/media-centre/releases/091012/#.V5afqC8kqUk (July 28, 2016).
Perera, S. (2012) "Sri Lanka's displacement chapter nears end with closure of Menik Farm," September 27, UNHCR. www.unhcr.org/506443d89.html (August 8, 2014).
Petrescu, D. (2007) *Altering Practices: Feminist Politics and Poetics of Space*, New York and London: Routledge.
Pieris, A. (2007) *Imagining Modernity: The Architecture of Valentine Gunasekara*, Colombo: Stamford Lake and the Social Scientists' Association.
Pieris, A. (2010) "South and Southeast Asia: the postcolonial legacy," *Fabrications (Journal of the Society of Architectural Historians of Australia and New Zealand)*, 19, 2: 6–33.
Pieris, A. (2012) *Architecture and Nationalism in Sri Lanka: The Trouser under the Cloth*, Abingdon and New York: Routledge.
Pieris, A. (2014) "Colombo to Sri Jayewardenepura: the schizoid subjectivities of postcolonial capitals," *Historic Environments*, 26, 3: 74–85.
Piyadasa, L. (1984) *Sri Lanka: The Holocaust and After*, London: Marram Books.
Plesner, U. (2013) *In Situ: An Architectural Memoir from Sri Lanka*, Copenhagen: Aristo Publishing.
Powell, R. (1993) *The Asian House: Contemporary Houses of Southeast Asia*, Singapore: Select Books.
Powell, R. (1996) *The Tropical Asian House*, Singapore: Select Books.
Powell, R. (1998) *The Urban Asian House: Living in Tropical Cities*, Singapore: Select Books.
Powell, R. (2001) *The New Asian House*, Singapore: Select Books.

Powell, R. (2015) *The New Sri Lankan House*, London: Laurence King Publishing.
Prematilleke, L. (ed.) (1994) *The Cultural Triangle of Sri Lanka, International Campaign*, Colombo: Central Cultural Fund.
Robson, D. (2002) *Geoffrey Bawa: The Complete Works*, London: Thames and Hudson.
Said, E. (1978) *Orientalism*, New York: Pantheon Books.
Shanaathanan, T. (2011) *The Incomplete Thombu*, Sri Lanka: Raking Leaves.
Sharvananda, S., Sahabandu, S. S., and Zuhair, M. M. (2002) *Report of the Presidential Truth Commission on the July Riots*, Colombo: Department of Government Printing.
Sieghart, P. (1984) *Sri Lanka: A Mounting Tragedy of Errors*, London: International Commission of Jurists and Justice.
Spivak, G. C. (2008) *Other Asias*, Oxford: Blackwell.
Stevens, Q., Franck, K. A., and Fazakerley, R. (2012) "Counter-monuments: the anti-monumental and the dialogic," *The Journal of Architecture*, 17, 6: 951–972.
Tambiah, S. J. (1996) *Levelling Crowds: Ethnonationalist Conflicts and Collective Violence in South Asia*, Berkeley: University of California Press.
Tamil Centre for Human Rights (Paris) (2004) Report published on Sangam.org, December 2, http://sangam.org/wpcontent/uploads/2014-/08/TCHR_Christian_Hindu.pdf (March 9, 2015).
Taylor, B. B. (1986) *Geoffrey Bawa*, Singapore: Mimar Concept Media.
Treanor, B. (2006) *Aspects of Alterity: Levinas, Marcel and the Contemporary Debate*, New York: Fordham University Press.
Tzonis, A., Lefaivre, L., and Stagno, B. (eds) (2001) *Tropical Architecture: Critical Regionalism in the Age of Globalization*, Chichester: Wiley-Academy, with The Netherlands: Fonds, Prince Claus Fund for Culture and Development.
van Horen, B. (2002) Planning for institutional capacity building in war-torn areas: the case of Jaffna, Sri Lanka, *Habitat International*, 26, 113–128.
Winslow, D. and Woost, M. D. (eds) (2004) *Economy Culture and Civil War in Sri Lanka*, Bloomington: Indiana University Press.

17

Recasting the Ethnic Retail Street

Analyzing Contemporary Immigrant Architecture in the United States

Arijit Sen

The village of Morton Grove in Cook County, Illinois has a population of 23,270 people. In 2010, the U.S. Census Bureau noted that 9.4 percent of this population, or 2182 residents, were of Asian Indian descent. Among them was Bashir Bozai, a Muslim immigrant from Pakistan who owns two South Asian restaurants in the city. Ghareeb Nawaz, his first and original enterprise is located on Devon Avenue, locally known as Little India, a pulsating ethnic retail street on the northern edge of Chicago (Figure 17.1).[1] The second store, recently opened and operated by Bashir's son Mohammad, is located on the University of Illinois Chicago campus, south of the Chicago Loop. The latter location primarily caters to university students and "mainstream" customers. As Bashir gets older, he hands over control of day-to-day running of both stores to his son. Consequently, his son moves between his home at Morton Grove, the store in Little India, and the outlet near the south campus (Bozai and Bozai 2013). If we consider a day in the lives of these two individuals, we find that their everyday world or home range—a term used by animal ecologists to describe a geographic range in which organisms spend most of their time—consists of multiple nodes across the geography of the Greater Chicago region (Powell and Michael 2012).

The world of immigrants has always animated American cosmopolitan imagination. During the first half of the twentieth century, in the United States, especially Chicago, fears of unassimilated or racially "unassimilable" hordes dominated popular perceptions of immigrant working-class neighborhoods or urban ghettos that housed ethnic and racial minorities. Simultaneously valorized and feared, the territorially bounded spatial character of enclaves garnered scholarly interest—more so, since the 1962 publication of Herbert Gans's *The Urban Villagers*, an account of Boston's Italian west end (Gans 1982). Today, cities proudly tout their Little Villages and Chinatowns as tourist destinations (Sen 2009; Ward 1998; Anderson 1987). With the emergence of diaspora studies the term has gained popularity globally. Researchers write about enclaves housing Chinese and Indians in Europe and South East Asia (Khan 2015).

The exact physical layout of an ethnic enclave may vary by its location. It could encompass one city block with a cluster of ethnic stores, strip malls, an entire ethnic retail street, or even multiple blocks with residential, cultural, and religious institutions within walking distance. Nevertheless, across the world, these ethnic geographies are purposely designed to look, feel, sound, and smell the same—a spatial facsimile rendered with consistent and instantly recognizable

Figure 17.1 Map of Chicago showing Morton Grove, Devon Avenue, and the University of Illinois campus

architectural branding essential for recognition, especially because many ethnic enclaves include transnational sites of commerce. In common parlance and mass media accounts, ethnic enclaves have become a shorthand for an exotic world of alien architecture, sights, and smells, a cacophonous babel of foreign tongues, lifestyles, and culture—a shibboleth for difference and alterity (Lautman 2011; Ghisolf 2015; Selvam 2018; Mai 2014).

If this singular narrative of ethnic space as a locus of distinction and difference affirms a city's tourism appeal, it also erases an aspect of urban ethnic spaces in global cities that points towards transcultural exchange and engagement. Bashir Bozai's suburban world tells us that ethnic enclaves, made famous by the Chicago School of urban sociology, are no longer the only form of immigrant settlement in twenty-first-century Chicago. On his way to Ghareeb Nawaz, Bozai stops at his suburban grocery store or shops at Walmart in Pointe Plaza, near his home. He takes a detour to visit his friends in Chicago's outer suburbs. His world is intertwined across mainstream and ethnic spaces. Separating ethnic and non-ethnic spaces no longer seems possible in our examination of ethnic geographies. The world of today's immigrants is territorially dispersed and networked—a community without propinquity. This condition, that Zelinsky and Lee call heterolocalism, explains that "members of certain newly arrived groups may be able to sustain their identity as an ethnic community despite immediate or rapid spatial dispersion" (Zelinsky and Lee 1998: 282). With the emergence of new settlement patterns, the human experience of heterolocal geographies has caught scholarly attention in geography and urban history (Li 2005).

Architectural research, however, lacks a method to study such dispersed but interconnected worlds because of a common tendency to focus on isolated buildings, culturally predetermined building types, and hagiographies of architects or builders. In other words, the unit of analysis in architectural scholarship is an individual building or its presumptive author. My work on embodied placemaking suggests that the human body and its experience of space can become an alternate entry point into the analysis of ethnic place (Sen 2012, 2013, 2015a, 2016).[2] I suggest a shift in our methodological focus towards process—*how sites are defined, reproduced, and negotiated*, as if in a complicated theatrical performance between individuals and larger sociospatial contexts of host culture, the city, and its history. My focus on embodied experience is not merely about an instantaneous engagement between the human body and its surrounding. It also accounts for historical time and cultural memory that produce, what Paul Connerton calls, incorporated bodily practices (Connerton 1989: 73). Such a method cannot ignore the *longue durée* of environmental time, because the human experience of the built environment is often framed by the ways land and water shift and sculpt our ecology.

Embodied placemaking also suggests that individuals and groups approach this common world from different perspectives. Hannah Arendt describes that the world we hold in common is also a site where difference is acknowledged, a place we approach from "differences of position and the resulting variety of perspectives" (Arendt 1958: 57). However, as a precursor, she argues that in a multicultural society difference is organized around something we share, that is

> to live together in the world means essentially that a world of things is between those who have it in common, as a table is located between who sit around it; the world, like every in-between, relates and separates men at the same time.
>
> *(Arendt 1958: 52)*

To Bashir Bozai, his son, and many customers, the architecture of Morton Grove, Devon Avenue, Ghareeb Nawaz, and the University of Illinois Campus may hold different meanings and interpretations, but it is nevertheless part of a social and physical common ground that they share. If ethnic spaces, rather than being mere sites of difference, are instead read as common grounds in a multicultural settler society, then the central question that confronts us is how this common landscape is organized, delineated, and experienced across considerable demographic diversity. This chapter focuses on uncovering how such a shared world is reproduced.

Indeed, on first glance, qualities that identify Ghareeb Nawaz as an ethnic space to its users include symbols of difference such as signage, scale, smells, sounds, the ubiquitous presence of ethnic bodies, and, a sequential and hierarchical organization of processional spaces by which the "seemingly alien" store interior is organized (Sen 2012). These symbols of difference help in the architectural staging of this ethnic space, allowing us to distinguish Ghareeb Nawaz from its next-door neighbor, an Italian pizzeria. This spatial experience is rendered by boundaries differentiating front and back zones, public and private domains, inside and outside territories. While boundaries mark out spaces, the place itself is contingent and ephemeral, reproduced during everyday activities and performances. Similar to a stage-set, Ghareeb Nawaz is more than an assemblage of walls, doors, and floors, more than a static building-type. Instead, as the dramaturgical metaphor of a stage suggests, architecture, senses, movements, atmospheres, activities, behavior, and emotions recreate a sense of place that is more than the sum of its parts. Personal histories and cultural memories play a part in this process, complicating the sense of place, triggering myriad affective responses and reactions from diverse users. This sensate and aesthetic experience of place, that sociologists Daniel Aaron Silver and Terry Nichols Clark call "scenes," then suggests an epistemological alternative in our quest to read ethnic places (Silver and Clark 2016).

Then, on second glance, talking about scenes allows us to perceive how ethnic spaces are also common grounds and sites of shared knowledge, where boundaries are not merely ways to separate but are turfs around which we come together. Here, I borrow from urban cultural landscape historian Grady Clay who explains that descriptions of places are embedded in everyday language by terms such as edges, fronts, centers, out there, back there, and border zones. Clay writes,

> The true language of cities deals with relationships rather than free standing objects.... Thus, with the objects and processes in a city: each makes sense in combination, in relation to, in context, in time. Standing alone, each, considered on its own merit, is bereft, uncomplicated, and uncommunicative.
>
> *(Clay 1980: 19)*

These terms outline a syntax by which humans cognitively orient their shared world. Clay uses these terms to analyze the urban scene, but these terms are equally useful to analyze a building. This chapter focuses on the term "edges" as a heuristic device to describe Ghareeb Nawaz and Little India. The word may refer to permanent boundaries, such as a storefront façade marking Ghareeb Nawaz or cross-streets defining the edge of Little India. It could refer to the ephemeral and somatic, such as an atmospheric ambience produced by the powerful smell of grated garlic and crackling cumin seeds on spluttering oil emanating from the restaurant kitchen and creeping into the quieter and staid alleyways of West Ridge, lined with middle-class residences. An edge could refer to a moment on a historical timeline when the city encroached upon the countryside in the twentieth century, marking the birth of Devon Avenue as a commercial strip. It may refer to an environmental condition between a marshy hinterland and the lake that determined, many millennia ago, the current high ground on which Ghareeb Nawaz sits. A complex story of edges will show how the current and the contemporary relate to spectral remains from the past, and how different edges overlap, concatenate, and intertwine to produce a world we share—in this instance, the world of Bashir Bozai.

Reading Buildings as Systems of Edges

The interior layout of Ghareeb Nawaz is divided into a front and a back zone (Figure 17.2). Its architecture reminds us of the spatial and dramaturgical metaphor used by sociologist Erving Goffman to explain social interactions in everyday life (Goffman 1956: 66–86). What strikes you as you approach Ghareeb Nawaz is its front edge, a wall of advertisements plastered over a relatively mundane storefront (Figure 17.3). The advertisements are not static. In the last ten years, the number of posters and signage reduced as the city came down harshly on unauthorized hoardings. Today the large placards are gone, replaced by authorized smaller signs on the windows. Nevertheless, the storefront remains evocative, written up in travel and food related websites as a sensory display of an alien culture, albeit tamed and made less unfamiliar, in order to be consumed by intrepid Chicago foodies. Ghareeb Nawaz was originally designed to cater to immigrant cab drivers from India, Pakistan, and Bangladesh. But soon it became a popular destination for people of the South Asian and Middle Eastern diaspora. On reading the storefront posters carefully one can discern a wider cross-section of food items (gyro sandwiches, falafel, hummus, and baba ghanouj) advertised to a targeted customer base from the Middle East, South Asia, and North Africa.

In the last decade, the restaurant has moved from being a hole-in-the-wall joint catering to immigrants into a foodie destination for a racially diverse clientele. In 2009, Ricardo wrote in Yelp.com about, "people from Pakistan and India eating there." He was comparing this place to "a lot of [other] India restaurants for white people," but his experience in Ghareeb Nawaz "was like I was on a real restaurant of India or Pakistan" (Ricardo, Yelp Reviews 2009). By July 2016, the clientele had diversified and Eddie wrote, "Came here with the gf on a random

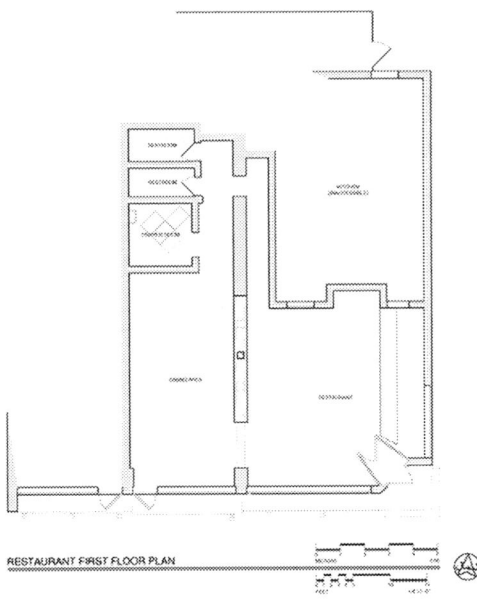

Figure 17.2 Interior layout of Ghareeb Nawaz, Drawing by Travis Olson, Center for Historic Architecture and Design

Source: Copyright Arijit Sen.

Figure 17.3 Exterior advertisements on the storefront, Ghareeb Nawaz
Source: Copyright Arijit Sen.

Saturday and the restaurant was packed with people of all races, including many Indians" (Eddie, Yelp Reviews 2016). Recent food reviews declare that the restaurant, with its new updated décor, caters to a very mixed clientele of all races and ethnicities who come from the Greater Chicago region to try out delicious and cheap Indian food (Wiviott, Chicago Reader Review 2016; Wiviott, Zabihah Review 2016). Groupon review pages warn foodies, "Ghareeb Nawaz's through-the-roof ratings prove that this Chicago hub serves some of the best Indian entrees in town ... Ghareeb Nawaz does not take reservations, so plan accordingly" (Wiviott, Groupon Review 2016).

If you carefully observe the rhythms of this place, a curious pattern of use and activities explains how a diversity of customers shares this space. Cab drivers, many practicing Muslims from Arab, African, and Asian countries, rush in during prayer hours for *salah* or *namaz* (prayers), entering the restaurant either from the parking lot at the back or from the front entrance. After prayers, some stay back for food but most rush out. A small prayer room, integrated within the store interiors, is tucked far back, away from the front counter, creating a relative unobtrusive back zone for this unexpected activity inside this restaurant. The room, approximately 9′ × 9′, is enough to hold two praying individuals. A rug, floor patterns, and framed images of *Al Kaaba Al Musharrafah* distinguish this room from the other spaces and from the hubbub in the dining areas (Figure 17.4). The family area is occupied by larger families while the front section serves predominantly men. But this gendered division of space, really only understood by the ethnic in-group, dissipates during crowded evening hours when the clientele is also more diverse.

Creating this front and back layout was not difficult for Bashir Bozai. The building he bought was one with a front–back layout already well defined by its previous owners. In the 1970s, Patel Brothers, the oldest Indian immigrant-owned grocery store in this strip opened in this location. Proximity to public transit and cheap rent were reasons why Mafat Patel and his brother set up their business in this corner building (M. Patel 2013). This store therefore marked

Recasting the Ethnic Retail Street

Figure 17.4 Prayer room inside Ghareeb Nawaz before new renovation
Source: Copyright Arijit Sen.

a historic moment of arrival of one of the first Indian food stores on this street. Patel Brother's store, explains Susan Patel, the daughter of one of the owners, was laid out haphazardly, but the back of the store was important because it was here that she and her brother played when they were growing up, their mother out in the front counter selling spices and food while keeping a watch on them (S. Patel 2013). The back room was an extension of their home since the family spent much time in their store. This public front and back interior layout continues to be a common spatial arrangement among immigrant-owned stores where family labor is an important part of the business. The relative "invisibility" of the back zone has its drawbacks too, for there are instances, elsewhere, where exploitative use of cheap immigrant labor may continue unabated in these spaces, ensconced away from the surveillance of the city and its enforcement agencies.[3]

Sensory ambience and insurgent re-adaptation of space into front and back domains are not something that is unique to Ghareeb Nawaz, Patel Brothers, or for that matter, South Asian immigrants. These are familiar strategies by which ethnic groups take over an old building and make it their own. Jewish storeowners who moved into the area after World War II took over this street using spatial strategies that were very similar to the current South Asian storeowners. By 1963 there were approximately 48,000 Jews in the West Rogers Park area (Cutler 1996). Adam Langer recounts how in the 1970s and 1980s, the smell of Jewish delis and restaurants along Devon Avenue selling spicy bean curds and *kichels* animated the street, transforming the old storefronts into public front rooms of the Jewish community. Langer describes a sense of loss when Jews moved out and new immigrants came in. He found that although the buildings remained, the familiar spaces and edges disappeared. The Levinson's Bakery remained a landmark but by 1981, "Knopov's bakery was gone as well, and its delcos, kichels, and kosher red-tinted, cream-filled chocolate cupcakes along with it." Then again,

> Across California Avenue, a major north–south street that runs perpendicular to Devon Avenue, the change continued. Gitel's Kosher Bakery and Lazar's Juvenile Furniture remained, but Bella Roma, and the Parthenon had moved—the former to Little Italy, the latter to Greektown. In their places stood two Indian restaurants.[4]
>
> *(Langer 2004: 398)*

By the late 1980s, as the now-aging Jewish residents and their children began moving to suburban locations such as Skokie, Buffalo Grove, Highland Park, and Deerfield, newer immigrants moved in. Ethnic geographies reorganized, moved, and reconstituted, dynamically recomposing Devon Avenue's sense of place, but the architectural grammar remained the same. The newcomers were immigrants of South Asian origin. Indians and Pakistanis set up businesses and replaced the world of the Jewish residents with sounds and smells from the Indian subcontinent. Initially few new stores were interspersed amid preexisting Jewish and other ethnic businesses creating a checkered multicultural street fabric and a confluence of cross-cultural currents. In order to distinguish themselves from the neighboring stores South Asian storeowners used bold signage, unique store names, and exotic storefront displays (Sen 2015b: 749–825). Steel beams, studs, stanchions, cantilevered hanger rods, and frames were all part of an elaborate mass-produced material culture that served as infrastructure to support this elaborate economy of signs to create a "front." Those stanchions still exist on top of Ghareeb Nawaz although Bozai has taken his lights and hoardings down.

Tracing this history of building edges takes us further back to the early decades of the twentieth century when Chicago grew northwards with the extension of the Western Avenue transit line. As we move westwards on Devon Avenue, we find, hidden behind the cacophony of store signs and product displays, distinctive commercial façades from the early twentieth century (Longstreth 1987: 68). These imposing façades, built by architects such as William Keller, A. E. Norman, Oldefest & Williams, Johnson & Anderson, Dewey & Pavlovich, Minkus & Gross, and Adolf Woerner, are among some of the finest examples of two storied terracotta street-front architecture (Archer and Santoro 2007; Koval et al. 2006). An economic slump during the Great Depression halted the building boom in this neighborhood, yet, these buildings were physical expressions of the expanding urban edge of Chicago. In addition, the unique footprint of buildings—narrow width and elongated depth, granular on the lower floors and expansive upstairs—is representative of its origins and explains how the buildings catered to clients.[5] In the past, larger institutions such as banks and offices occupied the upper floors, while real estate at the street level was rented out to stores and small businesses. Today the old office and bank spaces are gone, but cultural and health organizations, elderly apartments, tax, travel and legal services, and women and children-related services occupy the upper floors. New signage on the upper floors addresses residents and families while the street level signs cater to a diverse retail clientele (Figure 17.5).

Reading buildings by exploring the production of edges demonstrates how buildings are physically or symbolically subdivided to produce sequences of front, back, top, and bottom territories that sustain polyphonic rhythms of everyday life in synchronous harmony. The material edges remain, only to be reused and invested with new meanings as cultures change.

Figure 17.5 Front façade of commercial buildings along Devon Avenue

Source: Copyright Arijit Sen.

Ghareeb Nawaz and the other buildings in Little India, when read as a system of edges, open up that dynamic world in which old architecture mediates and gently contours the complexity of contemporary heterolocal immigrant worlds.

Reading Neighborhoods as Systems of Edges

Analysis of edges also opens new ways of seeing ethnic enclaves. Ghareeb Nawaz's location on Devon Avenue marks one edge of Little India. Although in reality there are more South Asian restaurants located east of Ghareeb Nawaz, majority customers, city reviews, and news articles refer to Ghareeb Nawaz as the "easternmost boundary of Little India." This condition is part of a longer history of urban imageability (Lynch 1960) and boundary formation.

A few blocks from Ghareeb Nawaz, Devon Avenue bisects Ridge Boulevard, a north–south public thoroughfare that connects the northern neighborhoods to Peterson Avenue, Bryn Mawr Avenue, and Lake Shore Drive. The street also connects to Clark Street and Ashland Avenue, high traffic thoroughfares appending the northern neighborhoods to South Chicago and downtown locations. Ridge Avenue became Chicago's urban edge long before current immigrants moved into this area. The street marks a geological high ground (ridge line) separating the once marshy lands next to Lake Michigan and the edge of a glacial valley. The area just east of this ridge used to be the ancient shoreline of a prehistoric lake formed by glaciers that geologists call Lake Checaugou. Known as the Greenbay Trail, the historic road along this ridge connected Chicago to the city of Greenbay in Wisconsin. It was a native American trail before 1800, then a military road, and later a stagecoach route with a stop a few blocks north of Devon Avenue. By the 1840s, Roman Catholic immigrants from Germany built fruit orchards and vegetable farms along this alluvial land. Between 1840 and 1870 Luxembourgians settled in this area. A large green space, the St. Henry's church and cemetery, diagonally opposite Ghareeb Nawaz, at the highest point in this neighborhood, marks this spot as a parish for immigrants from Luxembourg and Germany.

The ridge and its settlement history influenced subsequent land development and urban growth—east of this street became known as Roger's Park, and West Ridge grew on the western side. After annexation to Chicago in 1893 the two neighborhoods continued to maintain separate identities, political leanings, distinct architecture, urban density, land and property values. Lower rental costs and a denser built grid spurned the small businesses along the strip west of Ridge Avenue—today's Little India.

Ridge Avenue continued to serve as yet another significant edge for the ethnic Jewish settlement during the 1960s and 1970s. Still used today by local orthodox Jews, we find a white and black painted post located on the wall of a bridge near Ridge Avenue, just west of Ghareeb Nawaz. This is part of an *eruv*, which Isaac Cohen describes as "a physically constructed Rabbinic infrastructure that utilizes elements of the city, both civic and structural, to define public and private spatial" edges.[6] Cohen explains further that, an *eruv* extends the boundary of the private domain beyond the house "for the purposes of the Sabbath, to allow for Jewish ritual observance so that all individuals can fully participate in the life of the community." *Eruv* allows observant Jews to expand their domestic sphere beyond the boundary of their home into a larger territory. The post on Ridge Boulevard, part of the larger *eruvin*, extends upwards to meet steel wire strung overhead across Devon Avenue to the post opposite, creating an imaginary portal.

Therefore, multiple edges converge in this location and Ghareeb Nawaz is a site nested within a world that diverse groups and histories share, albeit seen and experienced differently. As a result, a highly localized and intimate prayer room in Ghareeb Nawaz becomes part of a shared geography. Its location, next to Ridge Avenue makes this space very accessible. The prayer room is part of a larger city-wide network of "free-standing prayer spaces" along major urban intersections and neighborhood edges that cater to practicing Muslim cab drivers who cannot drive to a mosque to conduct their daily prayers while driving passengers around. In their research in New York, Courtney Bender and Elta Smith found a similar network of alternative prayer rooms that allowed Muslim cab drivers to perform their rituals and prayers while on the move (Bender and Smith 2004). Bender and Smith argue that these edge-spaces represent "an organizational innovation within the existing field of American mosques and complicate the analysis of immigrant religious life that focuses solely on congregational participation" (Bender and Smith 2004: 76). Calling them spaces of everyday "lived religion," Bender and Smith show the creative role that "immigrants' activities play in reconstructing the boundaries of public and private, ethnic and religious identities" within heterolocal geographies (Bender and Smith 2004: 77). By examining the production of urban boundaries we realize that the *eruv*, the ridge, the church, and the prayer room are indeed part of a larger interconnected assemblage of lived worlds, landscapes, and edges.

New Geographies and New Methods

New geographies require new modes of analysis and novel ways of reading architecture. Contemporary immigrant landscapes are experienced as part of a larger, more dispersed, cartography of interconnected nodes and paths. Even Devon Avenue, a street that seems to resemble a twentieth-century ethnic enclave cannot be read as a hermetically sealed social and physical space. On the one hand, this street is a node within a larger immigrant landscape while on the other hand, the ethnic and cultural diversity among those who frequent this street questions the assumed social homogeneity of ethnic enclaves. The strategy to study the sequence of experiential, physical, and cognitive edges that orient the human body within these geographies helps shift our attention away from a description of the ethnic enclave towards focusing on the process by which ethnic spaces are produced within specific local contexts. An interpretive and multi-scalar approach suggests a new epistemology to understand ethnic space, not as a distinct and isolated site of cultural difference, but as one of many sites anchored by a common urban experience of place. As a heuristic device, an account of edges explains changes over a palimpsest of geological, cultural, social, and temporal processes.

Scholars from various disciplinary backgrounds—Jackson, Bourdieu, Chattopadhyay, and Herzfeld to name a few—demonstrate that our experience of time and place influences *habitus*, or a system of embodied dispositions and tendencies that help individuals organize, interpret, and participate in the social world around them (Jackson 1970; Herzfeld 1991; Bourdieu 2004; Chattopadhyay 2012). The way we use, engage, and experience place influences who we are, frames our action and structures our identity. Our focus on the social production of edges helps us see how immigrant worlds are experienced by the production, maintenance, and curation of boundaries. By focusing on how edges are marked, a process that has a history preceding the arrival of the immigrants, this analysis argues that the local landscape is not a *tabula rasa* that immigrants occupy and craft as their world. Rather landscape, as *habitus*, informs and influences how immigrant worlds are reproduced within an already shared syntax of space.

Proposing buildings and neighborhoods as a system of "edges" that produces a haptic and proprioceptic spatial experience also allows us to see immigrant architecture as a world anchored and mediated by a common urban experience of movement. In the case of Ghareeb Nawaz and Devon Avenue, we observe how time and memory—personal, cultural, and environmental—influence the way we know and viscerally experience this street. We see how global processes are articulated and inserted within a longer local story of place. Cumulatively, more such stories that explore how heterolocal spaces are defined by their edges, strung together, will produce a comprehensive history of contemporary immigrant cultural landscapes of mobility. This history of architecture, not focused on buildings and architects, will account for a reticulated landscape sustained by users and inhabitants who move between them.

Notes

1 For a more complete Devon Avenue ethnic landscape tour please visit the Intertwined Cultures public history website at www.intertwinedcultures.com.
2 Much of my work on immigrant spaces has focused on the performance of individual bodies in the production of ethnic spaces. See for instance, Arijit Sen and Lisa Silverman, *Making Place: Space and Embodiment in the City* (Indiana University Press, 2014). Also see Sarah Robinson's essay in this volume.
3 Berkeley's Pasand restaurant serves as a good example of how back zones could also become opaque spaces of exploitation. In the 1990s the restaurant owner, Lakireddy Bali Reddy exploited immigrant labor in these back zones. His unfair practices remained hidden from the state and law enforcement agencies, until one day in 2000, the police began an investigation for an unrelated incident (Russell and Poole 2003; Huddleston 2013).
4 The spectral remains of this Jewish past can still be observed if you visit the location of the Congregation Chevro Kadisha Machzikai Hadas at 2040 W. Devon Ave, a few buildings west of Ghareeb Nawaz. A good example of mid-century modern religious architecture from the 1950s, this space is currently occupied by a medical center and health care clinic and a community center catering to new Muslim immigrants. As a reminder and a remainder of its Jewish past the bright Star of David engraved on the stair landing and the stained-glass windows of the main prayer space are still visible.
5 A rich history of incremental growth and the resultant physical morphology of this street produce a feeling of visual density that urban planners call, "fine urban grain." This term refers to the high ratio of built area in comparison to open un-built space. Visual density also produces an overabundance of visual information and details such as signage, architectural ornaments, horizontal and vertical datum lines produced by cornices, walls, windows, sills, and parapets (McNeill 2011).
6 Architectural historian Jennifer Cousineau writes:

> An *eruv* is a space whose disparate areas are regarded as forming a single domain by virtue of the contiguity of its boundaries. An *eruv* can be built in a single street, uniting several dwellings on that street, or on a much larger scale, uniting many streets, households, and even neighborhoods. All *eruvim*, however, require real, physical boundaries. These boundaries tend to be minimalistic and are usually well integrated into the urban built environment.
>
> *(Cousineau 2014)*

References

Anderson, K. (1987) "The idea of Chinatown: the power of place and institutional practice in the making of a racial category," *Annals, Association of American Geographers* 71, 4: 580–598.
Archer, J. and Santoro, J. (2007) *Images of America: Roger's Park*, Chicago: Arcadia Publishing.
Arendt, H. (1958) *The Human Condition*, Chicago: University of Chicago Press.
Bender, C. and Smith, E. (2004) "Religious innovations among New York's Muslim taxi drivers," in T. Carnes and F. Yang (eds) *Asian American Religions: The Making and Remaking of Borders and Boundaries*, New York: New York University Press, 76–97.
Bourdieu, P. (2004) "Structures and the habitus," in V. Buchli (ed.) *Material Culture: Critical Concepts in the Social Sciences*, London: Routledge.
Bozai, B. and Bozai, M. (2103) Interviewed by Arijit Sen, Devon Avenue, Chicago, May.
Chattopadhyay, S. (2012) *Unlearning the City: Infrastructure in a New Optical Field*, Minneapolis: University of Minnesota Press.
Clay, G. (1980) *Close-Up: How to Read the American City*, Chicago: University of Chicago Press.
Connerton, P. (1989) *How Societies Remember*, New York: Cambridge University Press.
Cousineau, J. (2014) "Urban boundaries, religious experience, and the North West London eruv," in A. Sen and L. Silverman (eds), *Making Place: Space and Embodiment in the City*, Bloomington: Indiana University Press.

Cutler, I. (1996) *The Jews of Chicago: From Shtetl to Suburb*, Chicago: University of Illinois Press.
Eddie, C. (2016) Ghareeb Nawaz reviews on July 23, 2016. www.yelp.com/biz/ghareeb-nawaz-chicago?start=500 (October 29, 2016).
Gans, H. (1982) *The Urban Villagers: Group and Class in the Life of Italian-Americans*, New York: Free Press.
Ghisolf, L. (2015) "Tour Devon Avenue and Little India in an afternoon," *Time Out Chicago*. www.timeout.com/chicago/blog/tour-devon-avenue-and-little-india-in-an-afternoon (October 29, 2016).
Goffman, E. (1956) *Presentation of Self in Everyday Life*, Edinburgh: University of Edinburg, Social Science Research Center.
Herzfeld, M. (1991) *A Place in History: Social and Monumental Time in a Cretan Village*, Princeton: Princeton University Press.
Huddleston, T. (2013) *Slaves of Berkeley: The Shocking Story of Human Trafficking in the United States*, Absolute Crime Books.
Jackson, J. B. (1970) *Landscapes: Selected Writings of J. B. Jackson*, Amherst, MA: University of Massachusetts Press.
Khan, S. (2015) "'Otherness' of ethnic enclave attractions in multicultural cities: a study of Chinatown and Little India," *Asia-Pacific Journal of Innovation in Hospitality and Tourism* 4, 1: 63–76.
Koval, J., Bennett, L., Bennett, M., Demissie, F., Garner, R., and Kim, K. (2006) *The New Chicago: A Social and Cultural Analysis*, Philadelphia: Temple University Press.
Langer, A. (2004) *Crossing California*, New York: Riverhead Books.
Lautman, V. (2011) "A guide to Devon Avenue," *Chicago* magazine. www.chicagomag.com/Chicago-Magazine/January-2011/Guide-to-Devon-Avenue-in-Chicago/ (October 29, 2016).
Li, W. (2005) "Beyond Chinatown, beyond enclave: reconceptualizing contemporary Chinese settlements in the United States," *GeoJournal* 64, 1: 31–40.
Longstreth, R. (1987) *The Buildings of Main Street: A Guide to American Commercial Architecture*, Washington, DC: The Preservation Press, National Trust for Historic Preservation.
Lynch, K. (1960) *The Image of the City*, Cambridge, MA: MIT Press.
Mai, J. (2014) "The ultimate guide to Indian food on Devon Avenue," *Thrillist Chicago*. www.thrillist.com/eat/chicago/west-rogers-park/best-chicago-indian-food-devon-avenue (October 29, 2016).
McNeill, D. (2011) "Fine grain, global city: Jan Gehl, public space and commercial culture in central Sydney," *Journal of Urban Design* 16, 2: 161–178.
Patel, M. (2013) Interviewed by Arijit Sen, Devon Avenue, Chicago.
Patel, S. (2013) Interviewed by Arijit Sen, Devon Avenue, Chicago.
Powell, R. and Michael, M. (2012) "What is a home range?" *Journal of Mammalogy* 93, 4: 948–958.
Ricardo, E. (2009) Ghareeb Nawaz reviews on May 28. www.yelp.com/biz/ghareeb-nawaz-chicago?start=500 (October 29, 2016).
Russell, D. and Poole, P. (2003) "The Lakireddy Bali Reddy Case," Women Against Sexual Slavery. www.wassusa.com (October 29, 2016).
Selvam, A. (2018) "12 great Indian restaurants in Chicago that prove variety is the spice of life," *Eater Chicago*. http://chicago.eater.com/maps/best-indian-south-asian-restaurants-chicago (August 31, 2018).
Sen, A. (2009) "Creative dissonance: performance of ethnicity in banal space," *InTensions* 2. www.yorku.ca/intent/issue2/articles/arijitsen.php (October 29, 2016).
Sen, A. (2012) "Transcultural placemaking: intertwined spaces of sacred and secular on Devon Avenue, Chicago," in Jeff Hou (ed.) *Transcultural Cities: Border crossing and Placemaking*, New York: Routledge, 19–33.
Sen, A. (2013) "Staged disappointment: architecture and cultural contact," *Winterthur Portfolio* 47, 4: 207–244.
Sen, A. (2015a) "Awe and order: ethno-architecture in everyday life," in M. Lozanovska (ed.) *Ethno-Architecture and the Politics of Migration*, Abingdon, UK: Taylor & Francis/Routledge, 151–164.
Sen, A. (2015b) "Intertwined cultures along Devon Avenue, Chicago," in V. Price, D. Spatz, and B. Hunt (eds) *Out of the Loop: Chicago*, Chicago: Agate Midway Books, Agate Publishing.
Sen, A. (2016) "Food, place, and memory: Bangladeshi fish stores on Devon Avenue, Chicago," *Food and Foodways* 24, 1–2: 67–88.
Sen, A. and Silverman, L. (2014) *Making Place: Space and Embodiment in the City*, Bloomington: Indiana University Press.
Silver, D. and Clark, T. (2016) *Scenescapes: How Qualities of Place Shape Social Life*, Chicago: University of Chicago Press.

Ward, S. (1998) *Selling Places: The Marketing and Promotion of Towns and Cities 1850–2000*, New York: Routledge.
Wiviott, G. Ghareeb Nawaaz review on Chicago Reader. www.chicagoreader.com/chicago/ghareeb-nawaz/Location?oid=1024974 (October 29, 2016).
Wiviott, G. Ghareeb Nawaz review on Groupon. www.groupon.com/biz/chicago/nawaz-ghareeb-restaurant (October 29, 2016).
Wiviott, G. Ghareeb Nawaz review on Zabihah, June 5, 1998, www.zabihah.com/biz/Chicago/Ghareeb-Nawaz/iFp8kkMnaT (October 29, 2016).
Zelinsky, Z. and Lee, B. (1998) "Heterolocalism: an alternative model of the sociospatial behaviour of immigrant ethnic communities," *International Journal of Popular Geography* 4, 4: 281–298.

Part IV
Technologies

18
Obsolescence and Its Futures

Daniel M. Abramson

Architecture embodies modes of thinking about how forms and functions relate in space as well as how we imagine forms and functions might and should evolve over time. Traditionally, in Western culture, the temporal ideal has been that of permanence or very slow gradual change, symbolized in the ruinscape: architecture that endures for eons, only gradually degraded by nature and history.[1] However, in the twentieth century a radically different framework was invented to think about how to comprehend and manage time and change in the built environment. In the face of seemingly inexorable, accelerating developments in society and technology, architects came to believe that obsolescence had become the dominant paradigm for change: the new constantly out-performing and superseding the old, devaluing the latter and making it ultimately expendable. Obsolescence, it is argued in this essay, drove architectural imaginations in the mid-twentieth century leading eventually to today's dominant paradigm for comprehending and managing change in the built environment, namely, sustainability. Still, the history and lessons of obsolescence remain alive and pertinent for architecture in the twenty-first century.[2]

The term obsolescence was first applied in English to architecture about a century ago to help explain the unsettling phenomenon of American downtown skyscrapers recently built and still physically sound but now brought low by a process of what was first called "financial decay" (Bolton 1911: 73). So, for example, in 1910 the landmark Gillender Building at the corner of Wall and Nassau streets in New York City fell to the wrecking ball. At its birth in 1897, it had been the world's loftiest office tower. But now, only 13 years later, it was being rubbled for a taller, more up-to-date structure. Still physically sound, it was considered uneconomic and expendable, worthy only of destruction and replacement—in a word, obsolete.

Experts like the New York engineer Reginald Bolton in his seminal work, *Building for Profit: Principles Governing the Economic Improvement of Real Estate* (1911), identified causes for obsolescence's sudden losses of value with "the influence of fashion, change of habit, competition, development of new territory and shifting of the centres of population and business" (Bolton 1911: 75). Bolton tabulated obsolescence rates by building type—banks, for example, holding their value longer than hotels due to different rates of change in use and taste. Nevertheless, Bolton concluded, "The useful or economic existence of all classes of buildings, in the rapid march of modern conditions, is constantly shortening" (Bolton 1911: 68).

Daniel M. Abramson

After the Gillender Building's demise and Bolton's pioneering treatise, analysis of architectural obsolescence received further impetus with the introduction of the U.S. corporate income tax in the 1910s, which included deductions for the cost of obsolescence. The National Association of Building Owners and Managers (NABOM) conducted membership surveys and "autopsies" of demolitions in its Chicago home, to understand the phenomenon and establish building life span numbers for tax purposes.[3] Publicized widely, NABOM's discourse resonated with American popular imagination, then witnessing an epidemic of building demolitions and a flood of expendable consumer goods. A 1935 bibliography listed some 125 entries on the subject (Jameson 1953). "Blessed word," wrote the economist W. C. Clark, "which the income tax has forced upon our acquaintance and which we delight to roll upon our tongues because of its euphonious length and the impression of technical competence which its free use seems to convey" (Clark 1925). Chaotic architectural redevelopment in this capitalist context was thus given a logic and a name—obsolescence—a process of seemingly inevitable innovation and supersession, expendability and rebuilding; an architectural analog to the economist Joseph Schumpeter's famous mid-century definition of capitalism itself as Creative Destruction, new constantly superseding old (Schumpeter 1950: 83–84).

In the following decades of the 1930s through 1950s the idea of architectural obsolescence was extended by urban planners to the scale of the city. In the U.S., urban obsolescence indicated a district's sub-standard economic, health, and infrastructure performance thus primed for demolition and renewal, as in the infamous case of Boston's West End district, denoted an "Obsolete Neighborhood" in 1951 and thereafter nearly completely razed (Abramson 2012). In Europe, the term focused more on social than financial factors, appropriate where the state rather than private investment often led development. "In both the Eastern and Western blocs," writes urban historian Florian Urban, "obsolescence was the catchword of the time" (Urban 2009: 44). By the late 1950s the notion of built-environment obsolescence, in all its contexts, varieties, and scales—from capitalist to socialist, America to Europe, offices to cities—had become a dominant paradigm for comprehending and managing change. "The annual model, the disposable container, the throwaway city have become the norms," observed American preservationist James Marston Fitch (1982: 31).

How did architects respond? At first by denial. In the 1920s and 1930s, traditionalists stuck to classical forms embodying permanence and durability. Even avant-gardists like Le Corbusier continued to seek "a sure and permanent home" (Le Corbusier 1986: 263). There were exceptions. In Europe, the Czech shoe manufacturer Tomáš Baťa railed against "obsolete houses that will strangle and suffocate the next generation," and so projected 20-year life spans for the factories and dwellings of his famed company town of Zlín (Abramson 2009: 165–167).

It was not until the postwar years of prosperous consumerism that a younger generation of architects faced up to obsolescence's challenges. In the 1960s, University of London researchers produced in-depth studies discovering, for example, that hospital labs obsolesced faster than patient wards. From another angle, English architect Cedric Price promoted "an expendable aesthetic" and "planned obsolescence" (Price 1962: n.p.), characterizing some of his own designs, like the unbuilt Fun Palace, as "short-life toys" (Price and Littlewood 1968: 129–130). In Japan, the Metabolist group extolled evanescent form-making: "There is no fixed form in the ever-developing world" (Kawazoe 1960: 48).

But it was in design not words that architects engaged most deeply with obsolescence. The prime solution was the open-plan factory shed, widely adapted for schools and offices, hospitals and museums. Mies van der Rohe's New National Gallery in Berlin represented an apotheosis of the type: a perfect frame of infinite interior adaptability versus unforeseen change. Other architects, however, rejected the factory shed's monolithic exterior massing as too static for a dynamic age. Instead they promoted fluid, indeterminate design, like Northwick Park Hospital outside London (1961–1976, Llewelyn Davies and Weeks), the largest British medical complex of its day, which featured a loose-jointed site plan of demolishable blocks and extendable ends with demountable firestairs and removable metal infill panels (Figure 18.1). Permanence and impermanence harmonized in an age of obsolescence was the theme, too, of the megastructure, like Archigram member Peter Cook's Plug-In City project (1964–1965), featuring a long-term, infrastructural latticework supporting plug-in components of shorter lifecycles, from hotels to offices to shops.

At the same time in the 1960s evolved an impassioned counter-reaction to obsolescence, which refused its logic of supersession and expendability. Concrete brutalism, for example, initiated by Le Corbusier's Unité d'Habitation, became a worldwide vernacular in the 1960s and 1970s, embodying permanence against obsolescence's flux. The renewal of traditional expression by Aldo Rossi, Louis Kahn, Robert Venturi, and others, launching postmodernism, revalued historical imagery. Preservationism also witnessed a dramatic upswing in the 1960s, becoming more populist around the globe, and incorporating recent and vernacular structures. Preservationism revalues objects, otherwise destined for the discard pile, with historical and affective meanings, reversing the logic of obsolescence, which conceived the passage of time as purely corrosive. Adaptive reuse and gentrification also gathered steam during this period, fueled by activists like Jane Jacobs, who rejected urban obsolescence's wholesale destruction of city districts. The profligate waste of obsolescence also offended 1960s environmentalism, which led to ecological architecture. Indeed, what we call today sustainability could be said to encompass *all* the counter-tactics to obsolescence that arose in the 1960s, from adaptive reuse to postmodernism to preservationism to ecological design, which prioritized the conservation rather than expendability of resources, both natural and human-made.

The richness of 1960s architectural culture precisely reflected the passions of a contest over obsolescence still hanging in the balance, the two sides equally creative and fervid, Price and the

Figure 18.1 Northwick Park Hospital, growing end, Harrow (England), Richard Llewelyn Davies and John Weeks, 1961–1976

Source: Copyright Daniel M. Abramson.

Metabolists on equal footing with Jacobs and preservationism. But by the early 1970s the matter was largely settled, against designing for obsolescence. Financial constraint in the wake of oil crises dried up resources for replacement. Welfare state constriction eroded public patronage for renewal. Popular activism put an end to top-down bureaucratic planning. The grand dreams of a throwaway, expendable, plug-in future foundered on the shoals of economic, political, and cultural reversals. Instead, sustainability became the ruling paradigm. Notwithstanding some exceptions such as Asian urban development and several building types (e.g.,,, sports stadia and suburban teardowns), the dominant ideology of sustainability—who argues against it?—now generally inclines public opinion towards adaptive reuse or some other form of preservation over knee-jerk demolition. UNESCO's World Heritage rubric continues its global march; environmentalism is practically a secular religion.

Seeing obsolescence and sustainability in sequence points to obsolescence's part in the genealogy, the pre-history of sustainability. But we should not see obsolescence and sustainability as completely separate. The relation between the two is as much filial as agonistic. Adaptive reuse, for example, is a variation on the megastructure. In both, new components inserted into long-life frames accommodate change. Obsolescence and preservation are also mutually intertwined. Obsolescence's traumas are assuaged by preservation, while preservation feeds off fears of obsolescence. Both define the past as broken off from the present. They need each other to survive. As the historian David Lowenthal writes, "To expunge the obsolete and restore it as heritage are, like disease and its treatment, conjoint and even symbiotic" (Lowenthal 2004: 33). Obsolescence and ecological architecture mirror each other, too, in their dependence upon measurable performance. Today's tables of building energy use echo the data-mania of earlier obsolescence studies. In both approaches, architectural worth is reduced to experts' numbers.

In other words, we have not overcome the other side of the argument in the 1960s—belief in the promise of obsolescence—as much as a triumphalist narrative of sustainability might have it. Our time remains, as lived experience always does, polytemporal, in the sociologist Bruno Latour's phrasing. "The past is not surpassed but revisited, repeated, surrounded, protected, recombined, reinterpreted and reshuffled" (Latour 1993: 75). Obsolescence endures, even if not as a dominant worldview.

Today, obsolescence coexists with sustainability, though it is subordinate. The view is still heard that "if a building becomes redundant for the business it was originally built for it should be knocked down and replaced," as the head of the British Arts Council declared in the mid-1990s (Cunningham 1998: 4). "You know, our Arizona stadium will be torn down in 30 years because it will be useless," prophesies Peter Eisenman about a 2006 structure of his (Byles 2005: 298). Several building types seem especially susceptible to obsolescence today. In America's older inner suburban towns, Main Street preservation cohabits with ruthless domestic teardowns. Small but serviceable postwar homes on valuable land are replaced by large new residences featuring supersized kitchen-family rooms. These are both more lucrative for developers' profit margins and more compatible with the informal eating and gathering practices of contemporary life. American convention centers, casinos, and sports stadia have notably short lives, too, replaced by larger, up-to-date profit centers. Postwar public buildings around the world, especially of the concrete brutalist variety, suffer obsolescence as well, even if more aesthetic than functional. In Britain, Northwick Park Hospital's streaked gray blocks have been compared stylistically to a "Russian nuclear reactor" by hospital staff (Abramson 2005) (see Figure 18.1).

In China, capitalist modernization today sweeps away the past, echoing the American trajectory a century ago. "In both countries, older inner-city neighborhoods were viewed as obsolete," write the urban experts Yan Zhang and Ke Fang (Zhang and Fang 2004: 288). But the parallels extend only so far. The Chinese state steers development as much as the market does. Beijing is more like the top-down, nineteenth-century remaking of Paris than the capitalist free-for-all of Chicago. And the centralized urban form in China is hardly considered obsolete, outperformed by suburbs, as it was perceived to be in mid-twentieth-century America. "In China today, the city reigns supreme," declares the urban planner and historian Thomas Campanella (2008: 165). And even as Chinese cities undergo radical redevelopment, tactics of sustainability temper obsolescence. Shanghai effaces its working-class, alley-and-courtyard *lilong* housing precincts, but plans historic preservation and ecodistricts. Surviving tenements cluster beneath tower blocks alongside adaptive reuse and postmodern contextualism in gentrifying neighborhoods. The city's most popular tourist site is the reconstructed, high-end, *lilong*-style shopping district of Xintiandi. In China, a rich polytemporality exists in dynamic tension between modernization and conservation, obsolescence and sustainability.

Meanwhile, in the urban Western world, tens of thousands of obsolete dwellings have been razed on both sides of the Atlantic in the past generation—in the former East Germany, for instance, and in the city of Detroit alone some 161,000 (Byles 2005: ch. 8). Urban obsolescence persists. But it is not perceived as an existential crisis as it was in the mid-twentieth century. Artists and tourists now seek aesthetic and historical meaning in the postindustrial detritus of shrinking cities, discovering "admiration for its peculiar beauty," explains the pioneering photographer Camilo J. Vergara of his *American Ruins* project, "symbols of what led this nation into the twentieth-century" (Vergara 1999: 11, 206). Critics discern here nostalgia "for the ruins of modernity," observes the philosopher Andreas Huyssen (2006: 8). "The mammoth has changed from aggressor to victim and now earns our wistful affection," notes the architectural historian and theorist Robert Harbison (1991: 122). Some have taken the critique further, calling the aesthetic "ruin porn," thinking of work like the coffee-table tome *The Ruins of Detroit*, by Yves Marchand and Romain Meffre (2010) (Woodward 2013). Lush pictures of abandonment empty obsolescence of its menace.

In architecture, too, obsolescence has lost its edge. Once it energized discourse and design; now it is a minor chord. Architects remain interested in transience and flexibility, but their attention lacks the urgency that infused the last century. Technical solutions are occasionally offered to manage building life, like Designing for Disassembly (DfD), by two architects of the firm Llewelyn Davies Yeang (Durmisevic and Yeang 2009). Half a century ago this practice's founding principals, Richard Llewelyn Davies and John Weeks, wrestled strenuously with the theoretical, aesthetic, and practical implications of obsolescence, producing the idea of indeterminate architecture, a kind of "open work" in building resonating with contemporary artistic and cultural trends. Subsequently, the issue of obsolescence became more narrowly conceived. As a 1985 study concluded, "The question of hospital obsolescence is always a question of economic obsolescence" (DeChant 1985: 8). Gone are the broader cultural, technological, organizational, social, and philosophical facets supplementing the economic, which heightened the sense of excitement and urgency around obsolescence in the 1960s.

As such, obsolescence no longer drives design as it once did, when architects experimented imaginatively with factory-sheds and indeterminacy, megastructures and plug-ins. Only occasionally does contemporary architecture grant creative significance to obsolescence. Rem Koolhaas is an exception. Trained in late-1960s London, Koolhaas retains that moment's romance with obsolescence, particularly his admiration for Cedric Price. "He was a sceptic torturing a conservative discipline," Koolhaas proclaims about his generation's great teacher of expendability (Koolhaas 2004). Koolhaas' unrealized plan for Paris's La Défense district (1991), "declared that every building in this entire zone that is less than twenty-five years [old] has to be destroyed" (Koolhaas 1993: 53). In practice, Koolhaas expresses his understanding of obsolescence in smaller-scale details, as at the Illinois Institute of Technology campus center (1997–2003), whose elements look under construction, still provisional (Figure 18.2).

Figure 18.2 McCormick Tribune Campus Center, Illinois Institute of Technology, Chicago, Rem Koolhaas, 1997–2003
Source: Copyright Daniel M. Abramson.

Risk and uncertainty, off which the architectures of obsolescence thrived, are neutralized not only by the tactics of sustainability but also in the aesthetics of today's "supermodernism," a term deployed by the Dutch architecture critic Hans Ibelings. Taut glass boxes around the world by architects like Toyo Ito, Herzog & de Meuron, Jean Nouvel, and others convey an image of absolute finish (Figure 18.3). The skins of these buildings completely wrap the structures, symbolizing, in Ibeling's view, a monolithic timelessness. The effect is an image of architecture as "a safe container, a flexible shell," an inviolable treasure chest whose hermetic perfection transcends the flux of the world (Ibelings 2002: 62). Obsolescence is neutered as a critical factor of mutability in modern life, these jewel boxes suggest, obsolescence's power to move design negated.

If obsolescence was the dominant ideology of architectural change for mid-twentieth-century capitalism, giving a name to its process of wholesale expendability, then, arguably, sustainability performs the same function for current-day capitalism. Neoliberalism, as it is often called, seeks unfettered free trade, capital mobility, and modes of transnational production unrestrained by state regulation and local workers' rights. It idealizes a supranational global economy that is decentered and deterritorialized (for example, many companies in the American high-tech sector have headquarters on the West Coast and factories in Asia).

It may be going too far to declare that "sustainability culture is inherent to the logic of late capitalism," as does the philosopher Adrian Parr (2009: 4). But the symbiosis is evident. Both

Figure 18.3 Prada Boutique, Tokyo, Herzog + DeMeuron, 2003
Source: Copyright Daniel M. Abramson.

sustainability and neoliberalism manage risk with great operational sophistication. The challenges of financialized neoliberal capitalism are mediated through complex new technologies and techniques, from computerized trading to credit default swaps. Likewise, sustainability depends upon machine and managerial innovations to equilibrate change: green engines and preservation protocols. At the same time, sustainability is promoted as an economic growth machine to support capitalist accumulation. Ecobranding proves effective marketing. Sustainability's technophilia fuels corporate profits. Technology and administration are architectural sustainability's foci, not politics, transferring onto nature and away from the social. Not coincidentally, the neoliberal deregulation of capital flows and accumulation accompanies sustainability's hyperregulation of environments both built and natural. The latter, arguably, diverts attention from the former.

As much as sustainability promises a new, brighter future, can it ever break the current order? Sustainability advocates might excoriate capitalist exploitation of the environment and seek dramatic changes in consumption patterns, but its ethic is continuity and conservation. It is a privilege of the wealthy, who can afford to curb their consumption in the name of environmental salvation and to revalue obsolete objects as salvaged treasure. Unlike obsolescence, sustainability denies the promise of radical change. As the architect Ellen Grimes asserts, sustainability is an "inherently conservative term" (Grimes 2011). Sustainability suffers from an inherent contradiction: to change *and* to preserve the world. Its highest ideal is utopian equilibrium, an ideal net-zero perfection, in which all is stable harmony. Might, in fact, sustainability be merely an alibi of conservation, its practice in architecture as profligate as obsolescence; witness super-tall skyscrapers trumpeting their Leadership in Energy and Environmental Design (LEED) certification projected for Jakarta, Mumbai, and Shanghai. In other words, sustainability no less than obsolescence is ideological, productive for design to be sure, firing architects' imaginations as obsolescence once did, but nevertheless rife with illusion and contradiction.

What then are some lessons from the architectural history of obsolescence? First, the architectural history of obsolescence illustrates the flexibility of capitalism, its capacity to evolve from its own contradictions. What capitalism itself obsolesced—the industrial-age built environment—it then revalued through adaptive reuse, gentrification, and historic preservation. All that was solid need *not* melt into air, to be profitable again, architectural history teaches us.

The history of obsolescence also has lessons to teach architecture about time. Attend to the temporality of function, it suggests. This goes beyond architecture's usual temporal dimensions of historical association (looking like the past), natural mutability (changing like nature), or procession through space (movement in time). The temporality of use is remote to most architects and architectural historians, who mainly focus on the period of creation. At least since the Renaissance, the architect's ideal role has been to sire architecture: to beget a building by design, husband it through construction, then move on to further acts of procreation. "You know, I have designed buildings that I have never been to," Frank Gehry proclaims, "because the people I worked with weren't there at the end, so I didn't go see them" (Joyce 2004: xii). In this culture, the designing architect is neither encouraged nor paid to nurture a building through its useful existence. But the theme of obsolescence teaches that the life of buildings matters and implicitly makes this a high priority.

Taking obsolescence seriously teaches the value not just of sustenance but of transcendence, too. Expendability educates us to ends. Buildings are not forever. Yet the pendulum may have swung too far, from discarding to hoarding the past. We need to face buildings' mortality as we face our own, the authors of *Buildings Must Die* have argued, so "that death and waste can play their parts in architectural creativity" (Cairns and Jacobs 2014: 231). Obsolescence teaches letting go of the past—for worse and for better.

The history of obsolescence demonstrates the value as well in a vibrant architectural culture of the impulses both for extreme transformation and resistance to it. This was the characteristic struggle of the 1960s. Today the impulses stand imbalanced. Sustainability is in the ascendant, obsolescence eclipsed in architectural culture. "The current moment has almost no idea how to negotiate the coexistence of radical change and radical stasis that is our future," writes Koolhaas (2011: 119). The past is made a precious jewel. The contemporary most often bows delicately to the old, afraid to touch it, cleaned up and revered, as with many recent insertions into the historical fabric. In Hong Kong at the 2011 Asia Society Center building by Tod Williams Billie Tsien Architects, a new steel-columned walkway runs parallel at a respectful distance from the restored masonry wall of an old explosives magazine berm (Figure 18.4).

Less refined but more instructive, and expressive of the lessons of obsolescence, is the temporality of a renovated factory building in Zlín, Czech Republic. Here, a century ago, the shoe manufacturer Tomáš Baťa imagined 20-year building life spans. But in 2006 the frame of Building No. 23 was refurbished for a Business Innovation Center by Pavel Mudřík and Pavel Míček (Figure 18.5). The building has also been augmented with projecting bronze bays. But, more significant, something has been subtracted from the architecture. To lighten the structure, broad voids appear in the upper floors, shrinking the historical frame. Baťa's intention—a limited-life architecture—is honored unconsciously. Building No. 23 in Zlín embodies preservation, growth, *and* attrition all at once, treating the past flexibly, not reverentially. The past is visibly released. The present is open, as implicitly is the future, too.

The account here suggests a model of change of one cultural dominant succeeding another: obsolescence, then sustainability. But the historical progress was never predetermined. Rather, it proceeded through agency and circumstance, as much as through structural logic. History could have gone differently, we must believe. Without the U.S. tax code and NABOM, would the idea of obsolescence have taken such hold of architectural imaginations? Architectural obsolescence need not have become a dominant worldview; modernism was advancing without it. Le Corbusier and Gropius both believed in traditional, final, formal solutions, not the endless mutability of obsolescence—the former plumping for "a sure and permanent home" (Le Corbusier 1986: 48), the latter decrying "transient novelties" (Gropius 1965: 54). Likewise, sustainability need not have superseded obsolescence. The sides appeared balanced in the 1960s: Cedric Price and Metabolism as persuasive as Jane Jacobs and preservationism. But even as the critics of obsolescence pushed at the paradigm's contradictions—what to do with its remainders? how to account for unquantifiable values?—external crises brought to the fore obsolescence's top-down, resource-greedy nature, leading to its eclipse. Loss of faith in technocracy, a hallmark of 1960s counterculture and unrest, was followed by the 1970s oil crisis and recession, which put paid to dreams of endless abundance and expendability. By the time prosperity resumed in the 1980s, sustainability as we have broadly defined it, the desire to conserve rather than expend existing resources, occupied the heights in guises from postmodernism to ecologism. The architectural history of obsolescence is thus "*undetermined history*," in the phrase of the historian Joan Scott (Scott 2007: 25). By that Scott means a succession of events that are not predestined, tending towards a single present reality, but rather are contingent, matters of accident and agency, as much as underlying structure, logic, and teleology. History from this perspective appears as unpredictable as obsolescence itself. Radical change may or may not happen. The future unfolds in excess of our fondest projections.

Perhaps the most general lesson of the architectural history of obsolescence is that narratives of change are themselves changeable creations. Obsolescence preceded sustainability, and something else may come after sustainability, an as yet unformed, unnamed worldview for comprehending and managing change in the built environment. One candidate might be

Figure 18.4 Asia Society Hong Kong Center, Hong Kong, Tod Williams Billie Tsien, 2011
Source: Copyright Daniel M. Abramson.

Obsolescence and Its Futures

Figure 18.5 Building 23 rehabilitation, Zlín (Czech Republic), Pavel Mudřík and Pavel Míček, 2006
Source: Copyright Daniel M. Abramson.

resiliency, a contemporary byword related to sustainability that is beginning to impact architecture. Emerging in the 1970s in relation to ecologies, such as forests, and then applied to human social systems, resilience has more recently been taken up by urban planning in the wake of serial disasters, from Hurricane Katrina and the September 11 attacks to the housing bubble and global recession. A 2006 handbook defines resilience as "the capacity of a system to absorb disturbance; to undergo change and still retain essentially the same, function, structure, and feedbacks" (Walker and Salt 2006: 32). Resilience thinking thus conceptualizes change in terms of never-ending catastrophe, against which the resilient system must be designed with adaptability and diversity. Like sustainability, resilience presumes a fragile world, increasingly so, buffeted by hazard and risk. Different than sustainability, resilience thinking does not seek efficient, optimized control of an equilibrium state, but rather emphasizes redundancy and expects disaster, a series of constant crises throwing systems out of balance. Resilience thinking thus incorporates dramatic change much more than does sustainability. In this it perhaps approximates the earlier obsolescence paradigm in its acceptance or at least acknowledgment of radical change—though with resilience change is catastrophic, not beneficent. Resilience possesses a particular political economy, too, as the urban researcher Michael Quinn Dudley has pointed out, which "requires an interventionist state" to anticipate and manage the constant disturbance; in this way, resilience provides a kind of retort to neoliberalism's denigration of the public sector (Dudley 2011: 375–379). On the other hand, as Ross Exo Adams has argued, resilience thinking harnesses the state's powers in defense of capitalist investment against literally rising tides (Adams 2014). For architecture, it remains to be seen how much resilience thinking can be scaled down from the systems level to the built object *qua* adaptable, durable "safe haven," as architect Thomas Knittel puts it, generating new vocabularies of design forms and symbols (Knittel 2016: 48). But resilience, as a way to conceptualize change in architecture and design, may represent a hybrid of obsolescence and sustainability—incorporating the former's acceptance of radical contingent change within the latter's framework of systems crisis management.

Still the future is insusceptible to divination. No amount of imagination or analysis can pierce the fog of contingency veiling what will come. Ultimately, the outcome of a struggle to unseat a dominant paradigm is not preordained. Sustainability may persist. Capitalism certainly has survived, adapting to critique and crises. Yet worldviews *do* change, architectural history teaches us. Obsolescence waxed, then waned. Obsolescence preceded sustainability, and something else may come after sustainability, an as yet unformed, unnamed worldview for comprehending and managing change in the built environment. History does not proceed along a rigid path; accident and agency, along with the evolution of internal contradictions, helped invent obsolescence and then sustainability. The best lesson from the history of obsolescence may be to accept the essential *unmanageability* of change—the futility of so many efforts to manage obsolescence in design. Our futures ought not be considered iron-clad but rather malleable and contingent, as unpredictable and potentially liberating as obsolescence itself.

Notes

1 See Chapter 12 by Chattopadhyay in this volume.
2 This essay is adapted from my book *Obsolescence: An Architectural History* (Chicago and London: University of Chicago Press, 2016).
3 Earle Shultz, *The Effect of Obsolescence on the Useful and Profitable Life of Office Buildings* (Chicago: National Association of Building Owners and Managers, 1922); National Association of Building Owners and Managers, *Office Building Obsolescence: A Study of the W.C.T.U. Temple, Chicago* (Chicago: National Association of Building Owners and Managers, 1927); Paul E. Holcombe, "Depreciation and Obsolescence in the Tacoma Building," *Bulletin of the National Association of Building Owners and Managers* 137 (June 1929): 13–32; John Roberts, "Obsolescence in the Marshall Field Wholesale Building," *Bulletin of the National Association of Building Owners and Managers* 150 (September 1930): 41–45.

References

Abramson, D. M. (2005) Northwick Park Hospital, Conversation with P. Smith, A. White, and N. Hulme (December 19, 2005).
Abramson, D. M. (2009) "Obsolescence and the fate of Zlín," in K. Klingan (ed.) *A Utopia of Modernity: Zlín*, Berlin: JOVIS.
Abramson, D. M. (2012) "Boston's West End: urban obsolescence in mid-twentieth-century America," in Aggregate, *Governing by Design: Architecture, Economy, and Politics in the Twentieth Century*, Pittsburgh: University of Pittsburgh Press.
Adams, R. X. (2014) "Notes from the resilient city," *Log* 32: 126–139.
Bolton, R. P. (1911) *Building for Profit: Principles Governing the Economic Improvement of Real Estate*, New York: De Vinne.
Byles, J. (2005) *Rubble: Unearthing the History of Demolition*, New York: Harmony.
Cairns, S. and Jacobs, J. M. (2014) *Buildings Must Die: A Perverse View of Architecture*, Cambridge, MA: MIT Press.
Campanella, T. (2008) *The Concrete Dragon: China's Urban Revolution and What It Means for the World*, New York: Princeton Architectural Press.
Clark, W. C. (1925) "Obsolescence," in *Property Management: Proceedings and Reports of the Property Management. Annals of Real Estate Practice*, vol. 5, Chicago: National Association of Real Estate Boards.
Cunningham, A. (1998) *Modern Movement Heritage*, New York: E & FN Spon.
DeChant, T. (1985) *Detecting and Preventing Hospital Obsolescence*, Madison, WI: Institute for Health Planning.
Dudley, M. Q. (2011) "Resilience," in N. Cohen (ed.) *Green Cities: An A-to-Z Guide*, Los Angeles: Sage, 2011.
Durmisevic, E. and Yeang, K. (2009) "Designing for Disassembly (DfD)," *Architectural Design* 79, 6: 134–137.

Fitch, J. M. (1982) *Historic Preservation: Curatorial Management of the Built World* New York: McGraw-Hill.

Grimes, E. (2011) Untitled lecture, Future of History Conference, University of Michigan Taubman College of Architecture and Urban Planning, April 2011, www.youtube.com/watch?v=u6pcwH300Uw, accessed November 21, 2014.

Gropius, W. (1965) *The New Architecture and the Bauhaus*, trans. P. M. Shand, Cambridge, MA: MIT Press.

Harbison, R. (1991) *The Built, the Unbuilt, and the Unbuildable: In Pursuit of Architectural Meaning*, Cambridge, MA: MIT Press.

Huyssen, A. (2006) "Nostalgia for ruins," *Grey Room* 23: 6–21.

Ibelings, H. (2002) *Supermodernism: Architecture in the Age of Globalization*, Rotterdam: NAi.

Jameson, M. E. (1953) "Obsolescence in buildings: a selected list of references," in A. N. Lockwood (ed.) *Selected Readings in Real Estate Appraisal*, Chicago: American Institute of Real Estate Appraisers.

Joyce, N. (2004) *Building Stata: The Design and Construction of Frank O. Gehry's Stata Center at MIT*, Cambridge, MA: MIT Press.

Kawazoe, N. (1960) "Material and man," in K. Kikutake, N. Kawazoe, M. Ohtaka, F. Maki, and N. Kurokawa, *Metabolism: The Proposals for New Urbanism*, Tokyo: Bijutu Syuppan Sha.

Knittel, T. (2016) "Resilient design: modeling architecture's future in the face of climate change," *Arcade* 34, 3: 48–50.

Koolhaas, R. (1993) "Urban operations," *D: Columbia Documents of Architecture and Theory* 3: 25–57.

Koolhaas, R. (2004) In conversation with L. Cooke, "Architecture and the sixties: still radical after all these years," *Tate Etc.* 2, www.tate.org.uk/tateetc/issue2, accessed July 9, 2009.

Koolhaas, R. (2011) "CRONOAOS," *Log* 21: 119–123.

Latour, B. (1993) *We Have Never Been Modern*, trans. Catherine Porter, Cambridge, MA: Harvard University Press.

Le Corbusier (1986) *Towards a New Architecture*, trans. F. Etchells, New York: Dover.

Lowenthal, D. (2004) "The heritage crusade and its contradictions," in M. Page and R. Mason (eds) *Giving Preservation a History: Histories of Historic Preservation in the United States*, New York: Routledge.

Parr, A. (2009) *Hijacking Sustainability*, Cambridge, MA: MIT Press.

Price, C. (1962) "Activity and change," *Archigram* 2: n.p.

Price, C. and Littlewood, J. (1968) "The fun palace," *Drama Review: TDR* 12, 3: 127–134.

Schumpeter, J. (1950) *Capitalism, Socialism, and Democracy*, 3rd edition, New York: Harper & Brothers.

Scott, J. W. (2007) "History-writing as critique," in K. Jenkins, S. Morgan, and A. Munslow (eds) *Manifestos for History*, New York: Routledge.

Urban, F. (2009) *Neo-historical East Berlin: Architecture and Urban Design in the German Democratic Republic 1970–1990*, Farnham: Ashgate.

Vergara, C. J. (1999) *American Ruins*, New York: Monacelli.

Walker, B. and Salt, D. (2006) *Resilience Thinking: Sustaining Ecosystems and People in a Changing World*, Washington, DC: Island Press.

Woodward, R. B. (2013) "What a disaster," *ARTNews* 112, 2: 66–73.

Zhang, Y. and Fang, K. (2004) "Is history repeating itself? From urban renewal in the United States to inner-city redevelopment in China," *Journal of Planning Education and Research* 23, 3: 286–98.

19
Intelligent Architectural Settings

Christopher Beorkrem and Eric Sauda

It has long been an article of faith among architects that the design of buildings has a profound influence on the behavior of its inhabitants. But there has been at best only anecdotal evidence to support this claim. The spread of sensing technologies and data analytic techniques may hold promise for a more empirical approach. This chapter will outline important foundational issues for this field and will present contemporary examples of new techniques being applied to architectural settings.

Architectural theory has been interested in human occupation, particularly since the industrial revolution and the resulting proliferation of architectural production. In 1836, the English architect Augustus Pugin advocated for the Gothic style as a prescription for the dislocations of industrialization. In 1957 Sir John Summerson, searching for some basis for a theory of modern architecture to replace a reliance on history, claimed to find the "source of unity in modern architecture" in "the social sphere, in other words in the programme" (Summerson 1957: 307). The emergence of human environment studies in the 1970s and 1980s aimed to provide a structure to bring methods from the social science into architecture. Work by researchers such as Sanoff, Moore, and Hall seek to provide both a broad overview of methods as well as specific insights available to designers to better understand human behavior (Sanoff 2000; Moore and Golledge 1976; Hall 1966).

Other disciplines have also been interested in the relationship between individuals and their surroundings. Environmental psychology as an interdisciplinary approach that includes psychologists as well as architects, landscape architects, designers, geographers, anthropologists, have emphasized the study of behavior in the "wild," in environmental settings ranging in scale from single rooms to entire cities and landscapes (Gifford 2007; Mehrabian and Russell 1974). Methods in this field include complex problem solving as well as evaluation of common values leading to enhanced communal well-being. The goal of the field is a set of principles that can be applied to sets of similar environments.

An offshoot of this approach is POE (post-occupancy evaluation), which is a systematic gathering of information about the use of buildings after their occupation (Preiser, Rabinowitz, and White 1988; Zimmerman and Martin 2001: 168) Since it was never part of the architectural service contract, it was at best used only in rare circumstances. Recently, more structure has been brought within the purview of the field, particularly in health care facilities, which are under pressure to evaluate the use and performance of their facilities. Methods for conducting POE's generally involve researchers (typically ethnographers) spending considerable time on site and generalizing their observations for use in facility improvement and new designs.

Within computer science, the field of human computer interaction (HCI) has become interested in the ways in which computers are more frequently deployed not in isolated boxes, but rather in settings ranging from public displays to automobiles to refrigerators to ATMs. The subfields of inquiry emerging from HCI have been named ubiquitous computing, physical computing, and social computing; they all have in common the use of computing outside the graphic-user interface of a mouse, keyboard, and screen, as well as an understanding that the spatial and social setting are key design determinants (Weiser 1993: 75; O'Sullivan and Igoe 2004; Wang et al. 2007: 79). Recognizing these developments, Paul Dourish has proposed a new paradigm for human computing interaction that he calls embodied interaction (Dourish 2004).

Foundational Issues

There is a clear need for a systematic approach towards collecting and analyzing data about human occupation and architectural settings, and that there are techniques available that may make this more common and more useful in guiding decision making. Architects have long relied solely on precedent and assumptions to define how their designs impact human occupation and use. Before examining contemporary examples of approaches to this problem, we need to establish some foundational issues within the field, which we will call *intelligent architectural settings*. The goal of intelligent architectural settings is to employ sensing technologies of all types to collect large archives of data about human occupation and to employ data science analytic techniques to better understand and transform those settings.

Sensing devices have become relatively miniaturized, inexpensive, and common throughout architectural settings. These devices range from simple radio-frequency identification (RFID) tags to Bluetooth beacons to camera arrays. Issues concerning these devices include:

- *Wearable versus passive*: Specially designed devices such as identity badges offer individual user data, but are often difficult for settings without homogeneous user groups. *Passive sensing* such as motion detectors and cameras can gather information about a much wider group without the need to recruit participants.
- *Specific device versus user devices*: An overlapping choice is between specific devices engineered for a study versus connection to an existing device such as a smart phone. While smart phones are tempting as sensing devices, there are significant problems with differing platforms and low levels of participation.
- *Reliability versus flexibility*: Less intrusive devices such as Bluetooth beacons do not provide a consistent signal and have difficulty registering relative locations through walls as they rely on triangulation to locate an individual's device in a space.

Privacy has become a key concern for all systems that gather information about human occupants. Key issues include:

- *Information storage*: In many settings, users may have significant objection to the retention of data. In health care facilities, there are legal requirements that constrain the use of patient data, but such guarantees are scarce for employees, and can be a source of considerable concern. A strategy for protecting and engaging the users of the system and assuring them of the limits of the use of the collected data will be important to the success of any intelligent architectural

setting. Such safeguards are particularly important for sensing such as ID tags that are inherently connected to an individual.
- *Anonymize information*: One important method to maintain privacy is through strategies to anonymize information. For sensors that are intrinsically identified with a user (such as employee ID tags), this can require an affirmative decision to discard certain portions of the data to gain the confidence of the users. Interestingly, for computer vision systems, extraction of vector information from video footage is the only practical way to compress the enormous size of video files, and individual user identification is not intrinsic to the system. As a result, the data is for all practical purposes already anonymous.
- *Expectation of privacy*: There is considerable variation in the expectation of privacy in different settings. Within a home, the expectation of privacy is very high, and most employees have come to understand that they have limited privacy at work. Public spaces are a more nuanced setting, where expectations of privacy depend on the activities performed there and the timing of events. Finally, there are settings, such as memory care units and autism classrooms, where surveillance is an expectation and desire of the client, and privacy is a minor concern.

Inclusiveness is the flip side of concerns about privacy. Systems that are aimed only at specific, well-defined groups such as employees of a single company or students in defined classroom settings have a very different set of issues from those aimed at more heterogeneous groups such as people in public lobbies or using a transit system. Particularly with the distinction between wearable sensors and passive sensing, many sensors can be difficult to implement broadly across large groups of disparate users of a particular space. It is generally a goal to include as many users as possible in studies, but this constitutes particular challenges to approaches that emphasize custom sensors.

Analytic techniques are equally as important as sensing. While the results of studying architectural settings have progressed from simple counting and qualitative assessments of limited applicability, the flood of new data that will come from new sensing technology will require a more sophisticated understanding of the analysis of large-scale data. Issues include:

- *Counting*: Data returned from sensors can be analyzed for frequency and type using tabulations and comparison. There are many existing programs for comparing this data, which are typically built into the control software for the device.
- *Graphics*: In architectural settings, location is an obvious interest, and the use of graphics to identify spatial location is a particularly powerful tool. Work by researchers including Edward Tufte demonstrates how to use graphics as a powerful tool of understanding (Tufte and Graves-Morris 1983; Tufte 1991: 322).
- *Visualization*: In the field of visualization, the concept of graphics is expanded using powerful tools capable of sorting data between multiple linked windows showing different representations of the same data. Such visualizations enable one to see patterns in data differently, and to engage "visual thinking" (Card, Mackinlay, and Shneiderman 1999).
- *Interactivity*: The ability to interact with data visualization is a particularly powerful way to allow users at all levels of expertise to explore and question the meaning of the data. The field of visual analytics has made rapid advances that are particularly suited to the analysis of architectural settings.
- *Machine learning*: A technique used in computer science research allows supervised learning by machines that search for recurrent patterns across large time frames or large collections of data. No examples currently exist for architecture, but this method is clearly suitable for spatial analysis.

Research Goals for architecture settings can vary in significant ways and are likely to continue to evolve as new opportunities arise. Currently, the two main goals are:

- *Influence building design*: The most straightforward application of data from architectural settings is the evaluation and improvement of building design. This will require the analysis of multiple settings or a single setting over an extended period of time, both of which are currently feasible using sensing technology and analytic methods. It will also require the construction of data archives that hold the promise of reasonably anticipating human behavior in a variety of settings. As these archives expand, they hold the promise of improving performance in measurable ways. This could be particularly important in areas such as hospital and office design that have defined functions and measurable outcomes.
- *Interactive buildings*: Architecture may be conceptualized as a spatial volume containing human and technical elements. There is an implicit distinction between the active contents and the passive container. It is possible to instead place importance on the understanding of behavior and the idea of place as a construed setting: or, as Clifford Geertz describes it, the difference between "a wink and a blink" (Geertz 1994: 213). Such a paradigm proposes the creation of "intelligent" architectural settings that capture such meaningful behavior in real time and generate knowledge that is useful both in the real world as an interface with the users.

Contemporary Examples

The collection of data about human occupation has been explored in a variety of venues and contexts as technology has become more integrated. The so-called Internet of Things (IOT) has created a groundswell of cheaper and more reliable methods for interacting with our environment through wireless sensors. These sensors have often been adapted to monitor the comfort, use, and occupation of space. The following are a subset of some of the explorations undertaken by designers and ethnographers to better understand the occupation of our environment.

Human Sensing

Alex Pentland leads the Human Dynamics Laboratory at MIT whose mission is to use data to better understand human society (Pentland et al. 2005: 503). Ben Waber's work at Sociometrics Solutions grew out of this work and has been used by a number of large corporations to better understand and improve the performance of their employees. Waber coined the term "people analytics" to describe the use of individual sensing devices and the resulting data analysis in business organizations (Waber 2013).

Sensing: The current sensing technology used for this approach is the sociometric badge, which is about the size of a deck of cards and has an IR transmitter, a Bluetooth radio, an accelerometer and a microphone (Olguín et al. 2009: 43). The sociometric badge also has on-board data processing, which allows it to keep features of conversations (volume, duration, location, etc.) rather than complete audio files. The sensors are capable of recording 40 hours of activity between recharging. The data from the sensors are identified with individual users, and data from multiple individuals can be aggregated. Sociometric badges and their predecessors have been in use since 2000.

Privacy: Privacy is a particularly important issue within corporate workplace settings. Workers have rightly become anxious about their lack of privacy, and the adoption of sociometric data will rely on strategies that address this issue. Sandy Pentland proposes three concepts important to privacy (Pentland 2009):

- opt-in (no data collection without consent)
- individual control (no use of data for control of users)
- data for others only in aggregated form (allow management decisions only to improve working methods).

The studies conducted by Waber are at a larger scale than other research in this field, and his approach demonstrates the implementation of privacy standards without compromising the usefulness of the aggregated data. Indeed, the privacy standards help with the widespread adoption of the sociometric badges, enabling the data to provide a more holistic understanding of occupation and use than individual sensors can.

Inclusiveness: The corporate settings studied by Waber are all subject to considerable control by a central authority. The work settings open the possibility of uniform behavior and technologies across the entire population. It is not clear how they might translate to more heterogeneous, public settings or settings with less control.

Analytic technique: Pentland has demonstrated in a research setting how the use of sociometric badges would be useful in analyzing behavior. Waber's work in corporate settings is much more explicit about the ways tracking behavior can lead to better business outcomes. A good example is his work with a Bank of America call center, uncovering the ways in which changes to existing break structure led to increased retention and performance.

Research goal: The goal of this research at the human dynamics lab is broadly focused on the understanding of data and human behavior. As it has developed by Waber, it has focused on improving performance in complex settings through the analysis of behavior. The process emphasizes the collection of data followed by an analysis of meaning leading to proposed improvements. Waber presents profitability as the primary driver for improving employee comfort and happiness and therefore efficiency.

SUS/AECOM

AECOM is a multinational engineering and architecture firm with offices worldwide and approximately 95,000 employees.[1] The firm has a history of time utilization studies dating back to the 1990s that has resulted in a database of over ten million observations (Whitehead 2014). The data for this is a time log of the use of identified spaces in a variety of building types. Using this data with their clients has enabled them to compare sectors by country, work cultures, and use sectors.

Sensing: Space Utilization Study (SUS) is a proprietary tool to help clients understand how space is being used and to identify type of activities. There is no automated sensing associated with this approach. The methodology is an adaptation of POE techniques. A temporary worker is provided with a tablet and given a fixed route through a facility, with route stops identified for detailed recording. Typically, the observer walks these route eight times a day over two weeks. At each route stop, a record is entered from a preset list into the tablet of the:

- activity (empty, temporarily unoccupied, collaboration, individual work, pausing)
- equipment (desktop, laptop, telephone, paper, teleconference, tablet, projector)
- number of people (1–10).

Privacy: The data collected with SUS in inherently anonymous, so privacy concerns are not a major issue. Given the nature of the data collection, it is unlikely that this approach will raise any privacy concerns.

Inclusiveness: There is a tradeoff between the time required for data collection and inclusiveness with this approach. It requires no special technology by the user populations, but the manual nature of the data collection limits the number of spaces and the length of time that can be observed.

Analytic technique: Based on this data, it is possible to examine the change in utilization over time and between spaces. Data can be aggregated for multiple spaces.

Research goal: The major research goal is the development of a large database that can be searched for similarities and differences. The strength of this approach is the ability to make POEs routine so that it is possible to conduct them on a more regular basis and incorporate them into changes in the spatial arrangement and scheduling of spaces. This approach also allows customization of the study to include space, activities, or equipment that is of particular interest.

One shortcoming is the limit to the number of surveys that can be conducted; it is hard to imagine using this technique for more than an occasional survey. Another is the proscriptive nature of the investigations; the survey must be designed to find a precise form of behavior, with little opportunity to observe behavior and new metrics, nor can it provide interpretative data about the user's attitude towards the space or other users in the space.

CASE/WeWork

The firm CASE launched in May 2008 with a plan to bring better technology and information flow to the process of designing and constructing a building. Founders and architects Federico Negro, David Fano, and Steve Sanderson saw an opportunity to consult through the entire process (with the help of technology) to streamline efficiency and save money.

Sensing: CASE has recently studied the use of Bluetooth beacons as a method of providing positioning information inside the work space to create a better understanding of the ways in which people use space.2 Bluetooth beacons connected to a user's cell phone allow for the identification of position information, recorded at regular intervals, which can be varied by the systems operator or the user. The beacons are placed on walls throughout a work environment, typically at least three per room, to afford triangulation of a user's device while they are in a particular room. Beacons can calculate approximate distances and direction from the device and use those measurements from multiple beacons to triangulate a user's location. The signal strength can be distorted by walls, depending upon the density of their makeup, and this can often result in anomalies in the data. Placing more beacons throughout the space can allow for fewer anomalies and minimize their impact on the data collected.

Privacy: CASE has conducted experiments in their own offices with willing participants (which, given the emphasis of the firm, includes all employees). For a single employee on one day, they collected 3849 data points (which include spatial information), 589 feet of travel and seven hours and 55 minutes in the office. The resulting data can be aggregated and used to create graphic representations of an individual employee's day.

Inclusiveness: Because of the small scale of this approach, issues of privacy have not yet been addressed. It will probably be most effective in small to medium enterprises that have a common mission.

Analytic technique: The data gathered can be used to create timeline studies of individual users, aggregations of multiple users incorporating time and spatial location. Working with Mani Williams, a PhD student from RPI who held a research residency in the firm, they have developed a way to aggregate multiple users, and interactive using linked windows representing views of the data in spatial temporal and categorical views.[3]

Research goal: The goal of the research is to create a corpus of data about the movement of users within a space. This data can be used either to improve the efficient use of the space or at a large scale to compare spaces from their patterns of use.

The work at WeWork is currently experimental. The strength of this approach is the automatic way in which it collects information. The data is currently limited to user identification and a spatial location. The firm has not yet faced issues of privacy and widespread adoption within large, potentially heterogeneous settings.

VALSE

VALSE (Visual Analytic for Large Scale Ethnography) is a collaborative research group that includes computer scientists, architects, and anthropologists at UNC Charlotte and Temple. VALSE incorporates computer vision-based methods for the collection and analysis of ethnographic data in architectural settings. These methods have been tested in research settings and are currently being deployed in a school for autistic children.

Sensing: The SENSING toolkit is a framework for storing and providing access to long-term, large-scale human behavior data collected from a camera array. Analysis and visualization of data for extended time scales has required new approaches including the ability to use multiple cameras for tracking as well as the ability to track multiple occupants, including simple pose recognition and orientation (Spurlock and Souvenir 2012; 2014; Spurlock, Wu, and Souvenir 2014). The system can currently track an unlimited number of occupants in a very compact form, keeping records of human motion lasting weeks, months, or even years (Figure 19.1).

Privacy: VALSE does not record a user's image, but instead relies only on the movement pixel "silhouette" users create as they move through the field of view of the camera. This silhouette is triangulated with other cameras in the space to create a relatively accurate position of the user and also of their skeletal positions and glance. By not recording the image of the user, privacy is maintained but the complete monitoring of the position affords the ability to infer not only position and occupation but also potentially other activities with users and objects as well as behaviors over time.

Inclusiveness: VALSE is capable of monitoring several individuals in a space at a given time, limited only by the total number of people as well as by the number and locations of the cameras. The camera array must be able to see into a crowd from multiple vantage points on to each individual in order to be able to map their skeleton and monitor their movements over time. If a crowd is too dense relative to the camera array and angle, then the system is able to only see individual users that are closest to the cameras.

Analytic technique: As an extension of the SENSING toolkit, VALSE allows an expert to view avatars representing real-time motion and also visualizations of motion summaries, all controlled using a familiar DVR-style interface. VALSE combines tracking and activity recognition methods into an interactive, real-time system for visual data analysis in the study of motion behavior (Figure 19.2).

The current VALSE interface combines timeline visualization with spatial visualizations overlaid with the motion of occupants. The visualizations are linked and open to exploration by

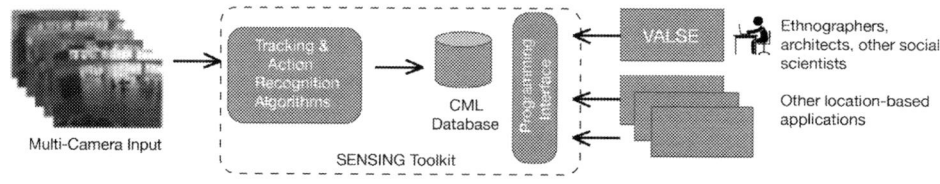

Figure 19.1 VALSE flowchart

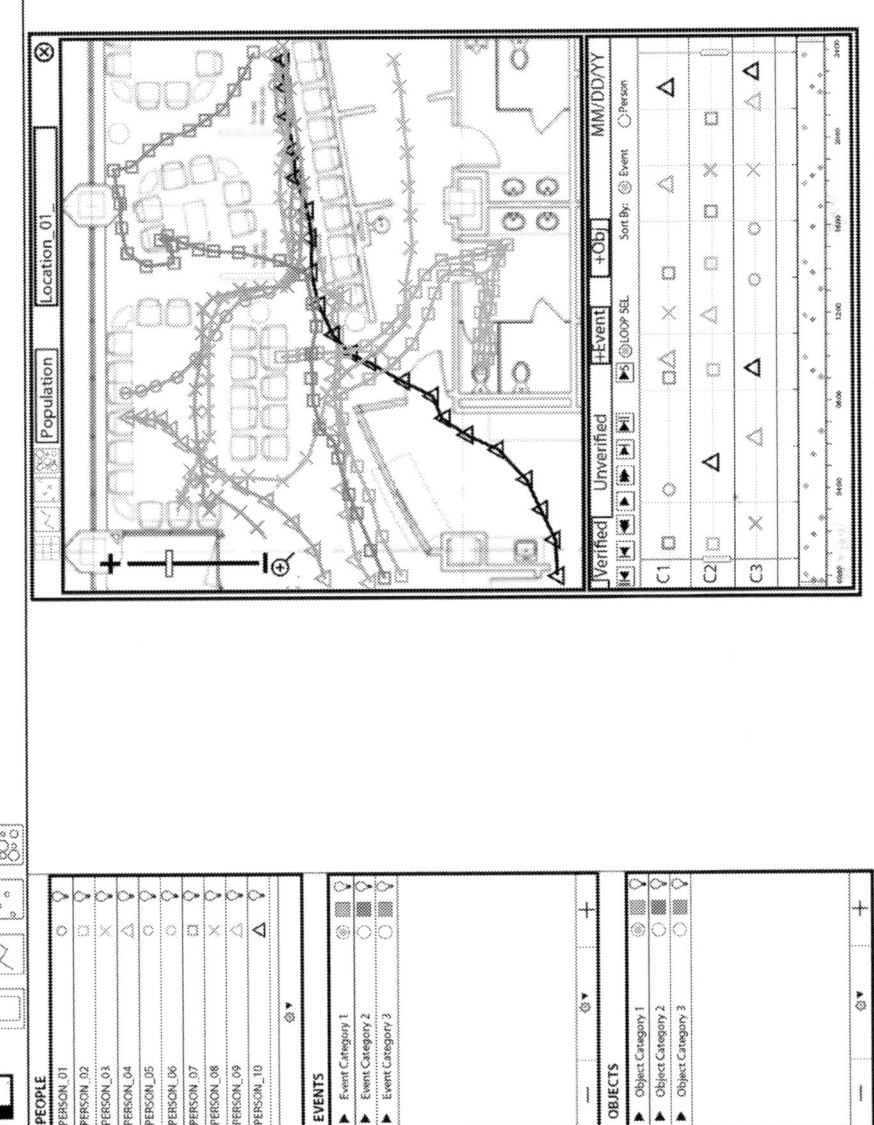

Figure 19.2 Top: Heat Map view. Bottom: Event Selection view

ethnographers or other domain experts. A critical part of the VALSE interface is the method of identifying meaningful behavior at the intersection of time, people (one or more), and objects. Once a meaningful event has been identified, the system can search for all incidents of this behavior over very long time periods. This approach leverages the ability of human ethnographers to recognize meaningful patterns of behavior with the computational ability to apply these insights for very extended periods of time.

VALSE was modeled from a combination of two different types of tools: drawing and annotation software. The drawing software (Adobe Illustrator, Rhinoceros, and AutoCAD) helped to lend methods for organization of elements as well as creation and selection processes. The annotation software (ELAN annotation, VCode, and Morae) lent itself to the control of the timeline and recording events. The expert interacts with VALSE through the Interaction Window with two main portions: the Visualization Panel and the Event Timeline. The Visualization Panel is the region that displays spatial information about the observed area, and the Event Timeline shows and allows the expert to interact with a list of the events that have occurred within the space.

Research goal: VALSE is intended to serve as a next level tool capable not only of providing location information for a user, but also of mapping behavior of users in a space over very long periods of time (Beorkrem et al. 2015a; Beorkrem et al. 2015b). The interface is intended to allow a researcher to identify a behavior that is important to the performance or use of a space and then search a database of the past movement to identify other iterations of this behavior. The tool can then report back frequency, duration, and location of those behaviors since the system was installed. Additionally, the system through machine learning could begin to identify other behaviors that researchers may not have noticed occurring in the space, because of a lack of frequency or because of the subtleness of movement (Figure 19.3).

Conclusion

Designers have long sought methods for understanding and creating relationships between the social life and the architectural spaces in which they occur, hoping to create meaningful or even fluid boundaries within architectural space. Until now, such strategies have relied on evidence collected through human observation for short-scale periods. Sensor-based information offers the opportunity to detect meaningful human behavior for much longer periods of time; it is not hard to imagine systems that collect data over the entire life of the building and even offer the opportunity to integrate data and space into a cohesive architectural setting.

To accomplish this goal, architects, computer scientists, and social scientists will need to cooperate to create new methods and paradigms for evaluating and designing architectural environments. POEs have until now been the exclusive domain of social scientists using individual human observers for short periods of time, limiting the scale of analysis, typically measured in hours. New methods from computer science, and in particular from data analytics and sensing technology, promise real-time and continuous observation of meaningful behavior, and performance focused on architectural spaces and organizational strategies.

There are two specific outcomes of the further development of sensor-based analysis of architectural space. First, the development of a fine-grained understanding of the uses that are made of facilities, which should lead to improved future design iterations and renovations. This will require methods of cataloging and comparing design alternatives, and detailed studies of the ways in which users occupy them. There are significant challenges in assembling such archives, ranging from competing file structures to legal restrictions and intellectual property conflicts. In addition, specific metrics will need to be developed to evaluate the usefulness of the data.

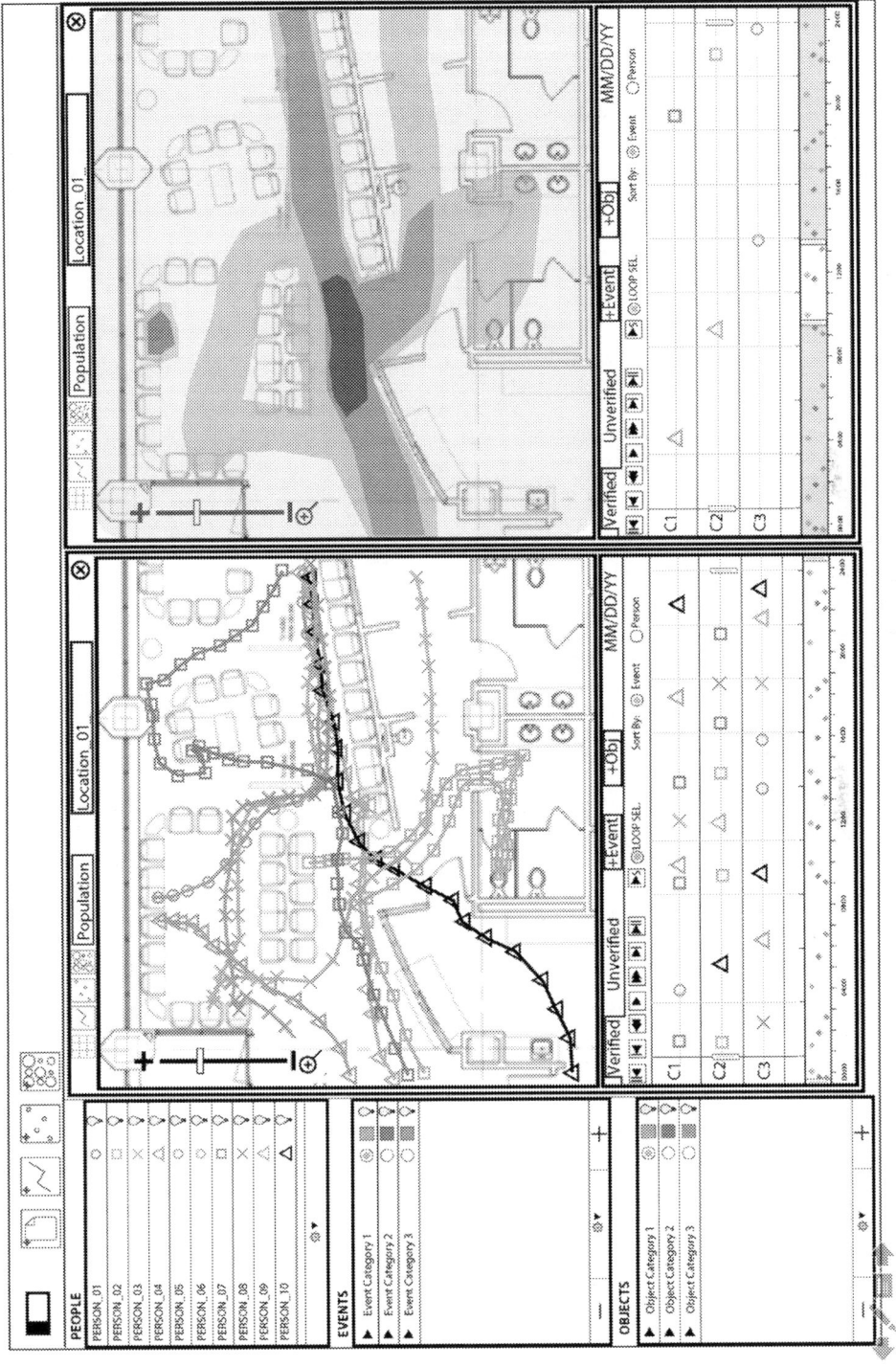

Figure 19.3 Prototype of the VALSE interface. Note the use of multiple windows which present multiple representations of the data from the setting. This interface is fully interactive and discoverable with the ethnographers studying the setting

Second, the generation of intelligent architecture settings that integrate architectural, ethnographic, and data analytic approaches can lead to settings that can adapt to both the individual and the group. Architectural settings could be designed to include both spatial elements and sensing techniques that help us to continuously understand how people are reacting. Using this information, we can understand individual performance in the space (for example how Alzheimer's patients are coping on a day to day basis) as well as how a larger group uses a space (perhaps leading to changes in spatial arrangement). We might be able to imagine settings, for example, as therapeutic instruments that could have a profound impact on comfort, happiness, and productivity. While we have long suspected that the built environment has had a tremendous impact on our lives, technology promises new ways in which those spaces can be continuously adapted to our needs.

Notes

1 www.aecom.com/about-aecom/history/.
2 www.case-inc.com/node/506.html; www.case-inc.com/node/514.html; www.case-inc.com/node/530.html.
3 https://vimeo.com/maniwilliams.

References

Beorkrem, C., Danilowicz, S., Lanclos, D., Spurlock, S., and Souvenir, R. (2015a) "Keeping an eye out: real time, real world modeling of behavior in health care settings," Design Modeling Symposium, Copenhagen.
Beorkrem, C., Danilowicz, S., Lanclos, D., Spurlock, S., and Souvenir, R. (2015b) "Intelligent architectural settings using a computer vision based visual analytic interface," CAAD Futures.
Card, S. K., Mackinlay, J. D., and Shneiderman, B. (1999) *Readings in Information Visualization: Using Vision to Think*, San Francisco: Morgan Kaufmann.
Dourish, P. (2004) *Where the Action Is: The Foundations of Embodied Interaction*, Cambridge, MA: MIT Press.
Geertz, Clifford (1994) "Thick description: toward an interpretive theory of culture," *Readings in the Philosophy of Social Science*: 213–231.
Gifford, R. (2007) *Environmental Psychology: Principles and Practice*, Colville, WA: Optimal Books.
Hall, E. T. (1990 [1966]) *The Hidden Dimension*, New York: Anchor Books.
Mehrabian, A. and Russell, J. A. (1974) *An Approach to Environmental Psychology*, Cambridge, MA: MIT Press.
Moore, G. T. and Golledge, R. G. (1976) *Environmental Knowing: Theories, Research and Methods*, Stroudsburg, PA: Dowden.
O'Sullivan, D. and Igoe, T. (2004) *Physical Computing: Sensing and Controlling the Physical World with Computers*, Boston, MA: Course Technology Press.
Olguín, D., Waber, B. N., Kim, T., Ara, K., and Pentland, A. (2009) "Sensible organizations: technology and methodology for automatically measuring organizational behavior," *IEEE Transactions on Systems, Man, and Cybernetics, Part B (Cybernetics)* 39, 1: 43–55.
Pentland, A. (2009) "Reality mining of mobile communications: toward a new deal on data," *The Global Information Technology Report 2008–2009*, World Economic Forum, 75–80.
Pentland, A., Choudhury, T., Eagle, N., and Singh, P. (2005) "Human dynamics: computation for organizations," *Pattern Recognition Letters* 26, 4: 503–511.
Preiser, W. F. E., Rabinowitz, H. Z., and White, E. T. (1988) *Post-occupancy Evaluation*, New York: Van Nostrand Reinhold Company.
Sanoff, H. (2000) *Community Participation Methods in Design and Planning*, New York: John Wiley & Sons.
Spurlock, S. and Souvenir, R. (2012) "Dynamic subset selection for multi-camera tracking," *Proceedings of the 50th Annual Southeast Regional Conference*. ACM.
Spurlock, S. and Souvenir, R. (2014) "Multi-view action recognition one camera at a time," *IEEE Winter Conference on Applications of Computer Vision*. IEEE.

Spurlock, S., Wu, H., and Souvenir, R. (2014) "Multi-view recognition using weighted view selection," *Asian Conference on Computer Vision*. Springer International.

Summerson, J. (1957) "The case for a theory of modern architecture," *RIBA Journal* 64, 8: 307–310.

Tufte, E. R. (1991) "Envisioning information," *Optometry and Vision Science* 68, 4: 322–324.

Tufte, E. R. and Graves-Morris, P. R. (1983) *The Visual Display of Quantitative Information*. Cheshire, CT: Graphics Press.

Waber, B. (2013) *People Analytics: How Social Sensing Technology Will Transform Business and What It Tells Us about the Future of Work*, Upper Saddle River, NJ: FT Press.

Wang, F.-Y., Carley, K. M., Zend, D., and Mao, W. (2007) "Social computing: from social informatics to social intelligence," *IEEE Intelligent Systems* 22, 2: 79–83.

Weiser, M. (1993) "Some computer science issues in ubiquitous computing," *Communications of the ACM* 36, 7: 75–84.

Whitehead, C. (2014) "Ten years of time utilisation studies," *People Place Performance*, www.aecom.com/blog/ten-years-of-time-utilisation-studies-2/ (August 30, 2016).

Zimmerman, A. and Martin, M. (2001) "Post-occupancy evaluation: benefits and barriers," *Building Research & Information* 29, 2: 168–174.

20

Future Architecture
Biohybrid Structures and Intelligent Materials

Ljiljana Fruk and Veljko Armano Linta

Flexible solar cells. Three words, many meanings. To a material science student, they might be an inspiration for a cool project, to a scientist a ground to test the boundaries of skill and knowledge, to an environmentalist a way forward, to an industrialist a profitable investment and to our grandparents the stuff of science fiction. To all of us, however, they represent a novelty accompanied by different levels of excitement depending on our professional and personal backgrounds. The scale of design and engineering is changing and today we are able to manipulate matter at the molecular level using a set of tools and strategies joined together within nanotechnology: molecular engineering at nanometer scale. Our new capabilities mean that novel properties can be introduced to already known materials by assembling atoms into larger structures in a controllable way, or by combining seemingly incompatible materials such as biomolecules and noble metals to obtain functional devices (Figure 20.1) (Hung et al. 2011). Nature uses the principle of nanotechnology continuously to produce bioscaffolds. Bones, our body's support beams are made of biomolecular and inorganic structures interwoven to provide porous, growing, and self-healing material. But they are not only a structural element, they interact with surrounding tissue and adapt to the changing environment by both receiving and sending chemical and mechanical cues. The idea of interfaces will be explored in later paragraphs, but one of the most challenging issues both at nano and macro scales is the design of functional interfaces. How do we manufacture materials which can perform desirable functions while keeping manufacturing cost and environmental impact low? How far can we go to imitate and engineer Nature, and when is it better just to use what has been given to us?

Before we dive into the world of nanomaterials and their applications in architecture, it is important to clarify what we mean by intelligent materials and biohybrid structures. Intelligent materials are defined as materials capable of responding to stimuli or changes in the environment and adapting their function accordingly. Clearly, materials found in Nature can be defined as such: previously mentioned bones, piezoelectric materials (they produce electricity under pressure) such as wood, or impact resistant, self-healing composites of insect and sea species shells, to name a few. Intelligent materials can be found in Nature in abundance, so can the bio-nano hybrids: combinations of biomolecules or even whole organisms (viruses or bacteria) and usually inorganic nanostructures. Such examples include mixes of collagen protein and hydroxyapatite

Biohybrid Structures and Intelligent Materials

Figure 20.1 Nanostructure (nanoflower) made of DNA biomolecule and gold nanoparticles used for design of light triggered memory devices

Source: L. Fruk and Y.-C. Hung, 2011.

particles in bones, or various bio-mineralized shells made of proteins, which guide assembly of carbonates and silicates into beautiful structures (think of simple algae called diatoms).

VELJKO ARMANO LINTA (VAL): So, what is the hype about, why are we talking about a new era of material design, when a lot is out there already?

LJILJANA FRUK (LF): Understanding how things behave at the nanoscale, the scale of proteins (typical protein will be around 3–10 nm in diameter) and molecules (size of water molecule is less than 1 nm) enabled by development of high resolution microscopes, help us to understand Nature's design and introduce new components, in ways that we are now capable of tuning functions to particular demand and producing multi-responsive materials that react to change of humidity, pressure, pH, light, temperature, magnetic field, or sound. All of these developments have already made a huge impact in medicine (Lehner et al. 2013) and electronics, and with the development of better manufacturing and scale-up procedures, it will change the architecture and construction industries as well. The advantage of nanostructured materials resides in the amounts needed to achieve a desired effect: often the properties can be tuned using a large amount of the carrier material and a small amount of the dopant nanostructures. This has already made a huge impact with regard to the preparation of better performing, nano-reinforced concrete (see later in the chapter).

VAL: When we talk about architecture and given that buildings are becoming increasingly more complex systems requiring ever more intensive maintenance, more frequent replacement of hardware, and more complicated user interfaces, what kind of interface between scientists and architects might be useful in design and maintenance? Perhaps it would be possible to satisfy the complex requirements with simple solutions. Is the integration of various engineers in the design process the key to simplifying the complicated, fragile and unintuitive systems buildings have become, or should we expand our view and look to science to try to make these systems more pliable, self-evolving, self-repairing, even life-like?

LF: Such systems can be designed with the help of new technologies, such as nanotechnology, which is an excellent example of the multitude of scientific expertise joining in synergy to create new molecular structures. Nanotechnology is driven by principles of molecular architecture, which can be manipulated, changed, and tweaked at the atomic level. In the 1980s when Richard Smalley and Harold Kroto got interesting data on an unknown compound formed by the laser-induced evaporation of graphite, the molecular structure eluded them. It was almost impossible to account for a high number of present carbon atoms all aligned in a symmetric geometrical structure. A solution was hiding in the work of architect Buckminster Fuller, known for his studies of symmetry, geometry, and experimentation with the stable stacking of geometric shapes. He was also known for the design of the geodesic dome (although other architects had played with this idea earlier), and Kroto and Smalley realized that the structure of the geodesic dome can be used to describe the molecular structure of the new carbon-based molecule. They named it fullerene (Kroto et al. 1985) and it marked the beginning of the nanotechnology era. C60 fullerene or buckyball was the first of many highly symmetrical large carbon molecules, which were later followed by the discovery of nanotubes (also successfully predicted by Fuller) and the atom-thick layer material called graphene (Figure 20.2) (Singh et al. 2011). All of these have attracted the interest of engineers and scientists alike, and were for long considered the next big thing, a solution to certain medical problems such as targeted delivery of drugs as well as a way to resolve the speed limitations of electronic devices. Due to their durability, flexibility, and lightness, new carbon materials could change the way we not only manufacture materials but, ultimately, how we think about architecture. Not all of the expectations have been met yet, but carbon-nanotube-enhanced steel, which is lighter and more elastic than ordinary steel, has already been made. The conductive and low-weight graphene, if the issues with the large-scale production can be resolved, might become a material of the future which will transform the way we think about intelligent buildings. In an interesting twist of history, an architecture-inspired structure could return to architecture.

VAL: Indeed, besides being a remarkable architect, Fuller was also dedicated to self-awareness that was reflected in his structures and deeply rooted in his view of a geometrically ordered nature. However, Fuller's architectural order was not rigid; it was adaptable and applied wherever it could serve. It is the type of order that has the capacity to organize evolving systems to the extent that it can even be considered purposeful. It is organic, just the way the *Oxford Dictionary* puts it: "it is denoted or characterized by a harmonious relationship between the elements of a whole." Curvilinear architectural forms are sometimes called organic even if they possess none of the structural efficiency natural curved forms have, and instead hide bulky, complicated, uneconomical load-bearing structures beneath the façade cladding. Calling this architecture organic tells us something about our perception of the world: we are sometimes too preoccupied with the surface. The moment architecture becomes just a matter of visual appearance, the focus is shifted both from its actual structure and from the way it shapes our physical, emotional and mental wellbeing, and our relationships with others and ourselves. We become, metaphorically and literally, out of touch.

Biohybrid Structures and Intelligent Materials

Figure 20.2 Molecular structures of carbon nanomaterials. C60 Fullerene (upper left), carbon nanotube (upper right), and graphene (bottom)

Source: L. Fruk and R. Mach, Future is here Exhibition material, Centre for Art and Media and Machidee, Karlsruhe, Germany 2015/2016.

LF: When we talk about materials, whether in architecture, medicine, or engineering, we ultimately refer to interfaces: how different materials interact with each other and the environment and how do we respond to them. Nanotechnology and molecular engineering are much about designing interfaces at the smallest scales to allow for different types of molecules to be joined together into new materials and structures. If we take an example of modern solar cells, they involve engineering of interfaces between various materials, some of them which used to be considered incompatible (various biomolecules such as proteins, polymers, and nanoparticles). The introduction of superior structures such as seen in flexible solar cells involves even more skill and molecular insight to enable doping of stable and durable polymers with light-absorbing and energy-converting organic or inorganic materials (Fu et al., 2018; Popola, Gondal, and Qahtan 2018). Successful engineering of interfaces is one of the biggest challenges at the moment and nanotechnology was successful in addressing part of the challenge, opening a way to doping traditionally used materials such as glass or concrete with nanostructures to enhance existing features and add new features such as thermal conductivity or a self-cleaning ability. Coatings containing titanium oxide nanoparticle have already been used to create a durable, self-cleaning façade that can better withstand the elements (Andaloro et al. 2016), and cellulose nanocrystals have been added to concrete to significantly improve strength, impact resistance, and flexibility (Cao et al. 2015). Needless to say, such materials also have the ability to significantly reduce our environmental impact by decreasing the amount of needed material and easing the manufacture and recycling of used materials. The experimental application of photocatalytic coatings on different surfaces has shown a reduction of nitrogen oxide pollutants up to 40 percent (Zouzelka and Rathousky 2017).

VAL: Nanotechnology will, without doubt, continue making an impact in the manufacture of enhanced materials also in the years to come. However, a more interesting aspect of "nanotech" architecture lies in its ability to go beyond improving traditionally used building materials and processes and introduce new routes to the dynamic relationship between buildings and the environment and buildings and their users. New materials might blur the lines between living and inanimate structures and would therefore change the way architects and engineers think about design and the longevity of their own designs.

LF: One can see architecture as the art of interface design on a macroscopic scale, an interface between us and the world, between the outer world and the inner. And rather than being a boundary, every well-designed interface is a responsive, ever-changing, and adaptable connector. Today's digital interfaces help us perform our tasks more efficiently (we hope), but they also take into account our need to experience the pleasure of the interfacing action. Touchscreens will readjust to the environmental light, and besides being practical, keyboards and mousepads take on the craziest shapes to give us both the aesthetic and physical pleasures of interaction.

VAL: Along this line, a house is an interface that protects us from the elements, but also responds to our needs and habits, and can help us change them. In a vision of nanotech architecture, a house turns into a multisensory unit which can act as a communication interface; it responds to the environmental changes, feeds on seasonal differences in light, wind, and rainfall, connects us with our friends and colleagues and keeps us informed. This, of course, can be done only by using innovative materials in combination with clever and timely design. Without getting into the old Modernist discourse on concealment and truth of materials, and admitting that the change of scale from macro to nano turns architectural interfaces into magical black-boxes, it will be important for architects of the future to also become educators. By positioning functional elements out in the open, not concealing them behind aesthetically appealing masks, such as in the case of the famous Lloyd Building in London by Richard Rogers (Figure 20.3), users can be invited to question the function, enjoy the process, and admire the beauty of high-tech materials. The change will not only be structural and tangible, but aesthetic and psychological.

LF: Indeed, changing the molecular nature of materials could ultimately make them more natural and easier to get used to. We do not question the nature and self-sufficiency of the tree, even though we do not see the structural element of its trunk. We are aware of complex interactions between various inanimate compartments, which joined together result in a living entity capable of oxygen and sugar production. Nanotech architecture, which relies on molecularly engineered materials, will be able to blur the distinction between artificial and natural, and create a link, not a boundary with the surrounding and our inner nature.

In the future, we could have walls, floors, and ceilings that resemble a plant's ability to convert carbon dioxide into oxygen and produce additional material to ensure self-healing of any wear and tear (Wang et al. 2017), integrated structures that serve as water, gas, and air conduits on-demand, or act as water harvesting nano-plants in arid climates (Kim et al. 2018).

VAL: Could we have structural elements that also collect, filter, and process fresh water and waste or produce and transmit electricity? Materials that could be water-resistant, breathable,

Figure 20.3 Night image of Lloyd's Building by Richard Rogers, London
Source: Photostevo, 2011.

thermally insulating, temperature and oscillation buffering, and humidity regulating, built into our houses without any need for additional surface layers?

LF: This could be realized using biohybrid polymers that grow and repair themselves when in touch with a humid, carbon-dioxide-rich atmosphere and sunlight. Photosynthetic roofs, anyone?

VAL: The minimalist appearance that architects are so fond of could finally become the outer layer of equally minimalist, yet remarkably intelligent structures, and not be only a mere mask.

LF: Intelligent, self-healing walls could repair themselves without our intervention, without drilling, hammering, plastering, and gluing. Researchers are working on various strategies to design bricks or concrete that could enable that. At Delft University scientists have already made concrete doped with *Bacilus pseudofirmus* or *Sporosarcina pasteurii* bacteria, which can produce calcium carbonate in the presence of nutrients and water, and in this way aide self-healing of cracks. Many more versions of such biohybrid materials have been reported (Vijay, Murmu, and Deo 2017).

VAL: The question is will we be able to make them using locally available materials, maybe even renewable ones? Will we be able to shape those materials by giving them instructions on the nano-level, and reshape them as many times as we need, ultimately recycling them safely and on the spot once the building is no longer required?

LF: New intelligent materials could transform the way we build and the way we think about our environment and our world troubled by various challenges: low use of sustainable energy sources, pollution, and social and economic gaps across the globe. Installing efficient solar cells or painting roofs with easy-to-apply photosynthetic coatings would allow the use of free and readily available solar energy for all, removing the reliance on expensive energy sources in the hands of few. The availability of clean energy will have a dramatic, positive effect on the global culture and although it might not rapidly lead to a decrease in social inequalities, it will contribute to the change of direction and remove the continuous struggle for energy. This will, in turn, lead to more time and resources left for further development and enhancement of social justice. Today, solar cells can already be made transparent, lighter than ever, and be attached to buildings, small devices, or clothes such are the flexible solar cells from MIT, Boston based on parylene polymer, commonly used as a coating for the protection of biomedical or electronic devices from environmental wear (Jean, Wang, and Bulovic 2016).

VAL: Polymers have long been the compounds that proved to be both a blessing and a curse for our civilization.

LF: They are characterized by a molecular structure made of repeatable small molecular units, and are actually abundant in Nature: cellulose, the structural building block of plants (and wood), and chitin, a component of beaks, insects' and sea creatures' shells, are both biopolymers made of sugar (glucose) units. Deoxyribonucleic acid, better known as DNA, the carrier of genetic information, is a polymer made of four different subunits (bases), phosphates and deoxyribose sugar, containing a sequence of bases which is unique to the species and individually distinguishable. Biopolymers, like all things natural, go through cycles of change, being continuously recycled by chemical processes and with the help of intricate molecular machinery (DeMartino and Gillette 2007). However, when polyethylene was made in the lab at the end of nineteenth century, a man-made polymer was invented, one that was robust yet flexible, malleable, cheap, and, unfortunately, also quite indestructible (Figure 20.4). Plastics, a term encompassing all synthetic polymers, have been used to replace the heavier materials traditionally used in architecture: glass, wood, and metal, and manufacture new generations of adhesives, foams, paints, and sealants. Polycarbonate (PC) is used in fittings

Biohybrid Structures and Intelligent Materials

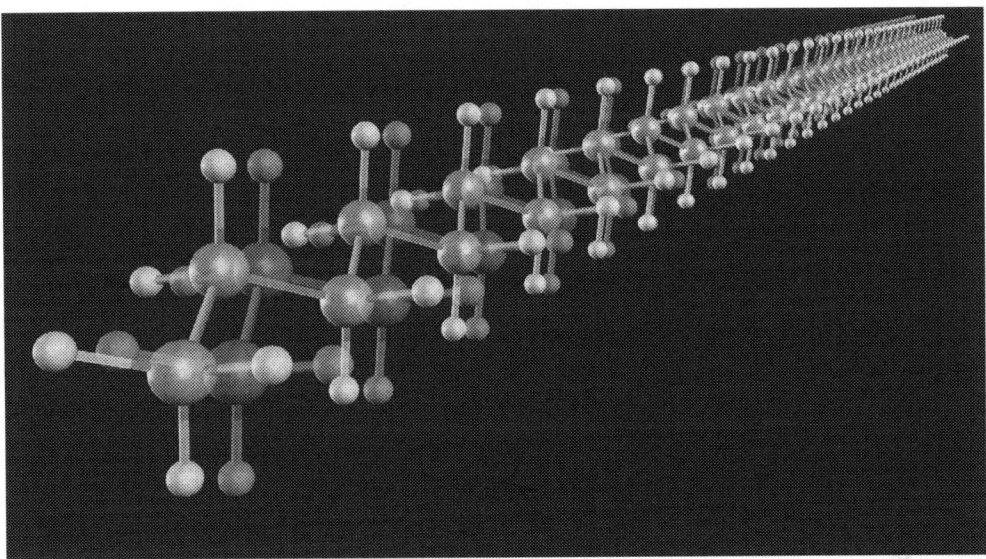

Figure 20.4 3D chemical structure of polyethylene made of repeatable carbon units
Source: Adapted with permission from Fruk and Weibel (2013).

    in hot water systems, polyester (PEST) for cladding panels, polypropylene (PP) for sound insulation, rubber and epoxy resins for flooring, acrylic glass can replace glass windows and polyvinyl chloride (PVC) aluminum or wood in window frames. This is to name just a few examples and although man-made polymers are lighter and more durable, that also means they are extremely environmentally stable with a lifetime of several centuries.

VAL: This alone does not make them exceptional: wood can have the same life span if treated properly: indeed the wooden house in Schwyz, central Switzerland was built in 1287 and is still standing. Mayan architects and engineers employed wooden beams in their monumental architectures, which, despite termites and jungle rot, are still intact thanks to the use of trees such as chico zapote that seem to last forever (Hellmuth 1989).

LF: The issue with plastics, unlike with wood (or glass and metal) is high stability, which makes recycling difficult, in particular the older, predominantly used types. Ultimately, this has led to islands of plastic debris floating in the oceans, to grains of polymers entering our food chain (microplastics), and, generally, a series of serious environmental issues (Sheavly and Register 2007).

VAL: Despite that, the influence of such materials on the development and the course of civilization cannot be disputed: they have provided cheap, durable materials to build structures and devices. They have remained cheap because their negative impact on environment and health has not yet been accounted for and reflected in increase of prices through improved taxation.

LF: Efforts are made to turn waste plastics into a construction material (Kamaruddin et al. 2017), but clearly it is time for a new materials revolution, one that has been initiated by nanotechnology already.

VAL: Human history is riddled with examples of technology creating at least as many problems as it solves, so this brings us to the issue of awareness. Utilizing locally available, biodegradable materials that are "tweaked" at the nano-level so that they can organize themselves into building blocks or even entire buildings, is a thrilling vision. Not only could such materials simplify the complicated systems within buildings, but they would remove the need for the construction and manufacturing industry as we know it: a polluting, traffic-intensive, energy-devouring, and corruption-prone business. Digital 3-D printing is already a fantastic step in that direction, although large-scale 3-D printers are still a financial and logistical challenge. Could intelligent, transformable, and self-assembling structures take construction to a whole new level, one that would resemble natural, living systems and do so in an economically viable way? Such construction principles could be applied everywhere, from temporary shelters for disaster victims and refugees to housing and other buildings in both the developed and developing worlds, removing the need for economic boundaries. With the economic system today proving to be unstable and unsustainable, the availability of more cost-effective and sustainable housing in the whole world would be a step towards building a healthy, aware, and dignity-based society.

LF: Some might argue about the number of lost jobs when the self-building houses are introduced, but new technologies have disruptive effects and many of the issues that might arise as a consequence of automation (robots) have already been extensively discussed.

VAL: One of the most interesting, although controversial proposals to deal with the consequences of job loss and poverty due to the technology-induced job market change is the universal basic income theory (Arnold 2018). Whichever way we take, the unsustainable cannot reach the steady state; it leads to destruction.

LF: Nature teaches us that anything that is not functional will perish and let us face it: Nature is an excellent architect. It does not only make renewable functional materials, but it can also evolve them to suit a particular function. Some bacteria, for example, under certain stress conditions such as change of temperature or lack of food, produce a whole bunch of proteins which assemble a protecting shield around the soft bacterial cell. Such shield, known as a spore, is almost unbreakable and selectively permeable: it allows the transport of nutrients and water through the shell, but keeps toxins out, allowing bacteria to survive thousands of years in the harshest of conditions. And we have just begun to understand how this whole process works (Leggett et al. 2012).

VAL: Maybe in the near future we will be able to use such bacterial processes on a large scale to prepare or direct the growth of protein-like hybrids to make breathable materials for intelligent and bio-friendly houses.

LF: This could be done with a little help from proteins, biopolymers made of smaller elements joined in linear sequences and then packed in 3D structures, important for their function. If we could enlarge them from the nanometer (1 billionth of a meter) to the meter scale, we would end up with majestic buildings of different structures, sizes, and functions, some of them self-repairing and all of them recyclable. The cell-city would contain proteins in the shape of barrels or spheres (catalytic enzymes or ion and oxygen transport proteins), resembling funnels allowing certain molecules to get into the city (ion channels spanning the cell membrane), machines (protein-making ribosomes or protein-degrading proteasomes) or have an elongated, rope-like structures keeping the fabric of the city together (collagen and elastin, which build our elastic, soft tissue) (Figure 20.5). The shapes of proteins often determine their function or the other way around, much like our buildings. They can also build bigger structures, in the process of self-assembly, as observed in the viral coat formation. Architecturally fascinating, viruses often have geometrically perfect capsids protecting the genetic material until the virus reaches a host in which it can reproduce (Figure 20.6). Being small, viruses do not have much space to store a large amount of genetic material, yet they need to perform such complex tasks like host invasion and replication. This

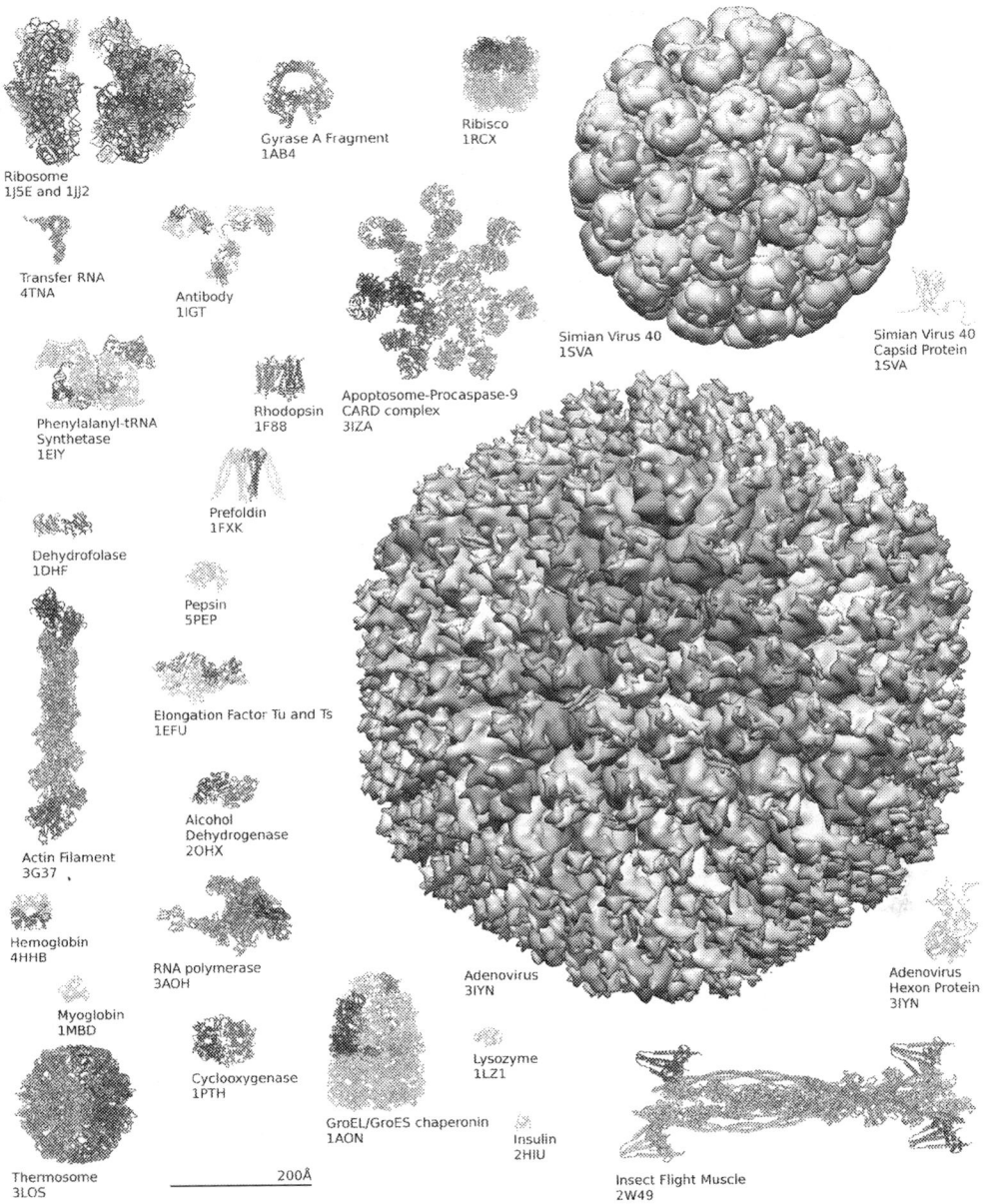

Figure 20.5 Variety of protein structures

Source: Image by Axel Griewel [CC BY-SA 3.0 (https://creativecommons.org/licenses/by-sa/3.0)], from Wikimedia Commons.

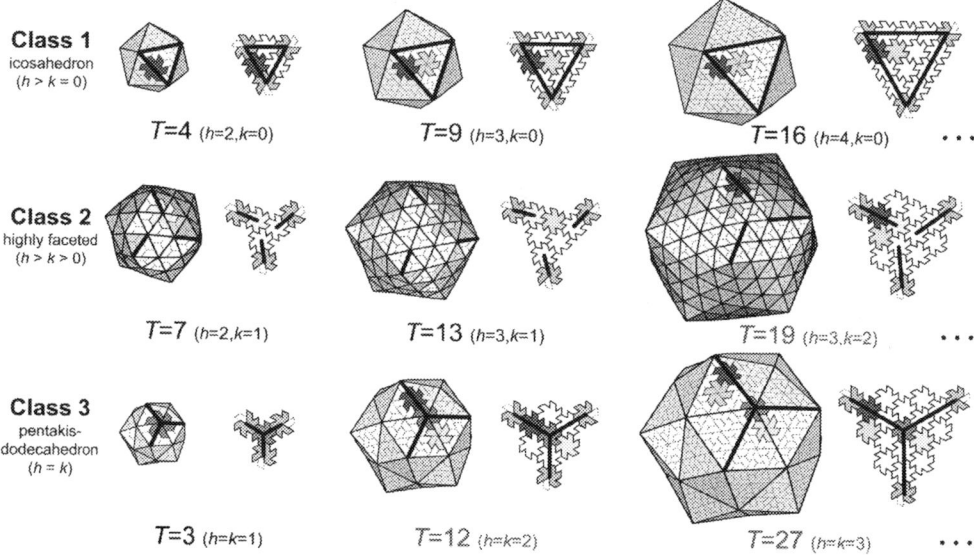

Figure 20.6 The three classes of virus capsids (shells). All canonical capsids made up from trapezoidal subunits can be built from a single type of pentagon and different hexamers (shown in distinct shades)

Source: Reprinted with permission from Mannige and Brooks (2010).

would normally require a large set of coded information stored in the genetic code carrier molecules, nucleic acids. But this is not the case, and they carry simple codes to instruct the formation of many copies of just a few smaller proteins, which then assemble into efficient protecting interfaces in various geometrical forms based on pentagonal and hexagonal spatial distributions (Mannige and Brooks 2010). For viruses it is all about architecture and efficiency. But proteins, structural and functional building elements of viruses and other cells could not be made without DNA, the molecule that encodes information for their synthesis and assembly.

DNA has one of the most striking structures in Nature: the famous double helix. It is stable enough to resist different environmental pressures, but flexible enough to allow for the repair of any damage. In Nature, physical and genetic flexibility, as well as the ease of adaptation, lead to a more successful species. A building with the structural properties of DNA would be both durable and flexible, and capable of evolving in line with environmental changes. Upon close study of the double helix structure, it is clear that everything is used efficiently. Not only the structural features such as the sequence of the building blocks, but also the topology, indents, grooves, and edges are equally important and can act as geometrical signaling points for information storage and read-out (Fruk, 2013).

VAL: Should new technologies enable us to build buildings that can compare with DNA in terms of durability and adaptability, the benefits could be immense, but we might actually face one big challenge: knowing what exactly we are to design. Design and construction are often driven by vanity, the need to show off and impress, be different and noticed. Expensive materials and solutions are often popular just because they are expensive. If we were to have one overwhelmingly popular technology that was quite affordable and characterized by a distinct visual style stemming from its basic structural properties, would we still be in need of architects?

LF: Indeed, we would. We might finally start putting the emphasis on the true purpose of architecture: creating places of wellbeing by thoughtfully enclosing spaces that can support our inter- and intra-personal world within the universe that surrounds us.

VAL: We could turn to the architect and monk Hans van der Laan for some guidance (van der Laan 1983). His lessons on things as fundamental as the relationships between inside and outside and between solid and void, as well as about proportions of architectural space, might seem too basic at first glance, but they are grounded in human nature and human perception and make us ponder things that are too important to be taken for granted. He compares the house to a sandal, whose purpose is to be the interface between the foot and the ground. It has to be harder than the foot in order to better endure the wear and tear of walking, yet softer than the ground in order for the foot to be more comfortable. Thus we have returned to the issue of interfaces. The "nanomaterial-house" might prompt us to re-think the house as the simplest artificial structure that we need in order to feel safe and balanced within our environment. We know now that we cannot achieve balance by accumulating things or by owning bigger and bigger spaces. But what is the right size, the right shape, and the right balance between open and closed?

LF: Nature has not given us exact instructions encoded in our DNA on how to build the right space in the right spot as it gave birds, which can build perfect nests from environmental material. So we just need to figure it out, and this process can lead us closer to our true nature. But even in the case of environmentally driven self-assembled houses, the fear of uniformity and occurrence of identical houses is unjustified. Adapting the Heisenberg principle to architecture: no two locations are identical. In fact, the challenge might be quite the opposite; our laziness or stylistic dogmas, dictates of politics and profits guide the design of the same model in different locations, with no regard for things such as sunlight and wind exposure, underground waters, rainfall or temperature oscillations, not to mention privacy and view.

VAL: The role of future architects might not be very different from today, but new materials might help us address our needs and express our characters in a more creative way. And we might not always need such complex actions as the change of molecular structure to achieve that. Sometimes tuning the topology of materials interfaces will suffice.

LF: Topology plays a huge role in architectural designs of this nature, and has already been used in architecture and the car industry to create clean and non-sticking surfaces. Today, we also know that the appearance of a color is not only a consequence of the light interacting with organic pigments, but also the result of the structural architecture at the nano-level. Butterfly wings, made of the tiny and regularly stacked biopolymer chitin, are an excellent example of nano-sized surface topology, which determines the interaction with light and therefore the observed color. Blue feathers of certain bird species have been shown to be composed of sponge-like materials filled with air bubbles, which absorb and reflect particular wavelengths in such a way that they appear blue (Figure 20.7) (Dufresne et al. 2009). Such discoveries, with a new and deeper understanding of old phenomena, lead to continuous developments of responsive materials, those that could one day enable us to efficiently tune our living spaces to our moods, personal health needs, or environmental changes.

VAL: Our worldview and the relationships we form with others are always co-shaped by the qualities of our living and working spaces. Living within a living being, a house that needs to be cared for, that requires adaptation as it itself adapts, and provides a two-way communication channel, would introduce a whole new level of experiences and a new, yet ancient and natural, sense of belonging. In turn, the house would take care of us, provide us with shelter, and maybe also with food, warmth, light, assistance when we get old or sick.

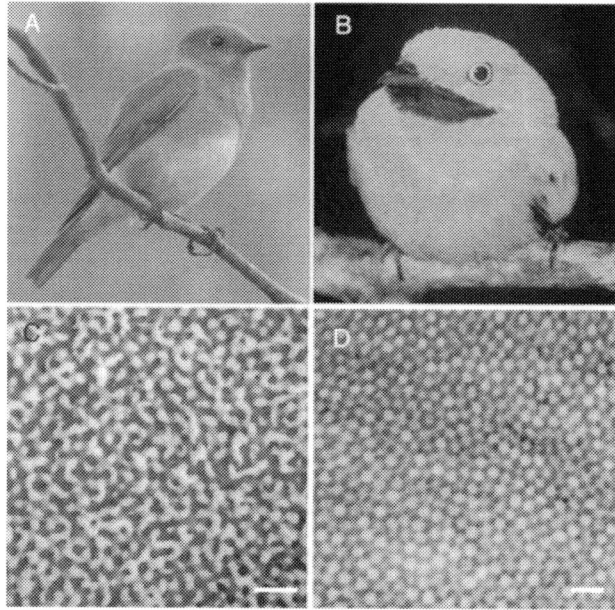

Figure 20.7 (A) A male Eastern Bluebird; (B) Plum Throated Cotinga; (C) and (D) Their respective keratin and air nanostructures

Source: Adapted with permission from Dufresne et al. (2009).

Perhaps we would be survived by it. So from day one we would be growing with it, literally and metaphorically. The level of (self-)awareness would be stunning.

LF: We would finally have an ever-changing and tangible architectonic interface built of self-assembling and self-repairing biohybrids tuned to and with our own nature.

References

Andaloro, A., Mazzucchelli, E. S., Lucchini, A., and Pederferri, M. P (2016) "Photocatalytic self-cleaning coatings for building façade maintenance: performance analysis through a case-study application," *Journal of Facade Design and Engineering* 4: 115–129.

Arnold, C. (2018) "Money for nothing: the truth about universal basic income," *Nature* 557: 626–628.

Cao, Y., Zavaterri, P., Youngblood, J., Moon, R., and Weiss, J. (2015) "The influence of cellulose nanocrystal additions on the performance of cement paste," *Cement Concrete Composites* 56: 73–83.

DeMartino, G. N. and Gillette, T. G. (2007) "Proteasomes: machines for all reasons," *Cell* 129: 659–665.

Dufresne, E. R., Noh, H., Saranathan, V., Mochrie, S G., Cao, H., and Prum, R. O. (2009) "Self assembly of amorphous biphotonic nanostructures by phase separation," *Soft Materials* 5: 1792–1795.

Fruk, L. (2013) "Double life of double helix: structural beauty of the molecule of life," in L. Fruk and P. Weibel (eds) *Molecular Aesthetics*, Cambridge, MA: MIT Press.

Fruk, L. and Weibel, P. (eds) (2013) *Molecular Aesthetics*, Cambridge, MA: MIT Press.

Fu, X., Xu, L., Li, J., Sun, X., and Peng, H. (2018) "Flexible solar cells based on carbon nanomaterials," *Carbon* 139: 1063–1073.

Hellmuth, N. M. (1989) "Wood that lasted one thousand years, report, Peabody Museum or Natural History," Yale University. www.maya-archeaology.

Hung, Y.-C., Hsu, W.-T., Lin, T.-Y., and Fruk, L. (2011) "Photoinduced write-once-read-many-times memory device based on DNA biopolymer composite," *Applied Physics Letters* 99, 25: 253–301.

Jean, J., Wang, A. V., and Bulovic, V. (2016) "In situ vapour-deposited parylene substrates for ultra-thin, lightweight organic solar cells," *Organic Electronics* 31: 120–126.

Kamaruddin, M. A., Abdullah, M. M. A., Zawawi, M. H., and Zainol, M. R. R. A. (2017) "Potential use of plastic waste as construction materials: recent progress and future prospects," IOP Conference Series: Material Science Engineering 267: 012011.

Kim, H., Rao, S. R., Kapustin, E. A., Zhao, L., Yang, S., Yaghi, O. M., and Wang, E. N. (2018) "Adsorption-based atmospheric water harvesting device for arid climates," *Nature Communications* 9, 1: 1191–1196.

Kroto, H. W., Heath, J. R., O'Brien, S. C., Curl, R. F., and Smalley, R. E. (1985) C60: Buckminsterfullerene, *Nature* 318: 162–163.

Leggett, M. J., McDonnell, G., Denyer, S. P., Setlow, P., and Maillard, J. Y. (2012) "Bacterial spore structures and their protective role in biocide resistance," *Journal of Applied Microbiology* 113, 3: 485–498.

Lehner, R., Wang, X., Marsch, S., and Hunziker, P. (2013) "Intelligent nanomaterials for medicine," *Nanomedicine* 9: 742–757.

Mannige, R. V. and Brooks, C. L. (2010) "Periodic table of virus capsids: implications for natural selection and design," *PlosOne* 5, 3: e9423. www.ncbi.nlm.nih.gov/pmc/articles/PMC2831995/.

Popola, I. K., Gondal, M. A., and Qahtan, T. F. (2018) "Recent progress in flexible perovskite solar cells: materials, mechanical tolerance and stability," *Renewable and Sustainable Energy Review* 82: 3127–3151.

Sheavly, S. B. and Register, K. M. (2007) "Marine debris and plastics: environmental concerns, sources, impacts and solutions," *Journal of Polymer Environments* 15: 301–305.

Singh, V., Joung, D., Zhai, J., Das, S., Khandakaer, S. I., and Seal, S. (2011) "Graphene based materials: past, present and future," *Progress in Materials Science* 56, 8: 1178–1271.

van der Laan, H. (1983) *Architectonic Spaces: Fifteen Lessons on the Disposition of the Human Habitat*, Leiden: E. J. Brill.

Vijay, K., Murmu, M., and Deo, S. V. (2017) "Bacteria based self-healing concrete: a review," *Construction and Building Materials* 152: 1008–1014.

Wang, Y., Li, S., Liu, L., Lv, F., and Wang, S. (2017) "Conjugated polymer nanoparticles to augment photosynthesis of chloroplasts," *Angewandte Chemie International* 56, 19: 5308–5311.

Zouzelka, R. and Rathousky, J. (2017) "Photocatalytic abatement of NOx pollutants in the air using commercial functional coatings with porous morphology," *Applied Catalysis B: Environmental* 217: 466–476.

21
Networked Urbanism
Definition, Scholarship, Directions

T. F. Tierney

The concept of the city as we know it is undergoing an enormous transformation. As wireless telecommunication services, locative technologies, and environmental sensor systems converge in physical space, new organizational logics are reshaping the geography and conditions of urban living.[1] Concurrently, confronting climate change urgently demands new policies governing carbon emissions, nuclear power, and the protection of specific natural resources.[2] As urban governance contends with these challenges, the incentives to investigate alternative solutions proliferate. Governments and industries must develop not only more efficient energy strategies but also the means to implement them: new forms of energy production, allocation, and infrastructure, as well as a more reliable and equitable system of resource distribution.

Although climate change is the most immediate threat, a host of lesser but nevertheless potentially destabilizing problems accompany and intersect with it. Internal and external factors, such as migration and population growth, materially influence contemporary urban form. In rapidly growing cities such as Los Angeles, Mexico City, and Manila, 700 or more new residents arrive every day (Figure 21.1).[3] While increased density may be seen as a temporary solution to urban growth, some critics cite planning policies themselves as problematic (Sclar 2012: 7–8). Formal, rigidly modernist agendas, previously established during a time of relative stasis, were not designed to respond nimbly to complex, constantly shifting problems. One solution proposed by social geographer Edward Soja (2000) suggests that, rather than focusing on built forms, architects and engineers study the connections and infrastructural systems that bind cities together, thus creating an advanced framework for improved growth and change. In this way, the discussion of networked urbanism can be framed around one key concept, *connection*, as it relates to the impact of information and communication technologies (ICTs) on urban infrastructure. Other topics, such as urban sociology, human–computer interaction, network resilience, and renewable energy, while worthy of further study, are discussed here only as subsets of the primary networked urbanism framework.

Intelligent Network Infrastructure

Although the field of urban studies is responding to rapid advancements in information communication technologies (ICT), the literature has not yet fully addressed the impact of wireless

URBAN POPULATION (% OF TOTAL)

Figure 21.1 Urban habitants shown as a percentage of total national population

Source: Image by Anthony Dombrowski, courtesy of URL: Urban Research Lab.

infrastructure on reformulating urban space (Amin and Thrift 2002; Graham 1997, 2000; Graham and Marvin 2001; Graham and Guy 2004; Greenfield 2013; Kitchin 2015; Kitchin and Dodge 2011; Moss and Townsend 1999; Picon 2015; Sassen 2006; Townsend 2000, 2013). Significant sociological research has emerged on the topic (Castells 2000; Latham and Sassen 2005; Sheller and Urry 2000, 2006; Urry 2012); however, it has mostly been confined to empirical studies, and consequently the findings are not aimed at urban design and planning. Examinations of sensor-enabled environments exist (Shepard 2011), but the implications of such environments have not been fully theorized. Other studies analyze transportation and sustainability (Cervero 2013; Tsay and Herrmann 2013) but are addressed exclusively to policy-makers. Some studies consider the territorial implications of global economies and free trade zones (Easterling 2014; Sassen 2001, 2008), while still others address specific newly developed smart cities but fail to integrate those into a wider theoretical perspective on existing cities where most urban dwellers reside. Importantly, much previous research was carried out before the widespread adoption of mobile technologies and the Internet of Things (IoT), defined as the integration of Web 2.0, mobile telephony, and sensing technologies (Gubbi et al. 2013). Overall, what is lacking in the literature is an updated and synthesized approach to the subject of networked urbanism.

The late William Mitchell (Mitchell, Borroni-Bird, and Burns 2010), architect, writer, and director of the MIT Media Lab, envisioned the modern city as an interconnected network of systems, an intelligent and responsive infrastructure imbued with self-awareness through sensors and computing.[4] And while Mitchell presents a compelling vision, the subject cannot be studied in isolation, inasmuch as cities are little without citizenry. In this debate, we intentionally stake out a holistic position by enfolding social practices into intelligent infrastructure. We choose to focus on the ways in which the human dimensions of networked infrastructure can be instrumental in shaping everyday mobility in urban space: how wireless technologies are being employed to connect transportation, commerce, and architecture, effectively reshaping the contemporary urban condition. In accord with Graham and Marvin's (2001) notion that cities are sociotechnical processes, we investigate the iterative effect of communication technologies: how social practices are enabled by technology and how technology in turn shapes new social practices. Written in the same belief that infrastructural networks are the ideal integrators of urban spaces, this chapter provides an examination of how they might bind neighborhoods and cities together into cultural wholes.

Definition of Intelligent Infrastructure

Intelligent cities can be defined as the ubiquitous layering of cellular communication networks and cloud computing with physical space. A quotidian example of intelligent infrastructure is a wireless mobile communication device—the smartphone—which connects people, places, and practices within an urban context. Other types of intelligent platforms cover the spectrum—from networked traffic signals that can be adjusted from afar to electric grids that respond to usage to location-aware apps such as Foursquare, which (among other things) combines restaurant reviews with health inspection data. In Hong Kong, an Octopus Card or in Zaragoza, Spain, a citizen card (electronic banking and pass card) offers access to a free citywide WiFi network, municipal bike-sharing, museum and library privileges, and free public transport (Townsend 2013). In Paris, networked resource sharing includes the Autolib' electric car-sharing and parking system. Vehicles can be reserved via mobile device or online by credit card; they can also be unlocked and allotted parking spaces. Other informal modes collectively known as mobility-on-demand (MoD) systems include Lyft, Uber, and Didi Kuaidi; similar services are emerging around the globe.

In addition to networked programs initiated by government institutions or private corporations, intelligent infrastructure also includes participatory practices. In this category we include civic hacking, crowdsourcing, urban games, and the open source/open data movement. Although space does not allow discussion of all aspects of the phenomenon, it is important to note that individuals and groups are creating their own platforms specific to their cultures and locales. An example is that of coders who volunteer hundreds of hours of their time in hackathons, designing and developing open source applications for public use; some of these apps, such as Weathersignal, Roadify, and Waze, use crowdsourced information. Also relevant to the discussion are municipal apps that leverage open public data—for example, the city of San Francisco's Rec & Park app or the Crimespotter app.

Other critical applications have been realized for communities under crisis in disaster or emergency situations. Currently, many humanitarian groups and NGOs are developing mobile platforms; for example, the Digital Humanitarian Network (DHN), a group of 16 volunteer technology organizations, acts as an interface between those groups and conventional humanitarian organizations. The DHN brings together expertise in geographical information systems, online mapping, data analysis, and statistics to assist hundreds of thousands of people enduring crisis situations in finding information, supplying aid, and coordinating disaster and recovery efforts—all through their mobile devices. In addition to nonprofit ventures, collective coding groups such as Code for America enlist volunteer developers to partner with contractors, entrepreneurs, and municipalities, in some cases leading to the creation of startup companies. Ad hoc software platforms developed by volunteers allow citizen users to combine best practices into user-friendly social media toolkits for risk mitigation and community response.[5] One of the best known is Ushahidi, a data management system and platform that utilizes SMS messaging and proved highly effective during the earthquake in Haiti and Hurricane Sandy (Tierney 2014).

These bottom-up efforts by coders and ordinary citizens are some of the more exciting aspects of intelligent infrastructure. Described as do-it-yourself (DIY) urbanism, these projects include installation of free neighborhood WiFi, as with the Detroit Digital Stewards,[6] and other community toolkits that foster equal access to information through the establishment of mesh networks—ad hoc networks that wirelessly connect computers and devices directly to each other without passing through any centralized organization such as an ISP. Mesh networks serve as a type of collaborative infrastructure and can automatically reconfigure themselves according to the availability and proximity of bandwidth and storage, which makes them more resistant to disasters or other interferences.[7] DIY efforts may also overlap with other movements, including Internet activism; some of the best known are the Independent Media Center and the Occupy movement. DIY differs in that although networked technologies may be employed for organizational purposes, the objective is to promote change directly within a neighborhood. These networked efforts may strengthen community and democratic efforts (Pagano 2013: 339).

Networked urbanism simultaneously encourages a reassessment of institutional foundations in planning and decision-making. In addition to using infrastructure-focused sites such as FixMyStreet or Fill That Hole, city governments are increasingly embracing networked technologies (online interfaces and smartphone applications) for involving constituents in land use planning and control. The prevalence and ease of use of these platforms offer citizens opportunities to voice their concerns and provide informational input on land use control through political participation. Crowdsourcing discussion and decision-making may avoid unexpected or unwanted land use changes. "The point is not to turn over land use authority outright to the public," says Lee Ann Fennell,

> but rather to find better ways to elicit, aggregate, coordinate, and channel the preferences, intentions, and experiences of current and future land-users.... Planners must begin shifting

their focus from the top-down regulation of land use to the development of information platforms for coordinating land use.

(Fennell 2013: 412)

As efficient and innovative as these new communication strategies are, they do not in themselves realize the smart city. What are the dynamics that make a smart city work? Social practices enabled by intelligent infrastructure—known as *near-field communication*—allow wireless radio communication between such things as phones, transit cards, and readers. These networked connections can enable payments through Google Wallet, the Clipper Card, or other bank and credit cards; they can also support data-sharing—on location information, songs, or photos. Such interactions are now common practice in everyday life, where the smartphone has effectively become the urban interface in OECD countries. In the developing world, where governments are slow or reticent to invest in fixed infrastructure, mobile phones have emerged as the primary method of data communication.[8] In place of expensive fixed transportation routes or linear communication systems, residents use mobile phones (and attendant connection to the Internet) to access political, consumer, and health information. Mobile telephony is being employed for everyday interactions: banking, making and receiving payments, and even medical consultations (Pew Research Center 2014).

Such a system is supported by four components: (1) software: Internet Protocol version 6 (IPv6), enabling the previously mentioned IoT, so that any object can access (and be accessed through) the Internet; (2) long-range broadband wireless connectivity: what used to be called radio communication;[9] (3) processing/transmission hardware: device connectivity via built-in radio communication;[10] and (4) sensors: mechanical devices sensitive to environmental conditions that transmit signals to measuring or control instruments.[11] This new experience of technology in the everyday is called *intelligent infrastructure*.

While the Internet has been in everyday use for decades, what is new about intelligent infrastructural systems is self-awareness. While the smartphone, the most ubiquitous intelligent device, incorporates sensors such as the accelerometer, compass, and GPS, the high cost of these sensors formerly prevented them from being used indiscriminately in the environment. That has changed. The recent affordability of sensors allows their widespread use in machines, devices, and transportation—and even on individuals (an example is the Apple Watch). Increasingly, inexpensive wireless sensors will be embedded in the urban environment, creating sophisticated large-scale sensor networks. Within these networks, smartphones will effectively act as wireless hubs for other devices, connecting the IoT (also known as the Internet of Everything or Cloud of Things) at the urban scale (Maulik 2014). Autonomous vehicles with embedded sensors will be capable of perceiving other automobiles, pedestrians, and road position, in addition to intra-car communication. Whether sensors are mobile or fixed, they are examples of infrastructural intelligence, enabling citizens and infrastructure to become hyperconnected to each other and their environments.[12]

Intelligent Assemblages

Within the conversation between people and devices, IoT describes an urban society enmeshed with technology in what social scientist Bruno Latour (1992) calls a *sociotechnical system*—a complex assemblage of human, computational, and physical resources. More recently, philosopher Graham Harman (2002) proposed a framework known as object-oriented ontology, or OOO. He reinterpreted the sociotechnical assemblage by focusing on relationships between entities by ascribing equal agency to things and beings. Further, OOO argues that objects such as robots or other devices exist independently of human perception, and thus all relations, human and nonhuman, are said to exist on equal ontological footing with one another.[13] While OOO disavows any totalizing thesis such as actor network theory (ANT), these notions need not be seen as contradictory. Considering the world and the interdependence of all its entities, a philosophical position such as OOO can undergird a broad ecological position frequently championed by Timothy Morton (2013), which I am calling "Equality among Entities" or EoE. Thus, along with the discussion of sensors, networks, and telecommunication devices, a larger theoretical conversation concerns the environmental implications of land use policy and non-renewable resources exemplified by sustainable directives.

A body of theories largely subsumed under the term *ecological urbanism* is accelerating an expansion in both the scope and scale of projects by environmental designers. Informed by postmodern, poststructuralist sensibilities, ecological urbanism suggests that the contemporary urban condition is too complex for any singular disciplinary perspective. As advanced by Mohsen Mostafavi, former dean of the Harvard Graduate School of Design, ecological urbanism "searches for a new basis of a performative urbanism that emerges from the bottom up, geared to the technological and ecological realities of the postindustrial world" (Mostafavi 2010: 65). Mostafavi's directive is straightforward. Climate change is related to carbon emissions produced by burning fossil fuels; thus, if we want to limit warming, those emissions have to be phased out (Kolbert 2014). Designers, whether architects, planners, or engineers, must address that fact in their research and practice.

Keeping in mind theories related to ANT, OOO, and EoE, urban policy can be viewed as moving in the direction of sociotechnical assemblages made up of human and nonhuman relations. What might this mean for urban residents and their neighborhoods? We cannot begin to presume that ICTs are a wholesale solution to complex urban problems. Furthermore, the development of more individualized and flexible forms of engagement within networked environments may actually counter the connective potential of the networks themselves by enabling a personalized infrastructure that stands in contrast with public works.[14] While the personal does not always undermine the public, infrastructure, as a meta-structure, is generally understood to be universally accessible and thus related to social equity. Nonetheless, in the debate over proliferation of sensors and telecommunication devices, a larger and more important discussion involves the governance of this technology. Policy-makers express guarded optimism that ICTs, including large-scale data analysis, can bring increased efficiency and order to urban processes. Before we can begin to examine that proposition, we must ask who (or what) is behind smart cities initiatives. The smart city conversation is currently driven almost exclusively by large IT organizations such as Cisco, IBM, and Siemens—corporations that are motivated to implement their proprietary business models and optimization strategies in economically challenged cities (Townsend 2013). Other corporations keen to participate in the connected car discussion specifically are well known: Google, Apple, Ford, GM, and others are attracted to the massive data-collection opportunities—and the lucrative sale of that data to third parties (Sterling 2014: 40–43). Cities, however, are not corporations—a point we will revisit later.

Recovery of the Technologically Augmented City

While the smart cities discussion is a fairly recent phenomenon, the interweaving of engineering technologies with the planning and construction of cities dates back to classical antiquity (and earlier). For our discussion, however, the postwar period of the OECD countries is particularly relevant to our concerns. The word *infrastructure*, according to architectural historian Mitchell Schwarzer (2016), is relatively new. In the mid-twentieth century, the term was used to describe the coordinated military actions of multiple nations in the NATO alliance. The concept was gradually extended to both building and transportation systems and later expanded further to encompass societal support systems (water and power and waste management) as well as telecommunications and the Internet.[15] The evolution of the word has paralleled the development of networks and globalization, further developing the notion of interconnectedness (Wigley 2007: 36–40).

The rise of network organization nonetheless marked a theoretical transition away from the notion of urban space as a neutral container and towards an understanding of it as a conductive medium for the movement of people, information, and objects. Spatial theorists envisioned relational structures as topologies that could be projected onto physical social space, in particular, in urban planner Melvin Webber's notion of "city as a communication system" (Webber 1963: 23–54). A vigorous discussion emerged out of the College of Environmental Design at the University of California, Berkeley, where Webber theorized that communication technologies would begin to define an urban realm that was "neither urban settlement nor territory, but heterogeneous groups of people communicating with each other through space" (Webber 1964: 116). Moreover, he argued, "A city is not described by the buildings, but by the social relations which bind the city together." Indeed, a community is defined by its social overlay—the interweaving of social relations and communications (Webber 1963: 29). A city, then, is a spatial adaptation to social practices and information exchange.[16] To borrow Webber's phrase, the contemporary city can be understood as an *information system* and conceptualized as a second-order abstraction in which the forces behind the form play a role in producing the form. Whereas technological determinists have perceived change as originating from advances in technology, spatial theorists have examined the specific economic and geographic forces driving those occurrences. Those theoretical frameworks positioned space as inherently caught up in social relations, thus producing and consuming them.

Webber's urban theories were influential not only in San Francisco but also in the planning of the new town of Milton Keynes in the UK (coincidentally, a test location for today's self-driving car).[17] The history of the 1960s also documents an escalating complexity in decision-making on transportation policy.[18] As postwar trends placed increasing pressure on the historical city, the demographic shift from rural to suburban was producing its own challenges, upon which space unfortunately does not allow elaboration.

Suffice it to say that by the early 1970s the restructuring of the market economy and advances within the field of information technology had created a complex emerging society organized on a diverse cultural base through ready access to information (radio, television, and later the Internet). What Castells (2000) terms the "network society" encompasses new forms of spatial and temporal organization, a type of space allowing for distant, synchronous, and real-time interaction (Castells 1989: 146). Sassen (2006) and Easterling (2014) describe this societal shift in terms of global flows of information networks that link distant locales around shared functions and meanings, reconceptualizing spatial arrangements under transnational economic and technological prerogatives.[19]

In developing countries, we are also seeing a new wave of infrastructures for extremely contrasting urbanizing territories understood through the concept of micro-infrastructure. In this context, the following questions arise: How small can we imagine infrastructure? And how does this change the way we have traditionally thought about urbanization, site selection and location, and environmental resources? As an alternative to traditional fixed infrastructure, the concept of microgrids holds possibilities for developing-world contexts and urbanizing territories that currently lack the ability to connect to centralized, existing sources of infrastructural energy or water. That also includes user-driven practices such as "autonomous infrastructure," defined as a new model of urbanism that considers the integration of multiple infrastructural subsets in a single cohesive system that harnesses energy from local renewable resources (Chehab and Makkouk 2013). The aim is to generate infrastructural frameworks in which the core organizational principles rely on alternative energy sources such as solar power, waste-to-energy, and passive design techniques, each of which has specific urban as well as architectural implications. Such a system has the potential to engender highly autonomous urban morphologies adapted to local climatic conditions and social practices that in turn influence future visions for mobility and the energy needs of horizontal city forms (Sousa 2007).[20] As envisioned here, autonomous deployment allows the network to grow organically, driven by network users, as with the evolution of the Internet. While an autonomous infrastructure might not be a long-term planning solution, in developing countries it may better serve the needs of the populace than traditional fixed, centralized models.

We can envision effective infrastructures as accomplishments of scale, growing as locally constructed, centrally controlled systems are linked or assembled into networks and "internetworks" governed by distributed control and coordination processes. This interweaving of bits and matter, Mitchell, Borroni-Bird, and Burns (2010) argued, is fundamentally changing the way that we use space, distribute resources, and design our communities.

Public vs. Private Ventures

Substantial investment to construct a comprehensive metropolitan networked system such as those proposed by private corporations (Cisco and Siemens, among others) raises larger issues about private and public investment. Many of those issues remain to be fully interrogated; nonetheless, within the smart city discussion there is a growing trend to conceptualize mobility as a utility or a service, one that is always on and available. Analyzing the effects of ubiquitous computing technologies on existing mobility practices should become instrumental for future urban planning and design. Townsend (2013) cautions that at the infrastructural level the fragility of an overarching wireless network system (WNS) coordinating the agent systems limits its implementation. Thus, the development of highly reliable and secure wireless network systems is crucial to the city's evolutionary development. Other concerns exist alongside that of WNS vulnerability. While the vision of a connected city allows for the expansion of differential pricing structures, it ignores the important issue of equal and universal access.[21] It cannot be overemphasized that a connected city needs to connect *everyone*.

While smartphones are an element of quotidian social practices, as they allow for messaging, coordination, navigation, and geotagging, thereby enabling individuals to reserve or hail rides electronically from their phones, they are not equally distributed. The smartphone is evolving into a form of highly personal infrastructure, which potentially conflicts with previous notions of what is held in common or public. That shift in what constitutes "the public" is destabilizing historic democratic principles related to *civitas* and the rights of access to the city.[22] With regard to transit, if microleasing and ridesharing assume computer literacy, will they continue to serve increased numbers of elderly or other underserved populations who are among the highest users of public transit? These are important questions, because mobility and access are integral components of the urban public realm; thus, along with the push for open data, which is to say data that is freely available for all residents, there exists a concurrent need for software research and development based on actual user needs rather than perceived market-driven objectives.

In sum, networked urbanism is an assemblage of diverse human actors, social practices, and computational and physical resources. If organizations, both societal and governmental, are moving in the direction of networked infrastructural models characterized by individuality, mobility, and affinity, what might this mean for urban environments? A critical realization is that the topics of sustainability, social equity, public space, urban infrastructure, and privacy can no longer be understood in isolation. Each entity is connected to the others through networked systems and wireless infrastructural integration.

Intelligent Land Use Planning

Discussions such as the preceding encourage designers to move beyond devices and system towards larger questions concerning land use planning and society. The invention and application of intelligent infrastructure are more than technical exercises: They have real-world implications. Simply replacing a fossil fuel-burning car with a smart electric one—even one that can drive itself safely and collaborate with other vehicles—will not be enough for a socially equitable and sustainable city unless we concurrently adopt new ownership models and fundamentally change settlement patterns (Chin 2013). Armed with what we know now about networked technologies, how can we apply that new knowledge to create more open, accessible, and sustainable cities? While academic research is examining questions assembled by disciplines ranging from transportation planning to sociology and cultural geography, design research is still insufficient to develop plausible responses addressing the social demand for access. In the effort to create greater access for urban residents, rethinking the automobile may not be enough.

The discussion of mobility extends beyond the notion of simply reaching a destination, of moving people from point A to point B. Mobility encompasses a more expansive definition, including the user experience of the public realm—the qualitative experience of moving along sidewalks, streets, and subways. Mobility is also related to user health, safety, and well-being, in addition to the many ways it contributes to urban cultural identity. Transit infrastructure, although intended to connect residents, may actually disconnect them from other sociocultural opportunities. That view is reinforced by Thün et al. (2014), who contend that transportation corridors often create physical geographies of disruption, since corridors act as barriers, simultaneously generating geographies of exclusion—economic, cultural, and health-related. For Brillembourg and Klumpner's Urban-Think Tank, the need to rectify existing social exclusions is a primary shaper of design decisions. Community involvement, including public workshops attended by architects, planners, activists, and neighborhood leaders, figures prominently in their research methodology.[23] Others, such as Thün and colleagues, also use participatory methods but integrate demographic data analysis related to factors of proximity, availability, and affordability of mobility into their proposals (Thün et al. 2014). Recognizing that urbanism/infrastructure is a field of study complicated by diverse situations and actors, Urban-Think Tank, as well as Thün et al., suggest that transit space itself could be reconceived as a novel social system.[24] Through the application of the logics of social connection, the reconfiguration of transit stations and corridors might result in new formal typologies, such that public transit stations might serve as more than mere functional transfer points, instead acting as information access nodes and cultural destinations by providing a broad variety of activities.

As the previous discussion demonstrates, there is no one universal smart city. Each city defines what is intelligent for its unique context. Unlike earlier high modernism, which assumed a tabula rasa condition, architectural programs derived through community workshops have the advantage of identifying user-generated programs specific to each unique culture and neighborhood. In these territories, responding to constituents' unmet requirements for access to health care, fresh produce and other foods, and learning opportunities uncovers significant untapped design potential. What can emerge at metro transfer points/transit nodes are other neighborhood-specific programs, which could also house medical clinics, farmers' markets, classrooms and libraries, public media studios, free public WiFi, or community meeting spaces (Thün et al. 2014). The exploration of architectural prototypes at multiple scales and time frames could be a productive means to create increased access to social and civic amenities within the space of smart mobility infrastructure.

As Ryan Chin (2013) of City Science Initiative explains, we must fundamentally rethink the urban structure of our cities, so that living and working are brought closer together, making us less reliant on the automobile. That approach requires walkable, high-density, mixed-use neighborhoods wherein the needs of every resident are met within a 20-minute walk. Indeed, such ideas are not novel but draw inspiration from the Russian Constructivists (1919), by way of the principle of "coupling," a strategy that combines multiple functionalities. Coupling has proven an effective strategy for advanced transit-oriented developments (TODs): mixed-use developments combining residential, commercial, and public space, which maximize access to public transport through proximity. TODs have existed since the 1950s and offer several advantages: increased urban density, lower car-to-resident ratios, and better pedestrian access to public transit. Moreover, because TODs are generally located within a radius of a quarter- to a half-mile from a transit stop, they solve the first-and-last mile problem mentioned previously. Today, networked shared mobility expands the parameters of TOD requirements, as well as their typological configurations, allowing TODs to be located almost anywhere (Tierney 2013b).

Innovative urban modes and models are required to make cities a more accessible and inclusive space for all inhabitants. Land use planners are reexamining current programs and pathways in various global contexts (in North American, European, and Asian cities, as well as southern hemisphere *favelas*) to discover new spatial possibilities and ways to bridge the socioeconomic divide of mobility (Audi Urban Future Initiative 2012). Through small-scale interventions, whether transit-oriented developments, networked resource sharing, or mobility zoning, it is possible to reduce environmental impacts while creating a stronger sense of place and community. Such investigations seek to imbue the spaces of mobility with activity, life, and purpose, thereby contributing to greater well-being in everyday experience (Figure 21.2).

Figure 21.2 Re-programmable surface, BIG Audi Urban Future Initiative 2010
Source: Courtesy of BIG: Bjarke Ingels Group ©.

Privacy and Data Collection

Although we have been considering the primarily positive effects of intelligent infrastructure, some less visible and more controversial problems increasingly compromise networked urbanism. As most are already aware, intelligent infrastructure translates into an expansion of networked standards of surveillance into our physical lives through WNS, global positioning systems (GPS), and other sensor networks. As a result, physical space is being increasingly measured, quantified, and circumscribed by data. What has become a matter of concern is that this future assemblage of WNS and urban space has the capacity to instantiate an extensive applied control topology that entangles sensors with data, personal information, and mapping—in other words, context (Tierney 2013b). The placelessness of the early Internet has come full circle such that every nodal point can be located, interconnected, and known.

If the entire city effectively becomes a wireless sensor network system with data spontaneously generated from each point, then individuals can be geographically located and monitored at all times.[25] Information gleaned from mobile wireless networks includes with whom we come into contact and for how long, and ultimately what value we, as individuals, offer as a node in the network. Moreover, the broad mobility dynamics concerning our movement as a group become all-important data for determining the reconfigurable topology and routing protocols implemented by the network, its efficiency, and overall performance (Townsend 2013: 273). At the same time, accurate information is crucial for allowing municipal transit planning agencies to schedule, maintain, and operate a transportation system, as well as to plan strategically for transit investment.[26] Nonetheless, the integration of networked communication into location-based protocols and the expropriation of that data to external sources, such as mobility providers, raise serious questions about individual privacy.

Furthermore, the mass popularity of location-based software has not gone unnoticed by commercial interests. Market forces embed software opportunistically for both political and commercial objectives. From game designers to online retailers, profit-seeking commercial entities are finding ways to leverage locative media through new cross-platform applications that pop up daily. Those applications and services concurrently seek increasingly sophisticated ways of collecting and monitoring personal data. In addition, location-based mobile applications record information about everyday sociality as the metadata collected through user-generated content running on proprietary applications also becomes commercially lucrative (Stalder 2012: 250). Just as geographic, social, and even biometric data form the economic base of fixed Internet conglomerates (such as Facebook and Google), the additional geospatial data retrieved from mobile devices is associated with a significant market value. These realities all have consequences for our individual privacy (O'Dwyer 2011).

What appears to be an emphasis on mobility customization at the user end is actually veiling the commercial practice of personal data mining on the provider end. Users perceive a gain in control but they are in fact being constantly monitored. "The extent, precision, and speed of this data gathering is unprecedented," according to Internet theorist Felix Stalder (2012: 50). As our notions of access and mobility are being reconfigured, so too is individual privacy. Concern about the surveillance of individual and collective actions (including racial profiling), communications, and movements by domestic security forces is warranted, both here and abroad.[27] As evidenced by WNS, technology has multiple dimensions and may be repurposed for different objectives. Networked systems can thereby be instrumentalized to increase urban access as well as to limit it.

Conclusion

The public aspect of intelligent infrastructure makes it inseparable from social issues. While most scholars agree that soft infrastructure—wireless technologies, the Internet, and social media—holds the potential to produce new kinds of space and enable new social practices, uneven accessibility remains a significant problem. Graham and Marvin's *Splintering Urbanism* (2001: 43–45) extensively documents uneven economic and technological development related to hard infrastructure—transportation systems, electrical grids, fiber optic networks—caused by a pattern of differential access to public services. Looking ahead to the integration of intelligent infrastructure into everyday practices, Picon (2015: 67) presents two contrasting visions: on the one hand, a neocybernetic ambition to steer the city in the most efficient way; and on the other, a more participative approach in which empowered individuals invent new modes of cooperation.

While these two positions may appear oppositional, upon further reflection, they might not be mutually exclusive. Viewed in combination, networked infrastructure can contribute to more open, accessible, and sustainable cities for all urban habitants. For example, crowdsourced transit information, which combines optimization algorithms *and* participatory practices, results in shorter commute times. Accordingly, technology can contribute to greater social equity, if planners adopt a holistic model. Vincent Roumeas of Paris Region Entreprises finds that a strategic urban design emerges from an overarching vision of what constitutes a thriving neighborhood (Tierney 2013a). Networked infrastructure is only one aspect of that vision; employment opportunities, affordable housing, and enhanced neighborhood culture and identity are others.[28] What unifies this vision is the conviction that social exclusion from access to resources (information, transit, or otherwise) is best addressed by raising awareness of the functioning of infrastructures and making that knowledge available to others. While many of the ideas set out herein are not fully realized, speculation on the future of cities does more than merely present possibilities. Alternative futures may spark discussion and create new participatory practices. For landscape architect and urban planner Kevin Lynch (1960), cultural imaginaries play a significant role in understanding context and influencing the decisions that either enable or limit possible futures. Thus, a discussion of future cities provides a space for urban residents to reflect on their daily experience and, more importantly, to participate in decision-making processes. For decades, planning decisions were based on an incomplete understanding of the consequences of the automobile and use of fossil fuels, not only with regard to climate change but also in relation to population growth, suburban development, and industrial expansion. While acknowledging these past shortcomings, we may find the adoption of networked participatory practices to be a productive way to involve all residents in decision-making processes. One aspect of DIY urbanism is that residents can enter into a collective conversation and deliberate on a city as an envisioned space different from what they inherited. Neighborhood discussions such as these can be one of the most important catalysts for fundamental change (Heynen 2003).

Collective intelligence, according to researchers Lévy and Kerckhove, is the capacity of networked information and communication technologies to enhance the collective pool of knowledge by expanding the range of human interactions (Flew 2007: 21). This is grounded by the historical notion of *civitas*, which encompasses particular sets of actions, relationships, and powers meant to ensure that *all* citizens can participate freely and fully in the life of their society. The objective is to look at these new conditions and reflect on how we can meaningfully engage with and change technology, including shaping it towards humanistic objectives. The processes of governance are complex, and ultimately there is neither a single method nor a simple technological solution for collective decision-making. How we, as a group, decide to plan for and adopt technology is what ultimately changes governance.

Networked technologies are restructuring urban practices; this observation, however, should not be confused with technological determinism. The integration of networked technologies into everyday social practices causes us to reflect deeply on their protocols, platforms, and interfaces. The production of space is increasingly dependent on code, and code is being written to produce space (Kitchin and Dodge 2011). Networked infrastructure as a form of code is thus actively shaping sociospatial organization, processes, and economies, along with discursive and material cultures. Those effects figure to become increasingly pervasive as more and more everyday practices are threaded through networked platforms.[29] With that in mind, designers, both urban and software, have a shared responsibility to concentrate not only on problem solving but also on the social, political, and environmental consequences of their design decisions (Katz 2008). While the focus of this project is not on policy-making per se, a humanistic approach—one that emphasizes the value and agency of human beings, individually and collectively—places responsibility for the quality of city life on everyone, design professionals, engineers, policy-makers, and average citizens alike. The future of networked urbanism depends on conceptualizing infrastructure not as a means of optimization, data collection, or control but as a connective tissue of social relations binding a city together. Thus, it becomes a collective venture, synthesizing public and private—one that must be inclusive and sustainable for the benefit of all urban dwellers.

Notes

1 Labels range from ubiquitous computing, pervasive computing, and urban informatics to the Internet of Things (IoT), from smart dust and ambient intelligence to sensor topologies. In 2012, the city of San Francisco commissioned Paradox Engineering to deploy a pilot industrial wireless network to manage urban infrastructure, effectively creating an IoT at the urban scale.
2 Transport systems have significant impacts on the environment, accounting for between 20 and 25 percent of world energy consumption and carbon dioxide emissions. Greenhouse gas emissions from transport are increasing at a faster rate than any other energy-using sector (Meyer and O'Kane 2013).
3 Regarding the debate on how to measure urban growth, refer to Brenner and Schmid (2014).
4 Questioning the primacy of personal automobiles, Mitchell outlined the ways a postcarbon landscape could reshape urban form. The sustainable city would integrate connected e-cars, mobility-on-demand systems, smart electric grids, and dynamically priced markets. See Mitchell, Borroni-Bird, and Burns, (2010). Ryan Chin, former director of the City Science Initiative MIT Media Lab is developing autonomous mobility-on-demand (MoD) systems—a network of self-driving, shared-use, lightweight electric vehicles (EVs) for cities.
5 According to Meier (2015), a dedicated interface was created to crowdsource disaster damage and geolocation, quickly mobilizing hundreds of dedicated volunteers.
6 The Detroit Digital Stewards Program was launched by Allied Media Project (AMP) in partnership with Open Technology Institute, which are global leaders in using wireless technology for human rights. The Detroit Digital Stewards are technologists, organizers, activists, and elders exploring and learning new technologies with the goal of supporting community-owned WiFi networks.
7 Refer to De Filippi (2014).
8 Fixed infrastructure represents a significant economic investment for countries—and what is constructed is often unevenly distributed, a topic explored in Graham and Marvin (2001).
9 There are two basic technologies used to operate mobile broadband (cell-phone) networks: Global System for Mobile Communications (GSM) and Code Division Multiple Access (CDMA). GSM is more popular in Europe and Asia and CDMA is more common in the United States. The major technical differences between the two systems have to do with the way each technology shares space on the radio spectrum. Without getting into the details, both GSM and CDMA use different algorithms that allow multiple cell-phone users to share the same radio frequency without interfering with each other. Mobile broadband is also known as 3G, or third-generation cell-phone technology. Now carriers are installing 5G, which will be a single global standard for delivering high-speed Internet access to mobile devices.

10 A cell-phone has a processor in it that converts the received digital information into an analog signal so that a voice can be heard. This occurs in an average time of four to eight seconds. Each cell-phone also contains its own transmitter to encode spoken information onto a radio wave.
11 Ultimately, these chips may even be able to "sip" energy harvested from their ambient environment, including stray electromagnetic radiation, thermal gradients, or even the rustle of a breeze. Maulik (2014). www.oracle.com/us/corporate/profit/big-ideas/012314-smaulik-2112685.html.
12 In 2012 San Francisco contracted Paradox Engineering to deploy such a prototype system. The intelligent unit is designed to be embedded in municipal light standards; it houses an environmental sensor, a small computer, and a camera. Promoted as an energy-saving method to control traffic flow and other operating costs, the system could effectively double as urban surveillance, invisibly monitoring the everyday activities of citizens by capturing their conversations and motions on cameras to be studied in some remote location.
13 OOO is not without its critics; see Galloway (2012).
14 Public works (or internal improvements) are a broad category of infrastructure projects, financed and constructed by the government for use in the greater community. They include public buildings (municipal buildings, schools, hospitals), transport infrastructure (roads, railroads, bridges, pipelines, canals, ports, airports), public spaces (public squares, parks, beaches), and public services (water supply, sewage, electrical grid, dams and other, usually long-term, physical assets and facilities).
15 See Schwarzer (2016). During the 1950s, the rapid rate of technological change characteristic of postindustrial societies called for new methods of organizing space that would facilitate an integrated flow of objects and information. At the 1958 Delos Summit, the Greek architect and planner C. A. Doxiadis launched the field of *Ekistics* (a complex term signifying settlement within ecological balance). In concert with architect Buckminster Fuller and cultural theorist Marshall McLuhan, he proposed an "invisible extension of the physical." The intention was to design at the largest possible scale by analyzing vast amounts of global information, what today we would call big data. Without access to computing, but inspired by systems theory, Doxiadis, Fuller, and McLuhan believed that spatial patterns could be detected in patterns emerging from flows of information. Their visionary proposals initiated a form of urban planning dependent upon a grid of networks and special-interest communities and all predating the Internet.
16 Never before in human history has it been so easy to communicate across long distances. Never before have men [sic] been able to maintain intimate and continuing contact with others across thousands of miles; never has intimacy been so independent of spatial propinquity, nor has the capability existed to unite all places within an almost equal time distance.

Webber also viewed the automobile as "an important instrument of personal freedom" (Webber 1964: 40–43).
17 Refer to www.miltonkeynes.co.uk/news/local/driverless-pods-to-ease-parking-and-travel-woes-in-mk-1-5636619?fb_action_ids=3767406519984&fb_action_types=og.likes&fb_ref=.UtwupzrQ6KY. like&fb_source=aggregation&fb_aggregation_id=288381481237582 (Accessed August 14, 2014).
18 After Britain passed the New Towns Act after World War II, the government quickly chose land for new developments to accommodate the increasing population, and several new towns were founded. Following the 1950s Baby Boom, during the 1960s a renewed interest grew for new towns; new propositions allowed the development of more innovative research.
19 See also Latham and Sassen (2005); Sassen (2006). Taken up by Easterling (2014), these new spatial configurations manifest as free trade zones without allegiance to any country.
20 According to E. S. Sousa (2007), advanced fourth-generation wireless networks are based on the concept of autonomous deployment of the network infrastructure. There is a requirement for self-configuration of the air interface to facilitate deployment by the users and the network operator has the task to manage the use of the spectrum by the networking elements (Sousa 2007). http://ieeexplore.ieee.org/xpl/login.jsp?tp=&arnumber=4299332&url=http%3A%2F%2Fieeexplore.ieee.org%2Fiel5%2F4299028%2F4299029%2F04299332.pdf%3Farnumber%3D4299332 (Accessed January 3, 2015).
21 Differential pricing structures are seen to encourage energy optimization towards greater sustainability. See Mitchell, Borroni-Bird and Burns (2010).
22 The Twelve Tables of Roman law defined the right to use a road as a *servitus*, or claim. The *ius eundi* ("right of going") established a claim to use an *iter*, or footpath, across private land, the *ius agendi* ("right of driving"), an *actus*, or carriage track.
23 Audi Urban Future Initiative (2012) *Urban-Think Tank's Research in Caracas, Venezuela and São Paulo Metropolitan Region, Brasil*. Available at: http://audi-urban-future-initiative.com/blog/urbanthink-tank.

24 Social geographer Jean Tricart contends that the "social content" of a city is the basis for reading it and the study of social content must precede the description of the geographical artifacts. "Social facts, to the extent that they present themselves as specific content, always precede forms and function and, one might say, embrace them" (Tricart 1963).

25 According to Dan Work, PhD, transportation engineer, University of Illinois Urbana Champaign, the concern is that individuals can be identified through any two repetitive location points, even if the data is anonymized.

26 Data may be deposited and stored anonymously in government/institutional facilities for use in related research studies.

27 While it is understandable for urban planners to collect and model data to understand the complex interactions of a city, this understanding would not apply to how repressive governments use those very same methods of data collection to discipline urban residents.

28 Conversation with Vincent Roumeas, as reported in Tierney (2013a).

29 As social geographers Rob Kitchen and Martin Dodge argue, urban policy-making requires an interdisciplinary approach. Geographical Information Systems (GIS), software, digital modeling programs, and wireless sensor information now make it possible to build a model of the city from user interaction and to understand movement and circulation patterns in novel ways. This enables designers and planners to study the city from the bottom up, that is, from the actual everyday social practices of urban habitants.

References

Amin, A. and Thrift, N. (2002) *Cities: Reimagining the Future*, Cambridge, UK: Polity Press.

Audi Urban Future Initiative (2012) *Urban-Think Tank's Research in Caracas, Venezuela and São Paulo Metropolitan Region, Brasil*. http://audi-urban-future-initiative.com/blog/urbanthink-tank.

Brenner, N. and Schmid, C. (2014) "The 'urban age' in question," *International Journal of Urban and Regional Research*, 38, 3: 731–755.

Castells, M. (1989) *The Informational City: Information Technology, Economic Restructuring, and the Urban Regional Process*, Cambridge, MA: Blackwell.

Castells, M. (2000) *The Rise of the Network Society*, 2nd edition, Malden, MA: Blackwell.

Cervero, R. (2013) "Transport infrastructure and the environment: sustainable mobility and urbanism," in *Urban Development for the Twenty First Century*, Second Planocosmo International Conference, Bandung Institute of Technology.

Chehab, L. A. and Makkouk, M. (2013) *Autonomous Infrastructures*, Unpublished March Dissertation, Architectural Association.

Chin, R. (2013) "Solving transport headaches in the cities of 2050," BBC. www.bbc.com/future/story/20130617-moving-around-in-the-megacity.

De Filippi, P. (2014) "It's time to take mesh networks seriously (and not just for the reasons you think)," *Wired*, January 2. www.wired.com/2014/01/its-time-to-take-mesh-networks-seriously-and-not-just-for-the-reasons-you-think/.

Easterling, K. (2014) *Extrastatecraft: The Power of Infrastructure Space*, New York: Verso.

Fennell, L. A. (2013) "Crowdsourcing land use," *Brooklyn Law Review*, 78, 2: 385–415.

Flew, T. (2007) *New Media: An Introduction*, Oxford: Oxford University Press.

Galloway, A. (2012) "A response to Graham Harman's 'Marginalia on Radical Thinking'." https://itself.wordpress.com/2012/06/03/a-response-to-graham-harmans-marginalia-on-radical-thinking/.

Graham, S. (1997) "Telecommunications and the future of cities: debunking the myths," *Cities* 14, 1: 21–29.

Graham, S. (2000) "Constructing premium network spaces: reflections on infrastructure networks and contemporary urban development," *International Journal of Urban and Regional Research* 24, 1: 183–200.

Graham, S. and Guy, S. (2004) "'Internetting' downtown San Francisco: digital space meets urban place," in O. Coutart, R. Hanley, and R. Zimmerman (eds) *The Social Sustainability of Technical Networks*, London: Routledge, 32–47.

Graham, S. and Marvin, S. (2001) *Splintering Urbanism*, New York: Routledge.

Greenfield (2013) *Against the Smart City: The City Is Here for You to Use*, Helsinki: Do Projects.

Gubbi, J., Buyya, R., Marusic, S., and Palaniswami, M. (2013) "Internet of Things (IoT): a vision, architectural elements, and future directions," *Future Generation Computer Systems* 29, 7: 1645–1660.

Harman, G. (2002) *Tool-Being: Heidegger and the Metaphysics of Objects*, Chicago: Open Court.

Heynen, H. (2003) "The need for utopian thinking in architecture," Berlage Institute paper presentation.
Katz, B. (2008) "Design and the human condition: an untimely meditation," The Hewlett Foundation Lecture, Menlo Park, CA, February 14.
Kitchin, R. (2015) "Data-driven networked urbanism," Programmable City Working Paper, Manooth, Ireland.
Kitchin, R. and Dodge, M. (2011) *Code/Space: Software in Everyday Life*, Cambridge, MA: MIT Press.
Kolbert, E. (2014) "Rough forecast: comment on climate change," *The New Yorker*, April 14.
Latham, R. and Sassen, S. (2005) *Digital Formations*, New York: Princeton University Press.
Latour, B. (1992) "Where are the missing masses? Sociology of a few mundane artefacts," in W. Bijker and J. Law (eds) *Shaping Technology, Building Society: Studies in Sociotechnical Change*, Cambridge, MA: MIT Press, 225–258.
Lynch, K. (1960) *The Image of the City*, Cambridge, MA: MIT Press.
Maulik, S. (2014) "Trends in infrastructure: the Internet of Things," *Profit Magazine*, 19, 1. www.oracle.com/us/corporate/profit/big-ideas/012314-smaulik-2112685.html.
Meier, P. (2015) *Digital Humanitarians: How Big Data Is Changing Humanitarian Response*, New York: Taylor & Francis.
Meyer, B. and O'Kane, B. (2013) "Strategic approaches to developing future mobility solutions by applying systems integration and thinking methodologies," Include Asia 13 Conference paper, Hong Kong.
Mitchell, W. J., Borroni-Bird, C. E., and Burns, L. D. (2010) *Reinventing the Automobile: Personal Urban Mobility for the 21st Century*, Cambridge, MA: MIT Press.
Morton, T. (2013) *Hyperobjects: Philosophy and Ecology at the End of the World*, Minneapolis: University of Minnesota Press.
Moss, M. and Townsend, A. (1999) "How telecommunications systems are transforming urban spaces," in J. O. Wheeler and Y. Aoyama (eds) *Fractured Geographies: Cities in the Telecommunications Age*, New York: Routledge, 31–41.
Mostafavi, M. (2010) *Ecological Urbanism*, Zurich: Lars Müller Publishers.
O'Dwyer, R. (2011) "Network media: exploring the sociotechnical relations between mobile networks and media publics," ISEA Conference paper, Istanbul.
Pagano, C. (2013) "DIY urbanism: property and process in grassroots city building," *Marquette Law Review*, 97, 2: 336–337.
Pew Research Center (2014) "Emerging nations embrace internet, mobile technology: cell phones nearly ubiquitous in many countries." www.pewglobal.org/2014/02/13/emerging-nations-embrace-internet-mobile-technology/.
Picon, A. (2015) *Smart Cities: A Spatial Intelligence*, Chichester: Wiley & Sons.
Sassen, S. (2001) *The Global City: New York, London, Tokyo*, 2nd edition, Princeton: Princeton University Press.
Sassen, S. (2006) *Territory Authority Rights: From Medieval to Global Assemblages*, New York: Princeton University Press.
Sassen, S. (2008) "Re-assembling the urban," *Urban Geography*, 29, 2: 113–126.
Schwarzer, M. (2016) "The conceptual roots of infrastructure," in T. F. Tierney (ed.) *New Urban Mobilities as Intelligent Infrastructure*, Charlottesville: University of Virginia Press, 39–62.
Sclar, E. (2012) "Urban professionals in the 21st century: challenges for pedagogy and professional practice," Paper presentation, Global Urban Summit, Columbia University.
Sheller, M. and Urry, J. (2000) "The city and the car," *International Journal of Urban and Regional Research* 24, 4: 737–757.
Sheller, M. and Urry, J. (2006) *Mobile Technologies of the City*, London: Routledge.
Shepard, M. (2011) *Sentient City: Ubiquitous Computing, Architecture, and the Future of Urban Space*, Cambridge, MA: MIT Press.
Soja, E. (2000) *Postmetropolis: Critical Studies of Cities and Regions*, Hoboken, NJ: Wiley-Blackwell.
Sousa, E. S. (2007) "Autonomous infrastructure wireless network," Mobile and Wireless Communications Summit, Budapest, July 1–5.
Stalder, F. (2012) "Between democracy and spectacle: the front-end and back-end of the social web," in M. Mandiberg (ed.) *The Social Media Reader*, New York: New York University Press.
Sterling, B. (2014) *The Epic Struggle of the Internet of Things*, London: Strelka Press.
Thün, G., Velikov, K., McTavish, D., and Zielinski, S. (2014) "Protean prototypes: developing access-enabling infrastructures for Chicago," presentation paper, University of Michigan. http://taubmancollege.umich.edu/research/research-city/protean-prototypes-developing-access-enabling-infrastructures-chicagoland.

Tierney, T. F. (2013a) "Is Paris a smarter city than New York?" PRIME, San Francisco, CA, August 8. https://blogprimehubtech21.wordpress.com/2013/08/23/is-paris-a-smarter-city-than-new-york/.

Tierney, T. F. (2013b) *The Public Space of Social Media: Connected Cultures of the Network Society*, London: Routledge.

Tierney, T. F. (2014) "Crowdsourcing disaster response: mobilizing social media for urban resilience," *European Business Review*, July 9. www.europeanbusinessreview.com/?p=4911.

Townsend, A. (2000) "Life in the real-time city: mobile telephones and urban metabolism," *Journal of Urban Technology* 7, 2: 85–104.

Townsend, A. (2013) *Smart Cities: Big Data, Civic Hackers, and the Quest for a New Utopia*, New York: W.W. Norton.

Tricart, J. (1963) Cours de geographie humaine. *L'habitat Urbain*, vol. 2, Paris: Centre de Documentation Universitaire.

Tsay, S. and Herrmann, V. (2013) *Rethinking Urban Mobility*, Washington, DC: Carnegie Endowment for International Peace.

Urry, J. (2012) "Social networks, mobile lives and social inequalities," *Journal of Transport Geography* 21 (March): 24–30.

Webber, M. (1963) "Order in diversity: community without propinquity," in L. Wingo (ed.) *Cities and Space: The Future of Urban Land*, Baltimore: Johns Hopkins University Press, 23–54.

Webber, M. (1964) "The urban place and the non urban realm," in *Explorations into Urban Structure*, London: Oxford University Press.

Wigley, M. (2007) "The architectural brain," in A. Burke and T. F. Tierney (eds) *Network Practices: New Strategies for Architecture and Design*, New York: Princeton Architectural Press, 30–53.

22
The Architecture of Water

Karen Piper

I grew up near the "banks" of the Owens River, which was really nothing more than a giant rusted pipe that ran along the hillside carrying water to Los Angeles. That pipe had the whole river diverted into it, flowing past my hometown of Ridgecrest, California. The water was not something I could drink or touch—or even see. If I followed the pipe north, I would eventually reach the murky, fishless depths of a concrete canal—the second half of the Los Angeles Aqueduct, extending 233 miles from L.A. to Owens Valley. This concrete canal is also behind a fence, its waters untouchable. That is what rivers meant to me as a child. Pipes and concrete.

In most of California's valleys, rivers have been turned into concrete channels. In some of them, the rivers now flow backwards. The San Joaquin River once flowed north to San Francisco Bay but now is diverted south into the Friant-Kern Canal, first to supply valley farmers and then to Los Angeles. The Sacramento River, which starts in Northern California, used to end at the Bay as well, but now continues south for hundreds of miles to Los Angeles. In California, rivers do not flow but are "wheeled"—or carried through aqueducts like water hauled to the desert in a wheelbarrow. The only real rivers are high up in the mountains where the wilderness is. Not down in the valleys.

Only protected by the Clean Water Act if deemed "navigable," most of California's rivers do not even count as rivers. For instance, a little water still flows in the old San Joaquin River, but not enough to reach the sea—not enough to be a "river." Instead, it stops in the middle of the San Joaquin Valley, unnoticed. Of course, the 200,000–500,000 salmon that used to run up the river each year did not realize their river had been replaced. Instead, they kept trying to run up the same river until they nearly went extinct, finding no place to lay their eggs. Today, as part of a restoration program, trucks move salmon up and down the river, connecting the still-impassable sections.

California is an experiment in the artificial, a place that, despite its elaborate water engineering, seems to be perpetually in drought, broken only by short periods of intense flooding. In 2016, at the tail end of an historic five-year drought, Donald Trump came to the San Joaquin Valley and declared, "There is no drought. You have a water problem that is so insane. It is so ridiculous where they're taking the water and shoving it out to sea." He was talking about the river restoration program (Colvin and Knickmeyer 2016). I understood this garbled speech only because I had heard a similar narrative, at another rally led by Representative Devin Nunes and

Sean Hannity for *Fox News* in 2009.[1] Nunes had called those who supported the fish conservation program "eco-terrorists" then. In his book *Restoring the Republic*, he further said they were members of a "Doomsday cult" and "followers of neo-Marxist, socialist, Maoist or Communist ideals." Their goal, Nunes claimed, was to "depopulate the land" (Doyle 2010). Clearly, Nunes had prepped Trump for this rally. Behind Trump, a sea of people held identical green signs that read, "Farmers for Trump." Trump concluded, "We're going to start opening up the water so that you can have your farmers survive. We're going to get it done quick. Don't even think about it. That's an easy one" (Ellis 2016).

Republican Nunes later took credit for Trump's talking points and organized a $50,000-per-head "meet and greet" with local farmers (Khan 2016). While Nunes represents the poorest district in the nation, with a large population of undocumented migrant workers, he works for its rich farmers. For instance, there is Mark Borba, who owns a world-class race horse breeding facility, the largest cattle feedlot in California, and a 9000-acre farm. He enjoys flying his private plane to the Santa Monica racetrack on weekends to watch his horses compete. Then there is billionaire Stewart Resnick, who owns the Franklin Mint, POM Wonderful, and a large percentage of the world's pistachios and almonds. He is known for putting Afghanistan out of the almond business. Now he lives in Beverley Hills, where he and his wife are renowned both for their glitzy soirees and the number of buildings named after them. These are the men from the Westlands Water District who literally pay Nunes' salary. To them, water is money.

Nunes has long been fighting against environmental regulations that keep water from getting to his constituents, these wealthy Westland farmers. In 2014, Mark Borba's emails to Devin Nunes and others were leaked to *The Fresno Bee*, giving us a rare glimpse into the private interactions between politicians and large campaign donors. In the emails, Borba is upset about the failure of a Nunes-sponsored bill called the Sacramento–San Joaquin Valley Water Reliability Act, which was sent to committee where it was killed by Senator Diane Feinstein. At the time, Borba was paying Nunes about $4000 a month, as well as paying Senator Feinstein. The bill would have stopped efforts to restore the San Joaquin River, as well as water allotments for endangered fish. After it died, Borba wrote to Nunes' Chief of Staff and others,

> [Feinstein's] the fucking Chair of the National Security Team, for Christ's sake! She should call OBAMA on the carpet and insist that he direct Interior to get real! If "Blackie" won't return her call, she should schedule a press conference on the steps of the Capitol or in front of Michelle's house![2]

After the bill's failure, Borba became a large campaign donor to Trump; a month after Trump was elected, his legislation got through Congress. Introduced by Devin Nunes, Kevin McCarthy, and Diane Feinstein, it was included in what is called a "poison pill" rider and was the first water-related legislation to have passed in Congress in a generation.

A few months later, Trump appointed Westlands Water District lobbyist and attorney David Bernhardt to be second-in-command at the Department of Interior under Ryan Zinke. At Westlands, Bernhardt's job had been to sue the Department of the Interior. Now, he would be in charge of it. At stake was a massive new water project for Central and Southern California, the $23 billion California Water Fix. The proposed project consists of two four-story-high tunnels that would travel 35 miles under the San Joaquin–Sacramento River Delta, routing northern California's rivers south. Trump included the project on his Top 51 list of urgent infrastructure projects, along with two private groundwater mining operations in the desert. One of these mining operations, Cadiz Inc., is partially owned by Bernhardt's company (Rowland 2017).[3] Cadiz's financer, Apollo Global Management, advised President Trump on

Figure 22.1 The Los Angeles Aqueduct

Source: Copyright Karen Piper.

infrastructure and, after Cadiz's approval by Trump, provided a $184-million loan to Jared Kushner (Hiltzik 2018).

Of course, rivers have long been used as the world's political footballs, promised as gifts by campaigning politicians to drought-stricken regions or wealthy campaign donors. This way of thinking about rivers is hardly limited to Trump or Nunes or Republicans in general. But what interests me is the way in which these private political moves—whether in emails or in secret $50,000 meetings—become written on the landscape. What interests me is what made that iron pipe show up in the desert where I grew up, a sign now posted to it reading: "No Shooting" (Figure 22.1). In short, I am interested in how backroom political dealings turn into touchable, built things, and how these things, in turn, become clues that can lead us back to secret email exchanges or dried up lakes. In the end, I will suggest it is time to leave behind the era of backroom political deals and instead fashion something fresh: a new architecture of water.

Two British Colonial Dreams

Long before Trump and Nunes were alive, people have been battling over the same rivers in California. Today, San Joaquin Valley farmers fight with environmentalists and politicians over the Central Valley and State Water Projects, aqueducts winding their way along the valley floor (Figure 22.2). A century earlier, the battle for this same water was between a British engineer,

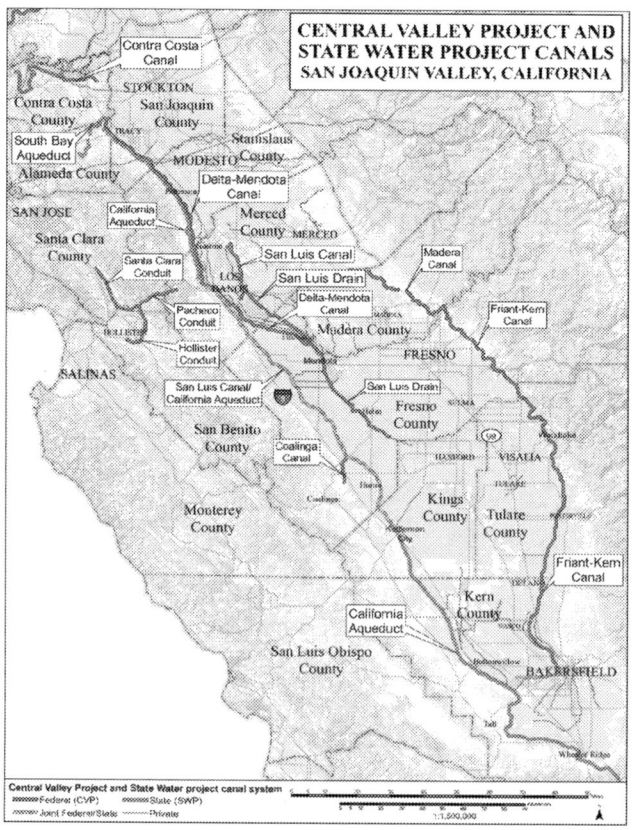

Figure 22.2 Map of Central Valley Project and State Water Project, San Joaquin Valley, CA. U.S. Bureau of Reclamation

The Architecture of Water

Bank of America, and Congress. In the early 1870s, engineer Robert Maitland Brereton came to California from British India to design an irrigation system for the San Joaquin Valley. Previously, he had designed the Indian Peninsular Railway System and so become friends with another famous British engineer, Sir Arthur Cotton. Cotton had another large water project in mind for India called the River Linking Project, and the two engineers kept in touch while working on these sister projects. Though they rarely get credit today, these two men helped initiate a new era of expansion and modernization in agriculture, and a tenuous thread could be drawn straight from their story to a rally in Fresno and the election of a far-right Prime Minister in India. It is this thread that I would like to trace, looking at how these two irrigation projects—in India and California—set the standard for over a century of planning in water infrastructure.

In 1871, Brereton was commissioned by the head of Bank of America, William Ralston, to design an irrigation plan for the entire San Joaquin Valley. For the next five years, he mapped and charted the valley's rivers and soils. He wrote,

> I made an extensive examination of all the natural water resources of the western slopes of the Sierras which commanded the San Joaquin Valley lands. For the purpose of showing Californians the benefits to be derived from a proper system of irrigation, I placed about 6,000 acres ... under cultivation.

Brereton's pilot project was a success, and so Ralston asked him to travel to Washington, D.C. to seek funding and building permits for the full-scale version. Before Congress and President Ulysses Grant, Brereton argued for "the importance of irrigation for the arid lands of the West" and proposed irrigating around eight million acres in the San Joaquin Valley (Figure 22.3).

Back in India, Arthur Cotton was paying close attention to Brereton's work, which he described as "a project for watering the valley of the San Joaquim [sic]; the advantage in

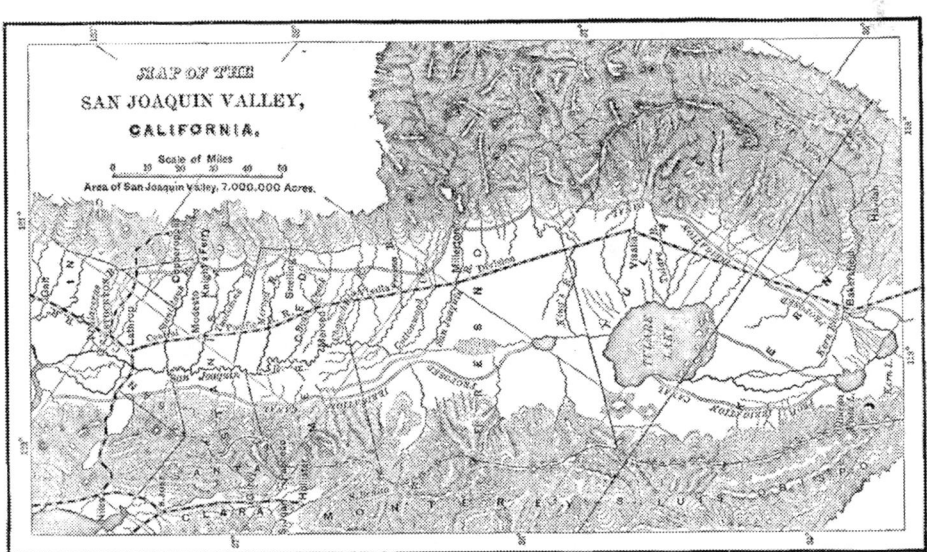

Figure 22.3 Robert M. Brereton's proposed irrigation canals, Charles Nordhoff, *California: A Book for Travellers and Settlers*, New York: Harper & Brothers, 1874

soil, facilities for storing, and distributing water, etc., are far beyond those of India." Flattered at Cotton's approval, Brereton wrote, "He took the warmest kind of interest in my California work, and wanted me to induce the government of India to use the labor-saving machinery I was using on my canal building." (The British colonial government in India was using *corvee* or indentured labor to dig the canals by hand.) Cotton, who had been building canals in India for decades, had more fame and expertise than Brereton at the time. In fact, Brereton had been inspired by Cotton's work in India to try to attempt the same in California. Brereton invested $40,000 of his own money in the California irrigation scheme, called the San Joaquin and King's River Canal Company. When Brereton finished his work in California, Cotton had hoped he would come back to India to help build the River Linking Project. "I have a great set of works in my head," Cotton wrote to Brereton, "being quite certain that India can be made a garden from the Himalayas to Comorin" (Maitland 1908: 25–28).

But in Congress, Brereton encountered his first hurdle. While intrigued by the project, Congress said they could not condemn the properties that stood in its path, citing the sanctity of private property. Subsequently, Bank of America declared bankruptcy and the project was abandoned. William Ralston fell into a long depression that ended with him dead in the San Francisco Bay. According to his friends, he simply went for a swim one day and did not come back. Brereton, who also lost all his money, was no longer considered employable in India. He never worked with Cotton again. Instead, he moved to Canada, where he wrote that Congress had "killed that great and first enterprise in irrigation in North America."

Cotton hit a brick wall in India around the same time. He too had to travel to British Parliament to seek funding and permissions, but Parliament had insisted the project was simply too expensive to build. Not only that, the Parliamentarians concluded, there was not enough water in India to keep the canal system up and running. Cotton had angrily replied, "There is water enough in India for every conceivable purpose ten times over; THERE IS NO WANT OF WATER" (Hope and Digby 1900: 213). Soon, both engineers' dreams of a world being "made a garden" had sputtered and stalled. Yet, ironically, neither project died.

In reality, Congress had not killed Brereton's project. Instead, it could be argued, they stole it. A month after Brereton's proposal failed, Congress set up a committee to look into irrigating the San Joaquin Valley, though it would be several more decades before construction began. By then, Brereton was forgotten. By the time the project (now called the Central Valley Project) was built, reinforced concrete had replaced dirt as the building material of choice. Today, the U.S. Army Corps of Engineers is given credit for these projects. Specifically, General Barton Alexander is said to have designed the Central Valley Project. Its history was thus Americanized.

As for Cotton, his plan lay dormant for almost a century, until it was dusted off by Indian engineer K. L. Rao in 1972. What appealed to Rao was not the steamship transportation system that Cotton said the canals could provide, which would benefit England by getting raw resources more quickly to Indian ports. Rao was interested instead in what he called a "national water grid," a system that could bring "water equality" to India. He set about calculating the per-capita water "availability" in each state, a figure that included every drop in their rivers. Then he labelled each state as having a "water surplus" or a "water deficit" in relation to a national average. Finally, he claimed that "link" the country's major rivers via canals could be used to transfer water from rivers with a "surplus" to those with a "deficit." It sounded like a Jeffersonian dream of equality but ecosystems do not operate according to the rules of grids and equal rights. A jungle wants to be a jungle, not a desert, and vice versa. There is not some universal "in between."

Perhaps not surprisingly, Rao's proposal did not go far, though an office named National Water Development Agency was set up to study it. The far-right Bharatiya Janata Party (BJP) or Indian People's Party, which is pro-development and pro-Hindu, also took an interest in it, which they have since maintained. As with Trump, it seemed the promise of free water to farmers was a useful campaign strategy. In 2014, BJP leader Narendra Modi became prime minister and Cotton's dream was on the verge of becoming a reality. By then, however, Arthur Cotton was largely forgotten, and the project was instead attributed to K. L. Rao. History was thus Indianized, marking the project a patriotic symbol for the state.

If employees at the Indian Water Development Agency or Prime Minister Modi had looked into the history of its sister project in California, they may have paused, since California's aqueducts had developed some costly problems. But projects like these have the tendency to develop a political momentum all their own, and transnational water history was not consulted. Instead, water infrastructure had become rhetorically, habitually, linked to the idea of "development" and nation-building. When California's aqueducts were mentioned in the many reports about the River Linking Project, they were referred to only as an example to follow. California's agricultural bounty was something that campaigning politicians promised like rupees to Indian farmers: "Look, California became rich through irrigation. You can be, too!"

Dream or Nightmare?

Back in California, unexpected problems occurred as soon as the aqueducts opened. One was that a layer of clay beneath the soil began trapping aqueduct water near the surface, particularly on the drier west side of the San Joaquin Valley where Westlands is now located. Over time, this led to water-logging and then, as the water evaporated, to salt build-up in the soils. Before long, land started to became saline and un-farmable. To halt these problems, farmers began installing tile drains beneath the soil to collect excess water and funnel it out to sea. The Bureau of Reclamation promised a 290-mile drainage canal to San Francisco Bay, so farmers' hopes hinged on this new plan. What followed instead was a series of problems that unraveled like comedy of errors ... and is still being dealt with today.

After the first 87 miles of the Bureau of Reclamation's drainage canal was built, drainage water was funneled into a series of temporary reservoirs near Kesterton Wildlife Refuge, where it was to be stored until the rest of the canal was built to the San Francisco Bay. But then the birds in the wildlife refuge began to die. At first, it was hardly noticeable, but soon a massive die-off of migrating birds was occurring at Kesterton. Scientists who investigated the problem found baby birds with no eyes, brains outside their skulls, and other mutations caused by selenium and other toxins in the reservoir. When photographs emerged, the public was mortified. The reservoirs were filled in to keep the birds away, and the Bureau abandoned the toxic canal. To this day, farmers are battling the U.S. Bureau to get their drainage canal built, but it would now cost an estimated $13 billion dollars to complete.

As for bringing utopian equality to farmers, the Central Valley Project and State Water Project that followed did precisely the opposite. Farms were supposed to be limited to 960 acres, but corruption followed in the wake of water and this law was never strictly enforced. Westlands Water District was slowly split into two demographics: a few wealthy farmers with up to 25,000 acres and a laboring population who, besides earning less that minimum wage, had to live with air pollution, toxic groundwater, and a lack of schools and hospitals. Many were undocumented so had few rights, and that same mix of salt, selenium, pesticides, and fertilizers that once killed the birds at Kesterton was now slowly killing them. People complained of breaking out in rashes when they showered. Babies were born blue due to lack of oxygen.

Cancer became far too common (Sager 2016). The cleaner aqueduct water of the California Aqueduct was reserved for almonds, pistachios, pomegranates, and cattle. Laborers drank polluted well water.

While benefits continue to accrue for those who hold senior water rights or have enough money to swing legislation their way, taxpayers are faced with new expenses. The burden of fixing the health and environmental consequences caused by aqueducts often, unwittingly, falls on them. In a state built by aqueducts and dams, of course, the problems of the San Joaquin Valley are not the only aqueduct-related burdens that taxpayers are facing today. East of the Sierra Nevada Mountains, that pipe that runs near my hometown with a river inside it is also responsible for drying up Owens Lake. As it dried, the lakebed began to emit dust filled with heavy metals, causing cancer, respiratory failures, and other ailments. Ultimately, it became the worst dust pollution problem in the Western Hemisphere. I still have its dust in my lungs. In an attempt to stop the dust, the City of Los Angeles has been forced to spend $2 billion to date. They have tried building a sprinkler system on the lakebed, planting saltgrass, laying gravel, and tilling the surface of the lakebed. Some methods worked, others did not, but the dust remains a health hazard for tens of thousands of people today. And the price tag keeps rising.

Despite the severity of this dust problem, it pales in comparison to another aqueduct-caused problem: the Salton Sea. Four times the size of Owens Lake, the inland Salton Sea was accidentally created when water diverted into a new aqueduct from the Colorado River broke through its banks in 1904. No one could stop that river, as hard as they tried, until it became a massive inland sea. Now this sea is slowly drying up, since the water that once flowed into it has been allotted elsewhere. Since farming occurred around the Salton Sea, the lakebed dust is even more toxic than that of Owens Lake. Besides heavy metals, the dust contains DDT and other pesticides and fertilizers. If it is not stopped, California's Pacific Institute has estimated the problem will cause $29–70 billion in damages to property values and health. The problem is that no one knows quite how to stop it. One idea is to create a smaller, "perimeter lake" around its edges, which emit the most dust. Estimates for fixes like this range from $2.5 to $10 billion, and only in the short term. Because the state claims this is unaffordable, it appears that regular people, hundreds of thousands of them, will pay the price with their health instead (Perry 2017).

In short, we are looking at $17 to $25 billion to *try* to fix the problems caused by aqueducts. Yet there is one more aqueduct-caused disaster that must be added to this pricey figure: the potential collapse of the Delta. The San Joaquin River and California's other major river, the Sacramento River, meet in an estuary and marsh region called the San Joaquin–Sacramento River Delta. There, the rivers slow, carving islands then erasing and re-carving them again. At least, that is what used to happen. Now the San Joaquin River is partially blocked and the Delta, which is three times the size of San Diego, has been settled by farmers who built levees around the islands over a century ago. Today, the majority of California's spawning fish still pass through the Delta and then attempt to head up rivers they know by heart, though they are largely blocked by dams or diverted. The freshwater that does reach the Delta from northern California is pumped out and into the California Aqueduct, part of the State Water Project. As in any delta system, when freshwater is removed, saltwater creeps in, leading to fears that the whole region could "collapse," or be flooded by the Pacific Ocean. If this were to happen, Southern Californians would find saltwater running from their taps.

These problems began as soon as the first Delta pump, which pumped water into the California Aqueduct, was turned on in 1951. Fish were sucked into the pumps and killed, a river reversed its course, and the ocean moved inland just a bit. Nevertheless, pumps kept being built. In the 1960s, Governor Jerry Brown proposed a "Peripheral Canal" be built around the Delta to side-step its problems, routing water directly from the Sacramento River north of the Delta into the California Aqueduct. The canal would not solve the problem of declining freshwater in the Delta, but at least it would mean that Los Angeles's taps would keep running in the case of a Delta collapse. Of course, northern Californians did not want the canal, nor did Delta farmers and fishermen. Today, the Delta is like the Netherlands, keeping the sea at bay with earthen levees and the force of freshwater. Two million people live in or around the Delta and would be at risk if it flooded, as would the freeways and railroads that crisscross the state. In 1983, Governor Brown submitted the Peripheral Canal to the test of a general vote. It was voted down.

The next Governor, Arnold Schwarzenegger, tried to resurrect the idea, renaming it the Bay Delta Conservation Plan and including some money and land for Delta habitat restoration in order to appease its critics. Nevertheless, the project did not get past the environmental review. Finally, in 2011, Jerry Brown was elected again as Governor and, as was tradition, renamed the project yet again. Now it would be the California WaterFix. This time, it would go *under* the Delta rather than around it, requiring fewer properties to be taken through eminent domain. "I want to get shit done," Brown said, and declared he did not need a vote to build it. Then Donald Trump appeared, promising to "open up" the water.[4] No one knew quite what he meant.

Water Grabs and Muslim Bans

Meanwhile, in India, the first link of the River Linking Project, which connects the Ken and Betwa Rivers, has already flooded a tiger preserve. It is estimated that around 20,000 people will also have to move to make room for this one link alone.[5] The Ken–Betwa link, like so many of these projects, was eagerly awaited by the people of the Betwa region, while farmers in the Ken River watershed complained that they did not have enough water to give away. In fact, both regions are bone dry outside of monsoon season, so there is a seeming randomness in this choice of rivers.

Though each link out of the 30 or so that will be built comes with its own problems, a particularly problematic one is the Brahmaputra–Ganges River link. The Brahmaputra River is one of three main rivers that supplies Bangladesh, a nation built on the deltas of these rivers and ending in islands called the Sundarbans in the Bay of Bengal. As in Louisiana and California, the delta keeps the sea at bay. It also is home to the world's largest mangrove forest, where the rare Bengal tiger and gangetic dolphins live. There, the border between India and Bangladesh is unmarked. Author Amitav Ghosh once described this area as "a meeting not just of many rivers, but a roundabout people can use to pass in many directions—from country to country and even between faiths and religions." There, Muslim, Hindu, and traditional religions and cultures meet and mingle—but the Indian far-right does not enjoy such mixings.

The Brahmaputra will be diverted in the tea-growing state of Assam before it reaches Bangladesh. There, religions have also ebbed and flowed with the population but are mainly a mixture of traditional, Hindu, and Muslim. One day, local people were surprised when the state organized "India's Biggest River Festival," flying in Hindu priests from Haridwar to officiate in April of 2017. What followed was an event resembling one of Prime Minister Modi's garish campaign rallies, with Bollywood-style videos, imported musicians, and colored floodlights on the river, where prayers and sacred dips took place. Not one of the local religious leaders was invited. "So basically, people from outside the state will teach us our customs now," said Rajib Sarma, who runs the local temple. Hafiz Ahmed, who runs a literary group for Muslims on the river's islands, concurred. "Our cultural identity is not even recognised," he said. "People on the [riverine islands] face the wrath of the Brahmaputra all the time, but a festival celebrating the river doesn't even feature us." He added that, lately, Muslims were being branded as "illegal migrants" there (Saikia 2017). Modi's style of Hinduism is pure political theater, with grand gestures of worshipping rivers while at the same time destroying them.

Today, Bangladesh is facing an arsenic poisoning epidemic due to water shortages and river pollution, which will only worsen if the river is diverted. This epidemic can be seen in the face of 36-year-old Kamala Mandal, who was banished from her home after nasty scars and wounds began to form on her skin. Her husband thought it was leprosy, which is a common assumption there. In reality, her illness was caused by drinking toxic well water. According to the World Health Organization, Bangladesh is facing "the largest mass poisoning of a population in history.... The scale of the environmental disaster is greater than any seen before; it is beyond the accidents in Bhopal, India, in 1984, and Chernobyl, Ukraine, in 1986" (Smith, Lingas, and Rahman 2000). Up to 77 million people suffer from arsenic poisoning; one in ten will die from cancer.

Yet a kind of arms race is occurring for control of the Brahmaputra River. Both the Indian and Chinese governments seem to think that they must grab it before the other does, each blaming the other for what will happen to Bangladesh if they do. If the Brahmaputra River is diverted, not only will the arsenic become more concentrated, but well water will also turn salty. Like the California Delta, Bangladesh is dependent upon flowing freshwater to keep the sea at bay, both above and below ground. Stopping this flow of fresh water would cause saltwater to rush into the void. According to activist Medha Patkar, it would invade aquifers across almost half the country, which would be catastrophic. Tens of millions would be displaced. The sea would creep inward as the country shrank in size, killing the mangroves and the Sundarbans.

Prime Minister Modi, rather than addressing this issue, is instead strengthening immigration laws. Months before Trump's so-called "Muslim ban," an Executive Order that would limit immigration for certain people, Modi had introduced his version, a legal amendment that gave immigration preference to "religious minorities" who faced "religious persecution" in Pakistan and Bangladesh. Clearly, it was intended to prioritize Hindu immigration. Trump's Executive Order was also directed as Muslim-majority nations, using exactly the same language about "religious minorities" in order to allow Christians in from Muslim countries while banning Muslims. Immediately, it was roundly denounced for its "Christian-only" language. Few seemed to notice its Hindu-only legal predecessor. Modi once went even further, saying that naturalized Muslim Bangladeshis would have to go back to Bangladesh if he was elected. He said, "You can write it down. After May 16, these Bangladeshis better be prepared with their bags packed" (Das 2016). Hindu Bangladeshis, in contrast, could stay.

Rather than ending water inequity, the River Linking Project seems to serve the purpose of keeping rivers *in* and Muslims *out* of India. Again, comparisons with the U.S. came to mind, specifically in the form of a "Wall." Trump's chanted campaign slogan, "Build A Wall!" neglected to mention that almost half the U.S.–Mexico border is in the middle of the Rio Grande River. This river moves, and the border moves along with it. Because of this fluid boundary, the 1970 Boundary Treaty states that the Colorado and Rio Grande Rivers cannot be impeded.

Trump also threatened Mexico's water supply with his list of "infrastructure priorities," which included two private groundwater mining operations that would affect the flows of both the Colorado and Rio Grande. According to the owner of the Cadiz project, it will store "surplus water" from the Colorado River underground until it is pumped and sold to the highest bidder in Southern California (Hiltzik 2015). But the Colorado River is one of the most parched and contested rivers in the United States. There is no surplus. In fact, the Mexican government has oft-complained that it does not receive its mandated allotment of the Colorado River. As for the Augustin Plains Ranch groundwater mining project, it would reduce water flowing into the Rio Grande River, according to a recent study.

Almost immediately after becoming president, Trump dramatically increased the deportation of Mexican undocumented workers, while simultaneously threatening the water supply of Mexico. Former Mexican President Vincente Fox warned Americans in a Tweet, "America, this is how dictatorship begins." Meanwhile, Trump's alt-right guru Steve Bannon bragged that he had come up with the infrastructure plan. "I'm the guy pushing a trillion-dollar infrastructure plan," he said. "We're just going to throw it up against the wall and see if it sticks. It will be as exciting as the 1930s, greater than the Reagan revolution—conservatives, plus populists, in an economic nationalist movement" (Wolff 2016). The "economic nationalists" of the 1930s were fascists, who also believed in large-scale infrastructure projects and deportation schemes.

Building with Rivers

So how do we combat politicians who view water as campaign promises or worse?

First, we need to work with watersheds, not against them, which means understanding how they work. This can mean simply knowing the way water naturally flows around your house, in your town, or across your state. We need to work with it, to help it to flow. While that should be such a simple thing, billions of dollars have been spent in doing just the opposite, in fighting the flow of water and separating it from the land it supports. That is what makes it complicated. Modern water infrastructure has served to centralize power in dangerous ways. It is the source of wars. It is old and colonial and outdated, but it is also the accepted norm around the world.

Next, we can start to think about alternatives to help unravel this narrative, this crumbling concrete nation. We can instead envision new ways of interacting with and thinking about water. This might mean hauling fish in a truck while waiting for the day that the river can do that work for us again. That simple act of hauling keeps alive the memory of a river long after its fate has been decided by politicians. That is why politicians find it so threatening, why they think that environmentalists are members of a "Doomsday cult." Memories *can be* extremely threatening. At the California Aquatic Science Center, a group of scientists and historians have tried to reconstruct what the San Joaquin River looked like before the Spanish arrived. They call it "historical ecology" and rely upon archival materials ranging from navigational charts to photographs and journals to try to recreate the Delta ecosystem of 200 years ago. Simply remembering, in this sense, is way of rebuilding.

Ancient aqueducts from Peru to India to Rome were designed both to follow water's natural flow and to be aesthetically appealing and complex. Today, we only have dams and canals endlessly punched out of the same modern blueprint, revealing a loss of system complexity. So how do we restore complexity, both biologically and aesthetically? In India, there is a movement to restore ancient community-built small dam systems, as well as the stunning stepwells of the old royalty. Making water systems visible and part of public life can help keep it out of dark, backroom political deals. In the U.S., fighting to end "dark money" in campaigns is another way to return water to the public. We need to restore the beauty of our relationship with water, to bring it into the light.

In short, we need twenty-first-century holistic alternatives, not nineteenth-century colonial dreams. For instance, a promising wild-crafting market is emerging in India in which high-value herbs and heritage seeds, grown in the wild, are marketed in tangent with Ayurvedic medicine through e-commerce. India's organic food industry is also growing at a rate of 25–40 percent a year. For architects, the challenge is to build for that, to wild-craft water for agro-forestry, knowing that bio- and human diversity is the key to healthy living. And to healthy rivers.

In his first week in office, Trump cut the Clean Water Rule, allowed coal ash to be dumped in the nation's waterways, and restarted the Dakota Access Pipeline, which threatens to contaminate groundwater. Now he wants to bring back the era of big dam-building, as he stated, "They don't even talk about dams anymore. You know hydropower is a great, great form of power," but "we don't even talk about it because the permits are virtually impossible" (Siciliano 2017). His solution was to cut the dam permitting time from ten years to one, which would make the Oroville Dam look like a model for dam safety, despite its catastrophic failure. Finally, Trump said he would only hire people who would "not seek to use their power to push an extreme environmental agenda" ("Presidential" 2016). For him, this means they cannot talk about climate change, since he has pulled out of the Paris Climate Accord.

Meanwhile in India, Modi developed his own list of "enemies," according to the *New Republic*, which includes "the beef-eaters [Muslims], the environmentalists, the university students, the feminists, the Dalits, the leftists, the dissenting writers, the skeptics, the 'antinationals'—anyone who will not declare, both fists clenched, '*Bharat Mata Ki Jai!*' (Mother India)." Modi's online mobs, which Salman Rushdie called "Modi Toadies," once attacked "libtards," "presstitutes," and "sickularists" in India, while Trump's trolls berated "libtards," "snowflakes," and "crybabies."

In times like these, I prefer to listen to rivers. Rivers are the ultimate symbol of border crossings—and deltas are their meeting grounds. Deltas are fragile places defined by an intimate dance between rivers and tides, yet they are also fortresses against a devouring sea. In the tangled web of deltas, there is a world that stops you in your tracks, a world full of life. There, you will find that rivers are committed to watersheds, not to "national water grids," flag-waving aqueduct openings, or large campaign donations. There, rivers speak the language of poetry, not the sound of stomping feet. Only in working with them, not against them, will any of us survive.

Notes

1 For a full analysis of this rally, see my California chapter in *The Price of Thirst: Water Inequality and the Coming Chaos* (2014).
2 A copy of the email was provided to me by Lloyd G. Carter, former UPI and *Fresno Bee* reporter, who has been covering valley agriculture and water for decades.
3 Rowland (2017) writes, "Bernhardt's lobbying firm owns 200,000 shares of the stock in Cadiz Inc, and stand[s] to earn nearly $3 million more if the Interior finalizes the decision."
4 There have been debates about who will pay for the WaterFix, but Trump continues—at least theoretically—to support the project (Lochhead 2017).
5 Most of the people displaced are Dalit or "tribal" people; we should remember that Americans did the same thing to indigenous people, actually setting a precedent for others to follow. See Hardikar (2013) for stories of displaced people in India.

References

Colvin, J. and Knickmeyer, E. (2016) "Trump vows to 'Open up the water' in drought-stricken California," *PBS NewsHour*, May 27. www.pbs.org/newshour/politics/trump-vows-to-open-up-the-water-in-drought-stricken-california (December 9, 2018).
Das, K. N. (2016) "Modi's BJP vows to strip Muslim immigrants of vote in Assam," *Reuters*, March 10. www.reuters.com/article/india-politics/modis-bjp-vows-to-strip-muslim-immigrants-of-vote-in-assam-idUSKCN0WC2WR (August 8, 2016).

Doyle, M. (2010) "California lawmaker's book pounds environmentalists," *McClatchy Newspapers*, September 30. www.mcclatchydc.com/news/politics-government/article24592231.html (December 5, 2016).

Ellis, J. (2016) "Trump belittles Clinton, whips Fresno crowd into frenzy," *The Fresno Bee*, May 27.

Hardikar, J. A. (2013) *Village Awaits Doomsday*, New York: Penguin.

Hiltzik, M. (2015) "The Cadiz Water Scheme: how political juice kept a bad idea alive for years," *Los Angeles Times*, October 7.

Hiltzik, M. (2018) "Loan to Jared Kushner raises questions about California water project," *Los Angeles Times*, March 7.

Hope, E. and Digby, W. (1900) *General Sir Arthur Cotton: His Life and Work*, London: Hodder and Stoughton.

Khan, D. (2016) "California growers' meeting with Trump draws Dem ire," *E&E Daily*, May 27. www.eenews.net/stories/1060038001 (November 15, 2016).

Lochhead, C. (2017) "Interior Department clarifies that it remains behind proposed Delta tunnels," *SFGate*, October 26. www.sfgate.com/news/article/Interior-Department-clarifies-that-it-remains-12306807.php (December 9, 2018).

Maitland, R. (1908) *Reminiscences of an Old English Civil Engineer, 1858–1908*, Portland, OR: Irwin-Hodson Company.

Perry, T. (2017) "Salton Sea inaction could cause 'catastrophic change,' report says," *Los Angeles Times*, January 12.

Piper, K. (2014) *The Price of Thirst: Water Inequality and the Coming Chaos*, Minneapolis: University of Minnesota Press.

"Presidential candidates answer farmers' and ranchers' questions" (2016) *FB News: The Official Newspaper of the American Farm Bureau Federation*, September 30. Online. Available (December 15, 2016).

Rowland, J. (2017) "Trump nominates Deputy Interior Secretary with serious conflicts of interest," *ThinkProgress*, April 28.

Sager, R. (2016) "Like Flint, water in California's Central Valley unsafe, causing health problems," *FoxNews*, March 8. www.foxnews.com/health/like-flint-water-in-californias-central-valley-unsafe-causing-health-problems (November 15, 2016).

Saikia, A. (2017) "The new Brahmaputra: a river festival in Assam draws criticism for promoting RSS brand of Hindutva," *Scroll.in*, April 5. https://scroll.in/article/833658/the-new-brahmaputra-a-river-festival-in-assam-draws-criticism-for-promoting-rss-brand-of-hindutva (May 1, 2017).

Siciliano, J. (2017) "Trump: hydropower is 'Great'," *The Washington Examiner*, April 4. www.washingtonexaminer.com/trump-hydropower-is-great (December 9, 2018).

Smith, A. H., Lingas, E. O., and Rahman, M. (2000) "Contamination of drinking-water by arsenic in Bangladesh: a public health emergency," *Bulletin of the World Health Organization* 78: 9.

Wolff, M. (2016) "Ringside with Steve Bannon at Trump Tower as the President Elect's strategist plots 'An Entirely New Political Movement,'" *The Hollywood Reporter*, November 16. www.hollywoodreporter.com/news/steve-bannon-trump-tower-interview-trumps-strategist-plots-new-political-movement-948747 (December 20, 2016).

Part V
Cityscapes

23
What Might Be
Re-describing Urbanscapes of the Global South

AbdouMaliq Simone

Reinventing Detachment

Does the Global South still exist? Had it ever existed? The clear lines once used to demarcate a developed from and an underdeveloped country, a First from a Third World, a metropole from a colonial world do not fit the extensive diversities of history and economy that characterize the countries of the "Non-West." Yet divides, exploitation, and vast disparities persist. Are there any clear ways to characterize them? These are questions we can deliberate forever. For now, I want to use the notion of the "South" as a tool for re-description. Where the hyphen between "re-" and "describe" points to a resistance to description—its making of narratives, orders, and connections between things—at the same time it performs this resistance through an incessant turning over of concepts and places, of constantly switching things around. Here the "South" is more important as a "wild card," a "joker," than being pinned down to specific values or meanings.

In urban studies today there is an intense obsession with describing what the urban actually is (Brenner and Schmid 2015). This obsession misses the extent to which the urban may exist as that which is somehow intrinsically immune to whatever we make of it. So instead of approaching particular spaces, built environments, or ways of living strategically as elements or evidence of particular principles, macro-forces, or structural arrangements, how can they be re-described as what Celia Lury (2012) refers to as n-dimension spaces, states of existence that *might be*.

This is not a matter of imagination, fantasy, or forward visualization. Rather, existent conditions are re-described as aspects of a process that might be taking place *right now*, but which is occluded or rendered inoperative simply because we are seeing and engaging the realities examined in a particular way. This is an "inventive method" in that it attempts to compose urban knowledge of *what can be as well as of what is* (Lury and Wakeford 2012). This is not a use of a method to establish or confirm knowledge of what the city or urban actually is, but knowledge of how different urban realities might be taking place at the same time, and what it would take to enact or experiment with them.

The Global South may not exist as a coherent political project, geographical region, sensibility or postcolony (Dabashi 2012; Sheppard et al. 2015). But I want to reiterate it here as a technology of detachment, inert, neither substance nor sense, that occasions the possibility of re-description (Agamben 2014). Samir Amin (1990) may have talked about the Third World detaching itself from global capital some decades ago, but the detachment I refer to here does not go anywhere in particular; it is a constant unsettling.

Somewheres Always Elsewheres

At the Venice Biennale of 2013, the Danish Pavilion presented a video installation of Jesper Just that portrayed three black men navigating a large exurban development, Tianducheng, some 200 miles from Shanghai. Tianducheng is built as an immense replica of Paris, or more precisely, an early modernist rendition of Paris. The city was initiated in the mid-2000s but remains largely under construction. Despite the aspirations for elegance, the rapidity and cheapness of the construction process renders much of the built landscape as already ruined.

Additionally, the inhabitants of the city have largely altered the supposedly Parisian characteristics of the place. They have removed the balconies and balustrades, and reworked the surfaces of buildings in order to make them more functional and long lasting. The black male characters assume different positions in relationship to this environment. One man is filmed walking through the expanse of the city as if carrying out some obligatory rite of passage that needs to be expeditiously experienced and then disposed of. Another presses his face closely to the surface of the buildings, inserting his body into their curvatures as if awaiting the words of some oracle, some secret to be revealed.

The exhibition demonstrates the simultaneously obdurate and exhausted imaginary of city form, the unyielding yet never kept promise of urban life. In contrast to the barriers and high costs entailed for Africans to access urban Europe—the supposed embodiment of "well-being"—the Chinese have mass-produced the surface representations of that well-being as cheap knock-offs. But instead of simply bemoaning the kitsch of such simulations or the ways in which simulations take on a reality more real than their referents, the "provision" of Paris in Tianducheng offers a way of activating different networks of urban comparison and thus potential.

Somewhere in between hyper-vigilance to the wisdom of Western urbanity and complete disattention to it, there might be a mixed bag of orientations that could inform serious experiments with the shaping of existent and emerging urban regions. First, it is increasingly possible to put up anything in the middle of nowhere. The results may not last, but the impractical is not a necessary deterrent to ciphers of elsewhere or to a past being instantiated anywhere. China, especially, has the money and political muscle to cite built environments anywhere and copy them at will. While such citation is a well-worn lesson of postmodernism, what is less considered is its inverse. In other words, what does exist does not necessarily have to function in the way it appears, is relegated, or conceived.

This applies not only to the now famous ghost towns of contemporary China, its vast underutilized and quickly ruined development projects, but to the seemingly haphazard, provisional constructions of urban districts whose sense of temporariness or imminent ruin has been much more long lasting. In cities across Asia and Africa residents constructed built environments that were not meant to last but have persisted long past their "expiration date," while, on the other hand, apparently definitive solutions to accommodate a particular population for a long-term future fall to ruin years before "their time" (Benjamin 2015; Sorace and Hurst 2015).[1]

What the comparison between Paris and Tianducheng, mediated by the images of African men, might also yield is the sense that the original Paris was built to be "messed with," defaced, and reworked. For the primary function of the surface of grandeur we associate with Paris was to get rid of the dingy well-worn, battle scarred, and largely impenetrable working-class neighborhoods and markets that made this city (Harvey 2005; Vidler 2011). In this way, Paris finds its actual realization in Tianducheng, particularly as the latter now acts as an available space of residence for both various aspirant and leftover populations. In a not dissimilar fashion, Paris, itself, endures in large part because so many different kinds of people from all over the world continue to pay attention to it as some kind of culmination of modernity even if they have to engage in practices and reside in dystopian landscapes that have little to do with that modernity (Garnier 2014).

Perhaps the critical dimension of this comparison is neither the real nor fake Paris, nor the permutations of their relationships, but the way in which Africa brings together France and China in this exhibition. They are brought together not only in the sense that destinations of sojourning and migration have shifted as Europe becomes more fortress-like or that more Africans will operate in China as an inevitable by-product of the enormity of China's presence in Africa.

But rather that the capacity of France to remain relevant as some kind of trope of modernity and for China to exemplify the capacity to mushroom urban landscapes anywhere largely depend on how Africans intersect, synthesize, or dispense with these capacities. This is because modernity could only initially consolidate itself in the violent renunciation of African human capability and where the financing available to develop a significant part of the infrastructure needed to accommodate a swelling African urban population is now contingent upon China's ongoing need to extract raw materials from the continent and generate multiplier effects from it (Chari 2015; Davies, Draper, and Edinger 2014). As many African cities depend upon men and women wandering through disposable, wasted, or thrown-together urban landscapes far from home, what will these aggregate exposures to a wider world of disparate cities, both copying and distancing themselves from each other, mean in terms of the ongoing shaping of African cities themselves?

For what after all is urban Africa? Far from being the last frontier or a largely rural region, Africa may seem like an elongated archipelago of disparate towns and cities punctuated by diverse morphological features and terrain, contested interstices, and consolidations of land for extraction or industrial agriculture. But to a large extent it operates as a near continuous stream of urban settlements of varied densities and built environments. While significant populations now residing in make-shift settlements will be pushed out as urban land prices increase, a more hopscotch, hodge-podge complexion will prevail, as settlements swell and contract, as higher-end built developments leapfrog over relatively immovable shantytowns.

Conurbations cross national borders; districts of enormous population densities will be interspersed with vast carpets of less dense, quasi-rural yet heavily populated regions. This landscape will be dotted by sporadic infrastructural articulations, replete with thousands of small connectors, buildings, and projects in various stages of completion. Any particular instantiation of settlement and work is likely to be insufficient to the processes of trying to sustain an individual or household over the long run and so the pursuit of urban livelihood will likely entail finding ways of being involved in projects elsewhere in this archipelago. It will entail mixtures of employment, entrepreneurship, cultivation, theft, borrowing, joint ventures, and speculation—where diverse activities act as hedges for each other (Fox 2012; Ernston, Lawhon, and Duminy 2014).

The salient comparison then will be of a Paris as if the Haussmann project never happened and to a Tianducheng that constructed itself as a Paris intentionally offered as a design meant to fall apart or never be completed. For an emergent urban Africa will be a landscape of hits and misses, of jumbled up textures and invisible edges, where different technical practices involving stitch, weave, solder, joint, hinge, fold, and glue will have to be elaborated in order to make disparate projects, buildings, practices, and populations go with each other. The African who presses his face to the wall in Jesper Just's video does so more to find ways of enjoining himself to this environment than he does to glean some secret beneath the surface.

Proliferating the Improper

These wanderings of African men through the half-ruined, half-to-be-built city of Tianducheng are certainly not unusual in African history, for the region has long experienced vast circulations of people, both volitional and involuntary. While not diminishing any sense of a person's right to place, a right to have a place to reside, there also needs to be what Corsin Jiminez (2014) identifies as a "right to infrastructure." This is a right to have access to the capacity to design the technical supports needed in order to cultivate place, even if place is only something temporary and where the activation of such a right might better enable people to move among places as a condition of both livelihood and aspiration. As Corsin Jiminez indicates, such right to infrastructure is materialized through the *prototype*, which is a continuous process of material and social elements acting on each other in open-ended fashion, what he calls the condition of being "beta."

Citing the example of open source hardware projects, the prototype is the concretization of the ability of people to shape their own "infrastructural being." In other words, an assemblage of codes, designs, patterns, maps, instructions, and drawings circulating in open source fashion gives rise to various experimental concretizations of tools, buildings, platforms, and conduits that need not take one particular shape or function. Rather, they vary according to the experimental conditions, participants, needs, and settings of realization. The material concretization of a hardware design gives rise to a specific social composition, as a specific social composition makes particular use of an open source hardware system. As Corsin Jiminez indicates, "prototypes are always, already 'pre-broken'." This is because their experimental conditions consist precisely in holding themselves up to deconstruction and reassembling. It is also in this sense that they work as "experiments in living," instantiations of the urban condition as a vital infrastructuring process.

Prototypes are detached from propriety, and if propriety plays a role it is not in the realization of specific designs but in the responsibility of thorough documentations of design processes. Thus in this reflection on Tianducheng, even its cheap imitation of a stereotypical image of Paris, while not a prototypical process as Corsin describes it, reflects the sense of models being "less than one and more than many." They are more than simply the replication of themselves across different scales. Rather, they proliferate in order to generate different forms and outcomes, where they are never complete in and of themselves. In this sense planning is something neither obsolete nor definitive, different models about how to build homes, handle waste, access water, or generate power can be designed and proposed without necessarily being imposed. While issues of affordability and financing are crucial, infrastructural rights as prototypes potentially open up the black box of how fundamental aspects of the urban actually work.

With a great deal of work trying to make cities smarter, through the implantation of sensors and WiFi networks, and the use of data tabulation marks and command models and the proliferation of various user interfaces providing information about services and locations, there are, at least theoretically, an increasing number of mechanisms for providing information about how the hardware of cities operates. While it is not expected that the enormity of scale and intricacy required for sophisticated material flow systems will be a matter of popular adaptation, there remain many domains of urban functioning that are at least matters of public concern and could be matters of public engineering.

The design and use of public spaces, distribution of goods, transport of materials and waste, reticulation of resources among local networks of residents and commerce, the design of public service facilities, recycling systems, and public information systems are potentially areas of not only social mobilization but of design and materialization in collaborations among fabricators, artisans, municipal officials, mechanics, artists, and craftsmen. These efforts might in turn bring into existence other formats of sociality through the very infrastructures that are produced (Thrift 2012).

At the same time, there is a pervasive sense of detachment in Just's depictions of these African men. This is a detachment supposedly remedied through more conscientious enactments of human interdependency with complex ecologies. Revivifying the importance of attachment to place, as an organic development would intensify demonstrations of responsibility to care for both the physical and social dimensions of the built environment, rendering them more sustainable and appropriate to the needs of those who inhabit it.

Yet as Claire Colebrook (2012) has incisively argued, such aspirations for a more organic attachment, one which downplays the centrality of human design as an overarching force in service of a more measured distribution of value across many different things, living and non-living, is always already infected by a violence that erases the specificity of everyday conditions in terms of a notion of life or the world in general. Getting beyond the condition where humans have such a hard time considering their own detachment and malevolence in relationship to an earth they continue to see as an environment *for them* always occurs through imagining some higher sense of "we," some greater collective good.

Given this, we may have to detach ourselves from convictions that the virtuous is restored through recognizing our proper place within complex ecologies. We may have to achieve this detachment in order to fully appreciate the ways in which cities are full of many different kinds of forces and that cities are not just for us. They are neither the embodiment of all that needs to be rescued or redeemed nor are they the launching pads for that very salvation. That cities are full of forces that have nothing to do with us does not rule out the ability of people to stay in place. But it means that any stability is a matter of constant recalibration, of ducking and diving, and riding waves, and not insisting upon particular grounds of propriety, property, or entrenchment.

Such a strategic sense of detachment is not an easy thing to consider, especially in light of what Saskia Sassen (2014) calls the proliferation of expulsions. Here new systemic "edges" are constituted in the midst of places with defined characteristics—homes, nation-states, cultures—and from which particular actors and practices are cast out of relevance. For example real things and the value they have for production and use often become irrelevant for the calculation of value through financial instruments, which use these things—their availability now and in the future—as the occasion to speculate on probable futures. Despite the brutality of such calculations they nevertheless point to the urgency of re-describing the ways in which we understand and engage the complexities of urban life and those that inhabit increasingly precarious cities.

The Uninhabitable as Strategic Essential

Khavn de la Cruz's film *Ruined Heart* is one example of how detachment ushers in new, albeit troubling, ways of seeing and re-describing. Set in Quezon City, the film is a prime example of the Filipino genre that some have called "the deep South," reflecting an atmosphere traumatized by systematic violence, of unsettled racial, religious, and political turbulence. Pointing also to the passions of the U.S. deep South and metaphorically to all of the unresolved ruptures and potentials still embedded in cities seemingly swept away in the dreary formatting of land-rent-inspired accumulation, "the deep South" is a place of both what Lucas Bessire (2014) calls "negative immanence" and insistent distinction.

AbdouMaliq Simone

Rather than sustaining the semblance of normative forms of the human in heroic but ultimately debasing struggles to survive conditions where you don't know where the next "assault" is coming from, residents self-consciously embrace various mutant forms of the inhuman, turning delirium into reason (and vice versa). Rather than seeing the urban poor and marginal as defeated shadows unable to resist systematic dehumanization, this new genre of Filipino filmmaking renders this detachment as a strategic indifference to the theft of their capabilities, and their appropriation of animal, spiritual, and other hybrid figures as a means to keep the city in their grip.

The film has no story or, rather entertains whatever narrative the spectator wants to make of it. The film's title is simply accompanied with the designation of "another love story between a criminal and a whore." Characters have no name, but at the outset are simply designated by their function—"criminal," "lover," "friend," "pianist," "whore," and "boss." It is a minimalist world, where one's fate comes down to the alignment of a few elements, but set against an urban background where all kinds of people are dealing with each other all of the time. While these deals are important, they also go nowhere except for another round of deal making. Even if everyone seems to be paying attention to what is going on and are always offering themselves up to be captivated by one scheme, one trickster, evangelist, patron, or politician after another, they, in the end, seem indifferent to the fierce battles of individuals to stay afloat taking place all around them.

In the film, the usual order of things—the by now banal, exhaustive hierarchies of social power—is once again interrupted by a usual array of passions. Or, rather, the interdictions concerning who can be with whom, who can do what to whom, are transgressed, even as all the parties know full well where this transgression leads. They may be exhausted with revenged betrayals and displays of disrespect. The bosses know full well that their power is a show that is over if it fails to entertain and are, at the same time, bored with the injunction that the "show must go on." Still, all the characters go ahead and play out the predictable scenario until the end. In this film, the relationship between the male criminal and the woman who is the boss's "property" comes seemingly out of nowhere, and only as they try to run off to avoid the unavoidable do they discover some "real details" about each other.

The film finds it hard to accord definition to any space, to determine whether something is inside or outside, as the frontiers between households, between political rally, church service, occult ceremony, carnival, sports event, musical show, and family gathering blur into each other. In doing so, residents lose their anchorage, but no one seems to mind. Everyone has some recourse to each other detached as they are from the bounds of propriety, which make the claims of property and events of betrayal all that more anachronistic. At one point, as the criminal and whore are in the midst of making love, the criminal reaches for a huge telephone book of Manila and smothers the whore's face with it as he rips it apart, page after page, as both head towards climax. Here, one of the city's basic catalogues of identification and location is torn apart, as if no one has a right to even the most bureaucratic attachment.

It is interesting that the place where the two lovers on the run are able to assume some kind of "normal" scene of intimacy—up until then played out in Fellini-like displays of street parties—is in an empty single room in a yet to be occupied boarding house—now seemingly detached from the world. The boarding house has become one of the key tropes for the circulation of youth in many cities of the South today. This cheap accommodation without long-term obligation acts as a node that enables youth to move from one job to another in different parts of the city, looking to hang on, quickly make their mark, or insert themselves into opportunities that are ever-more fleeting and nearly impossible to plan for. The key is how to be in the right place at the right time, and this means detaching oneself from as many obligations and fixed identities as possible. This requires an infrastructure, and here the boarding house plays an important role.

No matter how detached, it doesn't mean that residents don't engage. While they hide out in a lower-working-class suburb, bordering on a small and cheap amusement park, the whore, freed from enforced promiscuity, spends most of her time playing silly chase and tickling games with scores of local children and in the process makes sure that all of them are touched, all of them are recognized even though she has nothing else to offer, only passing through, and is soon to be shot dead.

The "deep South," although it may point to histories and tactics of detachment, is not something fundamentally apart. We may recognize it as something of particular parts of the world or of every city, but it points to the fact that force, whatever it is, can exceed the bounds placed on it. It leaks, radiates, and affects in ways that cannot always be anticipated and controlled. Thus any occurrences can ramify across each other, affecting and being affected in ways that exceed whatever infrastructure is available. The turbulence of the "popular quarters" of cities may be largely constrained but it does not go away, it is always there, as if nothing *really happens*. It is not that the residents of all the back alley universes of Quezon City have failed to resist or put all of their cards into futile acts of redemption. Rather, they endure through stealth, through acts of apparent compliance or insanity that cover up the fact that they are already elsewhere than where we expect them or have chosen to embrace the waste to which they have been relegated as a ruined heart still beating.

Across the world, the streets, the police, the social welfare institutions, the schools, the penal system, and the courts may have largely worn down the capacities of many residents to effectively improvise their existence, to wheel and deal their way into greater opportunities. Cooperation and collaboration may be precarious and short-lived. These same residents may largely be detached from any sense of aspiration and conviction. Instead of efforts to restore the marginalized and diminished into a fuller human existence, it may be necessary to concede to this detachment and envision ways of etching out a social fabric where the boundaries between the virtuous and destructive are erased; where there are no sustainable entities called households, schools, churches, or markets, and where bodies and lives are affixed to provisional structures, techniques, and practices that have no clear dispositions in advance.

It may be necessary to concede space to the inhabitation of the city by "creatures" who have been there in one way or another all along, even though there may be nothing healthy, worthy, or sustainable about them in the terms of efficacy long preferred. It is not that we claim the end of dignity or justice, but rather the need to take risks of new ways of seeing what might otherwise be abject or irrelevant. We might continue to wish for the equality of all, the fulfillment of everyone's human potentials. But the city may have pretended to have such aspirations in mind, but has never worked on this principle. As cities cease to work in many respects, it is important to engage what the variegated inhabitants of the urban actually do to each other, and find within the confusion and ambiguity lines to follow, cultivate, and re-describe.

Note

1 See Danny Hoffman's essay in this volume.

References

Agamben, G. (2014) "What is destituent power?," *Environment and Planning D: Society and Space* 32, 1: 65–74.
Amin, S. (1990) *Delinking: Towards a Polycentric World*, London: Zed Books.
Benjamin, S. (2015) "Cities within and beyond the plan," in C. Bates and M. Mio (eds) *Cities in South Asia*, London and New York: Routledge, 98–119.
Bessire, L. (2014) *Behold the Black Caiman: A Chronical of Auyero Life*, Chicago and London: University of Chicago Press.

Brenner, N. and Schmid, C. (2015) "Towards a new epistemology of the urban?," *CITY* 19, 2–3: 151–182.
Chari, S. (2015) "African extraction, Indian Ocean critique," *South Atlantic Quarterly* 114, 1: 83–100.
Colebrook, C. (2012) "A globe of one's own: in praise of the flat earth," *SubStance* 41, 1, 127: 30–39.
Dabashi, H. (2012) *The Arab Spring: The End of Postcolonialism*, London: Zed Books.
Davies, M., Draper, P., and Edinger, H. (2014) "Changing China, changing Africa: future contours of an emerging relationship," *Asian Economic Policy Review* 48, 2: 180–197.
Ernston, H., Lawhon, M., and Duminy, J. (2014) "Conceptual vectors of African urbanism: 'Engaged Theory-Making' and 'Platforms of Engagement'," *Regional Studies* 48, 9: 1563–1577.
Fox, S. (2012) "Urbanization as a global historical process: theory and evidence from sub-Saharan Africa," *Population and Development Review* 38, 2: 285–310.
Garnier, J.-P. (2014) "'Greater Paris': urbanization but no urbanity: how Lefebvre predicted our metropolitan future," in A. Moravanszky, C. Schmid, and L. Stanek (eds) *Urban Revolution Now: Henri Lefebvre in Social Research and Architecture*, Farnham, Surrey and Burlington, VT: Ashgate, 133–156.
Harvey, D. (2005) *Paris: Capital of Modernity*, London and New York: Routledge.
Jiminez, A. Corsin (2014) "The right to infrastructure: a prototype for open source urbanism," *Environment and Planning D: Society and Space* 32, 2: 342–362.
Lury, C. (2012) "Going live: towards an amphibious sociology," *Sociological Review* 60, Issue Supplement S1: 184–197.
Lury, C. and Wakeford, N. (eds) (2012) *Inventive Methods: The Happening of the Social*, London and New York: Routledge.
Sassen, S. (2014) *Expulsions: Brutality and Complexity in the Global Economy*, Cambridge, MA and London: Harvard University Press.
Sheppard, E., Gidwani, V., Goldman, M., Leitner, H., Roy, A., and Maringanti, A. (2015) "Introduction: urban revolutions in the age of global urbanism," *Urban Studies* 52, 11: 1947–1961.
Sorace, C. and Hurst, W. (2015) "China's phantom urbanisation and the pathology of ghost cities," *Journal of Contemporary Asia*. DOI:10.1080/00472336.2015.1115532. Accessed: January 12, 2016.
Thrift, N. (2012) "The insubstantial pageant: producing an untoward land," *Cultural Geographies* 19, 2: 141–168.
Vidler, A. (2011) *The Scenes of the Street and Other Essays*, New York: Monacelli Press.

24

Watching the City
A Genealogy of Media Urbanism

Joshua Neves

Media changed the flesh of infrastructure.

(Sundaram 2010)

In a well-known essay, Michel de Certeau laid out what has become a common distinction for understanding urban visuality. He distinguishes between "seeing" Manhattan from atop the former World Trade Center, on the one hand, and the embodied practice of walking in the city, on the other. As part of a larger project investigating *The Practice of Everyday Life*, the two examples are instructive. De Certeau rightly worries about the strange voyeurism of "seeing the whole," which offers spectators a god-like view of a seemingly coherent and transparent text. Or as he puts it: "the panorama-city is a 'theoretical' (that is, visual) simulacrum, in short a picture, whose condition of possibility is an oblivion and misunderstanding of practices" (de Certeau 1984: 93). In contrast to this view from on high, he stakes his own interest on ordinary practices of doing and making, in this case, walking. Walking, he tells us, occurs "below the threshold at which visibility begins."

I begin with this well-worn tale because it both continues to have a good deal to teach us, and overstates its case. The pairing serves as a good metaphor for de Certeau's interest in above and below, reading and writing, the monumental and the mundane. But it is just that: a rhetorical device that helps him to situate his intervention towards much overlooked and misunderstood aspects of everyday life. The problem with the dichotomy is that it both conflates the practical or micro with the concrete—other scales too can be textured—and forecloses other practices and possible points of reference. My interest here is not, however, to critique de Certeau so much as to signal how his earlier intervention casts a shadow onto contemporary debates in ways that may be out of sync with present concerns: the relationship between the seeing and the city has changed.

I think it is fair to say that de Certeau's critique of "imaginary totalizations" is also targeted at the kinds of pictures and "optical knowledge" circulated by cinema, TV, photography, among other media—and not, that is, the relatively uncommon practice of standing atop monumental towers. I linger on this point because it is this aspect of de Certeau's spectrum that I want to focus on in this chapter. While I remain committed to charting "microbe-like" spatial practices, and to their capacity to disrupt dominant epistemologies, I want to pursue another genealogy of seeing or, as I would have it, *watching* the city (de Certeau 1984: 96). This approach starts by rerouting de Certeau in a couple of ways. First, de Certeau's focus on "pedestrian speech acts" seems to overlook the basic and intensifying imbrication of media technologies and representations (panoramic to POV) within the field of everyday life—including walking (de Certeau 1984: 97). These domains cannot be so easily disarticulated and, in fact, to separate them is to misread the thicket of the ordinary. Second, de Certeau's critique of top-down visuality as a hegemonic force—"a picture, whose condition of possibility is an oblivion"—shuts out alternate practices of encounter. In this context, the *theoretical* is not simply the opposite of *practical*—as his example seems to suggest—but is another and entangled tool for engaging the kinds of subaltern and popular itineraries at the center of his own project.

Contrary to de Certeau's anxiety about the city-as-picture, the urban planner Kevin Lynch theorized the abstract *image of the city* held by residents to be constitutive of urban form. He emphasized, for instance, how the clarity of such mental images was crucial to quality of life—to occupying cities that are beautiful, meaningful, secure (Lynch 1960: 2–3). For Lynch, this posed important design problems: how to make cities whose physical organization and sensual cues were in tune with human communities and ways of life. What he called "legibility" was part of a feedback loop between urbanites and the city. As Lynch writes, "the environment suggests distinctions and relations, and the observer—with great adaptability and in the light of his own purposes—selects, organizes, and endows with meaning what he sees" (Lynch 1960: 6). Thus spaces that are too precisely ordered can also inhibit the co-creation of this mental picture.

Importantly, Lynch is interested not in individual but *public images* shared by many residents: "areas of agreement" that cohere in the "interaction of a single physical reality, a common culture, and a basic physiological nature" (Lynch 1960: 7). What he calls *imageability*—also, *legibility* or *visibility*—is the textures or qualities of the city that are likely to generate meaningful images in inhabitant-observers: "shape, color, or arrangement" and "a heightened sense, where objects are not only able to be seen, but are presented sharply and intensely to the sense" (Lynch 1960: 9–10). Writing in the late 1950s, he is caught up with the possibility of remaking the urban, and sees the *image of the city*, the capacity to clearly and meaningfully locate oneself, as a crucial part of reconfiguring the "total environment" (Lynch 1960: 13). This aspect of Lynch's argument will be familiar to many readers via its adaptation by Frederic Jameson as "cognitive mapping" (Jameson 1991)—an analogy to his own project of disalienation and the difficulty of locating oneself in the fast transforming world system (Figure 24.1).

These well-known formulations suggest both distinct ways of seeing the city—the big and small, cognitive and enacted—and, at the same time, have a good deal in common. For example, while Lynch's image of the city is tilted towards the bigger picture, he is also interested in how meaningful social pictures are co-produced in practice—and not only imposed by towering specularities or grand urban designs. Further, and like de Certeau, Lynch's focus on visuality in terms of perception, imagination, even ideology, does not take into account actual engagements with images, media artifacts, or media ecologies. What interests me about their influential approaches is this: each offers a model of urban visuality that is decidedly devoid of media forms and practices. To borrow a phrase from Ravi Sundaram, they seem to theorize an urban world *before media* (Sundaram 2010: 21). It is this entanglement, intensified by lo-fi and hi-tech digital practices, that I trace as *media urbanism* in this chapter. Put otherwise, I want to extend or adapt the abovementioned approaches in the context of our present dilemmas.

Figure 24.1 Images of the city increasingly from everyday urban architectures and experience. A construction site in Beijing's Doncheng District is fenced in with images of a future park, left, while cars and cyclists pass by, right

Source: Photograph courtesy of Graham Bury.

Joshua Neves

Media + Splintered Urbanism

These dilemmas are manifold, but let's begin this reorientation with two assertions. First, and most basic, engagements with urban visuality can no longer rely upon idealized images of Western cities and perambulations as their sole data. While thinkers like Lynch and de Certeau no doubt remain important, we also need to push beyond Franco-Anglo imaginaries and proscriptions—acknowledging the deeply political nature of these lingering postcards. This, of course, includes attending the massive inequity at the heart of the Northern metropolis. Second, the emphasis on cities as spaces of specularity and spectacle, leisure and consumption, has tended to make peripheral the politics of the *polis* itself: the architectonics of urban life push well beyond discussions of the *flâneur* and *flâneuse*, among similar preoccupations.[1] Such conceptualizations too often take for granted normalized conditions of (il)legality, (non)citizenship, displacement, segregation, and occupation, among other markers of difference and differentiation that are crucial to everyday urban encounters and city images, big and small.

My entry point into this splintered media urban domain is, perhaps counterintuitively, through photography. What Ariella Azoulay terms *the civil contract of photography* offers a generative aperture into the political relations animated by visual encounters. Her theorization stems from pictures of injury and displacement—such as photographs of Palestinians in the Occupied Territories—and the sense that such images show more than "what was being done to" those displaced (Azoulay 2008: 12). Instead, such images carve out a "civil political space." This civil political space, she observes, works against the image bank of dominant culture (what Azoulay terms "planted" pictures): "Because photographs, unlike planted pictures, have no single, individual author, in principle, they allow civic negotiations about the subject they designate and about their sense" (Azoulay 2008: 13–14). Her articulation makes two valuable points about engaging and unraveling visual fixity and address. First, such images belong to *no one* and as such the spectator is not simply addressed by the photographs, but is an "addressee" who can produce and disseminate her own meanings from the images. Second, the pictures shore up an entangled set of social relations that include the photographer, the spectator, and the photographed subject(s). Crucially, this ensemble restores the *captured subject* to a position of significance and capacity—and does not simply focus on the activities of photographers and viewers, as is the habit in many visual fields.

To trace this civil political space, Azoulay argues, we need to stop *looking at* photographs and start *watching* them. She writes:

> The verb "to watch" is usually used for regarding phenomena or moving pictures. It entails dimensions of time and movement that need to be reinscribed in the interpretation of the still photographic image. When and where the subject of the photograph is a person who has suffered some form of injury, a viewing of the photograph that reconstructs the photographic situation and allows a reading of the injury inflicted on others becomes a civic skill, not an exercise in aesthetic appreciation.
>
> (Azoulay 2008: 14)

This is to say that the civic skill of "watching" insists on more than the common idea that photography (cinema, TV, etc.) essentially represents something that *was there*. Rather it also testifies to the "fact that the photographed *people* were there." And assuming that the photographed people are *still there* at the time of watching, the photograph, Azoulay continues, reanimates the political relations of the governed (2008: 16–17).

She proceeds by reinstating a basic fact in political theory: citizens *too* are governed. This actuality is too often disremembered because the legal and ideological bonds between state and citizen seem to operate above and against non-citizens, and others acting outside of the formal spheres produced and policed by the state. Azoulay's aim is to disrupt the formal affinity between state and citizen, and instead to energize the space of relations *among the governed*—including both citizens and non-citizens. In this context, "political duty" is primarily a responsibility to one another, rather than "toward the ruling power" (Azoulay 2008: 17). This sense of social responsibility and connection flies directly in the face of the commonsense duty articulated by the nation-state, as well as the biopolitical and bourgeois pedagogical projects that pit citizens against non-citizens on issues ranging from migration, jobs, and illegal housing to health care, sexuality, piracy, and myriad ways of life pushed to the edge of the licit city.[2] In contrast, Azoulay's theorization of the civil contract uniting the governed instantiates a new mode of negotiation: the "demand not to be ruled in this way" (2008: 16).

To make sense of this mediatic relation, one thread of Azoulay's project is to examine the politics of the gaze in photographs of vulnerable subjects. She asks: "Does their use of photography express a civic skill that they possess?" and "Why are they looking at me?" Such questions recalibrate the politics of witnessing associated with images of displacement and disaster. It suggests a temporal shift that refuses the assumption that what is captured in such pictures is "over and done with"—an assumption that would foreclose the political assemblage at issue here (Azoulay 2008: 19). Thus, Azoulay argues, when a Hebron merchant whose business has been destroyed by occupying forces stares into the camera it is not primarily to demand remuneration for lost property. Rather, it is to refuse the position of noncitizenship imposed on him by the state, and to demand "participation in a sphere of political relations within which his claims can be heard and acknowledged" (Azoulay 2008: 20). Azoulay's theorization reinterprets the social duties of spectatorship and image making as a civil skill and matter of political will. Further, her understanding signals the political volatility associated with the distribution of images, including how they are embedded in the city itself. This includes the way that captured subjects utilize official media to transmit their own claims and to alter the ways they are governed.[3]

Here I want to extend Azoulay's *watching*, and "dimensions of time and movement," to the media city. For de Certeau, Lynch, and related scholars, engaging the city, of course, very much includes attending to the movement (e.g., walking) and temporalities that constitute everyday actions and imaginaries. What needs to be "reinscribed" is thus not a focus on ordinary spatial practices (though these spatial practices need to extend to the media field), but rather the interpretive modes connecting micro practices to the bigger picture. This relational approach expands the scale of agency beyond the extremely local and the pre-visible, and opens our attention onto media urbanism—including the ordinary inhabitations that must constantly shift between close-ups and panoramic views, the city and its images.

Media urbanism is a concept I import from Ravi Sundaram's provocative engagement with contemporary Delhi—*Pirate Modernity: Delhi's Media Urbanism* (2010). In particular, Sundaram is interested in the ways digital technologies, including their lo-fi, recycled, and piratical forms, have become imbricated in the fabric and experience of urban life. He writes, for example: "'media' now permeates not just the lives of Delhi's residents, but inflects political and cultural processes: court judgments, road deaths, video piracy, encounter deaths and terrorism, and the displacement of the urban poor from river-front settlements" (Sundaram 2010: xiv). In short, Sundaram draws our attention to the formal and informal technologization of the urban, including its new and contested role in everyday life, our dreams and desires, and techniques of governance. Contra the fabulation of New York, London, and Tokyo as the emblematic global media capitals, Sundaram insists that Southern cities too are *media cities*—and in ways not accounted for by current models of urban visuality or understandings of media environments (2010: 2).

Joshua Neves

Watching the Media City

Watching the media city is to see the city in a different way. Further it is to begin to articulate a critical vocabulary and mode of encounter adequate to the everyday textures and inhabitations of actually existing cities. This is significant for numerous reasons, not the least of which is the increasing illegalization of everyday life—from aliens, squatters, and the violently policed to cultural/economic pirates and normalized neoliberal disposability. In this context, Azoulay's formulation helps us to recalibrate urban specularity as a political assemblage—and not aesthetic appreciation. It emphasizes the common social project of the governed contra governmentality—against, that is, the biopolitical mechanisms that work to divide and immunize populations. This civil political space also insists upon tracing such relationships over time and in their mobilities so that variegated actors, including non-citizens, etc., are understood to make political claims on the social. Finally, this discussion also draws our attention to current tensions between representational and materialist methodologies. If recent decades have been marked by spatial, anthropological, and materialist "turns," in what follows I return afresh to the problem of representation, and the imbrication of urban images within the city itself.

To give texture to this proposal let us consider two entangled examples related to Beijing's media urbanism in the first decade of the twenty-first century. Each signals contemporary problems related to urban visuality, digital proliferation, and (un)civil political relations. I turn to these examples because I know them well and because they signal key textures of what I am calling *watching the city*. My aim is not to single-out China—which is too often the case in both popular and academic accounts—but instead to signal some of the ways media reconstitute urban experience and everyday politics. In other words, the contested or illicit urban formation at issue here is a structural problem across the world system. This chapter could have just as "easily" focused on media urbanism through the lens of murderous policing, social abandonment, and innumerable other structural violences that animate Western fantasy cities like New York or Paris, among many other sites.

China's New Documentary Film Movement offers a good illustration of new media's transformative relationship with the city. Alongside fictional filmmaking and other mediations, this often lo-tech and street-level documentary culture emerged in the late 1990s with the availability of cheap digital cameras and editing software, as well as easy forms of distribution like the VCD/DVD, informal exhibition sites, and the like. While broad in scope, New Documentary films have paid close attention to the textures of urban life and, in particular, developed observational techniques suitable to its focus on marginal lifeworlds and uneven development. Wang Wo's 2005 observational documentary *Outside* (*Waimian*) exemplifies this mode of watching the city. The work is interesting for its focus on outdoor and public spaces in Beijing, and neighboring cities (literal "outsides"), its interest in visually theorizing the everyday forms of marginality through which the city reproduces itself ("outsiders"), as well as its informal aesthetic. Shot over a period of five years (2001–2005), the film's perambulatory mode and unusual use of long shots and close-ups return us squarely to the issues of urban visuality with which we began.

The documentary opens in Tiananmen Square, China's most famous outside space, and immediately pressures the distinct forms of seeing possible in the Square—cutting between the official viewpoint of Tiananmen's lookout to a low-angle reverse shot peering back from the Square itself. Next, the camera-observer wanders through the concrete blocks of the Square. We see a young girl drinking a bottle of water while watching tourists and marching soldiers take up space in their unique ways. Visitors get their pictures taken in front of the Chairman's portrait; Wang's camera angle superimposes their faces over Mao's own image, also glimpsing the ubiquitous CCTV cameras. The camera then tilts upward 180 degrees across the sky, gazing at the sun (a common Mao symbol, and index of pollution), before resting on the upside-down image of the Monument to the People's Heroes and Chairman Mao's Mausoleum, and slowly tilting back. Soon after, we leave the familiar space of the Square and become lost in the city—far from Beijing's monumental images and sites. Much of the remainder of the documentary unfolds as if a walk through the margins of the city, focusing on a range of people at play, work, drunk, fighting, sleeping, pissing, waiting, or harassed by security guards, police, and rubbernecking crowds.

Of particular interest is the film's strategic use of zooms. Crucial to this mode of capture are scenes that begin with intimate, close-up shots of street life: a couple holding hands, a disabled man's attempt to steal rebar from a construction site, workers asleep along the railroad tracks. After lingering in proximate observation, the camera then slowly zooms out to reveal its position far from the action. In one scene on a train platform, we watch as migrants and others without appropriate urban registration (*hukou*) are loaded onto a train and out of the metropolis—a common occurrence in the lead up to the 2008 Olympics. The scene is captured from a hidden camera position, at once close to the action and out of the police's view. Young men in military uniforms and police officials fill the frame, guiding, sometimes with force, the "floating" workers (*liudong renkou*) onto train cars and out of the city. For several minutes we watch row after row shuffle onto the train, the camera occasionally lingering to accentuate a young woman in a pink tank-top, a Uighur man spitting, or onlookers attempting to make sense of the action. One worker, squatting in the line, recognizes the camera with a knowing look of complicity.

In another sequence, near the end of the film, a couple walks and argues in a small concrete square alongside decaying courtyard-style homes. The scene lasts several minutes and roughly 17 shots, and though the viewer inhabits a different sonic space from the action, one has the feeling of being *on the scene*. Half way through the segment, the argument abruptly subsides and the two begin to waltz. After some time in close observation, cutting and panning to keep the dancers in frame, the camera slowly peels back to reveal its hidden position high up in a building several hundred yards from the scene of action. An immense landscape is laid bare, including newly erected skyscrapers, building cranes, and a moving train bisecting the frame from right to left. This technologized vision literally penetrates the scene to represent daily acts that would otherwise be below the "threshold of visibility." It plays on surveillance to reveal fullness (Figures 24.2a and 24.2b).

What I want to emphasize here is how the poetics of these sequences, among many similar shots in the documentary, inscribe a new dialectic between street-level practices and the panoramic gaze. The extreme close-up, with its exaggerated focal length, wobbles, is soft in focus, and shallow depth, whereas the long shot is crisp, still, and captures the city in deep focus. But my interest here is in neither the visual verisimilitude of the close-up nor the panoramic shot, but rather the relationship between the two. In other words, what is crucial here is *the zoom itself*. The zoom signals a form of cognitive mapping shored up by digital urbanism. It suggests new capacities for penetrating the city and meaningfully locating oneself within and across a social spectrum. Here panoramic distance both takes on a new relation to spatial practice and allows for a kind of visual intimacy—a complex relation between videographer, spectator, the city, and its subjects—operating as a counter surveillance.

While some viewers, especially foreign audiences, have reacted to the film's voyeurism—the way it captures people from a distance and without their knowledge—the layered "watching" in *Outside* can also be understood to foster a civil political space of connection. At one level this includes the textual emphasis on the videographer and spectator, but it also extends to the way marginalized populations use and become entangled in such claims—as with the knowing look

Figures 24.2a and 24.2b Wang Wo's *Outside* focuses on street-level practices, like fighting or dancing, before zooming out to reveal the larger urban fabric and the cinematographer's distant position

from the deported migrant on the train platform. More than the digital affordances suggested by the New Documentary Movement, and the brief example of the zoom, this also signals a range of new publicities articulated by the production, distribution, and exhibition of media. For example, scholars and practitioners have emphasized how the *xianchang* (on the scene) mode of production, hand-to-hand forms of distribution, or informal networks for archiving and exhibiting such works are what gives them social meaning. What matters about independent video, in this view, are not the films themselves but the social infrastructures and affinities that they inaugurate: images of urban life seep into everyday urban practices and social imaginations.

If Wang's *Outside* emphasizes the informal and mediatic relations among the governed, a second set of examples tilts more towards the official operations of the technologized city. My focus here is on the explosion of screens across urban space—from terminals in buses, subways, and train stations, to sidewalks, elevators, and the large-format displays embedded in building façades. These screens draw our attention to the digital extension of media forms as an urban process. As I have argued elsewhere, what is significant here is the way that formal screen industries emerge both in response to the proliferation of informal devices and practices, as well as to substantive shifts in economic organization, mobility, urban living (see, for instance, Neves 2014; 2011). If televisual address has largely been theorized for its role in the home, and for its communicative function in a social formation based on what Raymond Williams has termed "mobile privatization" (Williams 2003: 19–21) my interest is to chart the explosion of TV sets and settings across the media urban field (Figure 24.3).

Two sets of examples are instructive. First is the rise of state-corporate non-domestic TV industries and consoles in the early 2000s in Beijing and across other major cities in China. Beijing All Media and Culture Group (BAMC), for example, formed in 2001 to support a range of out-of-home television ventures, including City TV (*chengshi dianshi*), Mobile TV (*yidong dianshi*), and Metro TV (*ditie dianshi*). This "outdoor video media platform" operates hundreds of screens across the city: in parks, shopping districts, historical sites, on building façades, buses, subways, train stations, and more (Neves 2011: 33–34). As suggested above, this explosion of formal TV screens into everyday city spaces both works against proliferating informal TV cultures (smart phones to sidewalk consoles) as well as other forms of self-programming shored up by alternative video/documentary, mobile media, and the Internet. Thus, City TV signals a new capacity by state-corporate media to engage a fractured TV audience across a wide range of daily itineraries: on the bus, sidewalk, bathroom, elevator, and so on. This proliferating urban footprint is quite distinct from informal TV sets and settings. Unlike sidewalk screens or mobile devices that might play a DVD, downloaded files, or simply be switched off, one has little control over the channel, volume, location, etc. of screens on the metro.

One way to understand the proliferation of non-domestic televisions is through the lens of China's massive and semi-permanent population of migrant workers—the so-called "floating" population. What I have termed *unhomely television* describes a mode of economic organization, everyday living, and televisual address where over 250 million people, many of them at work on new urban infrastructures or making screen devices in microelectronic factories, are not home at 7pm for China Central Television's nightly news (*xinwen lianbo*)—a broadcast carried by all stations (Neves 2014: 62–64). In contrast to Raymond Williams' notion of "mobile privatization"—which assumes a home centered living combined with daily commutes to work—this social address aims to court and reconnect a range of bodies not reached by domestic TV (Williams 2003 [1974]: 19–21). Strangely, the idea of "mobile privatization" holds in this context, only it needs to be resignified to describe the specificities of China's postsocialist neo-liberalism. Here privatization does not describe suburban nuclear family living, though, of course, this too exists, but rather an economic logic where workers must compete in a marketized

Figure 24.3 The LED Sky Screen at The Place shopping mall in Beijing's Chaoyang District shows looping nature videos and live TV broadcasts

Source: Copyright Joshua Neves.

Watching the City: A Genealogy of Media Urbanism

Figure 24.4 A migrant worker watches broadcast TV on a large screen attached to Beijing's Worker's stadium ahead of the 2008 Olympic Games

Source: Photograph courtesy of Graham Bury.

zone marked by both the withdrawal of state support and the persistence of centralized control (Figure 24.4).

Finally, a crucial aspect of urban TV systems is the way they frame images of the city within the city itself: on sidewalk screens, embedded within architectural forms, on public transportation, and so on. This shift asks us to reconsider the very idea of "tele-visuality"—the commonsense formulation of TV in English and many European languages, as well as de Certeau's understanding of urban specularity as constituted through distant panoramas. Instead, the city-within-the-city structure, shores up new forms of *paravisuality*, where what is pictured onscreen is not distant (tele-) but near (Neves 2014: 57). This includes watching an advertisement on the bus for a business or cultural site just outside the window, or news programs transmitting images and stories about the street or building you are "watching." This media urbanism draws our attention to the basic interpenetration of city scales (street-level to the panoramic), urban ontologies (distinct registers of urban experience, including their remediation across screens and the city), and everyday practices and imaginaries. Walking in the city can longer be understood as an activity below or before visibility. Instead, drawing on Azoulay and others, my argument here is that *watching the city* suggests a new genealogy from which to make sense of the city and its images, including the social infrastructures and assemblages such pictures make disappear or bring into view.

Notes

1 Ann Friedberg (1993), among many others, has taken up Walter Benjamin's urban stroller, including its feminine articulations.
2 This distinction between what constitutes the population, and what is outside of it, is crucial to Michel Foucault's understanding of biopower and racism. See, for example, Michel Foucault, *Society Must Be Defended: Lectures at the College de France, 1975–1976*, trans. David Macey (New York: Picador, 2003); also: Roberto Esposito, *Immunitas: The Protection and Negation of Life* (Cambridge, UK: Polity Press, 2011).
3 This discussion is expanded in Chapter 1 of my forthcoming monograph, *Underglobalization: Beijing's Media Urbanism and the Chimera of Legitimacy* (Duke University Press, 2020).

References

Azoulay, A. (2008) *The Civil Contract of Photography*, New York: Zone Books.
de Certeau, M. (1984) *The Practice of Everyday Life*, Berkeley: University of California Press.
Friedberg, A. (1993) *Window Shopping: Cinema and the Postmodern*, Los Angeles: University of California Press.
Jameson, F. (1991) *Postmodernism, or, The Cultural Logic of Late Capitalism*, Durham, NC: Duke University Press.
Lynch, K. (1960) *The Image of the City*, Cambridge, MA: MIT Press.
Neves, J. (2011) "Beijing en abyme: outside television in the Olympic era," *Social Text* 107, 29:2: 21–46.
Neves, J. (2014) "The long commute: mobile television and the seamless social," in R. Bai and G. Song (eds) *Chinese Television in the Twenty-first Century: Entertaining the Nation*, New York: Routledge, 51–66.
Sundaram, R. (2010) *Pirate Modernity: Delhi's Media Urbanism*, New York: Routledge.
Williams, R. (2003) *Television: Technology and Cultural Form*, 3rd edition, New York: Routledge.

25
The Singapore Flyer
View, Movement, Time, and Contemporaneity

Iain Borden

How do we understand fantastical architecture such as the Singapore Flyer observation wheel, overseeing the grandiose Marina Bay urban development in Singapore, and playing a major part of Singapore's substantial efforts to assert itself on the global stage as a contemporary and modern state? An undoubtedly magnificent engineering achievement, the Singapore Flyer is not a building, keeps moving, has no recognized designer, and consequently resists interpretation through the conventional conceptual schema used by architectural historians, theoreticians, and critics. The Flyer is also immensely popular, being visited by hundreds of thousands annually and is frequently offered up by the Singapore Tourism Board (STB) and others as one of the most visible symbols of Singapore's rapid modernization and globalization. How then do we interpret the Singapore Flyer both as a contemporary piece of architecture and as a way of perceiving and knowing Singaporean modernity? Above all, can it reveal something more general about how we experience contemporaneity as a pervasive and modern urban condition (Figure 25.1)?

To begin with, the Singapore Flyer is hardly unique as an observation wheel, despite being the world's tallest at 165 m on completion in 2008, and it therefore must be understood in the context of other recent creations around the world—including the London Eye (135 m, 2000), the Diamond and Flower Ferris Wheel at Tokyo (117 m, 2001), the Star of Nanchang (160 m, 2006), and the Melbourne Star (120 m, 2009)—as well in the context of earlier renowned examples such as the original Ferris Wheel at the Chicago World's Columbian Exposition (80.4 m, 1893) and Riesenrad at Vienna (64.75 m, 1897) (Anderson 1992). Yet the Singapore Flyer misses some of the magical qualities associated with these other wheels, and has never attracted the design kudos as that garnered, for example, by the London Eye via its entrepreneurial architects David Marks and Julia Barfield (Allsop et al. 2008). This is perhaps unsurprising given that the engineering-led Flyer has much of its creativity incorporated within hidden developmental aspects of its design, such as the innovative engineering calculations required to minimize the bulk of the 2-D ladder truss rim. It consequently lacks, to the untrained eye at least, those more evidently sophisticated characteristics such as the spider's web filigree construction of the Star of Nanchang, the iconic light shows of the Diamond and Flower, or the futuristic passenger pods of the London Eye and Melbourne Star.

Figure 25.1 Exterior view
Source: Copyright Chris Cheung 2013.

From Tower to Wheel

But rather than the design or construction of the Singapore Flyer, what of peoples' experiences of the wheel, particularly when riding on it? Through such considerations, we begin to reach into the realms of Henri Bergson's intelligent knowledge: "the faculty of constructing unorganized—that is to say artificial—instruments," wherein we may comprehend not only things as objects but also their systematic inter-connection, as well as our own place within this system (Bergson 1998: 150).

In his famous pre-9/11 remarks on the view across Manhattan from the 110th floor of the World Trade Center, Michel de Certeau contends that viewers gain an "optical knowledge" of the strategic organization of the city, but are also cut off from the everyday street-level dynamism of New York (de Certeau 1984: 91–95). Much of this correlates with the views from the Singapore Flyer—and indeed with the view from almost any high-level vantage point above any city worldwide—but there are also distinct modulations to de Certeau's model which can be discerned from the Flyer, as we shall see.

A tower with a high-level observation floor does not offer the same spatio-temporal and visual experience as that of a giant Ferris wheel, despite the apparent similarities of offering a fabulous high-level view. To begin with, to reach the observation deck in a tower, the viewer normally takes an enclosed, high-speed elevator from ground level, part of the joy deriving from the stomach-jolting accelerated ride in the elevator cabin itself, followed by a sudden emergence out of the dark and into the panoramas of the observation deck. On the Flyer, the journey is itself light-filled and far more gradual, the movement taking place both slowly and in a literally less straight-forward (or straight-upward) manner, the curvature of the wheel creating a steady unfolding of the view as the rotation unhurriedly sweeps round. At the tower summit, the viewer normally finds themselves peering down upon the architectural hustle and bustle of a densely developed city, whereas the Singapore Flyer is comparatively set further apart from its urban neighbors. And in temporal terms, the visitor to a tower can usually choose how long to stay on the observation deck, moving around the perimeter of the building as many times and in as many different ways as they like before choosing when to descend. At the Flyer, choices are far more circumscribed, for the time of the journey is entirely dictated by the wheel itself, while the spaces of the cabin—although of course allowing a wide-ranging 360-degree view—are far more constricted.

View

And what of this view itself? On the one hand, in general terms, the visitor's view from the Flyer is indeed similar to that of a panorama from the World Trade Center, where we observe space and the city as if it were an abstract map, where the whole city is rendered as if a giant model, where the messy, organic, and conflictual appears to be controlled, planned, and predictable, and where a masterly knowledge of all of this can, apparently, be provided by vision alone. This condition is what David Nye calls a "geometrical sublime," and the Singapore Flyer offers it in abundance (Nye 1994: 87–108).

On the other hand, the specific view from the Singapore Flyer is quite different to that from a New York or London skyscraper, and, as we shall see, so too is the kind of knowledge which it offers up. From the Flyer, while there is of course immediate urban architecture to be seen—such as when looking north-west across the East Coast Parkway highway towards the Millenia Tower, Suntec City, and out beyond to serried ranks of Housing and Development Board (HDB) residential blocks—this is neither the dense locality of Wall Street and the financial district seen from the World Trade Center nor the heart of London seen from the London Eye.

It is worth remembering here that although the Flyer itself is not a state-owned initiative but a private sector development-led project, it is nonetheless very much part of a government-controlled plan for Singapore's economic and spatial development (Allsop et al. 2008; Anon 2008; Henderson 2010; Pereira 2005; Rashiwala 2005; Sim 2005). The Flyer is above all an intrinsic element within Singapore's large-scale Marina Bay urban development, overseen by the Urban Redevelopment Authority (URA) and incorporating the Esplanade Theatres, renovated Fullerton Hotel, Waterfront Promenade, Promontory event space, ArtScience museum, The Sail @ Marina Bay exclusive residences, Helix Bridge, and extensive Gardens by the Bay park (Bishop, Phillips, and Yeo 2004: 2; Davey 2011; Davey et al. 2010; Lee 2008: 177). Marina Bay also forms the setting for many large-scale tourist attractions and events, such as the introduction of gambling at the Marina Bay Sands casino and integrated resort (Henderson 2007; Wong 2008), concerts by world-famous performers, and the city's annual Formula 1 motor race (Singapore Tourism Board 2012). The Flyer is, therefore, a highly contemporary project, an of-the-moment construction expressly intended to integrate with Singapore's most recent and most progressive attempts to create a powerful global presence.

The immediate view from the Flyer, therefore, directly equates with the Singaporean government's aims for the marina, using a relatively high degree of aesthetic design and an amalgam of residential, business, financial, and entertainment facilities to focus more on giving impetus and a "global face" to the country's strategic development imperatives, and less on the immediate and varied cultural needs of its diverse citizens (Bishop, Phillips, and Yeo 2004: 8–11; Dale 2008; Park 2007; Soh and Yuen 2010; Lee 2007; Yeoh 2005). It also accords with the same government's positioning of Singapore as the "hub of global culture as well as capital" and a "global city of the arts" through such facilities as the Esplanade's theatres (Arts and Culture Strategic Review 2008; Bishop, Phillips, and Yeo 2004; Chang 2000; Chang and Lee 2003; Hutton 2012; Kong 2009; Kong and Yeoh 2003; Park 2007).

Moving back to the Singapore Flyer, the immediate view from the wheel allows one to see all of these physical manifestations "writ large" upon the landscape (Hutton 2012: 44), and so suggests the Flyer as a kind of strategic spatial disposition within the planned modernity of Singapore rather than, say, a more localized placement of a tower among the comparatively unplanned bustle of London or New York. This is further emphasized by the mid-distance view to the south of the Singapore Flyer and over the Gardens by the Bay project. Here, Singapore is presented as "the world's premier tropical garden city" (National Parks Board 2008 quoted in Phua 2009), and from the high-level Flyer the utopian character of the project is emphasized by the expansive spread of 101 hectares of landscaping and by a series of unworldly 25–50 m high "Supertree" vertical gardens. The ark-like Flower Dome and Cloud Forest conservatories conjure up additional sci-fi allusions—including the environmental sci-fi film *Silent Running* (1972, dir. Douglas Trumbull)—through the complexly ribbed, curved glass structures which provide Edenic protection for natural habitats at risk from climate change.

But it is from the view beyond the mid-distance, in the broad 180 degree arc south of the Singapore Flyer, reaching east across the South China Sea and south and west across the Singapore Strait to Indonesia, that an even greater spatial expansivity emerges. First, the Flyer's visitor is faced with the skyscraper cluster of Singapore's 266-hectare Downtown Core to the west, including the Overseas Union Bank Centre, Republic Plaza, United Overseas Bank, Capital Tower, and Ocean Financial Centre (Figure 25.2). Once the viewer passes beyond their instinctive or relative knowledge of simply recognizing the names and other factual details of these buildings, then a more intelligent process of knowing—"a frame in which an infinity of objects find room in turn" (Bergson 1998: 149–150)—quickly reveals the presence of a major financial operation and its connectivity within networks of electronic communications and transaction,

Figure 25.2 View towards Downtown
Source: Copyright Chris Cheung 2013.

and more broadly within what Manuel Castells calls the "space of flows" (Castells 1989; 2010). Hidden from explicit view, but nonetheless intimated at by the splendorous verticality and grand opulence of the towers, are the presence of the 800 company listings on the Singapore Exchange (SGX), an average daily foreign exchange turnover of US$260 billion, the management of wealth assets totaling US$1.4 trillion, and the accommodation of over 600 financial institutions (Monetary Authority of Singapore n.d.).

Similarly, and second, the visitor is also presented with the hulking traffic out to sea—particularly the scattered field of massive container ships, including the 18,000 TEU Triple-E Maersk class of mega vessels—plying their trade from the Brani, Keppel, Pasir Panjang, Sembawang, and Tanjong Pagar terminals and Singapore's 561 km^2 of port waters (Lim 1991) (Figure 25.3). Compared

Figure 25.3 View over the Gardens by the Bay project towards the Singapore Strait
Source: Copyright Chris Cheung 2013.

to the relatively recent and immaterial nature of financial trade and the Downtown Core, these transporters disclose a more historic, geographic, and physical form of contemporary globality, with 130,000 vessels totaling 1.5 billion gross tonnes and conveying 30 million containers, 500 million tonnes of cargo and one million passengers every year (Maritime and Port Authority of Singapore n.d.). This immense shipping of goods around the world's highly dispersed yet interconnected supply routes and markets also reveals Singapore's long-held position as a major entrepôt for international maritime trade. And if the visitor swivels 180 degrees to face northeast, the aircraft serving Changi Airport provide similar indications of global transportation: 106 airlines flying to 250 cities in 60 countries, with over 320,000 flights and 51 million passengers per year (Changi Airport n.d.).

Third, and turning back to the view over the Singapore Strait, when looking to the southwest or east the visitor is confronted by something wholly new, something which cannot be seen from ground level: the horizon. This non-restrictive boundary, along which the deep blue Strait and azure Asian sky are conjoined by the gentle curvature of the earth, at once marks the limits of our vision but also tempts us into trying to see beyond it. In the words of philosopher O. F. Bollnow, the horizon "positively entices one into the distance" (Bollnow 2011: 73) and, as the "transcendental condition of the human being-in-the-world" (Bollnow 2011: 74), serves to remind us of our place within a much larger and extensive space which we cannot reach but know to exist. In short, the view of this horizon does not distance us *from* global space, but encourages to realize our position *within* it.

All of this serves as a simple yet hugely effective reminder both as to Singapore's position as a major global player and as to the Flyer viewer's positioning with that global context. These vertiginous towers and colossal ships placed within the expansivity of a global view provide no exact data or precise lessons, but they nonetheless serve as unmissable indicators of Singapore's role within both electro-magnetic and geopolitical networks (Bishop, Phillips, and Yeo 2004: 14), operating as the seventh most important city in the 2012 Global Economic Power Index (Florida 2012) and offering the world's second most open economy (Miller, Holmes, and Feulner 2012), second busiest container port (Adam 2011), fourth most important financial center (Z/Yen Group 2010), and seventh busiest airport (Airports Council International 2012). While not all these operations are by any means explicitly legible from the buildings, vessels, and horizon, their highly suggestive presence cannot help but be noticed by those viewing from the Flyer. If, as Bergson argues, "[t]he objects which surround my body reflect its possible action upon them" (Bergson 2004: 6–7), then here, at the top of the Flyer, viewers find themselves inescapably faced with the imposing scale and extent of Singapore's economy, and by their own corresponding powerlessness. The effect is akin to the sublime, the visitor encountering the presence of a terrifying power of such magnitude and character that it cannot be readily quantified, and within which they nevertheless know themselves to be existing. The Flyer thus allows a jumping of scales between the self, wheel, city, nation, and world, providing a glimpse of a global space in which we always live but do not often see or acknowledge; in short, the Flyer imparts—through its form, operation, and, in particular, view—an aesthetic symbol and experience for the visitor in relation to contemporary, globalized Singapore.

Architecture, Movement, and Time

Also of particular importance is the specific architecture of the Singapore Flyer itself. Most obvious here is the way in which the wheel's cabins operate as framing devices for the viewer, both composing the view into a series of pictorial compositions and also separating the visitor from that view such that the overall sense is of disconnection, distance, and unreality; it is as if

Singapore is being disclosed not as an immediate reality but as a cinematic representation of itself, as a distant land which can be viewed and understood in new ways (the framed camera-like view from the cabin), but which cannot be known intimately. The contemporary here becomes mediated, framed, and distanced from the viewing subject.

More subtle yet also more pervasive is the revolving movement of the Flyer. The Flyer rotates slowly, silently, and majestically, like a huge clock, and in this sense it could be held to correlate with the precision, accuracy, repeatability, and constant measuring of artificial machine-measured time, that is with the time of timetables, diaries, appointments, and meetings which Georg Simmel and others have identified as one of the conditions of urban modernity in the early twentieth century (Simmel 1903: 635–646), such that "[p]unctuality, calculability, exactness are forced upon life by the complexity and extension of metropolitan existence" (Simmel 1903: 638).

However, despite their superficial similarity, the spokes and cabins of the Singapore Flyer do not move like the hands of a clock, for they glide without jumps, chimes, or ticks, and without markers to indicate hours, minutes, or seconds. To use Bergson's distinction, this is not then a time of atomized dates, divisions, or schedules, of "one instant replacing another," but of duration, "the continuous progress of the past which gnaws into the future and which swells as it advances," that is of a more individual and subjective time by which we find ourselves in a continuous, lived condition (Bergson 1998: 4). In short, the Flyer's continuous rotation reveals not the operational and apparent qualities of modern time at an urban scale, that is Simmel's stopwatches and schedules, but the homogeneous, uniform abstract time of capitalism, whereby this kind of time is not only sub-divided, regulated, and controlled but is simultaneously treated as homogenous and universal. If then, as Fredric Jameson has argued, genuinely postmodern architecture introduces a new category of urban space, a "complete world" exhibiting a "placeless dissociation" from its locality (Jameson 1991: 40–42), then the Flyer does this also for time, for, through its continuous and jump-free rotation, it signifies not so much sub-divisions *of or within* time, but the constant movement *between and across* sub-divisions of time, or, in other words, the unending advancing nature of global time zones, economic cycles, stages of technological progress, and the lifetimes of individuals or, even, of entire cities or nation-states. The contemporary here becomes not a distinct moment or separate place, but a continual unfurling of time and space, a condition which is always changing and always connected to both past and present, a contemporaneity which is ever in flux.

The Singapore Flyer is then quite distinct to the individualized sub-divisions of Simmel's metropolitan time (one's own diary of meetings and appointments), providing instead a counter-balance to the "maelstrom of modern life" and the general speed-up which Marshall Berman and others have identified as one of the essential conditions of modernity (Berman 1988: 16). Thus where, in our everyday lives, we often feel the need to synchronize ourselves with the modern world through ever more intensive work patterns and fast-paced communications, the Singapore Flyer suggests another form of synchronicity, one in which we must yield in time, just as we do in space, to the larger patterns and operations of capitalist modernity; during the ride on the Singapore Flyer, for a few brief minutes, the visitor's body keeps in time with that of a utopian planned city, where all is at once constantly moving and eternal, where everything synchronizes beautifully and without error. The contemporary here is calming, settling, and even comforting.

Except, of course, as the visitor well knows, while the Singapore Flyer is seemingly endless in its rotation, for those riding on the wheel the journey in fact lasts for little more than half an hour. Even as the visitor might begin to feel a synchronicity with global capitalist time, perhaps during the middle of their journey, the impending and ever-nearing finality to their ride provides an awakening out of that reverie, and into a realization that Singapore as city and nation, and the global context in which it resolutely places itself and forever aims towards, will always outlive and out-last any single citizen or guest.

To return to the comparison with the tower, where the tower in effect tantalizes, promising to allow a view of everything but actually delivering very little, the Singapore Flyer initially promises much less, presenting itself largely as a fairground-derived entertainment ride, but, once experienced, discloses much more, revealing the systematic nature of Singapore, as both the city's plans, extent, and reach, and also our own position within that system. Unlike the tower, the Flyer never pretends to be about locality, and instead is a much more honest and, ultimately, revelatory disclosure of the nature of capitalist and global space–time, and, by implication, of how we are bound up in this modern condition.

From Present to Future

As the experience of riding on the wheel as described above shows, what begins to open up here is Bergson's understanding of a different form of knowledge from intelligence, that of intuition. Let us consider how this might be possible.

In Bergson's terms, intelligent knowledge "bears on relations" (Bergson 1998: 151) and more particularly on form (in the philosophical sense) as "the totality of the relations set up between these materials in order to constitute a systematic knowledge" (Bergson 1998: 148). By contrast, intuition, as a more highly developed and attuned form of instinct, is more open to alternative ways of seeing, doing, and creating. Where intellect is concerned with the "movement of matter" and with "the secrets of physical operations," intuition goes in the inverse direction, "in the very direction of life" (Bergson 1998: 176 and 268), a process which is "within the object" and "an immanent, temporal movement of part to whole, of phases of things to other phases, of parallel lives" (Bergson 2007: xiv). How then might we consider intuition or intuitive action at the Singapore Flyer? Surely this wholly constrained, controlled, and commodified environment would be the very last place at which we might expect to find such things?

Private Time

In *The Elementary Forms of the Religious Life* (1912), Émile Durkheim explores the relationship between time and social organization, and makes the distinction between "time in general" and private time, or "my time" (Durkheim 1915: 10). We have already explored the former in relation to the Singapore Flyer, particularly in terms of the correlations between its rotational continuity and the abstract time of global capitalism. But what of the latter, or, more correctly, what of the relationship between the two?

During the journey on the Flyer, one complete rotation does not signify the "present" or the "contemporary" as a discernible moment at which time stands still, but rather underlines how the past (where the wheel has been), the present (wherever the wheel is at any one instant), and the future (where the wheel is going) are all part of a continuum. All of this is readily visible to the visitor, who literally sees this longer duration of past–present–future whenever they turn towards other cabins, which give visible form to the realization in the visitor's mind of "that is where I have been, this is where I am, and there is where I shall be." Furthermore, this is not a timeline, a kind of scheduled linear temporality divided by distinct intervals and markers (Rosenberg and Grafton 2010), but a condition where time is thickened out into an amalgam of that which has occurred, that which is occurring, that which will occur, and even, allowing for more than one rotation, that which will occur again. The way in which the Flyer seems to move faster when riding at its base (where the ground-level architecture provides a static contrast to the wheel's rotation) and much slower at the top (where there are no such nearby points of reference) further adds to the sense of the contemporary as a morphing continuum, the seeming differential speed imparting a sense of the magical and of the illogical. Similarly, strange effects occur when looking from the Flyer down upon the construction sites below: during one ride I took in July 2011, the building work then taking place on the Gardens in the Bay structures looked, from the height of the wheel, to be proceeding at snail's pace and so gave the impression, to my mind at least, that I was watching the slowness of historical time from a vantage point from within the future. That the Singapore Flyer is a modern day interpretation of a century-long tradition of Ferris wheels adds yet another layer here, for the overtly mechanical nature of its "gear and girder" (Kane 2007: 216) aesthetic of motors, spokes, trusses, and creaking rotation is subtly brought into the twenty-first century by its white frame and air-conditioned silvered cabins, completing the impression that past and present are here being extended out into a single duration and, in Bergson's terms, making "of its past a reality which endures and is prolonged into the present" (Bergson 2004: 192). In short, the Flyer is a series of durations of past, present, and future, these durations being of different lengths and configurations.

Moving and Viewing

Significantly, these sightings of other cabins are not film stills, with each cabin somehow representing a static frame within a longer sequence, for the constant movement of the wheel prevents us from seeing the world, the city, and ourselves as being composed of spatial or temporal fixities, or as a set of discrete views. Despite the Flyer being marketed as a platform from which to view Singapore, the "view" here is not that from of a static tower, and instead is a constant condition of viewing, one which emphasizes change, relative position, and the intuitive knowledge of things which are no longer comprehensible solely through the intelligent knowledge of objects and systems. Indeed, much of the drama of the view from a Ferris wheel comes from the seeming immobility of the viewer, who is placed as a stationary subject within a moving apparatus, the effect of this being that it is the view, and not viewer, which appears to move (Dorrian 2006: 29). At the Flyer, the distance from the Marina Bay, Downtown Core, and other parts of the view add to this effect, such that, given that the wheel is moving so slowly that the viewer almost thinks that they are stationary, this viewer is constantly surprised that, having turned away from a certain view for what they think is just a few seconds, on turning back again that same view has changed as if of its own accord. Such seemingly surprising if not irrational effects accord with Bergson's view that, if intellectualization of consciousness strips us of energy and vitality, such that the "more consciousness is intellectualized, the more is matter spatialized" (Bergson 1998: 189), then movement here de-stabilizes intelligence, making it more temporal and dynamic, and seems to disrupt what it is that we know.

So what is it that we come to know or un-know? There are no specifics here—no exact thoughts, meanings, or associations which might be identified or prescribed. But there are certain qualities and conditions which the Singapore Flyer opens out, and by which an intuitive mode of consciousness might be encouraged. Perhaps above all, the Flyer may provide extraordinary visual drama, particularly during the uppermost stages of its rotation, but the very slowness of the wheel also creates something more reflective, where one externalizes one's body rhythms outward into the immense steel structure, and then returns to the privacy of the internal body of flesh and blood (Figure 25.4). Nor is this purely physiological, for the Flyer operates as a space and time of contemplation, of calm and suspended thought in which the visitor can

Figure 25.4 Cabin at top of the Flyer
Source: Copyright Chris Cheung 2013.

reflect on their position within both the architecture of the wheel itself and of the wider Singapore and world outside. It is a contemporary space–time of the mental mind as well as of the fleshy body.

Above all, the *moving* nature of the view is most important here. Indeed we should perhaps say not that "the" view changes during the ride but rather that the Flyer offers an ever-changing condition of viewing, the emphasis being here not on what-can-be-seen, on Singapore as a representation of itself through the framed screen-like sides of the cabins, but on the state of viewing that the visitor finds themselves within. Thus, literally, there is no single view, for the rotating wheel imparts a dynamic and three-dimensional quality via its ever-shifting movement in both the vertical and horizontal axes. The viewing condition is not then one of modernist montage—or contrasting or juxtaposed frames—but is anti-montage, anti-dialectic, and anti-discordance, having instead a gradually morphing, fluid, and evolving character. In this sense, the viewing condition invokes not so much Berman's modernity of moments of stillness and places of stability being rapidly interrupted by contrasts, upheavals, and destructions, all moving towards some kind of perfectly realized future (epitomized for Berman by Baron Haussmann's and Robert Moses' attempts to reconstruct Paris and New York respectively), as Zygmunt Bauman's "liquid modernity" of constant flux in which "change is *the only* permanence" and "uncertainty *the only* certainty," and in which there is no ideal end in sight (Bauman 2012: viii). For example, in the specific case of Singapore, here one constantly encounters an official ideology emphasizing "the need for agile and incessant transformation," and as evidenced, for example, by the HDB's sustained campaign to rehouse almost the entire population (Bishop, Phillips, and Yeo 2004: 3 and 36–37; Joo and Wong 2008). In short, it is a city where almost everything seems to be less than 50 years old, such that the intuitive visitor aboard the Singapore Flyer reads the wheel's—and their own—condition of constant movement and viewing as a correlation with this recent and liquid modernity, in which everything and everybody are forever subject to unstable, fluctuating change. Riding the Singapore Flyer intuitively is to be what the government has called "world ready" (Singapore 21 Committee quoted in Binnie et al. 2006: 149), to be fully immersed in what we might now call a "contemporary modernity."

The personal identity of each visitor is also caught up in this process. The sense of enclosure within the Flyer's cabin, of being at once thrust into yet held apart from the (liquid and contemporary) modernity of Singapore, creates a dream-like state of existence wherein the visitor, further intoxicated by sensations of detachment, vertigo, and the sublime, may find contemplative thoughts being nurtured. The Flyer is not of course a museum, scrapbook, or photo album, and it would perhaps be an unlikely place for Proustian moments triggered by paving stones or madeleine cakes, and nor does it celebrate a Proustian delight in the discontinuity of moments and transitory episodes which are remotely and distantly accessed. The wheel does not, then, tend to provoke specific memories, but our experience of it nonetheless continually reminds us of the fluid and constant nature of memory and time, that is for people personally as well as for modernity as a whole. This is particularly engendered by the wheel's curious sense of non-directionality, for when riding on the Flyer one has the peculiar sensation of moving backward as much as of moving forward. Once again, then, it is a duration of past and present that is being tilted at, a duration which is constantly being re-evaluated and re-established.

> We must, by a strong recoil of our personality on itself, gather up our past which is slipping away, in order to thrust it, compact and undivided, into a present which it will create by entering. Rare indeed are the moments when we are self-possessed to this extent: it is then that our actions are truly free (Bergson 1998: 199–200).

Bergson's last remark here makes clear that immersion in duration can be a way to find freedom, and this is perhaps why the Singapore Flyer (as with many other modern Ferris wheels) is a frequently favored location for marriage proposals or even marriages themselves, in that it helps to conjoin past, present, and future relationships within a peculiarly appropriate space–time. Local Singaporeans also often interpret the Flyer as a symbol of a prosperous life and as a source of good luck (Windfall Films 2009), for with 28 capsules on the wheel, 28 maximum passengers per capsule, 28 rotations per day, and eight being a lucky number in Chinese culture, the Flyer signifies "double prosperity" (Singapore Flyer n.d.). Indeed, the rotational direction of the whole wheel was also changed very late in its construction phase so that, on the advice of *feng shui* experts, it would bring fortune and good *qi* (energy) into Singapore (Chee 2008).

As this appearance of marriage, fortune, and prosperity suggests, there is a strong sense of the future at the wheel, but this is not a future in which the individual is making all the running, determinedly rushing headlong through decisions and actions into a world that is wholly of their own construction. Rather, as the visitor moves slowly around the Flyer, it is not so much the visitor who is moving towards the future as the future which is moving towards the visitor, the latter being able to use the thickened present of their journey in order to gather themselves, contemplate their position against the oncoming future, before then getting off the wheel, moving outwards and, once again, into their own immediate present and future.

As cultural historian Stephen Kern notes after psychiatrist Eugène Minkowski's *Lived Time*, this kind of experience of the future is a conflation of *activity*, where individuals move purposefully towards the future while in control of their lives, and of *expectation*, where the future comes towards the same individuals, and who consequently steel themselves against it (Kern 1983: 89–90; and Minkowski 1970: 6 and 87–88). At the Singapore Flyer we enter into both of these states, wherein the act of riding on the wheel tends not only to create a state of acquiescence to the oncoming future of Singaporean modernity, but also provides a space and time in which visitors may galvanize themselves towards that modern future. This is particularly evident in the change which frequently occurs in visitors as the wheel draws near to full circuit. Few visitors, except those suffering from an extreme attack of vertigo, are ever anxious to depart while experiencing the main journey, remaining quite calm, content, and almost unexcited during the slow but steady progress. Yet once the rotation nears completion, a change in mood often appears, the sense of calm and otherworldly time begins to melt away, and the thickened present of the Flyer becomes replaced by the normal time of the city—faster, more segmented, more impatient, more atomized. People become quick to leave, determined to re-enter the normal world, and eager to face what lies ahead.

And so we end at our final understanding of contemporaneity. The contemporary, we can say, is a morphing and fluxing continuum of past, present, and future, a spatial complexity encompassing scales from the bodily to the global, a condition experienced alternatively as both terrifying sublime and comfortingly calm. Above all, we experience and know the contemporary through intuition as much as by intelligence, and in such manner it galvanizes us in our attempts to deal with present and future urbanism.

Acknowledgments

Many thanks to Chris Cheung for providing the photographs.

Earlier versions of this chapter have been published as "The Singapore Flyer: View, Movement, Time and Modernity," in Kyriaki Tsoukala, Nikolaos-Ion Terzoglou, and Charikleia Pantelidou (eds) *Intersections of Space and Ethos* (Abingdon, UK: Routledge, 2015), 82–91, and "The Singapore Flyer: Experiencing Singaporean Modernity through Architecture, Motion and Bergson," *The Journal of Architecture*, 19(6) (2014), 872–902.

References

Adam, S. (2011) "Singapore miracle dimming as income gap widens squeeze by rich," *Bloomberg Markets Magazine*, August 10. www.bloomberg.com (accessed June 13, 2013).
Airports Council International (2012) *2011 World Annual Traffic Report*, Montreal: Airports Council International.
Allsop, A., Dallard, P., Hui, H. K., Lovatt, A., and McNiven, B. (2008) "The Singapore Flyer," *The Arup Journal* 2: 1–14.
Anderson, N. D. (1992) *Ferris Wheels: An Illustrated History*, Bowling Green: Bowling Green State University Popular Press.
Anon (2008) "Flyer facts," *The Straits Times*, December 25. www.straitstimes.com (accessed June 25, 2013).
Arts and Culture Strategic Review (2008) *Renaissance City Plan III*, Singapore: Ministry of Information, Communications and the Arts.
Bauman, Z. (2012) *Liquid Modernity*, Cambridge, UK: Polity.
Bergson, H. (1998) *Creative Evolution*, New York: Dover Publications. First published 1907, English translation 1911.
Bergson, H. (2004) *Matter and Memory*, New York: Dover Publications. First published 1896, fifth edition 1908.
Bergson, H. (2007) *An Introduction to Metaphysics*, Basingstoke: Palgrave Macmillan. First published 1903, English translation 1913.
Berman, M. (1988) *All That Is Solid Melts into Air: The Experience of Modernity*, Harmondsworth: Penguin.
Binnie, J., Holloway J., Millington, S., and Young, C. (eds) (2006) *Cosmopolitan Urbanism*, London: Routledge.
Bishop, R., Phillips, J., and Yeo, W.-W. (eds) (2004) *Beyond Description: Singapore Space Historicity*, London: Routledge.
Bollnow, O. F. (2011) *Human Space*, London: Hyphen.
Castells, M. (1989) *The Informational City: Information Technology, Economic Restructuring, and the Urban-Regional Process*, Oxford: Basil Blackwell.
Castells, M. (2010) *The Information Age: Economy, Society and Culture*. Volume 1: *The Rise of the Network Society*, 2nd edition, Chichester: Wiley-Blackwell.
Chang, T. C. (2000) "Renaissance revisited: Singapore as a 'Global City for the Arts'," *International Journal of Urban and Regional Research* 24, 4: 818–831.
Chang, T. C. and Lee, W. K. (2003) "Renaissance city Singapore: a study of arts spaces," *Area* 5, 2: 128–141.
Changi Airport (n.d.) www.changiairport.com/our-business/about-changi-airport/facts-statistics (accessed June 19, 2013).
Chee, F. (2008) "Flying with feng shui," *The Straits Times*, August 11. www.straitstimes.com (accessed June 24, 2011).
Dale, O. J. (2008) "The Singapore City Centre in the context of sustainable development," in T.-C. Wong, B. K. P. Yuen, and C. Goldblum (eds) *Spatial Planning for a Sustainable Singapore*, Dordrecht: Springer, 31–57.
Davey, M. (2011) "Gardens by the Bay: ecologically reflective design," *Architectural Design* 81, 6: 108–111.
Davey, M., Bellew, P., Er, K., Kwek, A., and Lim, J. (2010) "Gardens by the Bay: high performance through design optimization and integration," *Intelligent Buildings International* 2, 2: 140–157.
de Certeau, M. (1984) *The Practice of Everyday Life*, Berkeley: University of California Press.
Dorrian, M. (2006) "Cityscape with Ferris Wheel: Chicago 1893," in C. Lindner (ed.) *Urban Space and Cityscapes: Perspectives from Modern and Contemporary Culture*, London: Routledge, 17–37.
Durkheim, E. (1915) *The Elementary Forms of the Religious Life: A Study in Religious Sociology*, London: George Allen & Unwin. First published 1912.
Florida, F. (2012) "What is the world's most economically powerful city?," *The Atlantic Monthly*, May 8. www.theatlantic.com (accessed June 6, 2013).
Henderson, J. (2007) "Managing the planning and development of new visitor attractions: a Singapore model," *Managing Leisure* 12, 1: 24–42.
Henderson, J. C. (2010) "New visitor attractions in Singapore and sustainable destination development," *Worldwide Hospitality and Tourism Themes* 2, 3: 251–261.

Hutton, T. (2012) "Inscriptions of change in Singapore's streetscapes: from 'new economy' to 'cultural economy' in Telok Ayer," in L. Hee, B. Davisi, and E. Viray (eds) *Future Asian Space: Projecting the Urban Space of New East Asia*, Singapore: NUS Press for Centre for Advanced Studies in Architecture, 43–71.

Jameson, F. (1991) *Postmodernism, or, the Cultural Logic of Late Capitalism*, London: Verso.

Joo, T. T. K and Wong, T.-C. (2008) "Public housing in Singapore: a sustainable housing form and development," in T.-C. Wong, B. K. P. Yuen, and C. Goldblum (eds) *Spatial Planning for a Sustainable Singapore*, Dordrecht: Springer, 135–150.

Kane, J. (2007) "A whirl of wonders: British amusement parks and the architecture of pleasure, 1900–1939," PhD thesis, Bartlett School of Architecture, University College London.

Kern, S. (1983) *The Culture of Time and Space 1880–1918*, London: Weidenfeld & Nicolson.

Kong, L. (2009) "Making sustainable creative/cultural space in Shanghai and Singapore," *Geographical Review* 99, 1: 1–22.

Kong, L. and Yeoh, B. S. A. (2003) *The Politics of Landscapes in Singapore: Constructions Of "Nation,"* Syracuse: Syracuse University Press.

Lee, T. (2008) "Gestural politics: mediating the 'new' Singapore," in K. Sen and T. Lee (eds) *Political Regimes and the Media in Asia*, Abingdon, UK: Psychology Press, 170–187.

Lee, W. W. (2007) "Encoded histories: design review and regulations in Singapore, 1819–2006," MA Architecture thesis, Architecture Department, National University of Singapore.

Lim, K. W. (1991) "Management and utilization of Singapore's port waters: new directions," in C. L. Sien and C. L. Ming (eds) *Urban Coastal Area Management: The Experience of Singapore*, Singapore: Association of Southeast Asian Nations/United States Coastal Resources Management Project Conference Proceedings 7, 11–20.

Maritime and Port Authority of Singapore (MPA) (n.d.) www.mpa.gov.sg/sites/port_and_shipping/port/port.page (accessed June 19, 2013).

Miller, T., Holmes, K. R., and Feulner, E. J. (2012) *Highlights of the 2012 Index of Economic Freedom: Promoting Economic Opportunity and Prosperity*, Washington: The Heritage Foundation and The Wall Street Journal.

Minkowski, E. (1970) *Lived Time: Phenomenological and Psychopathological Studies*, Evanston: Northwestern University Press.

Monetary Authority of Singapore (n.d.) www.mas.gov.sg/Singapore-Financial-Centre/Overview.aspx (accessed June 19, 2013).

Nye, D. E. (1994) *American Technological Sublime*, Cambridge, MA: MIT Press.

Park, B.-G. (2007) "Imaginative construction of a global city as a strategy for the growth of knowledge-based economies: a critical evaluation of the place-marketing in Singapore," *Journal of the Korean Geographical Society* 42, 2: 280–294.

Pereira, M. L. (2005) "Singapore Flyer set to soar in 2008," *The Straits Times*, September 13. www.straitstimes.com (accessed June 25, 2013).

Phua, J. (2009) "Visual and sensorial innovations in urban governance: the Singapore landscape spectacle," Paper presented at Tenth Berlin Roundtable on Urban Governance: Innovation, Insecurity and the Power of Religion, Irmgard Coninx Foundation.

Rashiwala, K. (2005) "Singapore Flyer now slated for completion by end-07," *The Business Times Singapore*, April 1. http://newspapers.nl.sg/ (accessed June 25, 2013).

Rosenberg, D. and Grafton, A. (2010) *Cartographies of Time*, New York: Princeton Architectural Press.

Sim, G. (2005) "Giant wheel project delayed," *The Straits Times*, April 1. www.straitstimes.com (accessed June 25, 2013).

Simmel, G. (1903) "The metropolis and mental life," in P. K. Hatt and A. J. Reiss (eds) *Cities and Society: The Revised Reader in Urban Sociology*, New York: Free Press, 635–646.

Singapore Flyer (n.d.) www.singaporeflyer.com/visitor-guide/10-great-reasons-to-visit/ (accessed May 31, 2013).

Singapore Tourism Board (2012) *Annual Report 2011/12*, Singapore: Singapore Tourism Board.

Soh, E. Y. X. and Yuen, B. (2010) "Singapore's changing spaces," *Cities* 28: 3–10.

Windfall Films (2009) "Ferris Wheel," *Big, Bigger, Biggest* documentary television series.

Wong, T. C. (2008) "Integrated resort in the central business district of Singapore: the land use planning and sustainability issues," in T.-C. Wong, B. K. P. Yuen, and C. Goldblum (eds) *Spatial Planning for a Sustainable Singapore*, Dordrecht: Springer, 59–80.

Yeoh, B. S. A. (2005) "The global cultural city? Spatial imagineering and politics in the (multi)cultural marketplaces of South-East Asia," *Urban Studies* 42, 4/5: 945–958.

Z/Yen Group (2010) *Global Financial Centers 7*, London: City of London.

26

Bi-Space

The Original Social Networking Site

Craig L. Wilkins

In 2009, along with several other newly minted Kresge literary fellows, I was invited to read some work to an intimate crowd of urban, sub-, and exurban visitors as part of a large fundraiser at the Detroit Institute of Arts, one of the city's world-class cultural institutions. I was happy, and indeed honored to have been asked, but in accepting the invitation, raising funds was not *my* primary objective. I was more interested in raising awareness of those who might find the time to attend, myself included. What I read that cool October eve—a jeremiad on the city as badlands narrative, often constructed by those with little to no relationship to the city in question—was an invitation to begin interrogating disparate and incompatible notions of the urban realm in general, and Detroit in particular, with an audience greater than one. The performance was well received; there were many compliments and requests for copies, signed of course, but the content of that performance was rarely acknowledged. In fact, it seemed most attendees pointedly avoided any mention of it at all, my hopefully friendly invitations notwithstanding. Several years later, Detroit's always impending and inevitable implosion all but a slowly receding memory, the invitation remains open, as I am still wrestling with that profound disconnect; still trying to understand and give voice to why such stunningly divergent views concerning the urban environment persist and what such persistence might reveal about us as a society. For all the attention Downtown, Midtown, Corktown, and the Villages receive in Detroit's new post-bankruptcy narrative—it is considerable and for the most part, deserved—they alone do not make the city. Despite what the discourse around the new, new Detroit Renaissance would lead one to believe, there IS more to the D than those four lucky neighborhoods, and the lucky people who luckily live there. In this post-bankruptcy landscape, the D is increasingly being marketed as a *tabula rasa* for development and commerce, so it is even more critical to acknowledge the other places and people in the city—those who, should we accept the discursive framework above, must by association be considered unlucky. They live here too, and may have much to say about the notion of blank slates, their luck, and the implications thereof.

A designer with activist tendencies, I tend to view the built environment as a set of social, economic, and political acts that manifest ideological intent in physical form and, I have come to believe, one important yet unacknowledged factor in the persistence of the "lucky/unlucky" dichotomy: the assumption of a common urban aesthetic that is not really common or accepted at all. By aesthetic I am referring to ordering notions of the beautiful, the ugly, the valuable, the worthless, and the like; from whence they come, and upon what grounds such legitimacy is claimed. In fact, nothing could be further from the truth.

I have come to this realization honestly, but admittedly by a rather circuitous route. As a scholar and cultural critic who lives and works by choice almost exclusively in urban locales, it has been my experience that across the nation, there has been an increased obsession with producing environmental order—manicured landscapes at both the individual, municipal, and even regional level—for some considerable time, perhaps a century or longer. While the criteria for and method of imposing that order has changed over that time, the notion of order itself, and a particular ideal order at that, has not. This is not surprising; it is in the nature of nations to identify, categorize, prioritize, and plan. Indeed, it is part and parcel of their *raison d'être*. The Egyptians did it; the Greeks did it; the Romans, Ottomans, and colonizing Europeans did it. However, most recently, through our individual planning and economic development agencies at the state, regional, and local levels, we are doing it to ourselves and rather poorly to boot. As the representative of both people and place, publicly—and increasingly privately—sanctioned planning entities have assumed the authority, if not the duty, to impose a preferred order upon the places and spaces we as a civil society collectively engage. Through all manner of tools—grids, codes, permits, laws, regulations, restrictions, covenants, and associations are only the most common—they have divided, sub-divided, separated, categorized, labeled, prioritized, organized, and valued our shared realm, seeking a uniformity of expectations and behaviors in the built environment at almost every level. However, standing in contrast to these various, arbitrarily regulated hierarchical spaces are those that do not fit neatly into authorized explanations. These unplanned and uncategorized spaces, unintentional products of the cataloging process itself, tend to accommodate transgressive and unregulated activities by their very nature and to date have stymied most attempts at manicured order. For example, in the most recent past configuration of global economies, commercial interests are often the engines that fuel the physical form of cities (how fast can goods be moved, what's the easiest route, most efficient method, etc.); however, due to the cyclical nature of those economies, it is a logic that has at the very least, uneven results. Cities built upon functional divisions, be they determined by race, ethnicity, commerce, or some other constructed category, often position economic growth, social, cultural, civic development, and other objectives as separate, atomized entities locked in a zero-sum competition for resources (Perry 1995: 221).

It is a competition that has devastated many post-industrial cites both in America and abroad because inherent in this approach is the anointing of winners and losers; at best, the aforementioned lucky and unlucky, but perhaps more accurately understood as the worthy and unworthy.

In general, cities in the twenty-first century must undertake the difficult task of overhauling this idea of a zero-sum, economically determined, function-centric organization that supports an all-encompassing, universal planning narrative. Cities must rethink the very constructed nature and necessity of such singularly imposed narratives if they are to meet internal and external challenges posed by advancing technology and retreating work (Liggett 2006: 3).

In this, urbanists face a ridiculously difficult task: on the one hand, for the first time in history, there are more people living in urban areas than rural ones; a trend that's not likely to dissipate. Places like Mexico City, Sao Paolo, Shanghai, and Lagos are the most striking example of this phenomenon, but they are hardly alone. As more and more developmental resources are gathered in these locations, the more these concentrations of desires will continue to attract residents, the impact of which will be a landscape pockmarked with the visual indicators of whose desires are being satiated and whose are not, or so the argument goes. On the other hand, counter-arguments state such concern is overblown; that the explosion in, more than the access to (which is problematic) technology is the safety valve against such dire predictions; that, as more and more of our work, play, and commerce lives are spent in the boundless (but increasingly policed) space that is online, the less it matters the location of inhabitants. It is a position that sees the heretofore unheard-of phenomenon of shrinking cities as less catastrophic than otherwise presented. However, in my view both these diametrically opposed predictions are dead on arrival. Why? Because both have at their core one major flaw: each sees the problem—and thus, the solution—through the narrow lens of economics first and foremost, if not solely. I remain unconvinced by this framing of both problem and solution, as neither takes into account the dystopian effects on civil society that is the inevitable conclusion of their arguments. In opposition to such arguments, K. Anthony Appiah has countered with a praxis of "cosmopolitanism"—which at its base rejects the notion of economic determinism of societies and cultures, recognizing the fact that "the deepest problems facing cities today are not about physical boundaries but the issue of how to make the assembly cohere" (Liggett 2006: 3). Should he be correct, the work of urbanists today must be understood as an effort to facilitate that cohesion; and so for the remainder of this essay I will focus on providing a little insight into how urbanists might make such come about. And to do so, I am going to tell a little story—a couple of stories actually—of the everyday.

The Intentional Resident ...

Somewhere in the city, a slim, handsome man of medium height and advanced age closed the door to his 1927 3-bed, 1.5-bath residence on Conant Street behind him. Reaching into his pocket for the key to the home he and his wife of 40 years raised four children—three their own—he paused, glancing both left and right, apparently nonchalantly but in actuality, with deliberate purpose. Door secured, key in pocket, the casually dressed fellow descended the porch stairs and headed west, careful to not only peer ahead as far as possible, but at the same time keep a relaxed tab on the comings and goings off to his left and right. Walking carefully along the cracked and broken sidewalk, he noticed the grassy patches between the walk and the curb were growing more and more spotty. He sighed, stealing a momentary glace upward, taking stock of the trees; once again, the trees. Sitting on the porch or living room window, he and his wife would often talk wistfully about the trees. Because of the city's neglect, Conant was a less leafy street than it'd been in the past; a situation he often thought matched perfectly, if not intentionally, the population of his block and the homes there upon as well. It was a cause of gentle sadness for them both, as they vividly remembered a not too distant time when it wasn't so. The older gentleman and his family had only lived on Conant Street for about 20 years. They moved in just after their former neighborhood—a community block-busted only a few years before—had been determined by the city to be "impeding the progress" of a newly proposed highway. He'd been lucky; having been a homeowner, the city paid him a little something for his house, while at the same time paying him nothing for his home. Many of his neighbors faired about the same or worse; most were renters and sub-renters and so for them, the most they received was a 30-day notice, maybe a little assistance with moving expenses and a thanks, if that. There weren't very many places in the city his friends and neighbors were allowed to live in those days; many came to Conant; others formed little enclaves further east or west. Conant sported a lot fewer of those pioneers now.

Still, the trees, homes, and people that remained—both old and new—were fine enough as far as he could tell. Both he and his wife were friendly with them all—the people, I mean; well, maybe the trees too—and would occasionally stop to speak with them about things both past and present. His family was always invited to whatever planned or impromptu goings on that occurred in most neighbors' homes, back and side yards and they were similarly welcome to his also—at least, the ones he still knew well. There'd been much turnover on Conant Street over the last decade or so and well, he was not always familiar with the new faces. They seemed to change so much, so quickly, it was hard to keep track. His wife was better at that kind of thing than he but it was important for him to do so as well. Over his long years on earth he'd learned it was caution—or the lack thereof—that often separated the young from the old and the young from growing old. Thus, the increasingly open spaces between buildings on the once densely populated street were met with an odd mix of regret and relief.

Shaking free of the reverie, he moved on. There was pinochle and dominoes to be had, and being July, he and his card-playing, tile-tossing buddies would be handing each other lessons and lies outside. A little less able to do the kinds of outdoor activities they regularly engaged with reckless abandon in their thirties—softball, basketball, handball, sometimes golf—they often took advantage of agreeable weather to enjoy outside what few games they still played. New card decks in his pocket, he made his way off the sidewalk, taking the recently available shortcut between the homes of the former Mr. and Mrs. James Bailey and the longtime residence of momma Queen Ester Green; alas, all three only memories now. The Bailey home burned in 2012 and was razed a year later. Queen Ester's stood empty since her passing about four years before that. Both had been huge losses for the block, as each had been there almost as long as the neighborhood had been opened for workers from the South. The workshop that was once his garage was full of doors and railings salvaged from time to time from the fire, as the city had yet to remove the rubble. He'd been making tables, chairs, and the occasional garden railing, pet fencing, or animal coop as time permitted. Amongst his game-playing buddies, there'd been talk of doing something with Queen Ester's home—a clubhouse, griot circle, daycare, something—but it hadn't happened yet, primarily because of the talk about the city being consolidated. Up and down the block, everyone on Conant Street was afraid of being forced to do something with their homes no one wanted to do yet again. He hoped the rumors were untrue. He was too afraid to fight last time, and too old to fight this time.

High-stepping through lots that once held homes, families, cars, campers, and boats but now only wood, brick, memories, and opportunities, he first heard and then saw the Johnson twins, neighborhood artists, painting one of their locally famous murals on the other side of Queen's house. This one depicted the Queen herself and her open kitchen. The Queen had no children of her own but she had an entire cadre of kids that called her momma. Many of the young adults still here, the twins included, spent an inordinate amount of time in Queen Ester's front and back porch, parlor, and kitchen. In fact, he was sure his two oldest girls learned how to cook not so much from their mother but from Queen Ester; of course, he wasn't crazy enough to ever say so. He laughed heartily at the possibility his wife also suspected the same. There was something about the girls' chicken that was awfully familiar and seemed to make their mother awfully testy.

Still chuckling at the thought of his wife's vexation, he turned to watch a group of boys and girls of all ages—only a few of which he could recognize—play what seemed to be some odd combination of soccer and kickball behind the houses and alley. He laughed again and, in a youthful display of playfulness long lost, the old-timer reached down and removed a loose, damp pile of clothes and cardboard to grab one of the several discarded tires that tried to mark these lots—and much of his neighborhood, for that matter—a dumping ground. This one seemed to be from a large truck of some sort; once upright, it came up almost to his waist. The game wasn't far away, so he decided he'd move it and maybe give those kids more room to play. Henry Atwater lived a block or so over in a house next to the two, maybe three vacant lots where they played cards, and was always using old tires and stuff for things in those lots; in fact, most of the furniture there were just tires, crates, and door tops painted to make for seating, tables, and such. Henry would get the twins to nicely paint the stuff if he could, but other kids if not. He frequently said to all that would listen—and to the height of irritation of his game-playing buddies—he wasn't gonna spend good money for tables and chairs when they were right across the street for free. When the weather was good, the older, handsome man and many more like him would gather, talk, drink, play cards, fib, and generally enjoy their retirement in what they came to call Atwater Park, which of course, made Henry quite happy—and rightfully so. He'd done a lot to clean it up. They gathered almost daily except on Sunday. Sunday—mostly due to church, ball games, or hangovers; sometimes all three—Atwater Park became a kind of informal neighborhood trading post; a place to get fruits, vegetables, and bread that didn't sell at Saturday's farmers' markets as well as batteries, phones, pampers, and anything else that happened to find its way off a truck or out a side door and into the park. In fact, just last Saturday his wife brought home a slightly torn but full bag of white athletic socks along with several heads of cabbage. When he asked her why, she just laughed and said the smell of one made her buy the other, whatever that meant. Rolling that badly flayed, wobbly rubber tire down the alley, careful to avoid the sporty, speeding black SUV barreling down the street, he was still puzzling over his wife's remark. Finally, he figured he'd ask Henry—who'd been married almost as long as he—to explain once he got to the park.

Which had better be soon, he figured; since he was holding all the cards....

Competing Narratives …

Useable *(i.e., transactionable)* normative space is defined ultimately by its limits, or more accurately, its coordinates—be they measurable (inches, feet, meters, etc.), geographical (north, south, east, west, etc.), geometrical (circular, triangular, rectangular, etc.), organizational (symmetrical, asymmetrical, etc.), and/or some other structure—as they apply to a Cartesian 3D universal division of space. The simplest way to make visible the influence of this x, y, z framing of the world is to just look outside any city window. The street you see is one element of a massive grid system that allocates spaces in measurable chunks using uniform, if not universal, frameworks. We use this framework to communicate about space and place every day. One lives at the corner *(intersection)* of Conant (y) and Barnes (x); another resides on Conant (y) halfway between Barnes (x) and Blackard (x); a friend on the *east* side of town, next to Grand *Circle*, a mile away from Washington *Square*. The normative is predictable, expected, foundational; it is how space and place are understood and communicated. As an abstract, space can be what we claim it to be because we, as a collective body—a social order, if you will—have agreed on what constitutes it and have embedded that understanding within our common system of communication (textual, visual, aural, etc.) concerning space. However, this is not necessarily true in the Lefebvrian view. Indicators of a particular space are not definitive. From this perspective, what is determinate and undisputable is not what one is told a space is, but what one experiences a space as. In this perspective, the determining factor, what ultimately defines a particular space, is the actions of and/or between people. In fact, for Lefebvre, it is the interaction that creates space, not the other way around. Ultimately, the difference between the two is this: in the normative view, one comes into a spatial order—an organization, an operation, an aesthetic—that already exists. In the other view, one comes to a spatial order that is created by one's (many "one's" actually) encounter with it; it is "[t]he critical difference … between the defined and the not-yet-defined" (Papastergiadis 2010: 77–78). One is ready-made; the other ready to *be* made. One is locked; the other loaded.

Residents of uncategorized spaces like our elderly retiree realize there is a similar normative narrative that defines a city as well. It is a bounding that's clear and definitive; anything that does not conform to that understanding is considered an anomaly and thus suspect. To refer to the urban as anything other than what has been normatively established is to not only reject an agreed upon social order established by that criteria but one's standing in that social order as well. However, based on real, lived experience in such "normative" spaces, these residents also recognize the constructed ideological framework that undergirds the spatial narrative of what is normal is certainly not neutral; it only masquerades as such for very specific reasons. In other words, the creation, dissemination, and application of that particular framework allows for the consolidation, justification, and legitimization of the privilege to define what is right and proper—in effect, what is normal, universal—on terms favorable to itself and to determine the consequences for when such definitions are not strictly followed. It authorizes the power to name, to determine value, usefulness, and the like. In short, it grants the power to define a standard, ostensibly neutral, natural, and universal, by which all others are judged.

Intentions Revealed …

Knowing what they know about the standard, for our elderly tour guide and friends a certain amount of rejection of the normative narrative is not unexpected. In fact, it could be reasonably argued that not only is such rejection inevitable, it is indeed critical to their survival. With at best an always tenuous hold on, and at worst, no access to permanence at all, the residents of Conant have learned to see space as less a definitive abstract, but more a suggested application; one that remains open to both individual and collective appropriation.

Thinking spatially means seeing the various political and technologies of planning—its various discourses—in their contextual place(s) in society. They become examples of particular relations to power that constitute the conditions of freedom and dominance in the socially produced urban space (Perry 1995: 213).

They have learned to be comfortable, or at least flexible and to navigate spaces that, like they, are always in transition. It is a spatial strategy that has been employed so long in such spaces by such residents it's almost second nature. Created by a spatial logic that tends to prefer, if not require, the kind of stability authorized by a set of defined boundaries and allowable uses, these spaces rarely adhere to the logics of fixed stability—the kind with well-known rules of behavior, aesthetics, ownership, and economics that allow them to operate in the manner expected. I often liken these spaces—and the residents that inhabit them—to the film the *Matrix*. In it, the hero Neo, who due to particular lived experiences senses something's not quite right with the current narrative condition that he is expected to embrace, struggles to quell his uneasiness and in the process becomes aware of his own agency—ultimately battling to establish his identity on his own terms. To the authority that defines the standard, he becomes an anomaly; a consequence of the imposition of a normative narrative. In effect, he is their creation. Unable to do away with the unintended and unwanted byproduct of their all-encompassing ideological effort, the best that can be done is to minimize its destructive possibilities. In the urban realm, the residents of Conant are like Neo: an unwanted byproduct of an imperfect unifying logic; they, like the number Pi, are the variance that can be neither solved nor eliminated. For Henry and his friends, this variance, this unintended, unwanted space is where they live; this is their normative. Here, the normative spatial abstract is a beginning, not an end.

The irregularity of these spaces, the remnants of different kinds of history coexisting and decaying within the present, the complex play of light and darkness all contribute to what we pathetically call the "character" of a place, but more importantly, they serve as opportunities to discover wonder, and contemplate the weird patterns of history. These thoughtful zones—spaces in which a different kind of thought is possible—are so loaded with resonance and inspiration, partly because they were never intended as places of reverie … Such moments of spatial reverie are almost beyond the realms of urban planning and architectural design (Papastergiadis 2010: 78, 80–81). This is Conant Street; this is Atwater Park. This … is the urban aesthetic.

Intentions' History ...

Temporary moments—protests, parades, patriotic celebrations, etc.—aside, the people who frequent the Atwater Parks of the world never come at a city directly; head on. Their approach is always slightly askance. Where *can* I live? Where am I *allowed* to go? How far? Where *can* I shop? How long *can* I be in this space? This list, conditional and arbitrary, goes on. It's never where do I *want* to live, it's always where *can* I live. It is rarely a question of economics *only*; it is a condition of economics *also*.[1] They are always a group that moves through the city with one eye looking ahead, the other behind. They see the city sideways, askew, often weighing decisions as if life depends on it:

> When one has to improvise incessantly, it is difficult to predict the implications of one's own actions, and life becomes a gamble in which the stakes of guessing "right" and "wrong" are high.... These politics affect the use of urban knowledge in several ways. There is a hedging of bets in which the uses of various types of knowledge coincide and none takes precedence.
>
> *(Simone 1998)*

Thus, such movements must be hidden, disguised even, in frames that recall an acceptance of the normative to avoid detection and disruption. Like the John Canoe, Candomblé, Capoeira, Slave Codes/Songs—diasporian spatial practices that have centuries-long traditions—it is a world hidden inside another, quietly asserting and retreating as time and purpose demands. Both unpredictable and indecipherable to those without access to its coding, such spaces leave traces of itself on the landscape, recognized by those who speak the language; indecipherable to all others. It's the beginning of an urban aesthetic; everything remains in play, to be considered in its best and worse light as conditions change. Nothing can be ignored or truly discarded, for what is useless today might be extremely valuable tomorrow. Adaptability is key; making space—sharing, borrowing, adapting, salvaging, subverting, appropriating, finagling—may be the only strategy available. Regardless, it is often the most useful. Never in a position to impose their world vision on the city's landscape by fiat, subversion becomes a strategy to be acknowledged as still part of the civil society, to exert some control over the direction of their existence. And that kind of lived experience requires a different kind of aesthetic notion, a different idea of what is beautiful and valuable. People of color in particular, but perhaps all marginalized communities or ethnicities to varying degrees, are comfortable in this space. They have little choice. Helen Liggett refers to this spatial condition as an "excess of fact," which she describes as "the complexity and crowded nature of un-staged photography, where many factors aside from the single subject interact to create meaning" (Liggett 2006: 2). For her, "fact" can be understood as a relationship with the world that begins not as one imagines the world to be, not as some predetermined ideal of what it should be, but exactly as one finds it; everyday encounters that begin with difference and move towards a creation of value. It is a space that is both presented and unfinished, "pointing to the gap between the work and the audience's reading of it" (Liggett 2006: 2). Photography or architecture, what Liggett describes is at the foundation of an urban aesthetic.

To a certain degree, residents of the uncategorized spaces of the city have never been able to focus—at least, not in the way that allows the application of an excess of fact. For these residents, there is no such thing. Others safely ensconced in the normative narrative can afford to focus. They assume—and rightly so—they have the ability to make their (spatial, financial, political, etc.) dreams a reality; to force object and objective to align upon the world stage decidedly in

Craig L. Wilkins

their favor. It is rare the residents of the city's residual spaces have that opportunity, much less that power, and so they're perpetually left without the kind of stability and expectations (financial, political, cultural, spatial, etc.) that others might enjoy. They must keep themselves—and the spaces they inhabit—flexible, malleable, and easily adaptable, for they may have to make their environment, not to mention themselves, anything and everything in the blink of an eye. In a landscape that does not acknowledge who and what you are, the question is not how or why a distinct urban aesthetic develops, but why it does not develop every time, all the time.

The Accidental Tourist

"JEEZ! What the ..." he yelled at the very definition of last second. Catching a glimpse to his right of a man rolling a rather large black tire out of an alley and into the street, he yanked his three-year-old Lincoln Navigator sharply to the left, only narrowly avoiding a most serious collision, not to mention an equally serious roll-over by the slightest of hairs. Heart racing and palms sweating, he was chastened by his inattention. "Dammit! Keep your eyes on the friggin' road, idiot; you almost hit that guy. Jeez!"

He was completely lost—and in all honesty, a little afraid—so perhaps on some level he could be forgiven for his haste. No one likes to be lost; it's frustrating, time consuming, and to a certain degree, humiliating; the combination of which could make a driver a little inattentive to anything beyond getting un-lost, and doing so with all deliberate speed. He was no exception, and perhaps at the moment he might just be the very poster child for such discomfort. A simple venture into the city for a meeting and lunch had turned into his own personal episode of Survivor, *except he was desperately praying to get voted off the island, or in this case, off the street. Lost in the city proper was not where he thought he'd be when he left his home this morning. Somehow, somewhere he'd made a wrong turn—he suspected several wrong turns, actually—and, well ... here he was, nervously searching for a way, any way, back home.*

A middle aged, robust, and slightly balding man who liked to jog to keep in shape, the image of every evening when he stood in his front lawn—a lawn that looked much like every one to his left, to his right, across and down the street of his neighborhood; peering over that hedge he could never quite keep tamed preparing to run the 27.4 minutes it took for him to complete his route—came unexpectedly to mind. Maybe he thought he might have to resort to that training should this trip go bad. He thought of running down the canopied, long, narrow streets west of his West Bloomfield Hills neighborhood streets that seemed to stretch to infinity broken only by the occasional perfectly perpendicular scar marking the increasingly receding blocks—and how he was often struck on how similar the houses and lawns making up the various blocks in both directions actually were. It wasn't as if he'd never noticed before; in fact, that kind of consistency was one of the primary reasons he and his wife chose to settle there but it was always something that remained below the surface, in the background; something just understood between them. Having both grown up in similar kinds of neighborhoods, West Bloomfield Hills' "curb appeal" was what they'd come to expect in a community, if not how they ultimately defined community. Its appearance was simply the norm; just something that <u>was;</u> explanations of how or why were unnecessary, and on some level, unwanted. However, today, given his immediate experience in his unplanned location, he was struck by how much "given" there actually was back home. The "sameness" of his neighborhood, as well as the "difference" of his neighborhood compared to here, was stark. Yes, in his neighborhood the houses and house numbers on his block varied in size, shape, and color; some neighbors chose to outfit their stoops and porches with chairs scattered here and there and flowers both hanging and potted; yards were, for the most part, mowed and respected—he had yet to see a pet anywhere it shouldn't be; bushes were typically neatly trimmed—although a few ambitious neighbors had gone so far as to actually shape their hedges; some driveways shot right back to the garage or car port while others curved into and out of the front step of the little Tudor community; but despite these clearly differentiated individual elements, the no-longer-chubby hubby could swear there was a pattern in these disparate placements. Maybe he was imagining things that weren't there, but, in the search for a way home, somehow he found the apparent order to the chairs, flowers, bushes, and even the breaks in the curbs and lawns somewhat reassuring. Especially compared to this, his neighborhood looked nothing like where he found himself this afternoon; in fact, the two couldn't be more different if they were on different planets. None of the markers he understood as neighborhood or community were visible. He was clearly in a place he didn't understand and didn't want to be.

The initial views from any of the many tinted windows of his fully loaded Navigator offered nothing recognizable. It appeared each street had been reduced to its most fundamental elements: house, sidewalk, street, yard; not all in that order and certainly not in equal amounts. In fact, the saw-tooth result of that unequal distribution of houses, non-houses—be they burned, collapsed, or simply non-existent—and everything else on each block he drove past was simply stunning. Never could he have imagined a major urban metropolis could or would tolerate such. In some of the non-house spaces lurked cars, bikes, gardens, and even farms—complete with small livestock—filling the void. Other locations featured images perhaps less desirable: dumps and refuse of all kinds abounded, clearly outnumbering the other, more creative uses of these vacant lots. He quickly came to the conclusion that unless the residents in the area had decided to simultaneously purge their homes of unwanted this and that, these dumps were being seriously augmented by those more transient. Almost every street he ventured down dead ended at some point, cut off by the very highway he was growing increasingly desperate to enter. And at each dead end, his anxiety level rose considerably. He'd heard stories about what happens at these dead ends and quite frankly, he wanted no part of it. Apparently, it was not pretty and he had no intention of becoming a statistic.

"That way?" he wondered, "maybe I can get on there." It was damn near impossible to know without trying; there weren't a lot of landmarks he recognized. The highway feeders in this neighborhood were not lined by ugly, sandy-colored concrete sound walls sprinkled with various but innocuous designs to keep people from realizing they were indeed, ugly, sandy-colored concrete sound walls. It fooled no one, even when the ivy began to grow; they were still sound walls. There didn't appear to be anyone around to ask for directions. Each block was similarly deserted. The houses looked tired from holding up the weight of future expectations. Many had collapsed or burst into flames under such weight. There were so many vacant lots it appeared the houses were the anomaly, not the other way around. Many of the lots appeared to be makeshift junkyards. Clothes, chairs, boxes, tires, hats, blankets, diapers, even a refrigerator or two were routinely left in these uninhabited and apparently unattended areas.

Truly perplexed—and maybe a little angry—he wondered, "What the hell; Really!? This is kinda crazy."

Unexpectedly, he became increasingly drawn to the area and his frantic search for an interstate entrance less and less important. Like the images he found in the "Detroit Disassembled" picture book he recently paged through but didn't purchase at Barnes & Noble, the devastated landscape he was now seeing first-hand was really quite fascinating. The more he grew in awe of what was to him wholly implausible, the slower his pace. The effect was somewhat ironic; traveling through the neighborhood—surveying the landscape and the people in it from the distance provided by his large black SUV—his favorite Lincoln resembled something of its Chrysler competitor: a police cruiser, another vehicle frequently seen observing and surveying. But ... he'd never experienced anything like this up close, despite the numerous times he'd visited the city. This was hardly surprising; previous visits were limited to downtown, the ballpark, the bars, restaurants, galleries, pop ups, and various cultural institutions. He'd no real reason to venture any place else. In fact, all media reports indicated that there WAS no place else, at least no place worth thinking about. But ... here he was, in both that media-defined and administratively ignored no-place and, well, it was disconcerting to say the least. Like a bad highway accident, it both drew and repulsed him.

Shaking loose from his thoughts, he realized it was late and he did, in fact, have places to go. However, by that time, he'd gotten so turned around by the combination of his accidental tour as well as his GPS's rather irritatingly imprecise and occasionally confusing instructions (how could it not know that Alter is a one-way street?), that despite the alarm in his head strongly warning him against announcing his lost and subsequently easy pickings status to the world—well, at least the world he was unfamiliar with—he felt he had to ask for directions. He was getting more and more disoriented with each turn: each block was so similarly depopulated and dispersed to the point he could no longer distinguish between them, if he ever could. So, he decided to toss caution to the wind and ask for some friggin' help. If anything, it'd make for a good story later on, and he was a sucker for a good story. He wasn't getting out of his car to get one though; no, not hardly, not here. In his opinion, for the story to be really good, he had to tell it himself and to do that, he had to get home alive. In fact, any story written today indeed HAD to have that little detail as its most important theme.

No sooner than he'd made, what for him was this rather substantial decision, he spotted some activity, some people. Ahead on the right was a cleared lot where several men were sitting on brightly colored tires and crates arranged around what appeared to be doors on saw horses, maybe? Off to one side of the yard there appeared to be a ramp, again made of doors and mismatched wood, leading up to a platform upon which sat a few more tires along with benches and a metal container sawed down the middle and set sideways on cinder blocks. All of it was, well, neatly arranged and … imaginatively colored.

Seemed as good a spot as any to stop and ask for help. So, he pulled to the side, put his car in park and lowered the passenger-side window. But before he could get it completely open, he heard one of the men shout, "You can't get there from here!" The rest of the men, about eight or nine, broke into various levels of laughter. "Leave him alone, James," one said after a giggle or two, "You know as well as I do he don't wanna be here." James just looked at his friend and said again, "You can't get there from here!" Again the laughter; this time a little louder and a lot more uniform. Lost, embarrassed, and now suddenly annoyed, the accidental tourist was about to go, figuring that no help would be forthcoming. Not at all inclined to be the source of humor from a bunch of clearly unemployed men, he couldn't reach for the lever to raise the window fast enough. As he sat there, watching his window rise along with this temper—wanting to say something, anything—to that boorish clique, he saw one of the men wave, get up off a door/bench and, shaking his head with a trace of a smile, slowly walk his way. The driver guessed he was about in his late sixties. He was thin, but you could tell he'd worked with his hands at some point because his arms were still toned, even at his age. Maybe he still does. He wore a loose-fitting white short-sleeved shirt, and a pair of well-worn jeans and work boots. On his left arm sat a rather large and opulent watch—lots of golden sparkles—and his right hand was adorned with a couple of similarly sparkly rings. As he got closer to the car, the lost and angry driver could make out a small gold chain across his neck that shone rather brightly and deeply in contrast to his skin.

"Don't mind them," the elder man said, "They just live here. We were making bets on whether you would stop and ask for directions. James there just lost. Never play pinochle with him if you can help it. He's a sore looser."

Now, more confused than angry, the driver said, "You were making bets? On what; me? How? I just saw you guys!"

"Well, that may be true but we saw you about 15, maybe 20 minutes ago. First we were making bets on what you were doing 'round here. Then we seen you circling the block a couple times and figured you were jus' lost. No one wanted to bet after that."

The driver was somewhat taken aback. He could not recall having ever seen these men prior to this moment, but obviously they had seen him. It was disturbing.

"So how did you figure I was lost?" he couldn't help but ask.

"That was easy. Not too many people that come through here in a Navigator we don't know. You're not a cop; your ride's too nice. Besides, we know most of the police that come up here. You're not a developer 'cause you would've gotten out of your car. You're not a googler, 'cause you didn't take no pictures. Also, if you'd been any of those, you would've had a map with you. So, all that's left is that you're lost. I'm Henry, by the way. I figured you'd ask by now."

"I'm sorry," he said, actually embarrassed, "I'm just a bit out of sorts today," which was quite the understatement. "Yes, Henry, I'm lost. Can you tell me how to get to—"

"The interstate?" Henry interrupted. The driver could only nod.

"Sure. Go down a block, you'll see a church. It'll look like a corner store, but it's really Mount Olive Baptist. Go past the grassy lot they use for parking and make a left. That's Sampson. Follow Sampson about three blocks and you'll see the entrance."

As Henry was talking, the driver had time to regain his composure somewhat and he was ashamed at what he had wanted to say to these men only a few minutes before. It was unconscionable and he was glad, for many reasons, he hadn't the chance to be an ass.

"Thanks Henry, I appreciate the help."

"No problem; now, if you hit Martha's BBQ joint, you've gone too far."

"I think I've got it."

Henry smiled, nodded, waved, and headed on back to the group. The driver thought for a second and then called, catching the helpful Mr. Atwater before he'd made it halfway back to the game.

"Say Henry, how long have you lived here, if you don't mind me asking?"

Cocking his head, squinting, the recently helpful Henry responded, "As long as I can remember. Why?" in a tone decidedly less friendly than before.

The chance explorer thought for a second or two before deciding a truthful answer would perhaps, not be such a wise response.

"No reason," he finally said, "just wondering. Thanks again for the help." And off he went to find Jesus....

Tour Review ...

For the accidental tourist, this entire spatial experience is problematic. From his perspective, Conant rejects the fundamental element that makes the city a city; it is (common) legibility. It demonstrates contempt for normative rules of communication, defiance of common spatial logic, rejects categorization and is completely dependent on the user to make sense of both the space and actions within. A complete nullification of the normative narrative, locations like Conant are to be avoided at all costs; ameliorated if possible, policed if not. The normative narrative allows spatial value to be determined only by how well it fits into the gridded abstract of what a city is supposed to be, not by what it actually is or facilitates. For visitors such as our healthy runner, there's often an expectation that nonconforming, category-defying spaces like Conant are temporary and as such, less necessary to learn to read, adapt, and engage. The small but significant moment where it might occur to each accidental tourist to learn a new language is quickly filled by the more comforting belief that the path to something better, something ordered and ready to be inserted back into the common, overall unifying spatial and social identity is already preordained and in process; it's only a matter of time before reaching fruition shuts the door to any other kind of spatial reality. However, the residents of these spaces know better. They're spatially bilingual, or more accurately, bi-spatial. They understand that while moving from one spatial logic to another might be possible and even desired, it can in no way be expected, assumed, or believed to be in any way permanent. One must be spatially fluent.

Craig L. Wilkins

Aspirations are fine as far as they go but their conditions remain temporary, fragile; thus, the bilingual nature of their spatial language. It is the epitome of being in (at least) two places at the same time. On the other hand, that an entire swath of the urban core has abandoned that logic is inconceivable to our erstwhile monolingual Lincoln owner; that the grid—the most overt sign of universal conformity and spatial expectancy—might not signify the same social and spatial order here that it does elsewhere is not a concern until confronted with the very real possibility. It is a realization that perhaps is only the beginning of a frightening experience from which there may be no return. The thought that order as our balding driver has understood it lay abandoned anywhere in the city and something else to which he has little to no access has replaced it, an urban condition where visitors can never be sure he or she knows and understands what they are seeing, lies at the heart of the fear of the city by those not of the city.

It is indeed Stephen Hopkins' *Judgment Night* come to life; caught too deep in an unexplained logic, unable to navigate a way to safety before all hell breaks loose.

Conclusion

[S]ince power is what the powerless want, they understand very well what we of the West want to keep.

(James Baldwin)

Understand, the imposition of a singular, normative spatial narrative acts as the catalyst for bi-spatial communication "because not only does it specify the precise use of space but also it is an imposition of a limit on the identity of users" (Papastergiadis 2010: 112). For those to whom the normative spatial logic signifies marginalization and erasure, they do not—and indeed cannot—abide by such limitations. Thus, in the uncategorized spaces of the city they learn to be bi-spatial, and from this a particular urban aesthetic is born; a constantly moving, changing, developing, adapting, and integrating one that "not only reveals the hidden potential of space, but also extends the forms of interaction. [Its] use of space opposes the technocratic definition of the city" (Papastergiadis 2010: 112).

One might go so far as to say this urban aesthetic is the cultural product of people who have learned to spin hay into gold; to make something from what's typically considered nothing. Ironically, this nothing is part of an intense focus—one that works extremely hard to ignore, hide, contain, marginalize, problematize, and police it, lest someone recognize that it's a product of the normative's own making. However, those efforts at containing, if not eliminating, the creative places of this bi-spatial universe tend to squeeze so hard that such practices and products seep into places the normative would rather it not. Such practices and objects—such, aesthetics—when coupled to the place and conditions of their creation are often incomprehensible to those whom encounter them sans that lived experience, unwanted and thus deemed problematic. The invasion, infection; the spread of this foreign logic into their conventionally legible location is to be fought at all costs. However, once decoupled, purged of its most revealing formative elements, carefully pruned of any critique of the normative imposition and the conditions of its creation, an urban aesthetic is often considered extremely valuable; available for appropriation by others, to be bought and sold as something new. Like asphalt, an urban aesthetic is both undesirable waste and highly valued commodity. The most recent evidence of appropriation can be seen in the rise of Robin Thick, Justin Timberlake, and Sam Smith to the top of the R&B charts, Kreayshawn and the "White Girl Mob" in pop music, and Macklemore and Iggy Azalea in rap, which can be traced back to Elvis and indeed, beyond that. Once scrubbed mostly clean of any critical, criticizing context, the processes and products that seep out from marginalized, hidden, policed urban space—the most amenable space available for creative practices—are always coveted.

This is true even, if not particularly, in the built environment. With a history that spans centuries, continents, and countries, it is no coincidence that a bi-spatial urban aesthetic gave birth to both community design and participatory planning; it is also no coincidence each emerged in temporal tandem with another element of that lived experience, the black power/black arts movement. The objectives of all three—and others similar—were the same: to create a comprehensive concept of the world; a fundamental, life-affirming, and enabling spatial logic from which an aesthetic expression that makes sense to them, that values the unique experiences in space of people like themselves, can emerge. The phenomenon of hip hop is just the most recent manifestation of this praxis, one that continues to work towards "an aesthetics of existence that is not about a reach that may exceed our grasp, but is lodged in the capacity to inhabit indeterminacy and to participate in the construction of one's own identity" (Liggett 2006: 4). Both the trend of sustainability—the development of an entire area of practice that pushes reuse and adaptability, exploring new ways to use existing materials, not unlike hip hop's reuse of turntables and recoded music—and public interest design, critical practices that intentionally open up questions of social responsibility while resisting the erasure of identity, agency, and culture in the built environment, operate within this appropriative framework.

Through the dire material [and social] conditions that lead to its birth, the hip hop ethos transformed existing, often discarded, materials into new and creative uses. Such philosophies and strategies of reuse are now being used by architectural designers to develop structures for new communities. Innovative projects that challenge standard architectural aesthetics and functions include Rick Lowe's Project Row Houses in Houston, The One Small Project effort by Wes Janz, the Favela/Barrio program in Brazil and the Project Playhouse by the Detroit Collaborative Design Center (Wilkins 2008: 39).

At their intellectual core, all of the above, and other efforts both large and small not mentioned, owe a huge debt of gratitude to the principles, practices, and products of a bi-spatial, a *loaded* urban aesthetics.[2]

In a 2006 interview with Art21, the artist Kara Walker positioned her work as a response to the dilemma of, "How do you make representations of your world, given what you've been given?" (Walker 2006). Residents of Conant and similar spaces all across the globe—creators of a lived, loaded, bi-spatial urban aesthetic—know that predicament all too well and their experiential response might be most easily and accurately read as "How else? Any way you damn well can." Far from being embarrassed by it, it is my opinion they see such ability, and their capacity to create something from nothing and in the process imbue both person and product with value, as a source of individual and collective pride, not to be sacrificed easily in any kind of future spatial exchanges, real or imagined. They live here too, and they matter. A lot.

When thinking about how "to make the assembly cohere"[3] that is something urbanists should keep firmly in mind....

Notes

1 Yes, the dominant culture asks similar questions, sometimes; and yes, other marginalized groups do the same but for the dominant group, those questions are not part of their daily routine when traversing the city. They can avoid those questions entirely should they wish. The city is made to ensure that happens. Time has allowed all but the significantly—if not habitually—marginalized few to matriculate into the mainstream and thus, evolutionarily, lose that sense.

2 *Storyline*, International Movie Database (IMDb), www.imdb.com/title/tt0107286/ (accessed September 25, 2013).

Four pals are on their way to a boxing match, but get stuck in heavy traffic. To get to the boxing match in time they take the first exit they find to find another way to the venue. As they are driving around lost in gangland they get stuck and witness a brutal murder. The killer wants no witnesses and tries to kill them too. The four pals get away the first time, but the killer is soon back on their tail again while they are trying to find help in the middle of nowhere.

3 However, with notable exceptions, the creators of such value rarely benefit from such elevation themselves: Jean-Michel Basquiat and Keith Haring in art; Jay-Z, Sean Combs, and Russell Simmons in music; FUBU, Cross Colors, and Kari Kani in fashion, to name a few.

References

Liggett, H. (2006) "Urban aesthetics and the excess of fact," Great Cities Institute Working Paper, GCP-06-05.
Papastergiadis, N. (2010) *Spatial Aesthetics: Art, Place and the Everyday*, Amsterdam: Institute of Network Cultures.
Perry, D. (1995) "Making space: planning as a mode of thought" in H. Liggett and D. Perry (eds) *Spatial Practices: Critical Exploration in Social/Spatial Theory*, Thousand Oaks: Sage, 209–242.
Simone, A. M. (1998) "Globalization and the identity of African urban practices" in H. Judin and I. Vladislavic (eds) *Blank_____: Architecture, Apartheid and After*, Rotterdam: NAi Publishers, 173–187.
Walker, K. (2006) "The melodrama of 'Gone with the Wind,'" Art: 21. www.pbs.org/art21/artists/walker/clip1.html (accessed August 28, 2018).
Wilkins, C. (2008) "Architecture now," *International Review of African American Art* 22, 2: 39–42.

27

Urchins in the Infrastructure

Building with Hedgehogs in the Multispecies City

Laura McLauchlan

In and among human architectures, other architects are at work. Like us, they are engaged in vital and deadly works of re-forming, weaving, maintaining, and breaking-down structures, the everyday tasks of making a living (Figure 27.1). Despite the widespread impact and apparent dominance of humans over much of the world, we increasingly come to see that our abilities to build the worlds which we and others seem to need are greatly limited (Palmesino, Rönnskog, and Turpin 2013: 21).[1] While some critters thrive near to human lives (even, at times, despite our wishes), many others require us to find new ways of living and building if they are to live well, or even survive.[2] Building well in our current times may require that we develop new ways of creating and being—recognizing and working with uncertainty and precarity rather than attempting to maintain illusions of mastery (Tsing 2015: 5).

Figure 27.1 Hedgehog footprints from Redcliffe, Bristol
Source: Copyright Laura McLauchlan.

Questions of how to build with members of other species in mind become particularly vital as cities around the globe continue to expand, with 54 percent of the world—and rising—being categorized as urban by the United Nations (2018). Human-designed habitats are thus providing both unintentional and planned homes for a growing number of displaced critters. In this, European hedgehogs (*Erinaceus europaeus*) dwelling in the urban United Kingdom find themselves in a predicament shared by many other-than-human species of needing to survive in an increasingly urbanized world. In the company of urban hedgehogs and hedgehog champions in and around Bristol (UK), this chapter wonders about the ways in which we come to see our built environments differently when our attentions are trained on particular other-than-human lives. Thinking with Tim Ingold's recognition of architecture as a mode of inquiry into the nature of being alive—a practice of attending to the ways in which we shape, and are shaped by, built environments—I wonder about the emerging arts of hedgehog championing (Ingold 2013: 10). Such crafts seemingly require humans to develop new skills of attending to and working with the limits of our perception and—if we are to help shape viable homes for hedgehogs—to find ways to collaborate well with forces outside our awareness.

Noticing Hedgehogs and Re-visioning the City

Across the United Kingdom, people have been noticing the lack of hedgehogs for some time now. Largely beloved and once common critters in night-time gardens, hedgehogs are now a rare sight in many parts. Studies of road deaths of hedgehogs suggest the British population of *Erinaceous europaeus* has declined from a mid-1950s estimate of more than 30 million to perhaps less than a million today (Hedgehog Street 2016). Cars, poisons, and the reduction of habitat through concreting and gardening preferences for deathly tidiness and impermeable fencing seem to be key elements in this multi-factorial decline.[3] New buildings and roads further fracture hog populations. Hedgehogs typically roam up to 2 km a night in order to forage and find mates, and so a landscape can quickly be segmented beyond livability. And perhaps badgers play a part, too, though why they should be such a worry now, when the two species have long survived together raises further questions about the extent of habitat loss (Warwick 2014: 187–188). While other species may be lost without notice, hog declines have inspired action: Ecologists, rehabilitators, and concerned citizens are making moves to keep hogs around. Hedgehog-supporting organizations, including the nation-wide network of Wildlife Trusts, the Royal Horticultural Society, the Royal Society for the Protection of Birds, and, most particularly, Hedgehog Street—a program created by the British Hedgehog Preservation Society and the People's Trust for Endangered Species—encourage people to think about the drains, fences, roads, litter, paving, and poisons which hinder and, at times, preclude hedgehog lives (Figure 27.2).

Between August 2014 and November 2015, I located myself in several hog-focused worlds: one large multispecies center, staffed mostly by paid rehabilitators; one hog-only center, staffed by 50-something part-time volunteers; and the occasional day helping out at a rescue run by a single volunteer out of her home, which was tied into a network of individual volunteer rehabilitators across the greater Bristol area. I also interviewed and was instructed on hog lifeways by "hedgehog champions"—humans engaging in hedgehog-supporting environmental actions within their own gardens.[4] In spending time with champions and rehabilitators, I came to see the city differently. I found myself unsettled by cars on lonely roads as I walked or biked between hedgehog sites. I became anxious in the face of gap-less brick fencing. As champions pointed out what mattered to hogs, I found myself framing the world in these terms, so that streets without shrubs or leaf litter came to feel desolate despite the abundance of street art and

Figure 27.2 Hazards for modern hedgehogs: some of the many dangers hedgehogs face when living near humans

Source: Copyright Laura McLauchlan.

vibrant human community. But I also found new joys, breathing out at the sight of a good thick hedge or an unruly, vibrant, garden. I started to notice other possible hedgehog-supports in our surrounds—that ramp, that log pile, that heavy-bottomed shallow water bowl, that dry patch under the shed. The Bristol I noticed most closely was under 20 cm tall.

As we attend to the lives of other critters, whether human or otherwise, we come to notice our own surroundings differently, so that their very contents and meanings subtly shift (Hinchcliffe et al. 2005). Whether we intend hunting, caring for, conserving, or studying with that other, our worlds change through such attention. The hunter, Tim Ingold argues, comes to see the world in something of the manner of his or her prey (2013: 11). So, too, do ecologists and anthropologists, hopefully, come to glimpse something of the world of their subjects. In these instances of ever-partial attunement, we are reciprocally (though not symmetrically) re-done (Despret 2004). There is mystery in such becoming-with. Not every other we meet inspires us to that which Donna Haraway refers to as "the kinds of response and regard that change the subject—and the object" (2008: 287). Yet even apparent refusals to be open to other lives may shape us. One might not wish to become-with the mice entering one's home uninvited but, even in blocking up possible mouse entrance holes, putting our grains into jars, and keeping the kitchen bench crumb-free, we are responding to and being changed by mouse lives, as they respond to ours.

But for all the reorienting to the world which becoming-with hedgehogs brings, differences between human and hedgehog biologies ensure that we never come to see the world *as* hedgehogs. Attuning to hedgehog lifeways is full of limits and our offerings are often wild gestures into the unknown. For Jakob von Uexküll, though organisms might share the same surroundings, the particular environment which they perceive and on which they can act—their *umwelten*—may be radically different. Von Uexküll describes his now famous tick as having an *umwelt* centered on the perception of butyric acid emanating from passing mammals, the ability to move to connect with such a beast and a sense of warmth (suggesting a good place to begin to drill for blood). The tick perceives and acts in an environment markedly different from the dog it lands on (2010 [1934]: 50). Similarly, much of hedgehog worlds remain a mystery to humans, with the environments in which hogs sense and move being dominated by their keen smell and hearing—an *umwelt* which we can only catch glimpses of (Figure 27.3).

As I came to attune—ever partially—to something like a hedgehog view of the city, the often violent forces of our built worlds became increasingly apparent. Many aspects of our infrastructure fit poorly with the needs of those other species who find themselves in contact with them. Within our built environment, hedgehogs seem to be particularly accident prone. Their predilection for falling into almost any available cattle-grid or open drain is likely to be influenced by their poor eyesight. However, this tendency may also be partially due to hogs' relative lack of concern about falling, as their spikes are reasonably good shock absorbers for minor tumbles (Morris 2010: 156). Hedgehogs' habit of curling into a ball when frightened is also famously unhelpful in contending with cars and their combination of short legs and wide nightly range makes brick and concrete fencing particularly problematic. While hedgehogs can scrabble through gaps of about 5 square inches and haul themselves up steps (and sometimes stone walls), they are not agile like foxes or deer, or as forceful as badgers. This means hogs need help on the ground—gaps in fences, rot, roads which are passable. It also means that many of the emerging architectural interventions which offer homes for more mobile critters are impossible for hogs, who need ground support to access such offerings (see Campkin 2010).

However, it is not the fact of living in human-impacted worlds which makes life difficult for hogs. Indeed, hedgehogs will often actively seek out some human-built aspects of their surroundings, such as quiet sheds, chicken coops, compost heaps, wood piles, and, most famously,

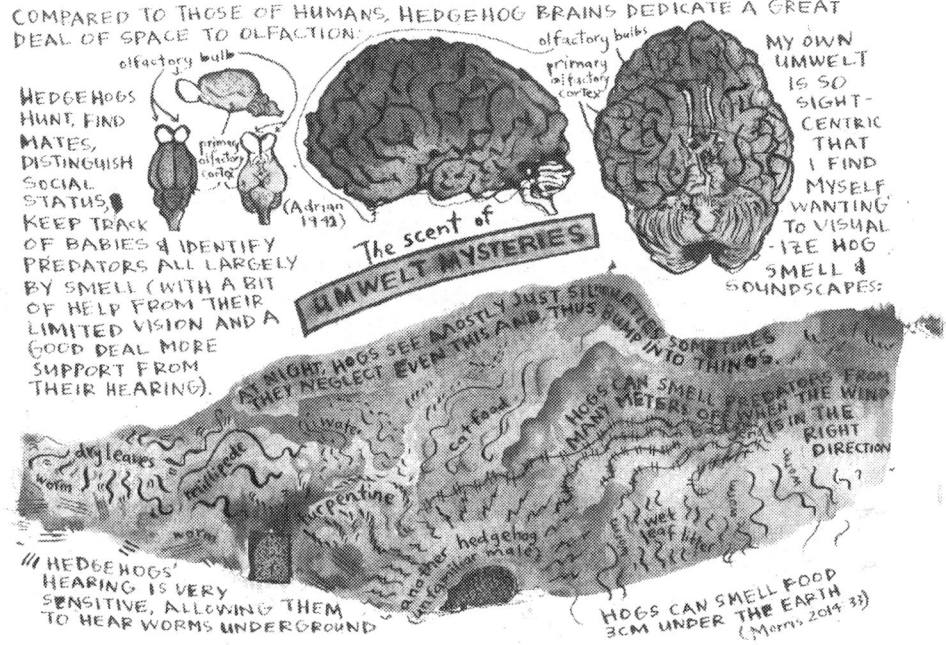

Figure 27.3 Umwelt mysteries: hog and human senses
Source: Copyright Laura McLauchlan.

hedges. For hedgehogs, a woodland edge-specialist, hedges can, in many ways, be seen as an extension of their habitat, with hedges approximating something like a woodland edge (Warwick 2014: 185–186). Far from acting as a barrier or marker of private property, for hogs, hedges provide not only shelter and nesting material, but also allow hogs to travel safely, close to cover from badgers (Hof, Snellenberg, and Bright 2012). Hedges of course also inspired the very name "hedgehog"—a name which seems to have first emerged during the Tudor period, during which hedge-cover increased due to hedges being used to segment previously commonly held land into smaller, privately owned paddocks. Previously, in Middle English, hedgehogs had been called "urchins" (Hoad 2003).

Rather than human-impacted worlds being inherently problematic for hogs, it is particular human-infrastructural paradigms which cause hedgehogs problems. Susan Leigh Star coined the phrase, "orphans of infrastructure" to refer to "those individuals, groups and forms of social and professional practice that fit uneasily or not at all within the emerging infrastructural paradigm" (cited in Carusi and Jirotka 2010: 293). Contemporary building practices in the UK have been widely hog-orphaning. Not only roads and concreting of the cities, but also agricultural industrialization in rural areas have made life hard for hedgehogs. Since the end of World War II, it has been estimated that almost half of Britain's hedges have been removed in order to create more efficient farms (Roberts, Atkins, and Simmons 1998). While small hedge resurgences are taking place all over the country, and hedging is currently subsidized by a range of national funds, hedge-laying and maintenance is labor-intensive, and hedge length in the UK is just holding even (RSPB 2015). Combined with increases in pesticide use, mono-cropping and the destruction of over 90 percent of wildflower meadows—vital sources of the larvae and beetles on which hogs feed—the infrastructural paradigms of industrial farming have left hedgehogs struggling in much of the contemporary rural UK, seemingly even more than in suburbs and villages (Warwick 2014: 186–187).

Even knowing the potential threat and promise of various aspects of our built environments, however, it can be difficult to avoid supporting hedgehog-harming infrastructure, even as we would have it otherwise. Sometimes even *thinking* against certain aspects of infrastructure can be a struggle. Untangling one's life from roading, for example, can seem almost impossible (see Koelle 2012). As human environments are built around roads, so too are hog-care networks. One needs to drive if one is to rescue injured hogs. Even champions who do not drive still support roads through other acts, whether buying food or going to the library to find books on hedgehog needs. Even leafletting on foot involves roads and cars in the shipments of ink, printers, computers, pens, and paper. At times, through the quiet, persistent directives of our infrastructures, we become vectors for that which we might not wish, the infrastructure building out through us.

Making Together (and Waiting Alone)

It is among and with such built worlds that hedgehog champions attempt to make space for hedgehogs. While a good deal is known about what makes a suitable hedgehog habitat, experienced rehabilitators and champions know that even the best studies aren't recipes or spells; following such guidelines to the letter is no guarantee that one will get hedgehog visitors. Championing hedgehogs seems to require crafts of offering hopefully helpful infrastructure to hogs and watching, waiting, and being willing to be surprised. At times, this also means letting hogs make the decisions. Hedgehog rehabilitator, Yvonne Cox, founder of Yate Hedgehog Rescue, regularly held a fundraising stall selling hedgehog merchandise, offering hedgehog-themed activities, offering fliers on hedgehog conservation supplied by the British Hedgehog Preservation Society, and answering people's hedgehog queries during local environmental events in Bristol. Tagging along with Yvonne on several such days, I quickly became familiar with one particular question: "How do I get a hedgehog?" Tirelessly, warmly, Yvonne would explain that you typically can't "get" a hedgehog. While, occasionally, rehabilitators might have a hedgehog who can't be released back to where he or she came from (perhaps because of dogs or badgers in the area), rehabilitators strongly prefer to release into areas where there are hogs already (though also with an eye to not over-populating any area). Who knows why hedgehogs aren't living in a particular quiet, leafy suburb which looks like it would be ideal habitat? What threats, what lacks, what blockages can't we see? Responding to hedgehogs' wisdoms about their own best place to be is a vital act of humility in hog championing. Concluding her response, Yvonne would encourage inquirers to just do all the right things and wait—put holes in your fences, get a log pile, make good compost, and stop using poisons. And encourage your neighbors to do the same. Sometimes I would add the joke, "if you build it, they will come," but few laughed—many had already been waiting for some time. But there really is little else that can be done but offer the best hog infrastructure you know of, and wait. Such is the patient, transgressive-infrastructural art of hedgehog championing.

Practices of wildlife gardening are central to hedgehog championing; human gardeners are typically encouraged to leave "wild" over-grown corners, to grow construction materials, such as hawthorn, apple and cherry trees, and leave piles of pruning for hogs to use (Wild About Gardens 2016: 13). While, in summer, hogs will often just sleep in long grass or under a bush, hedgehogs' winter homes—their hibernacula—however, are (usually) carefully constructed. Hedgehogs craft a hibernaculum by piling leaves, twigs, and sometimes paper and other materials into a relatively

Figure 27.4 An abandoned hibernaculum built inside a hedgehog house from the back garden of hedgehog champion, Kay

Source: Copyright Laura McLauchlan.

enclosed space (where the enclosure holds the material together). Entering into the pile, the hedgehog turns in circles, its spikes combing the materials into an orb with a hedgehog-sized cavity in the middle. Successful hibernacula have up to 10 cm of insulation, protecting hibernating hedgehogs from both cold and potentially disruptive sharp rises in temperature (Morris 2010: 134). Hibernaculum failures do happen, though. In spending six winters with West London hogs, Pat Morris noted that some hibernacula may fall apart during the winter, requiring the hogs to wake up and build a new nest: "building good nests needs practice" (2010: 133). Such building practices require hogs to become responsive to their materials, learning how to select and knit together the various elements of their nests—skills which hogs don't learn from their parents, but from engagement with materials (Ingold 2000: 354). In champions' backyards, these sleeping sites are often co-created, with hogs filling human-supplied nesting boxes with apparently very particularly-chosen items, including prunings and leaves from all over a neighborhood, such as an abandoned hibernaculum (Figure 27.4). In such homes, hedgehogs weave livable spaces from the forces and materials around them marrying together garden offerings and the forces of containment of the box (Ingold 2013: 42).

Human roles in wildlife gardening are often just about allowing hedgehogs—and other forces—to get on with the work of creating the spaces they seem to need, and looking out for and respecting their movements. Many champions would try to avoid using the space at night, lest they disturb the hogs and their night-time business. One hedgehog champion reported leaving a disliked bamboo patch which previous owners had planted, because it seemed to be a favorite sleeping spot of some of the hogs who visited his garden. Another left a broken piece of fencing which hedgehogs seemed to prefer as a thoroughfare over her carefully cut hedgehog-hole. Many human gardeners also give space for the liveliness of rot, appreciative of the curiously vital worlds it creates. Rot is actively encouraged in wildlife gardening, where mulching garden beds with compost is noted to encourage "plenty of earthworms, woodlice and beetles as it begins to rot down!" (Wild About Gardens 2016: 13). Just as fermentation helps us to see "that the chef may not always be human" (Radin 2015), attending to rot in built worlds allows us to recognize that those shaping our built worlds may be radically other-than-human. Encouraging rot shares much with composting practices in which, to compost well, one must learn to collaborate with "[c]reatures lurking in the cosmos beyond the narrow purview of our understanding" (Kirksey 2015: 201).

There can be great joy in working with such mystery. While, at times, champions laughed to me about the mess or worried about their human neighbors' take on their urban wilds, many people also spoke about the delight they took in the surprises offered by their wildlife gardens. In the 30th anniversary celebrations of Bristol's Avon Wildlife Trust, representatives spoke about how, initially, there had been complaints as local parks began to embrace wildlife gardening principles. Thirty years on, the messiness is generally seen as a sign of vibrancy, something to celebrate. This is the work of much of hedgehog championing and, rather than being cause for sorrow, realizing that we don't have control over (or even a sense of) everything that matters, can be curiously delightful.

Contested Spaces

For all this making-with, however, this is still a very human-centered story. Questions of which other critters might find themselves able to make a good living, or even exist at all, often comes down to their appeal to us. In many ways, hogs are a compatible, non-threatening, fit with human lives. The willingness of many British humans to share space with hedgehogs is not necessarily granted to other mammals, such as mice, rats, foxes, or badgers, all of which have greater tendencies towards encroachment. Unlike foxes, or even badgers, hedgehogs do not become tame easily and, while they often have something of a nonchalance around (quiet) humans, they do not become overly-familiar, such as by demanding food. Hedgehogs seem to have little or no desire to dwell in human homes, tending instead to build their nests in quiet corners of gardens, or under garden sheds. Hedgehogs don't proliferate, and, when frightened, wild hogs ball up or run off rather than bite. Despite their spikes, Jamie Lorimer describes hogs as having a "cuddly charisma" (Lorimer 2006: 23), a charm both enhanced and reflected by many fond hedgehog illustrations and stories.

Not everyone, however, is enamored with hedgehogs or notions of a multispecies city. While our anxieties, tolerances, and enthusiasms regarding living alongside other species are shaped by cultural contexts, our built environment also influences such questions. For those people living in poorly maintained homes, such as lower income renters, the threat of infestation tends to be higher (Wilbert 2010: 72). While many Bristolians who were not actively engaged in hedgehog championing did not mind the idea of hedgehogs being around, some worried about the others—the rats, foxes, and badgers, and possible diseases which might arrive along with hogs. Such boundary transgressions can be deeply unsettling and must be kept in mind alongside enthusiasms for multispecies cohabitation (Wilbert 2010: 76). Coming to care for other species might, in some cases, present too great a risk to one's preexisting cares, such as for ourselves and our families.

Although privately owned gardens can become safe havens for hedgehogs and other critters, the lack of a city-wide welcome makes connecting gardens and campaigning for wildlife-friendly open spaces difficult. Making public space for wildlife means contesting and unsettling human-centric meanings and control of such places (van Dooren and Rose 2012: 19). For people involved in the Hedgehog Street campaign, making holes in fences, a practice which requires negotiations of shared property, has been one of the greatest challenges to championing well. While, at times, such a task may mean working together with neighbors to chisel holes in garden walls—perhaps even forging friendships in the process—champions have found that it can also mean working against neighbors to create gaps or keep them open:

LAURA: Could you tell me more about the blocking and unblocking of the hole in the back fence?

DUNCAN: Yeah. So, behind me, it's a council—old people's—sheltered accommodation for older people. I don't know whether it was one of the older people—I think they worry about the cats—I think they worry about cats coming in and out. So, the fence—I have been keeping it free so that the hedgehogs can get in and out.

LAURA: And then they've blocked it up again, and then you'll kind of free it up again.

DUNCAN: They seem to have given up now because I keep unblocking it.

Throughout my time in Bristol, scores of people confided that they wished to make hog thoroughfares through their properties but that they'd been afraid of falling out with their neighbors or landlords and, accordingly, either hadn't pushed the matter or hadn't brought it up at all. Three champions—one in Bristol, one in Cheddar, and one in Portishead—had had astonishing success through forming street parties in which whole neighborhoods reconfigured around needs for hog pathways, opening access through their gardens, and refraining from putting out poisons. However, negotiating with other humans to create public space for hogs was often particularly difficult. Several champions who had been working to make (or keep) public space available to hedgehogs, explained the resistance that such campaigns can meet. One such champion, Joanna, invited me to see the green, hedgehog-occupied space at the center of the elegant housing estate on which she and her family live. Though the space had been pledged as a wildlife area, it recently became marked for over 50 new homes. Joanna, who had never previously been involved in any political movements, felt impelled to stand up for this space, which was home not only to hedgehogs, but also to bats and owls, as well as being a space which humans enjoyed. After speaking out at a public meeting and attempting to rally others to her cause, she was sent a letter by a neighbor accusing her of not caring for people and their needs for housing. Joanna spoke quietly as she showed me the cluster of oaks and the unruly, lively field that was to be built over. In becoming-with hedgehogs, the violent potentials of construction can become only too apparent.

My own street in Bristol was decidedly hedgehogless, a reminder of the force of our built world and our lack of collectives capable of redirecting such forces. Like many streets in the country, our rows of terraced houses sported paved front gardens and back gardens almost entirely closed-in by hog-impenetrable concrete walls (Low and Heyden 2015). One friendly pack of kids who lived on the street had never seen a live hedgehog, but had learned about hedgehogs in school. Their classes had encouraged them to care about hedgehogs and oriented them to what hedgehogs need to get by. They explained to me that all the cars around us and the lack of bushes and trees in our street meant we probably wouldn't have any hogs about. However, they still expressed longing that one day they might find a hedgehog in our neighborhood. Indeed, before I met these kids (or told any neighbors about my hedgehog project), I heard them from my upstairs bedroom one afternoon as they yelled "Hedgehog! Look, a hedgehog!" Elated that maybe there was an *Erinaceous* presence in the street, by the time I got downstairs, the kids had realized their hog was next door's bristly shoe-cleaner. From time-to-time the little team of kids left offerings of hedgehog nesting material at my front door, and once even a plastic-bottle hedgehog—likely to be the only hedgehog in St Agnes, unless we somehow find a way to become part of an urchin-welcoming infrastructural paradigm shift (Figure 27.5).

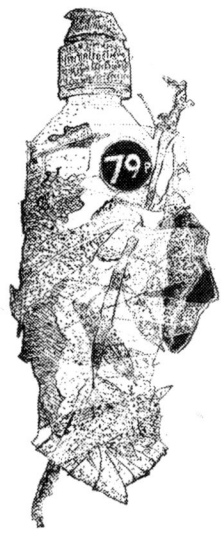

Figure 27.5 St Agnes hedgehog

Source: Copyright Laura McLauchlan.

Conclusion

We build in surroundings we can't fully know. This is not a case of "not yet"; it is not that if we only try harder or build better a day will come when we will finally comprehend the strange matter and lives among which we build. Though attunement and ever-developing technologies of attending to the lives of other critters *do* expand and shift what we notice and how we act, we can never be aware of all of our surroundings. Becoming-with a member of another species is always filtered and limited by our particular bodies and situated perspectives (Haraway 1988). In noting the curious movements and responses of hedgehogs, we see outlines, suggestions of scents and meaningful vibrations of matter which do not themselves enter our *umwelt*. Yet, these smells and movements and histories may be part of what makes hog lives possible. Outside of these almost-graspable worlds are realms of greater mystery, the vital matterings we can't even see the shadows of, the connections of which we are not aware. It is into such necessary mystery that we build.

While we live in a time marked by the expansion of human influence over much of the world, it is also becoming apparent that our ability to know precisely how to provide for our planetary others is greatly limited. Living and building well in our contemporary world, when other critters find themselves living closer to us than they might prefer, is no easy feat. While thoughts of hope always require asking "hope for whom?" (Kirksey, Shapiro, and Brodine 2014), among hedgehog champions and rehabilitators, I find myself encouraged by crafts of unmastery, of unknowing and learning, of attentive tinkering and making space for potentially vital unknowns. Such humans are only too aware that they don't know everything that matters to hedgehogs. Through this acknowledgment of limits, new ways of being and creating begin to emerge, practices of working with uncertainty, of humans learning to consciously collaborate with other architects and find ways give space to their interests, knowing that they might just be vital, even when we may never fully understand.

Notes

1 Throughout this chapter, I gather human persons up into "we" and "us," pronouns which are efficient but, unfortunately, also flatten the radical diversity of human practices of living alongside, making room for, and disbarring critters from human-built space.
2 I take the term critter from Donna Haraway, a term which she has re-defined to refer to all animals (including humans), as well as plants, fungi, aliens, and cyborgs (2008: 330). Rather than suggesting organisms as being located within a hierarchy of creation, the term "critter" is intended to sit within a world characterized by radical connection and contingency, in which all apparent organisms are shaped in radical concert with others.
3 In comparison there is a relative abundance of hedgehogs in my home country of New Zealand—despite practices of culling them. New Zealanders' relatively fence-wary tendencies and lower density of human housing may well be factors in these relatively high numbers.
4 The majority of hedgehog champions were signed up with Hedgehog Street who coined the phrase "hedgehog champion." Several people I came to interview and spend time with were not official Hedgehog Street hedgehog champions, but had been inspired to similar actions by other means, including other conservation agencies as well as television shows, such as BBC's *Spring Watch* and *Autumn Watch*.

References

Campkin, B. (2010) "Bugs, bats and animal estates: the architectural territories of 'wild beasts'," *Architectural Design* 80, 3: 34–39.
Carusi, A. and Jirotka, M. (2010) "Reshaping research collaboration: the case of virtual research," in W. H. Dutton and P. W. Jeffreys (eds) *World Wide Research: Reshaping the Sciences and Humanities*, Cambridge, MA: MIT Press.

Despret, V. (2004) "The body we care for: figures of anthropo-zoo-genesis," *Body & Society* 10, 2–3: 111–134.

Haraway, D. (1988) "Situated knowledges: the science question in feminism and the privilege of partial perspective," *Feminist Studies* 14, 3: 575–599.

Haraway, D. (2008) *When Species Meet*, Minneapolis: University of Minnesota Press.

Hedgehog Street (2016) "How many hedgehogs are left?" www.hedgehogstreet.org/pages/how-many-are-left-.html (June 16, 2016).

Hinchliffe, S., Kearnes, M. B., Degen, M., and Whatmore, S. (2005) "Urban wild things: a cosmopolitical experiment," *Environment and Planning D: Society and Space* 23: 643–658.

Hoad, T. F. (ed.) (2003) "Urchin," *The Concise Oxford Dictionary of English Etymology*, Oxford: Oxford University Press.

Hof, A. R., Snellenberg, J., and Bright, P. W. (2012) "Food or fear? Predation risk mediates edge refuging in an insectivorous mammal," *Animal Behaviour* 83, 4: 1099–1106.

Ingold, T. (2000) *The Perception of the Environment: Essays on Livelihood, Dwelling and Skill*, London and New York: Routledge.

Ingold, T. (2013) *Making: Anthropology, Archaeology, Art and Architecture*, Oxon and New York: Routledge.

Kirksey, E. (2015) *Emergent Ecologies*, Durham, NC: Duke University Press.

Kirksey, E., Shapiro, N., and Brodine, M. (2014) "Hope in blasted landscapes," in E. Kirksey (ed.) *The Multispecies Salon*, Durham, NC: Duke University Press.

Koelle, A. (2012) "Intimate bureaucracies: roadkill, policy and fieldwork on the shoulder," *Hypatia* 27, 3: 651–669.

Lorimer, J. (2006) "Nonhuman charisma: which species trigger our emotions and why?," *ECOS* 27, 1: 20–27.

Low, H. and Heyden, T. (2015) "The decline of the British front garden," *BBC Magazine*. www.bbc.co.uk/news/magazine-32780242 (June 16, 2016).

Morris, P. (2010) *Hedgehogs*. Stansted: Whittet Books.

Palmesino, J., Rönnskog, A.-S., and Turpin, E. (2013) "Matters of observation: a conversation with John Palmesino and Ann-Sofi Rönnskog," in E. Turpin (ed.) *Architecture in the Anthropocene: Encounters among Design, Deep Time, Science and Philosophy*, Ann Arbor, MI: Open Humanities Press.

Radin, J. (2015) "Rot: R for the ABCs of multispecies studies." www.multispecies-salon.org/rot/ (August 2, 2016).

Roberts, B., Atkins, P., and Simmons, I. (1998) *People, Land and Time: An Historical Introduction to the Relations between Landscape, Culture and Environment*, Abingdon, Oxon: Routledge.

RSPB (2015) "Advice and grant aid for hedge management and planting." www.rspb.org.uk/ourwork/conservation/advice/farmhedges/advice_aid.aspx (August 2, 2016).

Tsing, A. (2015) *The Mushroom at the End of the World: On the Possibility of Life in Capitalist Ruins*, Princeton: Princeton University Press.

United Nations (2018) "World urbanization prospects: the 2018 revision. Key facts." www.un.org/development/desa/publications/graphic/world-urbanization-prospects-2018-urbanization-around-the-world (September 16, 2018).

van Dooren, T. and Rose, D. B. (2012) "Storied-places in a multispecies city," *Humanimalia: A Journal of Human/Animal Interface Studies* 3, 2: 1–27.

von Uexküll, J. (2010 [1934]) *A Foray into the Worlds of Animals and Humans with a Theory of Meaning*, trans. J. D. O'Neil, Minneapolis: University of Minnesota Press.

Warwick, H. (2014) *Hedgehog*, London: Reaktion Books.

Wilbert, C. (2010) "Landscapes of not so distanced relatives," in B. Snæbjörnsdóttir and M. Wilson (eds) *Uncertainty in the City*, Berlin: The Greenbox.

Wild About Gardens (2016) "Get creative for hedgehogs this autumn." www.wildaboutgardensweek.org.uk/Downloads/Hedgehog-16pp-Booklet-FINAL (July 19, 2016).

28
Unsettling Formal Power Systems

Saskia Sassen

Cities are complex systems. But they are incomplete systems whose features take on urbanized formats that vary enormously across time and place. In this mix of complexity and incompleteness lies the capacity of cities to outlive far more powerful but formal and closed systems: many a city has outlived governments, kings, the leading corporation of an epoch. Herein also lies the possibility of *making*—making the urban, the political, the civic. Thus much of today's dense built-up terrain, such as a vast stretch of high-rise housing, or of office buildings, is not a city. It is simply dense built-up terrain. On the other hand, a working slum can have many of the features of a city, and indeed, some are a type of city—poor but deeply urban.

It is also in this mix of incompleteness and complexity that lies the possibility for the powerless to hack power in the city, in a way that they could not in a plantation, for example, and to hack particular features of the city. They are thereby able to make a history, a politics, even if they do not get empowered. Current conditions in global cities, especially, are creating not only new structures of power but also operational and rhetorical openings for new types of actors and their projects. In these cities, those without power can make themselves present: in the richest neighborhoods where they are the indispensable household support, in the corporate center where they are indispensable service workers, in their own neighborhoods where they make new economies and cultures. Thus powerlessness can become complex in the city. And this is, in itself, a transversal type of hacking. One way of conceiving of some of this is as instances of urban capabilities (Sassen 2013b, 2014).

In this essay I am particularly interested in two features. One is that the global city is a strategic frontier zone that enables those who lack power, those who are disadvantaged, outsiders, discriminated minorities—even though it decimates the modest middle classes. The disadvantaged and excluded can gain *presence* in such cities in a way they cannot in neat homogenous provincial cities. In the global city they become present to power and to each other, which may include learning to negotiate their multiple differences. They can hack power and they can hack their differences of origin, religion, phenotype. The second feature is the strategic importance of the city today for shaping new orders—or, if you will, hacking old orders. As a complex space, the city can bring together multiple very diverse struggles and engender a larger, more encompassing push for a new normative order. It enables people with different passions and obsessions to work together—more precisely, to hack power together.

Figure 28.1 Hilary Koob-Sassen, *When the Material Becomes Speech*
Source: Copyright Hilary Koob-Sassen.

Today's Frontier Zones

The large complex city, especially if global, is a new frontier zone. Actors from different worlds meet there, but there are no clear rules of engagement. The historic frontier resided in the creeping and expanding edges of colonial empires. Those edges of empires no longer exist. The frontier zone of the present day and the space of encounter of differences are deep inside our large messy global cities. Thus these cities are strategic for both global corporate capital and the powerless.

Much of the work of forcing deregulation, privatization, and new fiscal and monetary policies on governments actually took place in the corporate sector of global cities rather than in legislatures and parliaments. In this sense, then, the corporates hacked the city because the making of new fiscal instruments was a way of constructing the equivalent of the old military "fort" of the historic frontier: the corporate zone in our cities is a protected, de facto private space. And corporate actors have been doing this since the late 1980s in city after city worldwide to ensure they have a global operational space that suits their interests (Sassen 2001 [1991]). The global city is then also a frontier zone because it is where strategic spaces of power can be hacked, though they rarely are, which has always surprised me.

But global cities are also strategic for those without power. It signals the possibility of a new type of politics, centered in new types of political actors. That is one instance of what I seek to capture with the concept of *urban capabilities*. It is not simply a matter of having or not having power. In the case of the powerless, it is a strategic space because the political goes well beyond routinized voting and having to accept corporate utility logics, or the dominance of narratives that strengthen powerful actors. Urban space in powerful cities provides new hybrid bases from which also the powerless can act.

One outcome we are seeing in city after city is the making of new kinds of informal politics. For instance, there is a kind of public-making work that can produce disruptive narratives, and make legible the local and the silenced. Political work gets done this way: it becomes the work of making a new kind of contestatory public that uses urban space as a medium, a tool to hack power, even if it does not bring power down. The Occupy movements that rose in countries in very different parts of the world were momentarily disruptive but long-term educational. They rhetoricized inequality and provided a narrative to large sectors of the impoverished middle classes, usually a rather conservative/prudent sector. It has evolved as a politics that is making headway at the level of political speech and mobilization, not necessarily system change.

It also signals the possibility of making a new type of subject, one abundant in cities across time and place, but always somewhat rare: the urban subject that results from hacking ethnicity, religion, phenotype, inequality, physical disability. Old Baghdad and Jerusalem, industrializing Chicago and New York, early twentieth-century Berlin and Buenos Aires, were such cities. This is not to deny the specific histories and geographies that generated the urban subject. The urban subject is at home with enormous differences of religion, ethnicity, etc. A city's sociality can bring out and underline the urbanity of subject and setting, and dilute more essentialist markers. It is often the need for new solidarities (for instance, when cities confront major challenges) that can bring about this shift. Urban space, especially a city's center, can hack our essentialisms as it forces us into joint responses, into crowded public transport, into highly mixed work situations, into public hospitals and universities, and so on. From there it can move us onto the appreciation of an urban subject, rather than more specific individual or group identities that might rule in a neighborhood. The big, messy, slightly anarchic city enables such shifts. The corporatized city or the office park does not.

There is yet another type of hacking of long-time orders that is taking place today. It is the hacking of well established larger units, notably nation-states, that are beginning to lose the grip on domains where they once had considerable control. This is an important even if partial and not always desirable change. In *Territory Authority Rights* I identified a vast proliferation of such partial disassemblings and re-assemblings that arise from the remix of bits of territory, authority, and rights, once all ensconced in *national* institutional frames (Sassen 2008: ch. 8 and ch. 9).[1] In the case of Europe these novel assemblages include those resulting from the formation and ongoing development of the European Union (EU), but also those resulting in a variety of cross-city alliances around protecting the environment, fighting racism, and other important causes. These generate a European subject for whom protecting the local or global environment matters more than nationality. And they also result from sub-national struggles and the desire to make new regulations for self-governance at the level of the neighborhood and the city.

Against the background of a partial disassembling of empires and nation-states, the city emerges as a strategic site for making elements of new partial orders.[2] Where in the recent past national law might have been *the* law, today subsidiarity and the new strategic role of cities, makes it possible for us to imagine a return to *urban* law. We see a resurgence of urban law-making, a subject I discuss in depth elsewhere (Sassen 2008, ch. 2 and ch. 6). For instance, in the United States, a growing number of cities have passed local laws (ordinances) that make their cities sanctuaries for undocumented immigrants; other cities have passed environmental laws that only hold for the particular cities because they are far more radical than national laws, or developed currencies for local transactions that only function in those cities.

These are among the features that make cities a space of great complexity and diversity. But today cities confront major conflicts that can reduce that complexity to mere built-up terrain or cement jungle. The urban way of confronting extreme racisms, governmental wars on terror, the future crises of climate change, is to make these challenges the occasions to further expand diverse urban capabilities and to expand the meaning of membership. Yet much national government policy and the "needs" of powerful corporate actors go against this mode.

But how can the powerless hack power in the city?

When City Residents Hack Closed Intelligent Systems

To recognize openings for hacking power we need to appreciate the incompleteness of cities—that they can constantly be remade, for better or for worse, and that they are remade on their own terms in each case even when the technologies used are similar. Incompleteness and mutability has allowed many of the world's great cities to outlast kingdoms, empires, nation-states, and powerful firms. To take the imagery of incompleteness further: powerful actors can remake cities in their image. But cities talk back. They do not take it sitting. Sometimes this talking back may take decades, and sometimes it is immediate. A city's backtalk is one element of open-source urbanism: one way of describing this is to think of the myriad interventions and little changes from the ground up that contribute to shape a city's diverse neighborhoods and localities, each with its own problems and solutions, and each with its own potential for innovating and logics for claim-making. Together, such multiple, small, diverse, often inconspicuous interventions, generate localized knowledge about local issues and solutions, as well as specific claims and demands. All of these major and minor issues are also evidence of a city's constant evolution.

In sharp contrast to the above scenario, so-called "intelligent cities" seek to mobilize technologies to *eliminate* incompleteness. We need some of this. But one issue regarding the intelligent cities model is that it typically misses the opportunity to urbanize technologies. Instead it

Figure 28.2 Hilary Koob-Sassen, *Incompleteness*
Source: Copyright Hilary Koob-Sassen.

puts much technology in command rather than in dialogue with users, and flattens whatever the learning curve of a neighborhood could be.

Further, in negotiations with the global tech companies, city governments often may think they are at a great disadvantage when it comes to understanding the technologies they promote to solve a city's problems. But I argue that the city leadership need not think it has to bring to the table deep knowledge of the technologies. Most critical is that the city leadership know its city and its diverse needs—too often it does not. If it has detailed and thorough knowledge about all key aspects of its city it can interrogate the tech firms and ask them to show how it can benefit from whatever intelligent systems those representatives are trying to sell them. This turns the tables, and rather than the city leadership being put in the situation of audience to "brilliant" technologists (or, rather, sales people) it is pushing the tech companies to figure out how they can help the city. This would also mean that some of the techies would have to come to those meetings to address the questions/needs of an informed city leadership that knows what its city needs. Sales people alone would not be enough.

Let me briefly describe one form of deployment of impressive intelligent systems that does not quite contribute to the smart city; in the next section I then take the opposite example: an innovation that does not look so very smart but can actually contribute to the collective intelligence of the city.

One familiar instance of the intelligent city is the smart megaproject developed and managed by a private company that takes over a range of public control functions in a city. Generally, such projects are inserted in older urban tissues increasingly seen as of little value: narrow streets, small squares, rundown small buildings, and modest public offices. And yet, there is a loss here, albeit invisible to the average city resident, and regrettably also to its functionaries. The price is the loss of urban tissue with its embedded past and present knowledges. In the particular case of Rio de Janeiro, the residents knew, commented, and objected to the fact that IBM was running a key security and control system. While it enabled the police promptly to identify a disturbance in the city, by the time the police managed to get to the spot the guilty troublemakers usually were gone. The impressive set up became a joke. Indeed, even leaving aside the fact of multiple diverse worlds in a city, the ineffectiveness of the system must have taken the insiders by surprise as well. Developers, innovators, city governments, residents, all need to learn from these failures—understand how often an innovation does not work out as planned, or that it barely accomplishes what it was meant to do.

Would it not be smarter to enable residents who know their particular corner of the city: they could be furnished with devices for communicating with local civic associations or central authorities in case of danger or trouble? The intelligence, knowledge, intuitions of a city's residents should become part of the notion of a safe and smart city. And so should the fact that users can transform the putative aim of a technology as described by an engineer or techie, and make it work on their terms (Sassen 2012; 2017). An implication for cities is that if residents experience a city as "their" city, rather than the city of the rich or of the mafias, they will work at keeping it safe.

These are some of the vectors that can make residents into a constitutive element in the "smart city." And it is how learning curves become powerful precisely because they have got to factor in the diversity contained in a city. This is the challenge that smart systems need to confront and engage.

Open-Sourcing the Neighborhood: Hacking Codified Knowledge

How can we strengthen that positive scenario of the city's incompleteness invoked in the prior section? An open-source urbanism is an antidote. It would mean a deployment of open-source technologies in a variety of urban contexts. The question then becomes can we urbanize open-source technology? As a technological innovation, open source has not been about cities, but about collaboratively building tools. Yet the open-source approach resonates with what cities are at ground-level, as does the platform approach. To use an analogy, the park is made not only with the hardware of trees and ponds, but also with the software of people's practices.

Elsewhere I have suggested that the notion of open-sourcing neighborhoods could be a key instrument not only for solving problems that are neighborhood specific, but also as a first step in mobilizing neighborhoods into collective actions of diverse kinds, from urban farming to demanding better services from a city's government (Sassen 2013b).[3] A second, related fact is that every neighborhood is different and tends to confront slightly different problems of transport access, of flooding, of poverty and unemployment, and more. Hence every neighborhood has different types of knowledge about the city. Further, it also has a diversity of actors who spend time in the neighborhood and get to know it, e.g., the grandmother who sits at the window watching street life.[4]

These locally produced knowledges are different from the codified knowledge at the center of a system—the knowledge of governments, experts, elites. Connecting these diverse neighborhood actors to open-access networks, wikis, platforms, would circulate these bits of information across neighborhoods and across cities.[5] The effect would be to open up what are often closed systems of knowledge coming from the center or the top. Government agencies tend to verticalize their work, as do many leading urban civic institutions. We can hack this codified knowledge by bringing these bits of street and neighborhood knowledge into standard knowledge systems—and it might unsettle such organizations and push them to open up to local knowledges, including those of very poor neighborhoods. Central city government agencies could learn about aspects of the city they simply are not well positioned to access.

Eventually some neighborhood users are likely to experiment with developing versions, even if simple, of open-source technologies aimed at incorporating diverse bits of knowledge and diverse knowledge practices from the locality—via residents, friends, and also children, homeless people, grandmothers.[6] While none of them is an urban expert, each has specific knowledge about their angle into the neighborhood. All of this in turn might activate additional elements of both knowledge practices and technological practices, generate more engagement by city residents, and more cross-neighborhood projects and initiatives. Such scale-ups to other neighborhoods, and even the city level can enable exchanges and collaborations, and eventually enable neighborhoods to become fully mobilized and integral to a city's culture.

We must aim at such additional layers of tech space through new alignments and communication vectors. Urban space could be decentralized by bringing more action and initiatives to the diverse neighborhoods that constitute the city. New and unexpected intersections might emerge or be developed, with interesting economic, cultural, and political consequences. In this way, one aspect of open-sourcing the city may allow people increasingly to experience the city as theirs.

The processes that constitute, shape, and make the city dynamic can evolve also from the neighborhoods, rather than the center. The resulting technology may be more akin to an *urban WikiLeaks*. In an ironic twist, neighborhoods could begin to leak knowledge about specific conditions in their neighborhoods—knowledge that has the capacity to unsettle traditional hierarchical institutions. Neighborhood actors seen as marginal by authorities—a child or homeless person or grandmother—can bring their knowledge of place straight into the codified knowledge of the center. This is hacking the center via subjects that are the extreme "other."

Such an urbanizing of digital technologies contrasts with the standard model of the "smart city." One of my key arguments is that if the so-called "smart cities" do not mobilize the diverse intelligences and situated knowledges of their residents, they are missing out on a key component of what makes a city "smart." And they are also missing out on a potential for democratizing the smart city. Neighborhood knowledge is one key component of this larger "knowledge space" that a smart city should be able to help constitute.

Hacking Official Currencies and Making Autonomous Currencies

My final example concerns alternative local currencies, and the advantages for communities of using these whenever possible. What follows is part of the "Money Project" launched by Geert Lovink on alternative currencies, which gets at some rather deep issues—issues mostly invisible to the average person living in a city and rarely if ever explained by politicians (Lovink, Tkacz, and de Vries 2015; Sassen 2017).[7]

We need exchange mediums, such as money. But today's versions of money are mostly the official currencies of countries. And these are becoming extremely problematic. Why? Because they function less and less as an exchange medium and more and more as a tool for governments and corporations to extract household resources for their aims, often overriding the basic needs of a country's people. Taxation without citizen participation in how to spend those taxes is yet another such extractive mechanism. When corporations capture most of what consumers spend (and in that process destroy small family-owned businesses) then they also disproportionately control how that household money is invested and allocated (for instance, extreme increases in corporate salaries rather than investing in developing organic food).

Under these conditions, money is no longer simply an exchange medium. Nor is it a medium for ensuring large-scale investments—by either governments or corporations—into what a locality, a country, needs for its people—housing, infrastructure, clean energy, and so on. It becomes an instrument for implementing what governments and corporations want.

Yet not all alternative moneys are necessarily desirable. The key is a decentralized currency to enable the proliferation of non-corporate economies, and to do so at scales and with modalities that go beyond simple barter. Barter is fine for many operations, and it has thrived in certain settings, notably in parts of Latin America. But it is not enough. We need to scale-up if we are going to take back economic terrain now fully captured by large corporations. And we need to do this, even if some of the larger needs of a locality, notably transport systems, will have to be built by large corporations.

Digital currencies are clearly one option. Most recently Bitcoin has drawn a lot of attention. It has also become a destination for speculative investment, and for law suits! This has in turn raised some key questions, notably whether it is a decentralized currency. The challenge is to avoid the corporatizing of a currency, which is now the situation with most official currencies.

By corporatizing I mean that it serves to transform household resources (as measured by consumption capacity) into corporate profits, which can then be invested without any concern or knowledge about a locality's needs. Mostly, a modest firm that depends on a locality's choices is going to have to be responsive in a way that the large corporation is not. Further, the power of large corporations to set up franchises which might have to be a bit more responsive to a locality's needs, mostly winds up eliminating the locally owned businesses so the franchise can rule uncontested—a take it or leave it stance vis-à-vis the locality. Finally, and inevitably, the franchise has to pass on some of the locality's spending capacity to central headquarters. Ideally, a decentralized currency would favor local initiatives and redistribution inside localities (Sassen 2014: ch. 3).

In the last 20 years this shift towards the corporatizing of household debt has accelerated and become increasingly acute in more and more of the world (Sassen 2016; 2017).[8] Up to a certain point we need governments and corporations for some of our needs: vast transport systems, public buildings, airports, harbors, and so on. But much of this far too easily winds up using our money for their profit rather than our needs. One result is growing asymmetries of all sorts, marked by growing concentrations of wealth and expanded impoverishment at the other end. There are exceptions here and there, but they are not enough to obliterate these asymmetries.

Further, to some extent our governments have enabled the power of corporations to extract household money not just via consumption but also via their policies. The elegantly named "quantitative easing" is one such example: in the post-2008 crisis period, the U.S. became the most active government in transferring money to corporations, especially big banks and major financial firms (Sassen 2017). Only a small portion of this (US$320 billion) has been via proper channels—the legislature, which offers the chance of a public debate where we the citizens can, in principle, voice our acceptance or rejection of a government's proposal. But by far most of this transacting about the crisis was done secretly. We the people only found out via freedom of information requests (submitted by dedicated journalists) how our nation's money was spent: over $7 trillion dollars were secretly transferred from U.S. households to the global banking system. Several trillion more were transferred via quantitative easing, a public event, but one incomprehensible to the average household; this is language that does not spell out the fact that it is households and central bank money that is being transferred to private banks and corporations.

These types of abuses by powerful private actors is what leads me to argue that we need decentralized currencies that function as genuine exchange mediums to handle a vast range of the needs of households, modest firms, and localities. Such local currencies cannot handle all aspects of an economy, but they can handle quite a bit of the local economy of a city or region. It would mean avoiding franchises and establishing locally owned operations—the profits then recirculate in the community or city rather than partly being captured by corporate headquarters—that might be located in the same city or far away, including foreign locations. At the same time, we need national currencies to engage in the vast infrastructural and servicing projects that a country requires to address the needs of its people; and this may mean contracting with large engineering corporations. But this should not be necessary for many of our daily needs—food, furniture, and such.

Decentralized currencies should enable the return of significant components of our modern economies back into our cities and communities. And if these currencies are digitized, local initiatives and innovations can get replicated across a region or a country or a continent's localities. This is one way of constructing larger multi-nodal operational spaces that can cut across diverse types of boundaries without losing their local insertion.

What we do not need is what is happening today in a growing number of countries: the large-scale direct and indirect appropriation of the income of households and of modest firms to finance the profit-seeking aims of corporations.

Conclusion

Across time, cities have complicated the straightforward implementation of technologies. Cities are great hackers, though they mostly are so in ways we cannot quite capture in our language—cities have their own language. The mix of urban materialities and people's cultures in the city does not always lead to predictable outcomes, and hence can unsettle or disrupt the best designs. This holds at many levels—from advanced transportation systems to "intelligent systems" installed in buildings, to name just a few. Therewith the city also is a lens that allows us to understand the diverse interactions between users (whether systems, organizations, or people) and the design and implementation of the technologies used in cities.

The DNA of the city is more akin to open-source technology—the notion of the perpetual beta also comes to mind. An approach that takes open-sourcing into account would enable interactions between the technology and the user—beyond those already pre-programmed within these systems. This would strengthen an understanding of the city as a combination of incompleteness and complexity: it is this mix that has enabled cities to outlive enterprises, kingdoms, nation-states, and, yes, Cisco Systems. These are all rather closed formal systems, which has made them rigid and more susceptible to obsolescence. One implication is that the current practice of installing more and more closed, centrally controlled intelligent systems in cities puts those cities themselves at risk of becoming obsolete when the technologies become obsolete.

The city puts technologies to a test. It is one window into understanding successful technological innovations for urban systems and urban life. Powerful actors can remake cities in their image. But cities talk back as a type of open-source urbanism. There are diverse versions of this at local and immediate levels: do-it-yourself urbanism, tactical urbanism, urban guerilla tactics, urban acupuncture, urban prototyping. Each of these multiple small interventions may not look like much, but together they give added meaning to the notion of the incompleteness of cities and the fact that this incompleteness gives cities their long lives, thereby outlasting other more powerful entities.

Notes

1 The emergent landscape I am describing promotes a multiplication of diverse spatiotemporal framings and diverse normative mini-orders, where once the dominant logic was towards producing grand unitary national spatial, temporal, and normative framings (see Sassen 2008).
2 One synthesizing image we might use to capture these dynamics is the movement from centripetal nation-state articulation to a centrifugal multiplication of specialized assemblages, where one of many examples might be the trans-border networks of specific types of struggles, enactments, art, and so on.
3 In using the term neighborhood I refer to modest sections of a city; usually we do not use this term to name the places where the very rich live.
4 A great innovation along these lines is the healthcare project developed by Dr. Manmeet Kaur, to assist low-income workers in Harlem, in New York: www.cityhealthworks.com.
5 The simplest example of an implementation of this sort, albeit elementary, is the pot-hole application developed by the Boston municipal government: you hit or see a pot-hole, you click on the app, and the city government gets the information about its existence and the coordinates of its location. It saves the municipal government much wasted time trying to find potholes.
6 In a project on low-wage workers and digitization I found that what would most enable low-wage workers is the extension of digitization to the larger space within which these workers operate: not only the workplace narrowly understood, but also, and very importantly, their neighborhood. For a list of such innovations, see www.saskiasassen.com/PDFs/publications/digitization-and-work.pdf.
7 I thank Geert Lovink, Nathaniel Tkacz, and Patricia de Vries for letting me use this text here.
8 See Sassen (2017) for more details.

References

Lovink, G., Tkacz, N., and de Vries, P. (eds) (2015) *MoneyLab Reader: An Intervention in Digital Economy*, Amsterdam: Institute of Network Cultures.
Sassen, S. (2001) [1991] *The Global City*, Princeton: Princeton University Press.
Sassen, S. (2008) *Territory Authority Rights: From Medieval to Global Assemblages*, Princeton: Princeton University Press.
Sassen, S. (2012) "Interactions of the technical and the social: digital formations of the powerful and powerless," *Information, Communication and Society*. www.tandfonline.com/doi/abs/10.1080/1369118X.2012.667912.
Sassen, S. (2013a) "Does the city have speech?" *Public Culture* 25, 2 (April): 209–221.

Sassen, S. (2013b) "Open sourcing the neighborhood," *Forbes*, November 10. www.forbes.com/sites/techonomy/2013/11/10/open-sourcing-the-neighborhood/.

Sassen, S. (2014) *Expulsions*, Cambridge, MA: Harvard University Press.

Sassen, S. (2016) "The global city: enabling economic intermediation and bearing its costs," *City and Community* 15, 2: 97–108. http://saskiasassen.com/PDFs/publications/Sassen%2C%20City%20%26%20Community%2C%20The%20Global%20City.pdf.

Sassen, S. (2017) "Predatory formations dressed in Wall Street suits and algorithmic math," *Science, Technology & Society* 22, 1 (February): 1–15.

Part VI
Practice

29

Is It Really that Bad?

The Status of Women in Architecture and the Gender Equity Movement

Despina Stratigakos

Women currently make up 44 percent of architecture students in the United States and the United Kingdom (National Architectural Accrediting Board 2015a: 11; Duncan 2013).[1] These figures are perhaps the most hopeful sign of a more equitable future for American and British women in architecture. And yet they are also among its most troubling. How can they be both? Despite robust female enrollments in past decades, we have not seen a comparable rise in the number of women in practice, because female graduates drain out of the system. Questions about this pattern of attrition and why it continues have largely focused on women's entry into practice, particularly the early years of the transition. But the loss also suggests that not all is well in academia and that we need to better prepare female graduates for the professional conditions they will encounter. Moreover, schools themselves must be challenged on their discriminatory attitudes and practices, which architectural graduates carry forward into the workplace.

Today's enrollments in the United States would not have happened without much earlier efforts to dismantle educational barriers, including Title IX of the 1972 Education Amendments Act, which legally ended discrimination against women in federally funded education programs. Although some architecture schools, including Cornell University and the University of Illinois, began admitting women in the late nineteenth century, many did not open their doors until legally forced to do so. Architect Cassandra Carroll, interviewed by the *New York Times* in 1977, recalled that when she applied to architecture programs in the late 1950s, not a single architectural college was open to women in her native New Jersey, forcing her to move to Pennsylvania to pursue her education (Bonomo 1977).

Under the influence of the new legislation and the women's movement, female architectural enrollments began a steady climb. In 1972, women had made up less than 6 percent of all architecture students in the United States. By 1975, in the wake of Title IX, this figure had doubled to 14 percent. A decade later, in 1985, the percentage had again doubled and stood at a national average of 30 percent, although that number varied wildly at individual schools (from less than 7 percent to more than 50 percent). The pace of women's enrollments slowed thereafter, reaching 40 percent of all architecture students nationally by the end of the 1990s (Berkeley 1972: 47; Goldberger 1974; Futterman 1989; Anthony 2001: 12–13; Simon 2003). And there the numbers have largely remained, with only fractional increases in the intervening years.

In light of the enrollment gains made over the decades and antidiscrimination legislation, it would be easy to assume that architecture schools have wholly eliminated the deep and widespread discrimination against women that Ellen Perry Berkeley exposed in her 1972 "Women in Architecture" essay for *Architectural Forum*. She revealed a distressing picture of women discouraged by deans and faculty from pursuing architectural studies, critics refusing to engage with their work, male peers harassing them for taking jobs from men, and financial aid officers awarding them less funding than male students on the assumption that female students "probably" had husbands to support them (Berkeley 1972: 48). Title IX changed the situation for women in theory, but practice has been another matter. In the 1990s, a series of high-profile reports in Canada and the United States revealed the hostile and even abusive environment women continued to face in some architecture schools (Fraser 1992; Anthony 2001: 19). In January 2014, the *Architects' Journal* announced that a "shocking" 54 percent of the female students responding to an international survey on the status of women in architecture claimed to have experienced sexual discrimination at university (Mark 2014a).

Other forms of bias, equally widespread but more covert, are found in omissions or absences. For example, students are rarely exposed to the historic roles of women in architecture, whether as builders, clients, or critics. Admittedly, such accounts were slow to appear, emerging only in the late 1970s, under the influence of the feminist movement. But the next three decades saw a true efflorescence of writings about women in architecture, even if these remained a small branch of all architecture publications. Books and articles explored women's historical roots in architecture, surveyed their professional status, and offered feminist critiques of architectural design and urban planning (e.g., Matrix 1984; American Architectural Foundation 1988; Suominen-Kokkonen 1992; Weisman 1992; Greed 1994; Hughes 1998; Searing et al. 1998; Adams and Tancred 2000; Anthony 2001; Willis and Hanna 2001; Allaback 2008; Stratigakos 2008a; Horton 2010). Writings of this period generally moved away from essentialist ideas about the relationship of biology to design—for example, that men design phallic towers, while women are drawn to curvaceous and womblike shapes—although such views have not entirely disappeared, as recent criticisms of Zaha Hadid's Al Wakrah Stadium in Qatar as "a great vulvic bulge" reveal (Kennedy 1981; Birkby 1981; Lobell 1989; Wainwright 2013). The early 1990s also saw the emergence of an architectural theory of gender that examined gendered values in architecture's modes of analysis and its language, such as in the treatment of structure as masculine and decoration as feminine (e.g., Colomina 1992; Agrest 1993; Bloomer 1994).[2]

Today these many decades of research and publications amount to a substantial and significant body of literature on women and gender in architecture. Yet its impact remains limited because the knowledge and insights it offers rarely find their way into the curricula of architecture schools, where they are arguably most needed. The 1980s and 1990s witnessed a profound transformation of the humanities and social sciences curricula at North American and European universities. Today it would be shocking to find, for example, a survey course on the history of world art or on cultural theory that did not include a single female name. And yet this is routinely the case with history and theory courses offered in architecture schools (Kingsly 1991; Ghirardo 1996). In light of such glaring omissions, one can no longer argue that the necessary material is not available; it is there in abundance. But for it to find its way onto syllabi—to be lifted off the library shelf and actually put into use—there must be a desire to shift pedagogical gears.

Similarly, design studios that make gender or women their focal point are almost nonexistent in architecture schools. The studio curriculum, which is at the heart of any architectural program, is largely shaped by the interests and experiences of faculty members. Although it is simplistic to assume that female faculty will be interested in courses relating to women and that male faculty will not, nonetheless, the gender imbalance among design faculty at architecture schools has almost certainly contributed to the absence of such themes in studio courses. A female student responding to the 2014 *Architects' Journal* survey complained, "There aren't enough women teaching—it is very male dominated" (Mark 2014a). In the United States, about a quarter of all tenured professors in architecture schools are women (National Architectural Accrediting Board 2015b: 5). This percentage encompasses all specializations, including history and theory, which have a higher representation of women. In many schools, the presence of women among the ranks of tenured design faculty remains negligible. Because design studios, especially the more prestigious upper-level undergraduate and graduate courses, tend to be assigned according to seniority, the gender imbalance among tenured design faculty results in the overwhelming majority of such courses being taught by men (Groat and Ahrentzen 1997: 272, 277–279).[3] Moreover, nontenured female faculty who teach studio courses are much less likely to risk a "controversial" theme.

Several years ago, at one of the nation's top architecture schools, a female tenured design professor offered an undergraduate studio that addressed a pressing social need: housing for survivors of domestic violence. The theme was truly exceptional for an architecture school, a provocative gesture in a milieu where faculty and students typically shun courses perceived as feminist. And yet, although highly unusual, the material could hardly be said to be irrelevant: architects have an important role to play in creating environments that promote a sense of security and healing for the occupants, and the studio offered students a chance to combine design and social justice concerns. At the end of the semester, I participated in the final review as the only woman on a panel of five guest critics. Over the course of the three-hour review, the male critics discussed the formal aspects of the designs but did not once refer to the function of the proposed buildings or to their users. They could have been discussing anything—parking structures, fire stations, coffee shops, cinemas—take your pick. Whether from discomfort, ignorance, or a lack of interest, they thus removed the projects from their intention and context, abstracting them to an assemblage of architectural elements. The challenge of designing spaces for a highly vulnerable population suffering from severe trauma was left unexplored. It was almost as if there was no language in this architectural milieu with which to discuss it.

The conversations that do not happen in architecture schools also extend to public lecture series. These talks are an integral part of the pedagogy of architecture schools, a way to promote intellectual exchange and to expose students and faculty to "luminaries" of the profession. Additionally, they are a time for the school's community, both academic and beyond, to come together and engage in broader discussions. Lori Brown and Nina Freedman, co-founders of the New York City-based advocacy group ArchiteXX, surveyed the public lecture series at 73 architecture schools in the United States during the 2012–2013 academic year. They discovered that in the fall, 62 percent of the schools had invited just one woman or no women at all to speak (Brown and Freedman 2014). The following spring, over a third had no women on their lecture podiums. Privileging male voices in this way sends a strong message about who a school considers an authority and deems worthy of an audience. It also discourages female students. As one student-respondent to the 2014 *Architects' Journal* survey stated, "Women architects are never discussed or celebrated in school. It is almost perceived as a negative to be a woman in architecture" (Mark 2014a).

But even these statistics are misleading as indicators of exposure to gender issues per se in architecture schools. Most women architects invited to speak about their work choose not to discuss their experiences in the field as women. And one could argue, why should they? A male architect, after all, would not be expected to reflect on being a man in the profession (although it probably would be a good thing if he were). But if these women do not speak out, who will?

Lectures that specifically address women in architecture, whether in terms of contemporary issues or their histories, are in short supply on the architecture lecture circuit. This silence is particularly astonishing at a time when the status of women has become a public relations nightmare for the profession, with a deluge of negative stories appearing in the press and online blogs. You wouldn't know it, though, from the discussions happening—or rather, not happening—inside architecture schools.

Unsurprisingly, women leave architecture school poorly prepared for the gender discrimination they will face in the professional world. Recent studies support what women architects have been saying for years: in terms of job opportunities, pay equity, mentoring, and promotion, the deck is stacked against them. This contributes to an appalling and enduring phenomenon: the massive dropout of women architects from practice. Although the proportion of women has grown from a third to 42 percent of architecture school graduates in the United States in the past 15 years, their numbers in practice have climbed at a glacial pace. In 2000, women represented 13 percent of registered architects; today that number stands at 19 percent (Anthony 2001: 12; National Architectural Accrediting Board 2015a: 19; Lipowicz 2001; Chen 2014). If this rate of progress holds, we will have to wait until 2093 before we reach a 50–50 gender split. Although the numbers vary somewhat, this pattern of attrition also holds true for other countries, including England and Australia. More than a glass ceiling, there would appear to be a massive, choking bottleneck squeezing women out of practice. Since the 1990s, the question of "Where are the women architects?" has surfaced repeatedly in the media in response to this disappearance. Studies of the phenomenon that attempt to provide an answer, and that have been initiated by women themselves, suggest that the root of the problem is not what most people think.

In 1908, German architectural critic Karl Scheffler insisted that creative productivity and human reproductivity did not mix (Stratigakos 2008b: 293). The assumption lives on, and to the question "Where are the women architects?," the facile response has been "At home, having babies." This explanation has never been able to account for the women who choose not to have children but leave architecture anyway. Nor do mothers in architecture who leave necessarily do so because of their children. Nonetheless, the perception remains that having a baby will damage a woman's architectural career. The 2014 *Architects' Journal* survey revealed widespread anxiety among women about the professional consequences of maternity—88 percent believed it would have a negative impact. (By contrast, 62 percent of men believed that having children would have no effect at all on a father's career.) In an example of life imitating art, one of the respondents admitted that—like Michelle Pfeiffer's architect character in the 1996 film *One Fine Day*—"she had hidden the fact she had kids from her employer 'for fear it would hinder her career'" (Mark 2014b). Unfortunately, women's anxieties are not unfounded. Architecture perceives itself as an all-or-nothing profession, and part-time or flexible work schemes are discouraged, adding to parents' burdens in juggling family and work (Mark 2014b). Employers all too often expect pregnant architects to leave or lose interest in their work and demote or sideline them accordingly; women report returning from maternity leave to find their positions stripped of their former appeal and interest—not by their babies but by their bosses, who assume they are unable to continue with their usual responsibilities. Others discover that their jobs have vanished altogether (Richardson 2013; De Graft-Johnson, Manley, and Greed 2003: 17, 19; Mark 2014b). And yet, even taking into account these obstacles, only a fraction (3.8 percent) of the *Architects' Journal* survey's female respondents stated that parenthood resulted in their leaving architecture altogether (Mark 2014b).

Instead, it is the pervasive and deeply rooted inequality of professional opportunities and treatment as well as a male-dominated workplace culture that lie at the heart of most women's exodus from architecture. The factors are complex and tend to be multiple and varied—not a single event but, as architect Deborah Berke explains, the "recurring small blows" or "death by a thousand cuts" that pushes women out the door (Beck 2012). Moreover, recent studies suggest that, rather than one large bottleneck, there are various "pinch points" along the trajectory of a woman architect's career, such as in pursuing licensure or hitting the glass ceiling, where attrition is more likely to occur (AIA San Francisco and Equity by Design Committee 2015: 22ff.).

In an effort to understand and combat women's high dropout rates, in 2013 members of the San Francisco chapter of the American Institute of Architects (AIA) created "The Missing 32% Project," named after the percentage of female architecture graduates who are lost to practice. As part of its research mission, the project surveyed nearly 2300 male and female architects nationally and found that job satisfaction was notably lower among women (28 percent) than men (41 percent). The reasons are not hard to discern. There is, to begin with, a pronounced difference in what men and women earn. In a profession known for its long hours and low compensation, this issue hits hard. The pay gap exists at all levels, from entry-level positions to principals, but increases sharply at midcareer. For example, the Missing 32% Project reported that male architects with 15–20 years of experience earned on average $100,000, whereas women with the same level of experience earned $80,000 (AIA San Francisco and Equity by Design Committee 2015: 19, 21, 33). In 2014 the U.S. Bureau of Labor Statistics also found that, among full-time architects, men earn on average 20 percent more than women (U.S. Bureau of Labor Statistics 2014). The 2014 survey by the *Architects' Journal* suggests that the imbalance is even greater and calls the pay gap "the most effective barometer of gender inequality in the profession." But because salary transparency is rare in most firms, the extent of these disparities is usually hidden. As the journal noted, many women who responded to their survey grossly underestimated how much more their male colleagues were earning (Mark 2014c, 2014d).

Folded within this salary gap is another story about women architects and stalled promotions that also contributes significantly to job dissatisfaction and dropping out. According to national AIA records, the numbers of women principals and partners at firms quadrupled from 4 percent in 1999 to 16 percent in 2005 (American Institute of Architects 2013: 5). What seemed to be a breakthrough in women's professional ascent soon proved, however, to be another instance of stagnation: a decade later, the figure stands at 17 percent (Willis 2014: 122). The National Council of Architectural Registration Boards, which administers registration examinations and develops internship programs in the United States, reports that women represent only 13 percent of supervisors in architecture firms who are overseeing interns (National Council of Architectural Registration Boards 2014: 6). Stated differently, 87 percent of young architects working towards licensure are doing so with a male supervisor, at least according to the official record.[4]

Various factors contribute to women's slow professional climb up the architectural ladder. Maternity is often seen as the chief culprit, and many women with children do express frustration at the profession's "mommy track," with its diminished opportunities (Kaji-O'Grady 2014). But, as architect Diana Griffiths writes, "if family commitments were the only barrier to success then women architects without children should be thriving" and "flying through the ranks" (Griffiths 2012). That they are not indicates that there are other, broader impediments. Among them, women are less likely to receive the more glamorous types of projects that help to advance careers. This is often blamed on women themselves: they lack the ambition to go after the big jobs, it is said, or are unwilling to put in the long hours required to pay their dues. The underlying presumption here, deeply engrained in the professional culture, is that architecture is a meritocracy that rewards talent and hard work in a straightforward way (Clark 2014; De Graft-Johnson, Manley, and Greed 2003: 19). Women who share that belief and commit themselves to architectural practice without seeing professional returns are apt to lose confidence in their own abilities. As Denise Scott Brown has written, "On seeing their male colleagues draw out in front of them, women who lack a feminist awareness are likely to feel that their failure to achieve is their own fault" (Scott Brown 1989: 245).

Mentoring can make a critical difference: careers are advanced not just by ambition and sacrifice but also by having a sponsor to show you the ropes, make connections, and put your name forward for those career-enhancing opportunities. The first attrition pinch points for a woman come in the early years after she graduates from an architecture program, when she struggles to make the transition to practice. As an intern working towards licensure, she will rely for guidance and support on a pool of architectural supervisors that, as noted earlier, is 87 percent male. Later in her career, as she strives to break through the glass ceiling—another attrition pinch point—she will be dependent on finding mentors among a leadership that is 83 percent male (based on the gender breakdown of partners and principals). Women in male-dominated fields benefit from having a mentor, whether it is a man or a woman. But, as Sheryl Sandberg writes in *Lean In*, "Men are significantly more likely than women to be sponsored." Moreover, mentors tend to choose protégés who remind them of themselves (Sandberg 2013: 66–67, 71; Anderson 2014; Anthony 2001: 166–167).

A few years ago, I met with a group of women at a prestigious global architecture firm that has an almost exclusively male leadership. The women, despite degrees from the nation's top architecture schools and years of hard work—they ate not only lunches but also dinners at their desks (and none had children)—had not advanced significantly up the firm's corporate ladder. They described an office culture deeply shaped by an "old boys' club" mentality. It was customary, for example, for the male partners to informally select an incoming young architect to mentor and bring up through the ranks, a process that included plum assignments, invitations to important meetings, and introductions to prestigious clients. Among the women, the protégé was known as "the anointed one," and in their time at the firm they had never seen the honor bestowed on a woman. Meanwhile, the very few women in senior management offered little support. Speaking as a female executive who finds direct requests for mentorship "a total mood killer," Sandberg cautions young women not to be too aggressive in this pursuit and advises them instead to focus on excelling, which will draw mentors to them (Sandberg 2013: 65, 68). Yet women can excel day after day, year after year, and still remain invisible in a system that sees only men as leadership material.

Beyond low pay and stalled careers, job satisfaction for women architects is eroded by routine sexism in the workplace. The "Women in Architecture" surveys published annually by the *Architects' Journal*, beginning in 2012, suggest that the problem is widespread and getting worse. The survey asks: "Have you ever suffered sexual discrimination in your career in architecture? (this might include inappropriate comments, or being treated differently because of your gender)." In 2012, 63 percent of the 700 female respondents answered in the affirmative. Some online commenters have objected to the breadth and subjectivity of the question, arguing that holding a door open for a woman or giving her maternity leave could qualify under this definition. But the examples submitted by respondents indicate that they know what discrimination means. These include being given more secretarial work to do than male peers, being asked whether they are menstruating, and being told that pregnancy will result in a salary cut. In the 2014 survey, 66 percent of the 710 female respondents answered in the affirmative. These accounts cannot be dismissed as tales of the dark past: most respondents are young—80 percent are under the age of 40. Moreover, the discrimination continues, for some on a regular basis: 33 percent encounter it on a monthly or quarterly basis, while 11 percent say it is a daily or weekly occurrence (Waite and Corvin 2012; Minter 2014; Mark 2014e).

The more overt forms of sexism tend to occur in work with contractors, and two-thirds of the female respondents to the 2014 *Architects' Journal* survey felt that women's authority has yet to be accepted in the building industry, with half of the male respondents agreeing. When women first entered architecture in the nineteenth century, their opponents claimed that they would be defeated by their lack of authority on the construction site, a claim that is still used to justify women's lower promotion rates compared to men. But as Patricia Hickey, co-founder of Bubble Architects, stated in response to the survey,

> We need to be clear that women are being held back from promotion in architectural offices not because the practice directors think they will not be respected on site, but because the primarily male directors do not respect female leaders within the office; otherwise a gender pay discrepancy for the same roles would not persist.
>
> (Mark 2014f)

A number of studies suggest that it is easier for women architects to develop coping strategies for the overt sexism they may encounter at the building site. By contrast, the more subtle and pervasive forms of discrimination encountered in the architectural office do more damage because they are harder to counteract or defend against (Clark 2014; De Graft-Johnson, Manley, and Greed 2003: 21; Burns 2014).

As a historian, what alarms me about this picture—beyond the legacies that have been lost to us and the sheer injustice of it—is how familiar it all is. For well over 100 years, in one form or another, women architects have been fighting the same battle. In 1905, for example, Mabel Brown interviewed women architects for the *San Francisco Chronicle* to discover why they remained "something of a curiosity." She was told "that popular prejudice is against women architects—that it is next to impossible for one to get an opening in a regular office; and since experience means everything, it is impossible to make headway when denied a beginning" (Brown 1905). Resistance to their employment, as we know from other sources in this period, was based on fear that a female presence would disrupt a male environment, skepticism about their training and skills, the certainty that they could not exercise authority on the building site, and the assumption that their commitment to practice would evaporate as soon as they married (*Journal of the Society of Architects* 1912). If a woman did manage to get her foot in the door, Brown learned, she could expect menial duties and a "pittance" for pay. Architectural offices typically assigned women drafting or detail work, because they were believed to lack the "all-round" skills of their male colleagues (Brown 1905). To avoid such constraints, women architects advised other women considering the profession to open their own firms. But they also warned them to think twice about pursuing architecture at all if they lacked "the influence necessary to get on," meaning the personal and professional networks for success (*Journal of the Society of Architects* 1913). By and large, the hurdles to equity 100 years ago sound strikingly similar to those encountered today.

At the same time, 2015 is not 1905. Laws now protect against discrimination, even if they are not always enforced, and women architects have the numbers and allies to push for real change. The latter include male architects also dissatisfied with the status quo. The 2014 *Architects' Journal* survey revealed that 73 percent of the male respondents (and 79 percent of the women) believe the profession is too male (Mark 2014e). Moreover, although there have long been global forms of communication, the accessibility and reach of the Internet have both revealed how widespread the problem is and created the possibility for meaningful collaborations across borders and cultures. Finally, studies on gender discrimination in architecture, some of which have been cited here, have proliferated in recent years. In some cases, they provide us with concrete recommendations for tackling architecture's gender inequities, whereas in others, they highlight new areas of research that still need to be explored.

While money is not a panacea for architecture's gender inequities, it is a good place to start. Professional organizations must step up and exert pressure to end illegal pay practices. In the United Kingdom, architects are calling on the Royal Institute of British Architects (RIBA) to "name and shame" firms that pay women less than men for similar work, saying that it is no longer enough to issue general statements of condemnation. The demand arose after a report was released by the UK Office for National Statistics indicating that women architects earn 25 percent less on average than their male counterparts. Those denouncing the pay divide argue that change will not happen until the culprits are exposed and that inaction suggests indifference or even acquiescence. As Stephen Riley of Kiran Curtis Associates stated, "This issue has been raised constantly over the past 30 years and [the RIBA] is now looking rather foolish and damaging the image of the profession" (Mark 2014g).

Persuasion of a different sort has been explored by the Beverly Willis Architecture Foundation (BWAF) in encouraging large firms to take responsibility for promoting diversity among their leadership ranks. Beverly Willis, who opened an architecture office in San Francisco in 1958, founded BWAF in New York City in 2002 to advance women's status in the building industry. Since 2010, she and others at the BWAF have been holding round table forums with industry leaders as a means to educate them about the importance of diversity in senior management. The participants include principals or partners and human resource executives of the nation's largest architecture, engineering, and construction firms. In addition, the BWAF invites female executives from the organizations representing their most important clients. The mix is an effective one. When companies know that their clients are mindful of their lack of diversity, they become much more motivated to institute changes to protect their image and bottom line (Beverly Willis Architecture Foundation n.d.). Professional architecture organizations, such as the AIA, have an important role to play here in setting and promoting strong industry norms. Without such pressures, the status quo is likely to continue, with the anointed of one generation passing the baton to the anointed of the next.

Female role models can exert their own influence and need to be far more visible in classrooms, firms, and professional organizations. Having a personal relationship with a role model is not necessary; an effective role model may be a prominent figure in the profession or even a historical one. Role models boost self-esteem by countering negative stereotypes that cast doubt on a person's abilities to perform well in the profession. They increase motivation for career advancement and success. They foster a sense of identification with a field, combating alienation. The scarcity of female role models in architecture is thus profoundly damaging. According to the Missing 32% Project, almost a third of women who left practice gave the lack of role models as the deciding factor (AIA San Francisco and Equity by Design Committee 2015: 36).

To date, studies conducted on the status of women architects have largely focused on countries where attrition rates have been high, including Australia, Canada, the United Kingdom, and the United States. In addition to this national research, we need cross-cultural investigations that would allow us to compare places where women architects languish with those where they thrive. Among the latter is Greece, which by 1967 had seen women's architectural enrollments at the National Technical University in Athens reach 70 percent. That same year, women represented 50 percent of practitioners in Greece; today they are in the majority (58 percent). What makes Greece a welcoming environment for women in comparison to, say, Estonia, where 85 percent of architects are men (Meisels 1967; Mirza and Nacey Research 2015)? Along similar lines, what makes architecture different from other demanding and traditionally male occupations, such as medicine and law, in which women experience greater success? Women currently represent a third of all doctors and lawyers in the U.S., and those numbers are moving closer towards parity: half of the youngest doctors and lawyers are women (Mitchell 2012; Cohen

2012).⁵ Our understanding of what holds women back in architecture would benefit from comparative studies with other professions that have better integrated and retained their female practitioners. An extensive literature on gender diversity and women's leadership exists for other fields, but the lack of comprehensive long-term data for architecture has limited the ability to engage with it in order to determine what conditions are specific to the profession, and where it can implement successful strategies developed by others.⁶ Studies of this scale require considerable resources, however, and architecture's professional organizations have been slow to take the initiative.

That may change as their members become more vocal in demanding greater gender equity in architecture. Among the highlights of the 2015 AIA National Convention in Atlanta was a "hackathon" workshop organized by Equity by Design (formerly known as the Missing 32% Project) that brought together women and men from diverse backgrounds in a shared search for solutions. Many of those present had become interested in the issues through Equity by Design's social media outreach and were meeting for the first time at the convention, reinforcing the role that new forms of networking are having in knitting activist individuals and groups into a larger and more powerful movement. Equity by Design also displayed its research findings on gender equity issues, making visible, through its bold infographics, the impact of discrimination on the careers of women architects. Additionally, Rosa Sheng, the group's founding chair, co-authored a resolution for "Equity in Architecture," overwhelmingly passed by the convention delegates, that calls on "both women and men to realize the goal of equitable practice in order to retain talent, advance the architecture profession, and communicate the value of design to society" and states that "equity is everyone's issue." As the resolution points out, although the institute has recently called on the public to "look up" and value architecture and the service architects provide to society, the profession itself needs to look inward and to reflect on why it so devalues its own "human capital." The resolution calls on the institute "to develop an ongoing program to assess data, set a plan of action, track progress, and report on results. Now more than ever is the time for action both from grassroots and Institute leadership." As the resolution itself underscores, there have been many similar resolutions passed over the years—the first at the 1973 AIA convention in San Francisco, over 40 years ago (American Institute of Architects 2015: 15–16; Sheng 2015). Whether the leadership of the AIA and other professional organizations will finally take up their members' calls for action and address architecture's ongoing diversity problems through courageous and effective policy actions remains to be seen.

Notes

1 This chapter previously appeared as "The Sad State of Gender Equity in the Architectural Profession," in Despina Stratigakos, *Where Are the Women Architects* (2016), and is republished here with permission of Princeton University Press.
2 For a critique of the exclusion of this feminist theory in subsequent architectural theory anthologies, see Burns (2012).
3 Groat and Ahrentzen (1997) point out that the predominance of male faculty in upper-level design studios is not simply an outcome of the higher percentages of tenured male design faculty but also has to do with gendered perceptions that female faculty, including those in senior positions, are better suited to undertake the "nurturing" work of entry-level studios.
4 It is possible that an architect working towards licensure does so unofficially under a female supervisor, who does not have the authority to sign off as the National Council of Architectural Registration Boards (NCARB) supervisor. Even so, the degree of gender disparity in these figures leaves little doubt that male supervisors remain by far the dominant presence.
5 Cohen (2012) points out, however, that attrition—although at lower rates than in architecture—also exists in medicine and is slowing the progress towards parity.
6 For examples of promising work comparing architecture with other fields, see Adams and Tancred (2000), and Anthony (2001).

References

Adams, A. and Tancred, P. (2000) *"Designing Women": Gender and the Architectural Profession*, Toronto: University of Toronto Press.

Agrest, D. (1993) *Architecture from Without: Theoretical Framings for a Critical Practice*, Cambridge, MA: MIT Press.

AIA San Francisco and Equity by Design Committee. (2015) *Equity by Design: Knowledge, Discussion, Action! 2014 Equity in Architecture Survey Report and Key Outcomes*, report prepared by A. Pitts, R. Sheng, E. Evenhouse, and R. Hu, San Francisco: AIA San Francisco.

Allaback, S. (2008) *The First American Women Architects*, Urbana: University of Illinois Press.

American Architectural Foundation. (1988) *"That Exceptional One": Women in American Architecture, 1888–1988*, Washington, DC: American Architectural Foundation.

American Institute of Architects. (2013) "Women in architecture toolkit." http://issuu.com/aiadiv/docs/women_in_architecture_toolkit (December 3, 2014).

American Institute of Architects. (2015) "Resolution 15-1, equity in architecture," *2015 AIA National Convention and Design Exposition: Official Delegate Information Booklet*, Washington, DC: American Institute of Architects.

Anderson, L. (2014) "How women are climbing architecture's career ladder," *Curbed*, March 17. http://curbed.com/archives/2014/03/17/how-women-are-climbing-architectures-career-ladder.php (December 14, 2014).

Anthony, K. H. (2001) *Designing for Diversity: Gender, Race, and Ethnicity in the Architectural Profession*, Urbana: University of Illinois Press.

Beck, E. (2012) "Making the mold: the lack of diversity in architecture isn't a simple problem, but there are better and worse ways to approach the issue," *Architect*, July 2. www.architectmagazine.com/practice/best-practices/making-progress-with-diversity-in-architecture_o (December 20, 2014).

Berkeley, E. P. (1972) "Women in architecture," *Architectural Forum*, September: 46–53.

Beverly Willis Architecture Foundation. (n.d.), "Goals of the Industry Leaders Roundtable." www.bwaf.org/campaign/industry-leader-roundtable (August 8, 2018).

Birkby, P. (1981) "Herspace," *Making Room: Women and Architecture*, special issue, *Heresies* 3, 3: 28–29.

Bloomer, J. (ed.) (1994) *Architecture and the Feminine: Mop-Up Work*, special issue, *Any*, January/February.

Bonomo, J. (1977) "Architecture is luring women," *New York Times*, April 2.

Brown, L. and Freedman, N. (2014) "Women in architecture: statistics for the academy," *Indigogo*. www.indiegogo.com/projects/women-in-architecture (December 20, 2014).

Brown, M. (1905) "Women in profession: VII—Architecture," *San Francisco Chronicle*, September 24.

Burns, K. (2012) "A girl's own adventure: gender in contemporary architectural theory anthology," *Journal of Architectural Education* 65: 125–134.

Burns, K. (2014) "The elephant in our parlour: everyday sexism in architecture," *Archiparlour*, August 20. http://archiparlour.org/the-elephant-in-our-parlour-everyday-sexism-in-architecture (December 14, 2014).

Chen, S. (2014) "In architecture, a glass ceiling," *Wall Street Journal*, August 21. www.wsj.com/articles/in-architecture-a-glass-ceiling-1408633998 (December 20, 2014).

Clark, J. (2014) "Six myths about women and architecture," *Archiparlour*, September 6. http://archiparlour.org/six-myths-about-women-and-architecture (December 12, 2014).

Cohen, P. (2012) "More women are doctors and lawyers than ever—but progress is stalling," *Atlantic*, December 11. www.theatlantic.com/sexes/archive/2012/12/more-women-are-doctors-and-lawyers-than-ever-but-progress-is-stalling/266115 (December 21, 2014).

Colomina, B. (ed.) (1992) *Sexuality and Space*, New York: Princeton Architectural Press.

De Graft-Johnson, A., Manley, S., and Greed, C. (2003) *Why Do Women Leave Architecture?*, Bristol: University of the West of England—Bristol, and London: Royal Institute of British Architects.

Duncan, J. (2013) "Why are so many women leaving architecture," *Guardian*, August 7. www.theguardian.com/women-in-leadership/2013/aug/07/women-leaving-architecture-profession (December 20, 2014).

Fraser, G. (1992) "Architecture students abused, report says: teaching environment at Carleton School called discriminatory, unprofessional, sexist," *Globe and Mail*, December 23.

Futterman, E. (1989) "Women in architecture: 100 years and counting," *St. Louis Post-Dispatch*, May 7.

Ghirardo, D. (1996) "Cherchez la femme: where are the women in architectural studies?," in K. Rüedi, S. Wigglesworth, and D. McCorquodale (eds) *Desiring Practices: Architecture, Gender and the Interdisciplinary*, London: Black Dog.

Goldberger, P. (1974) "Women architects building influence in a profession that is 98.8% male," *New York Times*, May 18.
Greed, C. H. (1994) *Women and Planning: Creating Gendered Realities*, London: Routledge.
Griffiths, D. (2012) "A lost legacy," *Archiparlour*, April 18. http://archiparlour.org/authors/diana-griffiths (December 12, 2014).
Groat, L. N. and Ahrentzen, S. B. (1997) "Voices for change in architectural education: seven facets of transformation from the perspectives of faculty women," *Journal of Architectural Education* 50, 4: 271–285.
Horton, I. S. (2010) *Early Women Architects of the San Francisco Bay Area: The Lives and Work of Fifty Professionals, 1890–1951*, Jefferson, NC: McFarland.
Hughes, F. (ed.) (1998) *The Architect: Reconstructing Her Practice*, Cambridge, MA: MIT Press.
Journal of the Society of Architects. (1912) "Architecture as a profession for women," 5, 53: 188–189.
Journal of the Society of Architects. (1913) "Why not women architects? Great demand and no supply," 6, 70: 393–394.
Kaji-O'Grady, S. (2014) "Does motherhood + architecture = no career?," *ArchitectureAU*, November 20. http://architectureau.com/articles/does-motherhood-architecture-no-career (January 20, 2015).
Kennedy, M. (1981) "Seven hypotheses on female and male principles in architecture," *Making Room: Women and Architecture*, special issue, *Heresies* 3, 3: 12–13.
Kingsly, K. (1991) "Rethinking architectural history from a gender perspective," in T. A. Dutton (ed.) *Voices in Architectural Education: Cultural Politics and Pedagogy*, New York: Bergin and Garvey.
Lipowicz, A. (2001) "Architects make gains, but few elevated to top," *Crain's New York Business* 17, 25: 32.
Lobell, M. (1989) "The buried treasure: women's ancient architectural heritage," in E. P. Berkeley and M. McQuaid (eds) *Architecture: A Place for Women*, Washington, DC: Smithsonian Institution Press.
Mark, L. (2014a) "Bullying on the rise in architecture school," *Architects' Journal*, January 10. www.architectsjournal.co.uk/home/events/wia/bullying-on-the-rise-in-architecture-school/8657351.article (May 23, 2015).
Mark, L. (2014b) "88% women say having children puts them at a disadvantage," *Architects' Journal*, January 10. www.architectsjournal.co.uk/home/events/wia/88-women-say-having-children-puts-them-at-disadvantage/8657348.article (May 23, 2015).
Mark, L. (2014c) "Gender pay gap worst in America," *Architects' Journal*, January 10. www.architectsjournal.co.uk/home/events/wia/gender-pay-gap-worst-in-america/8657355.article (April 6, 2015).
Mark, L. (2014d) "Pay gap widens: women architects earn less than men," *Architects' Journal*, January 10. www.architectsjournal.co.uk/home/events/wia/pay-gap-widens-women-architects-earn-less-than-men/8657346.article (April 6, 2015).
Mark, L. (2014e) "Sexual discrimination on the rise for women in architecture," *Architects' Journal*, January 10. www.architectsjournal.co.uk/home/events/wia/sexual-discrimination-on-the-rise-for-women-in-architecture/8657345.article (April 6, 2015).
Mark, L. (2014f) "Survey shows shocking lack of respect for women architects," *Architects' Journal*, January 10. www.architectsjournal.co.uk/survey-shows-shocking-lack-of-respect-for-women-architects/8657343 retrieved (April 6, 2015).
Mark, L. (2014g) "Gender pay gap: 'beyond shocking'," *Architects' Journal*, May 2. www.architectsjournal.co.uk/news/gender-pay-gap-beyond-shocking/8662077.article (April 6, 2015).
Matrix. (1984) *Making Space: Women and the Man Made Environment*, London: Pluto.
Meisels, S. S. (1967) "Half of Greek architects are women," *Jerusalem Post*, December 24.
Minter, H. (2014) "Sexism in architecture: on the rise," *Guardian*, January 13. www.theguardian.com/women-in-leadership/2014/jan/13/women-in-architecture-sexism (December 15, 2014).
Mirza and Nacey Research. (2015). *The Architectural Profession in Europe, 2014: A Sector Study Commissioned by the Architects' Council of Europe*, Brussels: Architects' Council of Europe. www.ace-cae.eu/fileadmin/New_Upload/7._Publications/Sector_Study/2014/EN/2014_EN_FULL.pdf (April 3, 2015).
Mitchell, J. (2012) "Women notch progress: females now constitute one-third of nation's ranks of doctors and lawyers," *The Wall Street Journal*, December 4.
National Architectural Accrediting Board. (2015a) *2014 Annual Report from the National Architectural Accrediting Board, Inc., Part I: Programs, Students, and Degrees*, Washington, DC: National Architectural Accrediting Board.
National Architectural Accrediting Board. (2015b) *2014 Annual Report from the National Architectural Accrediting Board, Inc., Part III: Faculty*, Washington, DC: National Architectural Accrediting Board.

National Council of Architectural Registration Boards. (2014) *2014 NCARB by the Numbers*, Washington, DC: National Council of Architectural Registration Boards. www.ncarb.org/About-NCARB/~/media/Files/PDF/Special-Paper/NCARB_by_the_Numbers_2014.ashx (December 21, 2014).

Richardson, A. (2013) "Half the mothers I know have been driven from their jobs," *Guardian*, August 8. www.theguardian.com/money/2013/aug/08/workplace-discrimination-pregnant-women-mothers-common (December 21, 2014).

Sandberg, S. (2013) *Lean In: Women, Work, and the Will to Lead*, New York: Knopf.

Scott Brown, D. (1989) "Room at the top: sexism and the star system in architecture," in E. P. Berkeley and M. McQuaid (eds) *Architecture: A Place for Women*, Washington, DC: Smithsonian Institution Press.

Searing, H. et al. (1998) *Equal Partners: Men and Women Principals in Contemporary Architectural Practice*, Northampton, MA: Smith College Museum of Art.

Sheng, R. (2015) "Equity by design: AtlAIAnta! Convention recap," *Equity by Design: Missing 32 Percent Blog*, May 17. http://themissing32percent.com/blog/2015/5/17/equity-by-design-aia-convention-atlanta-recap (May 23, 2015).

Simon, C. (2003) "Women in architecture: what are we doing here?," *Contract* 45, 3: 94.

Stratigakos, D. (2008a) *A Women's Berlin*, Minneapolis: University of Minnesota Press.

Stratigakos, D. (2008b) "The good architect and the bad parent: on the formation and disruption of a canonical image," *Journal of Architecture* 13, 3: 283–296.

Stratigakos, D. (2016) *Where Are the Women Architects?*, Princeton: Princeton University Press.

Suominen-Kokkonen, R. (1992) *The Fringe of a Profession: Women as Architects in Finland from the 1890s to the 1950s*, Helsinki, 1992.

U.S. Bureau of Labor Statistics. (2014) "Household data annual averages." www.bls.gov/cps/cpsaat39.pdf (April 6, 2015).

Wainwright, O. (2013) "Zaha Hadid's sport stadiums: 'too big, too expensive, too much like a vagina'," *Guardian*, November 28. www.theguardian.com/artanddesign/2013/nov/28/zaha-hadid-stadiums-vagina (December 3, 2014).

Waite, R. and Corvin, A.-M. (2012) "Shock survey results as the AJ launches campaign to raise women architects' status," *Architects' Journal*, January 16. www.architectsjournal.co.uk/news/daily-news/shock-survey-results-as-the-aj-launches-campaign-to-raise-women-architects-status/8624748.article (December 21, 2014).

Weisman, L. K. (1992) *Discrimination by Design: A Feminist Critique of the Man-Made Environment*, Urbana: University of Illinois Press.

Willis, E. (2014) "Five firm changes," *Architect*, October: 116–124.

Willis, J. and Hanna, B. (2001) *Women Architects in Australia, 1900–1950*, Red Hill, Australia: Royal Australian Institute of Architects.

30
Where is the Social Project?[1]

Kenny Cupers

In the last decade, a range of participatory and activist practices has emerged as the self-proclaimed inheritors of architecture's social project. From Architecture for Humanity's aid in poor and disaster-struck regions to temporary urban interventions, many of these initiatives transcend conventional definitions of architecture (Borasi and Zardini 2008). A new generation of architects, designers, and urbanists are turning down office jobs to build shelters in Burma, reclaim the streets of Sevilla, guerrilla-garden in London, or study the *favelas* of Rio de Janeiro. Privileging activism, informality, and alterity over what is perceived as a dominant architectural culture of tired formalism and celebrity obsessions, such practices expand design from the manipulation of form and material to the development of procedures and the creation of models of engagement (Bell and Wakeford 2008; Zeiger 2011). Despite their potential for change, many critics remain skeptical about the ultimate results and repercussions of these initiatives. Those policing the disciplinary boundaries of architecture have been most readily dismissive of what they consider to be social work and not *architecture*. A clear challenge to such disciplinary rejection has been the 2010 MoMA exhibition *Small Scale, Big Change: New Architectures of Social Engagement* (Lepik 2010). With projects that include low-cost housing, community facilities, school building, access to public transportation, and the renovation of existing social housing, the exhibition claimed novelty for a socially relevant form of architectural practice. While this direction is far from unprecedented in the history of twentieth-century architecture (Cupers 2013), it is more rare in MoMA's curatorial tradition. Yet, despite this symbolic importance and the galvanizing effect of such exhibitions, contemporary architectural culture seems to be increasingly fragmented by a fundamental fault line: that between architecture as social process and architecture as formal object.

On which side of this split can we locate the social project of architecture today? Is it a matter of devising social procedures or designing novel forms? How can new imaginaries be produced through projection or activism? Can architects, if they wish to be socially responsible, remain designers or would they then become social workers, as some practitioners derisively claim? These questions are hardly new. And yet they tend to remain unanswered unless we can devise a more precise way to evaluate the effects of these new projects on their larger social and political context. To do so, we need an analytical lens other than that conventionally trained on architectural projects. Such a change in perspective is well underway, not only in the field of architecture but also in other humanities and social science disciplines. The following three propositions suggest how such shifting approaches might help us rethink the social project of contemporary architecture.

From Intentionality to Agency

A first, rather straightforward, shift in perspective is that from intentionality to agency (Cupers and Doucet 2009). Critics typically evaluate the stated intention of the designer in relation to the evidence of the architectural product, whether gleaned through its media representation or through personal experience. That approach may suffice to judge the aesthetic or experiential merits of a building, but does not prove very helpful in assessing the types of projects and practices mentioned above. Does Park(ing) Day—an annual event whereby designers and citizens temporarily transform metered parking spots into public mini-parks—constitute a fundamental shift in the sociality of the contemporary street or is it a mere sign of spatial conquest by the cappuccino-sipping urban class? Answering that question requires an analysis not only of the social or political intentions, but of the agents, constituents, and publics involved in such events, the ways they emerge and proliferate, and most importantly, their ultimate repercussions—spatially, socially, and architecturally.

A crucial weakness of many activist architectural practices today is not that they are divorced from the conventional tools of design but that they are often only rhetorically political. They share this tendency with the dominant culture of architecture that they claim so loudly to reject. If formalism can be easily dismissed for its fetishizing of intentionality through authorship, architectural activism often falls victim to the same temptation, even if the intentions are explicitly political rather than formal. The tone of the debate changes fundamentally when we focus instead on the effects rather than the intentions of such projects. Despite benevolent rhetoric and good intentions, some activist projects are rightly criticized for being vehicles of a new "humanitarian imperialism" or for engendering urban gentrification (Zeiger 2011). In basic terms, an analysis of the social project of architecture today can no longer remain within the realms of intent, form, or representation but needs to tie these to consequence and effect.

From Ideology to Materiality

A second and related proposition is to more carefully consider the materiality of the projects under scrutiny. The call to judge architecture on what it *does* rather than how it *represents* is commonplace in architectural culture and yet it is rarely answered. In some ways, this mirrors the recent calls across the humanities and social sciences for a "new materialism" (e.g., Coole and Frost 2010). This trend should logically find fertile ground in architecture. It is hard to imagine a discipline traditionally better placed to think through issues of materiality and their human ramifications. And yet, architecture's materialism is often as idealistic as the type of reductive Marxism Bruno Latour so cogently dismisses (Latour 2007). Architecture critics—even those with a so-called phenomenological interest—have a long tradition of evaluating architectural projects as if they were images rather than complex processes of policy, design, construction, and inhabitation. The tendency within the academy to treat architecture discursively does not always prove useful for gauging its social role. Architecture is too often understood as a realm of forms merely *representing* the social, rather than as a process of production that takes place within a larger social world and also helps shape that world. Shifting the lens thus means reconnecting architectural production with consumption and use.

The direct equivalence of architectural form with politics—a modernist contradiction given new life by an alliance of practitioners and theorists during the 1990s—has now largely been discredited.[2] But its withering has only laid bare an older and more fundamental fallacy of architectural theory, whose basic assumption is *pars pro toto*: singular works of architecture illuminate our contemporary condition to such extent that the larger production of the built environment is but a footnote of similitude. Such a lens freezes the complex materiality of building into ideology and representation. Only a more empirically attuned lens, which focuses on the relationships between the material and the social, can reveal that complexity. In order to illuminate such relationships, we need to approach architecture not as an *image* of the political, but as an integral part of a more messy politics in which the materiality of architecture matters as much as those actually producing and using it.

From Critique to Reflexivity

Discussing the social project of architecture requires contextualization against the horizon of contemporary capitalism. The social ambitions of architectural modernism did not exist in a vacuum and were tied to larger forces such as national economic development, militarization, systems of international trade, the development of the welfare state, etc. So too is contemporary architecture inscribed in a particular regime of production and consumption. If that regime is now predominantly referred to as neoliberal and urbanization continues to play a key role in its strategies of accumulation, the politics of architecture are certainly more complex than blanket categories of complicity or resistance allow. The fact that the social role of architecture is now more often understood in terms of individual agency than collective structure might itself be part of a broader shift in mindset accompanying the rise of neoliberal democracies over the past decades. Despite their entanglement in increasingly interconnected structures, architects often appear to be standing alone. That is the case for star architects, behind which are hidden not only droves of hard-working interns but an unwieldy network of media and other institutions. It is also true for the "critical practitioner," a figure in which dissent and entrepreneurship have become almost indistinguishable.

Much of the activist subculture of contemporary architecture is founded on Henri Lefebvre's critiques of capitalist urbanization (Stickells 2011). But with critique often comes recuperation. In France for instance, Lefebvre's theories and the work of the Situationists were quickly institutionalized by the bureaucratic state and selectively co-opted in urban development from the 1970s onwards.[3] To what extent can the critical and creative apparatus of today's DIY urbanism be recuperated for conflicting purposes, such as when flash mobs become marketing tools and corporations reclaim the streets for pedestrian shoppers? With its prioritizing of alterity, the fringes, the radical, and the small scale, "critical spatial practice" may no longer constitute the most appropriate strategy. We should be wary of the claim that such approaches are inherently progressive because they offer a critique of capitalism. Understanding and representing mundane yet complex processes or systems like trash collection or the urban economics of housing could be far more critical, both to the field of architecture and to society at large. Rather than spectacular critique, we need sustained attention and committed experimentation. That means appreciating failure as much as success, learning from doing, and analyzing as much as projecting. It is a long-term reflexive process, the patience for which is persistently lacking in many types of practice today, both activist and projective. If DIY urbanism continues to operate transversally rather than progressively, it may ultimately fail to accumulate social capital outside of a relatively small group of activists. Instead, more sustained, reflexive practices can fundamentally alter the ways architectural knowledge is acquired.

Recyclart

A useful example to consider these prepositions is Recyclart, a Brussels-based non-profit organization that has been extensively examined by architectural theorist Isabelle Doucet (2015).[4] Recyclart emerged during the 1990s, at a time when the inner city of Brussels became the arena for a range of urban activists intent on improving public space and urban life. These activists reacted in particular to the effects of urban renewal and redevelopment or what could be called "speculation by dilapidation," the then-common practice of speculators buying old houses and deliberately letting them rot so as to be able to sell the land for profitable development. In line with urban activists at the time, Recyclart challenged this politics of urban dilapidation and the predominance of private development as the primary agent in city building. Yet unlike most bottom-up urban initiatives at this time, Recyclart was established by the municipal government of Brussels with European pilot project funding. Rather than dismissing Recyclart because it lacks grass-roots radicalism or assessing it based on any stated or implicit intentions, however, it is more productive, as Doucet has done, to study its situated agency. Crucial to that agency is a continuous movement between government bureaucracy and activist urban practice.

In 1997, Recyclart settled in the abandoned railway station of the Chapelle-Kapellekerk station, a small commuter station in central Brussels close to the traditional working-class neighborhood of Les Marolles and the upscale area of the Sablon. The organization's move to this spatial interstice was crucial to the development of its urban and architectural agenda. Over the following decades, the repurposed train station became a key social and cultural facility for the neighborhood and the city at large. The organization developed an international artistic program as well as social programs that aim to re-insert local youths into the urban job market. The foyer of the old station was turned into a bar, which operates a training program for cooks and bartenders, with apprentices drawn from the local youth. Another program trains youth in Recyclart's metal and timber workshops to produce street furniture for the city. The impact of these programs goes beyond the production of material goods or the physical improvements to the station and its surroundings. Through skill-building and local job creation, Recyclart has long-lasting effects on the marginalized and impoverished communities of central Brussels. The strength of its approach therefore lies in its combination of the architectural/urban with the socio-economic (Doucet 2015: 87).

As a public venue, Recyclart's cultural programming has an international outlook, with performers and artists drawn from across Europe. Its realm of action remains nevertheless focused directly on the surrounding communities. Rather than being a one-off revitalization project, or an assemblage of disparate actions, the organization has worked continuously with local inhabitants and organizations, as well as with urban and regional government institutions. While activists would likely regard such collaboration as compromised in ideological terms, its concrete social and material effects constitute the realization of exactly the agenda many of these activists had set for themselves in the 1990s.

Perhaps the most important aspect of Recyclart in this regard has been its role in local urban design projects. The organization worked with local inhabitants and artists to transform neglected urban spaces into collective gathering and activity places, often by economical means. In one case, this transformation amounted to installing a large arabesque-shaped bench under a palaver tree, formalizing an already existing local hangout. The furniture was built in Recyclart's own workshop by local youth, those who are typically overlooked by gentrification projects. While working within the institutional frameworks of local government, this project disrupted conventional approaches to urban design, which merely embellish space regardless of already existing uses, and which tend to discourage activities that are perceived as unwanted—loitering in particular. Recyclart was also involved in creating a skate park on a nearby empty lot, in collaboration with a collective of Brussels skateboarders and with the Brussels Institute for Management of the Environment. The organization held workshops with local neighbors and prospective users, which led to design scenarios that encourage a multitude of uses for the space, beyond skating.

Rather than just celebrating these projects for their good intentions or dismissing them as mere instruments of gentrification, Doucet demonstrates that Recyclart's sustained commitment and multi-pronged approach ultimately led to a more durable and perhaps even more socially responsible urban change than the more immediate but short-term forms of activism prevalent in the 1990s and 2000s. She points in particular to the fact that "activists operating from-within are acquainted with negotiating their critical integrity on a continuous basis. For such practices, scrutinizing one's critical integrity under change is somewhat second nature" (Doucet 2015: 93). Rather than being compromised by having to work with municipal government institutions, this position allowed Recyclart not only to remain committed to its social project, but to create a reflexive form of practice, which entailed acquiring highly specific and situated forms of knowledge that are both social and architectural.

For much of the profession today, claiming a social role for architecture is nothing but a hollow gesture—naïve if not disingenuous. It is no longer commonly accepted that architects should have legitimate expertise about building or social life in its most basic forms. Such knowledge, which used to be both expected from and eagerly imported into the field of architecture, is now cause for disciplinary anxiety. Yet the persistent conviction that engaging external forms of knowledge threatens the discipline of architecture does not hold up against the multiplicity of contemporary practices. Architectural knowledge is not a closed realm internal to a single discipline. The vitality of architecture hinges on its engagement with foreign domains of knowledge. Architectural experimentation should include not only form, process, and production but also reception and use. The development of strategies for social engagement today cannot be imagined without such an open approach to the production of knowledge. They could play a crucial role, once again, in our understanding of architecture's situated agency in the world at large.

Notes

1 This article is an adaptation and expansion of Cupers (2014).
2 For a brief overview of this debate, see Dutton and Mann (2000). The observation itself is Frederic Jameson's, see Jameson (1985: 71).
3 This argument has been most convincingly made with regards to corporate management, see Boltanski and Chiapello (1999).
4 What follows draws directly from her analysis.

References

Bell, B. and Wakeford, K. (eds) (2008) *Expanding Architecture: Design as Activism*, New York: Metropolis Books.
Boltanski, K. and Chiapello, E. (1999) *Le nouvel esprit du capitalisme*, Paris: Gallimard.
Borasi, G. and Zardini, M. (eds) (2008) *Actions: What You Can Do With the City*, Amsterdam: SUN Architecture.
Coole, D. and Frost, S. (eds) (2010) *New Materialisms: Ontology, Agency, and Politics*, Durham, NC: Duke University Press.
Cupers, K. (ed.) (2013) *Use Matters: An Alternative History of Architecture*, London and New York: Routledge.

Cupers, K. (2014) "Where is the social project?" *Journal of Architectural Education* 68, 1: 6–8.
Cupers, K. and Doucet, I. (2009) "Agency in architecture: reframing criticality in theory and practice" *Footprint Journal* 4.
Doucet, I. (2015) *The Practice Turn in Architecture: Brussels after 1968*, Farnham: Ashgate.
Dutton, T. A. and Mann, L. H. (2000) "Problems in theorizing "the political" in architectural discourse," *Rethinking Marxism: A Journal of Economics, Culture, and Society* 12, 4: 117–129.
Jameson, F. (1985) "Architecture and the critique of ideology," in Joan Ockman (ed.) *Architecture Criticism Ideology*, New York: Princeton Architectural Press.
Latour, B. (2007) "Can we get our materialism back, please?," *Isis* 98: 138–142.
Lepik, A. (2010) *Small Scale, Big Change: New Architectures of Social Engagement*, Basel: Birkhäuser.
Stickells, L. (2011) "The right to the city: rethinking architecture's social significance," *Architectural Theory Review* 16, 3: 213–227.
Zeiger, M. (2011) "The interventionist's toolkit." http://places.designobserver.com/feature/the-interventionists-toolkit-part-1/24308/.

31

Collaboration

Unresolved Forms of Working Together in Contemporary Architectural Practice

Sony Devabhaktuni and Min Kyung Lee

In their decision to award the 2015 Turner Prize to Assemble, the award committee highlighted the collective's community-based work in Liverpool's long overlooked and disenfranchised Granby Four Streets (Tate 2015). It was the first time a group had been granted the prestigious art prize and the first time the Turner committee recognized an architectural practice.[1] The partnership that developed between the Assemble collective, residents of Granby Four Streets, and the community land trust continues today, as they work together on the design and construction of projects for the neighborhood. In their citation for the 2016 Pritzker Prize, the jury praised the method of social engagement underlying Alejandro Aravena's commitment to social housing. Drawing on the *mutirão* tradition, Aravena's Half a House project in Iquique, Chile, was discussed as a model for a participatory approach to architecture: a lot is equipped with basic housing infrastructure, then half built, the remainder filled in at the discretion of the inhabitants over time (Pritzker 2016). Highlighting the open-source ethos of the work, Aravena placed the housing plans online, relinquishing his claims to individual ownership and intellectual property. Coincident with the Pritzker, Aravena was named the director of the 15th Venice Architecture Biennale, where his curatorial proposal focused broadly on architecture's role in shaping the human condition in the face of increasing environmental and social precarity (Aravena 2016). These events signal an increasing valorization of collective and multidisciplinary practices in the shaping of the built environment. In all of them, an object-driven approach to the assessment of architecture is replaced by a recognition of process-driven strategies that emphasize collaboration.

Widely used and seemingly ubiquitous in discussions on architecture, "collaboration" has acquired numerous meanings, from the strategic, interdisciplinary marriage of professionals with different skills working together, the participation of users in design conception, to management and organizational structures.[2] In none of these cases is collaboration a new phenomenon in architectural practice (Kubo 2014). Architects have often developed close relationships with their clients and included them in the design process; architects have also developed collaborative methods among themselves and other designers and engineers. Furthermore, participatory design and its particular relationship to social housing projects have played a significant critical role in urban planning and geography since the 1960s (Cupers 2013). However, the current usage of the term in contemporary architectural practice spans socio-economic and political concerns about public spaces that are unbound by utopian modernist visions. Instead, collaborative practices today value heterogeneity, difference, and unknowability, holding in tension individual actions and shared spaces.

In a discussion about the Spreewald housing project in Berlin, Michael LaFond, director of id22, a multidisciplinary institute focused on "creative sustainability, emphasizing self-organization and local urban initiatives" proposed that he and his colleagues were "trying to move from DIY [do-it-yourself] to DIT [do-it-together]."[3] DIT reflects a phenomenon in contemporary architectural practice that foregrounds collaboration as a critical and constitutive part of the design process (Figure 31.1). In the transformation of DIY to DIT, there is a specific resonance to the ways in which groups are recasting architectural practice itself through the foregrounding of collaboration. The transformative potential of working together, not only as an agent for designing differently but also for fundamentally rethinking practice, has come to be

Figure 31.1 Community gardens, Spreefeld Spreeacker, id22, 2015
Source: Photo: Michael LaFond.

critically relevant as financial crises around the globe reveal long-standing models of architectural work to be unsustainable and undesirable (Awan, Schneider, and Till 2011). It is this double theme—of how collaboration can be enacted within the development of a project and of its generative potential for practice—that is the subject of this essay, focusing on a number of architects working in ways that cultivate intentional strategies of collaboration.[4]

Redefining Labor and Work

The recent attention to collaboration merits a closer examination of the specific meaning of architectural labor in current socio-economic and cultural contexts. Labor, its definition, organization, methods, and products have been a central concern in modern architecture, from debates over industrialization, craft practices, Fordist and Taylorist systems to questions around education, authorship, and participatory design (Deamer 2015). Examining architecture and the nature of architectural work through this lens resonates with Hannah Arendt's often cited and also criticized discussion of labor, work, and action articulated in *The Human Condition*. Arendt distinguishes labor and work by proposing that the former corresponds to biological processes and is associated with all things natural (*animal laborans*). Labor is constant and perpetual, linked to the maintenance of human life, of individual lives. On the other hand, the latter is related to *techné* and *poiesis*: the making of the world (*homo faber*). Work is part of the human project to fashion and create an environment in distinction to nature, that is durable and permanent. For Arendt, work is inherently public and represents the conditions for political and social life. She argues, nevertheless, that the expression of human freedom does not reside with the *homo faber*, because work is still driven and compelled by necessity and by a goal outside of the work itself. Instead, action in itself is freedom (*vita activa*) and it is through acts of doing that humans express their free will. This freedom, moreover, emerges through interactions with others and is inherently public and plural (Arendt 1958: 148).

The sharp decline in building construction following the 2008 financial crisis made visible an already expanding distinction between work and labor, as well as public and private life. The limiting premise was that architecture was equated to building, magnifying the commodification of architectural practice (Fulcrum 2014; Martin, Moore, and Schindler 2015). If work was valued as the completed building, then the crisis meant that the architectural commodity could no longer justify the labor involved, if it ever did. Building could not serve to give meaning to creative and physical labor, and moreover, the built object could not necessarily be the primary objective. Modern architecture's direct association to building had already weakened by the 1970s and 1980s with the "paper architecture" advanced by avant-garde architects.[5] Their ephemeral projects worked around the more traditional roles played by client, site, and program to advance strategies of architectural experimentation that came to be understood as forms of research as well as finished works in and of themselves. The response to this new configuration of architectural production is also reflected in the emphasis on "design research" in academic institutions, effectively normalizing modes of making architecture that reflect the limited number of traditional commissions. More recently, the proliferation of architecture exhibitions, biennials, and festivals, directly influenced by contemporary art practices and art markets in the form of installation and performance art, further moved architecture away from the goal of a built object. Thus, due to reasons extrinsic and intrinsic to the architectural profession, production became increasingly framed by processes, events, and actions.[6]

This decoupling between architecture and building often submitted to the cultural terms of austerity, ultimately accepting the alliance between capitalism and architecture, even if a built object was no longer possible. However, for some architects, the development of collaborative practices offered a means to subvert these terms and redefine fundamentally the categories of work and labor in architectural design, research, and analysis. On the one hand, community building, events, and programming, and social activities that required few material and capital resources gained traction because of the economic climate. On the other, architects appropriated critical strategies from art and urban planning into their participatory methods. These strategies resonated with those of political movements that formed in parts of Europe and the U.S. in response to what was seen as a failure of traditional parties to propose relevant solutions to economic crises. The movements, whose recent manifestations include los Indignados in Spain and Occupy in the U.S., and the horizontal, dialogic, consensus-building strategies that they employed became a model for architects to create public spaces.

One of the primary roles for the architect that developed as a result of these strategies was the design of social engagement; the challenges posed by making participation possible varied from project to project such that culturally specific, scale-specific, or means-specific responses were envisioned in order to maximize input from those who ultimately would be affected. The Berlin practice subsolar, co-founded by Saskia Hebert and Matthias Lohmann, understood participation as having the potential to reveal—both for the architect and for the participants—forms of "implicit knowledge"; the architects proposed that "people don't know what they know" and that the participatory exercises they put into place "make[s] us all more clever."[7] In speaking about their collaborative processes, subsolar suggests that "we are the person that can open some windows. That can show some other possibilities" so that the exchange between architects and participants becomes an exchange that is "horizontal" with an aim to look for "different kinds of knowledge" in light of a need "to rearrange preoccupations with specialized knowledge" (Figure 31.2). For Ecosistema Urbano, participation made it possible to tap into a kind of "collective creativity" revealed through the design of participatory processes that were "as open and transparent as possible."[8] Where this "fieldwork" involving community meetings and awareness-raising has long existed in disciplines such as urban planning (Jacobs 1961), Ecosistema Urbano—while also casting their work within an overtly political realm—spoke of how "collective creativity" could "open the black box of the creative process of designers so we have more tools to respond" thus linking participatory processes to an expansion of the disciplinary tools of architecture itself. Indeed, architecture's "black box"—the kind of specialized knowledge with which many of these architects entered the profession—was understood to be inadequate for their goals and desires. Describing the education they received first in Madrid and then in London before setting up their practice in the early 2000s, Ecosistema Urbano recalled:

> Both [schools] understood the disciplinary part of architecture in one way—linked to one person, linked to one brain. We started working with conventional ways of architecture. We started learning that what happened outside the buildings was more important that what happened inside—that the social part of architecture was quite interesting. We realized that this social space was completely neglected.

Where architecture is still taught and perceived as "linked to one person" who operates within an autonomous field, the move towards collaboration, sociality, and debate supplants isolation as a generator of architectural ideas. Architecture itself takes on a new character; no longer an object resulting from individual genius, it is understood rather as the creation of immaterial networks, infrastructures, and experiences that reflect the ever-changing nature of the social relations from which they are generated.

In Ecosistema Urbano's 2014 project for the historic central district of Asunción, Paraguay, socially collaborative processes, within the group and among the city's inhabitants, were made explicit; the architects called it not a "master plan" but a "master process." Their diagrams

Collaboration: Unresolved Forms

Figure 31.2 "Estimating value" workshop, Wittenberge Town Hall, subsolar, 2015
Source: Photograph by Anja Weber Kubota.

demonstrate an attention less on designing and fixing urban forms and more on mapping different interests in relation to each other, identifying ways in which institutions and citizens could intersect. They began by embedding a member of their team in the city for nearly a year; as a resident, they collected information from citizens and neighbors, speaking with different interest groups and developing knowledge on the contemporary conditions of the area over time. Ultimately for them, "the influence of societal tools are much more important for us than disciplinary tools." From an embedded vantage point, the office gained and created knowledge that gave them an unmatched qualitative expertise. By listening to various groups, it also allowed them to work as mediators, generating discussions between various interests who may otherwise not be aware of the issues others were facing.

Although architects have moved away from imagining an ideal man for whom a project is made, the nature of engagement with communities and individual lives is fundamentally different from even some of the methods that developed in response to a modernist universalizing of the inhabitant.[9] Saskia Hebert points to this transformation when she argues:

> Everything is not new in this discourse. We did it in the 1970s. We can ask the simple worker how he or she would like his house built. We can use statistics, we can use interviews to find out about the broad variety of life and find out what people might need. And then we can talk to them and I think that's more interesting.

The use of interviews and statistics, methods that were put in place by an earlier generation of architects, is one mode of engagement. Hebert distinguishes this approach from her own when she says "And then we can talk to them," suggesting a way of relating to individuals that is not scripted or framed as a method of scientific data collection. In a studio exercise Hebert initiated at the Technischen Universität Berlin, students studying a specific community invited local people on picnics as a chance to get to know each other through wide-ranging discussions. The mode of engagement that Hebert describes and enacts within her teaching studio resonates with Arendt's articulation of action as opposed to work: where work has a defined, synthetic output, the kind that might be possible through the analysis of data or interviews, action values instead the very process of taking part in a dialogue, regardless of whether this exchange has specific results. Indeed, it is the unfinished open-ended nature of action that distinguishes it from Arendt's understanding of work and that makes the mode of engagement that Hebert describes radically different from previous modes of collaboration.

Agonistic Practices

The social nature of these methods of working together implies a diversity of views where difference is understood as a key value in practice. In his study on cooperation, sociologist Richard Sennett argues that conflict is inherent to working together and its practice requires skill. Referring to *techné*, Sennett expands its association with craft to include the active work of dialectic and dialogic communication based on discerning divergences and distinctions among varying perspectives (Sennett 2012: 6). Sennett emphasizes the practice of exchange "in the subjunctive mood," in which one's individual position is balanced with and in correspondence to another (Sennett 2012: 36). In response to a question about decision-making, Jing Liu and Florian Idenburg of the New York-based firm SO-IL proposed that conflict was inherent to their communication process. "How do you make decisions?—By fighting" (Figure 31.3).[10]

Figure 31.3 Brainstorming discussion, New York, SO-IL, 2015
Source: Photograph by Naho Kubota.

Agonistic ways of working together are not merely tactical undertakings leading to an optimized solution or a more efficient process thus contributing to architecture's place in a liberal economic system of production. Rather they appreciate difference and dialogue as offering possibilities for new forms of agency and for the configurations of people and spaces—both material and immaterial—that emerge from those interactions and juxtapositions, regardless of how measurable the emergent qualities may be.

This emphasis on inherent as opposed to purely instrumental qualities of collaboration is also reflected in the way the architects understand their relationship to members of a project team. In describing their studios, Ecosistema Urbano and Berlin-based raumlabor spoke about encouraging each team member to cultivate personal interests so that they could be specialists in an area that was important to them. Of external specialists, they referred to creating an atmosphere in which a horizontal exchange can take place, so that technical and artistic specialists are engaged with a project and not simply contributing to serve the interests of the architect. In both cases, collaboration is understood as operating most effectively when the process recognizes the individual capacities and interests of all participants; the architect's role then is to create an environment where this kind of horizontal exchange can take place.

An important aspect of designing and managing these collaborative, participatory processes is treating conflict as generative and necessary. One way to manage the tensions that may arise is to make the process as transparent as possible so that participants understand and have a stake in the work. For several of the firms interviewed, dialogue engendered during a project period is in itself one of the products of the work, acting as it does to open up channels of communication within a given territory or neighborhood that may not have existed beforehand. That these communication channels can outlive the project itself is understood to be not only a welcome outcome but also an explicit goal, such that architecture is seen as having the potential of creating lasting social networks. Thus, temporal categories of a project also change, such that commitment to a project does not end with a completed structure but is sustained through the duration of its use.

This profound belief in the transformative potential of social relations is echoed by the interviewed architects who saw the basis of their collaborative work as located in friendships often established before they even decided to enter the profession. Markus Bader describes the formation of raumlabor at the particular moment after the fall of the Berlin Wall:

> So the origin was really this shop space where a sort of being together was first and doing things together was second.... We knew we were not so interested in entering a classical career. We didn't really know what to do instead, because this professional field we were working in didn't, wasn't so visible at that time, didn't exist so much. So we definitely needed time and space and this kind of togetherness to produce things.[11]

The original group took a fluid shape through the friendship of four members, but each were also part of at least three other artistic collectives. The low rents, open spaces, and stagnant economic conditions in 1990s Berlin provided an opportunity to pursue projects that were not tied necessarily to building structures. The space in which they met was significant:

> So we used the shop not only as a studio to work but also as a place for parties and presentations and film screenings. So to program. And this program was of course an opportunity to connect socially but also discuss. To bring our topics more immediately or in a more immediate way than if as you would be able to if following a classic architect's way of speaking, which means typically entering competitions.

In the context of friendship, they developed a method of working and decision-making that was not object-oriented but through a dialogic process of making things that was also not necessarily architecturally specific.

Friendship, however, is also founded on what philosopher Jacques Derrida has termed, not "facing" but "turning" (Derrida 2005). He offers this formulation as a means to conceive of a politics whose choreography implies an inherent vulnerability (Wills 2005: 7). There is an implied trust in the gesture that establishes difference. In this case, friendship is not a homogenizing relation, but one that perforce constitutes contradictions and divergences. Vulnerabilities are shared, differentiated, and unresolved through friendly discourse, and they form the basis of collaborative practices and of linking those practices between the private and public spheres. Derrida's concept of friendship does not assume resolution as its basis or its objective. Paralleling political theorist Chantal Mouffe's concept of agonistic politics, collaborative practices of these groups thus acknowledge inherent conflicting and incomplete perspectives, and accordingly, the impossibility of consensus without exclusion, ultimately imagining a relation without an aim other than to relate (Mouffe 2013: 92).

For Ecosistema Urbano, the quality of difference manifested in the various opinions shared at the community meetings as well as the ones not shared and unknown by people who could not or did not want to participate. This unknowability had to be accounted for. In the case of raumlabor's 2010 project in Anyang, South Korea, this unknowability arose from cultural and language differences. Markus Bader recalled,

> This sort of fundamental misunderstanding ... like did we talk about the same thing or not? Did we really agree on something? Is this agreement ... in these collaborative spheres, it is a lot about trust. And if you go out of a meeting and you feel like, yes we all agreed to something. We trust each other.

In these two cases, the respect is implied through their status as architects and experts, and explicit in the practice of communication that often times does not lead to building. For them, friendship is not a strategy to realize a building; not a means to an end that is extrinsic to the relation. Rather, what is proposed is that the project becomes the catalyst for the possibility of friendship. For subsolar's ongoing project in Wittenberge, Germany, Saskia Hebert said of their community meetings, "We didn't talk about form; we talked about values, issues."

Unresolved Forms

Nevertheless, form is ever immanent in architecture; it is never distinct from values and issues. Among the practitioners interviewed, the challenge has been to work against the bias in architectural practice that continues to privilege building insofar as ideas, research, and representations are in the service of the built form. Our research also revealed this teleological bias in our own inquiries about how these qualitative methods of research and social processes could lead to different types of forms. The question had to evolve in order to consider a different paradigm that might foreground and outline a more contingent process of producing spaces. "What role does form have in your processes?" became "how does form emerge through your processes?" because form is not autonomous from the media of its conception, production, and use. The inherent difficulty of posing and addressing the question of form when foregrounding collaboration is that architecture as a design practice demands coherence and resolution, while architecture as social practice rejects the conceptual possibility of reconciliation. For some theorists, the concept of spatial agency overcomes this contradiction (Awan, Schneider, and Till 2011: 53–56);

Collaboration: Unresolved Forms

architects are less shapers of form and more mediators of space and spatialized relations. In this formulation, architects are not the only privileged agents in the creative production of space, and the built object is but one among many media that generates social and public discourses and sites.

The possibility of collaboration as a critical practice then does not manifest in form as a predetermined concept, but rather through forms—not limited to the visual—that are necessarily unresolved. In the case of raumlabor and SO-IL, temporality was an integral means to articulate this incompleteness. *Fountain House* (2014) by raumlabor was a temporary installation for the Montreal Biennale that sought to make perceptible the municipal public service and infrastructure of providing drinking water (Figure 31.4). The pavilion was composed on a circular plan with two concentric circles forming an inner room and a covered outer arcade, which included a staircase that allowed access to a roof-top terrace. At the center of the room was the fountain, composed of a slow trickle of water that fell from a small hole in the roof, creating a humid atmosphere in the interior. In addition to using cheaply accessible pine for its structure, the wall skin was made from packed earth that grew plants and housed little organisms. The short-term project made visible a long-term public service. Pole Dance (2010) by SO-IL was also a temporary structure built for the MoMA and PS1 Young Architects Program. The courtyard of PS1 was transformed into a participatory environment fashioned from a large open net made of an interconnected system of poles and bungees. The pole's movement by a visitor or the wind activated the installation, reverberating through the entire net, generating dynamic and

Figure 31.4 *Fountain House*, Montreal, raumlabor, 2014
Source: Photograph by Markus Bader.

unplanned waves. People were invited to walk, jump, dance, move, or not. The architects all spoke about the indeterminate quality of their installations; there was no predetermined method of use and no prescribed behavior. As Mouffe explains in her description of agonistic politics, "it is always through insertion in a manifold of practices, discourses and language games that specific forms of individualities are constructed" (Mouffe 2013: 93). Form then functions as an opportunity for open interventions through actions taken or not whose contingent relations ultimately constitute a public. The short life of these projects revealed the durability not of the built form but of the social ground which these installations activated.

This openness was what allowed for certain borders to become visible, whether it was the relation between public good and private use or between public effects and private acts through "constructed situations" and to frame actions rather than objects (Debord 2002 [1957]). Florian Kossak, Director of Postgraduate Taught Programmes at the Sheffield School of Architecture referred to this as "spatial propositions."[12] Using the windowsill as an example, he proposed that the question for a student is to learn not how to measure and render the width of that ledge, but to ask how different forms create varying social opportunities that then produce other spaces for interrelationships. Collaborative practices thus necessitate an expanded concept of architectural form that subverts long-held binaries of form and function, private and public, design and building, and producer and user. It is to account for the enmeshed, heterogeneous, and incomplete social practices that interpellate all of us as collaborators in the making and remaking of spaces at each moment.[13]

Conclusion

Participatory works and collaborative projects, of course, can be (have been) easily perverted into our contemporary neo-liberal culture that makes labor invisible by making the minutiae of our lives increasingly visible, subsuming and neutralizing the critical acts of many of the architects with whom we spoke. In an economic climate of austerity, these socially oriented projects meet the demand for architects—or people in general—"to do more with less" (Aureli 2013). They rely on other people doing and making things, and assume that people will do so freely and willingly. They will "share" and provide their personal "content," and the architect merely provides the frame that might participate in the maintenance of biopolitical capitalism (Deamer 2013). This could allow for an abdication of responsibility on the part of the architect, leaving accountability diffuse and the subjectivity of users even more constrained to a consumerism that equates architecture to theme parks.

Yet, the critical difference in many of these intentional practices of collaboration is in the acknowledgment of the unknowable other in spatial production. To characterize this approach as agonistic is not to favor a situation of constantly warring interests. Rather, it is to value the struggles that emerge in any creative process of learning, for it is in these necessarily unresolved interstices of a friendly relation that yet unimagined acts can materialize. In their 2014 project for Payers Park in Folkestone, the art and architecture collaborative, muf stated their goal was "to make space for the unknown" (Creative Foundation 2015), "where there is space for difference and for the play and the things that you don't yet know" (muf 2016). The slope of the steep hill was retained and created an opportunity to emphasize differences in elevation, materials, views, terrain, and activities. Weaving past and present, "real and fictitious uses of the site," muf organized a landscape that would allow for individuals to imagine their own narratives connected in and through the physical site (muf 2016). Ultimately, an essential element in fostering relational participation is based on outlining the field of negotiation among inhabitants, visitors, funders, artists, and architects, whose struggles in turn activate and enliven the site. Collaboration in the making of public spaces is thus a practice of recognizing impasses and yet continuing to relate as an end in itself, whose actions offer the transformative possibilities of new social forms.

Notes

1 Like many studios analyzed in this essay, such as raumlabor and muf, Assemble is not a traditional firm employing only trained architects. It is a collective that includes architects and artists, and other participants.
2 Much of the recent popular literature on collaboration has been driven by management studies including recent titles such as Doorley, S. and Witthoft, S. *Make Space* (2012); Markova, D. *Collaborative Intelligence* (2015); Tett, G. *The Silo Effect* (2015); Karlgaard, R. *Team Genius* (2015).
3 Michael LaFond, Director of id22, in discussion with authors, April 8, 2016.
4 Discussions with the following architects helped to form the arguments in this essay: José Luis Vallejo and Belinda Tato at Ecosystem Urbano (http://ecosistemaurbano.com); Michael LaFond at id22 (http://id22.net); Markus Bader at raumlabor (http://raumlabor.net); Florian Edinburg and Jing Lui at SO-IL (http://so-il.org); Florian Kossak at the Sheffield School of Architecture; and Saskia Hebert and Matthias Lohmann at subsolar (www.subsolar.net). We are grateful to all of them for their time and thoughtful conversation and hope this essay justly reflects their input.
5 Important precursors are Bernard Tschumi's *The Manhattan Transcripts*, 1976–1981 and his propositions that architecture was concerned with event, action, and happenings, as well as the Situationists of the 1960s. For the other meaning of "paper architecture" as temporary structure see Andrew Herscher's essay (Ch. 3) in this volume.
6 See chapters in this volume by Jeremy White (Ch. 32), Rohan Shivkumar's (Ch. 33), and Arindam Dutta (Ch. 34).
7 Saskia Hebert, co-founder of subsolar, in discussion with authors, April 15, 2016.
8 Belinda Tato and José Luis Vallejo, co-founders of Ecosistema Urbano, in discussion with authors, April 16, 2016.
9 Some of the most important literature demonstrating the historical and ideological development of the universal norms for inhabitants has come from feminist and queer theorists of architecture. See Colomina, B. (ed.) *Sexuality and Space* (1996), and Danze E. and Coleman, D. (eds) *Architecture and Feminism* (1997).
10 Jing Liu and Florian Idenburg, co-founders of SO-IL, in discussion with authors, March 17, 2016.
11 Markus Bader, co-founder of raumlabor, in discussion with the authors, March 29, 2016.
12 Florian Kossak, Senior Lecturer and Director of Postgraduate Taught Programmes, Sheffield School of Architecture, in discussion with authors, April 22, 2016.
13 The notion of interpellation used here does not refer to Theodor Adorno and Max Horkheimer's definition in *Dialectic of Enlightenment* but to Chantal Mouffe's definition outlined in a 2001 interview.

References

Aravena, A. (2016) *Reporting from the Front: 15th International Architectural Exhibition*, Venice: Marsilio.
Arendt, H. (1958) *The Human Condition*, Chicago: University of Chicago Press.
Aureli, P. V. (2013) *Less Is Enough: On Architecture and Asceticism*, Moscow: Strelka Press.
Awan, N., Schneider, T., and Till, J. (2011) *Spatial Agency: Other Ways of Doing Architecture*, London: Routledge.
Colomina, B. (ed.) (1996) *Sexuality and Space*, Princeton: Princeton Architectural Press.
Creative Foundation (2015) *muf Architecture Art – Payers Park*. https://soundcloud.com/creative-foundation/11-muf-architecture-art-payers-park (April 19, 2016).
Cupers, K. (ed.) (2013) *Use Matters: An Alternative History of Architecture*, London: Routledge.
Danze, E. and Coleman, D. (eds) (1997) *Architecture and Feminism*, Princeton: Princeton Architectural Press.
Deamer, P. (2013) *Architecture and Capitalism, 1845 to the Present*, London: Routledge.
Deamer, P. (2015) *The Architect as Worker: Immaterial Labor, the Creative Class, the Politics of Design*, London: Bloomsbury.
Debord, G. (2002 [1957]) "Report on the construction of situations and on the terms of organization and action of the international Situationist tendency," in T. McDonough (ed.) *Guy Debord and the Situationist International: Texts and Documents*, Cambridge, MA: MIT Press, 29–50.

Derrida, J. (2005) *The Politics of Friendship*, trans. G. Collins, New York: Verso.
Doorley, S. and Witthoft, S. (2012) *Make Space: How to Set the Stage for Creative Collaboration*, London: Wiley.
Fulcrum (ed.) (2014) *Real Estates: Life without Debt*, London: Bedford Press.
Jacobs, J. (1961) *The Death and Life of Great American Cities*, New York: Random House.
Karlgaard, R. (2015) *Team Genius: The Science of High-Performing Organizations*, New York: Harper Business.
Kubo, M. (2014) "The concept of the architectural corporation," in E. Franch i Gilabert, A. R. Lawrence, A. Miljacki, and A. Schafer (eds) *OfficeUS Agenda*, Zurich: Lars Müller Publishers.
Markova, D. (2015) *Collaborative Intelligence: Thinking with People Who Think Differently*, New York: Spiegel & Grau.
Martin, R., Moore, J., and Schindler, S. (eds) (2015) *The Art of Inequality: Architecture, Housing, and Real Estate*, New York: The Temple Hoyne Buell Center for the Studies of American Architecture. http://buellcenter.org/research-programs/house-housing/art-inequality-architecture-housing-and-real-estate-%E2%80%94-provisional-re (April 4, 2016).
Mouffe, C. (2001) "Every form of art has a political dimension," *Grey Room* 2 (Winter): 98–125.
Mouffe, C. (2013) *Agonistics: Thinking the World Politically*, New York: Verso.
muf architecture/art (2016) *Payers Park*. www.muf.co.uk/portfolio/payers-park-current (April 19, 2016).
Pritzker Prize (2016) *Jury Citation*. www.pritzkerprize.com/2016/jury-citation (July 8, 2016).
Sennett, R. (2012) *Together: The Rituals, Pleasures and Politics of Cooperation*, New Haven: Yale University Press.
Tate (2015) *The Turner Prize 2015*. www.tate.org.uk/whats-on/tramway/exhibition/turner-prize-2015/turner-prize-2015-artists-assemble (July 8, 2016).
Tett, G. (2015) *The Silo Effect: The Peril of Expertise and the Promise of Breaking Down Barriers*, New York: Simon & Schuster.
Wills, D. (2005) "Full dorsal: Derrida's politics of friendship," *Postmodern Culture* 15, 3: 1–32.

32

Starchitecture

Starchitect

Jeremy White

She died on March 31, 2016. It happened in a hospital at the very end of Interstate 95. Time of death was pronounced in the early morning hours, inside a blocky hulk of a complex in Miami. It was so unlike the structures she built a career designing.

Suffering from bronchitis, at age 65 her heart failed, and within hours, responses on the Internet touted the event as the passing of a great architect and the demise of a visionary. Michael Kimmelman of the *New York Times* posted his pithy tribute in the afternoon: "Hadid embodied, in its profligacy and promise, the era of so-called starchitects who roamed the planet in pursuit of their own creative genius, offering miracles, occasionally delivering" (Kimmelman 2016).

News of Zaha Hadid's death seemed impossible to deliver without also lauding her genius. The many thoughts and gestures on Twitter and other corners of the Internet that day gave expression to the mythologizing project that marks the state of high-profile architecture in the second decade of the twenty-first century. In polite irony, Kimmelman implied doubt of the very idea of the starchitect category, and yet peddled it in the same sentence. Heroic and yet ironic, these affectations-verging-on-traits are foundational to the starchitect and their starchitectural work.

This essay lingers over the mythologizing project of the starchitect, endeavoring to provide some historical underlayment for its construction. Selective in scope, it focuses on the art and architectural ideas girding it, with an eye to the always present commercial potentialities of its dazzle. In doing so, this essay explores four aspects of the starchitect as a category, although it will frustrate those seeking an exhaustive definition (it is "so-called," after all). Each aspect is obvious, and yet we explain them anyway. First, that a starchitect is prohibited from copying the work of another. Think of this as the first bylaw of the starchitect's guild. Their work is their signature and forgery is a crime punishable by ejection from the guild. This first idea is as old as the hills, derived from art history, and is predicated on the rather peculiar and impractical definition of a building as an art object. Second are the hidden actors who make the starchitect possible. Third, the starchitect's work must express relevance of the now, which is to say, it may not copy work from the vault of the past. The guilded starchitect must embrace the now, and like the avant-garde artist, their work must be reflexively relevant. And fourth, perhaps the most obvious point to make, the starchitect's work must be visually striking. Glam is everything, measured by its photogenic promise, trumping even space. There is no conceptual or technological limit on what an aspiring starchitect may resort to in the service of the visual. Underlying these ideas is the premise that these aspects were not born of the twenty-first century, but were brought into the world of architectural discourse by previous generations.

We begin in the art gallery.

Relationship: Artist and Art Object

We have to imagine a visitor walking around inside the gallery, or maybe it is a museum, except we really don't need the whole visitor, just their eyes and feet. The visual quality of this space is nearly everything, so through them we will be able to comprehend this initial exercise. The eyes are in a space, and the space is lit but not bright, the beam from track lights draws attention to the walls, and to sections of the wall where art pieces are hung. The lighting as well as the arrangement of pieces are curated, forming a rhythm that goes something like this: object, negative wall space, object, negative wall space, so forth and so on. The art objects are foreground while the wall is background, and the wall is plastered smooth and painted white but not too brightly white. Although some galleries might leave little or no wall in view, covering every square foot with art object, that is a past practice, now rare. Many if not most curators and gallery directors allow the objects a distinction of space, allowing the eye to come to rest on the object with ease and without conflict. The eyes approach one panel on the wall and soon their peripheral vision contains nothing but wall, the negative space framing that one art object. This affords the object a momentary respite from its rivals in the room. The art object now occupies the center of vision, isolated from the rest of the gallery. Indeed, a truly engaged person inside that gallery may feel momentarily removed from the city in which the gallery is situated.

This curatorial space is not complete without words. They are printed, and share the wall with the art object, although they take up a miniscule area by comparison. They provide the person with information: title (if there is one), media (probably), and if it is a gallery, maybe price. This last item may be indicated elsewhere, at the gallery's desk perhaps. In a museum, it is hidden. The arrangement of the gallery space foregrounding its treasures helps persuade the person that the art object is indeed a treasure, bolstering its value, and ultimately that value must take the form of a price in dollars or some other currency. This same pattern of foreground and background, bolstered by the relationship of art object and words, can be found in museum spaces as well. In this regard, the gallery space emulates the museum space, legitimizing the gallery. Commercial gallery and art museum are mutually supportive partners in many urban landscapes, one increasing the attraction of the other.

In both spaces, something else is vital. The art label accompanying the art object contains one other piece of information, and it is important to art commercialization as well. It is the artist's name (see Scheme 1 in Figure 32.1). (In the screenspace on the Internet, the starchitect's name is the searchable keyword.) This is so crucial that, in a museum, even when absent a surrogate name is included anyway, as "anonymous" or "unknown." The name of the artist is the art object's companion, although other names may crowd in upon that intimate relationship. The name of the object's owner may be included, or if a portrait, the name of the subject depicted in the picture space of the object may also be included. Even so, the artist's name trumps them all. When art historian Suzanne Frank asked architect Peter Eisenman to design her a house that would also be a work of art, and the result was a house that sported a leaky roof, she made sure the repairs did not visibly alter the configuration of the roof. She preserved the art value of the house for over 30 years, selling it to a photographer in 2016 who did not even attempt to make a home out of it, using it instead to stage social events (*Architect's Newspaper* 2016).

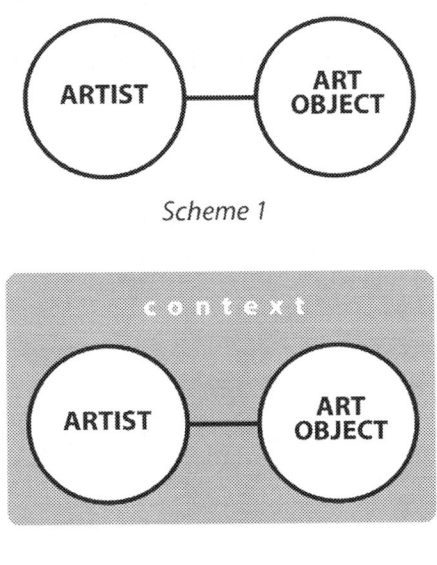

Figure 32.1 Scheme 1: Artist–Object relationship. Scheme 2: Artist–Object relationship in context
Source: Copyright Jeremy White.

    The artist's name elevates the value of the object, or devalues it, and vice versa. They are tied together in myriad ways. The curatorial space of the museum is organized by categories, such as time periods or periods of stylistic commonality; Impressionism or Abstract Expressionism, so on and so forth. Within those categories art objects are further organized by artist, one room devoted to Monet for example, a wall showcasing lilies, and the adjoining room containing works by the Pointillists. The north wall sporting a painting by Seurat and another by Signac, the east wall given over to Jean Metzinger to showcase the transition towards early-twentieth-century expressionism. This strategy of presentation is apparent in texts of art history, the monumental surveys by Gardner, Stokstad, Janson, and others follow the same pattern as art historian and art curator swim the same subculture and knowledge pool. They do not duplicate each other's work, however. The art historian may establish and deepen categorical schemes, they also contextualize the art object and its artist in their time, immersing the reader in information about the time and place in which the artist labored and was inspired. The curator separates and isolates the object from the contemporary fabric of the city, creating a space set apart in which the object, even one created in the contemporary world, can be viewed without distraction from that world. The historian endeavors to demonstrate how the object and its artist were a product of their time, emissaries from a particular time and place. The reader may thus come to some understanding of that time and place with the guidance of the art historian, as well as an understanding of the art object and the artist.

    This mission to appreciate operates in the gallery as well, where the appreciator may come face to face with the genuine art object. Inside the magic box of the exhibition space, absent the artist, the person can feel as though they appreciate not only the colors, textures, shapes, and techniques displayed in the picture space of the object before them, but they also may feel an appreciation for the instigator of those formal elements. In the eyes of the person, the object can stand in for the artist.

This is a foundational notion in art history. Scheme 2 illustrates this core principle (see Figure 32.1), diagramming the way the artist is embedded in culture (their context), which in turn is the context for the art object as well. There is nothing to interfere with the vector connecting them; nothing gets between the artist and art object. If the generic artist of the diagram is Eduard Manet, the generic context would be Paris of the tumultuous mid-nineteenth century. Both artist and object are embedded in that context, and the important point is the simple and strong relationship between the artist and the art object. That relationship is represented by the strength and clarity of the line. A single line with two simple ends. If we introduce a second artist into the diagram, say Vincent Van Gogh (Figure 32.2), we would need to make room for him alongside Manet, except his context would also deserve its own bubble (Scheme 3). Van Gogh knew Paris in the late-nineteenth century but the heart of his world was elsewhere in France and the Low Countries. Instead of Van Gogh, if the second artist was Monet, a fellow Parisian of the same period as Manet, we could place his bubble alongside Manet's within the same gray rectangle representing context (Scheme 4). Context can be a variable, it may or may not be shared, in no circumstance do we find the line connecting one artist to the art object of another artist. Artists may share context, but they remain tied only to their own art objects. This sharing of context allows us to study the work of Manet to discern features and references from those of Monet and Van Gogh. Regardless of how many artists crowd into the same context, the primacy

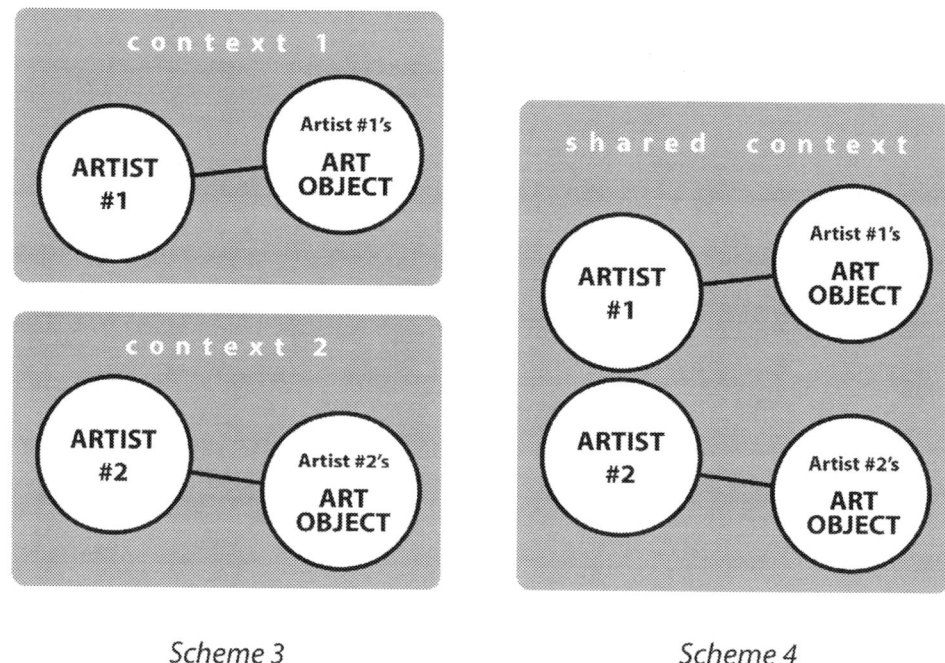

Figure 32.2 Scheme 3: Artist–Object relationships in separate contexts. Scheme 4: Artist–Object relationships in a shared context

Source: Copyright Jeremy White.

Starchitecture: Starchitect

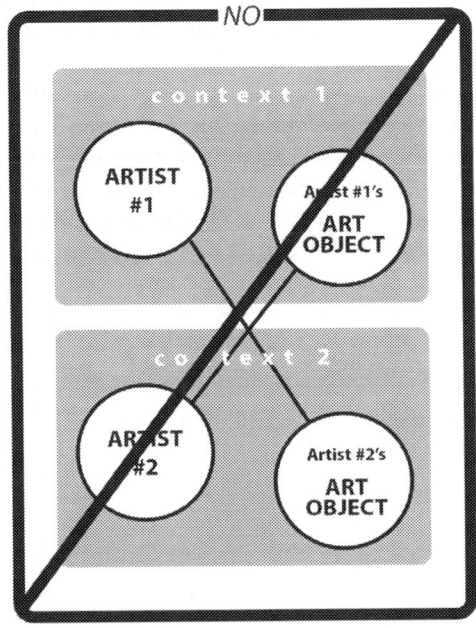

Scheme 5

Figure 32.3 Scheme 5: Impossible Artist–Object relationships
Source: Copyright Jeremy White.

of the line connecting artist and object remains true. It is the compelling line. The eyes scrutinizing the object on the gallery wall eventually comes to know that object, and soon, are incapable of confusing that object created by one artist for that of another (Scheme 5 in Figure 32.3).

Scheme 6 (Figure 32.4) illustrates an analogous relationship between the starchitect and their art object, the building they design. It is precisely the same diagram as Scheme 1. The structure of relationships and the number of bubbles are the same, but the terms are altered. Architectural magazines and websites regularly publish the work of Frank Gehry, Zaha Hadid, David Adjaye, and other high-profile architects, reifying the relationship of the diagram. They help draw the line connecting artist to art object.

The line connecting the two circles of Scheme 6 has an important implication. We can call it style, or perhaps in the case of the celebrity architect, signature. The Walt Disney Concert Hall in Los Angeles is the art object created by Frank Gehry, and it looks very similar to the art object he created shortly before in Bilbao, Spain: the Museo Guggenheim constructed at the end of the twentieth century. Likewise, the daring curves of the cultural center in Baku, designed by Zaha Hadid and yet canceled shortly before her death, shares the visually striking quality of Gehry's work, but there are too many uniquely Hadidian physical traits to confuse her work with Gehry's. Their signatures are distinct. Compare them to the sober work of Richard Meier, another celebrity architect, known for organizing the landscape in an all-encompassing grid such as that of the Getty Center on the Santa Monica Hills or his Sandra Day O'Connor Federal

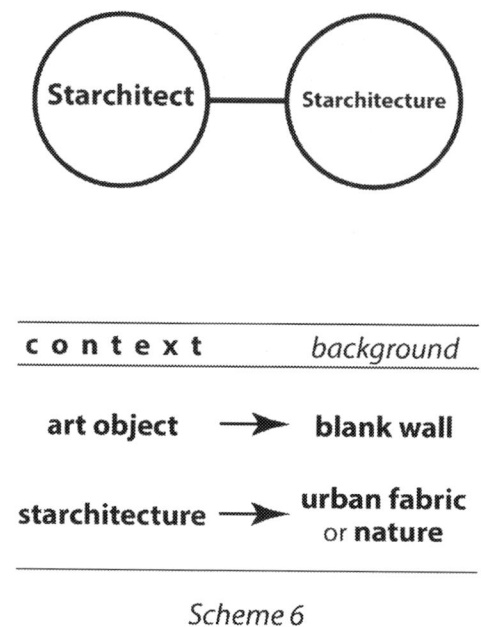

Figure 32.4 Scheme 6: Starchitect (artist)–Starchitecture (object) relationship. The table below indicates the background, or negative space, framing the object as a function of context

Source: Copyright Jeremy White.

Courthouse in Phoenix, Arizona. Each building is sufficiently consistent with others by the same starchitect that they evoke the hand and eye of the artist-designer in much the same way that an oil painting represents the artist. When the eyes leave the gallery and merge back into the urban fabric, to visit points of starchitecture scattered across the noise of the city's backdrop, they come to appreciate the visual traits of a starchitect's work. That signature will also become known with a few persistent clicks in the open browser, landing on the photographs of those buildings. A Gehry building is easy to spot a mile away. Literally.

Lies

The problem with the starchitect–starchitecture relationship is that it is a lie. The analogy in Scheme 6 is not valid: a building is not a painting, nor is it a sculpture. A building is not created by the hand of the architect, it is created by a team of builders and their machine tools, conforming to the rules and limitations imposed by code and ordinance. Many parts are fabricated in factories miles away, sometimes thousands of miles away, while others are assembled on site by teams of workers. The diagram is missing a bubble between the starchitect and starchitecture, representing builders (Arantes 2019) (Scheme 7 in Figure 32.6). But that is not the only omission.

When Gehry designed the Museo Guggenheim, he was not licensed to practice architecture in Spain, nor was he well-versed in zoning and building codes there, nor did he have relationships

Figure 32.5 The visually striking Walt Disney Concert Hall, 2016

Source: Copyright Jeremy White.

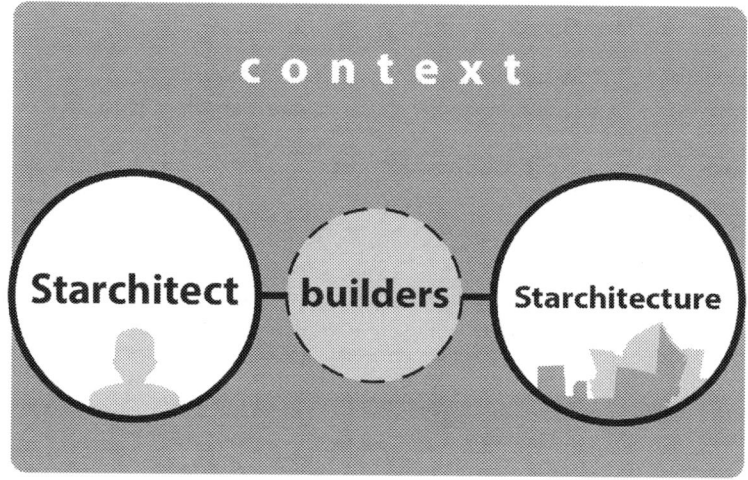

Figure 32.6 Scheme 7: Starchitect–Builders–Starchitecture relationship
Source: Copyright Jeremy White.

with builders and building officials in Bilbao. He did what most starchitects do, as they secure commissions in far-flung parts of the globe. He contracted with a local architecture firm to help negotiate that foreign social terrain. That extra architecture firm is usually referred to as the executive architect. Scheme 7 in Figure 32.6 hides that crucial partner, and a few other important designers as well. Gehry is not a one-man architecture firm. Based in Santa Monica, California, as of this writing Frank O. Gehry Partners, Ltd. employs over 400 people, many of them licensed and highly trained and skilled architects. Although he may be the driving creative force producing starchitectural designs, he relies on the teamwork (and ambition) of hundreds under his own roof to realize the daring complexity of that art. There are details to work out, and that job requires many designing hands. Much of the design is in the hands of engineers too. To put it bluntly, the game of producing the starchitectural object is a team sport. Scheme 8 illustrates the reality of the starchitect–starchitecture relationship, partially obscured by the glamour of the object–artist model (Figure 32.7).

The artist–object model is powerful, and not just useful for boiling down the complex teamwork of design to a single genius spirit, that magic trick of branding. The lie's persuasion is more convincing because of its deep roots in art historical culture. The discipline of architecture history largely derived from the parentage of art history, coming into its own on art historical terms in the late nineteenth and early twentieth centuries (Watkin 1983). The language of architecture history, and by extension, the language of architecture appreciation and criticism, derives largely from the history of art objects and its more limited relationship to artists (Vasari 2008).

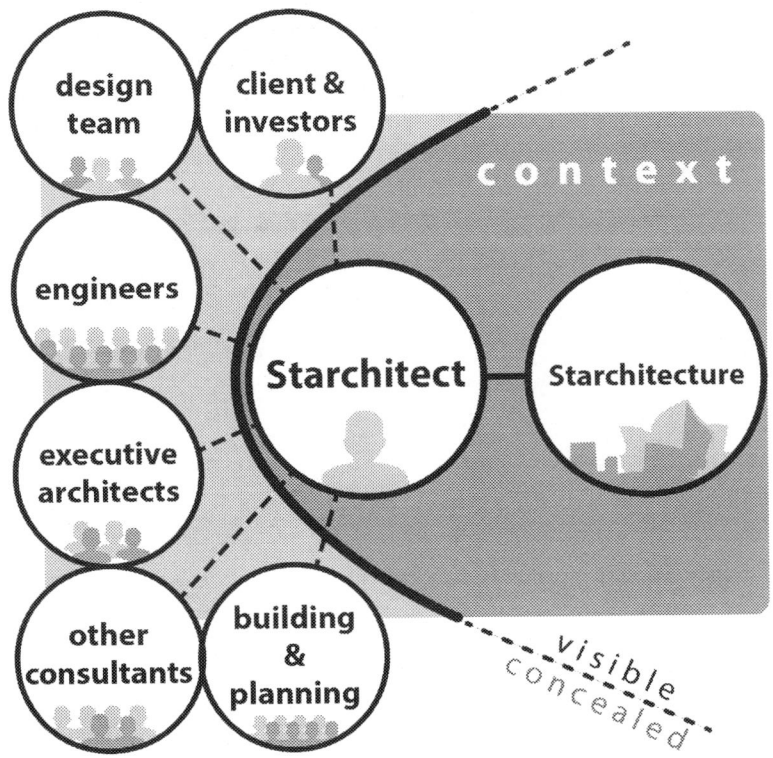

Scheme 8

Figure 32.7 Scheme 8: Starchitect–Starchitecture relationship (hiding other designers and design influencers)

Source: Copyright Jeremy White.

Through that language, starchitecture can be isolated from its urban context, or rural context, allowing an entire city fabric to melt away just as though all those buildings were the blank walls of the gallery. Architectural photography reinforces this trick, isolating the art object on the screen and the page of the monograph, strengthening with every frame the building's masquerade as an art object. Just as the problem of leaky roofs and electrical wiring has no place within the frame, the complexity of metal workers and masons, associate architects and accountants, building inspectors and building codes, all fade away in the glare of the shining starchitect standing beside his creation. He steps forward as sole genius. The monograph he cradles in his arm has but one name written on the cover, his own (Figure 32.8).

There have been attempts to see this lie as romanticism. Author and critic Michael Lewis located the starchitect phenomenon's origination with Frank Lloyd Wright and his conceit of heroism. Anointing him the "archetype of the celebrity architect," Lewis ascribed Wright's penchant for projecting himself as a supremely confident and gifted creative agent as the culmination of a deeper romantic trend in American history and letters. He saw in Wright the evolution of the Puritan spirit of self-reliance expressed in the writings of Ralph Waldo Emerson (Lewis 2007). This desire to find an essential root for heroic romanticism in early America obscures more mundane forces. Wright's talent for branding himself an artistic genius rode on a wave of professionalization in the nineteenth century, and that wave structured middle-class society in the twentieth.

In early eighteenth-century America, professionally trained architects were few and far between, and those scratching a living in the new republic competed against carpenters, masons, and designer-builders, most of whom hailed from the middling sorts or lower trade classes. In the late nineteenth century, elite non-builder designers leveraged their class by persuading state legislatures to impose licensing requirements that gave advantage to educated practitioners over their tradesmen competitors. They instituted a stark split between design and construction. This move to professionalize by academicizing architectural design paralleled the professionalization of law, medicine, and other fields, which was happening at the same time. Combined, this professionalization movement was a vital part of the construction of a powerful middle class in the United States (Ross 1972; Upton 1991). The heroic archetype was not monopolized by the architecture profession, however; it emerged in the larger swell of professionalization. Venues of popular culture, such as twentieth-century television in the United States, demonstrate the successful construction of the heroic doctor and the heroic lawyer, two other professions that managed to claim their own legal territory during the professionalization movement. Unlike doctors and lawyers, the heroic architect has not translated so easily onto the screen and other venues of popular culture, despite Ayn Rand's romantic figure of Howard Roark in *The Fountainhead*, an assertive novel of the 1940s that remains in print in the twenty-first century. Unlike the doctor fighting against human mortality in the dramatic theater of the hospital, and the passionate lawyer fighting for truth and justice in the dramatic arena of the courtroom, the architect is rarely depicted in a dramatic or cinematic space, a champion of art and good design. Compared to doctors and lawyers, the architect is rarely depicted at all in popular culture. Instead, in the contemporary landscape, the architect's drama manifests in their art objects. Those amazing, dazzling, sometimes glittering (literally) points in the urban fabric.

A city is not a museum any more than a building is a mere object. The reduction of a building to an art edifice allows the architect to stand apart from the team responsible for bringing that edifice into the world. Perhaps midwife is a more apt model than artist. It is possible to comprehend the built environment as the product of multiple and often competing agents: property owners, investors, residents, workers, realtors, building inspectors, and as demonstrated in this volume, even hedgehogs.[1] The architect is part of the team contending with those agents

Figure 32.8 Author's photograph of water damage on the underside of the roof inside Frank Gehry's Stata Center on M.I.T. campus, 2016

Source: Copyright Jeremy White.

and resulting forces. Although the art historical narrative dominates the discourse on starchitecture, reifying the mythic art–artist model, other approaches to architecture history developed in the late twentieth century to challenge that model. One such challenge emerged in the United States, culminating in the founding of the Vernacular Architecture Forum in 1979, an organization of architecture historians deriving their methods from a variety of disciplines including folklore studies, American Studies, geography, history, and only rarely from art history. When the vernacular architecture historian examines the so-called art object (a building), they include the architect as one agent among many, often of lesser importance than most other agents (Upton and Vlach 1986). The dividing line in Scheme 8, between the visible and the concealed, itself vanishes in that scholarly lens. The architect is one player among many, and often not the important player.

The sensational rebuilding of the World Trade Center can be trotted out as a case in point. Although Daniel Libeskind, starchitect of the Jewish Museum in Berlin, won the international design competition in 2003, it was Larry Silverstein, the developer and lease holder of the former twin towers who proved the most influential stakeholder. Despite winning a well-publicized design competition, by 2005 Libeskind was pushed out of the project. Reduced to the impressive sounding yet meaningless title of "Architect of the Master Plan," Silverstein awarded Skidmore Owings and Merrill the contract to redesign what would become a less daring but less expensive One World Trade Center, paid for primarily by Silverstein's insurance payout (Goldberger 2005). The rest of the World Trade Center site was divided among starchitects: the transit center awarded to the Spanish architect and engineer Santiago Calatrava; Two World Trade Center to the London architect Norman Foster; and Frank Gehry was slated to design the Performing Arts Center.

The insertion of a cultural building, an opera house or theater, was a vital element of Libeskind's original design, eventually conceptualized as a Performing Arts Center. It was intended to invigorate what was once a purely corporate environment of suits and ties that commuted out of the city every evening leaving the neighborhood a vacant space except for security guards. Reimagining the World Trade Center as a lively cultural space even after business hours was vital to Libeskind's conception, but languished due to financial considerations, finally given a boost in 2008 by a $75 million donation. The project gained renewed life and a new direction with the hiring of Maggie Boepple in 2012 to serve as the Performing Arts Center's president, and the appointment of a new set of board members. They were appointed by the governor and the mayor, and included other stakeholders such as Silverstein. Gehry had won the job to design the Performing Arts Center, but was later removed from the job by Boepple. REX architects were awarded the new contract, and their design features translucent marble and a price tag of $275 million (Pogrebin 2014; Cooper 2016).

Object as Text

REX architects envision the Performing Arts Center as a box, somber and austere by day but voyeuristically luminescent at night; background by day, art object at night. Its internal lighting is supposed to reveal the performance space through the stone. The principal considerations seem to have been how the building will fit in visually and sculpturally alongside its high-profile neighbors, turning the art object on at night is an imaginative tactic in that art saturated landscape. The World Trade Center is a highly symbolic site, dubbed "Ground Zero" ever since the destruction of the twin towers in 2001, a weighty term borrowed from Cold War nuclear rhetoric. Scrutiny over how the building will function, how it will deter rain and heat, are not publicized considerations for this high-profile building. Its visual character is paramount.

To say that the visual character of a work of high-profile architecture is crucial is perhaps obvious, but the historical legs beneath that obviousness are harder to see. It is not explained merely by reference to the founding of art history or the latter's profound and guiding influence on architecture and its visual appreciation, although those factors are vital. The explanation needs to take stock of a more recent past. The preeminence of plasticity and spatiality in architecture was solidified by the Modernist movement. It is now a maxim that architecture is spatial, both sculptural in the plastic sense as well as interiorized in the sense that space engulfs and encloses the human body.

This is not the place to present a history of heroic Modernism and its zeal to rid the built landscape of applied ornament, but a few preliminary notes are apropos. Austrian architect and essayist, Adolf Loos, expressed contempt for the meaning-laden imagery of the architectural façade, insisting that architecture is too easily associated with externally referenced ideas and predilections beyond the actual construction of the building. Freedom from decorative elements in useful manufactured objects was a mark of cultural progress, he argued, an idea laden with orientalist racism given Loos' disparaging example of Papuan tattooing (Loos 1998). Nonetheless, the disparagement of applied ornament took root in the architecture profession of the early twentieth century. This idea would prove foundational for Modernist practitioners of the mid-twentieth century, as many strove to remove the applied image from building façades, or, remove its ability to invoke references and allusions (Le Corbusier 1987 [1925]; Gropius 1965; Mies van der Rohe 1970; Wright 1901). In the hand of Modernists, the visual quality of architecture was therefore to be plastic rather than painterly. One way to ensure a building will not go out of style is to transcend style altogether, and banning applied ornament was a means of boiling a building down to its spatial and plastic truth. This ban would not last long. The Postmodernist critique of that position would be fueled by a different agenda, one more closely aligned to the art discourse of its day.

The painterly would make a triumphant return in the second half of the twentieth century. Robert Venturi's house for his mother and himself in New England would deliberately play with classical allusion as well as the stereotype of a suburban house using the gable as an image. His book, *Complexity and Contradiction* would call out this deliberate move to restore the richness of image to architectural design, finding a "mannerist" middle ground between applied ornament and its abolishment. The gentle manifesto appealed to architecture history for its persuasive support, while also suggesting tackiness was suitably decorative, poking ironic fun at his own creation. This both/and sentiment replacing either/or was developed further by his partner, Denise Scott Brown and co-author Steven Izenour in the book they wrote together with Venturi, *Learning from Las Vegas*, in the late 1960s. Their manifesto would revel in irony and provocation, reading:

> We shall describe how we come by the automobile-oriented commercial architecture of urban sprawl as our source for a civic and residential architecture of meaning, viable now, as the turn-of-the-century industrial vocabulary was viable for a Modern architecture of space and industrial technology 40 years ago.
>
> *(Venturi, Scott Brown, and Izenour 1972)*

"Meaning" was a keyword. Venturi and his co-conspirators took inspiration from the everyday landscape instead of ancient Rome. They borrowed this tactic from contemporary art, and also from the very Modernists they critiqued. The crux of their critique, and their manifesto, was relevance. In the 1960s in places like New York, London, and other metropolitan cities of the old colonial nations, some artists were taking popular images from advertising and elsewhere and making them reverberate in art galleries. Often transformed or stressed in a variety of visual ways, or merely allowed to work their magic in a new context, those images reflected contemporary values back at the viewer. This popular or "Pop Art" proved to be a reflexive approach to image production diverging from the prevalence for abstraction that marked the previous generation's concerns. Pop artists made the subject of their art the images around them. They drew attention to the cheap and the everyday, elevating popular culture to the status of high art. Their irony was inspired by the work of Dadaists, especially Marcel Duchamp (who, ironically, designated a urinal as a critique of the value of high art).

When Marilyn Monroe committed suicide in 1962, Andy Warhol created a series of silkscreen prints of the celebrity, taken from Bud Korman's photograph promoting the 1953 film *Niagara*. Irreverent and experimental use of non-traditional art production techniques, such as the lowly silk screening process, was typical of Pop Art practice, and Warhol emphasized the artificial character of the photographic image by applying lurid colors and multiplying the image in the same picture space, organized by a machine-evoking grid. One Marilyn or nine Marilyns organized in a grid pattern, or 100 silkscreen Marilyns presented as a diptych, the multiplicity reduced the captivating image of the celebrity to an obviously manufactured product. Warhol's pastiche made the viewer "see" the artificial quality of the image, and the celebrity, separating celebrity from subject. This approach to Pop Art subjectified the image itself, and it was this image-oriented or image-obsessed approach to art making that inspired Venturi and Scott Brown. A Las Vegas billboard graced the cover of their book, a rather unconventional image for an architectural treatise (Figure 32.9).

By studying the commercial landscape of Las Vegas and other everyday places, the team that wrote *Learning from Las Vegas* argued that image-making was vital to architecture. The commercial strip was an image-saturated landscape, not beautiful, but meaningful. In order to achieve relevance, they argued that architecture of the now had to make note of that saturation, draw attention to it and say something pithy or ironic about it. They critiqued their predecessors, "the Modern form givers," as fellow image makers who were ambivalent about the relationship between building and image. Where the Modern form givers eschewed applied symbolism or decorative surface treatment, the Postmodernists, as Venturi and Scott Brown would come to be called, played with it to say something about their contemporary world and its underlying commercial forces.

Even when designing what Venturi, Scott Brown, and Izenour playfully teased was "boring," or merely symbolized boring everyday buildings, the architects resorted to the writing of a manifesto attesting to their deliberate and artistic control over the art object. Applied image was the medium of control. Earlier manifestos penned by the Modern form givers, such as Walter Gropius, Le Corbusier, and Frank Lloyd Wright, spilled ink on the subject of the manufacture of machine materials, their transportation, and the process of industrial construction. Although they too were deeply concerned with the appearance of their art objects (perhaps that was their core concern), their Postmodernist successors seemed to have suppressed discourse on process and manufacture in order to locate their art exclusively in the visual quality of the object, and the associations triggered by those images. "We shall emphasize image—image over process or form," so state the authors of *Learning from Las Vegas*. They refer to this emphasis as something old, harkening back to nineteenth-century definitions of architecture as beauty applied to the box of the building. The mid-nineteenth-century manifesto by painter, architect, and writer John Ruskin established this precedent when he wrote:

> Architecture is the art which so disposes and adorns the edifices raised by man, for whatsoever uses, that the sight of them may contribute to his mental health, power, and pleasure.
>
> It is very necessary, in the outset of all inquiry, to distinguish carefully between Architecture and Building.
>
> *(Ruskin 1849)*

Figure 32.9 Architecture as Sign. Author's photograph of the 1977 edition of *Learning from Las Vegas* set against the blank screen of a local drive-through theater in Goleta, California (empty sign). Inset detail: Photograph adorning the first two editions of *Learning from Las Vegas*, depicting the "Tan Hawaiian with Tanya" billboard that became an iconic reference to the book (Vinegar 2008)

Source: Copyright Jeremy White.

His *Seven Lamps of Architecture* split architecture from building, allowing image its own existence, "adorning" that other thing called the building. A century later, architecture historian Nikolaus Pevsner began his famous survey of European architecture with the oft-repeated line, "A bicycle shed is a building; Lincoln Cathedral is a piece of architecture," solidifying the ontology of architecture and its existence as a separate category of landscape element (Pevsner 1983). By the 1960s, architecture with a capital "A" was free of building, both the noun and the verb. These predecessors gave Venturi and his team license to restore image to high architecture.

Emphasizing image and the associations that a referential image might evoke allows architecture to be thought of as a meaning-delivery system. The parts of a building that deliver meaning can be construed as a system for delivering meaning. Curiously, buildings are not necessary for delivery. Drawings can be architecture, or constitute an act of architecture (Kipnis and Zenghelis 2002). This was an important point made by the architect and architectural theorist Bernard Tschumi. In 1980 he wrote:

> The starchitect works at the limits, or edge, of the architecture profession, creating anomalous forms that have little bearing on the profession as a norm, but nonetheless establishing that "edge" of formal experiment; and in the case of the starchitect, this formal experimentation is intended to make the starchitect more apparent.
>
> *(Tschumi 1996)*

He goes on to say that formal experiments on paper, for in the 1970s that is how architects created form, with their hands and pencils and paper, do not need consummation as constructed buildings. Unlike a building, a drawing can be picked up, rolled, hung on a wall, but the design is still the intangible thing the drawing invokes. The drawing can convey the meaning of the architecture, without the three-dimensional building and its spatial experience. This seemingly radical obsolescence of three-dimensional space was consistent with architecture's divorce from building accomplished previously.

Tschumi pushed the idea of design's independence from building so far that he articulated the proposition that architecture is "text." Text is metaphorical, and yet architects of the late twentieth century played with the metaphor to the point that text seemed more substantial, even literal, if the pun will be excused. This manner of thinking about architecture was informed by critical theory and post-structuralism. Tschumi played with the idea of architectural syntax, partly inspired by the work of Jacques Derrida, designing large red function-free follies in a Parisian park, in his well-publicized and oft-cited Postmodernist project Parc de la Villette (Tschumi 2014). Each folly was a meaningless red dot in the landscape scheme organizing the park. Peter Eisenman also played with what he called "syntax" in the many plan oblique studies of his experimental house series (Frank 1994). In both cases, the massing of buildings and the arrangement of the parts within the massing could be likened to the conjugation tables of a language. Vocabulary does not influence the rules of syntax, it does not matter which verb is being conjugated because the rules of conjugation are mostly standard and these designers were interested in the ontology of the rule rather than how any particular rule influenced a sentence's meaning. The important thing is the structure of a rule, and the art-minded and image-oriented architect devised rules of formal conjugation, or transformation.

In this approach to form generation, the function of a building has little to do with the representative quality of a building's form. Eisenman's house series, with only one actually constructed and that for an art historian looking for an appreciating art object (Frank 1994), was not so much a building as it was a formal operation of lines, planes, and volumes. Once constructed, House VI did not need to look like a house, and indeed, in that regard it resembled the deliberate un-houselike work of Modernists, such as the steel and glass box of the Farnsworth House by Mies van der Rohe outside Chicago and Le Corbusier's Villa Savoye outside Paris, standing on its pipe columns. Daniel Libeskind's house in Connecticut, built in the first decade of the new millennium, was given the inscrutable name "18.36.54," corresponding to the number of planes, points, and lines determining the object's form, respectively. It too stood apart from other houses as well as their immediate surroundings. Standing apart was the point (again, pardon the pun), nature providing the negative curatorial space, and the reduction of architecture to text (in Eisenman's case) was a means to ensure the resulting buildings would bear little resemblance to their contemporaries and neighbors. When the roof leaked, the Franks gave up on the prospect of Eisenman designing a solution or even helping to solve the leak. They hired a regular architect to rethink the flashing. Eisenman was in charge of the text.

Glitter

A pixel is like a piece of glitter. Eisenman and Tschumi, and the other Postmodernists, did not work with pixels until the 1980s, and by then they embraced the moniker of Deconstructivist, a difficult term that referenced Soviet Constructivism of the early twentieth century while embodying the analytical claim of taking things apart. "Disjuncture" became a keyword. In the new century (the new millennium), in the age of the computer and its screen, Guy Debord seems strangely (perhaps simplistically) apropos. Both Tschumi and Eisenman were enamored with the work of Debord's colleague, Derrida, but in the era of Pop Art and Venturi, Debord wrote a book entirely organized by numbered theses, each an explosive shot aimed at contemporary capitalist society. This book, the *Society of the Spectacle*, included platitudes such as: "the spectacle is the *chief product* of present-day society," and, "The spectacle is *capital* accumulated to the point where it becomes image" (Debord 1967). In the new century of screens and software, apps and algorithms, standing on the shoulders of Postmodernists, the pixel presents a suitable motif for acts of architecture.

In the twenty-first century, drawings no longer precede buildings. The drafting table has been replaced by the computer, and although computer-aided design and drafting (CADD) initially followed hand-drawing in its preference for the line, building information modeling and form-based modeling are the medium through which the experimental architect designs their art objects. Patrick Schumacher, business partner and successor to Zaha Hadid, calls the work of contemporary art-minded architecture "parametricism," having jettisoned the unwieldy term Deconstructivism long ago. Germinated from the term parameter, a reference to algorithms central to form-generation software such as Rhinoceros, parametricism is a term also used by Greg Lynn. He asserted that the new form-generating design process is one of animation and coding (Lynn 1999). In the second decade of the new century, parametricism's sine curve has become the latest armature, the generic signature of the starchitect and their reach beyond the orthogonal. Instead of serving as a symbol or signal unlocking a bevy of associations sourced from architecture history, or from the everyday public commercial landscape, the sine curve organizes everything from the roof and terrace line of a wood-laminated structure in Seville to an imagined and unbuilt bank in London. Hadid even used it as a sinuous vertical axis in a limited-edition shoe she designed for United Nude in 2013, demonstrating how this armature transcends scale. Where the decorative line once adorned the box (Modernists railing against that lie), that flowing line now organizes three-dimensional form.

Parametric architecture bears little visual resemblance to the analog-manufactured design that once graced the Postmodernist's drafting table, as it revels in the serious business of generating striking and impossible form. Postmodernism is not dead, however, its legacy of irony bubbles to the surface not in the architecture of the Parametricist, but in other spectacles. The Greg Lynn Show is a case in point. It resides on YouTube where the architect serves as talk-show host in conversation with Schumacher and other prominent figures in the design world. Deadly serious discussions about the state of architecture in the second decade of the new millennium share air time with the banality of the talk-show video form. This campy wink alternates with Lynn's humorless Ted Talks and other video content where he asserts new form-generation techniques (parametricism and animation) as well as new material design (carbon fiber high-tensile furniture). Modernist romantic art heroism meets Pop Art inspired trickster rogue.

Lynn enjoys a privileged position as a United States white male designer and can afford to take such wildly different postures. His energy, abundant creativity, and zeal face no social limitations. The guild of the starchitect is generously populated by such white males, consistent with the architecture profession's bias for men. In the United States, one out of four architects is male (Sheng et al. 2015). Many commentators remarked that Zaha Hadid's death ripped a hole in the starchitect guild. One of the few women, an Arab woman, who commanded attention as a master architect, Hadid was a rare phenomenon, the exception to the rule.

Architects are licensed by the state and endure years of education and training, but a starchitect's ambition adds an additional layer to the recipe. Hadid spent her early career not working her way up from draftsman to job captain to project architect and then partner, helping to produce built projects every step of the way. She vied in design competitions instead, working out of what started as a tiny studio in London while creating one unrealized design after another, eventually winning modest competitions. She honed her craft via the production of drawings, paintings, and later, digital models expressing her designs (Futagawa 2014). What became a firm employing over 400 architects started in an artist's studio while Hadid experimented on Tschumi's proverbial "edge." As Arindam Dutta asserts in his essay in this volume, the university and boutique architect operates in a system of image production where actual buildings are not fundamental to a market of land value or to the construction of curricula vitae. While toiling to win competitions, Hadid taught at a prominent architecture school in London where she herself learned the trade, and likewise, typical of many a starchitect, Tschumi taught at an architecture school as well. The academic environment allows the production of monographs, gallery exhibitions, and appearances in biennales, all qualifying as architectural production, propping up an architect's career despite the paucity of actual buildings.

Conclusion

The art gallery anchors the art market. Ironically, the art–artist model, fundamental to art history and the appreciation of art today, describes only a segment of art production. Contemporary art, like architecture, is a team sport. The contemporary artist often works with others, assistants and fellow artists. Even when working solo, the artist relies on the recipient's engagement to complete the art experience. Installations can grow to the scale of a building, while performative aspects of an art piece flirt with other realms, such as theater, or sociology. When Ai *Weiwei* "installs" a piece, it can involve the population of an entire neighborhood. The professionalization of architecture may have been a long-term project to separate the designer from the builder, the contemporary artist has no qualm blurring distinctions of producer and appreciator. Identifying art as the most salient trait of design has been a particularly useful strategy for augmenting the architect's status as a professional. Once used as a means of distinguishing themselves from the carpenter-builder, the starchitect relies on art to separate themselves from the run-of-the-mill architect.

Digital technologies allow the starchitect to work at the edge of formal experimentation, leveraging the unexpected building form as a currency of image. Many shape their own image as well, as a design firm and as a celebrity. As with professionalization, the construction and reification of the starchitect as a master-artist enhances the brand of the architecture profession itself. This is old news (Upton 1991; Tschumi 2014). The brand's resilience is attested to by the resilience of Hadid's name. Two years on, the firm she left behind, manned (quite literally) by other architects, retains her name, Zaha Hadid Architects.

The object–artist model remains so robust for the starchitect, that even after removing the artist, the scheme still holds.

Note

1 See Chapter 27 by Laura McLauchlan in this volume.

References

Arantes, P. (2019) *The Rent of Form*, Minneapolis: University of Minnesota Press.
Architect's Newspaper (2016) "Peter Eisenman's iconic 1975 House VI finally sells," accessed December 15, 2018, https://archpaper.com/2016/09/peter-eisenman-house-vi-sells/.
Cooper, M. (2016) "Arts Center at Ground Zero has a new design, and, Barbra Streisand in charge," *New York Times*, September 8.
Debord, G. (1995) *The Society of the Spectacle*, New York: Zone Books.
Frank, S. (1994) *Eisenman's House VI: The Client's Response*, New York: Watson-Guptill.
Futagawa, Y. (2014) *Zaha m. Hadid: GA Architect 5*, Tokyo: ADA Editors.
Goldberger, P. (2005) *Up from Zero: Politics, Architecture, and the Rebuilding of New York*, New York: Random House.
Gropius, W. (1965) *The New Architecture and the Bauhaus*, Cambridge, MA: MIT Press.
Kimmelman, M. (2016) "Zaha Hadid, groundbreaking architect, dies at 65," *New York Times*, March 31.
Kipnis, J. and Zenghelis, E. (2002) *Perfect Acts of Architecture*, New York: Museum of Modern Art.
Le Corbusier (1987 [1925]) *The Decorative Art of Today*, Cambridge, MA: MIT Press.
Lewis, M. (2007) "The rise of the starchitect," *The New Criterion* (December), accessed December 15, 2018, www.newcriterion.com/issues/2007/12/the-rise-of-the-aoestarchitecta.
Loos, A. (1998) *Ornament and Crime: Selected Essays*, Riverside, CA: Ariadne Press.
Lynn, G. (1999) *Animate Form*, New York: Princeton Architectural Press.
Mies van der Rohe, L. (1970) *Mies van der Rohe: Library of Contemporary Architects*, New York: Simon and Schuster.
Pevsner, N. (1983) *An Outline of European Architecture*, London: Butler and Tanner.
Pogrebin, R. (2014) "Arts Center at Ground Zero shelves Gehry's design," *New York Times*, September 3.
Ross, P. (1972) *The Sociology of the Professions*, New York: Herder and Herder.
Ruskin, J. (1849) *Seven Lamps of Architecture*, London: Smith Elder & Co.
Sheng, R. et al. (2015) *Equity by Design: Equity in Architecture Final Report*, San Francisco: American Institute of Architects, accessed December 15, 2018, https://issuu.com/rsheng2/docs/equityinarch2014_finalreport.
Tschumi, B. (1996) *Architecture and Disjunction*, Cambridge, MA: MIT Press.
Tschumi, B. (2014) *Tschumi Parc de la Villette*, London: Artifice Books on Architecture.
Upton, D. (1991) "Architecture history or landscape history?" *Journal of Architecture Education* 44, 4 (August): 195–199.
Upton, D. and Vlach, M. (1986) *Common Places: Readings in American Vernacular Architecture*, Athens, GA: University of Georgia Press.
Vasari, G. (2008) *Lives of Artists*, Oxford: Oxford University Press.
Venturi, R., Scott Brown, D., and Izenour, S. (1972) *Learning from Las Vegas*, Cambridge, MA: MIT Press.
Vinegar, A. (2008) *I Am a Monument: On Learning from Las Vegas*, Cambridge, MA: MIT Press.
Watkin, D. (1983) *The Rise of Architecture History*, Chicago: University of Chicago Press.
Wright, F. (1901) "Art and craft of the machine," *Brush and Pencil* 8, 2.

33

A Eulogy for the Present
The Death of Architecture, c.2000 Exhibition

Rohan Shivkumar

Future historians of South Asian architecture may very well look back upon the period between 2016 and 2018 as an important period in the history of Indian architecture. In these years there have been four large-scale exhibitions examining the nature of architectural production in the country. Each of these was curated and presented by the architectural community as a public exhibition that would raise awareness and/or ask questions concerning the role that architects play in society, the history of the profession, and the possibilities and limitations of design.

The first of the events was the *State of Architecture* exhibition held in Mumbai in 2016 curated by Rahul Mehrotra, Kaiwan Mehta, and Ranjit Hoskote. According to the official website of the Urban Design Research Institute (2017), the organization that was central to planning, the curators "presented the state of contemporary architecture in India, mapping emerging practices and stimulating conversation on the different positions that characterize architectural production in India." This set off a series of exhibitions, as extensions or as responses to the arguments laid out by the show. *When Is Space?* in 2018 at the Jawahar Kala Kendra in Jaipur, curated by Rupali Gupte and Prasad Shetty, seemed to take the work of Charles Correa, the Indian architect who had passed away in 2015, as the object through which one could explore three different trajectories within Indian architecture: the urge toward mathematical transcendence, the exploration of typology, and the energies of the city. The *State of Housing* exhibition, again curated by the *State of Architecture* team in 2018 in Mumbai was an extension of their earlier show, this time examining the timeline of housing typologies and policy in India. The *Death of Architecture* exhibition curated by Aniket Bhagwat and Samira Rathod in 2018 at the Nehru Science Centre in Mumbai, on the other hand, was imagined as a space of rumination for the profession, to be able to seek out a meaning for itself and make itself relevant to the changing world.

In this paper I shall focus on the *Death of Architecture* exhibition, which was inaugurated in Mumbai and then traveled to 12 cities around the country, to sketch out some of these concerns and explore the possibilities that architects see for themselves in India. I shall be examining the rhetoric of the images and the texts of the curatorial notes and display panels produced by the participants, to excavate some of the paradigms and predilections of the contemporary architectural community. The motif of death in thinking about architecture in the present, I argue, represents not so much an aporia in the face of a rupture in the patron–client relationship that was nurtured in the milieu of a modernizing nation-state, as it serves as an alibi for inaction, non-intervention, and retreat.

Death of Architecture

In post-independent India, it was the middle-class professional who was presumed to be the champion of modernity. These professions had their roots in the institutions that the colonial administration had created to be the intermediaries between the colonial authorities and those they governed.[1] Professional education for these disciplines seemed to offer the burgeoning middle classes, often male, upper-caste individuals, access to the infrastructure of an education that could help them occupy the space between the rulers and the ruled. They had been the arms of the colonial government aiding and abetting the processes of domination. They were expected to distance themselves from their own experience of the world, and see themselves through the eyes of the colonial master. It was this class of people that became the leaders of the nationalist struggle, and eventually became the class that was entrusted with shaping the new nation from 1947 onwards. The educated middle classes occupied not only the bureaucracies that administered the machinery of the nation-state, including the Public Works Department, but also those occupations that were seen to be essential to the building of the new nation. These included the professions of law, medicine, engineering, and architecture.

Ever since, architects have framed their practices within the discourse of larger social transformations, doing so by providing housing for all or infrastructure for the poor, via scientific and rational thought, while also expressing the value systems of the Indian nation through evocations of history and tradition. These ambitions were thwarted by the developments in the latter half of the twentieth century. Architects struggled to find relevance in a country in which the process of modernization was never smooth, where mass migration, rural poverty, housing shortages, struggles over ideology and identity challenged the middle-class professional's imagination of the nation-state. Since the country's liberalization in the early 1990s this schism has become even more apparent. With the large-scale disappearance of the nation-state as client, architects have had to struggle to find relevance in the rapidly transforming landscape. With discourse, images, and influences now more easily streaming in from around the world, the profession is struggling to find itself. Who does it represent? What role does it see for itself? What are the determinants for the ethical and aesthetic choices it makes? It is this "death" that haunts most of the recent discourse concerning architecture and architectural education in India and the *Death of Architecture* exhibition.

For the exhibition, 13 "thinking and concerned design practices" (Bhagwat 2018: 6) were chosen to ruminate about the presumed "death" of the profession, ponder on concerns, tools, representation, and relevance. For the inauguration in Mumbai the large barrel-vaulted space of the Nehru Science Centre's temporary exhibition area was set up as the space for a mystical ritual. The floor of the room was filled with black river sand with strange sculptural formations. A naked light bulb hung low from the ceiling over concentric circles of white stones; a projector beamed images onto industrial residue arranged like a forgotten city. The overall effect seemed to evoke a sense of mystique, like encountering the totemic objects of some enigmatic tribal ritual. Along the walls, on dimly lit panels this tribe expressed its aspirations and frustrations with itself and the world.

The opening was attended mainly by architects and architecture students from Mumbai, curious about the provocation of the title. They meandered through the installations and tried to decipher the ideas and imaginations in the often abstruse text and drawings on the panels. This was a conversation within a circle and others had been invited to listen in. I am interested in this circle, from which I cannot excuse myself: after all I was invited to conduct a "court martial" of the participating firms at the opening of the exhibition. An investigation of this exhibition within the history of this circle of "concerned design practices," its genesis, presumptions, and concerns, reveals certain mythologies that shape contemporary architectural discourse in India.

The "Indian" Architect?

One of the first panels one encounters in the exhibition is the provocation of the curatorial note by Aniket Bhagwat. The date that this note sets for its purported death is the year 2000. Besides being the end of the millennium, it was also almost a decade after the Indian economy liberalized, allowing foreign direct investment in the country. Since then most of the practices represented in the exhibition have grown rapidly. Participants are provoked to ask themselves questions: What is it that they have been creating over the past 18 years? Is it "architecture," if indeed architecture died at the turn of the millennium? Did the promise of the new world order, emerging at the end of the 1980s with the fall of communism and the rise of neoliberal capitalism, reveal itself as a lie? The curatorial note asks these questions through a sketch history of the preoccupations of the profession since independence. The call is for the 13 firms to look within, to introspect on the "reasonably relevant causes amidst *select sections of society*" (Bhagwat 2018: 4, emphasis mine).

For his own exploration in the exhibition by the firm M/s Prabhakar B. Bhagwat titled "dissolving RE_TICENCE" Aniket Bhagwat traces the genesis of the "section of society" called the "concerned architect." The panels are divided across three sections, "Re-flect, Re-spond, and Re-view." Within the first section, a history of iconic "Indian" architecture is laid out in chronological order like bas-relief on the wall of an Indian temple. This includes the famous cave temples of India, temples from South India, Mughal monuments, colonial buildings, post-independent Indian experiments in modernism and later responses to create an "Indian identity" (Figure 33.1). In "Re-spond" we encounter a series of fingerprints, made out of texts exploring the nature of the nation-state, its possibilities and limitations. These are arranged chronologically from pre-independence texts by Mahatma Gandhi and Rabindranath Tagore through the famous texts of the birth of the Indian nation by Jawaharlal Nehru and B. R. Ambedkar, to utterances typical of current hyper-nationalism (Figure 33.2). The final section "Re-view" places architectural discourse within the landscape sketched above. Through the scars drawn on the surface of the panels one can read in fine print ruminations about architecture and the role of design culled from a variety of books and conversations over the past few years within the architectural community. The argument here seems to imply the close intertwining of the question of national identity with the role that architects see for themselves. It provokes us to delve into the history of the profession and study its genesis to understand its predilections and biases.

Tradition

This search for a particularly "Indian" identity is one that troubles "Watermarks" by Meghal and Vijay Arya in *The Death of Architecture*. Meghal and Vijay Arya begin their panel with the words "Indian philosophy sees death as a cyclical process, giving birth to a new spirit every time." They then proceed to describe the beauty of some of the traditional North Indian water systems in the country from the *ghat*s of Benares and the *kund*s of Rajasthan, and compare these with the "large scale, homogenous, mono-functional" water infrastructure that characterizes new

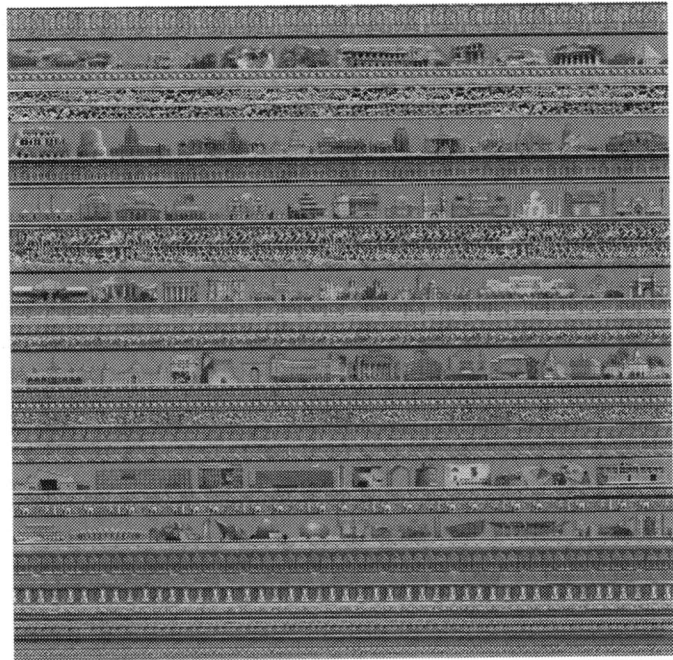

Figure 33.1 M/s Prabhakar B Bhagwat, bas relief, *Death of Architecture*
Source: Copyright M/s Prabhakar B Bhagwat.

Figure 33.2 M/s Prabhakar B Bhagwat, one of the fingerprints of texts concerning Indian nationalism, *Death of Architecture*
Source: Copyright M/s Prabhakar B Bhagwat.

communities "with people retreating into the banality and orchestrated publicness of gated communities" (Bhagwat 2018: 15). A series of experiential poems follows alongside abstracted cartographic drawings of traditional water systems. The poems belie a longing for the romance of the handcrafted and the sensuousness of the body in relation with water. As against the engineering mentality towards infrastructure they propose a poetic alternative (Figure 33.3).

A similar longing pervades the work of Edifice Architects and Navkar, as they look back at the towns of Thirupor in Tamil Nadu, and Pune respectively. While Arya Architects seem to be searching for the "eternal" and the "timeless," the two tropes of contemporary Indian architecture, both these firms want to address the question of the "local" and a "sense of place." Navkar Architects eulogizes the traditional architecture in the town of Pune with sketch drawings about the details of the way spaces responded to the specific culture and climate of the city.

By using reconstructions of historic buildings in Thirupor and juxtaposing them with contemporary photographs, Edifice Architects describe the disfigured body of the town in a feminized idiom: "Limbs at an angle, face distorted, identity lost, she sits heaving, clinging on to the temple that is now adorned by asbestos sheets, grills and tiled floors." This chaste and beautiful woman, in their reckoning, has literally been ravaged by the horrors of "development." Her, "cries are silent but still need to be heard. Her voice has not carried far as she is drowning in the flood of the gangrenous metropolitan" (Bhagwat 2018: 31). For their solution, they offer "non-intervention," not trusting contemporary society to intervene in sensible and sensitive ways to these kinds of architectural fabrics.

All of these examples seem to represent a certain longing for a time gone by—for a pre-industrial, pre-colonial, and pre-modern utopia where a balance between architecture, culture,

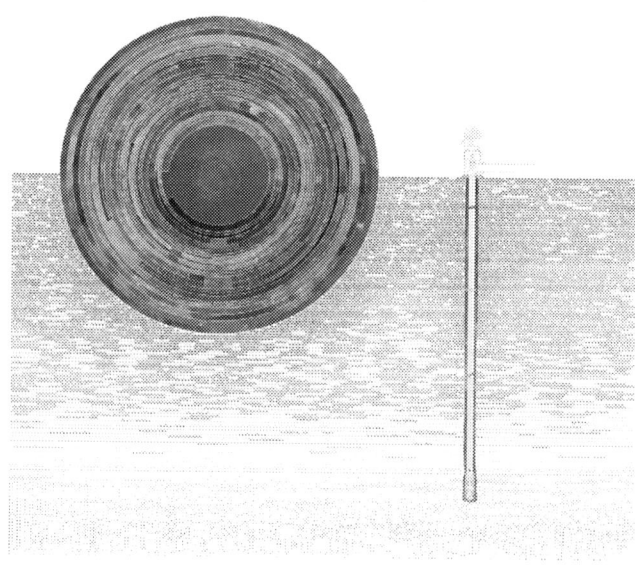

Figure 33.3 Arya Architects, panel showing ways of drawing water from the ground, *Death of Architecture*

Source: Copyright Arya Architects.

and climate is imagined. It is tempting to read this longing through Partha Chatterjee who in *The Nation and Its Fragments* speaks of the middle classes' urge to classicize tradition: such a "mode of classicization could comfortably incorporate as particulars the diverse identities in 'Indian tradition,' including such overtly anti-Brahamanical movements as Buddhism, Jainism, and various deviation popular sects" (Chatterjee 1993: 73).

In this version of Indian identity, the past is cleansed into a series of idealized relationships between Man and the Universe, Man and Nature. History is reduced to the subjective experience—to be pleasured in. A phenomenology without history is used to subsume violence. An abstracted past, an idealized world is projected in the sepia tone of nostalgia. The "timeless" and "eternal" are evoked as abstract imaginations that connect us to an imagined past—a continuum, unbroken by the ruptures of modernity. There could also be here a longing of the middle classes and upper castes to recapture their perpetual centrality in history.

Vernacular

But there is also another way in which the middle classes construct a tradition—the "vernacular."

Idealized as the opposite of the top-down "classical," this is imagined as a voice that emerges "from the people"—presumptively a more authentic expression of the local. The roots of this tendency within the Indian modern state are often seen within the Gandhian commonplace "The soul of India lies in its villages." In making this tradition the untutored is glorified as somehow more truthful and pure. A history of this approach in architecture is not too difficult to find, from the vernacular reifications in some of Tagore's buildings in Shantiniketan, to the romanticism of the Gandhian "return to the villages," to the appropriation of vernacular modes of building or ornamentation in so much self-consciously "Indian" architecture. Yet, this discourse of the vernacular as the crucible of culture is not limited to the architecture of the village or even that of traditional architecture in the historic cities of the country. One can see echoes of this, even in the way informal settlements in cities are discussed.

In every city in India the formal city is mirrored by an often larger informal one. This informal city is the place where most of the laborers reside, in slums on the outskirts or in the interstices of the formal city. The reciprocal relationship between the formal and the informal has often been spoken of in architectural discourse, although the line between the two is never clear. While in the early stages of nation building, the socialist state presumed a responsibility for the provision of shelter for those living in these slums, it turned out to be an impossible project largely due to the heavy-handed bureaucratization of the state, and in no small measure due to the lack of imagination among planners and architects about the nature of housing to be provided for these communities. Using antiquated and often irrelevant "standards" to imagine housing solutions, the projects built by state agencies were unable to meet the needs of those they claimed to serve. This frustration is apparent in some of the *Death of Architecture* projects, especially those by Mumbai-based Vikas Dilawari and Shabbir Unwala.

In both of these, the forces that shape the contemporary city are decried as inhuman. Dilawari rails against the "Shanghai-fication" of the city, the reduction of the city fabric to a mere game of numbers in the neoliberal economy. Both architects also complain about the regime of FSI (Floor Space Index) that determines the kind of architecture being built in this particular city: "In Mumbai today, the super built area is driving space-making. Architecture in the city has become redundant and merely endorses construction" (Bhagwat 2018: 133).

This is a familiar refrain. The "placeless-ness" of the neoliberal city and the inability for current systems of production to create truly relevant architecture. The slum is now seen as the crucible for popular knowledge in the heart of the city. Mumbai-based BARD studios also make such an argument for the popular. Claiming that the formal city does not have an architecture that enables "transactional capacities" they romanticize the architecture that emerges out of the informal processes in the city (Figure 33.4). These, they say, exist in the "blurred space" in between the lines of the formal city. They include

> extension to shops, folding shops of street vendors, porting devices, resting apparatus, fixtures fixed on boundary walls that help occupy them, things used to claim space, orphaned furniture left for wanderers, etc., are all transactional spaces. However, these spaces are not just utilitarian to facilitate transactions. They are *quirky, erotic, sedimented, and absurd*. In their absurdity these are instances of dreams trying to take shape and aspirations trying to get worked out.
>
> (Bhagwat 2018: 173, emphasis mine)

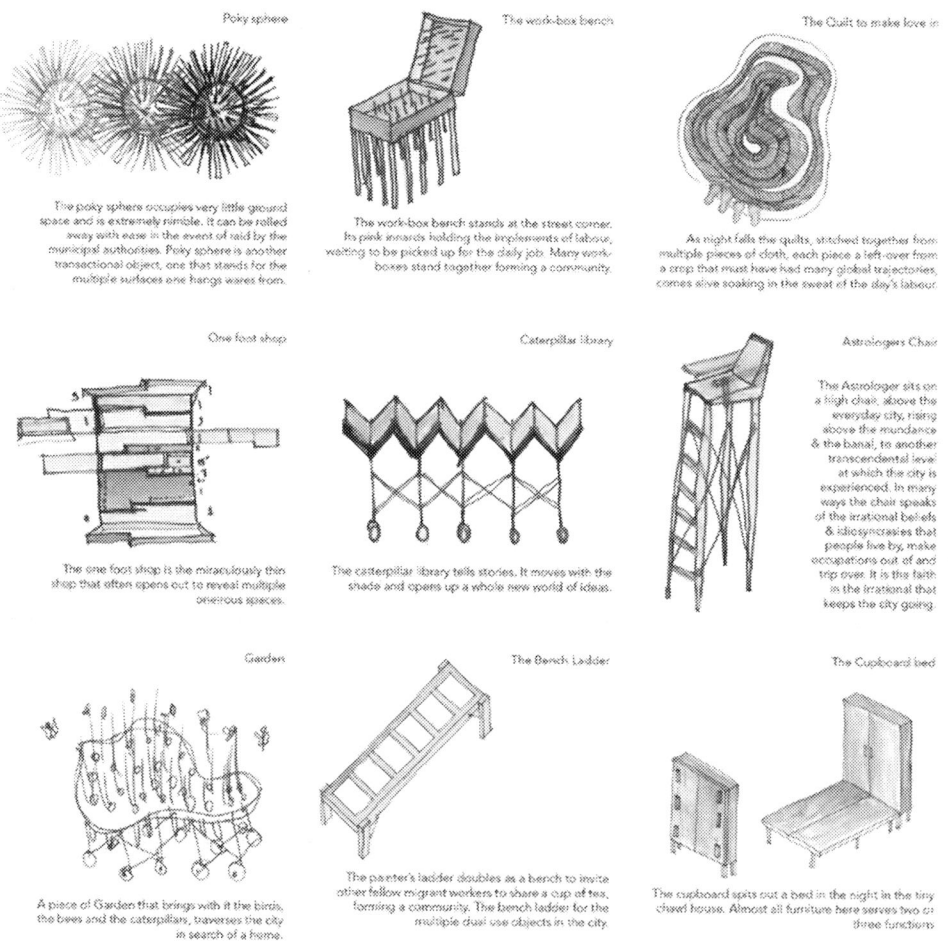

Figure 33.4 BARD Studio, drawings of some of the "Transactional Objects" proposed for the city of Mumbai, *Death of Architecture*

Source: Copyright BARD Studio.

A Eulogy for the Present

These evocations of the irrational seem to be incitements to rethink the moralities of the modernizing state, especially when the homeless are framed as "caretakers of wares left behind" by the formal city on the street (Bhagwat 2018: 179). The claims to quirkiness and absurdity reframe the popular as that lies outside the boundary of architectural knowledge, or the presumptions of the middle-class professional: "Design practices themselves will need to change their modalities to be able to participate in the creation of an architecture of transactional capacities" (Bhagwat 2018: 174). Another practice that celebrates this informality is the project by Hundred Hands Studio in Bangalore. Through a series of small design interventions, a proposition is made for micro-solutions to the issues faced by hawkers on busy market streets in Bangalore (Figure 33.5).

This turn to the urban popular, in which the vernacular and popular are conflated, may be usefully read through Chatterjee's discussion of the process through which the popular is appropriated by the nationalist elite:

> The popular becomes the repository of natural truth, naturally self-sustaining and therefore timeless. It has to be approached not by the calculating analytic of rational reasoning but by "feelings of the heart," by lyrical compassion. The popular is also the timeless truth of the national culture, uncontaminated by colonial reason.

Figure 33.5 INformalities, "Hundred Hands," *Death of Architecture*
Source: Copyright Informalities.

> The popular is appropriated in a sanitized form, carefully erased of all marks of vulgarity, coarseness, localism and sectarian identity. The very timelessness of its structure opens itself to normalization. Immediately, therefore, what is popular is unthinking, ignorant, superstitious scheming, quarrelsome, and also potentially dangerous and controllable. But with the mediation of enlightened leadership, its true essence is made to shine forth in its natural strength and beauty: its capacity for resolute endurance and sacrifice and its ability to protect and nourish.
>
> *(Chatterjee 1993: 73)*

The claims to "identity" evoked in the exhibition, in both the evocation of the classical and the popular seem to emphasize the exceptionalism of the "place" as the empirically determined territory within which particularities exist that architects have to address. However, as Saskia Sassen notes, a territory is "a complex condition that includes logics of power and logics of claim making, that cannot be reduced to land" (Sassen 2017: 128). In that sense the local is not merely

Figure 33.6 Busride, "End of the Local," *Death of Architecture*
Source: Copyright Busride.

a resistance to the purported equalizing forces of global capital, the place is also in many ways *produced* by the same forces. It is this difficulty in locating the local that Busride Studios struggles with in their contribution titled, "The Death of the Local" (Figure 33.6). Beginning with an image of King Kong poised to gobble up a traditional hut, their proposition decries the reduction of the local to pure iconography in contemporary architecture. With this image they neatly splice contemporary forces of capitalism and the ways in which it appropriates the global as a commodity: "Our local is a local seen from the outside" (Bhagwat 2018: 61).

With an analysis of projects lauded in the *State of Architecture* exhibition and in the Aga Khan Awards they also dismantle the discourse of relevance and resistance through which much of the architecture in India is framed: "Our resistance is as shallow as the cladding on our buildings," one proclamation reads in bold type (Bhagwat 2018: 58). Wittily dismantling the tropes of what stands as proxy for local architecture in mainstream discourse, they end with "The place has moved on. But we insist on being from there" (Bhagwat 2018: 67).

Ruin

If that is the state of place, what of time? Much architectural discourse seems to hinge on the unique nature of traditional Indian architecture's relationship to time. At one level is the evocation of the "timeless." The architectural theorist, Yatin Pandya notes:

> India's heritage does not confine to historic accounts of the events and objects frozen in their own time and space, but rather as cultural and architectural traditions which have *transcended the time and space* to remain alive and appropriate even in the present. In India, history stays alive as living traditions.... Tradition therefore survives and remains timeless.
> *(Pandya 2005: 10, emphasis mine)*

This call to look beyond the vicissitudes of history towards the eternal seems to imagine architecture that exists outside the realm of the everyday, and therefore able to transcend the social and the political. The search is one that can go beyond these everyday irritations in search of the eternal. Another trope of the framing of time within a uniquely "Indian" philosophy is the proposition that in India, time is cyclical. Again we turn to Pandya who explains this as, "the faith in reincarnations, the cycle of birth-death and rebirth, the unending chain of construction-destruction and reconstruction, all reaffirm the belief in the recurrence of time" (Pandya 2005: 12).

Both of these conceptions make their presence in the *Death of Architecture* exhibition, most vividly in the contribution by Anthill Architects. In a dense philosophical meditation on the nature of time, they propose four different, overlapping times in which we exist—Stellar Time, which architecture registers as "a Centred Geometry, an Axis Mundi and Ritual"; Terrestrial Time, where architecture is imagined as "the re-organization of the earth's crust" ("We dig material from here, process it, organize it, and put it there"); Historical Time, where "History organizes lines into Genealogies, Typologies and Grids"; and Momentary Time, where "real life" can inhabit space (Bhagwat 2018: 247, 248). Indian cities and therefore architecture is seen as an art that exists enmeshed in all of these and can address them all. An analysis of the way time is represented in four contemporary buildings follows, their architectural gestures and elements examined for the ways in which they address questions of Time and Space. The desire to create an architecture that can straddle all of the above times is apparent, as is the effort to be able to transcend the current modes of production shaping the architecture of the city (Figure 33.7).

This urge towards an architecture of transcendence can also be seen in the contribution by Vastu Shilpa Architects. Two cubicles are placed opposite each other, one with the sounds of

Rohan Shivkumar

Figure 33.7 Anthill Studio, illustration for "Terrestrial Time," *Death of Architecture*
Source: Copyright Anthill Studio.

the city and the other with sounds of nature. The attempt is to "represent two extremes, life and death," negotiated on a daily basis: "Paradoxically, being on the edge of death makes us alive and curiously, we become numbed by alive-ness and could be called dead. Our search as architects lies somewhere in between, negotiated, by our own desires, experiences, questions and hauntings" (Bhagwat 2018: 195).

The ruin testifies to the way that architecture can transcend the present:

> Ruins are stimuli allowing our minds to journey towards the indefinite, the distant, and the remote to satisfy the aspiration for the infinite, for something that vanishes in distant time or space whose measure is lost. The complexity, the richness of ruins lies within the deep temporal relationships revealed by the presence of reminders of mankind's building efforts accumulated over time.

(Bhagwat 2018: 196)

A Eulogy for the Present

Samira Rathod's contribution to the exhibition exults in the ruin as the possibility for beauty. The town of Bhadran on the outskirts of the city of Baroda is experiencing an exodus of its people. The architecture of the city thus lies abandoned and derelict. From the detritus of this dereliction, Samira Rathod constructs new beginnings. These assemblages "pay homage to the time that was, while looking to the future that can be" (Bhagwat 2018: 240). Meanings oscillate wildly within these assemblages. Their purpose is unclear and does not seem to solve any clear "problem." They exist for their own sake—as affective mnemonic oracles of the present: "Nostalgia for its own sake is valuable" (Figure 33.8).

The framing of time as this perpetually shifting marker, that consumes all, also informs the work of Abaxial. Using the narrative memories of middle-class residents of Delhi of important public spaces in the city—Connaught Place and Nehru Place—they make a case for an architecture that accepts change: "Based on shifting experiences, these memories build constructs

Figure 33.8 Samira Rathod Design Associates, some of the objects reconstructed from the residue of demolitions in the town of Bhadran, *Death of Architecture*

Source: Samira Rathod Design Associates.

that constantly alter the nature of relationships between the past and the present" (Bhagwat 2018: 109). These perspectives on time, these philosophical meanderings, can be seen as a luxury of those largely unaffected by the ravages of time. Anecdotes about remembered moments, the aestheticizing of history, can create a warm cocoon within which we can assume no responsibility for the consequences of our privilege, our presumptions, and our actions.

Guilt of the Modernizer

On the whole, the main preoccupation of the exhibition seems to be a reevaluation of the architects' relation to state modernization and their faith in modernity. This phenomenon is as old as the history of modernity and cuts across media and cultural spheres. Consider the 1954 film *Amar* by the director Mehboob Khan that stages an encounter between the modernizer and the subject of modernity. The city lawyer, played by that cinematic icon of modern India, Dilip Kumar, comes into the village as a savior, riding (quite literally) on a horse. In the forest he encounters this beautiful and enigmatic village belle. A mutual fascination begins, him for the purity and wildness she represents, and her for the clarity and modernity that he exudes.

One stormy night as she is wandering in the forest, she is pursued by the local goon. Not knowing where to go, she runs into the house of the modernizer, where she hopes she will be safe. The lawyer is caught off guard by this intrusion of the wild into his seemingly safe home. The intrusion brings out the inherent violence in him, and he rapes her. The rest of the film is concerned with the guilt of this modernizer, who knew that his action stood against everything that his value system represented.

This guilt of the modernizer, who presumed the responsibility to shape the new nation and saw this project fail looms large over architectural discourse. Faced with the undeniable evidence of the irrelevance of architectural practice to be able to intervene meaningfully in relationship with the popular, it chooses to gaze upon it enviously, ennobling it with a truth and beauty out of reach for the modernizing middle classes. This gaze/guilt also ennobles the one who was able to recognize these qualities. Once framed as such, it makes any action/practice irrelevant.

Architectural practice in India has been able to develop a strategy to reconcile itself with this schizophrenia—the presumption that the project of modernity (freedom, equality, and fraternity) was its burden to carry, and the evidence around that proves the failure it has been. A performance of "concern" allows the architect to split themselves across these with ease. One works as the alibi for the other. A belief in modernity would challenge the very foundations of what the profession is built on: the predominance of the nation-state (in the early years of the modern state) and capitalism (post-liberalization). These have not been easy to challenge as to do so would threaten the very position that they occupy in the socio-economic hierarchy.

Coda

The *Death of Architecture* exhibition was a response and an extension of the *State of Architecture* exhibition that preceded it. In the latter show, a survey was attempted to map the territory of the architectural profession in the country. In a series of maps across decades the locations of the primary practices in the country, the architecture schools and the projects chosen to be showcased as representative of the trends in architecture of the nation were mapped (Figure 33.9).

Over the past decade small towns and cities in India have experienced dramatic growth. Much of the production of built form in these cities is done by small town contractors or architects, or lie completely outside the formal economy. At the time of independence there were just two schools of architecture in the country, and by 1991 there were 45. Post liberalization

A Eulogy for the Present

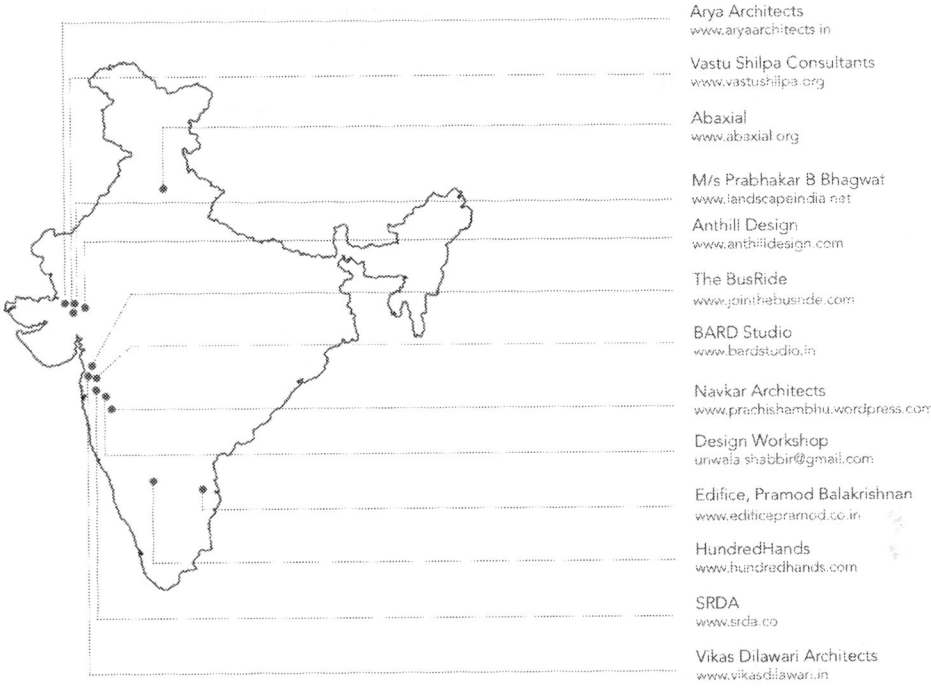

Figure 33.9 Location of the firms participating in the *Death of Architecture* exhibition
Source: Copyright M/s Prabhakar B Bhagwat.

witnessed a sudden increase in the number of architectural schools and by 1996 the number had almost doubled. As of October 2015, there are over 450 architecture schools that yearly send out over 24,000 architects into the country. This is an incredibly large number when compared to the current number of registered architects in the country—58,847 as per the issued enrolment numbers in December 2018 (Council of Architecture 2018).

In the *State of Architecture* exhibition, one was able to see the preponderance of projects in and around the three centers around which architectural discourse emerged: Mumbai, Delhi, and Ahmedabad. Besides these three, one can also see a smattering of practices in the cities that experienced the spurt of development post-liberalization: Pune and Bengaluru. These continue to be the centers for the places where magazines and journals, seminars and conferences on architecture take place. These are also the locations of most of the practices in *Death of Architecture*. As centers that determine discourse they seem to exert a hegemonic power over the rest of the country. There is much that is happening outside this realm of rarified discourse, but contemporary architectural discourse in India has not been able to find mechanisms to embrace these forces, and the architectural community recognizes this. This period of reconsideration within the architectural community in India, which includes the *Death of Architecture* exhibition, was an opportunity for reconsideration and hopefully recalibration within the architectural community. For this recalibration to be truly effective it would have to find a way not only to speak *to* this rapidly growing community, but to speak *from* it. This would necessarily need the community to reevaluate its presumptions of knowledge, its value systems, to rethink its own privilege that allows it access to the spaces and institutions of power, and perhaps even to rethink the structures through which it imagines its role in society.

Note

1 Thomas Babington Macaulay in his famous "Minute on Education" (February 2, 1835) considered it prudent to "form a class who may be interpreters between us and the millions whom we govern—a class of persons Indian in blood and colour, but English in tastes, in opinions, in morals and in intellect."

References

Bhagwat, A. (ed.) (2018) *DOA, Death of Architecture circa 2000*, Landscape Environment Advanced Foundation (LEAF).
Chatterjee, P. (1993) *The Nation and Its Fragments: Colonial and Postcolonial Histories*, Princeton: Princeton University Press.
Council of Architecture (2018) List of Enrolment Numbers Issued to Students Admitted in 1st Year B. Arch Course by the COA as on 02.12.2015 (Enrolment no. 40001 onwards), www.coa.gov.in. Accessed January 2, 2019.
Pandya, Y. (2005) *Concepts of Space in Traditional Indian Architecture*, Ahmedabad: Mapin Publishing.
Sassen, S. (2017) "Relocating global assemblages": an interview with Saskia Sassen conducted by Aneesh Tiwari, *Science, Technology & Society* 22, 1: 128–134.
Urban Design Research Institute (2017) *The State of Architecture: Practices and Processes in India*. www.udri.org/events/the-state-of-architecture/. Accessed January 2, 2019.

34
Architects "Getting Real"
On Present-Day Professional Fictions

Arindam Dutta

Theories of practice hold that the set of actionable knowables in a given situation need be, or rather can only be, a marginal subset of all the potential knowables in that situation. For Herbert Simon, to take one among many mid-twentieth-century gurus of practice, the concept-metaphor "design" presented the headland of this reduction, one opposed to the metaphysical vagueness of terms such as "nature." For Simon, the question "What is Nature?" amounted at best to prestige-seeking, with little to do with the needs of science itself (Simon 1969). Any discovery of so-called natural phenomena was in fact always a product of a more restricted epistemology of design (the "sciences of the artificial"), reductions that inevitably reflected economic interest. Rather than discover "nature," then, scientific discoveries responded to "task environments": criteria of use under which the qualities of matter became meaningful in new and specific ways. Matter is a performative entity; things were not things-in-nature as much as bundles of qualities that appear in the world because certain task environments become critical or purposive in a given socio-economic context. In other words, scientific programs do not unearth eternal, enduring truths, but rather represent a continually vanishing boundary of uncovering and refashioning the performative aspects of matter in response to a need, and moving on when the need has been met (Simon 1969: 131). "Nature" is here posed as a transactional field, a proto-market of sorts.

Since the 1960s, the humanities and social sciences have likewise tended to evade the constative question "What is …?" in favor of the performative: "How does …?" One discounts the obduracy of facts and truths, not because they are not valid, but rather because the brunt of the questions has shifted to the negotiational or the transactional. Design, construction, these appear more pertinent than ontology in modeling social behavior and cultural politics. There appears thus an unstated ideological convergence between the humanities, social sciences, and the sciences in the past half-century or so. For the humanities, design appears as the new grand narrative within which the predicaments of socialization, desire, and will can be thought through. Bruno Latour's exhortation towards a "parliamentarism" of knowledge and interest, towards so-called "matters of concern" rather than the putative inviolability of facts, might thus be described as a counterpart to Simon's ideal of a "boundary science" in that epistemic validity is seen in regional rather than universal terms, defined by need and context (Latour 2004).

Arindam Dutta

In any case, as the sciences focus more on securing commercial and state investments that keep research viable, there is a commensurate withering away of such "universal" metaphysical questions. What for Simon appeared in mid-twentieth century as a corrective against the bloviating of his contemporaries is now entrenched necessity: science *is* effectively product design. And rather than portend to discover the mysteries of nature, examining sociality and socialization, the erstwhile preserve of the humanities and social sciences, has now become, with the commensurate inroads into big data, a crucial feature in the market research that would render its products commercially viable. In every case, the invocation of design covers over a clandestine or not-so-clandestine premium on transactionalism as the driver of human affairs, a new utilitarian consensus creeping into political, economic, and cultural relations alike, from cognizance of rape in college dorm-rooms to disputes among nations about trade deficits and carbon emissions.

This essay charts the present-day ascendancy of design in terms of the effects that this tacit transactionalism may have, not so much on the arts and sciences, but on the auteur segments of the workforce that have traditionally called themselves designers, e.g., architects. In so doing, it charts three paradoxes that appear salient in this ascendancy. For the purposes of this paper, Herbert Simon's arguments cited above will serve for us as a useful foil, as symptomatic of mid-twentieth-century high modernism, wherein embracing the boundary games and cost–benefit calculus of the market sphere would entail the *secularization* of design, in that the "fall" or dissolution into economistic criteria would eliminate transcendental prerogative (nature, genius, truth, community, state, etc.), effectively transforming the designer from conjuring priest into a liberal, value-seeking vocation embedded at the heart of industrial capitalism. Today's designers, when called upon to assert a creed, I would argue, inevitably proffer some version of this rationalist faith—paradox intended—as their *raison d'être*, which suggests a tacit self-image or narrative hold that has still not fully run its course in the half-century following. The broad imputation of these three paradoxes, I will attempt to show, signals rather a devaluation of that self-image: I will argue that this self-image of the designer has *nothing to do* with the economic predicament in which they are placed and that the high-modernist view had sought to centrally orchestrate.

The first paradox that I outline is the following. *The present-day ascendancy of design connotes a reduced, if not marginal, role for the designer herself.* This is largely, I will argue, because design is not a singular activity. Narratives that singularize the figure of the designer on the lines that intending subjects occupy in novels or films profoundly mischaracterizes the fragmented games of legitimation that go into the creation of commodities, which involve a raft of value-additive activity, say, from incentive-seizing (e.g., greening) to investor-hunting, networking, intellectual property management, market research, locational constraints, supply chains, platform development, and so on. Rather than evolve into the equivalent of orchestra conductors, as the tacit liberalism of systems-thinkers in the 1960s had led them to hope, the designer represents a piecemeal, often inessential, node in a dispersed and ever-shifting division of labor.

As for those who traditionally called themselves designers, such as architects, this leads to a further, our second, paradox. *Rather than "modernize" into a liberal profession and skills commensurate with market rationale, there is a regression from the high-modern moment into a new feudality, in that their virtuoso creations best align with the appreciation and whimsy of (individual and institutional) wealth-holders and the powerful.* One cannot but reiterate that this regression is also a political one. Today this neo-feudal whimsy is bolstered by an intersecting network of academia, biennales, auction houses, museums, and galleries within which these auteurs or would-be auteurs circulate. There is a profusion of avant-gardist "projects," espousing a "criticality" that has less to do with critique in the epistemological sense than in conjuring up quixotic social utopias devoid of any actual social contract.

Architects "Getting Real"

The principal weight of my argument here will be to establish, and this is our third paradox, the following: *no boundary science can exist without a metaphysical kernel that grounds it*. Put differently, design remains through and through a vocation that essentially invokes transcendence of some kind in order to establish its legitimacy. The will to contingency embraced in design does not augur a path to freedom but rather the opposite, a submission to some ineluctable, sovereign spirit prone to arbitrariness and whimsy, which in the long run must be represented as the twisted workings of genius. The accentuation of design in the economic sphere corresponds not to an expansion of deliberative rationality but to a profession of faith.

If you do not know the story already, Google the words "Ordos 100," under Images. Somewhere between items 1 and 10, you should see pictures of a large architectural site model taking up a sizeable portion of a gallery space. The buildings are blocked out, low in resolution, presumably emulating the profundity of minimalist sculpture. Beyond the large floor model, on the periphery, you may see some drawing boards on the walls, dimly recognizable in the distance as renderings and drawings of individual buildings. Googling some more, you may chance upon some of these plates: photo-real pictures of these luxury residences as if already built. Further online browsing may throw up puff pieces, ruminations about the radical potentials of this speculative venture, and perorations about renewed ontological commitment. ("It's a big challenge for us, to think about what is a house, what is architecture."[1])

Ordos 100 was to be located in Kangbashi or New Ordos or Erdos (a southern Mongolian dialect/toponym, cognate with Urdu, the Mughal "camp language"), a new state-driven urban development in Inner Mongolia, conceived by local officials to cash in on a booming economy driven by the discovery of the region's huge coal and oil deposits, some 30 kms away from the city of Dongsheng. Now called Old Ordos, Dongsheng was in fact an unplanned boomtown dating back only to 2000, devoid of the laundered and consolidated amenities and services that new "planned" developments could offer to a burgeoning elite. The sponsors for Ordos 100 were two corporations owned by the Chinese businessman Cai Jiang,[2] a local entrepreneur who had made his career pursuing sundry local opportunities that the boom economy threw up, first selling cashmere and freshwater pearls to the Russian market for recycled steel, subsequently graduating to the regional dairy and coal industries, and eventually (and predictably) stepping into land speculation and real estate. Cai's proposal for a "creative district" in New Ordos was responding to new policy incentives from Beijing on creative economies and cultural districts; as with other such incentives that governments offer towards "green," "sustainable," "resilient," or other such tags, the kernel of these classifications consists in relaxed access to land and regulatory approvals. In the classic tradition of real estate kite-flying, Cai reportedly pledged $600 million of his firm's funds as seed to invite investments for the much larger amount required for the project, with little known about the source of these funds. To garner recognition, Cai approached, in 2007, the state-owned China Architecture Design & Research Group—one of China's Design Institutes mandated to technically supervise every built project—to carry out the overall schematics of the proposed development. A "creative district," composed of cultural venues, artists' studios, etc., was designated, as complement to a proposition to build 2500 residential units. Following yet another standard marketing strategy, an "Ordos Prize of Architecture" was announced for Asian architects, both to bring visibility to the project as well as to entice brand-recognized firms to the area. Of the residential units planned, Cai approached the team behind the Chinese state's biggest prestige project that year, the Olympics Bird's Nest, Ai Weiwei and Herzog and de Meuron (there are competing accounts about who was approached first) to help design the highest sliver of that market: 100 villas prospectively priced at $1.5 million each.

Rather than take on the project themselves, the trio—with Ai designated as master-planner—restructured the brief such that 100 architects from around the world would be invited to design each of the villas. Invitations were sent out from Ai's firm Fake Design, which caused some confusion among recipients about whether they were being spammed or pranked. In the event, the major players approached by the team passed on the offer. Since time was of the essence, the story goes, Herzog and de Meuron reached out to the smaller, hungrier outfits run by sundry adjunct and junior faculty in Western academia, the potential attraction being the radical cachet conferred by the "critical," more concept-driven, outlook professed by this cadre. Harvard's GSD, given Herzog and de Meuron's berth there, was heavily represented, as were other circuits—New York, Mexico, Switzerland, the United Kingdom—where the curators had professional interests. No Chinese architect was included.

Each firm was given 100 days to design their project, with very few program requirements. For some of these practitioners whose output had been more "mediatic" than in actual commissions, the temptation of building something was substantial. A camera team from Ai Weiwei's studio recorded the course of the two meetings in Ordos, and later posted the edited film on Ai's website.[3] It makes for uncomfortable viewing. Ai leads the proceedings with banal exhortations to the participants to put aside their individual/idiosyncratic approaches to arrive at some conceptual unity, perhaps even articulate a contemporary zeitgeist; the architects promptly respond by invoking the 1927 Weissenhofsiedlung or the 1893 World's Columbian Exposition. The effort is dropped almost as soon as it is considered, with the agreement that the outcome would be, in the words of Harvard's Preston Scott Cohen, "100 sculptures competing for attention" (Bernstein 2008). The conversation appropriately turns towards the virtues of pluralism. This "misfits" approach would result in a literal lack of fit: in final submission, when their models do not fit the holes cut out for them in the site model, the architects manually go to work, chamfering the edges of their site with X-Acto knives to wrest the few extra cardboard millimeters of space.

Many of the participants appear wary in terms of what they had gotten themselves into. Yale's Keller Easterling pointedly posed the question to the *New York Times* journalist filing the story: "Are we just performers in another of Ai Weiwei's pieces?" (Bernstein 2008). Ai's mannerisms lend to proceedings an ironic air, if not post-colonial schadenfreude at the scene of 100 Western architects scurrying across oceans to seek out any opportunity for a commission. (The year before Ai had sent 1001 Chinese subjects to live on cots during the Documenta art fair in Kassel, Germany.) The participants are made to line up to receive their compensation, doled out by suited accountants in wads of multiple currencies that some scramble to count. All appear uncomfortable with this naked descent into transactionalism.

After the two meetings, there were exhibitions where the models and drawing boards were carted from China to galleries in Europe, the stomping grounds of the curatorial team. Subsequently, the airwaves went silent. The New Ordos development faded away like many a venture: postmortem reflections, drawing more from cultural studies than economics, adduced timeworn Orientalisms about China's "overheated" economy, ghost-towns and asset bubbles, shady developers and non-transparent systems. Only a few of the buildings for the larger development were eventually built, along with five or so of the proposed projects on Ordos 100. None of the buildings were occupied. It took the anthropologist Michael A. Ulfstjerne three months after his arrival in March 2011 in Dongsheng/Kangbashi to find somebody who knew where the 198 hectares of the creative industries park or the Ordos 100 site was located. Ai Weiwei was in prison. Nobody seemed to know about the whereabouts of Cai Jiang; control over the property had gone to another local developer, the Liu Manshi group. It appeared that Cai may even have exited his ownership with a profit as land values continued escalating despite none of the projects being built. We are, we discover, a long away from the sovereign concept of territory espoused by Foucault or Lefebvre. Ai himself appeared to have been disenchanted with the perils of playing architect: "I dislike the entire process, and I could be doing something else … there are so many other things to do, like fold a man of paper or go skipping stones" (Ai 2006).

We note here the overlap of multiple realms of competence or speculation: the large architecture firm, the small architecture firm, the art firm, the curatorial circuit (from galleries to biennales), real estate developers, local chambers of commerce, construction firms, building materials lobbies, the Design Institutes, "formal" and "informal" financiers, not to rule out personnel manning the different nodes of jurisdictional facilitation and (de)regulatory procedures at the municipal, regional, and national levels across multiple bureaucratic ambits: finance, land-use and titling, environment, culture and creative industries, building codes, to name but a few. There is, of course, also that crucial transactional entity that displaces sovereign authority in the modern period, the political party system, in China ascribed as "monopolistic," but in more so-called competitive electoral arenas equally devoid of alternatives and increasingly defined today by a thrust towards "strong" decision-making powers and untrammeled by the imperative that Kant would substitute in the place of the sovereign, the exercise of "public reason."[4]

As the antipode within this decision-making power, we include the state's power to simply say "no," the domain of censorship. In its largest compass, this power comprises the wherewithal to curtail the rights of both domestic and international commerce and investment through the management of taxes, tariffs, and licenses. City planning is such a censorial power, in that it comprises a perpetual revision of what is allowable or not allowable in built space. In other words, censorship does not connote some obdurate limit beyond which speculation may not proceed, but rather constitutes a variety of devices in and *owing to which* speculation happens; indeed limits and boundaries determine the very texture of artistic, territorial, and financial speculation alike. Indeed censorship may derive from "democratic" imperatives, for example the putative rights of a putative civil society in zoning territorial space quite in the same way as they determine the visibility of, say, sex in public forums. A certain understanding of the aesthetic, even "art," is here critical to *establishing* the norms of censorship as much as the rights of speculation as well.[5] It is not coincidental that art galleries and art networks have proved instrumental in the gentrification of post-industrial areas. Ai's subsequent prosecution on alleged tax evasion, in a move that many inevitably saw as a crackdown on dissidence, in that sense simply represents the flipside of a long-existing bridge between art and commerce that Ordos 100, and Ai in his larger career, and in what amounted to the edge of his radicalism, had done much to underscore. If the aneconomic valuation of art confers to real estate speculation a higher price, should the artist/real estate speculator be granted tax immunity?

In what follows, it will be helpful to have the multiple circuits of interest or competence laid out above into two discrete precincts of legitimation. The first we provisionally name the realm of "critique," in that it refers to the norms of professional validation and expertise by which projects of various kinds can be assayed and judged. The second we could call "territory," which encompasses on the other hand the sum total of global contingency, the decisions, infrastructural outlays, and fragmented sovereignties that make up value in land. In the terms that we laid out at the beginning of this essay, the realm of critique may be described as roughly corresponding to the rubric of design, which is to say the finite set of actionable knowables that a discipline chooses to work in order to forge its ways in the world. Territoriality, by the same yardstick, we could define as the open-ended and potentially infinite set of maneuvers that define the relationship of land to markets. In the systems parlance of the 1960s that Herbert Simon would have well been familiar with, we can differentiate these two realms as "closed" and "open" systems respectively. As I have noted above, epistemologies of design subsist in the reduction of the latter to the former; more to the point, they would maintain that the reductive, closed system *must have* something of a predicative relationship (with so-called "margins of error") (Dutta 2007; 2008) with the so-called open system of which it is a putative part. It is in this kernel of the "must have," the Kantian *müssen* and the management of error that epistemology exposes itself as a faith, in the terms of various theologies of modernism, humanism, etc. It is also this faith, I would argue, that with the global spread of liberalism is inevitably being dressed over in the norms of transactionality. And it is here that I would like to place the principal brunt of my argument: all such reductions or transactions amount to nothing more than the profession of a faith. No system exists that can bridge the abyss between closed and open systems.

Consider the four corporate entities involved in the Ordos venture: the firm, the state, the art gallery, and the university. A half-century ago, Pierre Bourdieu had written about the closed circuits of social or cultural capital: seemingly extra-economic networks that interlock with institutional flows of capital, producing nodes of valorization such that value in one system is able to be indexed as value in the other (Bourdieu 1986). Bourdieu was speaking to a central paradox of post-war *dirigisme*, where expertise in planning and government decisions appeared to derive not, despite claims to the contrary, from some neutral regime of rational deliberation, but from extramural circuits of cultural legitimacy, both filiative and affiliative (e.g., old school networks), whose basis remained starkly *unmodern*.

In the Ordos saga, this pluralist terrain of capital is evinced in the developers' and curators' attempt to conflate the four circuits that we have identified above. For regional and municipal officers in Dongsheng (per capita income second only to Shanghai), urban development was an attempt to leverage and corral a runaway energy economy, where native raw materials were being siphoned off by large, monopsonistic, state-owned firms licensed from Beijing. In the official literature, the planning exercise thus characterized itself as the creation of "a new administrative centre due to existing ambiguities surrounding revenue streams and government restructuring."[6] For the provincial government, building new real estate was also a way of using up budgets (recently increased) sent down by the central government as part of a fiscal decentralization policy; local officials failing to spend an allocated budget risk "a reduction in future budget size, an appropriation of funds by central government, a series of political demotions and transfers, an adverse reputational impact, among other potential outcomes" (Chohan 2014). In the absence of other investment venues, new urban development appears as an allocative device, bundling together services that the state is required to provide (education, welfare, healthcare, security, etc.), with the hope that escalating land values from these rationalized and concentrated services would vouchsafe high revenue returns. Clarified property and tenurial rights would establish a smooth rent gradient (unlike older or cluttered/messy developments such as Dongsheng) that radiates outward from new city centers or so-called CBDs outward into residential districts: the so-called "Western urban land economics" (Hsieng 2010).

Since *any* place might acquire these attributes—indeed these new (de)regulated terrains are being laid out the world over—there is then an effort to supplement place with symbolic capital. Ordos officials thus routinely took to pronouncing various "art," "creative," or "green" zones dressed up with the "imminent" construction of important buildings (theaters, museums, art workshops) both to utilize central government incentives in these categories as well as maintain a certain programmatic indeterminacy aimed at capturing the next shift in policy or investor interest:

> After a secret permission, the [Creativity and Cultural Zone] might become a residential area, or something else. In these times, there is no way of saying. You say this is residential area, but it isn't; say these are villas, but at the same time they are not villas; say these are offices, but then again they might not be.
>
> (Ulfstjerne 2016a: 401)

Zoning, that protean instrument of twentieth-century bargaining, becomes an absurd game of predictive designation and unrealizable nostrums, on whose slippery deck governments and firms carry out a dance of continuous regulatory transgression and plays of interest, with moves writ from each side of the law. For example, eventually, the large villas planned for New Ordos suddenly began to face regulatory headwinds from Beijing officials wishing to cool down an overheated real estate sector. The developers who took over from Cai Jiang promptly redesignated the cultural district as a botanical or zoological garden instead. As a former employ of Cai, Xiao Bai, put it

> these are not villas, they are botanical gardens or maybe even zoological gardens.... All you really need is a piece of paper stating that they are this or that kind of construction, something in line with regulations, just don't mention luxury villas.
>
> (Ulfstjerne 2016a: 395)

"Culture" is not separable from this unstable play of signifiers. Art galleries and universities, other than simply *being real estate* (land was, and remains, a critical element in university endowments since their founding) of a kind in that they are routinely adduced as cores of various "innovation" or creative clusters or districts, similarly evince a delegitimation of terms, a shift in language games wherein claims to epistemic value necessitate simultaneous gambits in multiple, unrelated spheres of valorization. For instance, from much of the writing by and around Ai Weiwei, it becomes clear that a central image that Ai Weiwei seeks to project is to cast himself, the artist, as a business firm. Prominent mention is made of Ai's attention towards contracts, of his sub-contracting work to other firms or manufactories to realize his "made in bulk" projects; here, the Duchampian alienation from the aesthetic has transmogrified, by way of the mid-twentieth-century New York scene of white-collar artists (Jones 1998), into a figure of the artist as contracted professional. Inevitably this conflation of artist and firm returns liberalism to its eighteenth-century roots. The downside of this amalgam was made poignantly visible in the course of Ai's subsequent incarceration in 2011 by the Chinese government: the government insisted it was prosecuting Ai as a firm that had evaded taxes, while Ai took to describing himself as an artist whose free speech was being censored. Both claims were made against the background of the Chinese state's public relations challenges in relation to the global market: the negative signals posed by punishing the artist-firm vis-à-vis privileges promised to other firms seeking to invest in the Chinese market.

It is hard not to see these compound gambits as indeed firm-like behavior of a kind, in that they seek to mitigate the risks of investment by spreading meaning across multiple realms or circuits of capital, symbolic or otherwise. Lack of conceptual profundity can be mitigated if a work fetches a high sale commission price on the market; in such cases price itself can be drummed up to look like meaning. Conversely, a real estate speculation can always be dressed up to look like conceptual art, if the models and drawings lay claims to "critique," with a commercial afterlife in galleries and academic presses if the investors don't show up. We have not yet worked out the myriad potentials hidden in the question "Is this art?" which in the aftermath of Duchamp has largely been seen as an argument for the anti-aesthetic. Symbolic capital, as any anthropologist might tell you, is not a universal rubric but field-specific, coded, a kind of tribal or feudal behavior. The hyphenated, portmanteau construct of the artist-firm-critic thus produces the work of art as if a hedge, a gambit to secure value in varied spheres with the expectation that some may not catch. In the aftermath of the Ordos fiasco, for instance, Ai Weiwei's *film* on Ordos 100 received an Official Selection for the International Film Festival in Rotterdam in 2012. Here, the Ordos project is presented not as a real estate venture but as a performance art project, with the architects, and their conception of architecture, as the targets all along. In subsequent, "approved" monographs by/on Ai, a callow schadenfreude makes itself visible:

> Photographs depict scenes that appear satirical in the context of China's reputation as the Western architect's gold mine. *The architects play perfectly into Ai's conceit.* Descending upon the Mongolian frontier in search of a golden commission, the swarms of black-clad designers find only sand. Unwittingly, or perhaps to conceal their late-dawning suspicions, the architects carried out the performance for the cameras by surveying the sand-swept landscape, noting the contextual features of a site defined by its very placelessness.[7]

Keller Easterling's observation about the whole exercise being a performance piece, above, was thus prescient, but only in retrospect; had the Ordos 100 venture actually taken wing, "critique" would have had quite another valence altogether. In the event, Easterling appears to have matched play for play, insincerity by insincerity, by defining her building's program not in terms of recognizable architectural figures but as blank cultural commentary on media headlines reflecting various Chinese clichés. A nonsense architecture as it were, presuming architecture is about making sense: "A magician's box has extra space and trap doors. The rare Mongolian antelope stores fat in unlikely places. Big villas need home entertainment. Most of China's Olympic swimmers are girls" (Scharmen n.d.). At the same time, we note that this repartee, the critique of critique, circulates in *exactly the same circuits* in our description above of Ai's own plural gambits for validity. There is not a shift in type of game or in the rules of the game; the contest is rather one of big players and small players in the marketplace of wit.

Easterling's causticism nevertheless underscored the other participants' muted but equally evident credulousness towards the project: this too is evident in Ai's film (therefore not so "late-dawning" as Ai's ghost-written, chortling account above might have it). Rather, some of the architects take this "entrapment" as a sign of an existential problem, of their predicament in the world. For instance, as Alejandro Arevana, one of the participants, puts it to the camera: "I think [contemporary architecture] is irrelevant. Architects work with issues that only interest other architects." The architects know that they are the butt of a joke, but Ai is not the joker, or at least not the important one. The interlocutor whose intentions they struggle to descry is the *developer*, not the representative of a profession but a sort of hyphenated avatar—of a local warlord, a commodities trader, a political broker, or money launderer, it does not matter which—equally seeking to diversify its risk:

> Whenever you work for a big company that size, this is a big ... rich ... man, you never know exactly where the money comes from, if in the end he will really do it, if he will change his mind, or put your house somewhere else, or tell a Chinese architect to do it better, whatever, you have to jump and see in the end what happens, projects in China are not about absolute control, about absolutely knowing what will happen.[8]

The Mexican architect Francisco Pardo points out, in this context, the disappearance of what in the modernist era would be defined as the public interest: "We do a lot of developing in Mexico. We never meet the final client. We only meet the intermediary that is the developer."

The client-interlocutor represents the interlocutor of an interlocutor of an interlocutor, an incomprehensible morass of interests in which practice and/or truth has to forge its way. In such a situation, a transactionally derived "will to contingency" appears as both problem and solution, an unfathomable chess game played without the rules of chess:

> Mr. Ai, who is known as a provocateur, encouraged the architects to keep asking questions, though he rarely provided answers.
>
> But he did offer some specific comments on the houses by the first 28 teams. At one point, he told Mr. Meredith and Ms. Sample that a garage building on their property seemed a bit too big and would overpower a neighboring house. "Why don't you take some time and see if you can adjust it," he said gently.
>
> But they didn't need time. Mr. Meredith simply reached over to the cardboard model and ripped the garage off its base, exposing a patch of blue cardboard.
>
> "Good, a swimming pool," said Mr. Ai, smiling.
>
> (Bernstein 2008)

Such is "practice" in the *mise en abyme* of validation, the "task environment" in the field of flexible accumulation. Inevitably this has signal effects on the sphere from which so many of the Ordos 100 architects obtain their legitimacy: the university. If we remember, for regional officials and developers in Kangbashi, the air of "criticality" vested in inviting 100 international architects must be seen as itself a marketing strategy, aimed at garnering copious free ad copy in the myriad media columns devoted to following such cultural events and "provocations" across the world. "Assembling a … contingent of reputable, but relatively inexperienced designers whose potential as *critical* theorists and disciplinary practitioners [is still unfounded]" (Ai and Pins 2018: 287), with Ai Weiwei and Herzog and de Meuron as curators, was explicitly designed to lend land speculation an aura of speculative discernment, of sifting through diamonds in the rough, etc., with the premise that global investors might invest in properties as executives in an art investment fund might go around scouring the art fair or the biennale scene.

Criticality thus becomes a gambit for monetization. On the other hand, *within* academia, this engineering of minor fame—"We got a little taste of what it's like to be Zaha Hadid"[9]—is ironically cast by its recipients as a much-needed push towards "practice" and hard-nosed pragmatism, *against* critique seen as the preserve of seminars and scholars. A legerdemain takes place, where the "inexperience" adduced above, seen as value-additive for investments, is redescribed by the architects, by the very fact of participating in this curatorial venture, into a badge of experience. If Ai and Easterling's use of irony in their projects might be seen as hedges, with an express view to the reuse of their material in alternative venues, something similar might be happening with the other participants as well. Ines Weizman and Andreas Thiele's contribution might be considered the most pronounced in this respect, comprising a proposal to build Adolf Loos's phantasmatic Josephine Baker house, a provocation guaranteed to launch a few dozen term papers ("What does copying mean for architecture?") in "critical theory" seminars in Western institutions. The "project" was reinstalled in the Venice Architecture Biennale in 2012. The Ordos 100 projects will thus also have had a career in the participants' professional resumes, in the form of departmental lectures, self-published monographs, and exhibitions, not to rule out resumes and career portfolios; presumably they will be portrayed as examples of the architects' encounters with the "real world," of having what it takes, and so on.

In academia, curatorship or participation in exhibitions, totted up in self-published monographs, are now evinced strangely as examples of professional *practice*, which now appears as a nebulous category unencumbered by the methodological constraints either of falsifiable research or of project execution. In the case of the Ordos 100 architects, it is not hard to imagine, in tenure or other appointment dossiers, the obligatory supporting letter from Herzog and de Meuron testifying to the candidate's participation in the Ordos venture—"an honor to be selected"—as in itself a sign of professional and creative superiority. Curatorship here is thus like a currency note that can be cashed in at multiple venues. A private network—to quote Herzog: "We had to rely on our networks"[10]—thus becomes, in passing through the seemingly "objective" procedures of tenure and peer review, a public roster of genius. The neo-feudal, Bourdieuian world has not withered away.

In Ai's film, we nonetheless confront the architects' patent confrontation with what we might call the classic liberal predicament of the "pluralist aesthete": on the one hand, a well-meaning air of political innocence, even naivety, a wanting to do good, and on the other, the necessity to act, with the requisite suspiciousness towards outcomes, in what they (mis)cognize as their pragmatism or their "agency," terms that are taken to mean that what architects do in some way determines their power to effect change in the world. It is rather that today both the modernist conception of pragmatism and its postmodern critique or counter-practice appear to be increasingly undone in a universe where one does not quite know what one has to be pragmatic about, of the link between practice and its end. In such a situation, pragmatism returns to its Lutheran roots, as the practice of virtue without eschatological expectation. "You have to jump," take risks, see what happens; one cannot know the path to paradise. The fatalisms of the old feudal world more or less drew on the bias that things would turn out badly in this world no matter how earnestly one strives towards the good. By contrast, contemporary institutional ideology presses the reverse: that things must turn out well no matter how bad it gets. What Albert O. Hirschman once called "the bias for hope" is today exacerbated into a "fatalism of hope." One must enthuse at all times even if there is no joy in the proceedings. The authoritative cultural script for this unfree engagement is provided by Rem Koolhaas's *Singapore Songlines*, a text that maintains the legerdemain of Europe as the fount of an ecstatic *civitas*: "We think there can be no pleasure" (Koolhaas 1995: 1015). To quote Gayatri Chakravorty Spivak:

> But pluralist aesthetes of the First World are, willy-nilly, participants in the production of an exploitative society. Hence in *practice*, [the modernizing Third World anti-insurgency police] must destroy the enemy, the menacing other. He follows the contingencies of what he sees as his historical moment. There is a convenient colloquial name for that as well: pragmatism. Thus his emotions at killing [political insurgents] are mixed: sorrow (theory) and joy (practice). Correspondingly, we [i.e., liberal aesthetes in the First World] grieve for our Third World [counterparts]; we grieve and rejoice that they must lose themselves and become as much like us as possible in order to be "free"; we congratulate ourselves on our specialists' knowledge of them.
>
> *(Spivak 1987: 179)*

Matters are not thus much changed if we consider where this joyful rush to agency manifests itself as its opposite, in various forms of political radicalism or "resistance" movements in academia that mobilize the same institutional venues and biennale circuits. In its most limited sense, this presents itself as a kind of solipsism, disguised as an overconscientious regard for the "other." Take for instance Tatiana Bilbao, "I design the house for me, because I don't know the people who are going to live there, I don't understand the culture, how they live" (Ai 2012). This, from an architect. In its more strident variants, this radicalism can comport itself as a form of activism. A case in point could be the campaign, after a Human Rights Watch report (Human Rights Watch 2006) against the exploitation and abuse of South Asian emigrant labor in the

Persian Gulf Emirates, against major universities, museum corporations, and architectural brand-names such as Zaha Hadid, Jean Nouvel, Raphael Viñoly, Frank Gehry, and Tadao Ando, for their involvement in various business ventures there. In question was a development comparable to Ordos, building creative and cultural assets and districts to diversify investment patterns in a region buoyed largely by a single-resource, energy economy.[11] Quite like Cai Jiang and Ai Weiwei, corporate executives at New York University, at the Louvre, the British Museum, and the Guggenheim had partnered with sovereign wealth-holding corporations in the Gulf with the same assumption: that cultural/academic brands could be used to sell real estate in the desert, leasing out their name as well as personnel, at the requisite premiums, to provide academic/cultural services in a part of the world where such metropolitan goods were scarce.

We do not have the space here to offer a blow-by-blow account of the campaign, led largely by university-based academics and artists and architects, against these developments. Whatever their objectives, however well-meaning, it becomes clear that for the agitators, the equation wrought by the "relatively inexperienced" architects in the Ordos 100 equation might be said to be working here in reverse. If for the Ordos promoters, association with "critical" brand-names to create cultural content was good advertising strategy, in the case of the Gulf projects it was precisely the value of the brand, and the marketing element, that the agitationists approached as their sole point of "leverage," as the New York University sociologist Andrew Ross put it (2015: 15).[12] An article in the *New Yorker* spelled it out: "The country spends tens of millions of dollars—probably hundreds of millions—on P.R. firms to improve its image. A single human-rights report can undo the work of fifty million dollars" (Azimi 2016). Throughout the campaign, the fronts of activism remained almost hermetically sealed within the same intramural circuits, focused entirely on extracting concessions from *Western* institutions and figures. It seems not to have occurred to the campaigners that the appropriate legal forum for such a campaign was in fact the sovereign nations of South Asia themselves—such indeed was the point made to them by an Indian activist working in the field[13]—who were the only bodies constitutionally bound to protect the interests of their citizens, within their boundaries and elsewhere. If the architects in Ordos were deprived of an eventual contract, here we are confronted by a political activism equally devoid of an actual social contract.

In the end, Walid Raad's negotiations with the Guggenheim involved measures that had nothing to do with South Asia but a kind of score-settling about the New York art world itself, and *its* overlaps with real estate dynamics; quite in the fashion of Ines Weizman's proposal for the Baker House in Ordos. The artists proposed that the museum re-exhibit the exhibition it had notoriously cancelled in 1971, Hans Haacke's *Shapolsky et al*. (Haacke seems not to have understood his signing-on to the campaign as posing a conflict of interest.) Initially somewhat rattled and amenable to "negotiation," the museums soon enough came to the conclusion that the brouhaha would have little impact on investors and stopped talking to the protestors. The Guggenheim Abu Dhabi and Zayed National Museum were not realized not because of labor practices but because the market simply went in a different direction. The labor practices on Gulf building sites continue as before; for the artists, the biennales go on.

In the Kantian sense, to critique means to equip oneself with the means to judge. Thus, in the post-Kantian/Romantic university, knowledge production does not subsist in producing "truths" that literally mirror the external world; this is impossible, since externality or the universe *as such* is precisely what is unknown. Knowledge can only be reflexive. It can only be verified according to a procedure, one that it itself creates. This epistemic "finitude"—we can only test how we know, not what we know—thus inherently relies on, rather it launches, a pluralism of expertise invested in producing and testing these procedures, by which agreements as to various truths can be reached. As such, the Kantian system of the university was always fatally flawed: it promotes an institutional empowerment of knowledge-expertise based on consensus (quite like the liberal nation-state for which the university styles itself as a proxy), thus paradoxically rendering these privileged epistemic protocols vulnerable to capture by multiple tentacles of interest. The old arguments for postmodernity thus argued for a disempowerment of knowledge paradigms, calling our attention instead towards the political economy of research and knowledge systems: a "counter-practice" of observing *how* statements were used, and by whom, rather than what they said (Lyotard 1984; Dutta 2013).

The relationship between the state and the university in that post-Kantian imaginary was thus more than one of mere bureaucratic devolution or about the protection of academic privilege (on the feudal principle of the estates). Rather, these reflexive procedures unite them in a shared *telos*; state and university represent but two filiative outgrowths of an organum (among other such estates, the courts, the executive, the press, etc.) wherein knowledge and power—a claim and the legal right to make that claim—are both seen to derive from a methodological impetus for verification that, in its very establishment and in its institutionalization, *becomes* verification. The procedures of knowledge production provide the structural basis for authority in state and academic operations alike: in the post-Kantian imaginary, the stability of this reflexive structure posits as its counterpart the programmatic ideal of fostering various "experiments" as a way of rendering supple this knowledge/power bind, open to transformation and ontogenesis. It is in this sense of a failed experiment or failed speculation that the exhibition and films of the Ordos 100 project re-enter the validatory circuits of the university. The university thus epitomizes, or even provides, the crux of the state as a gambit for institutional and territorial continuism, a risk-managing maneuver aimed at bridging the abyss between the closed systems of knowledge and practice and the open, viral trajectories of capital. The knowledge-driven "expert" and the sovereign mechanisms of monetary and fiscal management would thus develop as two conjunct and contrapuntal organs of post-Kantian governmentality.

The contemporary crisis of expertise is thus primarily a crisis of the post-Kantian imaginary. As the celerity of liberated capital movements force commensurate real-time reaction (with the commensurate arbitrariness) by state authorities at all levels, there is an increased delinking of the state's monetary authority from its assumption of epistemic authority, since any "experiment" in the classic sense takes too long in comparison to the unpredictable and erratic terrain that investments are required to negotiate. There can be no planning, since at best plans are consigned to merely marking deliberative moments in a temporal universe of competing interest where such deliberation becomes just one more stake, another fount of interest. If in the post-Kantian frame epistemic reflexivity represented the countervailing moment of the state's propulsive behavior (the ideal of progress), there is now an unraveling of that contrapuntal arrangement. There is a change in ideology from, say, the Popperian dictum on falsifiability where statements are required to be amended in the face of counter-evidence that undoes the validity of a claim. By contrast, in the contemporary ideological conjuncture, the primary demand on a knowledge claim is that it be, like a real estate venture, equipped with an exit strategy: one must know when to pack up and capitalize on rising land values even if the buildings haven't even struck ground. Reflexivity and decision, traditionally posed in epistemology in terms of a tension, increasingly acquire the semblance of two unknotted threads no longer having anything to do with each other.

The university can no longer retain its germinational significance, as a redoubt of philosopher-princes tasked to mull over the *telos* of the nation-state and its people, defining goods, allocational ethics, narrative imaginary, and so on. Elsewhere I have typologized some other functions that equally, if not more substantially, describe the proliferating business briefs of the university:

as conduit for state-fiscal stimuli, as tax haven, as investment portfolio, as real estate developer, as advertising billboard, as entrepreneurial incubator, as labor sub-contractor, entertainment franchise (sports), as consulting firm, as biofinance (investment vehicle vested in the governance of life, such as National Institutes of Health), as vehicle of soft power (Dutta 2014, 2015). The predicament of a real estate developer or regional official in Inner Mongolia and a professor or dean in Cambridge, Massachusetts, is not so qualitatively far apart as we would have imagined. After all, universities serve as the exemplar for the so-called creative or innovational districts that the New Ordos would imitate. In the Ordos project, as in the university, it is not clear to what intent or effect statements are made or can be made: at best one *hopes* that a statement may have some effect, but a commitment to that outcome may itself prove to be counter-productive.

This essay began by positing theories of design that, in the mid-twentieth century and at the height of the power of the universities, explicitly sought to constrain knowledge production as an open-ended vocation and orient it towards more performative ends. On some level this amounts to nothing more than folk or karmic wisdom (know/talk less, do more); on the other hand, this served as a robust reminder of epistemic finitude that harks back to the metaphysics of the eighteenth century. Knowledge subsists in a perpetual state of incompletion, a principal consequence of which is that it cannot know its own ends. The radical incomprehension posited in Kant's "Critique of Teleological Judgment" thus resurfaces at the very moment when one portends to do away with romanticism. It is in the post-Kantian imaginary of incompletion that a regulatory "will to contingency" as the very essence of "the human" appears. The "events" or "happenings" celebrated by the *soixante huitards* thus resurrect a well-worn post-Kantian motif, placing it at the heart of design just as Kant had restructured the aesthetic within the heart of mimesis.

In this context, one facet of Ordos 100 presents itself as conspicuous, not so much in the context of this project per se but as a symptom of a more general, cultural shift present in both the profession and academia. Look back onto the images you chanced upon in the Google search, and consider what we have discussed above, whether in Ordos or in Saadiyat Island, regarding the extreme precariousness and provisionary nature of these ventures. Easterling's and Weizman's projects here go to the nub of the problem, in that architecture's value here is entirely discursive, an element of branding, rather than placed in its modernist self-image, of resolving programmatic challenges, since in any case one does not know what the program is. Given that systemic indefinition, what strikes one in the Ordos project renderings is the emphatic priority on formal *completion*. Each building is presented as a hermetic whole, its surfaces hyper-articulated in the most exquisite digital renderings, lit up to show considerable application of mind as to choices of material and texture. The response to programmatic indefinition, it would appear, is a high-definition aesthetics. In the absence of content, there is a premium on formal resolution, and the material finishes are wrought with little regard for supply chains, budgetary considerations, or operational and maintenance constraints. The architecture arrives as if fully resolved, even if nothing else is resolved. I would argue that this impetus towards phantasmatic completion is a reflection of the manner in which *land*—for architects, "site"—is being restructured in global economic movements today. Consider the behavior of the developers in Ordos: land is made available so that *anything* could be put there, if the right conditions obtain. Conversely, land itself becomes only one commodity in a basket of investment choices: investors can move investments from coal to real estate one day, and then, contingent on market movements, opt out as land prices rise to park investments in the media sector, and so on. There is a shift from the old, productivist universe, where land is a primary input, to a purely speculative territoriality: the availability of land is styled not in response to a production demand, but because it *could be* used in some way or another. The term "land-use" palpably becomes a nonsense designation, since use is precisely what must be kept fungible as a major feature of the stimulus. The relationship of part and whole are thus intrinsically changed: one has no organic relationship to the other. Apropos Tatiana Bilbao's "I don't understand the culture, how they live," in Ordos, like the land on which it sits, building is no longer an anthropological receptacle since there is no anthropos or ethnos to speak of. It is the designer who exemplifies the cultural subject, who is tasked with injecting place into a non-place.

Land must be seen as receptive to shifts of investment at a moment's notice, filled with infrastructural plenitude, ever ready to be installed and made operational in relation to investment decisions where tenurial rights are held not to be used but as leverage in larger bundles of investments. Correspondingly, form no longer corresponds to function, since they are not of the same time or place: there is an extirpation of program. And like the land itself, professional legitimacy in design lies in the projection of an air of perpetual readiness in the face of radical ignorance, ever prepared to instantly dress up the carapaces of space without any power over its contents. The aura of completion does not indicate an aesthetic choice, a design, but rather a resume, a performative demonstration that one *could* perform, *were* one asked. One would submit that this is not an exhibit of pragmatism but a rehearsal of the medieval Christian conception of guilt. There occurs, in the name of design, precisely what design claims to work against, a total disjunction between cause and effect. There is also a colloquial name for such expectation: faith.

Notes

1 Sou Fujimoto, quoted in Ai (2012).
2 Michael A. Ulfstjerne's field-studies conducted in the aftermath provide us with great anthropological insight and factual detail into the Ordos phenomenon, including Cai Jiang's role. See Ulfstjerne (2013, 2016a, 2016b).
3 Ai, *Eeduosi 100/Ordos 100* (2012).
4 The relevant texts on Kant's argument on public reason, put forth in his 1784 newspaper article, "What Is Enlightenment?" has been compiled in Schmidt (1996).
5 John J. Costonis's writing from the 1980s offers us an exemplary window into this role of aesthetics. See Costonis (1989).
6 *Erdos Urban Region Development Strategy*, 2005, Bert de Muynck, "Architecture on the Move," quoted in Ai and Pins (2018: 248).
7 Perhaps realizing the public relations risk inherent in this description, the article adds a caveat: "Ai remained a sincere host." Ai and Pins (2018: 293).
8 Interview with Simon Hartmann of HHF Architects, Zurich, in Ai (2012).
9 Michael Meredith, in Bernstein (2008).
10 Speaking to the *New York Times*, Herzog stated that the 100 architects selected for the project did not reflect any objective criteria, but rather, given the urgency pressed by the client, reflected who they knew and could call on (Bernstein 2008).
11 Details of this affair can be found in the following sources: Ross (2015), Azimi (2016), Gulf Labor Artist Coalition website (n.d.).
12 Andrew Ross, "Leveraging the Brand: A History of Gulf Labor," in Ross (2015).
13 See comments made by P. Naraswamy of the Palamoori Migrant Labour Union (PMLU) made to Paula Chakravartty and Nitasha Dhillon on their field visit to India on behalf of the campaign: "Indeed, they held government agencies directly responsible for failing to enforce ILO conventions on responsible recruitment practices" (Chakravartty and Dhillon 2015: 55).

References

Ai, W. (2006) "Here and now," blog entry posted May 10, 2006, trans. L. Ambrozy, republished in W. Ai and A. Pins (eds) (2018) *Ai Weiwei: Spatial Matters, Art Architecture and Activism*, Cambridge, MA: MIT Press, 119.
Ai, W. (2012) Film, *Eeduosi 100/Ordos 100*. https://vimeo.com/136530514 (December 20, 2017).

Ai, W. and Pins, A. (eds) (2018) *Spatial Matters: Art Architecture and Activism*, Cambridge, MA: MIT Press
Azimi, N. (2016) "The Gulf art war: new museums in the Emirates raise the issue of worker's rights," *The New Yorker*, December 19–26. www.newyorker.com/magazine/2016/12/19/the-gulf-art-war (December 28, 2017).
Bernstein, F. A. (2008) "In Inner Mongolia, pushing architecture's outer limits," *New York Times*, May 1. www.nytimes.com/2008/05/01/garden/01mongolia.html (January 5, 2018).
Bourdieu, P. (1986) "The forms of capital," in J. G. Richardson (ed.) *Handbook of Theory and Research for the Sociology of Education*, New York: Greenwood, 15–29.
Chakravartty, P. and Dhillon, N. (2015) "Gulf dreams for justice: migrant workers and new political futures," in A. Ross (ed.) *The Gulf: High Culture/Hard Labor*, New York: OR Books.
Chohan, U. W. (2014) "Erdos: the 'horde' that wasn't," April 24. www.mcgill.ca/channels/channels/news/erdos-city-e-er-duo-si-shi-horde-wasnt-235451 (January 3, 2018).
Costonis, J. J. (1989) *Icons and Aliens: Law, Aesthetics, and Environmental Change*, Urbana: University of Illinois Press.
Dutta, A. (2007) "Cyborg/artisan," in A. Dutta, *The Bureaucracy of Beauty: Design in the Age of Its Global Reproducibility*, New York: Routledge, 191–234.
Dutta, A. (2008) "Computing alibis: Third World teratologies," *Perspecta* 40 (Spring): 54–69.
Dutta, A. (2013) "Linguistics, not grammatology: architecture's *a prioris* and architecture's priorities," in A. Dutta (ed.) *A Second Modernism: MIT, Architecture and the "Techno-Social" Moment*, Cambridge, MA: MIT Press, 1–71.
Dutta, A. (2014) "Task environment: architecture and the 'creative economy'," interview with Janette Kim, *ARPA Journal*, May 15. http://arpajournal.gsapp.org/task-environment/.
Dutta, A. (2015) "The political economy of theory," in *2000+: The Urgencies of Architectural Theory*, New York: Columbia GSAPP, 71–87.
Erdos Urban Region Development Strategy (2005), in Bert de Muynck, "Architecture on the Move," in Ai Weiwei and Anthony Pins (eds) (2018) *Spatial Matters: Art Architecture and Activism*, Cambridge, MA: MIT Press, 248.
Gulf Labor Artist Coalition (n.d.) https://gulflabor.org/ (January 6, 2018).
Hsieng, Y.-T. (2010) *The Great Urban Transformation: Politics of Land and Property in China*, New York: Oxford University Press.
Human Rights Watch (2006) "Building towers, cheating workers: exploitation of migrant construction workers in the United Arab Emirates." www.hrw.org/report/2006/11/11/building-towers-cheating-workers/exploitation-migrant-construction-workers-united (December 22, 2017).
Jones, C. (1998) *Machine in the Studio: Constructing the Postwar American Artist*, Chicago: University of Chicago Press.
Koolhaas, R. (1995) "Singapore songlines," OMA, Rem Koolhaas, and Bruce Mau (eds) *S, M, L, XL*, New York: Monacelli Press.
Latour, B. (2004) *Politics of Nature: How to Bring the Sciences into Democracy*, trans. Catherine Porter, Cambridge, MA: Harvard University Press.
Lyotard, J.-F. (1984) *The Postmodern Condition: A Report on Knowledge*, trans. G. Bennington and B. Massumi, Minneapolis: University of Minnesota Press.
Ross, A. (ed.) (2015) *The Gulf: High Culture/Hard Labor*, New York: OR Books.
Scharmen, F. (n.d.) "ORDOS 38/100 (w/Keller Easterling Architects)." http://w-as.net/ORDOS-38-100-w-Keller-Easterling-Architects (January 5, 2018).
Schmidt, J. (ed.) (1996) *What Is Enlightenment: Eighteenth-Century Answers and Twentieth-Century Questions*, Los Angeles: University of California Press.
Simon, H. (1969) *The Sciences of the Artificial*, Cambridge, MA: MIT Press.
Spivak, G. C. (1987) *In Other Worlds: Essays in Cultural Politics*, New York: Methuen.
Ulfstjerne, M. A. (2013) "Un territorio creativo – creative land pad – The Ordos100: progettari in spazi fatasma (designing in ghost spaces)," *Cameracronica* 2: 20–22.
Ulfstjerne, M. A. (2016a) "Unfinishing buildings," in M. Bille and T. F. Sørensen (eds) *Elements of Architecture: Assembling Archaeology, Atmosphere and the Performance of Building Spaces*, New York: Routledge, 387–405.
Ulfstjerne, M. A. (2016b) "Taking part: the social experience of informal finance in Ordos, Inner Mongolia," *Journal of Asian Studies* 75, 3: 649–672.

Index

Page numbers in *italics* denote figures.

Abaxial 435
access: data 72–77, 250, 272–276, 278, 368; education 47, 175, 425; money and services 32–33, 192, 274, 278, 306, 338, 354, 359, 438, 441; security 38, 41, 196, 280; transportation 19, 41, 147, 150, 278, 368, 387; travel 304; visual 17, 21, 168, 343, 348; *see also* design
ADA (Americans with Disabilities Act) 103; *see also* design
Adams, Ross Exo 241
adaptation 49, 55, 71, 189, 221, 248, 266, 267, 276, 306, 312
Adjaye, David 16, *17*, 18, 22, 409
aesthetics 5, 37, 39–40, 42, 80–81, 107, 111, 113, 138, 143, 167–168, 171, 189, 208, 236, 342, 348–349, 451; *see also* urban
Africa 166–167, 219, 304–305
African 20, 103, 111, 165, 304–306; city 165, 167, 172, 305
African American 103, 111; *see also* black
Agamben, Giorgio 2, 4, 129, 131, 187–188, 196, 304
agency 5, 142–143, 149, 157, 239, 242, 274, 282, 315, 342, 349, 388–391, 399–400, 448
Ahmedabad (India) 437
alterity 4, 5, 22, 200–202, 204, 206, 208, 210–211, 217, 387, 389
American Institute of Architects (AIA) 379, 380, 382–383
Amin, Samir 304
ancestor hall 47, 50, 52, *53*, 55
Anthill Studio *434*
Anthropocene 6, 60, 77, 80–81, 86
Anthropocentrism 6
Anyang (South Korea) 400
Appiah, K. Anthony 339
appropriation 74, 129, 141, 149, 171, 308, 342, 348, 370, 429, 444
aqueduct 293–294, 298
Arad, Michael 59
Araeen, Rasheed 138, *139*, 140

Aravena, Alejandro 393
archaeology 204–205
Archigram 182, 184, 233
architecture: border 4, 27, 175–178, 182, 185, 207, 218, 296, 298; digital 3, 5, 13, 16, 32–33, 62, 71, 74, 107, 109–110, 113–114, 142, 422, 451; ephemeral 141–143, 157, 170, 187, 218, 395; excessive 166, 169, 172–173; and experience 16, 19, 21, 28, 59, 64, 72, 78, 81, 91–94, 97–99, 108–110, 113–114, 125, 165, 166, 191–192, 210, 217–218, 224–225, 260, 267, 278, 304, *313*, 315, 323, 325, 330, 333, 334, 341, 342–345, 347–349, 420; humanitarian 4, 25–30, 32, 189, 211, 388; paper 29–30, 74, 142, 151, 166, 211, 395, 420; performative 60, 62, 66, 275, 439, 452; tropical 170, 208, 326, 151; water 5, 47, 60, 80, 142, 257, 287, 290–294, 297–298, 326–327, 426, *428*; *see also* avatarchitecture; starchitecture
ArchiteXX 377
Arendt, Hannah 30, 217, 395
art: object 405–409, 414, 416, 418, 420–421
Arya Architects 428
Asunción 396
automaticity 117, 212–122, 124–126
autonomy 187, 189, 191, 196, 200
avatar 107–111, 250, 446
avatarchitecture 102, 107
Azoulay, Ariella 314–316, 321

Bachelard, Gaston 91, 93, 118
Bader, Marcus 399, 400, *401*
Ban, Shigeru 16, 25–30
Bangladesh 138, 141, 219, 295–296
Banham, Reyner 166
BARD Studio *430*
bathroom 21, 22, 103, 105, 112–115, 118, 130, 132, 319
Bawa, Geoffrey 201, *202*, 204, 208, *209*, 210, *211*, 212
Beigang (China) 49–52, *54*, 55

Beijing (China) 52, 234, *313*, 316, 317, 319, *320–321*, 441, 444–445
Beorkrem, Christopher 5, 244, 252
Bergson, Henri 325, 326, 328–331, 333–334
Berkeley (CA) 103, 276
Berkeley, Ellen Perry 376
Berlin 59, 62, 176, 232, 365, 394, 398–399, 416
Bessire, Lucas 307
Beverly Willis Architecture Foundation (BWAF) 382
Bhagwat, Aniket 424–426, *427*, 428–430, 433–436, *437*
bias 12, 94, 204, 206, 376, 400, 422, 426, 448
Bilbao (Spain) 409, 412
Bilbao, Tatiana 448, 452
biohybrids 268
biology 72, 376
bioscaffold 256
bi-space 337
black: people 87, 88, 103, 111, 112, 165–168, 172, 220, 288, 304–306; power 349
Black Rock City (NV) *190*, 191
blackness 87–88
body virtual 102, 107–111
Bollnow, Otto Friedrich 91, 94, 328
Bolton, Reginald 231
Borden, Iain 6, 323
border: walls 176–178
boundaries 4, 13, 16, 18, 21, 22, 32, 94, 103, 111, 113–114, 149, 175–176, 184, 218, 225, 252, 256, 309, 339, 342, 370, 387, 443, 449; and edges 5, 6, 102–114
Brahmaputra–Ganges River link 295
Bratton, Benjamin 86
breathing spaces 175, 178, 185
Brereton, Robert M. 291–292
Bristol (UK) 6, 351, 352–360
Brown, Denise Scott 380, 417, 418
Brown, Mabel 381
Brown, Wendy 176
Brussels (Belgium) 390–391
Brutalism 166, 170
Buddhist 203–206, 213
builders 78, 103, 138, 143, 181, 217, 273, 376, 380, 410, 412, 414, 436, 451
Building information modeling (BIM) 3, 110, 114, 421
Busride *432*, 433

California (USA) 20, 103, 107, 177–179, 189, 191, 222, 276, 287–292, 294–295, 412
camp: refugee 4, 15, 26–27, 30–33, 188–189, 191–192, *193*, 194, 196–197, 441; *see also* Dadaab; Kosovo
capitalism 29, 32–33, 75, 82, 84, 117, 128, 175, 192, 232, 236, 238, 329–330, 389, 395, 402, 426, 433, 436, 440; and neoliberalism 236, 238, 319; and obsolescence 5, 6, 142, 176, 179, 184, 191, 231–242, 371, 420
Caracas (Venezuela) 165, 171
Cartesian planning 341
Castells, Manuel 272, 276, 327
de Certeau, Michel 311–315, 321, 325
Chatterjee, Partha 429, 432
Chattopadhyay, Swati 1, 5, 138, 142, *144–147*, 150, *152*, *154–155*, 225
Cheddar (UK) 359
Chicago (USA) 6, 14, 215, *216*, 217, 219–220, 222, 224, 232, 235, *236*, 323, 365, 421
Chin, Ryan 278
China 2, 4, 6, 46–48, 50, 55, 84, *98*, 108, 198, 204, 234–235, 304–305, 316, 319, 441–443, 446
Choay, Françoise 65
CIAM 25
citizen 2, 6, 11, 25, 27, 31, 43, 44, 75, 111, 165, 176, 211, 272–274, 281–282, 314–316, 326, 330, 352, 369–370, 388, 397, 449
citizenship 27, 314–315
cityscapes 5, 65
civil contract of photography *see* photography
Civil Rights Movement (USA) 111–112
civil war *see* war
Clay, Grady 218
climate change 3, 38–39, 60, 78, 175, 182, 184, 270, 275, 281, 298, 326, 366
cognitive mapping 312, 317
cognitive science 93
Colebrook, Claire 307
collaboration 30, 103, 176, 248, 307, 309, 368, 381, 390, 391, 393–396, 398–402
Cologne 95, *96*
Colombetti, Giovanna 93
Colombo (Sri Lanka) 203–204, 210
colonialism 33, 192, 201
Colorado (USA) 37
Colorado River (USA), 294, 296–297
commemoration 57, 58, 60, 62, 64, 66
commons 5, 175–178, 180, 182, 184–185
communication: near-field 274; *see also* digital
community 5, 13, 16, 23, 26, 29, 32, 36, 37, 39, 43–44, 62, 65–66, 141, 143, 150, 157, 163, 171–172–173, 178, 180, 189, 205, 217, 222, 224, 273, 276, 278–279, 297, 339, 344–345, 349, 354, 370, 377, 387, 393, *394*, 396, 398, 400, 424, 426, 437–438, 440
computer-aided design and drafting (CADD) 3, 110, 252, 421
computer vision 246, 250
Connecticut (USA) 36–37, 41, 421
conservation 72, 188, 207, 233, 235, 238, 288, 356
consumerism 32, 82, 232, 402
contemporaneity 4, 197, 323, 329, 334

Index

contemporary architecture 1–6, 13, 15, 22, 25, 30, 39, 41, 46, 113, 165, 235, 388–389, 424, 433, 446; art 1, 80, 141, 157, 395, 417, 421
contingency 20, 119, 142–143, 149, 153, 158, 242, 441, 443, 447, 451
control 4, 32, 36–37, 44, 71–72, 75, 78, 80, 83, 87, 106–107, 129–130, 150, 167, 171, 188–197, 215, 241, 246, 248, 252, 273–274, 277, 280, 282, 296, 319, 321, 334, 343, 358–359, 365, 367, 369, 418, 442, 446
Cook, Peter 7, 182, 233
copyright 75, 178
Correa, Charles 424
Cotton, Arthur 291–293
counter-monument 4, 57–62, 66; *see also* monument
Couzens, E.G. 83
Cox, Yvonne 356
crisis 1–3, 6, 26, 106, 111, 179, 182, 191–194, 200, 215, 239, 242, 273, 370, 395, 450
criticality 440, 447
critique: Kantian 86, 444, 449–451
de la Cruz, Khavn 307
Cruz, Teddy 176–182, 184; *see also* Estudio Teddy Cruz + Forman
Cupers, Kenny 6, 387–388, 393
currencies: alternative local 365, 369–371; decentralized 369–370
Czech Republic 239, *241*

Dadaab (Kenya) 188, 192, *193*, 196
Dahlberg, Jonas 65–66
dam 297–298
data: analysis 244, 246–250, 252, 254, 273, 275, 278, 383, 398; center 110; digital 5, 22, 71, 73–77, 111, 114; collection 234, 245, 248–250, 252, 254, 273, 275, 280–282, 398; counting 246, 306; privacy 22, 246, 248, 275, 280–282; visualization 109–110, 246, *251*, *253*; *see also* infrastructure
Davies, Richard Llewelyn 233, 235
Davis, Heather 5, 80
deregulation 238, 364
Derrida, Jacques 400, 420, 421
design: landscape 37, 42, 44, 59; participatory 6, 393, 395; resilient 36–41, 44
designer 4, 6, 11, 15, 29, 42, 60, 78, 83, 103, 110, 147, 151, 153, 156, 157, 166, 244, 247, 252, 275, 278, 280, 282, 323, 337, 349, 387, 388, 393, 396, 410, 412, 414, 420, 422, 420, 446, 447, 452; fashion 50, 52
detachment 5, 303, 304, 307–309, 333
Detroit (USA) 235, 273, 337, 345
Detroit Collaborative Design Center 349
Devabhaktuni, Sony 6, 393
Dey, Purnendu Dey *145*, *148*
Dhaka (Bangladesh) 138, *139*, 140

digital: age 2; environment 3, 110, 114; network 4, 71; simulation 109; memory 76; technology 13, 26, 30, 142; communication 2, 13, 19, 74, 75, 260, 270, 272, 274–276, 280, 281, 326, 329, 368, 381; *see also* data
displacement 95, 196, 314; and populations 4, 5, 29, 165, 188, 191, 192, 204, 206–208, 315
DIY urbanism *see* urbanism
DNA *257*, 262, 266, 267
domesticity 4, 16, 20, 21; future of 22
Dongsheng (China) 441–444
Dourish, Paul 245
Dudley, Michael Quinn 241
duration 5, 6, 141–143, 147, 149–151, 155, 157, 187, 247, 252, 329, 330, 330–333, 399
Durgapuja 141, 143, 144, 147, 149, 150, 151, 153, 156, 157
Durkheim, Émile 330
Dutta, Arindam 6, 422, 439, 444, 450, 451
dwelling 91, 120, 122, 176, 178, 182, 189, 210, 232, 235, 352

Easterling, Keller 272, 276, 442, 446, 447, 451
Ecosistema Urbano 396, 399, 400
ecosystems 66, 84, 217, 292, 297
edges *see* boundary
education 42, 44, 47, 55, 103, 212, 375, 395, 396, 422, 425, 444
ejidos 178
Eisenman, Peter 59, 234, 406, 420, 421
Eliasson, Olafur 80
embedded security 4, 36–38, 41, 42, 44
embodiment 92, 98
embodied placemaking 217
emergency: punctual 28, 30, 33; protracted 28, 29
emotion 39, 72, 77, 91, 93–95, 98, 99, 218, 258
empathy 4, 91, 93–95
environment: adaptable 189, 241, 344
environmental: disaster 2, 27, 38, 39, 187, 188, 191, 241, 264, 273, 294, 296, 387; history 225; psychology 244; studies 1
epidemic 25: and arsenic poisoning 296; *see also* environmental disaster
ephemerality 142; *see also* architecture
equity: gender 6, 375, 378, 383; social 27, 275, 277, 281, 314; water 296
Equity by Design 381, 383
Estudio Teddy Cruz + Forman 176, 180, 182, 184
ethnic: community 217; enclave 215, 224, 225; minority 2, 215; retail street 215, 217; settlement 224; space 217–218, 225
ethnicity 338, 343, 365
ethnography 250; multispecies 352, 359; urban 245, 247
everyday life 2, 12, 28, 29, 103, 210, 219, 222, 274, 311, 312, 315, 316
exhaustion 88, 89

exhibition 6, 14–17, 29, 30, 31, 80, 138, 166, 181, *259*, 304, 305, 316, 319, 387, 395, 407, 422, 424–426, 432, 433, 435, 436, 437, 442, 447, 449, 450
experience *see* architecture
extinguishment 86, 87, 89

Fast, Omer 117, 118, *119–121*, 122, *123–124*, 125, *127–130*, *132–135*
Federal Emergency Management Agency (FEMA) 42
feminism 13, 15, 200, 376, 428
feminists 298, 377
festival 50, 141, 142, 147, 149–151, 157, 177, 189, 295, 296, 395, 446; camp 191
figure eight 127, 132–133
financialization 238
finitude 5, 86, 87, 89, 449, 451; *see also* duration
Flaherty, George 5, 175
fluidity 117, 118, 120–122, 124, 125, 127–129
France 194, 305, 389, 408
Frank, Suzanne 406
Friedman, Alice 4, 11, 12, 13, *14*, *17*
Friedman, Yona 182, *183*
frontier 308, 364, 446; *see also* strategic frontier zone
Fruk, Ljiljana 5, 256, *257*, *259*, *263*, 266
Fujimoto, Sou 18
fungibility 142, 149, 151, 452
future 5, 38, 44, 47, 66, 72–75, 78, 86–89, 114, 142, 167, 173, 184, 185, 189, 234, 238, 239, 242, 252, 304, 307, 329, 330–334, 349, 366, 375; architecture 165, 176, 256–258, 264, 267, 277, 281; *see also* domesticity; urban

Gallese, Vittorio 92, 93, 95
Garlington, Michael 190
Gehry, Frank 144, 238, 243, 409–410, 412, *415*, 416, 449
gender: bias 12–13; boundaries 113, 114; identity 102, 112; inequity 6; and sex 113; neutral 114; *see also* transgender
Germany 82, 95, *96*, 224, 235, 400, 442
Gerz, Jochen 62–63
Gihembe Refugee Camp *26*, *27*, *28*, 29–30, *31*; *see also* camp; refugee
global: city 326, 363–364; space 188, 328, 330; *see also* modernism
Global North 106, 176
Global South 142, 143, 149, 165, 166, 181, 303
globalization 29, 176, 200, 276, 323
Goleta (CA) 419
Gropius, Walter 239, 417, 418
grounding 127–128, 132–133, 196
Guangzhou (China) 46–48, *49*, 50, 52, 55
Gunasekara, Valentine 204
Gupte, Rupali 424

Haacke, Hans 449
habit 4, 13, 91, 109, 117–134, 150, 231, 260, 314, 354
habitat 98, 144, 170, 295, 326, 352, 355, 356
habitation 1, 3, 4, 118, 120–121, 123, 131, 140, 142, 211
habitus 4, 128, 129, 225
hacking 6, 13, 273, 363, 365–369
Hadid, Zaha 376, 405, 409, 421–423, 447, 449
Hailey, Charlie 5, 142, 187, 189, 191, 192, 194
Hall, Rachel 4, 36
Hamilton, Clive 86
Haraway, Donna 354, 361
Harbison, Robert 235
Hardt, Michael 175
Harman, Graham 274
Harvey, David 31, 165, 175, 305
Hawthorne, Christopher 40–41
Hebert, Saskia 396–398, 400
hedgehog 6, *351*, 352, *353*, 354–356, *357*, 358–359, *360*, 361
Hegel, G.W.F. 121–123, 126
Heidegger, Martin 91, 127, 167, 197
heritage 55, 75, 203, 204, 206, 207, 234, 298, 493
Herron, Ron 182, *184*
Herscher, Andrew 4, 25, 142
Herzog, Werner 87
Herzog + DeMeuron 236, *237*, 441, 442, 447, 448
heterolocalism 217
hibernaculum 356, *357*, 358
Hindu 141, 204, 205, 290, 293, 295, 296
Hirsh, Max 4, 46
Hoffman, Danny 5, 163, *164*, *168*, *169*, *170*, *172*, 173
Holocaust 57, 59
Hong Kong *98*, 140, 239, *240*, 272
Hoskote, Ranjit 424
hospitality 204, 208, 210, 211–212
hotel 49, 50, 52, 55, 163, 171, 172, 173, 204, 210, *211*, 231, 323, 326
house 11–23, 26, 28–29, 50, 52, *54*, 71, 83, 103, 113, 123, 126, 129, 130, 140, 151, 157, 173, 178, 181, 194, 197, 208, *209*, 210, 224, 232, 260, 262, 263, 264, 267, 278, 288, 297, 308, 339, 340, 344, 345, 357, 360, 390, 393, 397, 401, 404, 406, 417, 420, 421, 440, 441, 447, 448; tree 39–40
household 12, 13, 16, 20, 21, 22, 30, 305, 308, 309, 363, 369–370
housing 2, 3, 4, 12, 25, 27, 47, 50, 52, 149, 165, 167, 178, *180*, 181, 182, 191, 207, 211, 215, 235, 241, 264, 281, 315, 325, 360, 363, 369, 377, 387, 389, 393, 394, 424, 425, 429; affordable 32–33, 182, 281; market 30–33, 179; mass-produced 11; refugee 31; *see also* public
human behavior 41, 244, 247–248, 250, 252
humanitarianism 25–33

Index

Idenburg, Florian 398
identity 5, 13–14, 16, 18, 23, 72, 81, 83, 85, 86, 102, 103, 107–108, 113–115, 217, 225, 245, 333, 342, 347, 348, 349, 425, 428, 432; crisis 106, 111; cultural 278, 281, 291, 296; Indian 426, 429; national 204, 426; *see also* gender
Illinois (USA) 13, 215, *216*, 217, 235, *236*, 375
image of the city 312, 314, 321
image making 16, 418
imageability 224, 312
immigrant 2, 4, 5, 24, 194, 215, 217, 219, 222, 365; architecture 5, 6, 215, 225; communities 182; landscape 225–226; -owned 220–221
immigration 176, 205, 296
inclusiveness 60, 246, 248–250
incompleteness 184, 363, *366*, 367, 371, 401
India 6, 140, 141, 205, 206, 208, 219, 224, 290–291, 292, 295–298, 424–425, 429, 433, 436; Little 215, 218, 224
Indian: architecture 424, 426, 428, 433; farmers 293; food 220, 221; Indians 215, 220–222; nationalism *427*; Peace Keeping Forces 207–208; restaurant 222; subcontinent 205; *see also* identity
inequality 27, 33, 365, 378, 379
informality 5, 387, 431
infrastructure 6, 37, 38, 41, 71, 75, 76, 82, 141–143, 149–150, 155, 157, 165, 167, 171, 173, 178, 188, 197, 222, 224, 232, 270, 272–278, 281–283, 288, 290, 296–297, 306–309, 311, 319, 321, 351, 354–355, 369, 393, 396, 401, 425, 428; digital 71, 75, 77, 78; hedgehog-harming 356; orphans of 355; transit; water 5, 291, 293, 297, 426; *see also* intelligent; knowledge
inhabitation 120, 123, 143, 150, 309, 315, 316, 388
innovation 22, 26, 32, 47, 50, 55, 71, 82, 110, 142, 149, 151, 153, 225, 232, 238, 239, 367–368, 370, 445
installation 18, 60, 65, 80, *98*, *99*, 138, 140–141, 156–157, 181, *190*, 191, 194, 304, 395, 401, 402, 422, 425
intelligent: architectural settings 244–247; and bio-friendly 264; buildings 258; design 5; infrastructure 5, 272–274, 278, 280–281, 283; knowledge 325–326, 330–331; land use planning 278; systems 366–367, 370–371; *see also* materials
interior 12–16, 18, 20, 21, 22, 40, 52, 94, 102, *164*, 167, 169–170, 208, 218, *219*, 220–221, 232, 401
interiority 18, 123, 200, 210
Internet 74, 82, 247, 272–276, 280–281, 319, 381, 405, 406
Irigaray, Luce 86
irrigation 290–293

Ito, Toyo 236

Jacobs, Jane 43, 233–234, 238, 396
Jaffna (Sri Lanka) 201, 203, *207*
Jaipur (India) 424
Jameson, Fredric 171, 232, 322, 329
Janz, Wes 349
Japan 18, 27, 50, 72, 107, 108, 204, 232
Japanese garden 95, 97
Jensen, Michael 200
Jewish 221–222, 224, 416
Jiminez, Corsin 306
Johnson, Philip 13, *14*, 19, 22
Jordan 31–33
Joy, Rick *19*
justice *see* social; environmental

Kahn, Louis 233
kairos 196–197
Kenya 192
Kern, Stephen 334
Khan, Mehboob 436
Knittel, Thomas 241
knowledge 18, 71–77, 92, 175–177, 218, 247, 256, 278, 281, 303, 311, 317, 325, 326, 330–331, 343, 366–369, 376, 391, 396–397, 407, 438–439; architectural 389–391, 431; environment 4; infrastructure 71; and power 450; production 4, 449–451; systems 5
Kolkata 141, 143, 150, 155–158
Koob-Sassen, Hilary *364*, *366*
Koolhaas, Rem 16, 235, *236*, 239, 448
Kosovo 194, *195*
Kossak, Florian 402

Laan, Hans van der 267
land 47, 66, 72, 165, 175, 194, 210, 224, 234, 288, 291, 293, 297, 390, 393, 422, 443, 451; art 80; governance 46; ownership 171; speculation 441, 447; use 150, 181, 273–275, 278–279, 443, 451; value 422, 442, 444, 450
landscape 1, 2, 19, 21, 36–37, 40, 41, 42, 60, 65–66, 76, 102, 114, 163, 173, 178, 191, 192, 196, 218, 225–226, 244, 281, 290, 304, 305, 317, 326, 338, 343, 344, 345, 352, 402, 409, 414, 416, 417, 418, 420, 421, 425, 426, 446; architect 18, 244, 281; architectural 2, 103; artist 80; blighted 84; commercial 418, 421; cultural 218, 226; desert 19–20, 191; design 37, 42, 44, 59; dystopian 305; Durgapuja 143; global 76; immigrant 225; memorial 60; post-bankruptcy 337; post-disaster 187; social 172; urban 305, 406
Latour, Bruno 234, 274, 388, 439
Laugier, Marc-Antoine 11, *12*
Le Corbusier 11–12, 25–26, 102, 113–114, 166, 232, 233, 239, 417, 418, 421

Leadership in Energy and Environmental Design (LEED) 105, 238
Lee, Min Kyung 6, 339
Lefebvre, Henri 341, 389, 443
Leipzig 62, 101
Leslie, Esther 85
Levinas, Emmanuel 200
Libeskind, Daniel 416, 421
Liberia 163–173
library 21, 76, 201, 203, 272, 356, 376
Liggett, Helen 338, 339, 343, 349
lilong 235
Lim, William 201
Lin, Maya 57, 59, 80
Linta, Veljko 5, 256
Lipps, Theodor 93
Liu, Jing 398
Llewelyn Davies Yeang 235
Lohmann, Matthias 396
London *17*, 41, 42, 62, *64*, 80, 84, 118, 119, *120*, 138, 166, 232, 233, 235, 260, *261*, 315, 323, 325, 326, 358, 387, 396, 416, 417, 421, 422
London, Scott *190*
Los Angeles 80, 111, 171, 270, 287, 294, 295, 409
Los Angeles Aqueduct *289*
Lowe, Rick 349
Lury, Celia 303
Lynch, Kevin 224, 281, 312, 314, 315
Lynn, Greg 421, 422

McCarthy, Tom 117–120, 124–129, 132–133
Macedonia 58
machine learning 246, 252
McLauchlan, Laura 6, *351*, *353*, *355*, *357*, *360*
Maity, Snehasish *145*, *148*
Malabou, Catherine 84, 119
Maltzan, Michael 16, 20, *21*, 22
maquiladoras 179
marginalized 206, 309; communities 343, 390; populations 317; space 348–349
marketplace 50, *51*
Massey, Jonathan 37, 41, 42
materials 12, 14, 15, 19, 42, 64, 105, 114, 149, 150–151, 155, 156, 166, 170, 171, 178, 297, 305, 307, 330, 349, 358, 402, 418, 444; biohybrid 5, 262; building 5, 40, 147, 170, 443; construction 4, 151, 176, 356; intelligent 256–267; new 1, 259, 260, 263, 267; recycled 27, 178
materiality 4, 5, 69, 114, 126, 133, 388, 389; digital 76; urban 141; of plastic 86; of space 3, 98, 142, 165; and memory 76
matter 75, 76, 83, 85, 86, 87, 89, 92, 117, 119, 120, 122, 123, 125, 129, 131, 256, 315, 330, 331, 361, 439, 448; out of place 191; recalcitrant 5, 84–85, 130, 133; subject 117, 126–127, 133

Mbembe, Achille 168
media 1, 4, 6, 19, 36, 37, 71, 188, 191, 192, 211, 217, 278, 280, 311, 312, 314, 316, 319, 322, 345, 378, 388, 389, 400, 401, 406, 436, 446, 447, 451; digital 1, 64; social media 3, 13, 18, 23, 59, 62, 74, 109, 273, 281, 383; urbanism 6, 311–321
megacity 20, 142
megaproject 46–56, 367
Mehrotra, Rahul 142, 143, 424
Mehta, Kaiwan 424
Meikle, Jeffrey 82, 85, 87
memorial 4, 5, 44, 57–66
memory 4, 30, 36, 60, 64, 71–78, 118, 125, 130, 217, 225, 246, *257*, 297, 333; digital 76, 78; natural 73; third 73
mentoring 378, 380
Merleau-Ponty, Maurice 92, 94
Metabolism 239
Mexico 4, 176, *177*, 178, 296, 297, 442, 446
Mexico City 270, 338
Michael, Mike 85
migrant 2, 50, 52, 141, 171, 194, 317, 319; entrepreneur 52, 55; worker 46, 50, 55, 288, 296, 319, 321
military 41, 60, 74, 75, 163, 168–169, 179, 206, 207, 211, 224, 317, 364; action 275; camp 188, 194, 196; intervention 201; operation 194
militarization 176, 207, 389
Minkowski, Eugene 91, 334
Mitchell, William 272
mobility 5, 102–103, 105, 108–109, 157, 176–177, 189, 192, 226, 236, 272, 277–280, 319
Modern Movement 167
modernism 1–2, 5, 11, 14–17, 20, 25, 200, 204, 239, 278, 389, 417, 426, 440, 444, 435; global 165
modernity 4, 29, 82, 167, 172, 177, 178, 182, 201, 235, 305, 315, 323, 326, 329, 333, 425, 429, 436
modernization 166, 234–235, 290, 323, 425, 436
molecular structure 258, *259*, 262, 267
Mongolia 441, 451
Monrovia (Liberia), 163–173
Montreal (Canada) *401*
monument 57, *58*, 59–62, *63*, 64–66, 76, 204, 205, 207, 317, 426
Morton Grove (IL) 215, *216*, 217
Morton, Timothy 275
Mostafavi, Mohsen 166, 275
Moten, Fred 87–88
Mouffe, Chantal 400, 402
M/s Prabhakar B. Bhagwat 426, *427*, 430, *437*
muf architecture/art 402
multispecies city 351, 359
multispecies ethnography *see* ethnography

Index

Mumbai 238, 424, 425, 429, *430*, 437
Museum of Modern Art (MoMA) 15, 16, 29–31, 181, *184*, 387, 401
Muslim 203, 206, 207, 215, 220, 225, 295–296, 298
mVISA 30, *31*

nanomaterial *259*
nanotechnology 256, 258–260, 263
nation 5, 37, 57–58, 66, 72, 83, 175, 201, 204, 208, 211, 235, 275, 288, 293, 295, 296–298, 328, 330, 338, 352, 370, 377, 380, 382, 417, 425–426, 429, 436, 440, 449
national: average 375; border 2, 305; crisis 182; culture 431; currency 370; failure 37; focus 111; frames 365; funds 355; hegemony 212; history 66; identity 204, 426; law 365; memorial 57, *59*; outrage 37; park 57, *100*, 175, 326; population *271*; projection 201, 208; representation 65; space 203; success 59; tourism 60; water grid 292, 298
National Architectural Accrediting Board 375, 377, 378, 379
nationalist: elite 431; policies 201; privilege 6; movement 297; self-praise 60; struggle 425
nationalism 206, 426, *427*
nation-state 34, 206, 307, 315, 329, 365–366, 371, 425–426, 431, 436, 450
nature 20, 39–40, 42, 65, 71, 72, 77, 82, 83, 85, 87, 89, 189, 231, 238, 256, 257, 258, 262, 264, 266, 267, 342, 391, 429, 434, 439–440
Negri, Antonio 175
neighborhood 17, 39, 43, 144, 147, 150, 155, 157, 179, 182, 203, 208, 215, 222, 224–225, 232, 234–235, 272, 273, 275, 278–279, 281, 305, 337, 339–341, 344–345, 358–360, 363, 365–369, 390, 393, 399, 416, 422
neuroscience 4, 77, 92–94
Neutra, Richard 20–21
Neves, Joshua 6, 311, 319, *320*, 321
New Orleans 27, 39
New York 18, 29, *59*, 62, 111, 144, 147, 180, 181, 182, *184*, 192, 225, 231, 315, 316, 325, 326, 365, 377, 381, *398*, 417, 442, 445, 449
Noguchi, Isamu 95, 97
Nora, Pierre 64, 65, 66
Norway 66
Nouvel, Jean 236, 449

observation wheel 323
obsolescence: age of 233; and building type 231; and expendability 232–233, 235–236, 238–239; planned 179, 184, 191, 232; preservation 233–234; and sprawl 176; and sustainability 234–235, 238, 239, 242; unplanned 5; urban 232–233, 235
Occupy Movement 165, 273, 365

Ockman, Joan 13, 15
Ondaatje, Michael 123
open-sourcing 367–368, 371
organic 1, 43, 55, 84, 85, 105, 107, 120–121, 129, 258–259, 267, 298, 307, 325, 369, 452
Osaka 107
Oslo 65
Owens Lake 294

Palestinian 314
Palmyra 62, *64*
pandal 141, *144*, *145*, *146*, 147, *148*, 149–151, *152*, 153, *154*, *155*, *156*, 157
Pandya, Yatin 433
Paraguay 396
paravisuality 321
Parr, Adrian 236
participatory: design 6, 393, 395; methods 278, 396; planning 349; practices 273, 281, 387; process 396, 399
Pavel Mudřík and Pavel Míček 239
pavilion 18, 20, 95, 140–141, 143–144, 147, 149–151, 153, 304, 401
permanence 5, 57, 141–142, 171, 188–189, 231–233, 333, 342; *see also* impermanence
Pevsner, Nikolaus 420
Phoenix (AZ) 410
photography 76, 201, 311; civil contract of 314–315, 343, 414
Pieris, Anoma 5, 200, 201, *202*, 203, 204, *205*, *207*, *209*, 210, *211*
placemaking 217
planning 12, 13, 21, 46, 78, 142, 143, 149–150, 151, 165, 180, 185, 194, 214, 234, 270, 272, 273, 275, 276, 277, 278, 280, 281, 291, 306, 338, 342, 349, 424, 434–444, 450; landscape 41; urban 176, 178, 241, 277, 283, 342, 376, 396; *see also* land
plastic 5, 80–89, 92, 111, 114, 127, 151; sheets 27–28, 171, 262–263, 360, 417
plasticity 94–94, 417
Plesner, Ulrik 204, 208
pollution 262, 317; air 179, 293; dust 294; light 188; river 296
polymer 81, 84–85, 90, 259, 262–264, 267
Portishead 359
post-colonialism 192
postmodernism 1, 185, 233, 239, 304, 421
post-occupancy evaluation 5, 244
power systems 363
practice 4, 5, 6, 14, 26, 41, 49, 50, 59, 71, 77, 84, 89, 140, 149, 166, 191, 197, 203, 204, 205, 212, 234, 235, 254, 272, 273, 275, 276, 280, 282, 305, 307, 309, 311, 312, 319, 348, 349, 352, 358, 368, 371, 373, 388, 406, 431, 447; activist 387; aesthetic 200; agonistic 398; architectural 2, 3, 15, 27, 80, 97, 103, 114, 117,

184, 200, 235, 379, 387–392, 393–402, 410, 424–426, 436–437; art 80, 395, 418; bodily 217; of body modification 105; collaborative 394, 395, 400, 402; counter- 448, 450; critical 349, 389, 401; of defensive alterity 208; disciplinary 142; economic 47; embodied 43, 311; ethical 45, 211; everyday 281, 282, 321, 335; humanitarian 33; identities 189; labor 449; liturgical 150; material 178, 201; participatory 273, 281; social 3, 175, 272, 274, 276, 277, 281, 282, 355, 400, 402; street-level 317, *318*; theories of 439; urban 319, 390; and women 375–386; *see also* spatial practice
preservation 62, 71, 129, 234–235, 238–239; preservationism 233–234, 239; preservationist 4, 62, 232; *see also* spatial practice
Price, Cedric 232, 233, 235, 239
prison 37, 167, 173, 442
Pritzker Prize 25, 26, 27, 30, 393
privacy 2, 4, 11, 13, 16, 18–20, 22, 52, 112–113, 245–250, 267, 277, 280, 331
private: client 27; company 367; corporation 273, 277, 370; development 390; enterprise 75; firm 194; identity 225; interests 185; investment 232, 277; leisure 11; life 14, 395; network 448; organization 176; property 149, 292, 355; and public 17, 19, 23, 185, 218, 224, 277, 282, 400, 402; residence 149; retreat 19; sector 75, 326; space 11, 13–14, 16–18, 21, 23, 112–113, 364; sphere 16, 400; time 330; use 16, 402
privatization 30, 32, 75, 175, 178, 194, 319, 364
programming 109–110, 396; self- 319; cultural 390; urban 48
prosthetic 102, 106–107, 114, 129
prototype 5, 27, 107–108, 114, *253*, 278, 306
Proust, Marcel 99
Proustian: moment 118, 129, 132, 333; delight 333
public 2, 4, 11–24, 59, 75, 149, 157, 204, 273, 277, 293, 297, 365, 383, 388, 395, 402, 421; access 41; activity 208; art 59, 62, 67, 156; bathroom 103, 112–115; buildings 213, 234, 370; concern 156, 306; control 367; data 273; design 349; discourse 401; display 245; domain 75, 218; engineering 306; event 370; exhibition 424; expense 75; feeling 67; front 221–222; good 180, 402; health 74; housing 47; identity 225; images 312; infrastructure 149, 275, 281; interest 185, 446; institution 75; lecture 377; media 278; meetings 360; obligation 189; office 367; opinion 234; park 388; patronage 234; petition 111; policy 176; presentation 107; realm 277, 278; reason 443; reciprocity 208; relations 36, 378, 452; resistance 66; school 37; sector 241; service 281, 307, 401; setting 248; space 2, 13, 14, 16, 22–23, 55, 62, 103, 108, 109, 114, 149–151, 157, 175, 191, 227, 246, 277, 307, 316, 359, 390, 394, 396, 435; sphere 400; transport 272, 279, 321, 365, 387; transit 220, 277, 278–279; use 273; view 112; venue 390; works 275; workshop 278

queer 4, 13, 15
Quezon City 307, 309

racial: implication 37; politics 44; profiling 280; injustice 175; minority 215; turbulence 307
racialized: aesthetics 37, 40
Rathod, Samira 424–425, *435*
raumlabor 399–400, *401*
real estate 222, 231, 441, 444–445, 449, 451; crisis 3, 182; dead zone 179; developer 55, 210, 443, 451; dynamics 449; investment 6; speculation 443; venture 446
reality 65, 93, 97, 98, 114, 224, 239, 292, 293, 296, 304, 312, 328, 331, 343, 412; augmented (AR) 74, 77; spatial 347; virtual (VR) 74, 109, 114; political 23; of existence space 92, 94; of refugee life 30
recalcitrant matter *see* matter
recycled: biopolymers 262; emergency shelters 28; joists 180; materials 27, 29, 60, 178; and piratical forms 315; products 105; steel 155, 441
recycling 84, 184, 260, 262–263, 307
re-description 303–304
reflexivity 389, 450
refugee: camp 25, *26*, *28*, 29–30, *31*, 32, 191–192, 208; Syrian 31–33
Riegl, Alois 62, 64
religion 206, 225, 234, 295, 363, 365
repetition 118–120, 122–127, 130; of massing 48
reservoir 80, *81*, 85, 87, *88*, 293; of recalcitrant matter 130
resilience 43, 44, 45, 241, 270, 423; *see also* design
resiliency 36–39, 41–44, 45, 241; *see also* risk
restaurant 50, 55, 74, 182, 215, 218–222, 224, 272, 345
reversibility 142, 149, 156–157
REX architects 416
Rhodes, Lorna 167, 173
Rio de Janeiro 367, 387
risk 4, 75, 76, 78, 151, 191, 236, 238, 241, 295, 309, 326, 359, 371, 444, 445, 446, 448, 450; and resiliency 36–45; mitigation 273
river: Betwa 295; Brahmaputra 295–296; Colorado 294, 296–297; Ganges 295; Ken 295; Owens 287; Rio-Grande 296–297; San Joaquin 287–288, 294, 297
River Linking Project 290, 292–293, 295–296; *see also* Brahmaputra–Ganges River link
Robinson, Sarah 4, 91, 92, 94, *99*, *100*
robot 77, 108, 111, 264, 274; robotics 105–108, 111
Rogers, Richard 260, *261*

Index

Rohe, Mies van der 11, 13, 166, 232, 417, 421
role models 382
Ross, Andrew 449
Rossi, Aldo 233
Royal Institute of British Architects (RIBA) 382
ruin 72, 163–173, 203, 208, 210, 235, 304, 433, 435; ruinscape 231
Rumsey, Abby Smith 4, 71, 74
Russian Constructivists 2, 138, 279
Rwanda *26*, 27, *28*, *31*, 192

Sadler, Simon 184
Said, Edward 200
Salton Sea 294
Samanta, Bimal *146*, *151*, *152*, 153, *154*, *155*, *156*
Samira Rathod Design Associates *see* Samira Rathod
San Diego (CA) 176, *177*, 178–179, 180, 182, 184, 185, 294
San Francisco (CA) 19, 109, 111, 276, 282, 287, 292, 293, 379, 382, 383
San Joaquin–Sacramento River Delta 288, 294
San Ysidro (CA) *179*
Sanders, Joel 16
Sandy Hook (CN) 36–44
Saraceno, Tomás *98*
Sassen, Hilary-Koob *364*, 366
Sassen, Saskia 5, 29, 272, 276, 307, 363, 365, 367–370, 432
Sauda, Eric 5, 244
Savage, Kirk 57
school 112, 163, 232, 250, 293, 360, 444; architecture 6, 375–378, 380, 396, 422, 436–437; bathroom 112; building 40, 41, 44, 67, 147, 387; bus 108; gym 108; elementary 4, 36–44, 45, 67, 108, 112, 147; shooting 36, 112
Schwarzer, Mitchell 275
Scott, Joan 239
security 4, 196, 210, 317, 377, 416, 444; company 110; embedded 4, 36–44; food 2; forces 110, 280; measures 204; system 115, 367; threats 76; zone 110
seeing 108, 111, 142, 150, 151, 234, 276, 303, 308, 309, 310, 311, 316, 331, 342, 345, 365, 380; the city 311–312, 331, 348; ethnic enclaves 224; genealogy of 312; patterns 77; and re-describing 307; ways of 2, 330
segregation 4, 37, 93, 111, 204, 314
Sen, Arijit 5, 215, *219*, *220*, *221*, *223*
Sennett, Richard 398, 404
sensing: devices 245–247; passive 246; technology 5, 244–248, 252, 272
server farm 76
Shalev-Gerz, Esther 62, *63*
Shanghai 235, 238, 304, 338, 429, 444
shelter 11, 19, 25, 73, 110, 144, 188, 189, 193, 197, 267, 355, 387, 429; digital 30, 32–33; emergency xiii, xv, 25–29, 142; post-disaster 27; tax-sheltering 27; temporary 28, 31, 264
Shetty, Prasad 424
Shivkumar, Rohan 6, 424
de Silva, Minnette 204
Simon, Herbert 439–440, 443
Simone, AbdouMaliq 5, 142, 303, 343
Singapore 323–326, *327*, 328–334, 448; Flyer 323–334
Skidmore, Owings and Merrill 416
Skopje (Macedonia) *58*
Sloterdijk, Peter 89
smart: car 278; city 2, 114, 274–275, 277, 306, 367–369; design 38, 43; environment 100, 111; mobility; phone 73, 110, 245, 272–274, 277, 319; space 111, 114
social: act 337; behavior 17, 439; category 113; computing 245; concerns 3, 108; contract 440, 449; contradiction 182; convention 14; engagement 181, 387, 391, 392, 393, 396; engineering 13; equity 275, 277, 281; exchange 142; exclusion 13, 278; experiment 47; fabric 62, 157, 309; function 108; imagination 319; interaction 109, 113, 219; institution 309; justice 262, 377; life 22, 43, 60, 77, 252, 391, 395; mobilization 307; order 30, 128, 341, 348; policy 212; power 308; production 225; profile 49; project 6, 316, 387–391; proximity 200; relations 276, 282, 314, 396; responsibility 315, 349, 387, 391; setting 245; service 176, 179; sphere 244; status 16, 26; structure 178, 203; suffering 29, 32, 212; system 241, 278; transformation 109, 425; value 13; *see also* equity; housing; identity; media; practice; network; space
solar cells 256, 259, 262
softness 142, 153–155
SO-IL *398*, 401
space: existential 91–92, 94; gendered 113; kairotic 196; normative 201, 341; white 37, 43, 112; *see also* bi-space; gender; private; public
spatial practice 3, 4, 200, 311, 315, 317, 343
Spain 64, 272, 396, 409, 410
spectacle 13, 15, 66, 314, 421–422
Spivak, Gayatri Chakravorty 201, 448
Sri Lanka 5, 200–212
Star, Susan Leigh 355
starchitect 6, 405–423
starchitecture *see* starchitect
state 2, 27, 37, 40, 59, 141, 143, 149, 151, 157, 166–167, 171, 174, 192, 232, 234, 241, 292, 293, 294, 295, 297, 314–315, 323, 338, 389, 414, 422, 444, 445, 450; and capital 175–176, 184; formation 204; -funding 40, 41; investment 440; making 163; -owned 72, 326, 441, 444; regulation 236; response 2; sanction

462

Index

143; school 41; stateless 28, 30, 192, 199; support 321; welfare 234, 389; *see also* nation-state
stickiness 122
strategic: development 326; disposition 326; essential 307; frontier 363; location 188; move 203; organization 325; presence 194; role 365; spaces 364; urban design 281; *see also* detachment
Stratigakos, Despina 6, 375, 376, 378
street 17–18, 26, 94, 107, 109, 125, 141, 142, *144*, 147, 150, 153, 155, 157, 158, 182, 203, 231, 234, 278, 308, 309, 321, 339–342, 344–346, 387–390, 430–431; eyes on 43; food 50, *51*; life 317; -level 179, 188, 316, 318, 317, *318*, 321, 325; and hedgehogs 352, 359–360; *see also* ethnic retail
stuckness 123–124, 126
subsolar 396, *397*, 400
Sudjic, Deyan 18
Summerson, Sir John 244
Sundaram, Ravi 311–312, 315
surveillance 2, 13, 15, 16–17, 37, 41–43, 169, 196, 221, 246, 280, 317; counter 317; natural 43
sustainability 1, 5, 38, 40, 44, 191, 231, 233–236, 238–239, 241–242, 243, 272, 277, 283, 284, 336, 349, 394; *see also* obsolescence
Syria 2, 62; *see also* refugee

Tamil 201, 203, 205–207, 210
Tamil United Liberation Front 201
Tang, Dorothy 4, 46
technology 3, 5, 13, 15, 26, 30, 52, 71, 83, 86, 109, 118, 122, 133, 142, 151, 231, 238, 246, 247, 249, 252, 254, 266, 272, 274–276, 280–281, 303, 338, 339, 367, 368, 371; nano-, 256, 258, 260, 263, 264; *see also* digital
television 16, 74, 113, 276, 319, 414; unhomely 319
Téllez, Javier *177*
temporal: horizon 141, 149; polytemporal 234, 235; signifier 2; spatio- 249, 276, 325
territory 42, 64, 147, 165, 188, 189, 224, 231, 276, 365, 399, 414, 432, 436, 443
Thailand *100*
Thierfelder, Anja *99*
Tianducheng (China) 304–306
Title IX 112, 375, 376
Tijuana (Mexico) 176–179, 182, 184, 185
time 2, 15, 20, 60, 62, 65, 73, 76, 84, 86, 89, 91, 92, 94, 108, 123, 129, 130, 141, 149, 150, 153, 217, 225, 231, 233, 236, 238, 252, 304, 314, 315, 325, 328–334, 365, 428, 433, 435, 436; episodic 196; real-, 108, 109, 250, 252, 276, 450; timeless 428–433; utilization 246–248; *see also* contemporary; duration; finitude; temporal horizon

Tierney, T.F. 5, 270, 273, 279–281
Tod Williams Billie Tsien Architects 239, *240*
Tokyo (Japan) 16, 29, 108, *237*, 315, 323
topology 117, 132, 266, 267, 280
tradition 4, 19, 20, 22, 42, 46, 49, 50, 57, 64, 122, 140, 141, 143, 182, 191, 192, 196, 201, 204, 208, 231–233, 239, 262, 276, 277, 295, 331, 343, 368, 382, 387, 388, 393, 395, 396, 425, 426, 428, 429, 433, 441
transgender 112, 113, 115; *see also gender*
transience 182, 188, 194, 235
transnational 176, 200, 217, 236, 276, 293
transpace 111
transparency: material 11–13, 15, 18, 20, 39, 42, 127, 177, 262, 311; privacy 12–13, 127; process 396, 399, 442; social 13, 15, 39, 74, 177, 379
tropical architecture *see* architecture
Tschumi, Bernard 420–423
Tucson (AZ) 19, 20

umwelt 354, *355*, 361
uncertainty 75, 86, 333, 351, 361, 361; and newness 149; and risk 236
unhoused 25–26; *see also* house
uninhabitable, the 307
The United Nations Educational, Scientific and Cultural Organization (UNESCO) 204–206, 212, 234
The United Nations High Commissioner for Refugees (UNHCR) 27–28, 31–32, 33, 35, 191–192, 197, 198, 199
United States (U.S.) 3, 4, 11, 34, 42, 76, 105, 108, 167, 176–179, 182, 189, 194, 215, 232, 239, 291–293, 296, 297, 307, 370, 379, 382, 386, 396
university 206, 215, 298, 376, 422, 444, 445, 447, 449–451; city 47; town 4, 47–48, *49*, 50–52, 55
unsettling 5, 6, 119, 120, 133, 196, 231, 304, 359, 363–372
urban: aesthetics 349; capabilities 363–364, 366; design 46, 143, 165, 272, 281, 312, 390; development 46–47, 56, 234, 323, 326, 389, 441, 444; future 47, 173; infill 5, 144, 147, 153; intervention 149, 153, 387; life 159, 178, 304, 307, 314–316, 319, 371, 390; politics 165; registration (*hukou*) 317
urbanism: commons 178, 180, 184; DIY 273, 281; ecological 275; media 6, 311–322; networked 5, 270, 272–273, 277, 280, 282; open-source 6; splintered 314
urbanity 304, 310, 365
urbanization 6, 46, 49, 182, 210, 276, 362, 389
Utøya 65

Valkenburgh, Michael van 18
Vastu Shilpa Architects 433
Venturi, Robert 17, 233, 417–418, 420, 421

Index

Vergara, Camilo J. 235
vernacular: architecture 208, 416; building 181, 429; construction 138; innovation 55; and popular 431; precolonial 204; structures 233; tradition 429; worldwide 233
Vernacular Architecture Forum (VAF) 416
Vienna 59, 60, *61*, 323
village 46–47, *48*, 49–50, *51*, 52–53, *54*, 55–56, 84, 207, 211, 215, 356, 429, 436; houses 140
Vinegar, Aron 4, 117, *119–135*, *419*
violence 4, 5, 6, 15, 25, 26, 66, 93, 167, 201, 204, 206, 307, 429, 436; communal 165; domestic 377; gun 36–37, 38–39, 41, 44; slow 29, 84–85, 89; structural 32–33, 316
virtual: and artifact 72; body 102; building 110, 114; and digital 113; environment 4, 116; knowledge 76; and material process 120–121; object 132; of place 22–23; space 1, 76, 102, 111; structure 77; wallet 30; world 3, 111; *see also* reality
visuality 6, 311–312, 314–315
visualization 188, 246, 250, 252, 303; *see also* data
voucher humanitarianism *see* humanitarianism
voyeurism 4, 18, 23, 311, 317

Walker, Kara 349
Walker, Peter *59*, 60
war: civil 5, 27, 34, 192, 201, 204, 206–207, 210; zone 33, 206–207
waste 29, 75, 173, 175, 176, 179, *180*, 188, 233, 238, 260, 276, 306, 307, 309, 348; and plastic 89, 263
watching 43, 144, 311–322, 331, 346, 356, 368
water: supply 157, 296–297; surplus 296; systems 297, 426, 428
Webber, Melvin 276
Weeks, John *233*, 235
Weiwei, Ai 60, *61*, 65, 422, 441–442, 445–446, 449
Weizman, Ines 447, 449, 451
White, Jeremy 1, 4, 6, 102, 405, *407*, *408*, *409*, *410*, *411*, *412*, *413*, *415*, *419*
Widrich, Mechtild 4, 57, *58*, *61*, *63*
wildlife gardening 356, 358
Wilkins, Craig L. 5, 337, 349
Wittenberge 397, 400
women 50, 112–113, 222, 305, 375–383, 422
Wright, Frank Lloyd 414, 417, 418

Xiaoguwei Island (China) 47, *48*, 49–50

Yarsley, V.E. 83
Young, James E. 58–59

Žižek, Slavoj 29, 32, 117, 165
Zlín (Czech Republic) 232, 239, *241*
zones d'attente 194
Zumthor, Peter 95, *96*

Printed in the United States
by Baker & Taylor Publisher Services